The Oxford Dictionary of Sports Science and Medicine

Dose schedules are being continually revised and new side-effects recognized. Oxford University Press makes no representation, express or implied, that the drug dosages in this book are correct. For these reasons the reader is strongly urged to consult the drug company's printed instructions before administering any of the drugs recommended in this book.

The Oxford Dictionary of Sports Science and Medicine

MICHAEL KENT

Oxford New York Tokyo
OXFORD UNIVERSITY PRESS

Oxford University Press, Walton Street, Oxford OX2 6DP

Oxford New York
Athens Auckland Bangkok Bombay
Calcutta Cape Town Dar es Salaam Delhi
Florence Hong Kong Istanbul Karachi
Kuala Lumpur Madras Madrid Melbourne
Mexico City Nairobi Paris Singapore
Taipei Tokyo Toronto

and associated companies in
Berlin Ibadan

Oxford is a trade mark of Oxford University Press

Published in the United States
by Oxford University Press Inc., New York

First published 1994
Reprinted 1994 (twice), 1995

A catalogue record for this book is available from the British Library

Library of Congress Cataloging in Publication Data
Oxford dictionary of sports science and medicine / Michael Kent.
1. Sports medicine–Dictionaries. 2. Sports sciences–Dictionaries.
I. Kent, Michael.
[DNLM: 1. Sports Medicine–dictionaries. 2. Sports–dictionaries.
QT 13 098 1994]
RC1206.094 1994 617.1'027'03–dc20 93-23592
ISBN 0 19 262263 3

Printed and bound in Great Britain by
Biddles Ltd, Guildford and King's Lynn

Preface

Sports science includes any discipline which uses scientific methods to study sports phenomena. It is a relatively recent addition to the curriculum, but it is fast becoming an established area of study at schools, colleges and universities in Britain and many other countries, and it forms the theory base for national coaching courses.

Sports medicine first emerged out of the growth of the modern Olympic movement and the search for methods of improving athletic performance. It was originally concerned with the prevention and treatment of sports injuries, especially in the élite athlete. But modern sports medicine has grown in response to the demands of the large number of people who take part in sport for pleasure and for health. Many sports authorities recognize the need for sportspeople of all abilities to have access to adequate medical and scientific support, when and where they need it. Sports medicine has become accepted as an important aspect of preventative medicine and now takes its place among the other branches of medicine.

Sports science and medicine is truly multidisciplinary, covering topics such as anatomy, biomechanics, ergogenic aids, exercise physiology, nutrition, sport psychology, and sport sociology, as well as the cause and treatment of sports injuries. These topics have generated a wealth of specialist literature, each with its own language. The main aim of this dictionary is to make this literature more accessible to the nonspecialist: to help explain words and expressions found in textbooks used by the student, coach, athlete, or medical professional, who has a need for multidisciplinary knowledge.

This dictionary contains over 7500 entries covering all the main areas of sports science and medicine. Most terms are defined in a few short sentences with some longer accounts. The entries are extensively cross-referenced so that the dictionary is as self-contained as possible.

The entries cover words and expressions in current use and explain the meanings attached to them in the context they were made. Sports Science and medicine is a very dynamic and relatively new subject. However, it has drawn on older, established disciplines and has adopted many of their terms. Therefore, the dictionary includes some terms which have become obsolete or fallen out of fashion, but which the student is likely to encounter in the older literature.

The inspiration for this dictionary came from work done with Michael Allaby on The Concise Oxford Dictionary of Zoology and The Concise Oxford Dictionary of Botany. Michael has offered advice and encouragement throughout the project. I would also like to express my thanks to Simon Nicholas, Head of Physical Education at St Austell College, for his encouragement and comments, and to William D. Stanish MD who made some helpful criticisms concerning the original headword list.

Preface

The dictionary has been compiled with the help of a team of eminent advisers and contributors. They have worked extremely hard and kept to very tight deadlines. Their enthusiasm and support for the project has been greatly appreciated. This book would have been impossible without their expert knowledge. Any mistakes that have occurred are the editor's.

I would also like to express my thanks to the librarians at the School of Education, Exeter University, who allowed me free access to the library, and to the staff of Oxford University Press for their support.

There is absolutely no doubt that this book would not have been completed without the staunch support and contribution of my wife, Merryn. Her work went far beyond the demands of the marriage vows.

Michael Kent

St Austell College, Cornwall
January 1993

Contributors and advisers

Dr Stuart Biddle, Senior Lecturer, Exeter University; President, European Federation of Sport Psychology.

Dr Geoffrey P. L. Edwards, General Practitioner, The Health Centre, Wadebridge.

Dr Ken Fox, Lecturer, Exeter University; Fellow of the P.E. Association.

Dr Mike Hutson, Orthopaedic and Sports Physician, Park Row Clinic, Nottingham, and London Bridge Clinic.

Merryn Kent, MA(Oxon).

Dr Michael Kent, Senior Lecturer, St Austell College.

Greg R. McLatchie, MB, ChB, FRCS, Visiting Professor in Sports Medicine and Surgical Sciences, School of Health Sciences, University of Sunderland; Director of the National Sports Medicine Institute of the United Kingdom, St Bartholomew's Medical College.

Dr Andrew Sparkes, Senior Lecturer, Exeter University; Associate Director, Physical Education Association Research Centre.

B. D. Woods, Lecturer, Exeter University; Physiotherapist to the British Olympic Association.

Bibliography

Aldridge, J. A. and Pilgrim, N. (1984). *Prevention and rehabilitation of injury*. The National Coaching Foundation, Leeds.

American College of Sports Medicine (1971). *Encyclopaedia of sports sciences and medicine*. Macmillan, New York.

Armstrong, J. A. and Sparkes, A. (eds) (1991). *Issues in physical education*. Cassell, London.

Arnold, P. (1968). *Education, physical education and personality development*. Heinemann, London.

Astrand, P. O. and Rodahl, K. (1986). *Textbook of work physiology*, (3rd edn). McGraw-Hill, New York.

Badewitz-Dodd, L. (1991). *Drugs and sport*. Media Medica, Chichester, Sussex.

Baumann. W. (ed) (1983). *Biomechanics and performance in sport*. Karl Hofmann, Schorndorf, W. Germany.

Berridge, M. E. and Ward, G. R. (1987). *International perspectives on adapted physical activity*. Human Kinetics, Champaign, Illinois.

Biddle, S. (ed.) (1987). *Foundations of health-related fitness in P. E.* Ling Publishing Co., London.

Bull, R., Davis, R. J., Roscoe, D. A. and Roscoe V. J. (1990). *Physical education and the study of sport*. Wolfe, London.

Burke, E. R. and Newsom, M. M. (1988). *Medical and scientific aspects of cycling*. Human Kinetics, Champaign, Illinois.

Christina, R. W. and Corcos, D. M. (1988). *Coaches' guide to teaching sport skill*. Human Kinetics, Champaign, Illinois.

Cooper, J. M., Adrian, M., and Glassow, R. B. (1982). *Kinesiology*, (5th edn). C. V. Mosby, London.

Cooper, K. (1983). *The aerobics program for total well-being*. Evans, New York.

Corbin, C. B. and Lindsey, R. (1985). *Concepts of physical fitness with laboratories*. W. C. Brown, Dubuque, Iowa.

Cratty, B. J. (1981). *Social psychology in athletics*. Prentice-Hall, New Jersey.

Cox, R. H. (1983). *Sport psychology; concepts and applications*. W. C. Brown, Dubuque, Iowa.

Davies, D. (1989). *Psychological factors in competitive sport*. Falmer Press, Basingstoke.

Davis, D., Kimmet, T., and Auty, M. (1986). *Physical education: theory and practice*. Macmillan, Melbourne.

de Vries, H. A. (1986). *Physiology of exercise*. W. C. Brown, Dubuque, Iowa.

Dick, F. W. (1989). *Sports training principles*, (2nd edn). A. & C. Black, London.

Dirix, A., Knuttgen, H. G., and Tittel K. (eds) (1988). *The Encyclopaedia of sports medicine*. Vol. 1. Blackwell, Oxford.

Dunning, E. (ed.) (1971). *The sociology of sport*. Frank Cass, London.

Dyson, G. H. G. (1986). *Dyson's mechanics of athletics*, (8th edn). revised by B. D. Woods and P. R. Travers. Hodder & Stoughton London.

Edwards, H. (1973). *Sociology of sport*. Dorsey Press, Homewood, Illinois.

Elias, N. and Dunning, E. (1970). *Sociology of sport*. Frank Cass, London.

Elias, N. and Dunning, E. (1986). *The quest for excitement*. Blackwell, Oxford.

Eriksson, B. O., Mellstrand, T., Peterson, L., Renstrom, P. and Svedmyr, N. (1990). *Sports medicine: health and medication*. Guinness, London.

Faria, I. E. and Cavanagh, P. R. (1978). *The physiology and biomechanics of cycling*. Wiley, New York.

Fleishman, E. A. (1964). *The structure and measure of physical fitness*. Prentice-Hall, New Jersey.

Fox, E. L. (1979). *Sports physiology*, (2nd edn). W. B. Saunders, Philadelphia.

Fox, E. L. and Matthews, D. K. (1981). *The physiological basis of physical education and athletics*, (3rd edn). W. B. Saunders, Philadelphia.

Gill, D. L. (1986). *Psychological dynamics of sport*. Human Kinetics, Champaign, Illinois.

Green, J. H. (1986). *An introduction to human physiology*. Oxford University Press.

Greendorfer, S. L. and Yiannakis, A. (eds) (1981). *Sociology of sport*. Leisure Press, New York.

Harris, D. V. and Harris, B. L. (1984). *The athlete's guide to sports psychology*. Human Kinetics, Champaign, Illinois.

Harris, N., Lovesey, J. and Oram, C. (1982). *The sports health handbook*. Kingswood.

Hay, J. G. (1985). *The biomechanics of sports techniques*, (3rd edn). Prentice-Hall, New Jersey.

Hazeldine, R. (1990). *Strength training for sports*. Crowood Press, Wiltshire.

Howley, E. T. and Franks, B. D. (1986). *Health/fitness instructor' handbook*. Human Kinetics, Champaign, Illinois.

Humphreys, J. and Burke, E. (1982). *Fit to exercise*. Pelham, London.

Jary, D., and Jary, J. (1991). *Collins dictionary of sociology*. HarperCollins, London.

Jenkins, S. P. R. (1990). *Sports science handbook*. Sunningdale.

Katch, F. I. and McCardle, W. D. (1988). *Nutrition, weight control, and exercise*. Lea & Febiger, Philadelphia.

Klavora, P. and Daniel, J. V. (eds) (1979). *Coach, athlete, and the sport psychologist*. School of Physical and Health Education, Publications Division, University of Toronto.

Knapp, B. (1977). *Skill in sport*. Routledge & Kegan, London.

Krause, J. V., and Barham, J. N. (1975). *The mechanical foundations of human motion*. A programmed text. C. V. Mosby, London.

Kreighbaum, E. and Barthels, K. M. (1985). *Biomechanics: a qualitative approach to studying human movement*. Burgess, Minneapolis.

Lamb, D. R. (1984). *Physiology of exercise*. Macmillan, New York.

Leunes, A. D. and Nation J. R. (1989). *Sport psychology: an introduction*. Nelson-Hall, New York.

Loy, J. W., Kenyon, G. S, and McPherson, B. D. (ed) (1981). *Sport, culture and society: a reader on the sociology of sport*. Lea & Febiger, Philadelphia.

McArdle, W. D., Katch, F. I. and Katch, V. L. (1986). *Exercise physiology*. Lea & Febiger, Philadelphia.

MacDougall, J. D., Wenger, H. A. and Green, H. J. (eds) (1991). *Physiological testing of the high performance athlete*, (2nd edn). Human Kinetics, Champaign, Illinois.

McPherson, B. D., Curtis, J. E. and Loy, J. W. (1989). *The social significance of sport: an introduction to the sociology of sport*. Human Kinetics, Champaign, Illinois.

Marieb, E. N. (1989). *Human anatomy and physiology*. Benjamin/Cummings, California.

Martens, R. (1988). *The coach's guide to sport psychology*. Human Kinetics, Champaign, Illinois.

Martin, E. A. (1990). *Concise medical dictionary*. Oxford University Press.

Mottram, D. R. (ed.) (1988). *Drugs in sport*. Human Kinetics, Champaign, Illinois.

National Coaching Foundation (1986). *The Coach at work*. The National Coaching Foundation, Leeds.

National Coaching Foundation (1986). *Physiology and performance*. The National Coaching Foundation, Leeds

Nideffer, R. M. (1985). *Athlete's guide to mental training*. Human Kinetics, Champaign, Illinois.

Noakes, T. and Granger, S. (1990). *Running injuries*. Oxford University Press.

Noble, B. J. (1986). *Physiology of exercise and sport*. Times-Mirror/Mosby, St Louis.

Ottaway, P. B. and Haigh, K. (1985). *Food for sport: handbook of sports nutrition*. Resource, Cambridge.

Page, R. L. (1978). *The physics of human movement*. Pergamon, Exeter.

Paish, W. (1979). *Diet in sport*. E. P. Publishing, Wakefield.

Peterson, J. and Renstrom, P. (1986). *Sports injuries, their prevention and treatment*. Martin Dunitz, London.

Pitt, V. H. (ed.) (1977). *Penguin dictionary of physics*. Penguin, London.

Rasch, P. J., with contributions by Grabinier M. D., Gregor, R. J. and Garhammer, J. (1989). *Kinesiology and applied anatomy*. Lea & Febiger, Philadelphia.

Rees, C. R. and Mirade A. W. (eds) (1986). *Sport and social theory*. Human Kinetics, Champaign, Illinois.

Reilly, T. (1981). *Sports fitness and sports injuries*. Faber & Faber, London.

Reilly, T. Secher, N., Snell, P. and Williams, C. (1990). *Physiology of sports*. Chapman & Hall, London.

Roberts, G. C., Spink, K. S. and Pemberton C. L. (1986). *Learning experiences and sport psychology*. Human Kinetics, Champaign, Illinois.

Roy, S. and Irving, R. (1983). *Sports medicine: prevention, evaluation, management and rehabilitation*. Prentice-Hall, New York.

Rowett, H. G. Q. (1988). *Basic anatomy and physiology*. Murray, London.

Schmidt, R. A. (1988). *Motor control and learning: a behavioural emphasis*. Human Kinetics, Champaign, Illinois.

Sharkey, B. J. (1984). *Physiology of fitness*. Human Kinetics, Champaign, Illinois.

Sharkey, B. J. (1986). *Coaches' guide to sport physiology*. Human Kinetics, Champaign, Illinois.

Sharp, C. (1985). *Developing endurance*. The National Coaching Foundation, Leeds.

Silva, J. M. and Weinber, R. S. (eds) (1984). *Psychological fondations of sport*. Human Kinetics, Champaign, Illinois.

Singer, R. N. (1982). *The learning of motor skills*. Macmillan, New York.

Singer, R. N. (1980). *Motor learning and human performance*, (3rd edn). Macmillan, New York.

Sperryn, P. N. (1983). *Sport and medicine*. Butterworths, London.

Straub, W. F. and Williams, J. M. (1984). *Cognitive sports psychology*. Sport Science, New York.

Strauss, R. H. (1987). *Drugs and performance in sports*. W. B. Saunders, Philadelphia.

Thompson, C. W. (1985). *Manual of structural kinesiology*, (10th edn). Times-Mirror/ Mosby, St Louis.

Tucker, C. (1990). *The mechanics of sports injuries*. Blackwell, Oxford.

Tver, D. F. and Hunt, H. F. (1986). *Encyclopaedic dictionary of sports medicine*. Chapman & Hall, London.

Wasserman, K., Hansen, J. E., Sue, D. Y. and Whipp, B. J. (1987). *Principles of exercise testing and interpretation*. Lea & Febiger, Philadelphia.

Watkins, J. (1983). *An introduction to mechanics of human movement*. MTP Press, Lancaster.

Whitehead, N. (1985). *Conditioning for sport*. E. P. Publishing, Wakefield.

Williams M. H. (ed) (1983). *Ergogenic aids in sport*. Human Kinetics, Champaign, Illinois.

Williams, J. G. P. (1990). *A colour atlas of injury in sport* (2nd edn). Wolfe, London.

Williams, J. G. P. and Sperryn, P. N. (1976). *Sports medicine*. Arnold, London.

Wirhed, R. (1984). *Athletic ability and the anatomy of motion*. Wolfe, London.

Wooton, S., de Looy, A., and Walker, M. (1984). *Nutrition and sports performance*. The National Coaching Foundation, Leeds.

A

a Abbreviation sometimes used in *physiology references to indicate *arterial pressure.

Å Symbol for *angstrom.

A-band An area which appears as a dark band on images of *striated muscle produced by the electron microscope. The A-band contains interdigitating *actin and *myosin filaments and is located towards the centre of a *sarcomere. *Compare* I-band.

abdomen Lower part of the *trunk, between the *diaphragm and the *pelvis, containing *viscera which include the *stomach, *kidneys, *liver, and *intestines. The shape of a healthy abdomen varies. In children it may protrude, but if this is too marked it may indicate diseases such as *kwashiorkor. In young adults, the abdomen should be slightly indrawn or only slightly prominent with the outline of *abdominal muscles visible.

abdominal Pertaining to the *abdomen.

abdominal contraction An *isometric exercise in which the subject contracts anterior *abdominal muscles strongly, with no movement of the *trunk or *hips. Abdominal contractions may be performed sitting, standing, or *supine.

abdominal contusion Damage to the underlying tissue in the *abdomen due to a blow which does not break the skin. The degree of damage varies greatly and may not be clearly discernible. It is, therefore, wise to consider such injuries as serious until ruled otherwise.

abdominal hernia *See* inguinal hernia.

abdominal injury Physical damage to the *abdomen and its contents which are vulnerable to direct blows, particularly during *contact sports. Many injuries are superficial and involve bruising of the abdominal wall but *direct trauma can seriously damage the *intestines, *kidneys, *liver, *pancreas, and *spleen. The most common abdominal injury in sport is *winding.

abdominal muscles (abdominals) Consist of four muscle pairs: the *rectus abdominis, *external oblique, *internal oblique, and the *tranversus abdominis. They support and protect the contents of the *abdomen and contribute to *forced expiration. Well-functioning abdominal muscles unload the back during lifting and stabilize the *vertebral column. If weakened by lack of exercise, they become pendulous, forming a 'pot-belly'. Strengthening exercises include *sit-ups.

abdominal pain A feeling of acute hurt or discomfort in the region of the *abdomen. A severe, persistent abdominal pain is a symptom of several medical conditions which are potentially lethal if not properly diagnosed and treated. In such cases, medical advice should be sought, no medication or drinks given the patient, and physical exertion avoided.

abdominal rigidity An extreme tension of the *abdominal muscles over an area of localized tenderness or irritation. It may be due to an underlying pathological condition such as *appendicitis, but in sport, it is commonly caused by poor conditioning, poor protective gear, or a direct blow.

abdominals *See* abdominal muscles.

abdominal skinfold A *skinfold measurement which can be taken on a variety of places on the *abdomen, but which is commonly taken from a vertical fold of tissue 5 cm lateral to, but level with, the *omphalion.

abducens nerve *Nerve which supplies the lateral rectus muscle in each eye.

abduct To move away from the midline of the body.

abduction A movement of a body-segment, such as an arm or leg, away from the midline of the body. The term also refers to the movement of fingers or toes when they are spread apart. *Compare* adduction.

abductor A *muscle which causes *abduction during *concentric contractions.

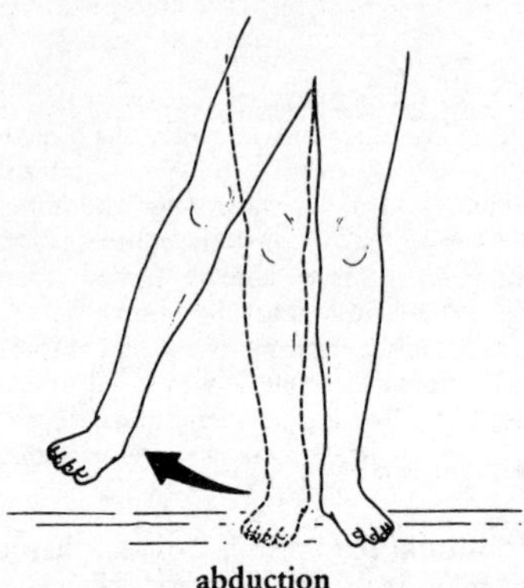

abduction

abductor pollicis brevis A small *intrinsic muscle which inserts onto the *proximal middle *phalanx of the thumb. It is active during *abduction and *extension of the thumb.

abductor pollicis longus A *deep muscle in the posterior fascial compartment of the *forearm; it causes *abduction and *extension of the *thumb. Its *origins are on the posterior surfaces of the *radius and *ulna, and the *interosseus membane. Its *insertion is on the base of the first *metacarpal.

aberration A behaviour which is a deviation from *normal.

abilities-to-skill transfer The effect of practising an *ability on the *learning and performance of a *skill. There is likely to be some *positive transfer, for instance, when a gymnast who has developed the abilities of *balance, *co-ordination and *flexibility, engages in the skill of dancing. *See also* transfer of training.

ability A general characteristic which contributes to proficiency in a number of *skills. *Balance, *co-ordination, and *flexibility are abilities used in the skill of trampolining, for example. Abilities are largely inherited. They may be extended and developed by experience but, unlike skills, they can not be learned. *See also* general motor ability.

ability-orientation The tendency of an individual to emphasize circumstances which reflect highly on his or her *ability while belittling circumstances which reflect badly.

Ablakov test A *power test in which an athlete jumps as high as possible from a half-squat position. An automatic stop-tape, one end attached to the athlete's waist and the other fixed to the floor, records the height reached by the subject.

abnormal Diverging more or less from the usual or typical. *Compare* normal.

abnormal quadriceps pull A condition due to an abnormally large angle of *insertion of the *quadriceps femoris muscle on the *patella (*see* Q-angle). When the muscle contracts it pulls the kneecap laterally resulting in *overpronation, excessive *internal rotation, and associated knee problems.

ABO blood groups The four natural human *blood groups (A, B, AB, and O) identified by Landsteiner (1868–1943). Each of the groups is characterized by particular *antigens on the *red blood corpuscles and *antibodies in the *plasma. Group A contains antigen A and antibodies to antigen B; group B contains antigen B and antibodies to antigen A; group AB contains antigens A and B but no antibodies; and group O contains no antigens but antibodies to both antigens A and B. *Agglutination occurs when incompatible blood groups are mixed, due to the antigen–antibody reaction. As an example, agglutination occurs when blood containing anti-A antibody (i.e., from groups B or O) is mixed with blood containing antigen A (i.e., from groups A or AB). Therefore, individuals belonging to blood group A can receive a blood transfusion only from other members of group A or group AB, or from a *universal donor in an emergency transfusion.

abrasion (graze) Injury in which the skin surface is broken but there is no complete tear throughout its depth. Such injuries are common in sport and, although they are often slight, they may allow the entry of dirt containing disease-producing organisms leading to the development of an *abscess.

Treatment includes thorough and immediate cleansing of the abrasion with soap and water followed by application of a sterile dressing. *See also* tetanus.

abrasive force A *force which can cause an *abrasion, such as the force between the ground and the foot of a runner.

abscess A localized collection of *pus surrounded by an inflamed area of tissue. *See also* inflammation.

abscissa **1** The horizontal, or x-coordinate, of a point in a two-dimensional system of *Cartesian coordinates. **2** The horizontal or x-axis of a graph.

absence A transient lessening of consciousness (e.g., as a result of *hyperventilation or a physical blow).

absent-mindedness Absorption in thought so as to be largely unaware of surrounding conditions.

absolute Not relative; independent of relations to other objects or factors. In sport, it often relates to units of *strength, *work, or *energy which are not adjusted for individual differences such as age, weight, and gender.

absolute error The average deviation of a set of scores from a target value; absolute error is a measure of overall error and does not take into account the direction of the deviation.

absolute frequency of knowledge of results *See* knowledge of results.

absolute humidity The total mass of water vapour present in the atmosphere expressed as kg (or g) of water in 1 m^3 of air. Generally, in sport, *relative humidity is the more important measurement of humidity because it has a greater effect on evaporation rate.

absolute load The total resistance to a movement, irrespective of the body-size of the individual involved. *Compare* relative load.

absolute outcome *See* outcome.

absolute refractory period A brief period following the stimulation of a *nerve cell or *muscle fibre during which no additional *action potential can be evoked no matter how strong the *stimulus; the nerve cell or muscle fibre remain completely unresponsive.

absolute strength The maximum force an athlete can exert with his or her whole body, or part of the body, irrespective of body-size or muscle-size. In many sporting activities, such as jumping and sprinting, the entire body is involved. *Compare* relative strength; *see also* strength.

absolute threshold *See* threshold.

absorbed dose The amount of a *drug which is taken up by the body. The vast majority of drugs are designed to be swallowed and absorbed into the bloodstream through the intestines. Not all of the drug ingested will be absorbed.

absorption Process by which products of *digestion pass from the *alimentary canal into the *blood or *lymph, or a *drug passes from its point of administration into the blood. *Compare* adsorption.

abstinence syndrome A group of unpleasant *symptoms which may include *anxiety, weakness, *nausea, vomiting, *tremor, and rapid heartbeat (*see* tachycardia), produced by the abrupt termination of the administration of a *drug. These symptoms, called withdrawal symptoms, are usually rapidly reversed after the readministration of the drug.

abstracting The process of discerning common elements in situations which are otherwise different. Abstracting is particularly useful in team-games when a player is said to have the ability to 'read a situation'.

abstract thinking Thinking in terms of concepts and general principles rather than in terms of specific objects or events.

acceleration The rate of change of *velocity of an object, measured as a change in velocity per unit time. It is usually expressed as metres per second squared ($m\ s^{-2}$).

acceleration due to gravity *Acceleration of a mass towards the centre of the Earth. *See also* acceleration of free fall.

acceleration, law of (Newton's second law of motion) A law which states that when a body is acted upon by a *force, its resulting change in momentum (*see* acceleration) takes place in the direction in which the force is applied, is proportional to the force causing it, and inversely proportional to its mass.It is expressed as:

$$a = f/m \quad \text{or} \quad f = ma$$

where *a* represents acceleration; *f* represents force; and *m* represents mass.

acceleration of free fall Constant *acceleration of a body falling freely under *gravity, in a vacuum or when *air resistance is negligible. It varies slightly in different geographical locations as a result of variations in the distance from the centre of mass of the Earth. The standard accepted value, usually referred to by the symbol *g*, is 9.80 665 m s^{-2}, or 32.17 feet per second per second. Sky-divers are sometimes said to be in free fall, but this is not strictly true since their downward *velocity is reduced by air resistance.

acceleration sprint A form of *sprint-training in which running speed is gradually increased from *jogging to striding and finally to sprinting at maximum pace. Usually, each component is 50 m long with a 50 m walk recovery. Acceleration sprints develop the *phosphagen system and they are particularly useful for emphasizing and maintaining the technical components of the sprint action as speed increases. The progressive nature of acceleration sprinting reduces the risk of muscle injury.

acceleration–time curve The graphical representation of *acceleration plotted against time. It is used in the analysis of a runner's performance at different phases of a run.

accelerometer An instrument which measures *acceleration.

acceptance A phase of *suggestion which consists in the acceptance of the idea, judgement, or belief suggested.

acceptor molecule A *molecule which has a high affinity for electrons. Acceptor molecules, such as the *cytochromes, are involved in *redox reactions in the *electron-transport system, and are vital in *aerobic respiration.

access 1 The extent to which facilities, including participation in sport, are available to people, whatever their social category (e.g., ability, ethnicity, gender, or sexual orientation). 2 The ability of a researcher to gain entry and acceptance to a social situation to gather data.

accessory bone A bone, such as the *os trigonum, which is not present in all people.

accessory digestive organ An *organ which contributes to *digestion but which is not part of the *alimentary canal. Accessory organs include the *gall-bladder, *liver, and *pancreas.

accessory nerve The eleventh *cranial nerve. It has a root emerging from the *cranium which joins the *vagus nerve and supplies the muscles of the larynx, and a root emerging from the *spinal cord which supplies the *sternomastoid and *trapezius muscles.

accident An untoward event without an apparent cause. Between 5–10 per cent of all attendances at casualty departments of British hospitals are the result of *sports injuries, but few could be strictly classified as accidents.

accident equation An equation which attempts to express, symbolically rather than mathematically, the factors which contribute to sports injuries. An example of an accident equation is expressed as:

$$I = CEprf/tms$$

where *I* represents the probability of an injury; *C* represents chance factors and *E* represents environmental factors, either of which may be favourable or unfavourable; *p* represents accident proneness, *r* represents risk acceptance, *f* represents personal failings, all of which tend to increase the chance of injury; *t* represents training, *m* represents maturity, and *s* represents safety precautions, all of which lessen the impact of an injurious situation and contribute towards the prevention of an injury.

accident-prone The tendency to become injured more than the average amount. An athlete may be accident-prone because of chance factors, but many injuries are due to preventable factors, such as a tendency not to *warm-up adequately, or poor training techniques. Young people have an increased risk of injury because, among other things, their bones are not fully developed. Older people may be more at risk because of fragile bones.

acclimation The response by an individual which increases his or her tolerance to a change in a single factor (e.g. temperature) in the environment. The term is applied most commonly to physiological experiments under controlled conditions. *See also* acclimatization.

acclimatization Reversible physiological response that enables an individual to tolerate environmental changes (e.g., a change in altitude or climate). *See also* altitude acclimatization; and heat acclimatization.

accommodation 1 Process by which the shape of the lens in the eye changes so that distant or near objects can be brought into focus. Accommodation, with *pupillary constriction and *convergence, enables an individual to retain focus of an object as it approaches. This ability is particularly important for players of ball games. 2 An effect produced on sense-organs by continuous and unvarying stimulation, so that eventually no sensation is experienced (*see* habituation). 3 A social process, sometimes encouraged by sporting links, in which different racial or political groups adjust to each other and coexist without necessarily resolving underlying differences. 4 A social process, analagous to biological adaptation, by which a *society, or an individual, adjusts to its environment. 5 In Piaget's theory, a mechanism by which a child develops from one stage to the next.

accommodation to competition Response of an individual to frequent exposure to competitive situations. If accommodation is positive, the individual will have optimal levels of *arousal so that performance can be maximized.

acculturation 1 A process which occurs when different cultural groups are in contact. Acculturation leads to the acquisition of new cultural patterns by one or more of the groups, with the adoption of some or all of another's culture which changes the group identitiy. Many argue that sport makes a major contribution to acculturation and is possibly one reason for support of national teams by governments which wish to encourage others to adopt their cultural patterns. 2 Any transmission of *culture between groups, including different generations. *See also* enculturation; and socialization.

accumulated feedback A form of *feedback in which information is presented to a performer after he or she has made a series of responses. The information represents a summary of all the responses, enabling the performer to determine how successful he or she has been.

accuracy 1 Ability of a performer to hit a target. 2 Ability of a performer, such as an ice-skater, to repeat movements successfully. 3 The ability to perform without making any errors. 4 The reliability of a measurement, often expressed in terms of the deviation (+ or –) of the measurment from its true value. *Compare* precision.

acebutulol A *cardioselective *beta blocker used in the treatment of *hypertension and *angina pectoris to reduce *anxiety. It is on the *IOC list of *banned substances.

acetabular fossa Rounded depression which serves as the attachment point of the *ligamentum teres from the *femur on the *acetabulum. It is perforated by numerous small holes.

acetabular labrum Horseshoe-shaped rim made of *fibrous cartilage which deepens the *acetabulum and makes the *hip-joint more stable (*see* stability).

acetabulum Deep cup-like socket on the lateral surface of each hip-bone (*see* coxal bone) of the *pelvic girdle, into which the ball-shaped head of the *femur fits.

acetaminophen The name used in the USA for *paracetemol.

acetazolamide A *diuretic on the *IOC list of *banned substances. It is a component of *medicines used to treat a number of conditions, including *oedema but it has been misused in sport to reduce weight artificially.

acetic acid (ethanoic acid) A colourless liquid which is the main *acid in vinegar. Strong acetic acid is corrosive and an irritant poison, but low dilutions can be of value in treating excessive *sweating. When sponged over the skin, it reduces perspiration and produces a cooling sensation. *See also* acetylcholine.

acetone An organic compound which is produced in the *liver and found in the *urine under certain conditions, such as starvation. *See also* ketones.

acetone bodies *See* ketones.

acetylcholine (ACh) A *neurotransmitter synthesized in the *synaptic knobs of some nerve-endings from *acetic acid and *choline. It is released by all *neurones which stimulate *skeletal muscle and neurones of the *parasympathetic nervous system. Acetylcholine sets off *action potentials in nerve and muscle cells by making them more permeable to sodium ions. Its effect is short-lived because it is destroyed by *acetylcholinesterase. Acetylcholine was the first neurotransmitter to be identified.

acetylcholinesterase An enzyme that breaks down *acetylcholine (ACh) into choline and acetic acid. Acetylcholinesterase is released onto the *sarcolemma of *muscle fibres and destroys ACh after the ACh has combined with receptors on the muscle fibre. Thus, acetylcholinesterase prevents continued muscle contraction in the absence of additional nervous stimulation.

acetylcoenzyme A An important intermediate in the *aerobic respiration of *carbohydrates, *fats and *proteins. When oxygen is present, pyruvic acid (formed from glucose during glycolysis), fatty acids (from lipids) and amino acids (from proteins) form acetylcoenzyme A which is then fed into the *Krebs cycle in the *mitochondria.

acetylcysteine A *drug used in the treatment of chronic *bronchitis, fibrocystic disease of the pancreas, and *paracetemol-poisoning.

acetylsalicylic acid (aspirin) A white crystalline powder which is a *nonsteroidal anti-inflammatory drug also usd as an *antipyretic to treat headaches and as a mild *analgesic to relieve pain. It is widely used for the treatment of muscle and joint injuries, *arthritis, and *cardiovascular disorders. It tends to increase clotting time and therefore increases the tendency of a person to bleed. Consequently, it can be harmful to individuals with stomach ulcers. A few individuals are allergic to aspirin and its ingestion could result in an *anaphylactic condition. It is a permissible drug, not on the *IOC list of *banned substances.

ACh *See* acetylcholine.

achieved status A high *social status acquired by individual effort or open competition (e.g., through winning at sport), rather than from the status the person is born with. *Compare* ascribed status.

achievement **1** The level of performance attained by an athlete, particularly in a standardized series of tests. **2** In *sociology, the acquisition of *social position or *status as the outcome of personal effort in open competition with others (e.g., in the Olympic Games).

achievement goals The personal targets that a performer sets himself or herself to achieve in a performance. Achievement goals are subjective and are based on what the individual regards as being successful outcomes. *See also* goal.

achievement motivation A *motivation which predisposes an athlete to engage in or avoid achievement-related situations. Achievement motivation is affected by a number of factors, including an individual's desire for success and fear of failure. It is a fundamental drive that may motivate athletes to commit large proportions of their lives to achieve particular personal *goals. *See also* achievement need; fear of failure; and fear of success.

achievement need A *drive which is related to how hard an athlete tries to gain success, and his or her capacity to experience pride in accomplishments. In sport, success may be self-evaluated or externally evaluated; it may be viewed in terms of winning a contest, improving the quality of a performance, or gaining approval from people whose views the performer values. Athletes with a high achievement need may require constant information and reassurance about their performance. *See also* achievement motivation.

achievement situation A situation in which an individual believes that his or her performance will be evaluated. *See also* competition.

achievement test A test which measures what has been accomplished, as in a *sargent jump or *Ablakov test; it contrasts with tests of potential such as aptitude tests.

Achilles bursitis An *inflammation of the *retrocalcaneal bursa in the heel. It is associated with tenderness in the anterior aspect of the *Achilles tendon, often in combination with some *fluctuation.

Achilles tendinitis A *stress injury of the *Achilles tendon, characterized by *inflammation, *pain, and tenderness. It is particularly common in long-distance runners who train on hard surfaces. Treatment usually includes rest, medication, such as *aspirin to reduce the swelling, and appropriate *physiotherapy. Relief may be obtained by using a heel pad to restrict the range of movement. In severe cases, *surgical decompression may be required. An acute inflammation of the Achilles tendon, if not treated properly, can develop into a chronic condition which is very difficult to resolve.

Achilles tendon A large *tendon situated at the back of the *ankle which connects the *gastrocnemius and *soleus muscles to the *calcaneus in the heel. It is very susceptible to injury.

achyllodonia A pain felt in and around the attachment of the Achilles tendon in the heel-bone.

acid A substance which dissolves in water and, in solution, liberates hydrogen ions. An acid reacts with a *base to give salt and water only.

acidaemia A condition in which the concentration of hydrogen ions in the blood plasma is higher than normal. *See also* acidosis.

acid–base balance The relatively stable relationship between the concentration of acids and bases in the body. An equilibrium is usually maintained by *buffering but this may be disrupted by certain conditions such as heavy exercise and *hyperventilation. An acid–base imbalance can adversely affect some functions in the body, such as *muscle contraction and the conduction of a *nerve impulse.

acidosis A state of acidity or abnormally high hydrogen ion concentration in the *extracellular fluid of the body. *See also* acidaemia; metabolic acidosis; and respiratory acidosis.

acquired Applied to a condition contracted after birth and not due to an inherited disease.

acquired ageing The possession of characteristics commonly associated with *ageing but that are, in fact, caused by other factors, such as lack of mobility. *See also* hypokinetic disease; *compare* time-dependent ageing.

acquired immune deficiency syndrome (AIDS) An incurable disease caused by a blood-borne virus (called human deficiency virus or HIV) that disrupts the body's normal *immune response. There is considerable controversy concerning the participation of AIDS sufferers in sport, but the general medical consensus is that, since the HIV virus is transmitted via body fluids, primarily through sexual relationships, parenteral transmission, and by infected blood and plasma products, there is very little risk of infection in sports in general. However, the risk of infection is slightly greater in those sports, like boxing, where blood contact may occur. Athletes, and others, who share needles and syringes to administer drugs are at risk.

acquired motivation (secondary motivation) *Motivation which is not inborn and does not satisfy a basic physiological need. An example of an acquired motivation would be the desire to win an Olympic medal.

acromial In anatomy, pertaining to the point of the *shoulder.

acromiale (acromial point) **1** An anatomical *landmark which is located at the *superior and external border of the *acromion process when the subject is standing erect with arms relaxed. **2** The most lateral point on the *inferior border of the acromion process.

acromial height A measurement of body height from *acromiale to the *base.

acromial point *See* acromiale.

acromial spur A bony projection from the *acromion.

acromioclavicular joint A small *gliding, *synovial joint between the *lateral end of the *clavicle and the *acromion. The *deltoid muscles attach to the anterior of the joint and the *trapezius muscles to the posterior. Together with the *sternoclavicular joint, it forms the *pectoral girdle. Its movements are *elevation, *depression, *protraction, and *retraction.

acromion *See* acromion process.

acromion process A process of bone which projects forward from the *scapula and combines with the *clavicle to form the *acromioclavicular joint, an arch of bone protecting the shoulder-joint.

acropodion (akropodion) An anatomical *landmark located at the most *anterior point on the toe (the first or second *phalanx) of the foot when the subject is standing. The subject's toe-nail is sometimes clipped before making the measurement.

ACTH *See* corticotrophin.

actin A contractile, *fibrous protein of *muscle fibres and *microfilaments. *See also* sliding-filament theory.

actin–myosin cross-bridge *See* cross-bridge.

action **1** Any unit or sequence of social activity or behaviour. The term is sometimes restricted to social activities which are intentional and involve conscious deliberation, rather than merely being the result of a behavioural reflex. **2** In *biomechanics, the product of *work and time. *Compare* power. **3** *See* muscle action.

action knowledge Knowledge which has practical applications, such as knowledge acquired by applied sport scientists which can be used to improve the performance of an athlete.

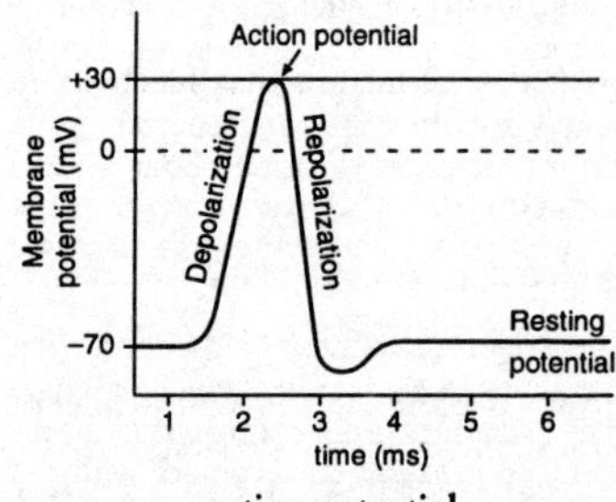

action potential

action potential A transient feature of membranes of *neurones and *muscle fibres during which the electrical potential inside the membrane becomes temporarily positive with respect to the outside. This *depolarization is an *all-or-none phenomenon and lasts about one millisecond, after which the *resting potential is re-established. The action potential at one site of a neurone provides a *stimulus to the next membrane patch, resulting in the propagation of the *nerve impulse.

action research Form of *research which aims, not only to study changes in social activities such as sport, but also to introduce such changes usually with the full involvement and awareness of participants.

action theory A method of approaching sociological analysis which regards the purposive social actions of individuals as the basis on which to seek explanations for social reality.

activation The state of readiness of an individual to respond to a *stimulus. It is an internal state which occurs immediately prior to an activity. Activation may be elicited by exposing an athlete to an *audience, by verbal exhortation, or by exposure to competitive situations. *See also* arousal.

activation energy The *energy that must be supplied to a system in order to increase the incidence within it of reactive molecules, thus enabling a particular chemical process to occur. *Enzymes lower the activation energy of specific chemical reactions.

activation system Body systems, such as the sensory system, *memory, and *perception, which effect *activation.

activator A metal ion that functions in conjunction with either an *enzyme or its *substrate in order to bring about a reaction.

active centre *See* active site.

active force A contact *force, occurring during activities such as walking, and which reaches its maximum level more than 50 ms after the foot makes first contact with the ground. Active forces are responsible for all the movements in which an individual, standing on both feet, bends his or her knees, and returns to the upright position. *Compare* impact force.

active immunity *Immunity produced by a person's own body cells after encountering an *antigen following disease or deliberate stimulation (*see* immunization).

active insufficiency The inability of a muscle which spans two joints (*see* biarticulate muscle) to exert enough tension to shorten sufficiently to cause a full range of movement in both joints at the same time.

active mobility exercise Movements used to improve mobility which are under the total control of the exerciser. *Compare* passive mobility exercise.

active movement A movement brought about by a person's own efforts. *Compare* passive movement.

active recovery *See* exercise recovery.

active rest A type of treatment which may be prescribed for over-use injuries. Active rest involves performing light exercise (often swimming or cycling) that does not impose undue stress on the injured part of the body.

active site Part of an *enzyme molecule that interacts with, and binds to, the *substrate when a complex between the enzyme and substrate is formed. The specificity of an enzyme for particular substrates is believed to depend on the shape of the active site being complementary to that of the substrate. The conformation between the enzyme and substrate is not absolute and may alter according to the reaction conditions. *See also* denaturation.

active stability The contribution of *forces exerted by muscle activity to the *stability of a joint.

active state Condition of a muscle immediately before, and during, contraction that makes it nonextensible. It is caused by the attachment of *myosin cross-bridges to *actin filaments.

active transport The net movement of a substance against a concentration gradient; that is, from a region where its concentration is low to a region of higher concentration. Active transport requires the expenditure of *energy. It takes place especially through cell membranes where the energy is provided by the breakdown of *adenosine triphosphate.

activity 1 The ability of a substance to react with another. 2 The attitude which is expressed in behaviour. 3 *See* basic movement.

activity fragmentation The breakdown of a *skill into components in such a way that the meaningful relationship between components is lost.

activity theory (substitution theory) A *gerontological theory of adjustment to old age which has been applied to retirement of athletes. It maintains that an athlete's adjustment to retirement is most successful when the *role lost upon retirement is replaced by new roles, so that the athlete's total activity level declines only slightly, if at all. A positive correlation between *mental well-being and involvement in sport supports this theory.

actomyosin A *protein formed by the coupling of *actin and *myosin during muscle contraction. *See also* sliding-filament theory.

actor (social actor) Any person involved in a social action. The person may or may not be playing a role. *See also* role theory.

actual leader behaviour The behaviour a coach or other leader exhibits, irrespective of the *norms or preferences of those who are led.

actual mechanical advantage *See* mechanical advantage.

actuarial age Age in years nearest to the subject's past or next birthday. It is used by many insurance companies, and in the *CP-index.

acuity Sharpness of vision; the ability to see detail.

acupuncture An ancient Chinese therapy, gaining popularity among sportspeople in the west, for the relief of *pain, particularly ailments such as *arthritis, back-pain, and *depression. It may also be used as an aid to recovery from sports injury. Needles are inserted through the skin and muscle tissue at certain points plotted on lines along the body determined by tradition. These lines do not correspond to any other single system. *See also* transcutaneous electrical nerve stimulation.

acute Applied to a condition which develops rapidly and is usually of brief duration.

acute angle An angle of less than ninety degrees.

acute compartment syndrome *See* compartment syndrome.

acute injury An injury with a rapid onset which may develop into a *chronic injury if untreated.

acute mountain sickness A condition which occurs at high altitudes due to lack of oxygen. It is characterized by symptoms which include shortness of breath, fatigue, headaches, and *nausea. *See also* altitude sickness.

acute muscular soreness A *pain that occurs in muscles during and immediately following exercise. It is thought to be due to an inadequate blood flow to active muscle which results in the accumulation of metabolic waste products such as *lactic acid. *Compare* delayed onset muscular soreness.

acute pyelonephritis *See* pyelonephritis.

acute strain A *muscle strain usually resulting from a single violent force which forcibly stretches a contracting muscle. It occurs most commonly in muscles passing over two joints (*see* biarticulate muscle).

acute stressor A situation or condition which elicits an immediate and temporary physiological response in excess of that required to complete a task.

ad- A prefix used in anatomy that denotes to, next to, or towards.

Adam's apple (laryngeal prominence) A prominence at the front of the neck formed by *cartilage overlying the *thyroid gland.

adaptability The ability of an individual to adjust to different conditions. It is applied especially to a member of a sports team who can successfully modify his or her style of play to suit a number of different playing situations.

adaptation 1 A persistent change in structure or response to suit a change in conditions. In sport, adaptation applies especially to the *training effects of *overload, when the athlete's capacity for physical exertion is progressively increased. 2 In sociology, the manner in which any social system, such as a sports club or sporting body, responds to its environment in order to survive. 3 A decline in the transmission of a *sensory neurone when a receptor is stimulated continuously with a constant *stimulus strength; *see* sensory adaptation.

adaptation energy A hypothetical measure of an individual's capacity to resist stress. According to protagonists of the concept, each individual has a finite amount of adaptation energy which is used to cope with different forms of stress. If the adaptation energy is expended on activities such as staying up late, less energy will be available to cope with the demands of training, resulting in either a reduction in training or feeling *run-down.

adapted physical activity Exercise and sport performed by people with physical disabilities and/or severe learning difficulties.

adaptive achievement pattern Pattern of behaviour in which success is achieved through adapting to the environment. This is accomplished by developing new ways of coping with challenging situations; by actively seeking challenges and persisting in overcoming them; and through satisfaction felt in tackling challenges. Hence an adaptive achievement pattern of behaviour is an important factor in the making of a successful athlete.

adaptive learning *See* adaptive training.

adaptive training (adaptive learning) A form of *training which progresses from easier to more difficult task demands as the learner improves. Adaptive training may use equipment designed to provide automatic adjustments of task difficulty according to the learner's level of performance, with the learner's errors maintained at a constant level as difficulty varies.

addiction to exercise (exercise addiction; exercise dependence) Physiological or psychological dependence on a regular regime of exercise, characterized by unpleasant symptoms if withdrawal from exercise occurs. The addiction may be for any exercise, but is most commonly associated with running. The term is often used in a pejorative sense to imply that the individual has an uncontrollable craving for exercise which can damage his or her functioning in other activities. *See also* exercise adherence.

addictive drug A *drug, such as a *narcotic analgesic, for which a user may develop an uncontrollable craving. Continued use of an addictive drug can result in an increasing *tolerance to its effects, a physical dependence, and harmful effects on the user and *society.

Addison's disease A severe disorder of the *metabolism, caused by the degeneration of the *adrenal cortex and an inadequate secretion of *corticosteroid hormones. This results in impairment of sodium reabsorption from the *urine, *anaemia, weakness, and low *blood pressure.

additive principle The notion in sports psychology that *intrinsic motivation and *extrinsic motivation combine to create the *need for achievement. Recent research suggests that they are not necessarily additive, but that intrinsic motivation can decline with certain aspects of extrinsic motivation. *Compare* multiplicative principle.

adduct To move away from the midline of the body.

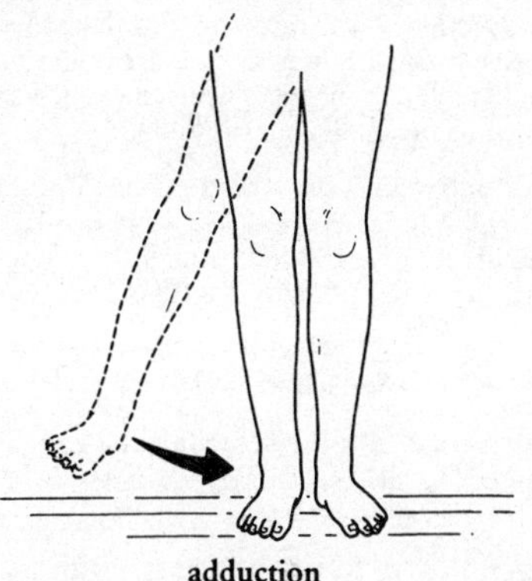

adduction

adduction A movement of a body-segment, such as an arm or leg, away from the midline of the body. The term also refers to the movement of fingers or toes when they move towards each other after being spread apart.

adductor brevis One of three *adductor muscles in the *thigh. The adductor brevis is a short muscle in the medial compartment which has its *origin on the main body and inferior ramus (lower border) of the *pubis, and its *insertion on the *linea aspera, above the insertion of the *adductor longus. The adductor brevis adducts and laterally rotates the thigh.

adductor longus The most anterior of the three *adductor muscles in the thigh. The adductor longus has its *origin near the *pubis symphysis and its *insertion on the *linea aspera. The adductor longus adducts, flexes, and laterally rotates the thigh.

adductor magnus One of the three *adductor muscles of the *thigh. The *origin of the adductor magnus has two parts, one on the *pubis and the other on the *ischial tuberosity. It has a broad *insertion on the *linea aspera and adductor *tubercle of the *femur. Its anterior portion adducts, laterally rotates, and flexes the thigh, moving the leg towards the midline of the body. Its posterior part is a *synergist of the *hamstrings in thigh extension.

adductor muscles 1 Muscles which cause *adduction. 2 The three anterior thigh muscles (*adductor brevis, *adductor longus, and *adductor magnus) which move the leg towards the midline of the body.

adductor muscle strain A muscle strain of the *adductor muscles; it particularly applies to the group in the thighs which pull the knees and thighs together. *See also* rider's strain.

adductors *See* adductor muscles.

adenine A nitrogen-containing base found in *DNA, *RNA, *ATP, and *NAD. It has a double-ringed structure.

adenohypophysis (anterior pituitary) A glandular, anterior part of the *pituitary gland.

adenoids *Lymph tissue in the back of the post nasal space. Adenoids may become enlarged and interfere with breathing. Enlarged adenoids are a cause of mouth breathing in track athletes and may contribute to poor *ventilation.

adenosine A *nucleoside occurring in *ATP and consisting of the *base, *adenine, and the sugar, ribose.

adenosine diphosphate (ADP) A *nucleotide containing *adenine, a *ribose sugar and two phosphate groups. ADP occurs in all cells and is involved in energy transformations.

adenosine monophosphate (AMP) A single *nucleotide consisting of the base, *adenine, *ribose (a sugar), and one phosphate group. AMP can be converted to *ADP and *ATP by the addition of one or two extra phosphate groups respectively. *See also* cyclic AMP.

adenosine receptor Neural receptors which use *cyclic AMP as an intracellular messenger. *See also* caffeine.

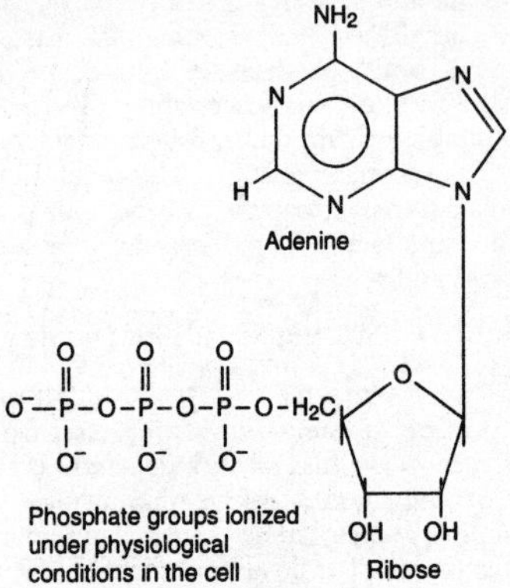

adenosine triphosphate

adenosine triphosphate (ATP) A *nucleotide containing *adenine, *ribose, and three phosphate groups. ATP is a complex organic compound formed from the addition of a phosphate group onto *adenosine diphosphate. The process is *endergonic, with the energy for the process being obtained from *respiration of food. ATP is stored in cells, especially muscle cells. The *hydrolysis of each molecule of ATP to ADP and inorganic phosphate is accompanied by the release of a relatively large amount of *free energy (34 kJ at pH 7) which is used to drive metabolic functions, including muscle contractions. An active cell needs more than 2 million ATP molecules per second to drive its biochemical machinery. The store of ATP in the body is sufficient to supply its needs for only a few seconds; therefore, it needs to be continuously replenished. ATP is the only form of energy which can be used directly by the cell for its activities.

ADH *See* antidiuretic hormone.

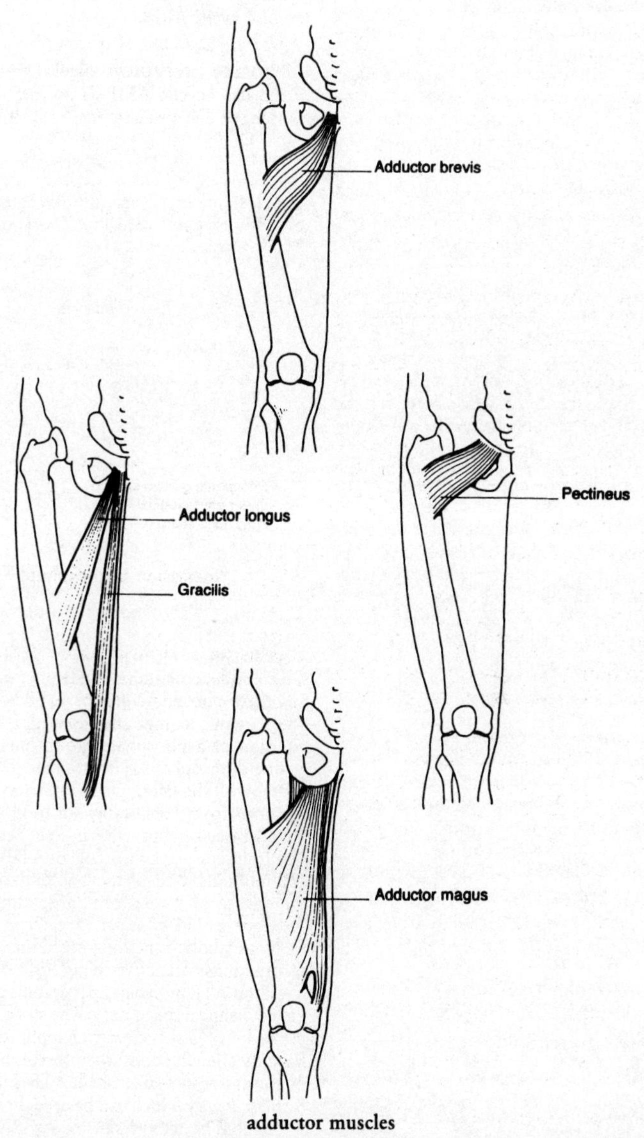

adductor muscles

adhesion 1 The sticking effect produced by forces between molecules of different materials. *Compare* cohesion. 2 An abnormal union of separate tissues, commonly as a result of *inflammation or *haemorrhage. Adhesions may involve the *synovial membranes of *joints, or form in and around *muscle. *Manipulation is often necessary to break down the adhesion and prevent the loss of normal function.

adipocyte (fat cell) A cell containing a glistening oil droplet composed almost entirely of *neutral fat. The droplet occupies most of the cell's volume, compressing the *nucleus to one side. Mature adipocytes are among the largest cells in the body. Although they can take up and release fat, becoming plumper or more wrinkled respectively, they are fully specialized for fat storage and are unable to divide.

adipose tissue Fairly loose *connective tissue containing large numbers of fat-storing *adipocytes which make up 90 per cent of the tissue. Adipose tissue is richly vascularized and has a high *metabolic activity. It may develop anywhere, but tends to accumulate in *subcutaneous tissue where it can act as a shock-absorber and insulator. Women tend to have more adipose tissue than men.

adiposis *See* liposis.

adolescence A period in the *life cycle between childhood and adulthood which begins after the *secondary sexual characteristics appear and continues until complete sexual maturity. It is a period during which bones are still growing and there is a high incidence of *epiphyseal injuries in contact sports. The physical changes are accompanied by important psychological changes relating particularly to the adolescent's self-concept. A sports coach needs to be very sensitive to both the physical and psychological changes taking place during this period.

ADP *See* adenosine diphosphate.

adrenal cortical hormones *Hormones secreted by the *cortex of the *adrenal glands. They include *aldosterone, *cortisol (*hydrocortisol), and *sex hormones, particularly the *androgens of both males and females.

adrenal cortex The outer part of the *adrenal glands.

adrenal glands (suprarenal glands) *Endocrine glands located superior to each *kidney. The inner part of the adrenal gland, the medulla, secretes the hormones *adrenaline and *noradrenaline, and its activity is controlled by the *sympathetic nervous system. The outer part, the cortex, secretes *adrenocorticoid hormones and its activity is controlled by *adrenocorticotropic hormone.

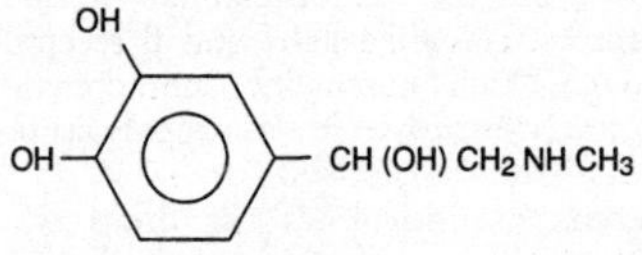

OH
OH
$CH(OH)CH_2NHCH_3$

adrenaline

adrenaline (epinephrine) A hormone secreted by the *medulla of the *adrenal gland. It has widespread effects on muscles, circulation, and *carbohydrate metabolism, preparing the body for action or what is commonly referred to as the 'fight or flight' response. Adrenaline increases *heart rate, depth and rate of breathing, and *metabolic rate. It also improves the force of muscular contractions and delays the onset of *fatigue. Adrenaline is a *stimulant which is on the *IOC list of *banned substances.

adrenal medulla The central part of the *adrenal gland which secretes *adrenaline and *noradrenaline.

adrenal virilism A condition found in females in whom the adrenal gland produces male hormones at high enough concentrations to give rise to considerable *masculinization. *Compare* testicular feminization.

adrenergic A *drug that exerts the same effect as *adrenaline.

adrenergic agonist *See* adrenergic stimulant.

adrenergic anatagonist A *drug (an *alpha blocker or *beta blocker) which blocks or inhibits the activity of *adrenoceptors.

adrenergic receptors *See* adrenoceptors.

adrenergic stimulant (adrenergic agonist; sympathomimetic amines) A *drug, such as *adrenaline, *noradrenaline, or *isoprenaline, that stimulates *adrenoceptors. Adrenaline and noradrenaline are sometims called stress hormones and prepare the body for action (e.g, when danger threatens or before competition). Their effects tend to improve the blood supply to the skeletal muscles.

adrenoceptors (adrenergic receptors) Two types of *catecholamine hormone receptors, classified as α and β receptors, through which *adrenaline, *noradrenaline, and the *sympathomimetic drugs exert their effects. The classification is based on the receptors' sensitivity to the drugs which stimulate them. Noradrenaline combines mainly with the α receptors and has little effect on β receptors; *adrenaline affects both equally.

adrenocorticotropic hormone (ACTH; adrenocorticotropin hormone; corticotropin) A *polypeptide *hormone, secreted by the anterior lobe of the *pituitary gland, that stimulates the production and release of hormones from the adrenal cortex. A *negative feedback mechanism ensures that secretion of ACTH is stimulated by a shortage of *corticosteroids in the blood and suppressed by a surfeit. *Stress stimulates the *anterior pituitary to secrete more ACTH and thus increase the secretion of *cortisol.

adsorption The taking up of a liquid or gas by a surface or interface. *Compare* absorption.

adult onset obesity *Obesity which first develops in adulthood. Individuals who become fat as adults usually have a normal number of fat cells (*see* adipocyte) but each fat cell is enlarged. Slimming leads to the fat cells returning to normal size. If an obese adult was obese as a child, he or she may have an excessive number of fat cells. Slimming then leads to the formation of abnormally small fat cells which have a tendency to fill up again until they reach normal size. Consequently, recurrence of obesity is significantly greater than among those who have sufferred adult onset obesity.

advancement The surgical detachment of a *muscle or *tendon and its reattachment further forward.

aerial perspective Change in depth perception of objects when viewed under different atmospheric conditions. Objects with clear details appear nearer than hazy objects.

aerobic Applied to conditions or processes which occur in the presence of, or requiring, oxygen.

aerobic capacity The total amount of *work that can be performed by the *aerobic energy system.

aerobic endurance The ability to sustain exercise that is predominantly *aerobic. The degree of aerobic endurance is reflected by the duration an *aerobic exercise can be performed.

aerobic energy system A *metabolic system involving a series of chemical reactions which require oxygen to breakdown food and produce *adenosine triphosphate. *See also* aerobic respiration.

aerobic exercise Relatively low intensity and long duration exercise using large muscle groups of the body and dependent on the *aerobic energy system. As the intensity of the exercise gets less and the duration gets longer, *fat becomes the preferred fuel. Aerobic exercise increases the body's demand for oxygen, thereby adding to the workload of the heart and lungs, and raising the heart rate. Such exercise, if performed regularly over an extended period of time, will strengthen the *cardiovascular system and help develop *endurance. Aerobic exercises include walking, jogging, swimming, cycling, and cross-country skiing. *See also* aerobic training.

aerobic fitness *See* cardio-respiratory endurance.

aerobic glycolysis *See* glycolysis.

aerobic power (aerobic work capacity) The maximum amount of energy that can be produced from the *aerobic energy system per unit time; that is, the rate at which energy is provided by *aerobic respiration. *Aerobic power is dependent on the ability of tissues to use oxygen to break down metabolic fuels, and the combined abilities of the various systems (*pulmonary, *cardiac, *vascular, and *cellular) to transport oxygen from the air to the *mitochondria. Aerobic power is usually measured in terms of oxygen consumption (*see* maximal aerobic power).

aerobic respiration Cellular *respiration requiring oxygen. Aerobic respiration involves *glycolysis, which takes place in the *cytoplasm; the *Kreb's cycle; and the *respiratory chain (including the *electron-transport system), which takes place in *mitochondria.

aerobics 1 A form of aerobic exercise popularized by Kenneth C. Cooper in the 1960s. He evaluated the demands of particular exercises for oxygen and their consequent effects on the heart and lungs. He then devised exercise programmes which have different point values dependent on their frequency, intensity, and duration. To develop *cardiovascular fitness, a person is expected to earn at least thirty points per week. 2 A type of *aerobic exercise consisting mainly of continuous *callisthenics performed to music.

aerobic threshold The minimum intensity of training below which there is no observable *training effect. The aerobic threshold is usually expressed as a percentage of a person's *maximal oxygen consumption or, more conveniently, as the *heart rate which correlates approximately with this percentage. Karvonen suggested the following formula for the heart rate at which the aerobic threshold is reached:

$$\text{THR} = 0.7(\text{max HR} - \text{resting HR}) + \text{resting HR}$$

where THR is the heart rate at the aerobic threshold; max HR is the maximum heart rate (taken as 220 – age); and resting HR is the heart rate at rest.

aerobic training Physical *training involving *aerobic exercises aimed at improving *aerobic capacity, *aerobic endurance, and *aerobic power. The minimum *training intensity which will usually result in an improvement requires an oxygen uptake of 50–55 per cent *maximal oxygen consumption which corresponds to approximately 70 per cent *maximum heart rate. The most effective training intensities are usually at 90–100 per cent maximal oxygen uptake, but sessions of long duration and low intensity can be as effective as those of shorter duration and high intensity. *See also* aerobic training zone.

aerobic training zone The range of *training intensities between an individual's *aerobic threshold and *anaerobic threshold. *See also* training heart rate.

aerobic work capacity *See* aerobic power.

aerodynamic drag force *See* air resistance.

aerodynamic force A *force acting on a body due to the relative motion between the air and the body.

aerodynamic lift The component of the total *aerodynamic force which acts perpendicular to the undisturbed flow of air past a body which has a lift-producing shape (*see* aerofoil), or past a spinning ball.

aerodynamics The mathematical and physical study of the *forces which affect the motion and control of a *body (e.g., a javelin or the human body) in air.

aerofoil A *body which has a surface shaped so that it produces *lift as air flows past it. The typical aerofoil shape is that of an aeroplane wing, but projectiles such as javelins also share this property.

aerophagia (aerophagy) A condition characterized by extensive swallowing of air.

aerophagy *See* aerophagia.

aerosol administration 1 A technique used to treat acute muscle injuries and involving the application of a spray from a pressurized can. The spray contains volatile compounds which evaporate on contact with the skin surface causing rapid chilling which may reduce *inflammation. 2 A method of administering *drugs in extremely small liquid or solid particles in a pressurized spray which is inhaled. The method is commonly used to administer drugs to individuals suffering from *asthma. The drug, such as *salbutamol, can be applied directly to the *bronchi and *bronchioles, thus reducing the risk of unwanted side-effects accompanying *systemic therapy.

aesthetic 1 Relating to pure beauty rather than other considerations. 2 Pertaining to *aesthetics.

aesthetic activities Activities, such as ice-skating, dance, and gymnastics, which have elements related to pure beauty rather than to other considerations.

aesthetic appreciation An emotional or mental response to beauty, or to something which is pleasing to the senses.

aesthetics The study of the nature of pure beauty.

aetiology A branch of *medicine dealing with the study of the cause, or causes, of a disease or injury.

affect An individual's emotional response to a situation. In sports psychology, it is often used synonymously with *emotion.

affective characteristics The emotional and temperamental characteristics, such as *confidence, which influence an individual's responses to a situation. They also include characteristics, such as the desire to learn, which are important in acquiring a *skill.

affective disorder Disorders of mood or *emotions such as excessive *anxiety and depression.

affective response The emotional response to a situation. The feeling of pride and satisfaction a person experiences when winning a competition and the feeling of disappointment on losing are examples of affective response.

affective sport involvement The emotional involvement of an individual in a sport which the individual does not play. It is typified by followers of a sport who experience mood changes when their teams win or lose.

afferent blood vessel A blood vessel which carries *blood towards an organ or tissue.

afferent nerve A *neurone which carries sensory impulses from a *receptor to the *central nervous system.

affiliation incentive A factor which motivates an individual to join a group. Affiliation incentives include opportunities to make friends and *personality traits, such as an individual's need to feel wanted.

aflatoxin A *toxin which may injure the liver if ingested in large quantities. Aflatoxin is produced by a *fungus (*Aspergillus flavus*) which grows on some crops including peanuts, wheat, corn, beans, and rice. It occurs especially in foods, such as muesli, which have been stored for a long time.

after discharge The continuation of the contraction of a muscle for a second or more after cessation of the *stimulus from an *afferent neurone. The afferent neurone has a network of connections with a number of *interneurones which transmit impulses along a number of different routes to the *motor neurone and then to the muscle. A strong stimulus results in impulses arriving at the *neuromuscular junction at different times, resulting in the muscle having a prolonged contraction.

after hyperpolarization The condition of a *neurone immediately following an *action potential when the potential difference across the membrane is reduced to a level lower than the *resting potential.

age 1 The period of time a person has lived. 2 A period or state of the human *life cycle. *See also* actuarial age; and chronological age.

ageing process A process accompanying an increase in *chronological age. Ageing is often associated with degenerative processes which include a reduction in muscle strength, weakening of the bones (*see* *osteoporosis), longer *reaction time, an increased difficulty in breathing, an increased tendency towards *obesity, and a decrease in both *aerobic capacity and *anaerobic capacity. A number of authorities believe that many of these degenerative processes may be due to habitual inactivity (*see* hypokinetic diseases) rather than disease or any irreversible process, and that regular physical exercise can retard the degeneration.

ageism 1 Any process or expression of ideas in which *stereotyping of and/or discrimination against people occurs by virtue of their age. Ageism applies particularly to such actions directed against older people, but the term may also be employed to refer to unreasonable discrimination against anyone where this occurs because of the person's *chronological age. 2 Values, beliefs, and norms that support the proposition that the value and capability of an individual is determined by the age group to which he or she belongs. Ageism also refers to the practices which support these beliefs, and leads to reduced expectations and opportunities for some age groups.

agency In sociology, a human action which is purposive and intentional, carried out at the volition of the individual or group concerned and not because of constraints imposed by social structure.

agglutin A type of *antibody causing *agglutination.

agglutination Clumping together of cells, usually resulting from the reaction between an *antigen and an *antibody; part of the body's defence system.

agglutinogen A surface *antigen that induces the formation of *agglutins.

aggregate A collection of individuals with no internal social structure or basis for persistence. *Compare* group.

aggression A form of *overt behaviour intended to harm a living person either physically or psychologically. It includes physical attacks and verbal abuse. The aggression may be against another person (extropunitive behaviour) or against oneself (intropunitive behaviour). It does not include unintentionally harming another person, or doing destructive violence to inanimate objects. Attempts at explaining aggression include the *frustration–aggression hypothesis, the *instinct theory, and the *social learning theory. *Compare* assertiveness. *See also* hostile aggression; and instrumental aggression.

aggression–approval proposition A proposition which suggests that aggressive behaviour (*see* aggression) and the results of such behaviour become more valuable the more they are rewarded. When an aggressive person receives rewards he or she expects, or does not receive the punishment he or she expects, the person will be more likely to repeat the behaviour.

agility The ability to change the position of the body in space rapidly and accurately without loss of balance. Agility is important in sports where obstacles or opponents have to be avoided (e.g., slalom events). It is recognized as a basic component of motor performance, but its exact nature has not been determined. Agility depends on muscular power, reaction time, co-ordination, and dynamic flexibility.

agonal contest A ritualized contest in which an individual or a team attempts to establish physical superiority over the opposition. Agonal contests offer the means of determining social rank, recognizing excellence, and according honour to an individual, an institution, or even a nation. The success of a national team in a world championship or the Olympic Games, for example, is held by many to reflect national character and to serve as an index of moral superiority. All sports are to some extent agonal contests, but the amount of honour won depends on many factors including the status and ability of the opponents, the importance of the contest to the peer group of the participants, and the value of the prize.

agonist 1 A prime mover muscle that, as a result of its active contraction, makes a major contribution to a particular joint movement. Some muscles are agonists for more than one action on two or more joints. The *biceps brachii, for example, is an agonist for *elbow flexion, radioulnar *supination, and several movements of the shoulder-joint. 2 A *drug that interacts positively with receptors to produce a response in a tissue or organ.

agranulocyte A type of *leucocyte which is nongranular and has a large spherical nucleus. Agranulocytes are produced in *lymph nodes and *bone marrow. They comprise about 30 per cent of all leucocytes and include *lymphocytes and *monocytes.

AIDS *See* acquired immune deficiency syndrome.

aim A skill-orientated ability in which a person aims a body part (e.g., a boxer jabbing with his fist) or a projectile at a target. Aiming underlies tasks in which the subject attempts to hit a target with a pencil or stylus using very quick movements. Such tasks have often been used to study motor control.

airfoils *See* aerofoils.

air force The *resultant of lift and *drag acting on a projectile as it is moving through the air.

air pollutants Substances, such as vehicle exhaust fumes or airborne industrial wastes, which reduce the quality or life-supporting capacity of the environment. High pollution levels adversely affect performances in endurance events, but little is known about the effects of pollutants on power events.

air resistance (aerodynamic drag force) Frictional forces which tend to reduce the speed of a body moving through the air and cause the body to fall to the ground before it has completed its parabolic flight path (*see* parabola). Air resistance increases with speed and lightness of the body. It is also increased by motions, such as the quivering of an arrow or spinning of a ball, when the motions are in a direction other than the direction of flight. Air resistance is affected by the surface covering and shape (*see* streamlining) of the body. *See also* drag; and fluid resistance.

airways Parts of the body through which air enters and leaves the *lungs.

akropodion *See* acropodion.

ala (pl. alae) Wing-like portion of the *ilium. Its thickened margin is called the iliac crest, which is the part of the hips on which one's hands are usually rested.

alactacid oxygen debt That portion of the recovery oxygen used to synthesize and restore the phosphagen stores (*ATP and *PC) in muscle following exercise. Most of the alactacid oxygen debt is paid off in the first few minutes after exercise. It has a *half reaction time of about 15 min and a size of approximately 2–3 l. It is independent of lactic acid removal. *Compare* lactacid oxygen debt.

alactic anaerobic system *See* ATP–PC system.

alanine A nonpolar, relatively insoluble *amino acid which occurs in two main forms: Laevorotatory-alanine, which is involved in *gluconeogenesis, and β-alanine, which is a component of *coenzyme A. Alanine production is increased in exercising muscle.

albumins Water-soluble, simple, *globular proteins that are the most abundant plasma proteins. Albumins occur in other tissue fluids including *synovial fluid. They transport materials and help maintain the *osmotic pressure of the blood.

alcohol Any of a large group of organic compounds derived from hydrocarbons in which the hydrogen atom has been replaced by a hydroxyl (–OH) group. The alcohol commonly used in drinks is ethyl alcohol (C_2H_5OH), a colourless, tasteless liquid formed during the fermentation of yeast. In medicine, alcohol has been used as a solvent (*see* tincture) and as an *antiseptic. It is rapidly absorbed into the bloodstream from the buccal cavity and stomach. After absorption, alcohol acts as a *depressant of the central nervous system, reducing feelings of *fatigue but also adversely affecting judgement, self-control, and concentration. Reactions are slowed and muscular coordination impaired. Alcohol is broken down in the liver into acetate, a potential energy substrate for cardiac and skeletal muscle, which has an energy value of about 7 kcal g^{-1}. Alcohol interacts harmfully with some drugs, including *antihistamines and *analgesics. A moderate intake of alcohol may reduce the risk of *coronary heart disease but excessive, chronic use may result in *cirrhosis of the liver, and harmful effects on the kidneys and heart. In sport, it has been used as a mild *tranquilizer by archers, and as an energy source by cyclists. Alcohol is banned from some sports venues (such as soccer grounds in Scotland) because of its association with crowd violence. It is not on the *IOC list of *banned substances, but breath or blood alcohol levels may be determined by governing bodies of particular sports and it is banned in certain sports including the modern pentathlon, fencing, and shooting. It is generally accepted that heavy drinking is not compatible with serious athletics.

aldosterone A *mineralocorticoid hormone, released from the adrenal cortex, which regulates the body's salt balance. Aldosterone increases the reabsorption of sodium and the secretion of potassium by the kidney tubules. It plays an important role in controlling the volume of body fluids. Aldosterone release is increased during and after exercise.

alertness A person's awareness of environmental *stimuli and the ability to respond quickly to those stimuli. Alertness is reflected by an increase in electrical activity of the *reticular formation and *cerbral cortex in the brain.

alfentanil A potent pain-killer belonging to the *narcotic analgesics and on the *IOC list of *banned substances.

algebraic sum (sum) The total number of quantities of the same kind with due regard to the positive or negative value of each quantity. Thus the algebraic sum of 2, –6, and –3 is –7.

algorithm of reflexes A set of *central nervous system reflexes which can produce a movement pattern after a period of training.

alienation 1 The process of being made to feel remote from a situation, *group, or *culture. 2 A sense of not belonging to a group.

alimentary canal (gut; enteric canal) The tubular passage extending from the mouth to the anus, differentiated into regions of *ingestion, *digestion, *absorption, and *egestion.

alkalaemia A reduction in the concentration of *hydrogen ions in the blood. *See also* alkalosis.

alkali A soluble *base or a solution of a base; it is often applied to any substance that has an alkaline reaction in solution (i.e., turns red litmus blue and neutralizes acids).

alkaline Having the properties of a *base or containing a base.

alkaline excess *See* base excess.

alkaline reserve *See* alkali reserve.

alkalinizer A substance, such as *sodium bicarbonate, that raises the *pH of the *blood. Alkalinizers are sometimes used prior to exercise in the belief that they will enhance performance by increasing resistance to lactic acid. They may, by raising pH, reduce the excretion of metabolic by-products of some *stimulants, thereby masking them.

alkali reserve (alkaline reserve) The amount of *base (mostly bicarbonate ions) available in the body for *buffering. The alkali reserve is a metabolic parameter used to estimate *acidosis induced by maximal exercise. A high alkali reserve is particularly important for athletes in sports which predominantly use the *lactacid system, producing high levels of lactic acid. Average values are between 22 and 26 mmol l^{-1}; lowest values (5–10 mmol l^{-1}) occur in middle- and long-distance runners. In sports medicine, the alkali reserve is also known as standard bicarbonate.

alkaloid A member of a group of nitrogen-containing compounds found in plants. They include *cocaine, *morphine, and *nicotine.

alkalosis A condition of abnormally high pH (pH > 7.45) or low hydrogen ion concentration in extracellular fluid. Alkalosis may cause an exaggerated reactivity of muscles which go into cramp-like spasms. *See also* metabolic alkalosis; and respiratory alkalosis.

allele (allelomorph) One of two or more different forms of the same *gene, only one of which is carried on a *chromosome.

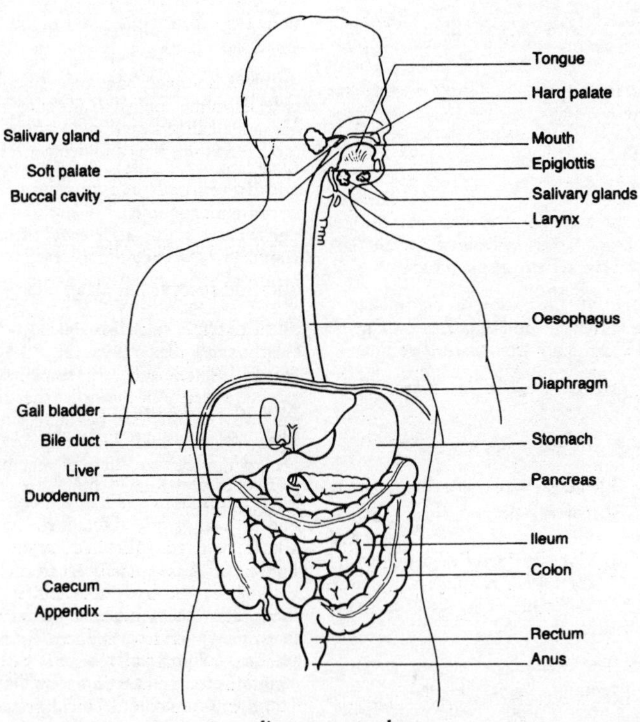

alimentary canal

allelomorph *See* allele.

allergen A substance, foreign to the body, that provokes an immune response. *See also* allergy.

allergic rhinitis *See* hay fever.

allergy An abnormal response of the skin or mucous membranes resulting from an overzealous *immune response and heightened sensitivity to a substance that is, in normal amounts, innocuous to the majority of people. Causes include house dust, fungi, and drugs. Of particular interest in sport is the susceptibility of some athletes to adhesive tape, antibiotics (such as penicillin), and *hay fever.

allometry The relationship between the rate of growth of one or more body-part with another part, or to the whole body. The relationships may be described by allometric equations which have been used to compare the functions of individuals of different sizes. For example, in Huxley's allometric equation ($\log Y = \log a - b \log X$), structural variables such as mass or stature are usually represented in the equation by X, with Y representing a functional variable such as *strength, *maximal aerobic power, or another performance measure. The obtained b values are then compared to theoretical expectancy (e.g., for a geometrical system in which size and shape are constant).

all-or-none law A law that states that certain structures, such as *neurones and *muscle fibres, either respond completely (all) or not at all (none) to a *stimulus. Thus there is no partial *nerve impulse or partial contraction of a muscle fibre. *Compare* graded potential.

allosteric enzyme An *enzyme which has its activity regulated by molecules other than its substrate, which bind to its *allosteric site. Such binding may inhibit or activate the enzyme.

allosteric inhibitor A substance which combines with the *allosteric site thereby inhibiting the activity of an *enzyme.

allosteric site A region on an *allosteric enzyme to which molecules other than the substrate can bind. *Compare* active site.

α-adrenoceptor blocker *See* alpha blocker.

α antagonist *See* alpha blocker.

alpha blocker (α antagonist; α adrenoceptor blocker) A *drug which is used in the treatment of *hypertension and other *vascular disorders. Alpha blockers inhibit *α receptors. Examples are indoramin, phentolamine, phenoxybenzamine, prazosin, and tolazoline.

α helix The twisted, helical configuration of a *polypeptide chain; it is a characteristic feature of fibrous proteins such as *collagen and *keratin. Successive turns are strengthened by *hydrogen bonds which make helically-coiled polypeptide chains more stable than untwisted ones.

α motor neurone A type of large, *efferent neurone that innervates *extrafusal fibres of *striated muscle.

α receptor (α adrenoceptor) An adrenoceptor which may be either an α_1 receptor, which when stimulated causes *vasoconstriction, or an α_2 receptor, which inhibits the release of *noradrenaline from postganglionic sympathetic nerve fibres.

altered state of consciousness A condition, different from the normal state of being awake, which may be induced by *hypnosis, *drugs, a *peak experience, or *fatigue. It can also be induced by *trauma (especially to the head), *hypoxia, and metabolic disorders.

altitude The vertical distance above sea level. A medium altitude is between 1829 m and 3048 m above sea level, and high altidude is over 3048 m above sea level. Altitude increases are associated with reduced barometric pressure and reduced oxygen partial pressure which lowers *aerobic capacity. Consequently, both medium and high altitude can adversely affect the performance of athletes in endurance sports, particularly those athletes accustomed to training and competing at sea level. Short-term *anaerobic capacity is not adversely affected by high altitude and the reduced air density may be beneficial to sprinters, jumpers, and throwers. *See also* altitude acclimatization; altitude-training.

altitude acclimatization Reversible physiological adaptations which improve a person's tolerance to the reduction in oxygen partial pressures at high *altitude. Early adaptations include *hyperventilation and increases in submaximal heart rate which raise the *cardiac output. Major long-term adaptations affecting the oxygen-carrying capacity of the blood include an increase in *haemoglobin content and *haematocrit, *polycythaemia, and a decrease in plasma volume. Effects on the muscle include an increases in capillarization, *myoglobin content, and *2,3-diphosphoglycerate concentration. There is also an increased secretion of excess base which reduces the buffering capacity of the blood. Acclimatization at medium altitudes takes about two weeks, but it may take much longer for high altitudes. Effects persist for about three weeks on return to sea level.

altitude hypoxia The lack of adequate oxygen due to the reduction in *oxygen partial pressure as *altitude increases.

altitude sickness (mountain sickness) A condition resulting from exposure to high *altitude, characterized by symptoms which include muscular weakness, headache, rapid pulse, *nausea, loss of appetite, feelings of lassitude, and possibly unconsciousness. Shortage of oxygen is the main cause. It can be fatal, and deaths attributed to altitude sickness occur each year in high mountain regions such as the Himalayas. Individuals differ in their susceptibility to altitude sickness, but nearly everyone suffers when a height of over 4900 m is reached. Symptoms are rapidly lost on return to a lower altitude.

altitude-training Training undertaken at moderately high altitudes in order to benefit from the effects of altitude *acclimatization and thus enhance performance in competitions. It is used particularly by athletes accustomed to low altitude conditions who are going to compete at higher altitudes. To be effective, the training must take place at least 1500 m above sea level and for a period of not less than three weeks, with the first week consisting of light exercise. It takes three to six weeks at sea level to lose all the training effects. Many athletes undertake altitude-training to improve performances in endurance events at low altitudes; opinion is divided as to its efficacy.

altruism Concern for the welfare of others rather than oneself. *Compare* egoism.

alveolar-arterial oxygen partial pressure difference The difference between the partial pressure of oxygen in the *alveolus and the mean arterial pressure of oxygen, measured in mmHg or kPa. It indicates efficiency of gaseous exchange in the lungs.

alveolar–capillary membrane The layer of *tissue dividing the *alveolus from the *pulmonary capillaries. It is the site of *gaseous exchange in the *lungs.

alveolar ventilation The volume of air which enters the *alveoli for *gaseous exchange. It is usually expressed as volume per minute and is given by: alveolar ventilation = (tidal volume − anatomical dead space) × respiratory frequency.

alveolus (pl. alveoli) A minute air-filled sac at the end of the finest divisions of the *bronchioles through which *gaseous exchange in the *lungs takes place. The wall of the alveolus is one cell thick and lined on the outside with *capillaries. Millions of alveoli occur in each lung to provide a very large surface area.

ambient Pertaining to the surrounding environment.

ambient temperature and pressure saturated *See* ATPS.

ambivalence A state of experiencing two opposing *emotions at the same time. It may be produced by being pulled psychologically in opposite directions by two *significant others. A coach may encourage an athlete to win at all costs, for example, while a parent encourages the athlete to believe that taking part and developing good *sporting behaviour is the most important consideration.

ambivert An individual who has neither pronounced *introvert or *extravert characteristics.

amblyopia (lazy eye) Poor vision which is not correctable with lenses. It may be due to an inability to focus with both eyes simultaneously, a condition known as lazy eye.

amenorrhoea Absence of periods (*see* menses). The condition is linked to *stress and loss of body fat. It is relatively common in middle- and long-distance female runners in whom it has been regarded as a harmless physiological variation of the gonadal rhythm; it does not affect long-term fertility. However, failure to menstruate for long periods is associated with changes in *oestradiol secretion and an increased risk of *stress fractures and *osteoporosis. Many questions remain to be answered regarding the long-term effects of amenorrhoea on the skeletal integrity of female athletes.

amfepramone A *drug, known in the USA as diethylpropion hydrochloride, which belongs to the *stimulants on the *IOC list of *banned substances.

amfetaminil A *drug belonging to the *stimulants on the *IOC list of *banned substances.

AMI *See* athletic motivation inventory.

amiloride A *drug belonging to the *diuretics which are on the *IOC list of *banned substances.

amino acids Organic compounds with two important functional groups: an amine group ($-NH_2$) and an organic acid group

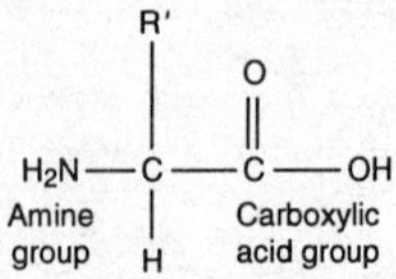

$$\begin{array}{c} R' \\ | \\ H_2N - C - \overset{O}{\overset{||}{C}} - OH \\ | \\ H \end{array}$$

Amine group — Carboxylic acid group

amino acid

(–COOH). There are about 80 naturally occuring amino acids, but only about 20 are used as the building blocks of *proteins. They come in two forms: *essential amino acids and *non-essential amino acids. Amino acids may be important respiratory substrates during endurance exercises, but they probably supply no more than 10 per cent of the total energy demands. Some amino acids, such as *γ-aminobutyric acid and glutamate function as *neurotransmitters.

amino acid supplements Pure, single amino acids (free amino acids) taken in the belief that they will act as an *ergogenic aid. It has been claimed, with little evidence, that at least two amino acids, arginine and ornithine, increase the secretion of *growth hormone.

aminophylline A water-soluble *drug belonging to the *methyl xanthines and related to *caffeine. It is a derivative of *theophylline and has been used as a *bronchodilator to relieve *asthma attacks. It is not on the *IOC list of *banned substances although it can have harmful side-effects on the cardiovascular system.

amiphenazole A *drug which belongs to the *stimulants on the *IOC list of *banned substances.

ammonium carbonate A salt of ammonia found in smelling salts (used as a restorative from fainting).

ammonium salts (smelling salts) A group of salts derived from ammonia. They are used as mild *diuretics and *stimulants.

amnesia Loss of memory. Amnesia can occur after a blow to the head during a contact sport such as boxing.

amortization phase The phase during which a limb is being forced to yield prior to the *amortization point. The duration of the amortization phase is critical to the efficient contribution of the combined forces from contractile and elastic components of the limb.

amortization point The point, during the movement of a limb (such as that of the take-off leg in the high-jump) at which *eccentric contraction stops prior to *concentric contraction.

AMP *See* adenosine monophosphate.

amphetamines (pep pills, uppers, speed) A group of *drugs belonging to the *stimulants. Amphetamines include dextroamphetamine, methamphetamine, methyl phenidate, and phenmetrazine. Although their effects are inconsistent, amphetamines act as powerful stimulants on the *central nervous system producing feelings of euphoria, aggression, and alertness which may be achieved at the expense of judgement and self-criticism. They suppress feelings of hunger and are components of some slimming pills. Amphetamines tend to increase *metabolic rate, *cardiac output, *blood pressure, *blood glucose levels, and *arousal. Claims that they produce an improvement in athletic performance have not been supported by scientific evidence. They are potentially very harmful. Administration may be followed by severe bouts of depression and dependence. Several fatalities have been attributed to the ability of amphetamines to suppress feelings of fatigue, permitting individuals to over-exert themselves to the point where they suffer *heat stroke and cardiac failure.

amphiarthrodial joint *See* amphiarthrosis.

amphiarthrosis (amphiarthrodial joint) A body *joint in which movement is very limited, as in the case of the *vertebral column where movement is accomplished by the compression of *intervertebral discs. *See also* pubic symphysis; and sacroiliac joint.

amplitude The maximum displacement from a zero or equilibrium position of an alternating quality, such as a vibration.

ampoule A small vessel one end of which is drawn out into a point and which is capable of being sealed for the storage of sterile solutions, such as medications used for injection.

amygdala Structure in the *limbic system of the *brain thought to control *motivation and *emotion.

amylase A digestive *enzyme that breaks down starch or glycogen to glucose, dextrin, or maltose in the alimentary canal. Amylases occur in saliva and the pancreatic juice.

anabolic steroids A class of synthetic *drugs related in structure and activity to the male hormone *testosterone, but which have less androgenic effects (*compare* androgenic steroid). Anabolic steroids are taken in tablet form, or by intramuscular injection, to improve muscle strength, power, and size. They encourage retention of nitrogen, potassium, and phosphate, increase protein synthesis, and decrease amino acid breakdown. They may also increase tolerance to hard training by improving tissue repair and tolerance to fatigue. Doped athletes may also feel stronger, more agressive, and more confident. Among teenagers and children, the use of anabolic steroids can adversely affect skeletal growth, leading to premature fusion of the *epiphyses. In adults, anabolic steroids may produce psychological changes, liver damage, and cardiovascular malfunctions. In males, use may reduce the size of the testes and affect sperm production. In females, use may cause *masculinization. Anabolic steroids are responsible for much drug abuse in sport. They are on the *IOC list of *banned substances.

anabolism Chemical reactions in the body concerned with the synthesis of large molecules from small ones, as in body-building, growth, and repair. Such anabolic reactions require energy. *Compare* catabolism. *See also* metabolism.

anaemia A condition in which the amount of *haemoglobin in the blood or the number of red blood cells is below the normal range for a healthy population of comparable age and sex. The standard varies according to country, but in women it is normally greater than 12 grams per decilitre and in men greater than 13.0 grams per decilitre. Anaemia may result in a reduced oxygen-carrying ability of the blood (*see* sports anaemia) and is characterized by tiredness, shortness of breath, and headaches. *See also* iron-deficiency anaemia; and sickle-cell anaemia.

anaerobic Applied to conditions or processes not requiring oxygen; in the absence of oxygen.

anaerobic capacity The total amount of *energy that can be obtained from the *anerobic energy systems, (the combined capacity of the *phosphagen system and the *lactacid system).

anaerobic capacity test A test of the ability of an individual to undertake anaerobic exercise using the *phosphagen system and the *lactacid system. *See also* intermediate anaerobic tests; long-term anaerobic tests; and short-term anaerobic tests.

anaerobic energy systems Metabolic systems which manufacture *adenosine triphophate without the need for oxygen. *See also* ATP–PC system; and lactic acid system.

anaerobic exercise Exercise of short duration that requires the use of *carbohydrates, particularly *muscle glycogen, but does not depend on the availability of oxygen. Anaerobic exercises include weight-lifting, sprinting, and throwing.

anaerobic glycolysis The incomplete breakdown of *carbohydrate to form *pyruvic acid. During anaerobic respiration, there is a net production of only two molecules of *adenosine triphosphate for each molecule of *glucose. *See also* lactic acid system.

anaerobic power The maximum amount of *energy that can be generated by the *anaerobic energy systems per unit time.

anaerobic power tests Tests which measure the explosive power of an individual. They include the *Margaria staircase test, the *Sargent jump, and the *Wingate anaerobic power test.

anaerobic respiration *Respiration not requiring oxygen. *See* ATP–PC system; and lactacid system.

anaerobic tests *See* anaerobic capacity tests; and anaerobic power tests.

anaerobic threshold (AT) The level of activity at which the *aerobic energy system can no longer supply most of the demands of the body for *adenosine triphophate. As the intensity of activity increases above the threshold, an individual becomes increasingly dependent on *anaerobic respiration. A number of different methods have been used to determine the anaerobic threshold, such as measuring changes in *minute ventilation and *blood lactate levels, but these methods have not been standardized. However, all methods indicate that the threshold is higher in endurance-trained athletes than untrained people.

anaerobic training zone A range of training intensity, commonly taken as being above the *anaerobic threshold, for developing *cardiovascular fitness using anaerobic exercises.

anaesthetic A substance that produces partial or complete loss of sensation either in a restricted area (regional and *local anaesthetics) or in the whole body (general anaesthetic). Use of local anaesthetics are permitted by the *IOC, but only under certain conditions, the details of which must be submitted in writing to the *IOC Medical Commission. Only local or intra-articular injections may be administered. *Cocaine must not be used.

analeptic A *drug used to stimulate the nervous system and restore consciousness to a patient in a coma or a faint. Analeptics act mainly on the cardiac and respiratory regulatory mechanisms. They include *adrenaline, *caffeine, *camphor, *ephedrine, and *strychnine.

anal fissure Crack-like sore in the anal region. Causes include constipation resulting from dehydration and trauma. Anal fissures do not preclude physical activity, but they may cause problems to horse-riders and cyclists. Anal fissures are painful and bleed moderately.

analgesia Reduced sensitivity to a normally painful stimulus, with no loss of consciousness. Analgesia can be induced by hypnosis or an *analgesic.

analgesic *Drug used as a pain-killer. Analgesics can be taken orally or, in some cases, as a *local anaesthetic by injection. Analgesics are subclassified into *narcotic analgesics, such as *morphine, and *non-narcotic analgesics, such as *aspirin and *paracetemol.

analogue A *drug which differs in minor aspects of molecular structure from its parent drug. Analogues may be synthesized so that they have more potent effects, less side-effects, or are more difficult to detect than the parent drug.

analogy A comparison, (e.g., between social phenomena or events and mechanical phenomena or events) made to show a degree of similarity, but not an exact identity, between the events or phenomena.

analyser The left *cerebral hemisphere which, in sport, is concerned with the learning of new skills, correcting flaws in technique, and developing strategy. The term is based on an oversimplified idea that the cerebral hemispheres of the brain exhibit a division of labour between the left and right sides. *Compare* integrator.

analysis An explanation of a process or phenomenon in terms of its component parts. Analysis of chemicals, such as *drugs, involves breaking down the substance in order to determine the kinds of constituents present (qualitative analysis) or the amount of each constituent (quantitative analysis).

analysis of variance (ANOVA) A statistical technique for analysing the total variation of a set of observations as measured by the *variance of the observations multiplied by their number. Analysis of variance is used to determine whether the differences between the *means of several sample groups are statistically significant.

anamnesis (case-history) A statement of the past history of a particular person's injuries or diseases. Anamnesis acts as an important starting point in the diagnosis of many *sports injuries.

anaphylactic shock An immediate over-reaction of the *immune system, following the administration of a *drug or other agent, in an individual who has been previously exposed to the drug and who has produced *antibodies to that drug. Anaphylactic shock is characterized by *nausea, lowered *blood pressure, irregular heart beat, vomiting, and difficult breathing. It may lead to coma or death. *See also* anaphylaxis.

anaphylaxis A hypersensitivity exhibited in certain people to some substances (e.g., injected foreign material). The condition commonly results in pain, swelling, feverishness and general prostration. A slight form of anaphylaxis occurs in individuals who suffer from nettle rash (*see* urticaria) or *asthma, and similar symptoms occur in those who take some food of which their system is intolerant. A potentially fatal, acute form of anaphylaxis is called *anaphylactic shock.

anastomosis (pl. anastomoses) 1 A union or joining of *blood vessels or other tubular structures. Anastomosis usually refers to the direct connection between arteries, veins, venules, and arterioles without any intervening capillaries. If an artery is blocked with a blood clot, anastomoses form a collateral circulation which enables other arteries to take over the blocked artery's work. If no anastomoses exist, the tissue beyond the artery is likely to die. *Endurance-training is believed to increase the anastomoses of *coronary arteries. 2 A surgical union of two tubular structures, usually by sutures or staples.

anatomical dead space (respiratory dead space) The volume of air that remains in the respiratory passages (nose, mouth, pharynx, trachea, bronchi, and bronchioles) during *ventilation and which does not participate in *gaseous exchange. A typical resting value for the anatomical dead space is 150 ml. *See also* dead space.

anatomical landmark *See* landmark.

anatomical position Position of an individual standing upright with feet together, arms hanging by the side with palms facing forwards and the thumbs pointed away from the body.

anatomical short leg Condition in which one leg is shorter than the other. As with *functional short leg, it can cause complications such as *lower back pain and joint dysfunctions.

anatomical snuffbox The triangular area formed when the thumb is extended and defined laterally by the raised *tendons of the *abductor pollicis longus and the *extensor pollicis brevis, and medially by the *extensor pollicis longus.

anatomical task analysis The analysis of the role of different muscle groups in a specific movement or *motor skill.

anatomy The science dealing with the form and arrangement of body-parts.

anconeus Short, triangular arm *muscle closely associated with the *distal end of the *triceps brachii on the *posterior of the *humerus. It has its *origin on the *lateral epicondyle of the *humerus and its *insertion on the lateral aspect of the *olecranon process. The anconeus *abducts the *ulna during forearm *pronation and it acts as a *synergist of the triceps brachii during *elbow extension.

androcentrism A tendency towards male bias in institutions, or generally to disregard the female contribution to society and culture.

androgen Any substance, such as *testosterone and some *steroid drugs, which promotes the development of male secondary characteristics.

androgenic Pertaining to an *androgen.

androgenic steroid A *drug belonging to the *steroids which has strong masculinizing effects (see masculinization). *See also* chorionic gonadotrophin.

androgenital syndrome *See* masculinization.

androgyny A condition in which an individual possesses both masculine and feminine sex-role perceptions or characteristics. *See also* BEM sex-role inventory; and personal attribute questionnaire.

android fat distribution The distribution of *adipose tissue, predominantly around the abdomen and trunk, and within the abdominal cavity. Excess fat of this type is often called 'apple-shaped' obesity and is far more common in obese males than in females. Regardless of the level of obesity, this type of fat storage carries an increased risk of *diabetes and heart disease. *Compare* gynoid fat distribution.

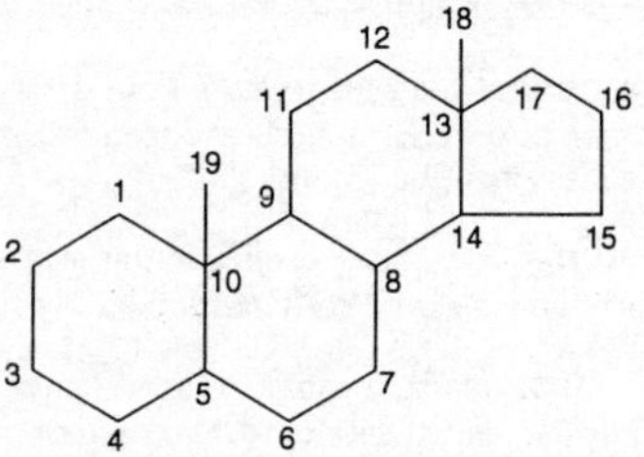

androstane

androstane A *steroid drug which is closely related to *testosterone. The structure of androstane is used as a reference when naming most compounds related to, or derived from, testosterone.

androstenedione A *steroid produced with *testosterone in the *testis. It is also formed in the liver by the metabolism of testosterone. Androstenedione has weaker *anabolic and *androgenic actions than testosterone.

androsterone A *steroid which is formed by the breakdown of *testosterone in the liver and is present in plasma and urine. It has a relatively weak androgenic action.

androsterone

aneurine *See* vitamin B_1.

aneurysm A baloon-like, blood-filled sac in an *artery wall that exposes the artery to the risk of rupture. It may reflect weakening of an artery by chronic *hypertension, *arteriosclerosis, infection, or *trauma. An aneurysm may also occur in a vein or ventricle after *myocardial infarction.

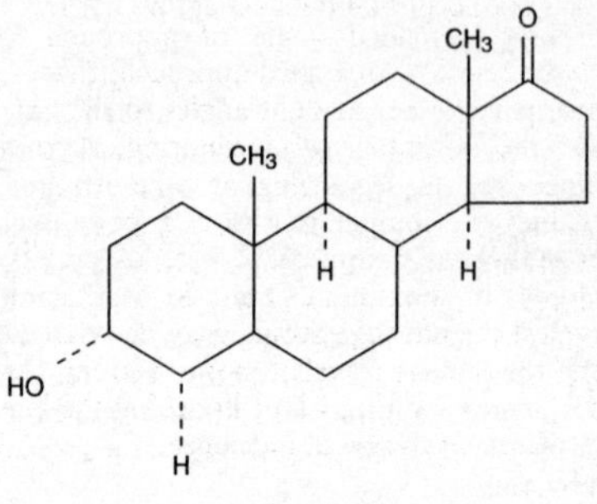

anger A strong feeling of displeasure or antagonism which is often elicited by a sense of injury or insult, and coupled with a desire to retaliate.

anger self-report test A *Likert-type questionnaire (*see* Likert-type scale) which yields separate scores for awareness of anger, expression of anger, guilt, condemnation of anger, and mistrust.

angina pectoris A pain in the chest which sometimes extends down the left arm; it is induced by increases in physical exertion and relieved by rest. The pain usually lasts about 15 min. Angina results from a reduced oxygen supply to the heart muscle and is a symptom of *coronary heart disease. A controlled programme of physical activity can be of benefit to angina sufferers, provided it is performed under medical supervision and is at a safe level. The appropriate level is usually determined by the subject exercising on a *cycle ergometer or a treadmill in the presence of a doctor.

angiotensin A substance circulating in the blood which reacts with *renin to raise *blood pressure.

angle The space between two intersecting lines or *planes; measured in *degrees or *radians.

angle of approach 1 The angle, in relation to the horizontal plane, of the paths taken by two bodies before they collide. 2

The direction of approach of an athlete about to perform a jump. For high-jumpers, the recommended angle of approach is about 20–30°. An angled approach (that is, one which is not at right angles to the bar) has the advantage of facilitating a great range of free leg swing at take-off, and enables the jumper to throw a body-part over the bar before the centre of gravity reaches its maximum point. At very acute angles, the effective spring may be reduced and the jumper travels too much along the bar, increasing the risk of knocking the bar off. *Compare* angle of incidence.

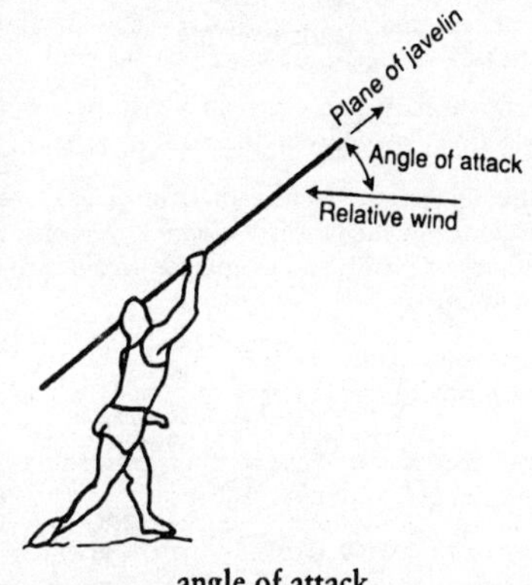

angle of attack

angle of attack The angle between the direction of relative flow of a fluid and the main plane of a body moving through the fluid. The angle of attack affects both *lift and *drag. No angle of attack combines maximum lift and minimum drag; a zero angle produces minimum drag but zero lift; lift is increased as the angle of attack increases, until a critical angle is reached (*see* stall angle) when drag exceeds lift and the object stalls. *See also* lift:drag ratio.

angle of entry The angle between the path of a body before impact and the surface with which it collides. It theoretically equals the *angle of rebound.

angle of gait During locomotion, the angle formed by a line drawn from the midpoint of the *calcaneus to the midpoint of the second toe of the same foot, and the line of progression.

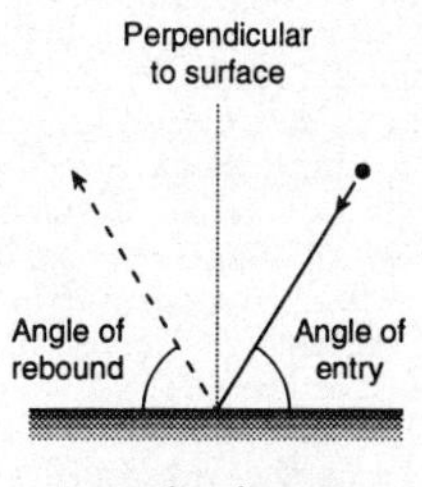

angle of entry

angle of impact The angle between the tangent to the flight path of a projectile at the point of impact, and the plane tangent to the struck surface at the point of impact.

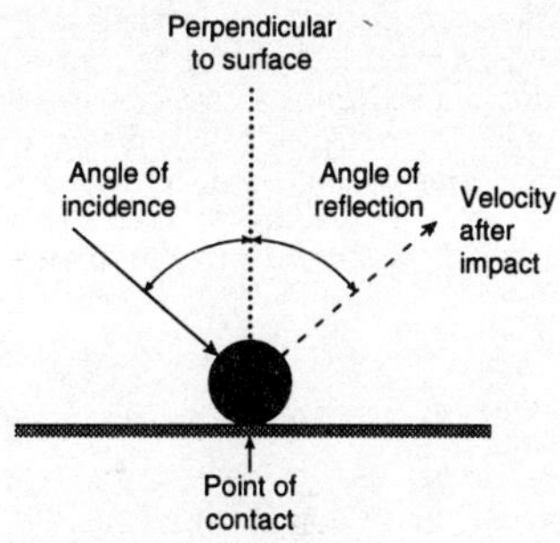

angle of incidence

angle of incidence The angle, in relation to the vertical, at which two bodies collide. When applied to the behaviour of colliding bodies, it is the angle formed by the direction in which the body is travelling before impact with a surface, and the line perpendicular to that surface at the point of impact. *Compare* angle of reflection.

angle of projection (angle of take-off) The angle between the line of flight of a projectile and the horizontal. For the projectile, it is the angle of the *centre of gravity's *instantaneous velocity vector at release, measured in relation to a stated frame of reference, usually the horizontal plane.

angle of pull The angle formed between the line of pull of a muscle and the long axis of the bone which the muscle moves. The angle of pull is usually indicated by the joint angle and it is a crucial factor in the strength of a muscular contraction: at only certain angles of pull can the muscle exert maximum *tension. Some weight-training machines have *variable resistance exercise machines which compensate for variations in muscular tension at different joint angles. *See also* Q-angle.

angle of rebound The horizontal angle between the surface with which a body collides and the path of rebound. It is theoretically equal to the *angle of entry.

angle of reflection **1** For colliding bodies, the angle that the direction of *velocity makes with the perpendicular to the surface at the point of impact. **2** When applied to the behaviour of balls, it is the angle formed by the direction in which the ball is travelling after impact with a surface, and the line perpendicular to that surface at the point of impact. *Compare* angle of incidence. **3** The angle between a ray of light reflected from a surface, and the *normal to the surface at that point.

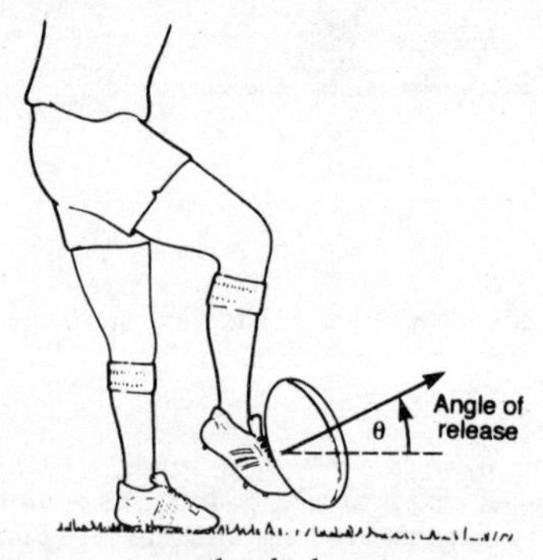

angle of release

angle of release The angle, relative to the ground, at which a body is projected into the air. The angle of release is an important factor affecting the flight path of a projectile. For any given speed of release, the angle of release which produces maximum horizontal displacement is 45 degrees, assuming the release and landing occur at the same vertical height, and that there is no spin or air resistance. In sport, the most common angles of release are between 35 and 45 degrees because of the affects of *height of release, aerodynamic effects, and *air resistance.

angle of stall *See* stall angle.

angle of take-off *See* angle of projection.

angstrom (Å) A unit of length equal to 10^{-10} m. Ten angstroms equal one nanometre.

angular acceleration The rate at which *angular velocity changes with respect to time. Angular acceleration = (final angular velocity – initial angular velocity) / time.

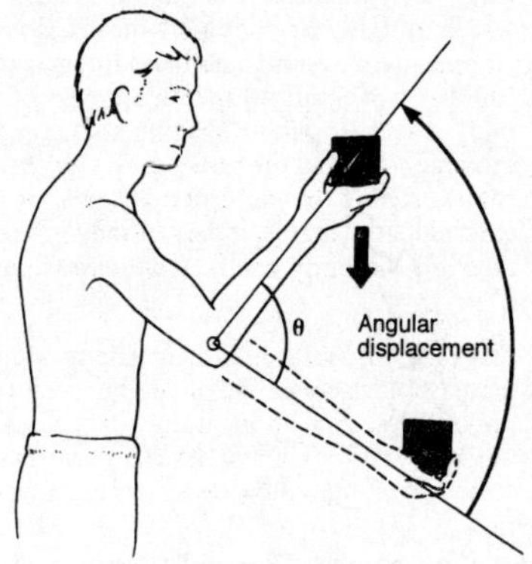

angular displacement

angular displacement **1** The angle through which a point, line, or body has been rotated in a specific direction about a specific *axis. It is designated by the Greek letter theta (θ). **2** The smaller of the two angles between a rotating body's initial position and its final position. The angle is measured in *radians and is described as being positive if the rotation is clockwise and negative if the rotation is anticlockwise.

angular distance **1** The angle described by the path taken between the intitial position and the final position of a body. **2** The distance between two bodies, measured in terms of the *angle subtended by them at the point of observation.

angular equilibrium *See* equilibrium

angular impulse The product of *torque and its time of application. *See also* impulse.

angular momentum The product of the *moment of inertia of a rotating body, or a system of bodies, about the *axis of rotation and the *angular velocity about that *axis. It is a *vector, possessing both magnitude and direction. The angular momentum of a system remains constant (*see* conservation of angular momentum); therefore, if the moment of inertia is changed, the rate of rotation, indicated by angular velocity, also changes. Angular momentum is an important concept in analysing turning movement in sport.

angular motion A form of motion in which a *body or body part moves along a circular path about some fixed line in space (the *axis of rotation) so that all parts of the body travel through the same angle, in the same direction, in the same time. The axis of rotation may be an internal axis or an external axis (that is, it may or may not pass through the body itself). *Compare* translation.

angular movements Movements which increase or decrease the angle between two bones. They can occur along any *plane of the body and include *flexion, *extension, *abduction, *adduction, and *circumduction.

angular speed A measure of how fast a *body, rotating around an *axis, is changing its angular position. The average angular speed is obtained by dividing the *angular distance through which the body rotates by the time taken: $w = \theta/t$, where θ = angular distance and t = time taken in seconds.

angular velocity The rate of *angular displacement of a rotating body in a specified direction (either clockwise or anticlockwise as determined by the *right-hand thumb rule). Angular velocity is measured in *degrees, *radians, or *revolutions per unit time; average angular velocity = angular displacement/time.

angular vibration A form of motion which occurs along the arc of a circle, such as the motion of a gymnast during a giant swing on a high-bar.

angulus inferior The *inferior angle of the *shoulder-blade. It is the *origin of the *teres major muscle.

anhydrosis (anidrosis) A condition characterized by the absence, or abnormal diminution, of sweating. Anhydrosis may occur as part of the failure of the normal thermoregulatory mechanisms, and result in *hyperthermia and *heat-stroke.

anidrosis *See* anhydrosis.

animal fats *See* saturated fats.

animal starch *See* glycogen.

anion An *ion carrying one or more negative charges and therefore attracted to a positive pole.

ankle The whole region in and around the *ankle-joint, including the *distal part of the *tibia and *fibula, and the *tarsus.

ankle-bones *See* tarsus.

ankle dorsiflexors Muscles of the anterior compartment of the lower leg which effect *dorsiflexion. They include, in descending order of importance, the *tibialis anterior, the *extensor hallucis longus, the *extensor digitorum longus, and the *peroneus tertius.

ankle evertors Muscles which effect ankle *eversion. They are, in descending order of importance, the *peroneus longus, the *peroneus brevis, the *peroneus tertius, and the *extensor digitorum longus.

ankle girth The circumference of the narrowest part of the lower leg, *superior to the *sphyrion. *See also* body girths.

ankle injuries The ankle is particularly susceptible to *sports injuries since the stresses and strains of balancing, checking, turning, and running are all focused there. It is second only to the knee in vulnerability. *See also* footballer's ankle; and Fosbury flop ankle.

ankle instability A predisposition for *fractures, *dislocations, and *sprains in the ankle-joint.

ankle invertors Muscles which effect ankle *inversion. They include the *tibialis anterior (the *prime mover), the *extensor hallucis longus, the *flexor digitorum longus, and the *flexor hallucis longus.

ankle-joint A synovial hinge-joint (*see* synovial joint) formed by the *tibia and *fibula articulating with the *talus. The ankle-joint is *diarthrotic and performs *uniaxial movements.

ankle-joint mortice The articular surface of the ankle-joint, formed by the *tibia and *fibula, that engages with the *talus.

ankle-sprain A soft-tissue injury of the ankle common in sports. It is often caused by the foot turning over and tearing the lateral *ligaments (inversion injury). Ankle-sprains are characterized by pain on movement and engorgement of the soft tissues with fluid in and around the joint. *See also* internal sprain; and sprain.

ankle-swelling The engorgement of the ankles with *lymph or other fluid following joint injury. Ankle-swelling may also be associated with other problems such as heart or kidney disease.

ankylosing spondylitis A *collagen disorder in which the vertebrae become squared and connected by fibrous tissue, causing the spine to become rigid (known as bamboo spine). Ankylosing spondylitis usually begins in the *sacroiliac joints and progresses superiorly up the spine. It is a disease which mainly affects young men between the ages of 20 and 40. It is characterized in the early stages by lower back-pain which is relieved by exercise and *non-steroidal anti-inflammatory drugs, and is aggravated by rest. Physiotherapy, including development of good *posture, constitutes an essential part of the treatment. *See also* spondylosis

ankylosis Loss of movement in a joint, usually from *arthritis, but also from *sports injuries such as *fractures which involve the *joint surfaces. During the healing of the fracture, the moving parts may fuse together with the broken parts. Ankylosis may also result from prolonged immobility. Good rehabilitation includes keeping the joints supple.

annulus fibrosus The outer ring of *fibrous cartilage in an *intervertebral disc.

anode Positive electrode towards which *anions are attracted.

anodyne Treatment or medication which tends to soothe and ease *pain or discomfort.

anomie A social condition, affecting individuals or society, in which a lack of moral or social direction leads to a loosening of the moral framework and the breakdown of *norms governing social interactions.

anorectic agent *See* anorexiant drug.

anorexia nervosa (anorexia) A potentially fatal illness, on the increase in western societies, in which there is a loss of appetite or desire for food. Although it can affect adults, both male and female, it occurs most frequently in adolescent girls and is usually accompanied by a distorted body image. Sufferers sometimes go to great lengths to restrict eating and to lose weight because they perceive themselves as being obese. Anorexia nervosa may also be associated with an inability to accept growth into adulthood, or a desire to be autonomous. The persistent anorexic becomes malnourished, suffers a variety of medical complications (including hair-loss and *amenorrhoea), and is at risk of death due to starvation. Anorexia nervosa may be preceded by eating disorders such as *bulimia. Gymnasts, cheerleaders, and dancers are prone to anorexia nervosa because of pressures on them to remain slim. The illness requires medical treatment and may respond to psychotherapy.

anorexiant drug (anorectic agent) A *drug that reduces the *appetite through an action on the *central nervous system. Anorexiants, such as *amphetamines and other *sympathomimetic amines, are sometimes included in slimming tablets. They should only be used under strict medical supervision. Dexfenfluramine has been used successfully in the treatment of obesity.

ANOVA *See* analysis of variance.

anoxia A state in which there is an inadequate oxygen supply to the tissues of the body. *Compare* hypoxia.

anoxic conditions Conditions in which there is an absence of oxygen.

antacid A medicine that neutralizes the hydrochloric acid in the *gastric juices or corrects general acidity.

antagonist 1 A *muscle that opposes or reverses the action of another muscle. Antagonistic muscles may also help regulate the action of an *agonist by partially contracting to provide some resistance, helping to prevent damaging overload, or to slow or stop the action. **2** A *drug that occupies a receptor site without producing a response, but which prevents the action of *endogenous substances or an *agonist drug.

antebrachial In anatomy, pertaining to the *forearm.

antecubital In anatomy, of, related to, or near the front (anterior) of the *elbow.

anterior (ventral) The front of a person, an *organ, or a part of the body.

anterior compartment A muscle *compartment of the lower leg which contains the *tibialis anterior, *extensor digitorum longus, *external hallucis longus, and *peroneus tertius.

anterior compartment syndrome (anterior tibial syndrome) A potentially dangerous form of *shin splints characterized by feelings of severe pain and burning with swelling, *erythema, and *induration at the front of the lower leg. Its exact cause is debated but it may result from muscle hypertrophy following prolonged training. The anterior tibial compartment is bounded medially by the *tibia and laterally by the *fibula, posteriorly by the posterior *interosseus membrane, and anteriorly by the *deep fascia. All of these are ungiving structures. During exercise or *trauma, increased blood flow or muscle swelling and *oedema lead to an increase in the pressure of the compartment and potential *ischaemia. Anterior compartment syndrome requires radical treatment: elevation, compression (bandages and massage), and anti-inflammatory and *diuretic drugs to increase urine flow and reduce *interstitial fluid. If very severe, acute surgery may be necessary to divide muscle fascia and give the enlarged muscle more space, thereby preventing the muscle from dying for want of oxygen.

anterior crest *See* tibia.

anterior cruciate ligament A major *ligament which attaches the *femur to the *tibia. It passes posteriorly, laterally, and upward from the *anterior intercondylar area to the medial surface of the lateral *condyle of the femur. It prevents backward sliding of the femur and overextension of the knee. It is lax when the knee is flexed and taut when the knee is extended. *See also* cruciate ligament.

anterior fascial compartment of forearm A *compartment in the forearm which contains muscles acting on the *wrist and fingers. The muscles are the *brachioradialis, *flexor carpi radialis, *flexor carpi ulnaris, *flexor digitorum profundus, *flexor digitorum superficialis, *flexor pollicis longus, *palmaris longus, *pronator quadratus, and the *pronator teres.

anterior horn of spinal cord Area of *grey matter in the *spinal cord containing bundles of *motor neurones.

anterior pituitary *See* adenohypophysis.

anterior–posterior chest depth In *anthropometry, the depth of the *chest at the *mesosternale level.

anterior–posterior plane *See* sagittal plane.

anterior superior iliac spine Blunt process on the anterior aspect of the *iliac crest. An important anatomical *landmark. It is easily felt through the skin and may be visible.

anterior talofibular ligament The external lateral *ligament of the *ankle-joint between the *fibula and *talus. Its main function is to prevent the *foot from slipping forward in relation to the *tibia. It is the most commonly damaged ligament in the ankle.

anterior tibial artery A major *artery which commences at the lower border of the *popliteus muscle and runs quite deeply in the front of the lower *leg, resting on the *interosseus membrane between the *tibia and *fibula. It then becomes more superficial and branches to supply the upper part of the foot.

anterior tibial nerve A *nerve in the front of the lower leg with branches supplying muscles of the ankle and foot, including the *tibialis, extensor digitorum longus and the *peroneus tertius.

anterior tibial syndrome *See* anterior compartment syndrome.

anterior tibial vein A principal *vein in the lower leg.

anthropometer An instrument for measuring the dimensions of the human body.

anthropometric tape A special tape, usually non-extensible but very flexible, for the very accurate measurement of parts of the human body.

anthropometry The measurement of the size and proportions of the human body and its different parts.

anti-arrhythmic A *medicine used to correct disturbances to the rhythm of the heart beat.

antibiotic A substance produced by a microorganism that can inhibit or kill other microorganisms, particularly bacteria and fungi (e.g., *penicillin from the fungus *Penicillium notatum* kills some bacteria by preventing cell-wall synthesis). Antibiotics have no effect on viruses such as those for the *common cold and *influenza.

antibody A type of *protein formed in the body called *immunoglobin that attacks foreign substances. Antibodies are produced in *lymph tissue by *lymphocytes called *B-cell lymphocytes. Most antibodies are produced in response to specific *antigens (*see* active immunity). Babies have a limited capacity to make antibodies and derive most from their mother (*see* passive immunity). Antibodies include antitoxins which are produced in response to *toxins; *agglutins which cause clumping of foreign cells; and lysins which cause the disintegration of invading cells. Other antibodies (opsonins) facilitate uptake of antigens by *phagocytes, while precipitins cause soluble antigens to precipitate.

antibrachium *See* forearm.

antibruise cream A *medicine that contains an anti-inflammatory drug to reduce *inflammation. Most are not very effective.

anticholinergic A *drug, such as *atropine, that inhibits the function of the *cholinergic (parasympathetic) nervous system by blocking the action of *acetylcholine. Anticholinergics are used to treat stomach *ulcers and *gastritis. They can cause temporary visual impairment with reduced ability to judge distances which can be a serious disadvantage in some sports.

anticipation The ability to look forward and judge correctly what is going to happen next. Anticipation is a *skill; thus a sportsperson can learn what to expect teammates or opponents to do in certain situations. *See also* perceptual anticipation; receptor anticipation; and selective attention.

anticipatory socialization A process in which an individual tries to change his or her social behaviour in the expectation of joining, and being accepted by, another social group which may or may not have a higher *social status than that which the individual currently occupies. *See also* socialization

anticoagulant A medicine that slows down the rate of blood *coagulation.

antidepressant A *drug, such as amitryptiline or imipramine, which improves mood and often reduces *anxiety, alleviating the symptoms of *depression.

antidiuretic hormone (ADH) A *hormone secreted by the posterior *pituitary gland which stimulates reabsorption of water through the distal *convoluted tubules and collecting ducts of the kidney, thus conserving water and resulting in reduced urine production. The secretion of ADH is usually increased in response to exercise so that the plasma volume may be conserved.

anti-emetic drug A *drug used to treat *motion sickness and to prevent or overcome *vomiting and *nausea.

antigen A substance (usually *protein or *carbohydrate) that is recognized as foreign by the *immune system and induces an *immune response including the production of *antibodies. Antigens may be living or nonliving and include *toxins (e.g., snake venom) or molecules on the cell surface (e.g., AB antigens of blood—*see* ABO blood groups).

antigravity muscle *Muscle which contracts, often through the *stretch reflex, in order to counterbalance the pull of *gravity and to maintain an upright *posture. Many antigravity muscles are of the *slow twitch fibre type, and are often called *tonic muscles

antihistamine A *drug which counteracts the effect of *histamines and relieves the symptoms of some allergic conditions, such as hay fever, but not of others, such as asthma.

antihypertensive drug A *drug which reduces *blood pressure and is used to treat *hypertension. *Beta blockers have antihypertensive properties.

anti-inflammatory medicine A *drug which reduces the tissue's *inflammation response to injury. They include *nonsteroidal anti-inflammatory drugs such as *salicylates, *enzymes (e.g., *hyaluronidase and *heparinoid ointment), and *steroids.

antinaturalism In *sociology, an approach to analysis opposed to the sole use of models drawn from the physical sciences to explain or study human social actions.

antioxidant A compound, usually organic, that prevents or retards *oxidation by molecular oxygen of materials such as food. Some antioxidants, such a *β-carotene, *selenium, and *vitamin C, may provide some protection against cancer because they neutralize free radicals.

antipsychotic drug A *drug, such as *dopamine, which reduces *aggression.

antipyretic A *drug, such as *aspirin, which can reduce an elevated body temperature.

antirachitic factor *See* vitamin D.

antiseptic A substance which counteracts putrefaction. Antiseptics are usually applied to the body to prevent *infection of a wound.

antispasmodic drug A *drug which relieves *spasms of *smooth muscle.

antispastic drug A *drug which relieves *spasms of *striated muscle.

antisterility factor *See* vitamin E.

antitetanus serum *See* tetanus.

antithrombin A substance in *blood plasma that inhibits coagulation by inactivating *thrombin.

antitussive A *drug which suppresses coughing either by a local soothing action or by depressing the cough centre in the *central nervous system. Great care must be taken by athletes when purchasing and using a cough or cold remedy because many contain antitussives, such as *sympathomimetic amines and *narcotic analgesics, which are on the *IOC list of *banned substances.

anus The posterior opening of the *alimentary canal; the outlet of the rectum.

anxiety A subjective feeling of apprehension and tension. The term is often used synomonously with *arousal, but anxiety is usually restricted to high arousal states which produce feelings of discomfort. The condition is closely associated with the concept of *fear, but is more a feeling of what might happen rather than a response to an obviously fear-provoking situation. Anxiety can be viewed as an enduring personality trait (*see* A-trait) and also as a temporary state (*see* A-state). Anxiety in sport may be affected by the *objective competitive situation and the *subjective competitive situation. Generally high levels of precompetitive anxiety depresses the level of performance by its affects on selectivity and/or the intensity of *attention. The detrimental affect may be due to *cognitive state anxiety (also known as task irrelevant cognitive activity) impairing a person's ability to discriminate between relevant and irrelevant information, resulting in time being wasted doing irrelevant tasks. There is evidence that regular exercise may reduce anxiety levels.

anxiety-blocking *See* relaxation procedure.

anxiety hierarchy A person's ranking of a class of situations from least to most *anxiety-producing, which is then used as a basis of systematic *desensitization.

anxiety-prone *See* A-trait.

anxiety–stress spiral The circular effect of *anxiety causing poor performance which results in even more anxiety.

anxiolytic A *drug that reduces *anxiety levels.

aorta The major *artery in the body; it carries *blood from the left *ventricle of the *heart.

aortic arch Part of the *aorta which arches from the ascending aorta up and over the heart to descend down as far as the fourth *thoracic vertebra.

aortic body A *receptor area in the wall of the *aortic arch near the *heart, sensitive to levels of *carbon dioxide, *oxygen, and *pH in the *blood. Information from the aortic body is conveyed by *sensory neurones to the *respiratory centre.

aortic stenosis Narrowing of the opening of the *aorta due to fusion of the *cusps of the *aortic valve or other parts of the aorta.

aortic valve A semilunar *valve which prevents the backflow of blood from the *aorta to the left *ventricle of the *heart.

apartheid An institutionalized discriminatory system of restricted contact between races, as in the Republic of South Africa where the population was separated and defined by law into 'whites', 'blacks', 'coloured', and 'mixed racial'. This separation was reflected in restrictions on sport participation.

A–P chest depth *See* anterior–posterior chest depth.

apnoea Cessation of the breathing impulse (e.g., through *hyperventilation).

apneusis A condition marked by prolonged inspiratory spasms.

apneustic Pertaining to *apneusis.

apneustic centre *See* inspiratory centre.

apocrine gland A type of sweat-gland which secretes *water, *salts, *proteins, and *fatty acids. Apocrine glands are less numerous than *eccrine glands. They occur particularly in the *axillae but they are not important in *thermoregulation.

aponeurosis Flattened ribbon-shaped or sheet-like tendinous connective tissue which replaces a *tendon in muscles that are flat and have a wide area of attachments.

apophyseal joint A *synovial joint between the arches of *vertebrae. Such joints are not supplied with nerves; therefore, injury may not result in *pain and the damage may go unnoticed.

apophysis A prominent process projecting from the surface of a bone from which it has never been separated, nor been able to move upon (*compare* epiphysis). Apophyses often act as attachment sites of *tendons.

apophysitis An *inflammation of an *apophyseal joint.

apophysitis calcanei *Inflammation and breakdown in the attachment of the *Achilles tendon to the *calcaneus. The condition is characterized by pain, swelling, and tenderness in the calcaneus when running or walking. Apophysitis calcanei tends to occur in active individuals between 8 and 15 years and usually resolves spontaneously when the afflicted athlete reaches 16 to 18 years, when *ossification of the skeleton is complete.

apoplexy *See* stroke.

apparent depth of water The depth of the water as perceived by an observer viewing it from above the surface. This depth appears to be less than the true depth owing to the refraction of light. The ratio of the true depth to apparent depth is equal to the refractive index of the water.

appendicular skeleton The *bones of the *limbs and limb *girdles that are attached to the *axial skeleton.

appendicitis An acute inflammation of the appendix. Appendicitis is the commonest cause of emergency abdominal surgery; it develops suddenly and is potentially very dangerous because the appendix may burst and cause a spread of infection resulting in inflammation of the *peritoneum which can be fatal. Symptoms include persistent abdominal pains and *nausea. Athletes who have had surgical removal of an appendix without complications can usually return to training a few weeks after the operation. Complications may prolong the need for convalescence and avoidance of physical exertion.

appendix The worm-like extension of the large *intestine. The appendix opens off the *caecum and is closed at one end. It is a vestigial organ which does not seem to have any function.

apperception The perception of a situation in terms of past experience rather than in terms of the stimuli which are immediately present. In sport, apperceiving may result in a team player misreading a situation and making inappropriate anticipatory movements.

appetite A psychological desire to eat. Unlike *hunger, it is probably a learned response associated with pleasant-tasting and satisfying food. It is an agreeable sensation which is undoubtedly necessary for good digestion and is accompanied by secretion of saliva and digestive juices. It also provides the desire to eat enough food to maintain the body and supply it with sufficient energy to carry on its functions. However, as with other body functions, disorders of appetite occur. Excessive appetite may result in *obesity, while diminished appetite is a sign common to many illnesses and in some cases may be a manifestation of *stress. *See also* amphetamines; anorexia nervosa; and bulimia.

applicability The degree to which data acquired by a *naturalistic approach may be applied to other studies and situations.

appositional growth Process by which *bones increase in thickness rather than length (*see* epiphyseal growth.)

approach–approach conflict A situation in which an individual is confronted with a choice between equally attractive alternatives. *Compare* approach–avoidance conflict.

approach–avoidance conflict A situation in which an individual is confronted with a single object or event which has both attractive and aversive features. When two or more such objects or events are involved, the situation is called a double approach–avoidance conflict.

approximations, method of A procedure in *operant conditioning, which may be adopted as a coaching strategy, by which an individual learns a certain behaviour in a step-by-step manner, each step involving a response slightly more complex than the one preceding it. The correct behaviour at each step is reinforced until that step is mastered, then the next step, which is still closer to the final criterion, is reinforced and so on. *See also* learning method.

apraxia A disorder of the *cerebral cortex, commonly caused by disease, which results in an inability to make precise skilled movements.

aptitude The capacity to learn readily and to achieve a high level of *skill in a specific area, such as a sport. Aptitude refers to an individual's potential rather than actual accomplishment. *See also* ability.

aqueous Pertaining to water.

aqueous humor Clear, watery fluid in the anterior chamber of the eye, through which the *cornea and lens receive nutrients.

arachidonic acid A 20-carbon, straight-chained, *polyunsaturated, *fatty acid formed from *linoleic acid. Arachidonic acid is found throughout the body in low concentration in free form, but an abundant supply occurs as a form bound with *phospholipids on cell membranes. It is released from damaged cells and is the basic molecule from which a number of biologically active molecules (including *prostaglandins and *lekotrienes) involved in the *inflammation response, are formed.

arachnoid The soft, web-like middle layer of *tissue surrounding the *brain and *spinal cord.

arc Any unbroken, curved portion of the circumference of a *circle.

arccos An inverse trigonometric function. If $y = \cos x$, then the inverse trigonometric function of x is $\cos^{-1} y$ (or arccos y) where $\cos^{-1} y$ is the angle whose cosine is y.

arc, flattening of A movement pattern of the arm which improves accuracy when throwing or hitting a *projectile. It involves a flattening of the centre of the arc of the curve in which the arm is travelling and in the direction which the projectile is to follow.

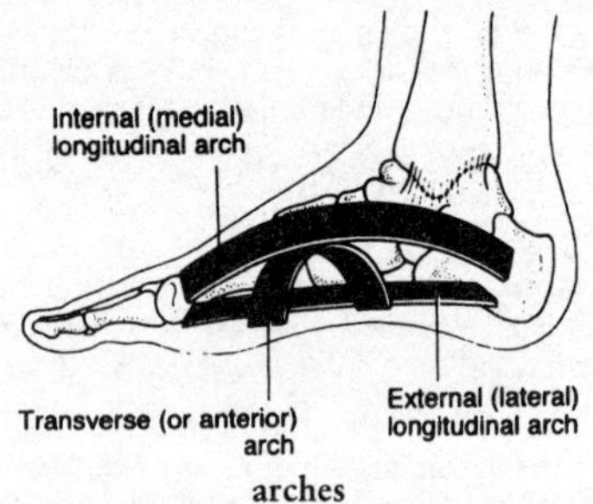

arches

arches Curved structures, arch-like in profile, which span the foot. There are three arches to each foot: two longitudinal (the medial arch and the lateral arch) and one short, anterior, transverse arch. Together the three arches form a half-dome shape which is essential for efficient load-bearing and locomotion. The arches distribute about half of our standing and walking weight to the *heel-bones and half to the heads of the *metatarsals. The shape is maintained by the combined action of footbones, strong *ligaments, and the pull of some muscles during muscle activity. *See also* flat feet; and high arches.

Archimedes' principle A principle which states that a body that is wholly or partly submerged in a fluid is buoyed up by a force equal to the weight of the displaced fluid.

archival research Research which relies on historical documents, ranging from official government statistics to the letters and diaries of individuals.

arch sprain A disorder characterized by pain in the *arches of the foot. There are two main types of arch sprain: static and traumatic. Static arch sprain is marked by pain and tenderness along the *plantar ligament and is commonly caused by prolonged stress on the feet which may result from changing footwear (e.g., from flat training shoes to spiked track shoes). Traumatic arch sprain is due to overstretching of the ligaments supporting the arches.

arch support Extra material inside a *training shoe which provides mechanical support for the *arches.

arcsin An inverse trigonometric function. If $y = \sin x$, then the inverse trigonometric function of x is $\sin^{-1} y$ (or arc sin y) where $\sin^{-1} y$ is the angle whose sine is y.

arctan An inverse trigonometric function. If $y = \tan x$, then the inverse trigonometric function of x is $\tan^{-1} y$ (or arctan y) where $\tan^{-1} y$ is the angle whose tangent is y.

area Measure of a surface in square units of length (e.g., m^2).

areolar tissue Loose *connective tissue which has a semi-fluid ground substance formed mainly of *hyaluronic acid with a loose arrangement of fibres. It provides a reservoir of water and salts for surrounding body tissue. If extracellular fluid accumulates in the areolar tissue, the affected area swells and becomes puffy, contributing to the condition known as *oedema.

argot A specialized language or jargon, shared by members of a *subculture.

arithmetic mean *See* mean.

arm Region of the body extending for the length of the *humerus bone.

arm abduction Movement of the *arm away from the midline of the body. *See also* arm abductors.

arm abductors Muscles which effect the movement of *arm abduction. They are the *deltoid muscle, which acts as the prime mover, the *latissimus dorsi and *pectoralis major being the antagonists.

arm adduction Movement of the arm towards the midline of the body. *See also* arm adductors.

arm adductors Muscles which effect the movement of arm adduction. They are the *latissimus dorsi, the *pectoralis major, and the *teres major muscles (which act as *prime movers) assisted by the *teres major and *subscapularis, while the *rhomboideus, *serratus anterior, and *trapezius act as *fixators of the *scapula.

arm curl A weight-training exercise using a barbell. With the subject in a standing position, the barbell is held in the hands with the palms to the front and the forearm extended. The barbell is curled upward and forward until the *forearm is completely flexed; the barbell is then returned to the starting position.

arm extension An angular, backward and downward movement of the *arm at the shoulder-joint. It is effected by the *arm extensors.

arm extensors Muscles which effect *arm extension. They include the *latissimus dorsi and the posterior fibres of the *deltoideus muscles (which act as *prime movers), assisted by the *infraspinatus, *pectoralis major, *teres major, and *teres minor. The *serratus anterior, *trapezius, and *rhomboideus act as *fixators of the *scapula.

arm flexion An angular, forward and upward movement of the *arm at the shoulder-joint which moves the arm anteriorly, usually in the sagittal plane; effected by *arm flexors.

arm flexors Muscles which effect *arm flexion. They include the anterior fibres of the *deltoideus and the clavicular head of the *pectoralis major, which act as *prime movers.

arm–hand steadiness A skill-oriented ability which underlies tasks such as archery and riflery. It is believed to exist within the movement control area.

arm horizontal extension Movement of the *arm from the front horizontal position to the side horizontal position. The *prime movers are the *infraspinatus and the *teres minor muscles.

arm horizontal flexion Movement of the *arm from the side horizontal position to the front horizontal position. The *prime mover is the *pectoralis major.

arm inward rotation (arm medial rotation) Movement of the *arm around its axis towards the midline of the body. It is effected by the anterior fibres of the *deltoideus and the *latissimus dorsi muscle assisted by the *teres major, while the *rhomboideus acts as a *fixator of the *scapula.

arm lateral rotation *See* arm outward rotation.

arm length In *anthropometry, the difference between *acromial height and *radial height.

arm medial rotation *See* arm-inward rotation.

arm movements Movements of the upper *arm.

arm outward rotation (arm lateral rotation) Movement of the arm around its axis towards the lateral side (away from the midline of the body). The *prime movers are the posterior fibres of the *deltoideus, the *teres minor, and the *infraspinatus, while the *rhomboideus acts as a *fixator of the *scapula.

arm preference A person's tendency to favour the use of a particular arm when performing a task. *See also* handedness.

arousal The intensity dimension of behaviour ranging from deep sleep to extreme excitement. Arousal refers to the state of general preparedness for action in the body and it involves the activation of the various organs under the control of the *autonomic nervous system. The term arousal is often used incorrectly as being synomonous with *alertness or *anxiety, although the latter is confined to situations of high arousal accompanied by unpleasant sensations. Physiological indicators of arousal include *blood pressure, *EEG brainwave patterns, *galvanic skin reaction, *heart rate, *muscle tension, and respiration rate. Biochemical indicators include *adrenaline and *noradrenaline blood concentrations. There is not a perfect correlation between these indicators. Different sports have different optimal arousal levels. The relationship between arousal and performance is often described by the *inverted-U hypothesis. This hypothesis is based on the assumption that arousal is unidimensional, but there is evidence that there are two or more arousal systems in the brain. Some researchers distinguish between psychological arousal (the readiness of an individual to respond to stimuli) and physiological arousal (as indicated by heart rate, sweating, etc.).

arousal reaction A reaction which occurs when an individual is confronted with sudden, usually threatening, environmental situations which stimulate the *reticular activating system. Other brain structures are then activated along with the *sympathetic nervous system, resulting in large quantities of *adrenaline and *noradrenaline being released into the bloodstream.

arrector pili Tiny, *smooth muscles attached to hair follicles which cause the hair to stand upright when activated.

arrested progress (plateau) A period during training or the *learning of a *skill when there is no apparent improvement in performance; the trend towards further gains ceases even though practice continues. This has been called the 'plateau of despond' because it is very discouraging. However, if the training effort continues for long enough, this period invariably passes and it is often followed by a period of accelerated improvement. *See also* physiological limit.

arrhythmia An irregular rhythm of the *heartbeat. It may be produced by various heart diseases which affect the mechanism controlling the beating of the heart. Sinus arrhythmia is a normal deviation in the rhythm of the heartbeat which accelerates slightly during inspirations.

artefact In the microscopic examination of tissues, a structure which is not present in the natural state but that appears during the preparation or examination of the material.

arterial Pertaining to arteries.

arterial and tidal pCO_2 differences The difference, measured in mm Hg, between the mean arterial *partial pressure of carbon dioxide and the *end-tidal partial pressure of carbon dioxide. It is positive when arterial partial pressure of carbon dioxide is higher than the end partial pressure of carbon dioxide.

arterial plaque Deposits of fatty substances, such as *cholesterol, on artery walls which can lead to *atherosclerosis.

arterial pO_2 The *partial pressure of oxygen in the arteries.

arteriole A small *artery that supplies *blood to the *capillaries.

arteriosclerosis A pathological condition involving the thickening and hardening of the arterial wall, and reduction in elasticity of the vessel. *See also* atherosclerosis; and hypokinetic disease.

arteriovenous anastomosis A small blood vessel with a relatively thick muscular coat which provides a direct connection between an *artery or *arteriole, and a *vein or *venule thus bypassing the capillaries. It plays an important part in *shunting.

arteriovenous oxygen difference The difference between the oxygen content of *arterial and *mixed venous blood. It is a measure of the ability of tissues to extract oxygen from the blood. Usually, the arterial oxygen concentration is determined for blood from the *femoral, *brachial, or *radial arteries, and the oxygen content of mixed venous blood is determined using blood withdrawn from the *pulmonary artery. The arteriovenous oxygen difference increases with exercise intensity and with training. The maximum difference in a trained athlete is about 160 mmol l^{-1}, compared to that of 140 mmol l^{-1} for a sedentary person. This indicates that the tissues of trained athletes are able to extract more oxygen from the blood, enabling them to be more active. The training effect may be due to adaptations in *mitochondria, increased *myoglobin content, and an improved *capillarization of the muscle.

artery A large, muscular blood vessel conveying *blood away from the *heart.

arthalgia A pain experienced in the region of the joints.

arthritis A term which covers a number of conditions characterized by inflammation of the joints. The most common is *osteoarthritis which results from degeneration and wearing away of *articular cartilage. This may gradually progress to involve underlying bones. Osteoarthritis may result from *trauma, incorrect loading of the joint, or disease. Knees and hips are most commonly involved and the ankles only very rarely. Athletes who suffer repeated joint injuries may accelerate the onset of arthritis. Arthritis sufferers should choose physical activities which put the least stress on the affected joint. Cycling and swimming are often suitable for individuals with arthritis of the hip, for example. Severe arthritis may preclude participation in sports. *See also* rheumatoid arthritis; and traumatic arthritis.

arthrodesis The surgical fusion of bones across a joint which eliminates movement of that joint.

arthrodial joint *See* arthrosis.

arthrogram An image of a joint produced on a photographic plate using *arthrography.

arthrography An *X-ray technique for examining joints, using air and/or a dye injected into the joint, which facilitate the detection of defects, such as torn cartilage.

arthropathy A disease or disorder of a joint.

arthroscope An instrument for probing into complex joints such as the knee. The arthroscope is inserted through a small incision into the joint. It incorporates a light source, fibre-optics, and a television camera. These enable the contents of the joint to be viewed directly for signs of injury.

arthroscopy A surgical operation which involves making a small incision so that an *arthroscope can be inserted into a joint.

arthrosis (arthrodial joint) Technical term for a nonaxial *gliding joint, such as an *intercarpal joint, which allows gliding or twisting movements.

articular capsule (joint capsule) A double-layered capsule composed of an outer fibrous layer lined with *synovial membrane; it encloses the joint cavity of a *synovial joint.

articular cartilage *Cartilage which covers the *joint surface, usually at the end of a bone. It is *avascular. Its main functions are to provide a smooth surface for articulation, to absorb shocks, and to distribute forces. Articular cartilage contains *collagen fibres which are continuous with the bone beneath. It plays an important role in the nourishment of the underlying bone. *Synovial fluid is forced in and out of the articular cartilage with changes of pressure produced by movements. The fluid penetrates into the bone supplying it with nutrients. *See also* hyaline cartilage.

articular discs *See* menisci.

articular surface fracture A *fracture which involves an adjacent articular joint surface.

articulating surface Surface of *bone which forms a *joint.

articulation A *joint; a point where two bones meet.

artificial respiration Any device or method used to re-establish breathing.

artificial resuscitation (cardiopulmonary resuscitation; CPR) Restoration of normal breathing and pulse, usually by mouth-to-mouth (or mouth-to-nose) respiration and rhythmical compression on the chest.

ascetic A person who practises great self-denial and abstains from worldly comforts

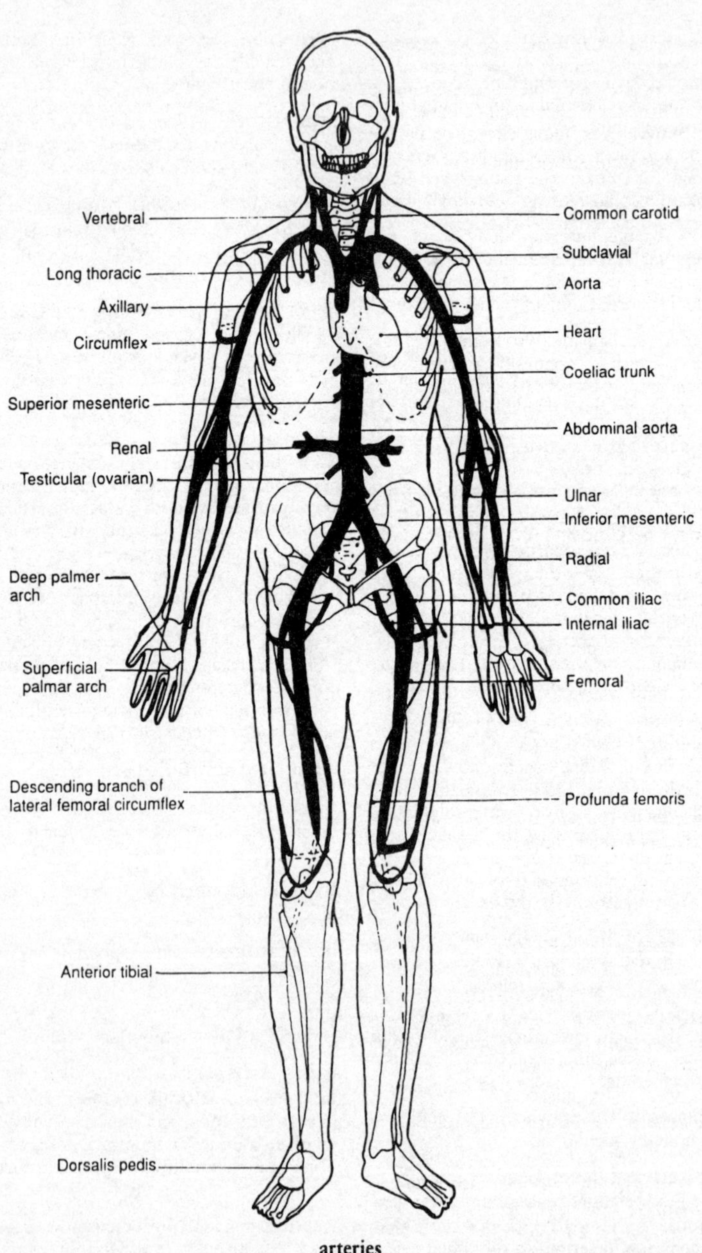
Vertebral
Long thoracic
Axillary
Circumflex
Superior mesenteric
Renal
Testicular (ovarian)
Deep palmer arch
Superficial palmar arch
Descending branch of lateral femoral circumflex
Anterior tibial
Dorsalis pedis
Common carotid
Subclavial
Aorta
Heart
Coeliac trunk
Abdominal aorta
Ulnar
Inferior mesenteric
Radial
Common iliac
Internal iliac
Femoral
Profunda femoris

arteries

and pleasures, usually for religious reasons but sometimes for sport. Percy Cerutty, the famous coach of Herb Elliot, advocated the practice of self-denial as an essential ingredient of training.

ascorbic acid *See* vitamin C.

asocial Applied to an individual who is unconcerned about the welfare of others.

ascribed status *Status in *society which depends on the position into which an individual is born. *Compare* achieved status.

aseptic techniques Procedures free from disease-causing organisms. When open wounds are being treated in hospital, for example, the air is filtered, instruments are autoclaved (sterilized by heat), and operators wear protective clothing.

aspartates *See* aspartic acid salts.

aspartic acid salts (aspartates) Salts of the amino acid, aspartic acid, which is an intermediate in the *ornithine cycle. Aspartic acid and aspartates are used as *ergogenic aids in the belief that they delay *fatigue by accelerating the conversion of ammonia to urea. Experimental results provide conflicting evidence of their usefulness.

asphyxia (suffocation) A term which means loss of pulse, but is applied to a whole series of conditions which follow cessation of breathing and the heart's action. If not treated quickly, asphyxia will result in insufficient oxygen reaching the tissues, loss of consciousness, and death. It can be caused by inhaling water, food (especially chewing-gum) being stuck in the trachea, or by equipment blocking the airway. Contact sports may result in a person losing consciousness because of a blow. The unconscious athlete is in danger of asphyxia if he or she is not in the correct position (*see* recovery position) since the tongue may fall back and block the airway, or the sufferer may choke on his or her own vomit.

aspiration The drawing off of fluid from the body by suction.

aspirational level (level of expectation) Expectancy of success or failure. Aspirational levels act as an important *motivation, determining the actual performance. People with high aspirational levels expect to succeed and often perform well, while those with low aspirational levels expect to fail and often perform badly. *See also* self-efficacy.

aspirin *See* acetylsalicylic acid.

assertion *See* assertive behaviour.

assertive behaviour (assertion) In sport, the use of legitimate, acceptable physical force and the expenditure of an unusually high degree of effort to achieve an external goal, with no intent to injure (although another person may be injured accidentally). The goal may be offensive and designed to acquire a valued resource, such as yardage in American football; or it may be defensive. There is considerable confusion between the terms *aggression and assertion. Sometimes assertive behaviour has been labelled *instrumental aggression, adding to the confusion. *See also* proactive assertion.

assessments of performance Measurements of the qualitative and/or quantitative value of a performance. The phrase is often related to physiological measurements of the ability of an individual to perform physical tasks. To be meaningful (*see* meaningfulness), assessments of performance should be conducted with the same rigour as other scientific investigations and follow the same rules of experimental design.

assimilation 1 In physiology, the incorporation of new materials into the internal structure of an organism. **2** In sociology, a process by which a minority group adopts the values and behaviour patterns of a majority, or dominant, group and eventually becomes absorbed into the majority group. *Compare* accommodation. **3** A *cognitive process in which children incorporate new experiences into their present interpretation of the world. The new experiences become part of the child's current *conceptual schema which therefore becomes fuller and more elaborate. If the new experiences cannot be assimilated then the conceptual schema is changed (*see* accommodation).

assistant movers Muscles which, by virtue of their small size or disadvantageous *angle of pull, are not *prime movers but may, by their contractions, contribute to the effectiveness of a particular movement.

association 1 An *attentional style which is consistent with internal focus. It is illustrated by some distance runners who tend to be very aware of their own emotions and internal body sensations, such as how their legs feel during performance. *Compare* dissociation. 2 Used synonymously with *correlation in *descriptive statistics. 3 A form of *learning which establishes the relationship between different events. The basic elements are connections between the stimulus and response, and the strength of the association is influenced by the frequency with which the events are presented together. An association area in the anterior of the *cerebral cortex is assumed to integrate previously stored information with incoming information. *See also* conditioning.

association area *See* association processes.

associative coping style A technique for managing *stress where the subject focuses internally on thoughts and body sensations, but ignores external stimuli. A golfer, for example, may focus on the muscle groups required to execute the swing while ignoring the noise from spectators.

association neurone *See* interneurone.

association processes Cognitive processes which establish relationships between, or among, events and which enable *association to occur. An association area in the anterior of the *cerebral cortex is assumed to integrate previously stored information with incoming information.

associative stage A stage in the *learning of a *motor skill in which the performer refines movements by detecting and correcting errors.

associative strategy A method of focusing on internal body sensations and thoughts which enables performers to monitor their internal condition continuously. *See also* associative coping style.

associator An individual who internalizes or adopts a narrow and internal attentional focus (*see* narrow attentional focus). Élite marathoners tend to be associators focusing on bodily sensations and so allowing for self-regulation. *Compare* dissociators.

A-state A temporary state of *anxiety evoked by a particular situation. *See also* state anxiety.

asthma A respiratory disorder characterized by recurrent attacks of difficult breathing, particularly on exhalation, due to an increased resistance to airflow through the respiratory bronchioles. Sufferers are hypersensitive to a variety of stimuli which cause the airways to narrow by contraction of their *smooth muscle, by a swelling of the *mucous membrane, or due to an increased mucus secretion. Asthma may be induced by exercise (*see* exercise-induced asthma). Sports vary in their tendency to induce asthma with running having a high tendency, cycling a moderate tendency, and gymnastics and swimming a low tendency. Paradoxically, many sufferers gain relief from their bronchospasms by regular exercise, and exercise is now seen as important in the management of asthma. Many drugs help to control asthma, but some are on the *IOC list of *banned substances. Several athletes, including the 400 m men's freestyle swimming champion of the Olympic games in 1972, have been disqualified because of pre-race ingestion of an oral anti-asthmatic drug.

astigmatism A defect of the *cornea or lens of the eye that leads to variable blurred vision.

astringent A *drug which shrinks cells. Astringents may be used to harden and protect the skin.

asymmetry The lack of *symmetry.

AT *See* anaerobic threshold.

ataxia The shaky movements and unsteady gait of a person lacking muscle co-ordination. Ataxia may be due to a failure of the *cerebellum to regulate the person's postures and movements.

ataxiagraph *See* ataxiameter.

ataxiameter An instrument used to assess *balance by accurately measuring the anterior to posterior, and lateral movements of

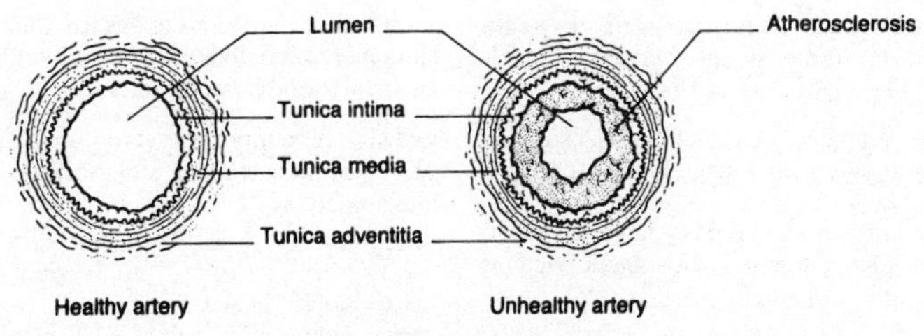

atherosclerosis

the head. Where a graphic record is obtained, the instrument is called an ataxiagraph.

atenolol A *cardioselective *drug belonging to the *beta blockers which are on *IOC list of *banned substances.

atherosclerosis A type of *arteriosclerosis characterized by the accumulation of fatty materials within the arterial walls. This results in a narrowing of the arteries and reduced blood flow which can encourage the formation of a blood clot and lead to a *stroke or heart attack.

athlete An individual who, by virtue of special training or natural talent, is fit to compete in a physically demanding sport. The term athlete is derived from the Latin word 'athleta' which referred to a person who competed in physical exercises for a prize.

athlete's foot A contagious infection caused by the fungus *Tinea pedis* and characterized by peeling skin and an itchy, and sometimes sore, feeling between the toes. It may be rampant where there is poor hygiene and communal washing, such as in changing rooms. The condition can be avoided by scrupulous care in washing the feet and the use of antifungal ointments and powders.

athlete's heart A non-pathological enlargement of the heart which is a physiological adaptation to endurance types of exercise. It is accompanied by *bradycardia. There is no evidence that the condition is detrimental to health.

athlete's kidney An abnormality of the kidney associated with repeated episodes of microtrauma, as might be caused by boxing or other contact sports. It is characterized by recurrent *haematuria and structural changes in the upper region of the major calyx.

athletic motivation inventory (AMI) An inventory designed to measure personality traits thought to be related to athletic ability. These traits include *aggression, conscience development, determination, drive, emotional control, leadership, mental toughness, responsibility, self-confidence, and trust. Although the inventory is much used, its ability to predict athletic success has been seriously questioned.

athletic pseudonephritis A non-pathological condition caused by severe exercise which mirrors the symptoms of acute *nephritis. The syptoms include *haematuria and *proteinuria, which make differential diagnosis difficult. But in athletic pseudonephritis there is an absence of sepsis, *anaemia, and *hypertension, and there is usually a normal white blood cell count.

atlantoaxial joint The *synovial joint between the *atlas and the *axis, which allows rotation of the head.

atlas The first cervical vertebra which articulates with the occipital bone of the skull and the axis. It has no *centrum and no spinous process.

atmosphere **1** Gases enveloping the Earth consisting of, at sea level, approximately 78% nitrogen, 20.95% oxygen, 0.36% carbon dioxide, and variable amounts of water vapour. **2** A unit of pressure; one normal atmosphere equals 101,325 newtons per square metre.

atmospheric pressure The pressure exerted at any point by the Earth's atmospheric gases above that point

atony A condition in which muscles are flaccid and lack their normal elasticity.

atopy The acquisition of hypersensitivity to various environmental substances such as pollen and house dust.

ATP *See* adenosine triphosphate.

ATPase An enzyme involved in the breakdown and synthesis of ATP.

ATP-PC system (phosphagen system) An *anaerobic energy system in which ATP manufacture is coupled with the exergonic breakdown of phosphocreatine stored in the muscles. It is the quickest source of ATP for muscle movement. Athletes in power events, such as the 100-metre sprint, performed at maximum intensity for about ten seconds, derive most of their ATP from this system.

A-trait An enduring personality factor indicating an individual's pre-disposition to experience *anxiety under stress.

atrial systole Contraction of the atria of the heart forcing blood into the ventricles during the *cardiac cycle.

atrioventricular bundle (AV bundle; bundle of His) A bundle of modified heart muscle fibres which conduct impulses from the atrioventricular node to the ventricles.

atrioventricular node A specialized area of tissue located in the right *atrium of the heart which receives the impulse to the contract from the *sinoatrial node and transmits it through the atrioventricular bundle to the *ventricles.

atrioventricular valves The mitral valve or bicuspid valve between the left atrium and the left ventricle.

atrium (auricle) **1** Either of two upper chambers of the heart. The right atrium recieves deoxygenated blood from the body via the venae cavae and the left atrium recieves oxygenated blood from the lungs via the pulmonary veins. **2** An anatomical passage or chamber such as the terminal saccule of the bronchioles of the lungs associated with alveoli.

atrophy Reduction in size or wasting away of an organ or tissue from lack of use or disease.

atropine A *drug, extracted from belladonna (the juice of the deadly nightshade), which blocks most actions of the *parasympathetic nervous system by preventing *acetylcholine from carrying out its function as a *neurotransmitter. With the parasympathetic system out of action, the *sympathetic system is left to function unopposed, thus atropine mimics some actions of the sympathetic nervous system and *adrenaline. Small doses of atropine cause a marked increase in the heart rate. Belladonna is used in some cough-mixtures for bronchitis and whooping cough.

attending Readiness to perceive, as in looking or listening for relevant *stimuli. *Focusing of the sense-organs is involved.

attention The selection of information so that the mind can concentrate on one out of several simultaneously presented objects or trains of thought. Attention involves withdrawal from some things in order to deal effectively with others. It enables a person to concentrate on the task in hand. *Information-processing models hypothesize that a selective filter in the brain restricts the amount of information that can be attended to at any one time. Attention can be measured by the extent to which interference occurs between two tasks which a person is performing simultaneously (*see* structural interference; and capacity interference). In the early stages of skill acquisition, more attention is required than when the skill is fully learnt. *See also* attentional style.

attentional focus The ability to focus attention on cues in the environment which are relevant to the task in hand. Attentional focus includes the ability of an athlete both to narrow and broaden his or her attention when necessary (*see* focus). It also refers to the ability to maintain concentration over the course of a game or event.

attentional narrowing *See* narrowing.

attentional skills *Cognitive processes affecting *attention, which can be developed and improved by training. The types of attentional skills which can be learnt for specific sports include the ability to select the correct stimuli to attend to; the ability to shift attention, when appropriate, from one set of stimuli to another; and the ability to sustain attention. These skills are needed for success in most sports.

attentional style An athlete's characteristic manner of attending to stimuli. Sports psychologists often refer to a two-dimensional model of the direction (external to internal) and the width (broad to narrow) of attention. *See also* broad internal; broad external; external overload; focus; internal overload; narrow focus; reduced focus; and scan.

attention span The period of time a person is able to sustain *attention on selected stimuli.

attenuation A weakening of the strength of a *stimulus.

attitude 1 A relatively stable characteristic that predisposes an individual to certain behaviours. Attitudes, unlike *personality traits, are not general dispositions but are directed towards specific objects, people, events, or ideas. In addition to behavioural components, attitudes have cognitive, and affective components. Thus, they may include beliefs, such as agreeing with the proposition that jogging is good for health; and they may involve having negative or positive feelings, such as liking or disliking, a person. A coach may have a great influence on the attitudes of an athlete. A particular attitude may be acquired by direct instruction, *classical conditioning, and *modelling. Once an attitude is established, it may be very difficult to change. Attitudes can be measured by using an *attitude scale. *See also* belief; conviction; opinion; prejudice; and view. 2 The orientation of the axis of a projectile in relation to a *plane or the direction of motion. *See also* attitude angle.

attitude angle The angle formed between the main *plane of a projectile and the horizontal ground. *Compare* angle of attack; and angle of projection.

attitude scale A method of measuring attitudes which is based on the assumption that holding an *attitude leads to consistent responses to particular persons, objects, or ideas. The scale presents statements about the topic of interest and the respondent states a degree of agreement or disagreement with the statement. Attitude scales include the *Likert scale, *Osgood's semantic differential scales, and the *Thurstone scale.

attraction force The attraction all objects have for one another. The only force of attraction strong enough to affect human movement depends on the Earth's gravity.

attraction, law of *See* Newton's law of gravitation.

attribute *See* variable.

attributions The perceived causes of events and behaviours, such as the outcome of a performance. Attributions may be classified along certain dimensions, such as internal/external, or stable/unstable. *See also* attribution theory; and locus of control.

attribution theory (causal attribution theory) A theory of *motivation which postulates that individuals formulate common-sense explanations for their own behaviour which can affect future behaviour. Inherent in the theory is the belief that an athlete is not a passive performer but actively processes information about a performance and constantly reflects on why he or she is losing or winning. The attributions that athletes select to explain their performance outcomes may reveal much about their motivation. Attribution theory assumes that athletes postulate reasons for their success or failure in a performance in a way which influences their future level of performance. These reasons, or attributions, may be arranged on several scales including attributions which are internal or external to the athlete (*see* locus of control); and causes that are stable (such as ability) or unstable (such as effort). It is generally agreed that successful athletes tend to attribute success to relatively stable, internal causes. *See also* cognitive theory.

Atwater factor The energy value per unit weight of food expressed as kcal g^{-1}.

audience In sport, passive observers or spectators of an athletic event. *See also* coaction; and hidden audience.

audience anxiety A feeling of *anxiety brought about by the presence or the anticipated presence of an audience. *See also* audience effect.

audience density The number of spectators in relation to the capacity of a stadium or sports arena into which they are crowded.

audience effect The effect of an *audience on the performance of an athlete. The relationship between the audience and the performer is complex, and is determined by the interaction of the particular factors pertaining to any specific sporting situation. The general effect of an audience is to raise the *arousal levels of participants but for some competitors the audience will be a source of considerable *stress and can cause anxiety.

audience hostility The level of ill-feeling that an *audience expresses towards officials and the visiting team.

audience intimacy The closeness of an audience to the performers. The *psychological presence of an audience tends to increase with audience intimacy.

audience size The number of spectators in an audience. *Compare* audience density. *See also* audience intimacy.

audience sophistication The level of knowledge the members of an audience have about the sport they are watching. An audience with high levels of knowledge tends to have beneficial effects on performance.

audiograph A graph of the minimal level of sound that a person can hear at various frequencies. Separate audiographs are obtained for each ear.

audiometer An instrument for measuring the level of human hearing.

audition The act or power of hearing. Sounds can provide important *feedback. The sound of a ball against a cricket bat, for example, may indicate how well the ball was hit.

auditory acuity (auditory discrimination) Keenness or acuteness of hearing. Auditory acuity may refer to the ability to perceive sounds of low intensity, the ability to detect differences between two sounds on a characteristic such as frequency or intensity, or the ability to recognize the direction from which a sound proceeds.

auditory discrimination *See* auditory acuity.

auditory nerve (vestibulo-cochlear nerve) The *nerve responsible for carrying *nerve impulses from the inner *ear to the *brain. It is the eighth *cranial nerve.

auditory ossicles Three small bones (called the malleus, incus, and stapes) which transmit vibrations in the middle ear.

auditory tube (Eustachian tube) A tube that connects the middle ear and the *pharynx.

Auerbach's plexus A network of *motor nerves forming a nerve *ganglion between the longitudinal and circular muscles of the intestines.

augmented feedback (extrinsic feedback) *Feedback which athletes would not normally receive as a natural consequence of their performance. Augmented feedback is added to the *intrinsic feedback which is typically received during the task and it is provided by a source (such as a coach, teammate, or videotape) external to the athlete.

augmenter An individual who tends to exaggerate the intensity of incoming stimuli. This makes augmenters hypersensitive and easily distracted by extraneous stimuli. They also tend to have low *pain tolerances.

auricle **1** The pinna, or flap, of the ear. **2** *See* atrium.

auricular haemotoma Collection of blood in the *auricle of the ear which can cause swelling and pain. It is often the result of a physical injury which, if repeated, can result in a distortion of the external ear known as a cauliflower ear. Urgent treatment, consisting of draining the *haematoma of blood and the application of a firm pressure bandage, is needed to prevent permanent deformity. The ear can then be protected from further damage by covering it with a few layers of two-way stretch strapping wrapped around the head.

authoritarian leadership A *leadership style which can best be explained in terms of *initiating structure. A coach exhibiting authoritarian leadership will expect strict, nonquestioning obedience of athletes to the training regime that the coach lays down. *See also* autocratic leadership.

authoritarian personality A person who prefers, or believes in, a system in which some individuals control while others are controlled. Those with an authoritarian personality usually exhibit deferrence to those in higher authority, and hostility to those with less authority. The term applies particularly to the personalities of some sports officials, coaches, and physical education teachers.

authority **1** The established ruling body (e.g., of a sport) which can legitimately exert power. **2** The power or right to control and judge the actions of others. This may be through the personal authority of a strong leader (charismatic authority); the established authority, known as traditional authority, (e.g., the authority of governing bodies of individual sports which can impose and enforce their own rules and regulations); or legal authority (e.g., of the state).

autoconditioning *See also* biofeedback training.

autocratic behaviour Coaching behaviour which involves independent decision-making and stresses the personal authority of the coach but not of the athlete.

autocratic leadership A task-structured form of leadership that discourages coach–athlete interaction. Autocratic leadership tends toward behaviour which is best explained in terms of *initiating structure. *See also* authoritarian leadership.

autogenic training A relaxation technique, involving self-suggestion, in which an athlete learns to associate a series of verbal cues and visual images with feelings of warmth and cold in different parts of the body; and with certain physiological responses, such as heart rate, and depth and rate of breathing. Once learnt, these responses can be self-generated when required. Autogenic training has been found to be particularly useful in reducing *anxiety before competition.

autohypnosis *Hypnosis of oneself rather than being hypnotized by another person.

autoimmune response (autoimmunity) An *immune response in which a person produces *antibodies or effector *T-cells that attack the individual's own tissues. Autoimmunity is associated with some degenerative processes such as *rheumatoid arthritis.

autoimmunity *See* autoimmune response.

autolysis The destruction of cells by the body's own *enzymes.

autonomic arousal *See* physiological arousal.

autonomic nervous system (involuntary nervous system; visceral motor system) The *efferent division of the *peripheral nervous system which controls what are normally involuntary activities, such as *heart rate, *respiration, body *core temperature, *blood pressure, and urinary output. The autonomic nervous system includes the *sympathetic nervous system and the *parasympathetic nervous system which innervate *cardiac muscle, *smooth muscles, and glands.

autonomous stage A late stage in the acquisition of a *skill when performance is habitual and requires little *attention.

autoregulation In circulatory physiology, the automatic adjustment of blood flow to a particular body area in response to its current requirements. *See also* shunting.

autosuggestion The acceptance by an individual of a suggestion arising in the individual's own mind.

autotraction *Traction using a person's own body-weight or muscle strength.

autotransfusion *See* blood doping.

auxology The study of growth.

auxotonic muscular activity The *neuromuscular pattern of activity which dictates the correct sequence and strength of different muscular contractions for a given sports technique.

avascular Applied to body structures that do not have blood vessels.

AV-block Delayed or blocked transmission of impulses from the *atria to the *ventricles in the heart.

average A vague term which refers to the normal or typical amount. It sometimes refers more specifically to the *arithmetic mean. *See also* measures of central tendency.

average angular velocity The arithmetic mean of all *instantaneous angular velocities obtained by a body in rotation during a given period of time.

average speed The *distance travelled by a body divided by the time taken: $s = l/t$ where s = average speed, l = distance covered, and t = time. *See also* speed.

average velocity The *displacement of a body divided by the time taken: $v = d/t$ where v = average velocity, d = displacement in a specified direction, and t = time taken.

aversion therapy A type of behaviour modification which relies on punishment or negative reinforcement. The subject learns that by doing something or behaving in a certain way, an unpleasant consequence can be avoided. The *reinforcer is the avoidance of pain or unpleasantness.

aversive event A *stimulus which results in behaviour which terminates the stimulus.

AV node *See* atrioventricular node.

avocational sport subculture A group of people, including players, coaches, and spectators, pursuing a sport interest that they value highly, but which they do not pursue as an occupation. *Compare* occupational sport subculture. *See also* deviant sport subculture.

avoidance–avoidance conflict A situation in which an individual is confronted by two unattractive alternatives.

avulsion fracture A *fracture in which a portion of the bone is pulled off by the attached muscle, tendon, or ligament. It commonly occurs suddenly following heavy, rapid loading of the muscles.

axial skeleton Part of the *skeleton that forms the central, longitudinal axis of the body. The axial skeletion includes the *hyoid bone, *ribs, *skull, *sternum, and *vertebral column.

axilla The space between the upper part of the arm and the side-wall of the chest, commonly called the armpit. The axilla is enclosed by the *pectoral muscles in front, and the *latissimus dorsi and *teres major muscles behind.

axillary In anatomy, pertaining to the *axilla or armpit.

axillary artery A major *artery which runs from the *subclavian artery into the upper arm.

axillary nerve (circumflex nerve) A nerve which runs close to the *shoulder-joint. It supplies the *deltoid and *teres minor muscles.

axillary vein A principal *vein which runs into the branchiocephalic vein (which in turn connects with the heart via the *superior vena cava) and returns blood from the arm into the *subclavian vein.

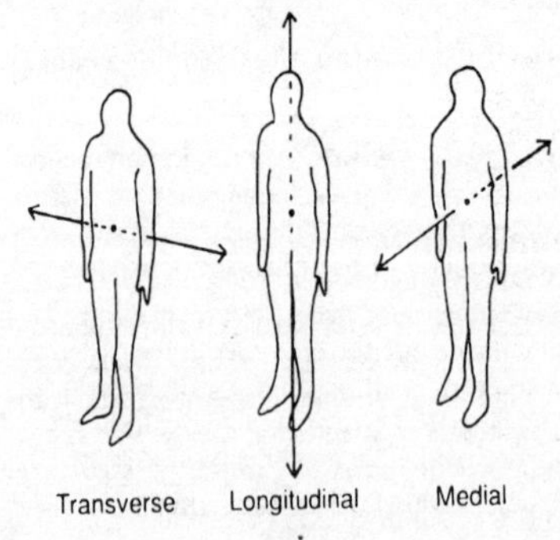

axis

axis 1 An imaginary line, sometimes called an axis of rotation, about which a given body, such as a joint, rotates. **2** The second *cervical *vertebra which has a vertical, superior process called the odontoid process, around which the *atlas rotates.

axis of rotation *See* axis 1 .

axle *See* wheel and axle.

axolemma The plasma membrane of an *axon. *See also* neurilemma.

axon A single, long, relatively unbranched process projecting from a *cell body of a *neurone which transmits *nerve impulses away from the cell body. An axon may or may not be myelinated (*see* myelinated fibres).

axonotmesis An injury to a nerve causing disruption of the *axon and *myelin sheath. It results in degeneration of the axon distal to the point of injury, but regeneration is spontaneous.

Ayalon test A test of *explosive power consisting of measuring the time required to perform a half pedal turn of 180° with the left leg on the pedal of a cycle ergometer, braked by a load which can be set at either 2.9 kg or proportional to the subject's bodyweight. *Power is estimated as the product of the *force (equal to the resistance applied to the flywheel) and the distance (equal to half the circumference of the pedal), divided by the time taken to perform the half pedal turn.

B

Babinski reflex An abnormal *plantar reflex involving an upward movement of the toe when a blunt object is drawn along the outer border of the side of the foot. It may occur in normal infants, but its presence after the age of two years usually indicates a disorder of the *central nervous system.

back Region of the body consisting mainly of the *vertebral column and the hinder parts of the *ribs, the *iliac bones, and the *sacrum. The bones are covered by thick and powerful muscles, the chief of which is the *erector spinae. Muscles also pass upwards to support the head and downwards into the lower limbs.

backache A pain in the back which may result from a number of causes. A large majority of backaches are the result of mechanical *back injuries. In a small percentage of cases, pain may be referred to the back from diseases in deep-seated organs (*see* referred pain).

backbone *See* vertebral column.

back extension *See* trunk extension

back flexion *See* trunk flexion

back injuries Physical damage to structures in the *back. As a result of our bipedal gait, humans are very susceptible to back injuries which cause *backache. Mechanical and traumatic causes which may result from participation in sport include muscular tenderness and ligament strains, *fractures of the *spine, *prolapsed discs, and *spondylosis. Injuries to the spinal column and spinal cord are very serious. In the USA, more working days are lost because of back problems than from any other single cause. However, most of the common complaints are the result of poor *posture, lack of fitness, (including poor *flexibility, and lack of strength and muscular endurance) and inappropriate load-carrying techniques.

back-pain Discomfort in the back region which is caused by an irritation of one kind or another affecting sensory nerves. Back-pain may be induced by a direct blow, a referred source which is not immediately obvious (e.g., from an abdominal or pelvic organ), or from a pre-existing condition awakened by a blow. *See also* backache.

back region 1 The private part of a social organization which is not normally accessible to non-members (e.g., the team changing room). 2 *See* back.

backspin An angular rotation of a projectile such as a ball, in which the top of the ball travels backwards relative to its centre, and the bottom of the ball travels forwards relative to the centre. A backspin is imparted by a bat or other implement being brought downwards and forwards across the path of a ball or other projectile. On landing onto another surface, the backspin tends to make the ball slow down and to increase its *angle of reflection.

backward chaining method A method of *learning a *skill which consists of several actions. The actions are learnt in reverse order with the final action being learnt first, and so on. It is a variant of the *part method. *Compare* chaining.

bacteria A group of microorganisms all of which lack a distinct nuclear membrane. Most are single-celled and bounded by a special cell wall. Some are *pathogenic, causing diseases such as *pneumonia and *septicaemia. Pathogenic bacteria thrive on organic matter in warm, moist locations.

Baker's cyst A *bursitis or *hernia occurring in the posterior of the knee, causing the patient to complain of a mass behind the knee. It is relatively common in athletes and may or may not reduce mobility.

balance 1 The ability to maintain a stable and specific orientation in relation to the immediate environment. Static balance refers to the ability to maintain a constant position while stationary, while dynamic balance refers to the ability to maintain equilibrium while moving. Multiple reflexes involving the eyes, the *semi-circular canals and other structures of the ear (*see* labyrinth), pressure receptors in the skin (particularly on the soles of the feet), and muscle *proprioceptors are fundamental mediators of balance. Good balance is necessary for the successful performance of many sports, especially those which require sudden changes in movement, such as gymnastics and tennis. 2 The harmonious development of physical, mental, and spiritual aspects of a person. A philosophical ideal of the ancient Greeks who thought that sport played a key role in the acquisition of balance. 3 An instrument used in weighing.

balanced diet The intake of various nutrients in sufficient quantities and in such proportions as to promote good health. Nutrients are classified into *proteins, *fats, *carbohydrates, *vitamins, *minerals, and water. Although the quantities of a balanced diet will vary with the age, sex, and activity of an individual, the diet should consist of about 50–60 per cent carbohydrate, no more than 35 per cent fats, and 15–20 per cent protein. Vitamins and minerals are needed in relatively small amounts (*see* recommended daily allowance). In addition, *roughage has been shown to be a necessary component of a healthy diet. In the past, athletes in training ate large amounts of protein, such as eggs, meat, and milk, but it is now generally accepted that carbohydrate, and not protein, is the best source of energy. Pasta parties have become almost a ritual for marathon runners on the day before competition (*see* carbohydrate-loading).

balanced tension theory A theory related to the behaviour of groups which suggests that a degree of *stress between groups can be productive if it is controlled and channelled. *Compare* conflict theory. *See also* channelled aggression.

balance tests Methods of evaluating the ability to maintain a *stable equilibrium. There are many different tests of *balance. One of the simplest involves testing an individual's ability to stand quietly on two feet with the eyes open or closed. This may be combined with an *ataxiameter which quantifies head movements, or made more elaborate by using the stick-lengthwise test. In this test, an individual stands with the ball of the foot, or length of one foot, on a stick measuring about 1 inch by 1 inch by 12 inches (or 2.54 cm by 2.54 cm by 30.5 cm). Some investigators increase the height of the stick above the floor. In addition to these simple tests, *teeter boards are used to measure static balance.

ball-and-socket joint (enarthrosis) A *joint (e.g., the *hip-joint or the *shoulder-joint) in which the ball-shaped *head of one bone articulates with the concave, cup-shaped socket of another. Such joints are sometimes called universal joints because they allow movements along three axes (i.e., they allow *abduction, *adduction, *circumduction, *extension, *flexion, and *rotation).

ballistic mobility exercise (kinetic mobility exercise) A *mobility exercise in which the subject uses his or her own body movements to extend *joint range. Arm swings and leg swings are forms of ballistic mobility exercise. *See also* ballistic movement; and ballistic stretching.

ballistic movement A forced movement initiated by active muscular contractions. The final stretched position is not held but the movement continues under the momentum of the limbs without any more muscular contraction. Ballistic movements have three main phases: an initial phase of *concentric muscle contraction which begins the movement, a coasting phase, and a deceleration phase accompanied by *eccentric contractions of *antagonist muscles. *See also* ballistic stretching.

ballistic response A task accomplished by a movement which is performed so quickly that the movement cannot be voluntarily changed, except for minor peripheral corrections, once it is initiated. The fast movement usually takes less than 0.2s. The ballistic response explains why a ball-player does not have to keep his or her eye on the ball during the last quarter second before hitting or catching the ball, as the movement is already committed. Of course, the movement may still cause the player to lose balance and miss the ball.

ballistics The study of the flight-path of projectiles.

ballistic stretching A potentially injurious type of stretching in which an individual performs quick, bouncing contractions of *agonist muscles which force *antagonist muscles to lengthen. The antagonists react by reflexively contracting (*see* stretch reflex), thus shortening and increasing the likelihood of muscle-tears. *Compare* static stretching.

ballistocardiograph An instrument which records the displacement of the body produced by the pumping action of the heart. The record may be altered by disease.

ballistocardiography A *cardiovascular functional test in which the subject's cardiovascular responses while at rest and during different activity levels are recorded on a *ballistocardiograph.

balneotherapy The science of treating disease and injury by the giving of baths. *See* baths; and contrast baths.

bamboo spine *See* ankylosing spondylitis.

bandage A pad or strip of material which may be wrapped around an injured or diseased part to stop bleeding, or to hold a dressing or splint in place.

bandaging *See* taping.

Bandura's self-efficacy theory A theory of situational self-confidence which proposes that *self-efficacy is fundamental to initiating certain behaviours necessary for competent performance. According to the theory, self-efficacy is enhanced by four factors: successful performances, vicarious experiences, verbal persuasion, and emotional arousal. Successful performance, which can be achieved by participatory *modelling, is regarded as the most important factor.

Bankart's operation A surgical procedure, named after the British surgeon A. S. B. Bankart (1879–1951), to repair the *glenoid cavity of a person suffering from repeated shoulder dislocation.

banned substance A performance-enhancing *drug which is subject to doping controls. The *IOC list of banned substances is generally accepted by the governing bodies of most sports. The 1986 list includes the following doping classes and methods:

Doping classes
*Stimulants
*Narcotic analgesics
*Anabolic steroids
*Beta blockers
*Diuretics

Doping methods
*Blood doping
*Pharmacological, chemical and physical manipulation

Classes of drugs subject to certain restrictions
*Alcohol
*Local anaesthetics
*Corticosteroids.

It is not a comprehensive list of individual drugs; the ban applies to all compounds related to those in the list. In addition, individual sports federations may have their own list of banned substances.

bar Unit of pressure equivalent to 0.986 923 atmospheres, 100000 $N m^{-2}$ (pascal), or 1 000 000 dynes per square metre.

barbell A long bar with adjustable weights at each end, used as *free weights in *weight-training.

barbiturates A group of drugs derived from barbituric acid. Barbiturates act as depressants of the *central nervous system and have powerful *anxiolytic and sedative properties. They have been commonly used in sleeping pills. Their effects are likely to disturb complex *motor skills. Barbiturates are habit-forming and habitual use may result in true *addiction.

bar chart (bar graph) Diagrammatic representation of information, such as frequency distributions. Bars of equal width are drawn to represent different categories, with the length of each bar being proportional to the number or frequency of occurrence of each category. *Compare* histogram.

bar graph *See* bar chart.

barometer Instrument for measuring atmospheric pressure.

barometric pressure *See* atmospheric pressure.

baroreceptor *Receptors consisting of nerve-endings, mainly in the *carotid sinus and *aortic arch, which are sensitive to changes in blood pressure.

barotrauma A tissue injury caused by pressure changes (e.g., during diving or after the explosive discharge of a gun). Any part of the body can suffer but the eardrum, sinuses, and lungs are particularly vulnerable. A torn eardrum can lead to infection and deafness; burst lungs can be fatal.

Barr body Particles found in the interphase nucleus of certain non-dividing cells in the *buccal *epithelium in females. The particles probably derived from the inactive *X chromosome; therefore, there is one less Barr body than X chromosome. Presence of a Barr body is used in *sex determination; females usually have one Barr body while males usually have none.

barrier In psychology, an insurmountable obstacle which interferes with the satisfaction of a *need. The barrier may be environmental or within the individual.

basal ganglia (basal nuclei) Cluster of nerve cells in the base of the *cerebral cortex of the brain. Basal ganglia are involved in the control of voluntary movements at the subconscious level. They appear to be particularly important in initiating slow, sustained, stereotyped movements, such as arm-swinging during walking. They form important relay stations between the cerebral cortex, the *thalamus, and the *brainstem nuclei.

basal metabolic rate (BMR) The minimal rate of *metabolism for an individual at body temperature who is not digesting or absorbing food. The BMR is usually expressed in units of energy per unit surface area per unit time. It is estimated from a subject resting quietly after at least 8 hours sleep and 12 hours since the last meal. BMR for adults is between 1200 and 1800 kcal day^{-1}. It is relatively constant for individuals (although it may be increased by regular, intensive exercise) but varies widely among individuals. Factors affecting BMR include age, body-size, body composition (amount of muscle), and sex.

basal nuclei *See* basal ganglia.

base 1 A *proton acceptor; a substance capable of binding with *hydrogen ions. 2 In *anthropometry, a firm horizontal surface on which an individual stands during body measurements. *See also* base of support

baseball finger An injury resulting from a hard, moving object impacting the tip of an extended finger forcing its distal end or middle *interphalangeal joint to be suddenly stretched, sometimes tearing the collateral ligament. The injury results in swelling, immobility, and pain. It occurs most commonly in baseball, but also in cricket, volleyball, and other ball games.

base excess (alkaline excess; BE) A parameter which indicates the acid–alkaline balance in the body. BE is affected by *blood lactate, with which it has a high correlation ($r = 0.98$), and the accumulation of other organic acids which occurs during and after exercise. It may, therefore, reflect adaptation to exercise. Normal BE values are between –2.3 and +2.3 $mmol l^{-1}$.

baseline A level of performance or fitness, prior to training, which is used as a standard to evaluate the effects of the training.

basement membrane Extracellular material consisting of *mucopolysaccharide and fibrous material between the *epithelium and underlying *connective tissue. It supports the epithelium and probably acts as a barrier controlling the exchange of molecules between the epithelium and the underlying tissues.

base of support The region bounded by body-parts in contact with some resistive surface, such as the ground, that exerts a counterforce against the body's applied *force. The outline of the foot is the base of support when standing on one foot.

base unit An arbitrarily defined unit of the *SI system. There are seven base units. They are: *ampere, candela, *kelvin, *kilogram, *metre, *mole, and *second. *Compare* derived unit.

basic movement (basic skill; fundamental skill) A movement or *skill (such as walking, running, hopping, stretching, or twisting) which forms the basis of other, more complex skills.

basic skill *See* basic movement.

basilic vein A principal *vein in the arm extending from the hand, along the forearm to the inner side of the elbow.

basking in reflected glory phenomenon *See* BIRG phenomenon.

basophil A white blood cell whose granular *cytoplasm is stained a deep blue by a basic dye. A basophil has relatively pale nuclei.

bather's itch A skin condition occurring among swimmers bathing in water infested by trematode worms known as Schistosomes. The larvae of the worm penetrate the skin giving it a blotchy rash.

baths Form of treatment used as a relaxant after activity and as a therapy for sports injuries. There are many types of baths, but they all act mainly by either extracting heat from, or adding heat to, the body. *See also* contrast baths.

B-cell (B-lymphocyte) A *lymphocyte formed in the bone marrow. After stimulation by an *antigen, B-cells divide to produce identical daughter cells which manufacture large amounts of the same *antibody.

B complex water-soluble vitamins which function mainly as *coenzymes. *See also* vitamin B.

BE *See* base excess.

bearing The direction of a point (*B*) from a fixed point (*A*) described either as the angle that a line *AB* makes with the line running due north and south through *A*, or as the angle the line *AB* makes with the line running due north through *A* considered in a clockwise direction.

beclomethasone A *corticosteroid, used as an inhaled *steroid by many people suffering from *asthma. Beclomethasone is unlikely to have an ergogenic action (*see* ergogenic aid) and its use is permitted by the *IOC.

bee pollen A mixture of bee saliva, plant pollen, and nectar; it is taken by some athletes in the belief that it is an *ergogenic aid, but claims of ergogenic effects are not supported by scientific studies. Bee pollen can cause allergic reactions in some people.

behaviour 1 The alteration, movement, or response of an object, person, or system acting within a particular context. 2 The externally observable response of a person to an environmental *stimulus. In sociology, an important distinction is made between automatic forms of behaviour which can be analysed in terms of reflexes, and intended action, where social meaning and purposes are also involved. The behaviour of sportspersons can involve a complex mixture of both.

behavioural anxiety A form of *anxiety reflected by an individual's *overt behaviour such as social avoidance.

behavioural coaching A coaching strategy which emphasizes the use of positive *feedback. Typically, the coach breaks down a *motor skill into specific parts which are then modelled for the athlete to copy. The coach supports and encourages the athlete during and after the athlete's attempts to perform the skill.

behavioural kinesiology The study of the structures and processes of human movement and how they are modified by inherent factors, by environmental events, and by therapeutic intervention.

behaviour checklist A means of categorizing and recording behaviours of interest as they occur during an activity. The behaviours are usually clear and specific. The observer records the frequency and/or timing of the behaviours, such as incidents of fighting in a game of soccer.

behavioural sciences The scientific study of individual human and social behaviour.

behaviourism A school of *psychology which stresses an objective natural science approach to psychological questions. Behaviourists usually study the principles of *learning, for example, through animal experiments then apply these principles to understanding and manipulating human behaviour. The main tenet of behaviourism is that only observable behaviour can be scientifically studied. Although this observable behaviour may include verbal behaviour which expresses thoughts, behaviourists tend to ignore mental functions, and concentrate their studies on *stimulus–response relationships and the circumstances under which *conditioning takes place. Behaviourism has influenced sports psychology in procedures such as *behaviour modification and the use of *rewards and *punishments in coaching.

behaviouristic leadership A style of *leadership, adopted by coaches, which applies the principles of *psychology to training. It assumes a close relationship between an athlete's behaviour and performance.

behaviour modification The intentional alteration of human behaviour by various psychological techniques. As an example, certain kinds of behaviour may be rewarded when they occur with the result that the rewarded behaviour is repeated and the unrewarded behaviour dropped. Some coaches see behaviour modification as an important means of motivating athletes; others are very opposed to it and view behaviour modification as a corrupt means of manipulating people; yet others see it as a useful tool to be used only in certain situations.

behaviour therapy Any technique for changing problem behaviour. Behaviour therapy includes *relaxation procedures requiring the subject gradually to approach a feared situation while maintaining physiological arousal at a low level.

belief 1 An *attitude which is based subjectively on emotions rather than on objective evidence. There are many beliefs in sport, particularly concerning diet, ergogenic aids, training, and injury. Some of these beliefs are based on empirical evidence, others are based on superstition or misunderstood theory. An important task of the sports scientist is to examine these beliefs, to support those which are beneficial and have scientific validity, and to give rational explanations for those that are harmful or useless so that they are abandoned. **2** A socially constructed and shared view about what should or should not be, or what is, was, or will be. Beliefs have been classified as either a descriptive belief or a normative belief. A descriptive belief is concerned with what is, or was, or will be; a normative belief is concerned with what should be or ought to be.

belief systems The entire body of knowledge and *beliefs which exist in a particular society or culture. The term may be used to describe patterns of belief and values in sport, and the central principles underlying these which give distinctiveness and coherence to the attitudes towards sport within a society or culture. The belief system of a culture has important implications for the development of sport within that culture.

belladonna The poisonous substance obtained from deadly nightshade (*Atropa* *belladonna*) from which *atropine is obtained.

Bell's palsy Paralysis of muscles on the side of the face and an inability to close one eye due to pressure on the facial nerve.

belly 1 The fleshy middle part of a muscle which forms the main, actively contractile part. 2 The *abdomen or cavity of the abdomen.

Bem sex-role inventory (BSRI) An *inventory in which the subject indicates on a seven-point scale how well each of sixty masculine, feminine, and neutral items describes him or her. On the basis of the responses, the subjects receive a masculinity and femininity score. Subjects scoring low in both femininity and masculinity are labelled undifferentiated, whereas those high in both are classified as *androgynous, or flexible, in their sex-role.

bench A step used in tests of *cardiovascular efficiency. The height of the bench and rate of stepping determines the effort intensity.

bending moment The algebraic sum of the *moments of all the vertical forces to one side of any point on a loaded beam.

bendrofluazide A *drug belonging to the *diuretics which are on the *IOC list of *banned substances.

bends Pain in the joints and limbs occurring as the result of a rapid reduction in atmospheric pressure which causes bubbles of nitrogen gas to accumulate in different parts of the body. *See also* caisson disease.

benign Applied to a condition, such as a tumour, which is not malignant.

benign hypermobility A condition, characterized by a generalized *hypermobility, which is not associated with increased risks of musculoskeletal complaints. *Compare* hypermobile joint disease.

benzocaine A local *anaesthetic available as an ointment and contained in some cough lozenges. It may alleviate a particularly troublesome cough.

benzodiazepines Widely prescribed, and therfore easliy obtainable, *tranquillizers and *anxiolytics. Benzodiazepines are used by some sportspeople for their claimed calming effect. It is generally accepted that they have a low toxicity and low incidence of serious side-effects. They are not, at present, prohibited drugs in sport.

benzphetamine A *drug belonging to the *stimulants which are on the *IOC list of *banned substances.

benzthiazide A *drug belonging to the *diuretics which are on the *IOC list of *banned substances.

beriberi Deficiency disease caused by lack of *thiamine (vitamin B_1). Beriberi leads to a decreased appetite; gastrointestinal disturbances; peripheral nerve changes indicated by weakness of legs, cramping of calf muscles, numbness of the feet; heart enlargement and tachycarditis; and mental confusion.

Berkowitz's reformulation A modification of the *frustration–aggression hypothesis which states that although frustration creates a readiness for aggression, aggressive responses can be modified by *learning.

Bernoulli effect The effect an object has on the layers of a fluid as it passes through the fluid. The pressure on the object by a stream of fluid is decreased as the velocity of fluid flow is increased. Thus fluid pressure is lowest where the relative velocity is greatest. A low pressure zone is created in a region of high fluid flow velocity and a high pressure zone is created in a region of low fluid flow velocity. The Bernoulli effect enables wings to fly, and can be applied to spinning and swerving balls in flight. *See also* magnus effect.

β-adrenergic receptors Receptors in the heart and lungs which respond to *catecholamines.

β_2 agonists (β_2 stimulants) *Drugs which belong to the *sympathomimetic group of *stimulants. They are used in medicines to treat *asthma and other respiratory ailments. The use of certain brands, such as *orciprenaline, is permitted by the *IOC in aerosol form. All oral forms are banned.

beta blockers 1 A *pharmacological class of agents which are banned by the *IOC. They are misused to reduce tension in some sports (e.g., snooker) where physical activity is not of great importance but in which *motor skills can be affected by muscle tremor caused by *anxiety. 2 *Antagonists of the *β receptors which reduce the activity of the heart. They have a wide range of clinical uses, principally in the treatment of *angina and *hypertension.

β-carotene A *nutrient converted by the body to *vitamin A. There is evidence that β-carotene provides protection against some forms of *cancer. Valuable sources include orange fruits and vegetables such as apricots, canteloupes, and carrots as well as leafy green vegetables such as broccoli and spinach. β-carotene lacks the toxicity of vitamin A.

betamcthasone A *drug belonging to the *corticosteroids. It is on the *IOC list of restricted drugs but inhaled preparations, used by asthmatics, are unlikely to have any ergogenic effects and are permitted by the IOC.

β-oxidation Series of reactions by which *fat is broken down from long *carbon chains to two *carbon units in preparation for entry into the *Krebs cycle.

β receptor *Adrenoceptors which are subdivided into β_1 receptors and β_2 receptors. β_1 receptors increase the rate and force of contraction of heart muscle and increase cardiac output. Stimulation of β_2 receptors causes *branchodilation, and *vasodilation of blood vessels in *skeletal muscle. Action of these receptors is blocked by inhibiting drugs called *beta blockers.

β_2 stimulants *See* β_2 agonists.

betaxolol A *beta blocker which has more affinity for β_1 receptors than β_2 receptors. Betaxolol is a commonly used *cardioselective drug which is on the *IOC list of *banned substances.

biacromial breadth In *anthropometry, the distance between the most lateral points of the two *acromion processes when an individual is standing upright with arms hanging loosely at the sides. It is a measurement of shoulder width. *See also* body breadths.

biacromial : biliocristal ratio The ratio of shoulder width (*see* biacromial breadth) to hip width (*see* biliocristal breadth). The biacromial : biliocristal ratio gives an indication of trunk build. Males tend to have a higher ratio than females.

biarticulate muscle A *muscle which spans two *joints.

bias 1 In research, the distortion of data or findings by the research method employed, or by the rearcher's suppositions. Bias results in a loss of accuracy, reliability, and validity of the research. 2 In statistics, a difference between the hypothetical 'true value' of a variable in a population and that obtained in a particular sample.

biased sample In statistics, a population sample which is not a true reflection of the parent population.

biaxial movement A movement in two *planes.

bicarbonate Ions which are formed as a by-product of carbonic acid. Bicarbonate ions are the main form by which carbon dioxide is carried in the blood. Some physiologists advocate the use of bicarbonate ions as an *ergogenic aid in the belief that the ions increase the *alkali reserve and neutralize *lactic acid, thereby forestalling the onset of *fatigue during heavy prolonged exercise.

biceps A two-headed muscle. *See also* biceps brachii; and biceps femoris.

biceps brachii (biceps) A two-headed *fusiform muscle which bulges when the *forearm is flexed. The *origin of its short *head is on the *coracoid process, and that of the long head is on the *tubercle above the *glenoid cavity and on the lip of the glenoid cavity. Its *insertion is by a common *tendon onto the *radial tuberosity. Contraction of the biceps flexes the *elbow joint and supinates the forearm (*see* supination). It also acts as a weak *flexor and *abductor of the arm at the shoulder.

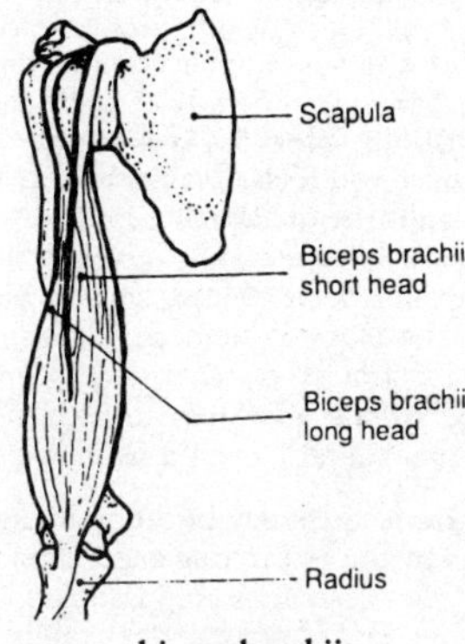

biceps brachii

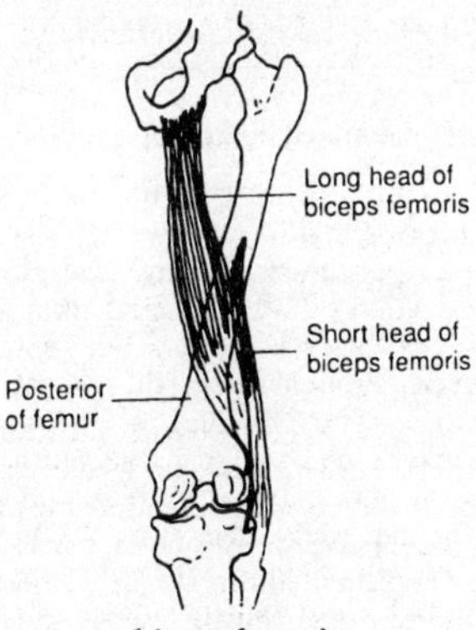

biceps femoris

biceps femoris The most lateral of the three *hamstring muscles. The biceps femoris is a two-headed muscle with the *origin of its long *head on the *ischial tuberosity, and the origin of its short head on the *linea aspera and *distal part of the *femur. It has a common *insertion onto the head of the *fibula and the lateral *condyle of the *tibia. Contraction of the biceps femoris extends the thigh and flexes the knee, and enables lateral *rotation of the leg, especially when the knee is flexed.

biceps groove *See* intertubercular groove.

biceps skinfold A *skinfold measurement of a vertical fold of tissue midline between the *acromiale and the *radiale on the anterior surface of the arm.

bicipital groove *See* intertubercular groove.

bicondylar breadth In *anthropometry, the distance between the *distal *condyles of the *femur, giving a measure of breadth across the knee.

bicuspid valve (mitral valve) The *valve preventing backflow of blood from the left *ventricle into the left *atrium of the heart.

bicycle ergometer A static cycle which has the drive wheel removed; used for the estimation of work output during exercise. The workload is adjusted by changing the gearing or by adjusting weights attached to a flywheel. Many of the modern cycle ergometers are computerized to give direct readouts of workloads, etc.

bifurcation Division into two branches; often applied to branching *blood vessels.

bigeminy Alternating normal and premature *ventricular systole, as revealed by an *electrocardiogram.

bilateral Pertaining to both sides of the body or body-part.

bilateral integration The simultaneous co-ordination of both sides of the body to perform a smooth movement.

bilateral transfer Transfer of a *skill learned on one side of the body to the other side. The acquisition of a particular skill involving the left hand is accelerated, for example, if that skill has already been learnt for the right hand. *See also* transfer of training.

bile *See* bile salts.

bile salts (bile) A greenish-yellow or brownish fluid produced in the liver from the breakdown products of *cholesterol, inorganic salt, and red blood cells. Bile is stored in the *gall-bladder and released into the *small intestine where it aids digestion and *adsorption of fats through its alkaline, emulsifying action.

biliocristal breadth The distance between the most lateral points on the surface of the *iliac crest. It is a measure of hip width. *See also* body girths.

binding site An area of an *enzyme to which other molecules can attach themselves. *See also* active site; and allosteric inhibitor.

binocular vision Vision in which the image of an object falls on both *retina at the same time, facilitating depth perception and stereoscopic, three-dimensional vision. The slightly different positions of the two eyes are important in allowing the object to be viewed from slightly different angles.

bioassay A technique in which the presence of a chemical is quantified by comparing its effects on living organisms with the effects of a known standard.

bioavailability The proportion of a *drug that reaches its site of action in the body.

biochemistry The study of the chemistry of living organisms.

bioenergetics The study of energy transformations in living organisms.

biofeedback Continuous visual or auditory information supplied to a subject concerning his or her physiological responses, such as heart rate and blood pressure, at the same time as they occur. *See also* biofeedback training.

biofeedback training (autoconditioning) A relaxation technique which depends on the subject receiving a continuous and immediate flow of information about some of his or her physiological functions that are commonly considered involuntary. The subject then attempts to modify these functions by a conscious effort; the results of the attempt are fed back to the subject. As an example, an athlete may be presented with a visual display of heart rate and muscle action potentials (indicating muscle tension) and learn progressively to control these variables.

biogenic amines A class of chemicals which can function as *neurotransmitters. They include *catecholamines and *indolamines.

biological rhythm *See* biorhythm.

biomechanics The application of physics and mechanics to the study of movement of organisms. In sport, biomechanics is especially concerned with how the human body applies forces to itself and to other bodies with which it comes into contact, and how the body is affected by external forces. A sound knowledge of biomechanics equips a coach or athlete to choose appropriate training techniques, and to detect and understand faults that may arise in their use.

biophysics The study of the properties of matter and energy in living organisms.

biopsy The removal and examination of tissue from a living body. A biopsy (e.g., to determine the proportion of fibre-types in muscle) is performed by taking a small sample of muscle, usually from the thigh or calf. The sample is sectioned and stained, and then examined microscopically.

biorhythm (biological rhythm) Cycles of human biological activity. It is claimed that each person has negative and positive periods within a 23-day physical cycle, a 28-day emotional cycle and a 33-day intellectual cycle. Proponents of the use of biorhythms as a means of predicting performance potential compile biorhythm charts which plot the cycles. Although there are wide individual differences, the correlation between changes of athletc performance and biorhythm has generally been found not to be strong. *See also* circadian rhythm; and diurnal rhythm.

biotin A vitamin of the B complex, also known as vitamin H. Biotin is found in small amounts in the tissue, combined with protein. It acts as a *coenzyme for *enzymes important in the metabolism of carbohydrates, fats, and proteins. Deficiency results in scaly skin, muscular pain, pallor, loss of appetite, nausea, fatigue, and elevated cholesterol levels. Some biotin is synthesized by bacteria in the *alimentary canal; sources in food include liver, egg yolk, and legumes.

bipennate *See* pennate muscle.

BIRG phenomenon (basking in reflected glory phenomenon) An individual's positive identification with a successful sports team in order to escape from a normally mundane lifestyle.

bisopropol A *drug belonging to the *beta blockers which are on the *IOC list of *banned substances.

bit A unit of information used in computers. The term is derived from BInary digiT. One bit is the amount of information required to reduce the original amount of uncertainty by half.

bitolterol A *drug belonging to to the β_2 agonists. Its use in aerosol form is permitted by the *IOC, subject to written notification, for the treatment of *asthma and other respiratory conditions. It may not be taken orally.

black box model A model of *information-processing in which an individual is considered to be the black box into which information flows from the environment. The information is processed in various ways inside the box until it is output as observable behaviour. Researchers using this model have been concerned mainly with what went into the box (the information or stimuli) and output (behaviour). Nothing of the structure of the box is known beyond what can be deduced from behaviour.

black bulb thermometer A thermometer placed in a black globe to measure *radiant energy or solar radiation, one of the three temperatures required to complete the *WBGT index.

black eye Bruising of the eye producing discoloration. The area around the eye is well supplied with blood and a blow to the eye or surrounding structures can cause internal bleeding which usually causes the discoloration. A black eye may indicate a more serious injury, such as a fractured cheek-bone.

black nail (runner's toe; soccer toe; tennis toe) Blackening of the toe-nail near its base. It may be very painful and accompanied by swelling of the joint. Runner's toe is commonly caused by the shoe being too short or too wide so that the foot slides forward and jams against the end of the shoe, especially on dry, artificial turf. Black nail may also be caused by a direct blow to the toe. The nail later dies and grows out with the black area growing away from the nail-bed eventually to drop off. The condition can be prevented by wearing well-fitting shoes, and it can be treated by inserting a heated, sterilized pin through the nail to create a hole which releases the blood. *See also* turf-toe syndrome.

blackout A temporary loss of consciousness. This has many causes, including a direct blow which occurs quite commonly in contact sports. *See also* concussion.

blind trial A method for testing the effectiveness of a *drug or any other treatment. Only the subjects are prevented from knowing whether the active drug or a *placebo has been administered. *See also* double-blind trial.

Bliss–Boder hypothesis An early, largely unsubstantiated hypothesis, that claims that attention devoted to well-practised movements will result in their disruption.

blister An injury to the skin in which the top layer is detached from the underlying layer; the gap between becomes filled with a watery fluid extruded by damaged cells. The blister is usually painful because the thick, outer *epidermis is lifted away to expose nerve-endings. It is caused by friction and is common among athletes who compete in brand new shoes without wearing them in properly. The prophylactic application of surgical spirit to the feet is a time-honoured tradition which may help prevent blisters. The blister can be treated by releasing the fluid with a sterilized needle, snipping away dead skin, and then applying a sterile dressing.

blocker's exostosis Deposition of bone in muscle of the upper arm which occurs commonly in defensive blockers in American football who suffer severe blows to the arm. *See also* myositis ossificans.

block rotation Lateral rotation of both trunk and pelvis at the same time.

blood *Connective tissue consisting of *erythrocytes, *white blood cells, and *blood platelets, with a liquid matrix called *plasma. It is the main transport medium in the body. *See also* lymph.

blood–brain barrier The layer of cells, covering the capillaries in the brain, which inhibits the passage of molecules, particularly those which have poor lipid-solubility, from the blood into brain tissue. It is important to consider the blood-barrier when designing *drugs, since the drug's ability to cross this barrier can affect the balance of its therapeutic and toxic effects.

blood chemistry tests Blood tests that measure the levels of naturally occurring circulating chemicals, such as *glucose and *lactate, or ingested drugs in the blood.

blood clotting *See* coagulation.

blood doping The administration of a *blood transfusion to a competitor other than as a legitimate medical treatment. Blood doping is carried out in the belief that it will increase the oxygen-carrying capacity of the circulatory system and therefore improve endurance. The blood may have been obtained from the competitior (autotranfusion) or from another individual. In autotransfusions, the blood is usually extracted from the competitor some time before the competition so that the body has a chance to replace the lost blood. Then, the stored blood is put back just prior to competition to boost the red blood cell count. In addition to contravening the ethics of medicine and sport, this procedure carries a number of risks. These include the possibility of increasing the blood viscosity which may overload the heart, the transmission of infectious diseases, kidney damage, and overload of the circulatory system. Blood doping is banned by the *IOC. *See also* erythropoietin.

blood flow The volume of blood flowing through a vessel or organ at a particular time. *See also* shunting.

blood glucose *Glucose dissolved in the blood. Too much glucose in the blood results in *hyperglycaemia and too little results in *hypoglycaemia; both conditions are harmful. Blood glucose level is controlled mainly by *insulin. Other hormones, especially *glucagon, *adrenaline, and *glucocorticoids, also affect the blood glucose concentration. Blood glucose level is a crucial factor in *diabetes mellitus.

blood group Any one of the many types into which a person's blood can be classified on the basis of the *antigens on the surface of the red blood cells. One of the most important is the *ABO blood group.

blood lactate *Lactate dissolved in the blood. Blood lactate concentration is used as a biochemical measurement of *anaerobic capacity and *aerobic capacity. Normal values are between 0.7 and 1.8 $mmol\,l^{-1}$.

blood plasma *See* plasma.

blood platelets (platelets; thrombocytes) Disc-like components of the blood; blood platelets are non-nucleated fragments of large *bone marrow cells which play an important role in blood *clotting.

blood pressure The *force exerted by blood against a unit area of blood vessel. It is the driving force which moves the blood through the circulatory system. Usually two measurements are made: systolic pressure and diastolic pressure. Systolic blood pressure is obtained when the blood is ejected into the arteries from the heart, and is the highest blood pressure. The systolic pressure in children is approximately equal to that of a column of mercury about 100 mm high; in young adults the value is about 120 mm, and it tends to rise with age as arteries get thicker. A systolic pressure of 180 is not uncommon and it may be as high as 280. The value varies according to the subject's body position (*see* postural hypotensive drop). Mental worry combined with lack of exercise may contribute to high blood pressure (*see* hypertension). The diastolic blood pressure is obtained when blood drains from the arteries, and is the lowest blood pressure. A typical value for diastolic pressure is 80 mmHg.

blood pressure cuff *See* sphygmomanometer.

blood retransfusion *See* blood doping.

blood serum The blood *plasma from which *fibrinogen has been removed.

blood transfusion The intravenous administration of red blood cells, or related blood products that contain red blood cells. *See also* blood doping.

blood volume Volume of blood in the circulatory system, typically about 5 l.

B-lymphocyte *See* B-cell.

BMI *See* body-mass index.

BMR *See* basal metabolic rate.

board-and-scale method (reaction board method) A method of calculating the *centre of gravity of a living person by weighing the person in different positions on a large *reaction board and applying principles of *static equilibrium in the calculation. The reaction board is supported on two thin edges, one of which rests on a block of wood and the other on the platform of a set of scales.

bobo doll An inflatable plastic doll used in the research of *aggression. The doll provides reinforcement when acts of physical aggression are made against it; when punched, the eyes light up and marbles are dispensed from the doll's stomach.

body 1 The human body. **2** In *biomechanics, a term which refers to both animate objects, such as the human body, and inanimate objects, such as a projectile or other item of sports equipment. In some cases, it is convenient to consider the human body in its entirety; in other cases it is better to consider the human body as a system comprised of separate bodies (*see* body-segments).

body awareness The recognition of different parts of one's own body, their relative position during movement, and their relationship to the environment. Body awareness is dependent on sensory information from the muscles and joints, and is essential for smooth, co-ordinated movement. *See also* kinaesthesis.

body breadths Measurements of the linear extent from side to side of a part of the human body. Those commonly used in *anthropometry are *biacromial breadth, *biliocristal breadth, *femur width, and *transverse chest width.

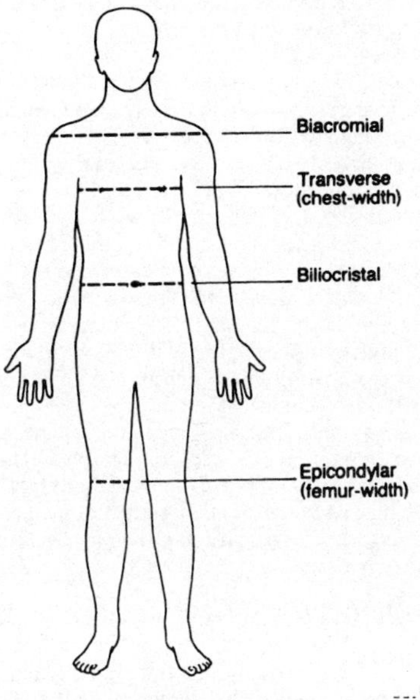

body breadths

body build *See* somatotype.

body building The use of exercises, such as *weight-training, in order to develop the size, shape, and symmetry of body muscles and make them more conspicuous. Body-builders compete by posing in front of judges who assess them subjectively.

body composition The relative percentage of *fat, *muscle, *bone, and other tissue in a human body. The most common approach to analysis of body composition has been to estimate percentage *body fat and *lean body-mass. *See also* body-mass index; cadaver dissection analysis; and obesity.

body culture An emphasis on body-shape in the light of the prevailing cultural preferences or fashions of society (e.g., the cult of slenderness).

body density The weight of a body per unit volume, usually expressed as $kg l^{-1}$ or $g cm^{-3}$. Body density requires the measurement of body volume. This is usually done by applying *Archimedes' principle and weighing the subject in air, then weighing the subject fully submerged in water, and making a correction for the residual volume of air trapped in the lungs and the air trapped in the digestive tract.

body fat A measurement of the amount of fat in the human body, usually expressed as a percentage of total body-weight. The percentage body fat of an average adult male is between 15 and 17 per cent, and that of a female about 25 per cent; values for athletes tend to be less. The fat and non-fat components of the body can be measured directly by *cadaver dissection analysis. The percentage body fat can be estimated from *body density using the *Siri equation: percentage fat=(495/body density)−450. Other methods include *skinfold measurements, *ultrasound, *nuclear magnetic resonance, and *computer-assisted tomography. The absolute body fat is the total weight of fat in the human body; it is the product of the percentage body fat and body-weight. *See also* adipose tissue.

body fluids The watery solutions in the human body which include *intracellular fluid, *tissue fluid, *blood, and *lymph. The body fluids make up more than half the body-weight of a person; most metabolic reactions (*see* metabolism) take place in the body fluids.

body girths Measurements of the circumference of different parts of the human body. Body girths commonly used in *anthropometry are *ankle girth, *chest girth, *gluteal girth, *head girth, *neck girth, *relaxed arm girth, *thigh girth, *waist girth, and *wrist girth.

body heights (body lengths) A measurement of the human body from the bottom of a structure to the top of the same structure, or a measurement taken at standardized points which indicate body stature. A number of different measurements of body height are used in *anthropometry. These include *acromial height, *dactylion height, *radial height, *spinale height, *stylion height, *tibial height, and *trochanterion height. *See also* sitting height.

body image (body schema) The *perception, both conscious and unconscious, of one's own body and physical dimensions. *See also* self-concept.

body language A form of non-verbal communication using movements and positioning of body parts. *See also* kinesics.

body length *See* body heights.

body-mass In *anthropometry, the mass of the human body measured to the nearest tenth of a kg when the subject is nude, or with clothing of known mass so that a correction to nude mass can be made.

body-mass index (BMI; Quetelet index) An estimate of *body composition used especially in epidemiological studies:

$$\text{BMI} = \text{weight in kg}/(\text{height in metre})^2$$

The index has insignificant correlations with *stature, but has a positive correlation with *skinfold measurements. It has been used as an indicator of *obesity on the assumption that the higher the index, the greater the level of *body fat. However, this assumption is not always true. When applying the index to some very lean individuals, such as weight-lifters, they can be falsely classified as obese because of muscle bulk.

body mechanics Application of physical laws to the human body at rest or in motion. Body mechanics once referred to postural activities only. The term has been largely replaced by *biomechanics.

body of vertebra *See* centrum.

body part identification The ability to name different parts of the body in response to a label. A component of *body awareness.

body schema *See* body image.

body-segments The division of the body into regions. There are eight main body-segments: the head, trunk, arm, forearm, hand, thigh, leg, and foot.

body-size A characteristic determined by both height and weight; often quantified by using the *ponderal index.

body sway The slight postural movements an individual makes in order to maintain a balanced position. It is also called postural sway.

body temperature The temperature of the human body as measured with a clinical thermometer. *See also* core temperature.

body temperature and pressure saturated A reference point for making gas volume corrections (e.g., from *ATPS), when it is necessary to know the volume of air that is ventilated by the lungs, and not the number of gas molecules present. Body temperature is 37°C and the body pressure is the same as *ambient pressure. When air at room temperature (20°C) is inhaled, its volume will expand in the lungs as a result of the increase in temperature from (from 20 to 37°C) and the addition of water vapour molecules because of the increase in temperature. Corrections to BTPS are necessary, therefore, for all respiratory gas measurements dealing with volume only (e.g., *vital capacity, *tidal volume, *minute volume, and *maximal breathing capacity).

body volume Body-mass divided by body density. It may be measured hydrostatically by weighing a subject in air and then weighing the subject completely immersed in water (*see* body density).

body-weight The gravitational force that the earth exerts on a human body at or near its surface. Body-weight is the product of body-mass (in kg) and *acceleration due to *gravity (9.81 ms^{-2}) measured in newtons (N).

Bohr effect *See* Bohr shift.

Bohr shift (Bohr effect) A shift to the right of an *oxygen dissociation curve due to an increase in carbon dioxide or acid in the blood. At most partial pressures of oxygen in the body, this results in a reduced effectiveness of haemoglobin to carry oxygen which makes unloading oxygen in the tissues more efficient.

boil (furuncle) A tender, inflamed, pus-filled area of skin usually caused by infection with the bacterium *Staphyllococcus aureus*.

bomb calorimeter A thick-walled container in which organic material is burned in an oxygen-rich atmosphere to estimate the *energy content of the material. It is used for measuring the calorific value of food. The food is placed in the chamber and ignited with an electric spark. Its combustion results in the liberation of heat which causes a change in the temperature of water surrounding the chamber.

bond That which links or holds one person to another.

bond energy The *energy characterizing a chemical bond between two atoms; it is measured by the energy required to separate the two atoms.

bonding The development of close interpersonal relationships; such as that which results from the attachment process between a parent and infant.

bone The hardest *connective tissue in the human body, it consists of a hard calcified matrix, mainly of *calcium phosphate, and *collagen fibres. Over 200 bones make up the *skeleton of the human body. Bone is living material and is very well vascularized (*see* Haversian system). Bones support and protect soft parts of the body; they act as levers for muscles during locomotion; they store calcium and fats; and they are involved in the production of *blood cells. Bones fall into four main classes according to their shape and size: *short bone, *long bone, *flat bone, and *irregular bone. Bone may also be classified according to its density as either smooth, dense, *compact bone or less dense *spongy bone.

bone injury Bone is very strong, but it is also relatively rigid so that if it yields at all, it tends to fracture. Sensation is confined to the *periosteum, so unless this structure is damaged, disorders of the bone are painless. However, pain is severe if the periosteum is even slightly stretched (e.g., by a *stress fracture). A number of bone injuries common in sport are: stress fracture, Osgood–Schlatter disease, and *epiphysitis.

bone marrow Modified *connective tissue of a *vascular nature found in the *long bones and some *flat bones. Bone marrow fills the tiny spaces between the *trabeculae of *spongy bone and in the cavity of the shaft of *long bones. It is red between the trabeculae, and yellow in the *medullary canal.

bone-remodelling The ability of *bone to respond to mechanical demands placed on it by changing its size, shape, and structure; the process involved in bone formation and destruction in response to hormonal and mechanical factors. Bones have to be mechanically stressed to remain healthy. They become heavier and stronger if gravity and muscle contractions impose forces on them. If a person is inactive and the bone is not stressed, it will atrophy (*see* osteoporosis). *See also* Wolff's law.

bone scan Use of scintigraphy (*see* scintigram) to examine the condition of bone. The differential distribution of radioactivity in the bone after introduction of a small dose of a radioactive substance (e.g., technetium-99 complexed with a diphosphonate derivative) may be used in the diagnosis of some sports injuries.

bony spur An abnormal projection from a bone due to bone overgrowth.

bony thorax (thoracic cage) Bones that form the framework of the *thorax; they include the *sternum, *ribs, and *thoracic vertebrae.

boredom A condition characterized by wandering attention, impaired efficiency, and low levels of *arousal. It is sometimes confused with *fatigue, but boredom can be viewed as the result of an underload on a system where there is lack of stimulation, motivation, and interest. It is commonly caused in sport by monotonous training routines.

born athlete A term commonly applied to an individual who exhibits great proficiency in a range of physical activities, apparently after very little practice. Many dispute the validity of its use and argue that athletes acquire their proficiency through *training rather than through *inheritance. *See also* genetic endowment.

bottleneck In structural models of *attention, a certain point in the *central nervous system through which the passage of information is restricted.

bouncing breast syndrome A condition in females who run with breasts not fully supported. Running causes the breasts to move, damaging the suspensory ligaments, and possibly resulting in a form of mastitis (inflammation of the breast). A simple preventative procedure is to wear a well-fitting sports bra.

boundary layer The layer of fluid closest to a *body over which the fluid is flowing. The boundary layer is subjected to viscous stresses (*see* viscosity) due to *adhesion between the water and the body surface which reduces its velocity relative to the body and thereby increasing *drag.

boundary-layer separation point The point at which the *boundary layer of a fluid passing over a *body separates from the surface of the body. It often coincides with the point of *eddy formation, the breakdown of *laminar flow, and the development of *turbulence.

bow legs *See* genu varum.

bowler's hip A condition characterized by a chronic pain deep in the hip. It is caused by inflammation of the *iliopsoas tendon and its *bursa at the attachment point of the tendon on the inner part of the *femur just below the hip. Bowler's hip may occur in any sport but is common in those which include repeated hip extension coupled with a twisting actions of the lower back.

bowler's thumb An injury at the base of the thumb to either the tendon or to the *ulnar nerve, causing a *perineal fibrosis. Bowler's thumb is found commonly in tenpin bowlers who attempt to put spin on the ball by retaining the thumb within the thumbhole until the last possible moment before release. The bowling action puts great strain on the tendons and the ulnar nerve. It may be a transient condition with the symptoms subsiding with the cessation of bowling, but it sometimes results in permanent damage to the nerve. It can be avoided by widening the thumbhole, changing technique, or padding the thumb.

Bowman's capsule A small sac at the end of the *kidney *nephron involved in the *ultrafiltration of *blood from the *glomerulus.

boxer's arm An injury resulting from a direct blow detaching a small spur of bone which has developed just above the elbow in some boxers. After extended rest, the spur usually reattaches itself.

boxer's fracture A *fracture of the neck of the fifth *metacarpal bone. The fracture usually produces a *flexion deformity. It commonly results from a mistimed punch.

boxer's knuckle An injury of the soft tissue of the knuckle. It is common in boxers who have their outstretched hands bandaged before a fight. This results in the bandages being too tight when the hand is flexed to make a fist, damaging underlying tissue. The damage may result in a *bursitis over the metacarpal head or a *distraction of the intermetacarpal ligaments.

boxer's muscle *See* serratus anterior.

Boyle's law The law that relates pressure and volume of a *perfect gas. It states that at a contant temperature, the volume (V) of a given quantity of gas is inversely proportional to the pressure (P) upon the gas; that is, V is proportional to $1/P$. Thus, increasing the pressure of a gas causes a proportional decrease in its volume.

brace A support used to hold parts of the body in the correct position.

braced knee-support An external, metal, hinged support, sometimes used by those with damaged *cruciate ligaments of the knee in order to play a non-contact sport.

brachial In *anatomy, pertaining to the arm.

brachial artery A major *artery in the upper arm. Because of its large size, the brachial artery is relatively easy to locate and is used to take measurements of the *pulse (the brachial pulse) and to take *blood pressure measurements using a *sphygmomanometer.

brachialgia A deep and widespread pain radiating into the arms. It is commonly caused by compression of the cervical nerve. Treatment includes supporting the neck with a cervical collar, heat treatment, and physiotherapy.

brachialis A strong *muscle lying immediately below the *biceps brachii in the upper arm. It has its *origin on the *humerus and its insertion on the *coronoid process of the *ulna and the *capsule of the elbow joint. It is a *prime mover of *elbow flexion.

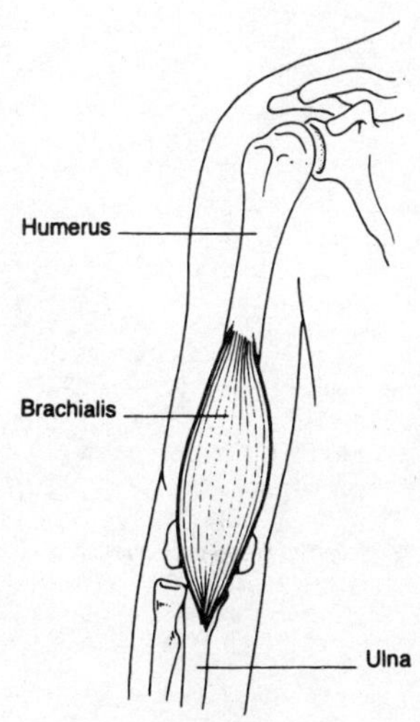

brachialis

brachial plexus A network of nerves at the base of the neck which supplies the arm, forearm, hand, and parts of the shoulder-girdle.

brachial pulse *See* brachial artery.

brachioradialis A *superficial *muscle in the forearm which has its *origin on the lateral supracondylar ridge at the *distal end of the *humerus and its *insertion at the base of the *styloid process of the *radius. The brachioradialis is a *synergist, helping to stabilize the elbow during *flexion of the forearm. It is also a prime flexor when the arm is in midposition.

brachium (pl. brachii) The arm, especially the part between the shoulder and elbow.

bracketed morality In sport, the suspension, during competition, of the high level of ethical morality necessary for everyday life.

bradycardia A decreased or slowed heart rate, sometimes taken as being less than 60

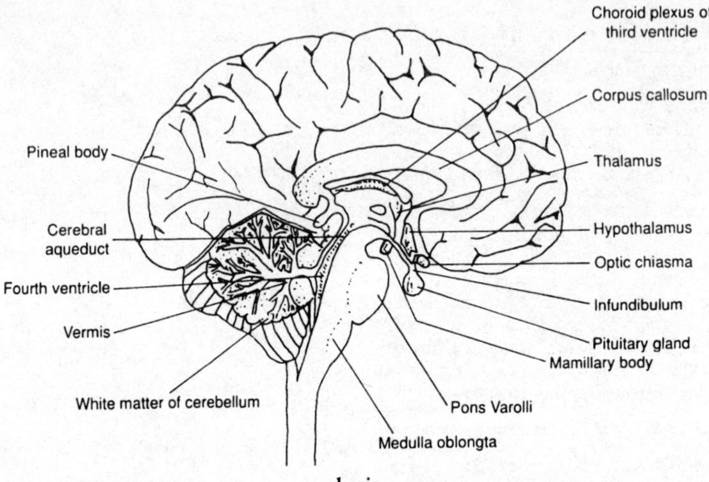

brain

beats per minute. It is a usual and normal effect of *endurance-training. *See also* athlete's heart; and heart hypertrophy.

bradykinin A potent, pain-eliciting chemical produced wherever body tissue is damaged. Bradykinin triggers the production of other chemicals such as *histamines and *prostaglandins. Some researchers believe that bradykinin attaches to pain receptors, causing them to send impulses to the *central nervous system. During exercise, bradykinin may be released in response to the increased acidity which occurs in active muscle, causing *vasodilation of the tissues and promoting sweating. There is strong evidence that it contributes to the inflammation response, particularly the early stages.

brain The part of the *central nervous system which is contained within the *skull. The main regions of the brain are the *cortex, *cerebellum, and *medulla oblongata.

brainstem Part of the *brain positioned between the *cerebrum and the *spinal cord, and which includes the midbrain, the *pons, and *medulla oblongata. The brainstem is responsible for many autonomic functions (*see* autonomic nervous system).

brain ventricles The fluid-filled cavities of the brain.

brainwaves Patterns of electrical activity of the *neurones of the brain which can be recorded with an *electroencephalogram.

breastbone *See* sternum.

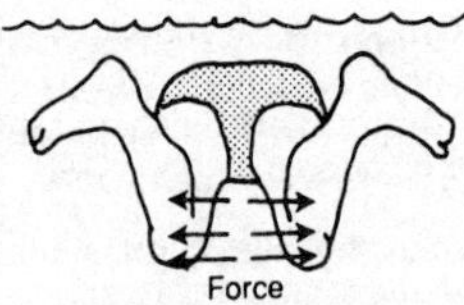

breast stroker's knee

breast-stroker's knee An injury, characterized by tenderness on the medial side of the knee, often caused by the hydrodynamic forces produced by swimmers using a breast-stroke action. In the propulsive phase, the knee extends and rotates medially with the foot in a pronated position. Hydrodynamic forces tend to abduct the leg at the knee-joint. The tender spot often coincides with the adductor tubercle and the associated medial collateral ligament. It is possible that swimmers who perform whip-kicks are more prone to the condition because of extensive *abduction–*adduction at the hip. Strong contractions of the stabilizers,

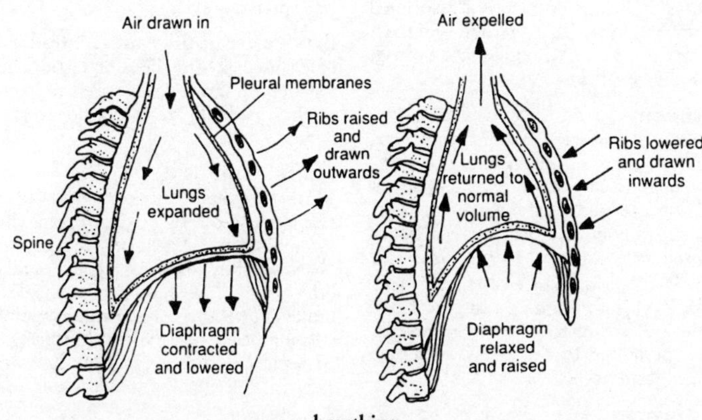

breathing

the quadriceps and the hamstrings, may limit abduction and adduction of the lower leg and reduce the risk of this injury.

breathing The process by which air is drawn into, and expelled from, the *alveoli (the specialized region of gaseous exchange in the body) of the lungs.

breathing reserve *See* ventilatory reserve.

breathlessness An inability to breathe easily. Breathlessness may indicate a *pulmonary or *cardiac malfunction if it occurs with mild exertion.

bregma Point at the top of the *skull where the coronal and sagittal sutures join.

British thermal unit (BTU) Quantity of heat required to raise the temperature of one pound of water by one degree Fahrenheit at, or near, its point of maximum density. One BTU equals 0.252 kcal.

Broadbent model A model of *selective attention based on the proposition that irrelevant stimuli are eliminated before they reach the *memory. Therefore, most of the information received by the senses is *gated out and never analysed. *Compare* pertinence model; and Triesman model.

broad cross-fibre stroke A massage administered with the thumb slowly stroking across a muscle at an angle of 90°. This massage stretches the muscle across its breadth.

broad external An *attentional style in which an individual has an ability to deal effectively with many external stimuli at the same time. *Compare* external overload.

broad internal An *attentional style in which an individual has the ability to integrate several ideas at the same time. *Compare* internal overload.

broken bone *See* fracture.

bronchial tree *See* respiratory tree.

bronchiectasis Sac-like dilations of the smaller divisions of the *bronchi and *bronchioles which may be *congenital or arise from infection.

bronchiole One of the smaller air tubules branching off the *bronchi (*see* bronchus) into the *lungs. Each bronchiole terminates in an elongated saccule called an *atrium. Bronchioles lack *cartilage and have *smooth muscle within their walls which controls the *lumen size. *See also* bronchodilator.

bronchitis *Inflammation of the *bronchi resulting in restricted airflow to the *lungs. It is marked by a hacking cough which attempts to clear the tubes. Acute bronchitis is due to viral or bacterial infections and is aggravated by physical activity. Therefore, a premature return to sport may exacerbate the illness. *Chronic bronchitis is associated with tobacco-smoking; *aerobic exercise, particularly in those who give up smoking, is generally beneficial.

bronchodilator A *drug which relaxes the *smooth muscle in a *bronchiole, thereby dilating its *lumen and easing the passage of air in and out of the *lungs. Bronchodilators are used to treat *asthma. Many are *sympathomimetic drugs which act as *agonists on β_2 adrenoceptors. They are regarded as performance-enhancers and, therefore, subject to doping controls. However, the use by athletes of some bronchodilators is permitted by the *IOC, subject to certain conditions.

bronchogram An *X-ray photograph taken of the *bronchial tree after the introduction of a substance which is radio-opaque.

bronchospasm A sudden contraction of the *smooth muscles which causes narrowing of the *bronchi. It may be induced by an *allergen, as in *asthma, or it may be associated with *bronchitis.

bronchus (pl. **bronchi**) One of the pair of tubes leading from the *trachea into the *lungs. A bronchus is reinforced with an incomplete ring of *cartilage to prevent it collapsing. It is lined with ciliated glandular epithelial tissue (*see* cilia) which propels small solid particles, such as dust, towards the mouth.

brown fat cells A highly vascularized layer of fat-containing cells, found particularly around the shoulder-blades and kidneys, which are involved in *thermogenesis. The cells are rich in *mitochondria which cause them to appear brown. The mitochondria contain large amounts of pigmented *cytochromes which enable them rapidly to generate large amounts of heat which is transported by the *vascular system. High metabolic activity of the brown fat cells is stimulated by ingestion of food and by *noradrenaline. Some forms of *obesity may be linked with a lack of brown fat cells.

Brozec formula A formula for determining percentage *fat composition from *body density. The formula is: percentage fat$=(4.570/\text{body density}-4.142)\times100$. *See also* specific gravity.

Bruce's treadmill test A *treadmill test much used in the USA for testing cardiac function. In this test, the speed and gradient of the treadmill are increased every third minute.

bruise (**contusion**) Seepage of blood, which gradually decomposes and is absorbed, into a tissue. The bruise changes colour, first to blue as the red pigment of *haemoglobin loses its oxygen, and then brown to yellowish as the haemoglobin is broken down and reabsorbed. Prevention of effusion of blood from small bruises can be achieved by applying a firm pressure for 3–5 min, followed by a cold compress. *See also* haematoma.

BSRI *See* Bem sex-role inventory.

B-TAIS A specific baseball and softball test of attentional and interpersonal styles. It is derived from the general *TAIS but uses sport-specific questions. It is thought to have a greater validity for the above sports than the general test.

BTPS *See* body temperature and pressure saturated.

BTU *See* British thermal unit.

buccal In *anatomy, pertaining to the cheek.

budesonide A *steroid used in the treatment of *asthma. Inhalation by aerosol is permitted by the *IOC, subject to written notification.

buffer A chemical substance which resists abrupt and large changes in hydrogen ion concentration (*see* pH) of the body fluids on addition of an acid or an alkali. Buffers bond to hydrogen ions, removing them from solution when the hydrogen ion concentration rises and releasing the ions when the hydrogen ion concentration falls. Many *proteins, such as *haemoglobin, are good buffers. *See also* renal buffering; and ventilatory buffering.

bulimia An eating disorder characterized by sequences of excessive eating followed by self-induced vomiting. *See also* anorexia nervosa.

bumetanide A *drug belonging to the *diuretics which are on the *IOC list of *banned substances.

bundle of His (atrioventricular bundle) Specialized fibres in the *heart which carry electrical signals for contraction from the *atrioventricular node down the *septum, between the *ventricles, and eventually into the *Purkinje fibres.

bunion A deformity found at the base of the big toe, commonly caused by ill-fitting footwear. The skin over the big toe is thickened and the head of the *metatarsal bone becomes unduly prominent. Treatment may involve simple *orthotics, or the use of a soft spongy pad to straighten the big toe. Occasionally surgery is needed.

buoyancy The upward, vertical thrust exerted upon a body which is wholly or partially immersed in a *fluid. The thrust is equal to the weight of the fluid displaced by the body. Therefore, a body weighs less in water than in air; the apparent loss in weight being equal to the weight of water displaced (*see* Archimedes' principle). In humans, buoyancy is affected by *lean body-weight, *body fat, and air in the lungs. If the buoyant force exceeds the weight, the body will float.

buprenorphine A *drug belonging to the *narcotic analgesics which are on the *IOC lst of *banned substances.

bureaucracy 1 An administrative organization based on a hierarchical structure, and governed by written rules and established procedures. The authority attached to an official, and the position of an official within the hierarchy, depends on the office held rather than the personal attributes and status of the incumbent. **2** A term used pejoratively to describe any official process which is deemed inefficient or unnecessarily obstructive.

burnout A complex psychophysiological syndrome characterized by feelngs of *anxiety, tension, *fatigue, exhaustion, and a loss of concern for the people with whom one is working. It appears as a result of chronic *stress, especially in jobs which are highly stressful. Burnout comprises the complex interaction between a number of physiological and psychological components. It has been conceptualized as an imbalance between the psychological resources of an individual and the demands being made on these resources. It has been used with reference to a decrease in the psychological capabilities of athletes, coaches, and managers to deal with stressful situations.

burns Damage to the skin or other tissue as a result of excessive heat. In sport, burns are seldom caused by direct heat. They are usually caused by friction when the skin rubs against another surface. The ability of a burns sufferer to participate in sport is determined largely by the extent and location of the burns. Even with minor burns, activities which involve the risk of friction against the affected areas should be avoided. In the case of more severe burns, activities which could promote infection should be avoided. *See also* blister; and mat burn.

bursa A small fibrous sac, lined with *synovial membrane and containing *synovial fluid. Bursae are usually found where soft tissues, such as muscles or tendons, move over bony prominences. They decrease friction during movement and act as shock-absorbers. *See also* bursitis.

bursa iliopeginea A *bursa at the front of the hip-joint.

bursa semimembranosa-gastrocnemia A *bursa at the back of the knee.

bursitis An inflammation of a *bursa which results in a form of internal blistering causing the bursal sac to become inflated with fluid. Bursitis may be caused by repeated mechanical irritation (frictional bursitis), substances formed as a result of inflammation or degeneration of tissue (chemical bursitis), or bacterial infection (septic bursitis). Treatment may include *diathermy and the topical application of anti-inflammatory drugs. *See also* calcification shoulder; housemaid's knee; and retrocalcaneal bursitis.

Buss aggression machine (shock-box) A machine allowing an experimenter to record a subject's level of state *aggression in terms of the duration and intensity of an electric shock that the subject is prepared to give an accomplice. No shock is actually given, but the accomplice behaves as if he or she has received one. Such research has declined in recent years because of the risk of psychological damage to the subject.

Buss–Durkee hostility scale A pencil and paper questionnaire designed to measure a subject's *aggression. It includes the measurement of seven aspects of hostility: assault, indirect hostility, irritability, negativism, resentment, suspicion, and verbal hostility.

butterflies An uncomfortable body sensation in the stomach associated with high levels of *arousal and arising from excessive muscular tension. Butterflies may be distracting and worrying, and therefore detrimental to performance. They can be controlled by relaxation techniques. *See also* visceral reaction.

buttocks The two prominences at the lower posterior part of the trunk formed mainly by the flesh-covered *gluteal muscles and *fat.

C

c An abbreviation sometimes used in physiological literature to indicate capillary blood.

C Chemical symbol for a carbon atom.

cable tensiometer A device, designed to measure the tension of aircraft control cables, which has been adapted to measure the tension of muscle during an *isometric contraction.

cadaver dissection analysis A method of measuring body composition by dissecting a fresh, dead human body, and determining the percentage fat in each of the body parts.

cadence The stride rate during locomotion.

caecum A blind-ending sac, between the *small intestine and the *large intestine, from which the *appendix arises.

caffeine A moderately addictive, *analeptic and *psychotonic drug belonging to the *stimulants. It is a constituent of chocolate bars, coffee, tea, and cola-type drinks. A cup of non-decaffeinated coffee contains 100–150mg of caffeine. Low to moderate consumption of caffeine is permitted by the *IOC, but urinary concentrations of more than 12 $\mu g ml^{-1}$ are regarded as a positive indicator of doping. Caffeine improves endurance by mobilizing *free fatty acids as fuel, so sparing *glycogen stores; it has a positive ergogenic effect on large muscles and on short-term intense exercise which requires strength. Reaction time becomes shorter and the user is more alert than usual. Intake may be followed by mild fatigue and depression. Excessive caffeine intake can lead to sleeplessness, diarrhoea, fluid loss, irritation of the stomach, ulcers, and hypertension. *See also* caffeinism.

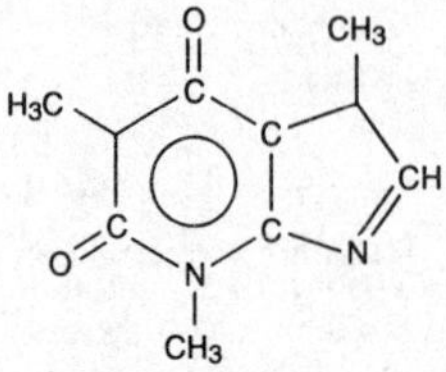

caffeine

caffeinism A medical condition resulting from a high intake of caffeine and characterized by anxiety, mood changes, sleep disruption, and other psychological and physiological abnormalities. Abstinence following high intake can lead to *withdrawal symptoms. There is evidence that an intake higher than 600 mg per day produces depression and negative effects. Caffeine intoxication is a recognized condition in the USA.

caisson disease A syndrome occurring in people breathing air at high pressure. It was quite common in those who worked deep underwater in caissons, watertight chambers open at the bottom and containing air at high pressure. On returning to the surface and normal atmospheric pressure, nitrogen dissolved in the bloodstream forms bubbles, which can cause pain (*see* bends), and circulatory blockage in the brain and elsewhere (decompression sickness). Symptoms are relieved by returning the patient to a high pressure.

cal *See* calorie.

Cal *See* kilocalorie.

calcaneal In anatomy, pertaining to the heel.

calcaneal apophysitis *See* Sever–Haglund disease.

calcaneofibular ligament A *ligament which runs between the *calcaneus and the *fibula.

calcaneomedialis nerve A *nerve on the medial, or inner, side of the heel-bone.

calcaneum *See* calcaneus.

calcaneus (calcaneum; heel-bone) The large bone that forms the projection of the heel behind the foot. It forms part of the *tarsus, articulating with the *talus and the *cuboid bones. The *Achilles tendon attaches to the calcaneus.

calciferol *See* vitamin D.

calcification The deposition of calcium salts in tissue. Calcification is important in bone formation.

calcification shoulder A chronic inflammation, with calcium deposition in the *subacromial bursa. Calcification shoulder may result from impingement of the subacromial bursa between the *acromion and the *supraspinatus tendon of the *shoulder-blade. Degeneration of this tendon, associated with ageing, may contribute to the condition.

calcitonin A *polypeptide *hormone formed in the *thyroid gland which regulates blood calcium levels.

calcium Metallic element essential for normal development and functioning of the human body. Calcium is the most abundant *cation in the body (over 1 kg is contained in the average adult) and is mostly stored as salts in the bones. It is also found in muscle and nerve tissue. Calcium is necessary for blood *clotting, growth of bones and teeth, muscle and nerve activity, and cell permeability. The recommended daily amount in the UK is 500 mg and in the USA, 800 mg. Sources of calcium include milk, meat, fish, poultry, legumes, nuts, and wholegrains. Its absorption is aided by *vitamin D. About a third of the dietary intake of calcium is excreted in the faeces. Long-duration activity and high temperatures result in loss of calcium through perspiration and urine excretion. The loss is believed to justify the use of calcium supplements for replacement, especially among *élite athletes. Excess calcium depresses neural and motor functions, and can lead to the development of kidney stones. Calcium deficiencies can cause retarded growth and *rickets in children, and lead to *osteomalacia and *osteoporosis in adults.

calcium antagonist (calcium channel blocker) A *drug which reduces the inflow of calcium ions into cardiac muscle and *smooth muscle, thereby reducing the strength of contraction of these muscles. Calcium antagonists are administered to treat *angina pectoris and *hypertension.

calcium carbonate An *inorganic salt in bones.

calcium channel blocker *See* calcium antagonist.

calcium fluoride An *inorganic salt found in bones. *See also* calcium.

calcium phosphate An *inorganic salt in *bones. *See also* calcium.

calf Region at the back of the lower leg formed mainly of the skin-covered *soleus and *gastrocnemius muscles.

calf girth The maximum circumference of the *calf of an individual standing erect with legs slightly apart and weight distributed equally on both feet.

calf muscle The *gastrocnemius and *soleus muscles, which have a common point of *insertion on the *calcaneus.

calf muscle strain A *muscle-tear in the *gastrocnemius and *soleus muscles common in squash and tennis players, particularly those who are unfit.

calibration The determination of the accuracy of an instrument by measuring its variation from a known standard.

California psychological inventory *See* CPI.

calliper A two-pronged instrument for measuring diameters. *See also* skinfold calliper.

callisthenics Systematic, rhythmic, light exercises, such as sit-ups, that are usually performed gracefully and without equipment. Callisthenics are designed to tone and strengthen muscles, and to promote general fitness.

callosity (callus) A thickening and hardening of the outer horny layer of skin. A callous protects the skin from rubbing, but it does tend to crack (*see* spinner's finger).

callus **1** Tissue containing blood and bone cells that form around a bone following a fracture. Callus formation is an esssential part of healthy bone repair. **2** *See* callosity.

calorie (cal) Unit of *work and *energy. One calorie is the amount of heat required to raise the temperature of 1 g of water by 1 °C. Although it is replaced by the joule in the *SI system, calories are still widely used, especially in describing energy values of food. Physiologists tend to use the *kilocalorie (equal to 1000 calories), sometimes referred to as Calorie and abbreviated to Cal, to distinguish it from calorie.

calorific balance A condition reached when intake of *calories from food equals expenditure of calories because of body activities. *See also* energy balance.

calorific equivalence *See* heat equivalence.

calorimeter A device for measuring heat production. In exercise physiology, *direct calorimetry is used to estimate heat production of a subject who is placed in a calorimeter consisting of a chamber supplied with air and surrounded by a jacket of circulating water inside an insulating boundary. Heat production is estimated from changes in the temperature of the surrounding water. *See also* bomb calorimeter.

calorimetry Measurements of *energy production and energy consumption in terms of heat. *See also* closed-circuit spirometry; direct calorimetry; indirect calorimetry; and open-circuit spirometry.

camphor A crystalline substance obtained from the tree *Cinnamomum camphor* . It is an *analeptic used in some ointments as an anti-irritant.

Canadian home-fitness test A safe, simple, self-administered test, the purpose of which is motivational rather than to define fitness levels accurately. The subject completes a questionnaire prior to the test to ensure basic fitness. Then, after warming-up, the subject climbs two steps of a standard staircase (each step 8 in or 20.3 cm high) at a rhythm set according to the age and sex of the subject for one or two periods of 3 minutes. The stepping rate approximates to 70 per cent maximum *aerobic capacity. A fitness score is obtained from the duration of the exercise and *heart rate.

canaliculus (pl. canaliculi) A very fine tubular channel found in the *liver and in the *Haversian system of *bone. Canaliculi in the bone contain fluid which transports nutrients and oxygen to the bone cells, and waste-products away from them.

cancellate bone *See* spongy bone.

cancelli *See* trabeculae.

cancellous bone *See* spongy bone.

cancer A group of diseases characterized by the uncontrolled growth of abnormal cells which have the ability to spread throughout the body or body-parts.

canine tooth Particularly prominent, sharp tooth between the *incisors and *premolars.

cannabis *See* marijuana

canreonate potassium A *drug belonging to the *diuretics which are on the *IOC list of *banned substances.

capacitance A measure of the ease of blood flow through a vessel; it is the inverse of *peripheral resistance.

capacitance vessels Vessels, mainly *veins, capable of holding and storing blood. Between 60 and 70 per cent of the body's blood volume is usually contained in the veins.

capacity The maximum amount something can contain, absorb, or produce independent of time (*compare* power). The term is often used in relation to the total amount of *ATP that can be produced by an energy system.

capacity interference Interference between two or more tasks performed at the same time, caused by limitations of *attention. That is, there is competition for the limited information-processing capacity of the brain. *See also* structural interference.

capacity model A model of *attention based on the notion that each person has a limited space in the *central nervous system for information-processing.

capillarity The action by which a liquid, usually water, is elevated when in contact with a solid surface by attraction between the molecules of liquid and the solid surface.

capillarization The development of a *capillary network to a part of the body. Improved capillarization of *cardiac muscle and *skeletal muscle occurs as a result of prolonged *endurance-training.

capillary The smallest of the blood vessels, located between an *arteriole and a *venule. The capillary wall consists only of an *endothelium which, because of its permeability and extreme thinness, enables the relatively easy exchange of gases, nutrients, and waste products between the *blood and *tissue cells.

capillary bed An area where there is a high density of capillaries forming a network.

capitate The largest bone of the *wrist which articulates with the *trapezoid and *hamate laterally; the second, third and fourth *metacarpals in front; and the *scaphoid and *lunate bones behind (*see* *carpus).

capitellum The lateral, ball-like condyle at the elbow end of the *humerus which articulates with the *radius.

capitulum A small, rounded end of a bone which articulates with another bone. *See also* capitellum.

capsular ligament A localized thickening in the capsule of a *synovial joint.

capsulitis Inflammation of a *joint capsule.

carbamino compound An organic compound formed from the combination of plasma proteins or *haemoglobin with carbon dioxide.

carbaminohaemoglobin An organic compound derived from the combination of *carbon dioxide and *haemoglobin: it plays a small part in the transport of carbon dioxide in the blood.

carbohydrates Organic compounds composed of carbon, hydrogen, and oxygen, sharing the chemical formula $C_x\ (H_2O)_y$. They are major sources of energy, each gram of carbohydrate yielding approximately 4 cal of energy. Carbohydrates include the simple *sugars, *glycogen, and *starches. Sugars are called simple carbohydrates and are found in fruits and table sugar. Starches are complex carbohydrates found in legumes, potatoes, and other vegetables. Carbohydrates are classified according to size as monosaccharides, disaccharides, and polysaccharides.

carbohydrate-electrolyte drink A drink which combines the properties of an *electrolyte drink and an *energy drink.

carbohydrate-loading (carboloading; glycogen overshoot; muscle glycogen loading) A procedure followed by some athletes to raise the glycogen content of *skeletal muscle artificially by following a special diet, usually combined with a special exercise regime. It is based on the assumption that depletion of *muscle glycogen stores results in stimulating the body to take up and store more *glycogen than normal. A typical carbohydrate-loading procedure for a marathon runner starts seven days before a race when the athlete depletes muscle glycogen by running a long distance, usually about 20 miles. For the next three days, the athlete eats a high protein, low carbohydrate diet and usually continues exercising to ensure glycogen depletion and sensitization of the physiological processes which manufacture and store glycogen. For the final three days before the race, the athlete eats a high carbohydrate diet and takes little or no exercise. Carbohydrate-loading can more than double the glycogen content of muscle which, it is believed, will enable the athlete to delay muscular *fatigue and to perform much better in long-distance events. However, the procedure is not without its risks. The period of carbohydrate depletion can be accompanied by *diarrhoea, *dehydration, and disruption of normal sleep patterns. Carbohydrate-loading also results in more water being stored, (with each g of carbohydrate stored, there are 2.7 g of water) sometimes making the athlete feel heavy and stiff. If persistently used, carbohydrate-loading can result in *myoglobinuria, chest pains, and heart irregularities.

carboloading *See* carbohydrate-loading.

carbon dioxide A colourless gas which occurs in the atmosphere as a result of oxidation of carbon and carbon compounds. Carbon dioxide gas is more dense than air and does not support combustion. It is produced as a waste-product of *aerobic respiration throughout the body and is carried in the veins, mainly as bicarbonate, to the lungs for excretion. Inspired air contains only about 0.04 per cent carbon dioxide, but expired air contains approximately 4 per cent. The concentration of carbon dioxide in the blood is the main stimulus to breathing. Concentrations above 6 per cent are toxic.

carbon dioxide output The amount of carbon dioxide expired from the body into the atmosphere. It is usually expressed as litres per minute. Under steady state conditions, carbon dioxide output equals carbon dioxide production by *respiration.

carbon dioxide transport The movement of carbon dioxide from the tissues to the lungs. From 60 per cent to 80 per cent is carried in the *plasma as bicarbonate ions, formed from *carbonic acid under the action of *carbonic anhydrase. A small amount of carbon dioxide is carried as *carbamino compounds. A series of chemical reactions enable carbon dioxide to be unloaded from the blood at the lungs. The carbon dioxide then diffuses into the *alveoli along a concentration gradient and is expired into the atmosphere.

carbonic anhydrase An *enzyme that accelerates the reaction between carbon dioxide and water to form *carbonic acid in red blood cells.

$$CO_2 + H_2O \xrightleftharpoons{\text{carbonic anhydrase}} H_2CO_3$$

carbon monoxide A poisonous, colourless gas which is produced from car exhaust fumes and from most smoke (tobacco smoke is almost 4 per cent carbon monoxide). It reduces the oxygen transport capacity of the blood by combining with *haemoglobin to form *carboxyhaemoglobin, taking the place of oxygen and adversely affecting the ability to perform *aerobic exercise. The affinity of haemoglobin for carbon monoxide is about 230 times its affinity for oxygen.

carboxyhaemoglobin A stable compound which forms when *carbon monoxide combines irreversibly with *haemoglobin. When carboxyhaemoglobin is formed in the blood, maximum exercise performance is reduced and attention declines.

carboxylation The addition of a carboxyl group (–COOH) or carbon dioxide into a molecule.

carcinogen Any substance capable of causing a cancer.

cardiac Pertaining to the heart.

cardiac arrest The cessation of the effective pumping action of the heart. The heart may be beating rapidly without pumping any blood, or it may have stopped beating entirely. Cardiac arrest is marked by an abrupt loss of consciousness and absence of breathing and pulse.

cardiac centre A mass of nerve cells, found in the *medulla oblongata, which adjust the force and rate of heart contractions to meet the varied demands of the body.

cardiac cycle Sequence of events which take place during a single heartbeat. *See* diastole; and systole.

cardiac diastole *See* diastole.

cardiac dysrhythmias A disturbance of the rhythm of the heartbeat which may lead to severe cardiac problems. Regular exercise may reduce susceptibility of the heart to rhythm disturbances.

cardiac hypertrophy Increase in size of the heart. In endurance athletes, it is characterized by large ventricular cavities and normal thickness of the ventricular wall, enhancing *stroke volume capability. Also, the cardiac hypertrophy is associated with an increased capillariization of the heart (*see* athlete's heart). In non-endurance athletes who regularly do high *resistance-training and *isometric-training, cardiac hypertrophy is characterized by normal sized ventricular cavities and thicker ventricular walls; the stroke volume is not affected. In non-athletes, cardiac hypertrophy may be the result of a number of pathological conditions including heart-valve disease.

cardiac impulse An electrical impulse which originates from the *pacemaker region in the *sinoatrial node and initiates contractions of cardiac muscle.

cardiac index The cardiac output divided by the estimated body surface area; an index which relates *cardiac output to body-size.

cardiac massage *See* external cardiac massage.

cardiac minute volume The amount of blood pumped out by the heart per minute.

cardiac muscle (cardiac striped muscle) *Muscle found only in the *heart. The cells are *striated, contain a single *nucleus, and branch so that they fit together tightly at junctions called *intercalated discs. Although cardiac muscle is *myogenic it has a contractile mechanism similar to that of striped muscle (*see* sliding-filament theory). However, cardiac muscle does not *fatigue and it cannot sustain an *oxygen debt. Consequently, it needs a continuous supply of oxygen.

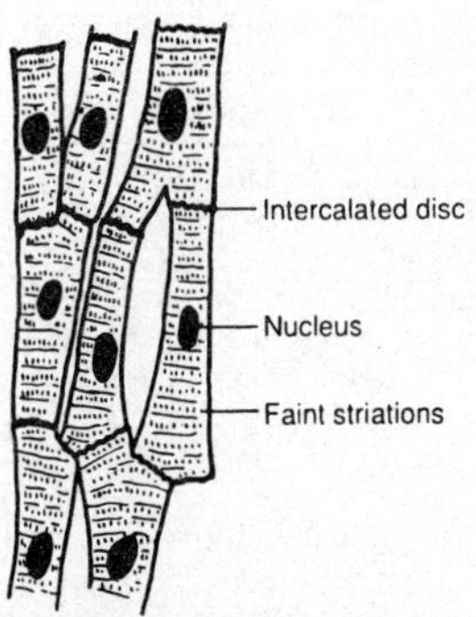

cardiac muscle

cardiac output (Q) The volume of blood pumped by the left *ventricle of the heart in one minute; the product of *stroke volume and *heart rate. The average cardiac output of a person at rest is 5–6 l; that for a trained endurance athlete can exceed 30 l min^{-1} during exercise.

cardiac rate The number of heartbeats per minute. *See also* heart rate.

cardiac rehabilitation A programme designed to help patients who have suffered heart disorders to return to normal activity without additional health problems.

cardiac striped muscle *See* cardiac muscle.

cardiac systole *See* systole.

cardinal reference plane A rectangular plane through the *centre of gravity of the human body. *See also* frontal plane; sagittal plane; and transverse plane.

cardiology The study of the heart and its functions.

cardiopulmonary resuscitation (CPR) *See* artificial resuscitation.

cardiopulmonary index (CPI) An index of cardiorespiratory endurance which uses seven parameters, expressed in the basic formula:

$$CPI = \frac{VC+MBH+MEP+age}{(SP+DP+PR)}$$

where VC = vital capacity in 100ml quantities, (i.e., 4400ml is recorded as 44); MBH = maximum breath holding time in seconds; MEP = maximum expiratory pressure in mmHg; age = *actuarial age; SP = *systolic blood pressure in mmHg; DP = *diastolic blood pressure in mmHg; PR = *resting pulse rate per minute. In tests, scores range from 0.8, for healthy non-athletes, to 1.825 for Olympic competitors. Those with heart disease score as low as 0.348. The CPI can also be used to indicate fitness by recording the time required to restore all parameters back to normal resting level after a standardized exercise.

cardiopulmonary resuscitation *See* artificial resuscitation.

cardiorespiratory endurance (aerobic fitness) The ability of the lungs and heart to take in and transport adequate amounts of oxygen to working muscles. Cardiorespiratory endurance allows activities involving large muscle groups (such as running, cycling, and swimming) to be sustained for long periods of time.

cardiorespiratory endurance test A test of the ability of the heart and lungs to supply oxygen to large muscle groups, thereby allowing them to sustain activity for long periods. There are a number of different tests. Some, such as the *cardiopulmonary index, are quite simple, while others are very complicated and use formulae with up to a hundred physiological indicators (*see* Cureton table). All the tests involve comparing physiological measurements during a rest period with those directly after exercise and after a specified recovery period.

cardioselective beta blockers *Antagonists which selectively inhibit the action of β_1 adrenoceptors (*see* β receptors). The heart is a major site of these receptors, therefore cardioselective beta blockers tend to exert a strong inhibitory action on the heart.

cardiovascular Pertaining to the heart and blood vessels.

cardiovascular disease Diseases of the heart and blood vessels. *Risk factors include *hypertension, *obesity, *smoking, *psychological stress, and *hypokinesia.

cardiovascular fitness The ability of the heart and the blood vessels to supply nutrients and oxygen to the muscles during sustained exercise.

cardiovascular system The body system, including the *heart and the *blood vessels, which is concerned with the circulation of *blood in the body.

career Sequence of positions an individual holds throughout his or her profession or life.

carnitene A *coenzyme involved in the transport of *fatty acids into *mitochondria for metabolism by the *β-oxidation pathway.

carotene A yellow unsaturated *hydrocarbon which is converted into *vitamin A in the *liver. Carotene is present in butter and carrots.

carotid artery The main *artery supplying oxygenated blood to the head. There is one common carotid artery on each side of the neck.

carotid body A small *gland in the carotid arteries which contains *chemoreceptors sensitive to changes in carbon dioxide, hydrogen ion, and oxygen concentrations in the blood. Its main function is to control breathing so that an adequate supply of oxygen is maintained to all the tissues of the body.

carotid sinus A small swelling in the wall of each *carotid artery containing sensory nerve-endings which respond to changes of pressure in the blood. It is concerned with maintaining a constant *blood pressure, particularly to the brain. Squeezing the *sinuses (e.g., in a wrestling stranglehold) causes the blood pressure to fall and the heart to slow by a reflex action, possibly resulting in the victim losing consciousness. Conversely, compression of the carotid artery below the sinus produces a fall of

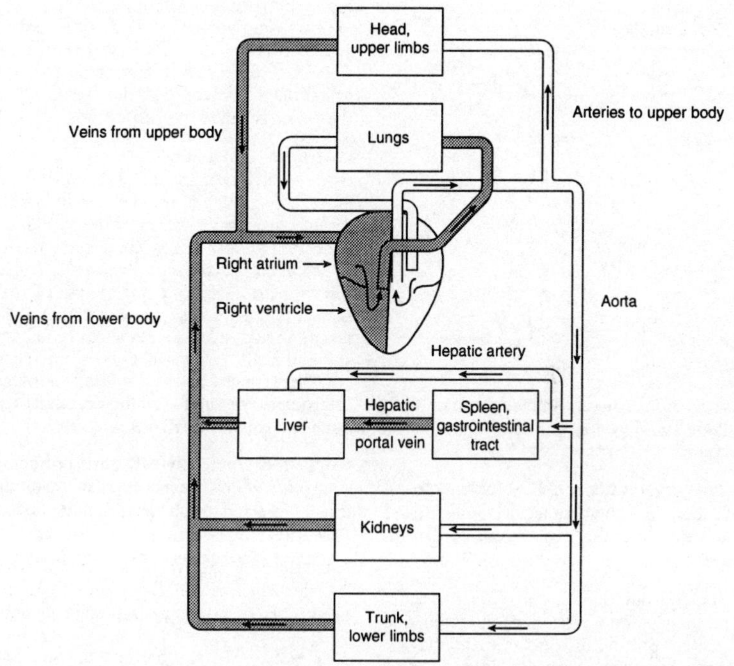

cardiovascular system

pressure within the sinus, a reflex rise in blood pressure, and an acceleration of *heart rate.

carpal In anatomy, pertaining to the wrist.

carpal bones (carpals) Eight marble-sized short bones (the scaphoid, lunate, triquetral, pisiform, traezium, trapezoid, capitate, and hamate bones) closely united by ligaments to make up the wrist. The carpus as a whole is very flexible, but movement between the carpal bones is restricted to gliding.

carpals *See* carpal bones.

carpal tunnel A narrow tunnel at the base of the palm of the hand, through which the *tendons and the *median nerve pass from the wrist to the hand.

carpal tunnel syndrome A condition characterized by pins and needles, pain, and numbness in the thumb and first three fingers of the hand which arises from compression of the *median nerve in the *carpal tunnel. *Arthritis or injury to the wrist may produce this syndrome. Most cases respond to rest and *hydrocortisone treatment, but sometimes surgical relief is needed.

carpometacarpal joint A *synovial joint between the *carpals and the metacarpals of the four medial fingers and the thumb. The carpometacarpal joint of the thumb is a *saddle-joint, able to undergo *flexion, *extension, *abduction and *circumduction. The carpometacarpal joints between the other fingers are *gliding joints.

carpus The Latin word for wrist, the *proximal part of the hand consisting of the

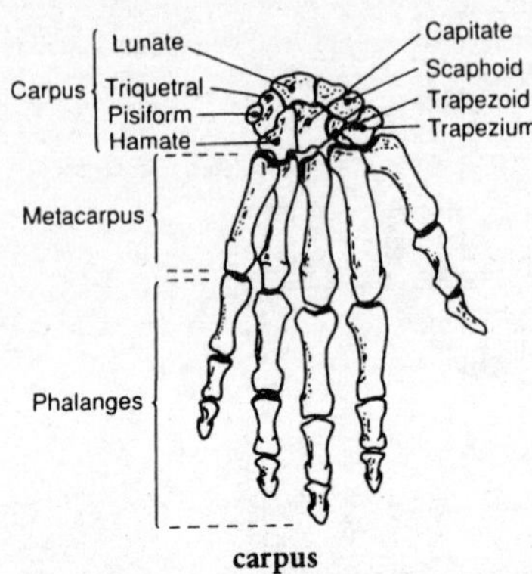

carpus

*carpal bones firmly joined together with *ligaments, but capable of some gliding movements over one another.

carrier molecule A lipid-soluble molecule that carries other molecules with lower lipid-solubility through biological membranes.

cartel A group that agrees to operate under common rules to restrict competition and maximize profits. In sport, a cartel may be formed by teams within a league which share rules, particularly those relating to the acquisition of players, revenue and advertising.

cartelol A *drug belonging to the *beta blockers which are on the *IOC list of *banned substances.

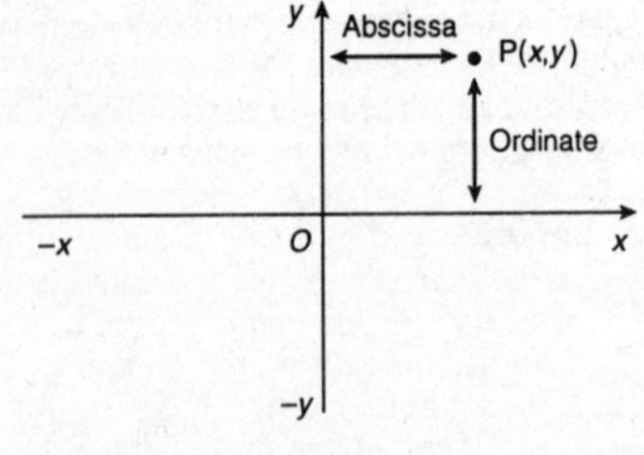

cartesian co-ordinates

Cartesian co-ordinates A system for locating and describing a point (*P*) on a graph by specifying its distance from two axes at right angles to each other which intersect at a point (O), called the origin. The distance from the horizontal or *x*-axis is called the *ordinate of *P*; the distance from the *y*-axis is called the *abscissa.

cartilage Tough and flexible connective tissue which forms the skeleton of an embryo and much of the skeleton of infants. As the child grows, much of the cartilage is converted to bone. Cartilage is characterized by rounded cartilage cells (*see* chondrocytes), surrounded by a mucopolysaccharide matrix (*see* chondrin) which is rich in *collagen. Cartilage has no nerves or blood vessels and heals slowly when damaged. There are three main types: *hyaline cartilage, *fibrocartilage, and *white fibrocartilage. *See also* articular cartilage; and menisci.

Cartwright's model of team cohesion A model which proposes that there are forces, referred to as determinants, which strengthen *team cohesion, and certain outcomes, referred to as consequences, associated with effective team cohesion.

case history *See* anamnesis

case study The study of a single example of something for its own sake (e.g., the study of the life of a famous sportsperson) or as an exemplar or *paradigm of a general phenomenon.

catabolism Metabolic reactions which result in the breakdown of compounds. *Compare* anabolism. *See also* metabolism.

catalase An iron-containing *enzyme found in all human cells, but particularly abundant in very active cells such as those of the *liver. Catalase helps to breakdown hydrogen peroxide, a poisonous by-product of *aerobic respiration, to water and oxygen.

catalyst A compound which is able to increase the rate of a chemical reaction by lowering the *activation energy for the reaction. Catalysts do not themselves become chemically changed by the reaction. *Enzymes are biological catalysts.

catalytic validity The degree to which a critical research process reorientates, focuses, and energizes participants to engage with, and transform, the situation or situations that oppress them

catastrophe theory A model of the relationship between *anxiety and performance which posits that performance decrements will be large and catastrophic under conditions of high somatic anxiety (physiological *arousal) and high *cognitive anxiety. *Compare* inverted-U hypothesis.

catecholamines A group of chemicals belonging to the *biogenic amines which can act as neurotransmitters and have other important physiological effects. Catecholamines include *dopamine, *epinephrine, and *norepinephrine.

Cattell 16PF A *personality inventory that measures sixteen *source traits of *personality. Many *personologists have adopted the Cattell 16PF for the personality assessment of athletes.

catharsis 1 The purging or cleansing of emotions by evoking pity or fear. 2 A psychoanalytical method incorporating free association by which repressed emotions are brought to consciousness.

catharsis hypothesis 1 The suggestion that *play affords an opportunity to discharge natural impulses, such as *aggression. 2 The suggestion that pent-up emotions, anger, and frustrations can be purged by expressing one's feeling's through aggression. *Compare* circular effect of aggression. *See also* instinct theory.

catheter A long, slender, flexible, hollow tube for inserting into a body cavity or artery so that fluid can be extracted, drugs can be administered, or blood-pressure monitored.

catheterization The use of a catheter to administer drugs or extract body fluids. Catheterization is banned by the *IOC because it has been misused to alter the integrity of urine samples so that *banned substances may avoid detection by doping controls.

cathine A *drug belonging to the *stimulants which are on the *IOC list of *banned substances.

cathode ray oscilloscope An instrument which enables a variety of electrical signals, including those from nerves and muscles, to be analysed visually.

cation An *ion with a positive charge.

cauda equina The bundle of *coccygeal, *lumbar, and *sacral nerve roots that descend from the *spinal cord to pass through their respective openings in the *vertebrae.

caudal Pertaining to the lower, tail-end of the body.

cauliflower ear A permanent distortion of the external ear produced by repeated injury common in contact sports. *See also* auricular haematoma.

causal attribution model A model used to describe how a performer attributes outcomes to particular causes. The model has at least three dimensions (depending on the researcher's preference) with one dimension referring to stable–unstable causes, another to whether the *locus of causality is internal or external, and a third referring to whether the causes are controllable or not. Therefore, causes may be internal, stable, and controllable (e.g., ability), internal, unstable, and controllable (e.g., effort) and so on.

causal attribution theory *See* attribution theory.

causal dimension scale A scale which assigns *attributions to one of three dimensions: *locus of causality, *stability, and *controllability. The causal dimension scale has been used by athletes to determine what they believe are the causes of the success or failure of a performance. The athletes rate each perceived cause relative to nine questions, three for each dimension.

causal explanation An explanation which identifies an immediate precipitating *cause or causes of a particular occurrence. Causal explanations usually depend on a number of assumptions concerning physical laws. *See also* cause-and-effect relationship.

causalgia A very unpleasant burning pain felt in a limb in which a *peripheral nerve has been traumatized.

causality 1 The relating of causes to the effects they produce. 2 The presumption that the occurrence or presence of an event or phenomenon is necessarily preceded, accompanied, or followed by the occurrence or presence of another event or other events. *See also* cause-and-effect relationship.

causal model A theoretical *model of the causal relationship (*see* cause-and-effect relationship) between *variables used in *causal modelling.

causal modelling A method used in sports sociology and statistics to test causal relationships underlying correlations between a number of variables. Causal modelling involves formulating and testing different theoretical models of the causal relationships betwen the variables, and selecting the model which best fits the data. *Compare* experimental method. *See also* log-linear analysis; and path analysis.

causal relationship *See* cause-and-effect relationship.

causal schema A person's relatively permanent set of *beliefs concerning the relationship between observed events and what the person perceives as causing the event.

cause A person, thing, or event which produces an effect. *See also* cause-and-effect relationship.

cause-and-effect relationship A relationship between one variable and another or others such that a change in one variable effects a change in the other variable. A cause-and-effect relationship is claimed where the following conditons are satisfied: the two events occur at the same time and in the same place; one event immediately precedes the other; the second event appears unlikely to have happened without the first event having occurred. Many phenomena exhibit close association, but they may not have a causal relationship. *See also* correlation.

cause variable *See* independent variable.

cavus foot (clawfoot; pes cavus) Condition characterized by a rigidity of the foot, decreased motion of the *subtalar joint and a decrease in internal rotation of the *tibia during locomotion. After the foot stikes the ground, the heel remains in *varus, the longitudinal arch (*see* arches) is maintained and the midtarsal joint does not unlock. During running, the foot remains rigid, decreasing its ability to conform to underlying surfaces and therefore absorbing the full force of ground contact. Cavus foot is associated with a number of lower leg injuries, including *Achilles tendonitis.

CBAS *See* coaching-behaviour assessment system.

cell The unit of structure and function in living organisms. The cell components usually consist of a *nucleus and *cytoplasm enveloped by a *plasma membrane. The cytoplasm contains a number of *organelles, such as *mitochondria which are involved in *aerobic respiration.

cell body An enlarged region of a *neurone containing a *nucleus.

cell cycle Series of stages through which an actively dividing cell passes.

cell membrane A biological membrane within or surrounding a cell. Cell membranes have a number of functions including providing a protective barrier, regulating the movement of materials in and out of the cell or its *organelles, and recognizing foreign substances. *See also* plasma membrane.

cell nest A group of *chondrocytes within the matrix of *hyaline cartilage.

Celsius A temperature scale, formerly called the centigrade scale, in which the melting point of ice is 0 °C and the boiling point is 100 °C at standard pressure. Each degree Celsius is 1/100 of this temperature interval and is equal in magnitude to 1 degree kelvin.

cellular respiration The breakdown of food within the cell to release energy which is used to manufacture *ATP. *See also* respiration.

cellulose A fibrous unbranched *polysaccharide that is the main structural component of plant tissues and constitutes *roughage in the diet.

ceiling effect A limitation that places a maximum level to the score that a performer can achieve in a task. The ceiling effect is imposed either by the scoring system or by physiological and psychological limitations. As an individual's level of performance improves towards the ceiling, it becomes more difficult to improve. In a sport which gives 10 marks for a 'perfect' performance, therefore, it is easier to improve a score from 6.0 to 6.5 than from 9.0 to 9.5.

cellulite A term created by the diet industry to describe the bulged, rippled, waffled appearance associated with subcutaneous fat often found on the hips, thighs, and buttocks of women. Cellulite is merely an effect created by *connective tissue and overfull fat cells, and is reduced by regular exercise and dieting.

cellulitis Bacterial infection of the skin which becomes inflamed but does not block blood vessels.

centering procedure *See* centring procedure.

centigrade *See* Celsius.

central group-member A member of a group who plays a pivotal role in the success of the group. The central group-member of a sports team is usually very concerned about the team's success, highly motivated, highly talented, and plays in a position where he or she is involved in much of the action of the game.

centrality The degree to which the spatial position of a team-member occupies the centre of the team formation. It is argued that central positions (such as quarterback in American football, or sweeper in soccer) are more highly interactive than those in peripheral positions which have independent tasks. A high proportion of managers and coaches are recruited from players in central positions.

central nervous system (CNS) The main mass of nervous tissue, lying between sensory *receptors and *effectors, which acts as an integrating centre. The CNS comprises the *brain and *spinal cord.

central pattern generator (pattern generator; spinal generator) An hypothesized complex neural circuitry in the *central nervous system containing a set of commands which, when activated, produce a co-ordinated movement sequence. The central pattern generator is thought to govern rapid motor actions and genetically-defined actions, handling the details of the individual muscle contractions, thus freeing the stages of processing for other tasks. The central pattern generator is capable of producing a rhythm or oscillation in the output from motor neurones to the different muscles involved in a movement pattern. For example, experiments on *spinal cord preparations of cats have shown that this oscillatory output first activates motor neurones to the flexors of the leg, and then activates the extensors, then flexors again, in a pattern similar to that displayed in locomotion. *See also* motor program.

central tendency *See* measure of central tendency.

centre of buoyancy (centre of volume) The point at which the *buoyant force acts on an immersed body's volume; it is the *centre of gravity of the water displaced by the body. In a symmetrical body, the centre of buoyancy coincides with the body's centre of gravity, but in asymmetrical bodies they may not coincide. In the human body, for example, the centre of buoyancy tends to be at chest level which is higher than the centre of gravity.

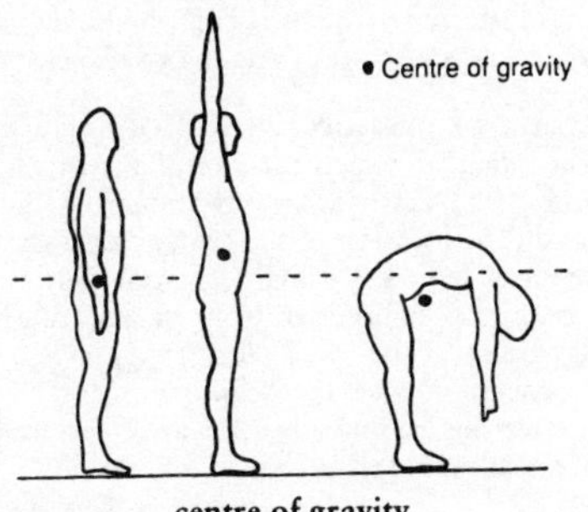

centre of gravity

centre of gravity The point at which the whole weight of an object can be considered to act; it is the point at which all parts of the object are in balance. The position of the centre of gravity varies depending on the shape of the object. If an object is a regular shape, the centre of gravity is also the geometric centre of the object. If the object is an irregular shape, as in the human body, the centre of gravity cannot be defined easily and it changes with every change in position of the body; it need not even lie within the physical substance of the body. Once in flight, a projectile cannot alter the path of its centre of gravity although movement may raise or lower the body parts around the centre of gravity. In this way it is possible to jump differing heights even though the centre of gravity reaches the same height. *See also* sacral promontory.

centre of inertia *See* centre of mass.

centre of mass: (centre of inertia) The point at which the *mass of a body may be considered to be concentrated and the sums of the *moments of inertia of all components of the body is zero.

centre of oscillation The point on a pendulum, on the line through the point of suspension and the *centre of mass, which moves as if all the mass of the pendulum was concentrated at that point.

centre of percussion The point on a striking implement that produces fewest vibrations on hitting another object. A ball hit at the centre of percussion of a bat will produce few vibrations and more force will be transferred to the ball. This point on a bat or racket is also known as the sweet spot.

centre of pressure (centre of surface) The point at which the *resultant of *lift and *drag acts on a body immersed in a fluid. The location of the centre of pressure changes with the *angle of attack. If the centre of pressure is in front of the *centre of gravity, the projectile experiences a *torque, known as a pitching moment, that rotates the leading edge upwards, resulting in a stall (*see* stall angle).

centre of rotation The point about which a *body rotates.

centre of surface *See* centre of pressure.

centre of volume *See* centre of buoyancy.

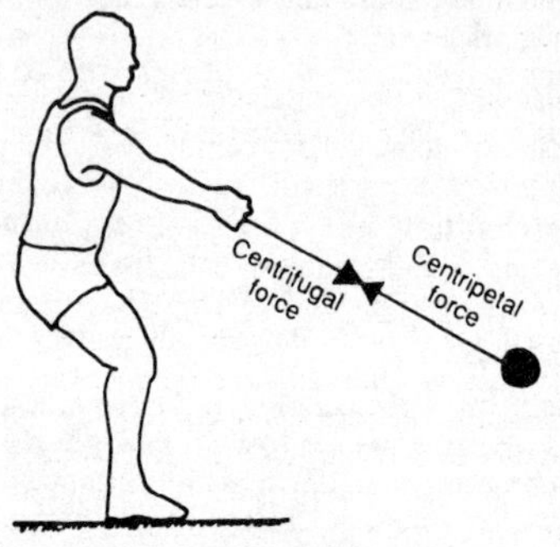

centrifugal force

centrifugal force The outward force acting on a body rotating in a circle round a central point. The centrifugal force acting on a body of mass m, moving in a circular path with radius r and velocity v is mv^2/r. *Compare* centripetal force.

centring procedure (centering procedure). A procedure adopted by athletes to control *attention and concentration. When the athletes feel they are losing control, they consciously centre attention on the most relevant cues. *See* refocusing; and thought-stopping.

centripetal acceleration The component of *acceleration of a body moving through a circular path which is directed to the centre of the circle.

centripetal force An inward force acting on a body rotating in a circle round a central point. The centripetal force acting on a body with a mass m moving in a circular path with a radius r, and with velocity v is mv^2/r. *Compare* centrifugal force.

centrum (body of vertebra) The central, discoid, weight-bearing part of a *vertebra. The centrum lies *ventral to the *spinal cord and is embryologically derived from the notochord, a cartilaginous rod.

cephalic In anatomy, pertaining to the head.

cephalic vein A principal *vein in the upper arm.

cephalins A group of *phospholipids which are important constituents of cell membranes.

cerclage A steel wire applied surgically to fix bone alignment internally following a fracture.

cerebellum Part of the brain situated behind the *medulla and *pons. It is involved in producing smooth, co-ordinated, locomotory movements; the control of *muscle tone; and the maintenance of *posture. The cerebellum continuously and subconsciously integrates information from the *primary motor cortex, other motor areas of the brain, and sensory receptors, especially *proprioceptors. *See also* vestibular apparatus.

cerebral cortex The outer, surface layer of *grey matter in the *cerebral hemispheres of the forebrain. The cerebral cortex contains motor areas which control complex *motor skills and some involuntary movements; sensory areas which receive incoming information from the *sense-organs; and association areas, which are responsible for thought, *learning, memory, language, and personality. *See also* prefrontal cortex; premotor cortex; and primary motor cortex.

cerebral dominance There are two cerebral hemispheres, the left and right. Cerebral dominance refers to the side which has the main responsibility for the development of language. In 90 per cent of people, it is the left hemisphere, while the right hemisphere is usually concerned with other tasks, such as *motor activities, visual-spatial skills, intuition, and *emotion. Most individuals with left cerebral dominance are also right-handed.

cerebral hemisphere A pair of large lobes in the forebrain which together make up the *cerebrum. The left and right hemispheres are connected by the *corpus callosum. Each hemisphere is concerned with *motor and *sensory functions, mainly of the opposite side of the body. The surface of the hemispheres constitute the *cerebral cortex. *See also* cerebral dominance.

cerebral perfusion imaging A scanning method involving the injection of small amounts of radioactive tracer substance into the blood. A special camera is used to view bloodflow through the cerebrum to assess functional damage. The technique is very sensitive and reveals microtrauma. It has been used to monitor brain damage in boxers.

cerebral spinal fluid *See* cerebrospinal fluid.

cerebral thrombosis A blood clot in the brain.

cerebrospinal fluid Body fluid formed from blood *plasma which circulates the spaces in and around the *brain and *spinal cord. Cerebrospinal fluid differs from plasma in having few cells and little protein. The fluid supports, cushions, helps to nourish the brain and spinal cord, and to remove metabolic wastes.

cerebrotonic trait A psychological characteristic of temperament which is said to be strongly correlated with *ectomorphy. Cerebrotonics tend to be solitary and adverse to crowds. They also tend to have an overfast reaction time and to be hyperactive.

cerebrum Part of the brain which expands to form the *cerebral hemispheres and the structures of the *diencephalon.

cervical Anatomical term designating the neck region; pertaining to the neck.

cervical curvature *See* spinal curvature.

cervicale A *landmark located on the most *posterior point of the *spinous process of the seventh *cervical vertebra.

cervical plexus A nerve network formed by the four upper cervical nerves situated opposite the upper cervical vertebrae, resting on the *levator scapulae and *scalenes muscles, and covered by the *sternomastoid. The *motor neurones supply the anterior muscles of the neck and the *diaphragm via the *phrenic nerve.

cervical rib A short extra rib which sometimes occurs on the seventh *cervical vertebra. It may cause problems by pressing against a *nerve or *artery.

cervical vertebra One of seven bones, identified as C1–C7, which are the smallest and lightest of the *vertebrae. Each is characterized by a *transverse process containing a transverse foramen through which the large vertebral arteries ascend to the neck to reach the *brain. The first two cervical vertebrae are the *atlas and *axis.

CGS system Centimetre, gram, and second system of physical units which is now replaced by the *SI system.

chafing (intertrigo). Abrasion caused by mechanical friction where two areas of skin rub together (e.g., in the groin) causing reddening and tenderness of the skin. Chafing is particularly prevalent among *obese people. Sweating may exacerbate the condition. It can lead to bacterial infections.

chaining 1 A concept that suggests that in a movement consisting of a number of components occurring in a sequence, termination of early components results in sensory *feedback which acts as a *stimulus to initiate the next component, and so on until the movement is completed. 2 A method of learning a *skill consisting of several actions linked in a series in which the completion of each action initiates the next action, as in a floor routine in gymnastics. The components are learnt in the same sequence as they are performed. *Compare* backward chaining.

challenge 1 An invitation to engage in a contest. 2 A demanding or stimulating situation.

channel capacity A concept based on the idea that *information has to pass through channels of limited capacity as it is processed in the brain. It is suggested that the channels act as bottlenecks restricting the amount of information going from the sense-organs to the brain, and limiting the ability to attend to environmental stimuli (*see* attention).

channelled aggression Feelings of *aggression which are diverted into positive, productive actions.

character 1 The personality structure or relatively fixed traits of an individual. 2 Attributes of personality deemed culturally valuable or appropriate by society, such as determination and will to succeed. Sport is often said to develop character, but data supporting this assumption are sparse.

charismatic authority Authority based on the special personal qualities claimed by and for an individual which make the individual attractive to, and capable of influencing large numbers of people. Originally used purely in a religious context, the term is now applied to individuals in many spheres.

Charles's law A law named after J. A. C. Charles (1746–1823) which states that a gas at constant pressure will expand by 1/273 of its volume at 0 °C for each 1 °C rise in temperature. Thus, the volume of a fixed mass of gas at constant pressure is proportional to the *absolute temperature.

charley horse A *muscle *haematoma of the *quadriceps femoris marked by severe and prolonged pain. It is caused by direct trauma and is a common injury in contact sports such as American football. The condition may develop into *myositis ossificans. The term has also been used for similar hamstring injuries.

chemical bond Means by which one atom is linked to another in a chemical compound. The chemical bond represents an energy relationship that occurs between electrons of reacting atoms.

chemical bursitis *See* bursitis.

chemical dependence *See* drug dependence.

chemical potential The amount of energy a molecule yields when broken down into simpler molecules. It is the *potential energy possessed by a molecule.

chemical reaction A chemical process by which molecules are formed, changed, or broken down.

chemical synapse *See* synapse.

chemoreceptor A sensory *receptor stimulated by contact with molecules and which is capable of reacting to, and differentiating between, different chemical stimuli. Chemoreceptors are found on the tongue and in the nose.

chemotherapeutics Artificially-manufactured medications and natural antibiotics used in the treatment of infections.

chest cavity The cavity within the *thorax.

chest girth The circumference of the *thorax, around the *mesosternale. *See also* body girth.

chest-pain Discomfort and soreness in or around the chest. Chest-pains may result from physical over-exertion and muscle strains. However, a constant pain in the centre or left side of chest, especially if felt in the arm, neck, or back requires urgent medical attention particularly if combined with shortness of breath, cold sweat, and fatigue. Such pains may be associated with a heart disorder. A stabbing pain in the chest may be caused by a lung infection.

Cheyne–Stokes respiration A pattern of breathing characterized by a few shallow breaths followed by increasingly deeper breaths which then fall off rapidly. Breathing may then cease for a few seconds and the pattern repeated. Cheynes–Stokes breathing occurs in most individuals at altitudes higher than 13 000 feet, but in some cases it may be a sign of a serious illness. The condition is also seen in terminal illnesses.

chicken-pox (varicella) An infectious disease caused by a herpes virus transmitted by droplets. Symptoms include a pustular rash and moderate fever in children which may be more severe in adults. Physical exertion should be avoided until the scabs have healed.

child development Changes in physical appearance, and psychological and social behaviour that occurs systematically throughout *childhood.

childhood Stage in the life-course characterized by a dependent status usually, but not necessarily, due to biological immaturity. Attitudes towards childhood vary considerably in different cultures.

childhood onset obesity *Obesity which first develops in childhood. Childhood onset obesity usually results in the development of an excessive number of fat cells (*see* adipocytes) which predisposes the sufferer to obesity in later life. *Compare* adult onset obesity.

chin-up Exercise used to develop upper-body muscles. The subject grips a horizontal bar with the palms of the hands towards the face. From a hanging position the subject pulls himself or herself up until the chin is over the bar. The starting position is then resumed.

chiropractic The treatment and correction of bodily ills by mechanical means. The spine is regarded by many chiropractors as the nerve-centre of the body so that many ailments, such as headaches, can be treated successfully by correcting faulty alignment of the backbone. The established medical profession in western countries has expressed reservations about chiropractic treatment.

chi-square Value obtained from a *chi-squared test, a statistical test comparing observed frequencies with the frequencies expected from a given hypothesis. The larger the difference between observed and expected frequencies, the more likely it is that a statistically significant difference exists between the categories.

chi-squared test Statistical routine which is a test of *significance comparing the observed results of an experiment or sample against the numbers expected from a theory of prediction. The test produces a value called *chi-square. It can be used only with data which falls into discrete categories.

chlamydial infection Infection caused by *Chlamydia* , a genus of virus-like bacteria. Some strains are transmitted from birds to humans while others are sexually transmitted. Symptoms include pain on passing urine. Infection can spread and cause sterility. Treatment is with a course of *tetracyclines. The severity of the symptoms determines the intensity of physical exertion possible, but activity should be avoided during the feverish stages.

chlordiazepoxide A *benzodiazepine derivative widely used as a tranquilizer; introduced into the USA in the mid-1950s under the trade name of Librium.

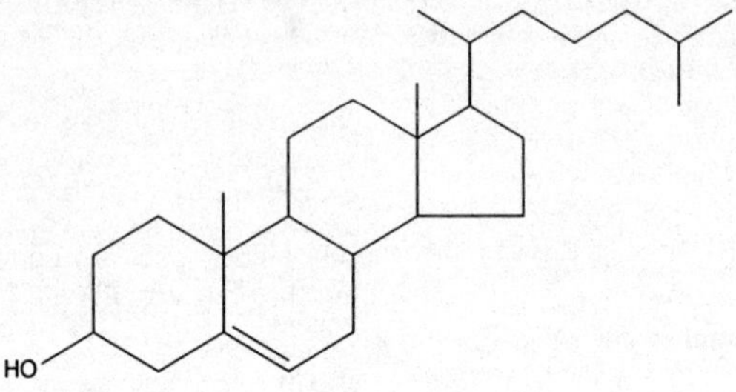

cholesterol

chloride shift Movement of chloride ions into red blood cells. The carriage of carbon dioxide in the blood is associated with the formation of bicarbonate ions in red blood cells. These negative bicarbonate ions diffuse out of the cells creating a net positive charge which is neutralized by the influx of chloride ions.

chlorophentermine A *drug belonging to the *stimulants which are on the *IOC list of *banned substances.

chlorothiazide A *drug belonging to the *diuretics which are on the *IOC list of *banned substances.

chlorthalidone A *drug belonging to the *diuretics which are on the *IOC list of *banned substances.

choice reaction time The *reaction time for a task in which a performer has had to make a choice in his or her response. The performer may have to respond to one of several different stimuli (e.g., the time it takes to choose which ball to hit with a racket when confronted with several balls at the same time), or may have to choose one of several responses to the same stimulus (e.g., the time it takes to choose which shot to attempt in a racket game when the stimulus, a returned ball, is the same each time).

choking 1 Difficulty in breathing due to any interference causing blockage or partial blockage of the airway. The condition may have internal causes, such as emotional disturbance, as well as external causes, such as a direct blow to the throat. 2 Colloquially applied to athletes whose performance deteriorates under stress, such as before and during important competitions. Such athletes may actually feel as if they are physically choking because of tightening of the bronchial muscles. An athlete who chokes may be one who, through poor pacing or excessive enthusiasm, develops a significant *anaerobic effort too early in the competition. Consequently, the accumulation of *lactic acid induces *hyperventilation and an uncomfortable tightening of the airway. Alternatively, the fear of competition may induce excessive hyperventilation.

cholecalciferol *See* vitamin D.

cholecystitis Inflammation of the gall bladder, often associated with the formation of *gallstones.

cholecystokinin A *peptide, secreted in the *cerebral cortex, which acts as a *metatropic *neurotransmitter.

cholelithiasis *See* gallstones.

choleric Applied to an individual who is easily angered or aroused. In the Middle Ages, such a person was thought to have an excess of choler, or yellow bile, in the body.

cholesterol A *lipid-related compound found in tissue and manufactured in the *liver. Cholesterol is important for body tissue repair; it is an essential compound of cell membranes which it strengthens; it forms the basis of *steroid manufacture in the body and is involved in the formation of a number of hormones; it forms bile salts; and it is the raw material for *vitamin D.

Extraneous sources of cholesterol include animal products such as eggs, meat, and cheese. A high-fat diet can increase the levels of cholesterol in the body and nicotine increases its deposition in the walls of blood vessels, but hereditary factors are also important determinants of blood cholesterol levels. There is evidence that a high blood cholesterol level increases the risk of *coronary heart disease and *atherosclerosis. Levels of cholesterol in the body can be decreased through exercise and a low-fat diet. A deficiency of cholesterol is rare. *See also* high-density lipoproteins; and low-density lipoproteins.

choline A compound important for the synthesis of *lecithin and other *phospholipids, and of *acetylcholine. Choline is also involved in the transport of fat in the body. A deficiency is rare because choline can be synthesized in the body, but where a deficiency does occur it causes damage to the liver. Choline is sometimes classed as a *vitamin but cannot really be considered one because it is not obtained from the diet.

cholinergic Term used to describe nerve fibres which secrete *acetylcholine as a *neurotransmitter.

cholinesterase *See* acetylcholinesterase.

chondrin A protein-rich material, resembling gelatin, which is produced when cartilage is boiled.

chondroblast Actively dividing cell which develops into a *chondrocyte and forms *cartilage.

chondrocyte Specialized, mature, non-dividing cell which secretes *chondrin which forms the matrix of *cartilage.

chondromalacia Roughening of cartilage (e.g., *chondromalacia patellae).

chondromalacia patellae (patello-femoral pain syndrome) Deterioration and softening of the articular cartilage of the kneecap. Pain is felt after, and sometimes during, exercise, or while sitting for prolonged periods. The *Q-angle is above 20° and there is malalignment of the lower limbs, increased pronation of the foot, *genu valgum, and increased rotation of the *femur. Treatment includes rest, the application of heat, and the restoration of the proper balance of muscles in the front of the thigh by exercising the *vastus medialis in a straight leg position. Chondromalacia patellae is relatively easy to treat in its early stages but it may require surgical realignment if it becomes established. The condition accounts for about 10 per cent of knee pain and is particularly common in young athletes. *See also* Clarke's sign.

chordae tendinae String-like, tendinous cords which prevent the *bicuspid and *tricuspid valves of the heart from turning inside out.

chorionic gonadotrophin *See* human chorionic gonadotrophin.

choroid plexus The network of *blood vessels lining the four large cavities in the *brain. The choroid plexus secretes *cerebrospinal fluid.

chromatography A technique for separating and analysing the components of a mixture of liquids or gases. Chromatography depends on the selective absorption of the different components in a column of powder (column chromatography) or on a strip of paper (paper chromatography). Chromatography is one technique used to identify specific *drugs in a urine sample.

chromium A metallic element, essential in the diet for proper *carbohydrate metabolism as it enhances the effectiveness of *insulin. Chromium may increase *high-density lipoproteins while decreasing *low-density lipoproteins. Sources of chromium include liver, meat, cheese, wholegrains, brewer's yeast, and wine.

chromosome Coiled structure found in the nucleus which contains *DNA, basic *proteins called *histones, and non-histone proteins which may regulate DNA.

chromosome test A test used for determining sex. It involves staining a thin scraping of cells from inside the cheeks using a nuclear dye and a fluorescent compound. The former stains a dense X chromatic body (*see* Barr body) present in X chromosomes, while the latter reveals the Y body associated with the Y chromosomes of males. *See also* sex determination.

chronic Applied to conditions which are of long duration and are usually slow to develop. *Compare* acute.

chronic arousal Basic arousal levels of individuals thought by some to be a function of personality (e.g., introversion–extraversion). Extraverts have lower chronic arousal levels so, in order to feel more comfortable, they often seek out exciting or stimulating situations. Introverts are the reverse.

chronic cerebral injury *See* encephalopathy.

chronic fibrosis Scarring which may occur after repeated damage to *connective tissue.

chronological age 1 Actual *age from birth regardless of developmental level. Chronological age is a measure of the time the developing person has been interacting with the environment (that is, the amount of time spent outside the womb) and is, therefore, inseparably associated with biological growth and experience. Since growth-rates vary widely with individuals, children of the same age show marked variations in strength, motor proficiency, etc. 2 In *anthropometry, the difference between the date of observation and the date of birth in years, months, and days.

chronometric approach An approach to the study of *information-processing which concentrates on *temporal aspects, considering the duration of the various processes. The approach makes large use of the study of *reaction times.

chronoscope A device which measures speed of reaction.

chronotropic Applied to a factor which affects the time or rate of a heartbeat.

chunking Grouping units of information into larger units or chunks in order to facilitate memorizing them. For example, if there are 15 different telephone numbers to learn they could be placed together in groups of three giving, in effect, five numbers to learn; the three letters C, A, and T could be grouped into one word, CAT, which also has a meaning attached to it. Chunking has been used to improve *learning, *memory, and *retrieval, and acknowledges that the human brain can process only a limited amount of information at any one time.

chylomicron A microscopical globule consisting of an outer *protein coat enclosing a fatty substance (*cholesterol, *phospholipid, or *triglyceride). Most *fat is transported in the *lymph and venous blood system as chylomicrons to be deposited in the *liver or in *adipose tisse under the *skin.

chymotrypsin A *proteolytic enzyme. Preparations in tablet-form have been claimed to be useful in treating soft-tissue sports injuries such as *sprains and *haematomas, and so to reduce recovery time. Not all injuries respond and there is some toxicity since serious hypersensitivity reactions occur. Chymotrypsin is used post-surgically to reduce *oedema.

cicatricial Pertaining to scar tissue.

cicatrix A scar tissue that forms in a wound during healing.

cigarette smoking *See* smoking.

cilia Microscopic hair-like projections on cell surfaces. Cilia occur in the *respiratory tract where they beat rhythmically in a wave-like motion and move *mucous upwards to the mouth. *Smoking impairs the normal action of cilia.

ciliary body Thickened rim of the *choroid of the eye containing the *ciliary muscles and secreting *aqueous humor.

ciliary muscle *Muscle in the *ciliary body concerned with *accommodation.

circadian rhythms The approximately 24-hourly pattern of some physiological activities. Circadian rhythms have been demonstrated in humans for changes in *heartrate, *metabolic rate, wakefulness, and *flexibility. Rectal temperature shows distinct rhythmic changes in the course of 24 hours with temperatures being at their lowest at about 4 a.m., increasing during the day with a peak in the afternoon. Circadian rhythms are also associated with some changes in levels of performance in sport:

for example, swimmers tend to perform better in the evening than early morning.

circle A plane figure contained by a line, called the circumference, which is everywhere equidistant from a fixed point within it, called the centre.

circuit-training 1 A form of weight-training designed to improve *strength, *flexibility, *endurance, and *aerobic capacity. Weight-machines are established in a circuit, each designed to involve a different set of muscles. Individuals move from machine to machine completing a set of exercises, usually in a given time, as they go. Generally, there are between six and fifteen stations to be completed in a time ranging from 5–20 min. Aerobic benefit is obtained by moving swiftly between machines and completing the circuit in a continuous flow of activity. The heart rate is kept at a steady, fairly high rate. 2 In athletics, a series of about eight to ten exercises chosen from a large variety of possible exercises. Typically, at the first training session the athlete is tested to a maximum number of repetitions completed, either to a point of exhaustion, or within a given time. The score achieved is divided by three to determine the training rate for each exercise. At each subsequent session the participant performs three circuits of all the exercises at the training rate. This rate can be adjusted as the athlete improves.

circular effect of aggression The notion that aggression begets aggression. *Compare* catharsis hypothesis.

circular motion The motion of a body about a circle. Circular motion is, more precisely, a movement that traces an arc at a fixed distance (the radius) from a fixed point or line (the axis). *See also* angular motion.

circulation 1 The flow or motion of a fluid in or through a given area. 2 The flow or motion of blood through the blood vessels.

circulatory vessels The vessels (*arteries, *arterioles, *capillaries, *venules, and *veins) which carry blood. *See also* lymph vessels.

circumduction 1 A body movement which consists of the angular movements of

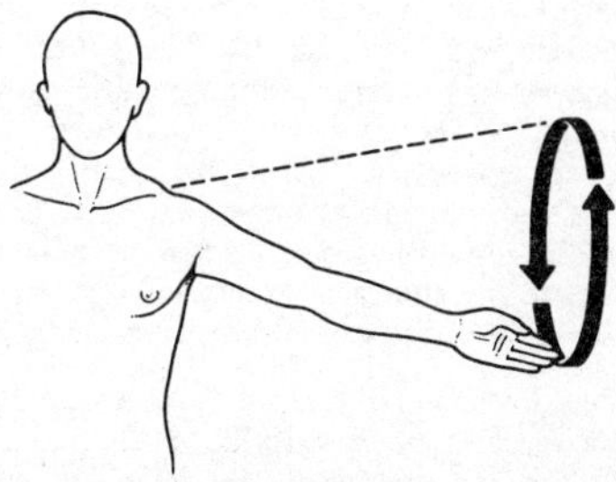

circumduction

the *flexion, *abduction, *extension, and *adduction of a limb performed in succession so that the limb describes a cone in space. The *distal end of the limb moves in a circle while the joint which forms the point of the cone is relatively stationary. Circumduction encompasses all possible movements of the hip or shoulder and is the best and quickest way to exercise the muscles which control the movements of *ball-and-socket joints.

circumflex humeral artery An *artery in the upper arm which passes around the *humerus and supplies the *head of the bone.

circumflex nerve *See* axillary nerve.

cirrhosis The hardening of an organ. It is often applied to degenerative changes in the liver.

cisterna A cellular, fluid-filled space enclosed by a *membrane.

citric acid A six-carbon organic acid found in fruits. It plays an important role in the *Krebs cycle.

civilizing process The historical process by which people have acquired a greater capacity for controlling their emotions. Associated with the civilizing process has been a lower tolerance of anti-social behaviour such as football hooliganism. This may explain why, although football-associated violence has a long history, it has received increased attention in recent times.

Clarke's sign A diagnostic test suggestive of *chondromalacia patellae. The patient lies in a relaxed position with the knee extended while the upper pole of the *patella is pressed distally. The patient is then asked to contract the *quadriceps as the articular condyle of the lower end of the *femur is pressed. If the patient can complete and maintain the contraction without pain the sign is negative. In chondromalacia patellae the contraction elicits sharp retropatellar pain and cannot be maintained.

class 1 A group of persons sharing a similar social and economic position. 2 The pattern of divisions that exist among individuals and groups in society on the basis of rank, economic status, etc.; it equates to the term social class. In western societies, class is usually based on occupation and socioeconomic grouping, (e.g., manual and non-manual workers). 3 A particular position within a system of social stratification or class system, such as middle class, bourgeoisie, or proletariat. 4 A group of students who are taught together; for example, a physical education class.

class consciousness The awareness among members of a particular social *class that they have interests in common with other members of the same class, and that these interests may be antagonistic to the interests of other social classes.

classical conditioning (Pavlovian conditioning) A form of learning in which a *neutral stimulus becomes a *conditioned stimulus capable of eliciting a given response after being repeatedly presented with an *unconditioned (significant) stimulus. In Pavlov's experiment, a bell was rung (conditioned stimulus) whenever a dog used in the experiment was fed. Eventually the dog would salivate (response) when it heard the bell ringing, even when the smell of food (unconditioned stimulus) was absent. Conditioning is more effective if the conditioned stimulus and unconditioned stimulus occur simultaneously, and are presented in the same location. *Compare* operant conditioning. *See also* principle of contiguity.

claudication Limping. Intermittent claudication is a cramping pain induced by exercise and created by temporary constrictions of the blood vessels which supply skeletal muscle. It occurs most commonly in the calf muscles.

clavicle (collar-bone) Slender, doubly-curved, long bone extending horizontally across the upper *thorax. The clavicle forms the *anterior part of the *pectoral girdle, and is attached anteriorly to the *sternum and laterally to the *acromion of the *scapula. The clavicle is the attachment point for many thoracic and shoulder muscles. It transmits forces from the arms to the *axial skeleton. However, it resists compression poorly and is easily fractured especially if the arms are outstretched during a fall. The clavicle is very sensitive to mechanical loads and is larger and stronger in those who perform exercises using shoulder and arm muscles.

clavicular Pertaining to the clavicle.

claw foot *See* cavus foot.

clinical examination A medical examination of a person to ascertain the extent to which he or she is suffering from an illness, condition, or injury.

clinical finding The findings of a doctor following a *clinical examination.

clique A small social unit within a *group.

clobazam A derivative of *benzodiazepine which does not seem to impair *psychomotor performance but does retain anti-anxiety properties. This may make it attractive as a tranquilizer in sport and exercise contests.

clobenzorex A *drug belonging to the *stimulants which are on the *IOC list of *banned substances.

clonidine A *drug which inhibits the release of *noradrenalin from *postganglionic neurones of the *sympathetic nervous system and which is used in the treatment of hypertension and migraine. Its use is permitted by the *IOC.

clopamide A *drug belonging to the *diuretics which are on the *IOC list of banned substances.

cloprenaline A *drug belonging to the *stimulants which are on the *IOC list of banned substances.

closed-circuit spirometry A method of *indirect calorimetry. The subject inspires via a face mask from a container filled with oxygen. Expired air goes back to the container of oxygen via soda lime which absorbs carbon dioxide. Changes in the volume of oxygen in the container are recorded as the volume of oxygen consumed. *Compare* open-circuit spirometry.

closed fracture *See* simple fracture.

closed interview Type of *interview in which the interviewee is asked questions and picks answers from a limited range. *Compare* open-ended question. *See also* fixed-choice questionnaire.

closed kinetic chain A movement sequence, starting with the free segment of the body such as the arms and trunk, and finishing at a fixed segment. An example is a dive which starts with movement of the arms and finishes with the feet.

closed-loop system (servo; servomechanism) A control system which appears to be self-regulating. Closed-loop systems employ *feedback and a reference of correctness (norm or set point). Deviations from the norm are detected and corrections made in order to maintain a desired state in the system. Closed-loop systems provide the homeostatic mechanism of many physiological functions (*see* negative feedback) and also control some movement patterns, where feedback from *proprioceptors and other receptors plays an important part. *Compare* open-loop system. *See* cybernetics; and information theory.

closed skill Skill that is performed in stable or largely predictable environmental settings. The movement patterns for closed skills can be planned in advance. Examples of closed skills are trampolining, golf swing, discus-throwing, performing a handstand, and diving from a platform or board. *Compare* open skill. *See also* self-paced tasks.

closure The formation of a bony union between the *diaphysis and *epiphysis after the *epiphyseal plate ceases to proliferate and the bone has reached maturity. *See also* epiphyseal bone.

clotting *See* coagulation.

clo unit Basic measurement for the thermal properties of clothing. One clo unit is the thermal insulation which will maintain a resting man comfortably at 21 °C where relative humidity is less than 50 per cent and air movement is $6\,\mathrm{m\,min^{-1}}$; it equates to a man wearing a three piece suit and light underclothes. At –40 °C, twelve clo units are required; light activity lowers this to 4 clo units.

cluster analysis A technique used to differentiate subgroups within a single collection of information about a group, people, or objects.

cluster sampling A sample from a representative group when it is not practicable to sample the entire *population. For example, if samples of students from universities were required, one university could be selected randomly then a random selection of students made from within the one establishment.

coach Motivator and teacher of an *athlete. Ideally, a coach is a moulder of theoretical and practical training, and a translator of technical information. *See also* coaching; and coaching behaviour.

coach–athlete compatability Situation in which the coach's behaviour is compatible with the *athlete's desires, and vice versa. It is a critical factor in the success and satisfaction of individuals and teams.

coaching The organized provision of assistance to an individual *athlete or group of athletes to help them develop and improve in the performance of their chosen sport.

coaching behaviour The *behaviour of a *coach. It is a function of the coach's own characteristics such as personality, ability, and experience, as well as of the influences of the situation in which the coach operates. There are many styles of coaching behaviour including *training and instruction behaviour, *democratic behaviour, *autocratic behaviour, *social support behaviour, and *rewarding behaviour. A coach may use one type of behaviour exclusively but is more likely to use different styles for different situations and individuals.

coaching-behaviour assessment system (CBAS) A system developed to permit the direct observation, analysis, and coding of a *coach's behaviour in a natural setting. It consists of twelve behavioural classes divided into eight kinds of reactive behaviour and four of spontaneous behaviour. Reactive behaviour of a coach occurs in response to the athlete's behaviour and level of performance. Spontaneous behaviour is not provoked or directly linked to the observed performance of the athlete and the behaviour may be either relevant or non-relevant to a game or performance. In one major study, approximately two thirds of all observed behaviours fell into the categories of *positive reinforcement, general technical instructions, or general encouragement. The observed behaviour of the coach can be compared with athlete's perception of the coach's behaviour and the coach's self-perception. Coaching behaviour can be modified with training.

coaching competencies *See* managerial competencies.

coaching stereotype The relatively rigid role which has been assigned to coaches and PE teachers by popular belief. A coach is perceived as one who strives for excellence and conditioning, and who otherwise presents a tough and relatively inflexible front to both team and supporters. Some studies have shown that coaches tend to be rather dominant, able to express aggression easily, and are not interested in the dependency needs of others. However, it is unclear whether this pattern of behaviour is a true reflection of personality or an attempt to act out the role imposed by society since other studies indicate that coaches do not differ from other members of society in the way and extent to which they exploit situations and people.

coaction 1 A situation in which a number of individuals are engaged in the same activity at the same time. The general affect of coaction is to raise *arousal levels. Individuals who are optimally aroused for a sporting event may become overaroused when joined by other individuals. This may lead competitors to perform less well and spectators to become aggressive. The larger the number of people engaged in an activity and the closer their proximity to one another, the greater the coaction effects will be. 2 The interaction between two or more individuals which produces a motivating effect on performance. *Compare* audience effect; and social facilitation. *See* social interactive forces.

coactive audience An *audience of one or more people who are performing the same task as the subject, but independent of the subject.

coactive sports Sports, such as archery or sprinting, in which athletes perform side by side with little interaction. *Compare* interactive sports.

coactor An individual who is performing the same task as the subject, but independent of the subject.

coagulation *Precipitation of suspended particles from a dispersed state (e.g., the clotting of blood). Blood coagulation involves the interaction of a variety of substances (coagulation of factors) which leads to the conversion of soluble *fibrinogen into insoluble *fibrin fibres, and the formation of a solid mass called a blood clot.

coagulation vitamin *See* vitamin K.

co-amilofruse A drug belonging to the *diuretics which are on the *IOC list of *banned substances.

co-amilozide A *drug belonging to the *diuretics which are on the *IOC list of *banned substances.

coasting *See* inertial movement.

cobalamin *See* vitamin B_{12}.

cobalt A metallic element resembling *iron. Cobalt is found in all cells but occurs in large quantities in *bone marrow. Sources include liver, lean meat, poultry, fish, and milk. Cobalt is a constituent of *vitamin B_{12}, required for *red blood cell formation. An excess of cobalt can result in heart disease.

cocaine An addictive *drug belonging to the *stimulants which are on the *IOC list of *banned substamces. Cocaine is an *alkaloid derived from the leaves of the coca plant, *Erythroxylon coca*, which grows in the Andes. Because of the dangers inherent in administering the drug there are no studies of cocaine's effects on athletic performance. Cocaine abuse is known to exist among some American football players and cyclists. Its effects include euphoria, increased alertness, and a feeling of increased mental and physical power. Side-effects include serious *cardiovascular problems such as *arrhythmia, *tachycardia, and *hypertension. Cocaine abuse has also caused *coronary occlusion, almost certainly the cause of death of at least one basketball and football player in the major leagues.

coccydynia (coccygodynia) Pain in and around the region of the *coccyx.

coccygeal Pertaining to the *coccyx.

coccygeal vertebrae *See* coccyx.

coccygodynia *See* coccydynia.

coccyx (coccygeal vertebrae) Vestigial tail-bone consisting of four, or less commonly three or five, fused *vertebrae. The coccyx gives slight support to the pelvic organs but is of no use otherwise except as the *origin of the *gluteus maximus.

cochlea Part of the *inner ear concerned with the detection of the pitch of sound. In humans, it is a coiled tube consisting of three parallel canals and containing the *organ of Corti which responds to sound.

cocktail party phenomenon The ability of a person in a crowded, noisy room to attend selectively to a single conversation (often containing personally-relevant information) while excluding other inputs. Some individuals lack this ability.

cocktail party problem The problem of being unable to distinguish one voice from another in a crowded room. *Compare* cocktail party phenomenon.

co-codamol A *drug belonging to the *stimulants which are on the *IOC list of *banned substances.

co-codaprin A *drug belonging to the *stimulants which are on the *IOC list of *banned substances.

co-contraction The concept that movement usually involves the simultaneous contraction of *antagonistic muscle groups. The contribution which each member of the group makes to the forces exerted may differ and varies with the type of contraction. For example, when the external resistance to the *agonist is great, the contribution of the antagonist will be minimal. *See also* reciprocal innervation.

code A set of rules or guidelines intended to govern or control behaviour.

codeine A *drug belonging to the *narcotic analgesics which are on the *IOC list of *banned substances. Codeine is present in a large number of medicines, including non-prescriptive preparations to treat colds and coughs when it may be combined with aspirin, a permitted drug. Care must therefore be taken by competitors if they are taking a cold cure while competing.

coefficient A factor that measures some specific property of a given substance and is constant for that substance under specific conditions.

coefficient of drag An index which indicates how streamlined an object is in a fluid flow. The higher the coefficient of drag, the lower the *streamlining. The coefficient of drag for the human body, and other asymmetrical objects, is found experimentally in a wind tunnel. The value of the coefficient depends on the shape of the body, the way the body is presented to the fluid, and how fast the body is moving relative to the fluid flow. As the shape becomes more streamlined, the value is lowered.

coefficient of friction The ratio of the magnitude of the maximum force of friction to the magnitude of the perpendicular force pressing two surfaces together; it is a measure of the roughness of two surfaces in contact with one another where one is moving, or has a tendency to move, against the other. Surfaces with a coefficient of friction of zero, are perfectly smooth and frictionless. The coefficient of friction depends on the nature of the surfaces, such as their hardness and texture, and the type of friction involved. *See also* coefficient of limiting friction; coefficient of rolling friction; and coefficient of sliding friction.

coefficient of kinetic friction *See* coefficient of sliding friction.

coefficient of lift A *coefficient which indicates how well a body can create a *lift force in a flow of air. It depends on the shape of the body and its *angle of attack. For example, the coefficient of lift for a discus during flight is about 1.2 for an angle of attack of 26°, 0.1 for an angle of attack of 2°, and about 0.7 for an angle of attack of 3°.

coefficient of limiting friction A measure of the roughness of two surfaces in contact with one another when they are static in relation to each other but with a tendency for one surface to slide over the other. *See also* coefficient of friction; and limiting friction.

coefficient of restitution The ratio of the relative velocity of an object before impact to its relative velocity, in the opposite direction, after impact. The coefficient of restitution is a measure of an object's *elasticity upon striking a given surface. For a ball, it is the measure of the ball's ability to return to its original shape after being deformed on impact. The coefficient of restitution of a perfectly-elastic sphere is unity (one), and zero for a perfectly-inelastic sphere. The coefficient of restitution is affected by the nature of the surface (using the same ball, astroturf may produce a coefficient of restititution twice as great as that of grass), speed of impact, *temperature and *elasticity of the striking object, and composition of the object.

coefficient of rolling friction A measure of how easily a ball will roll on a surface. The coefficient of rolling friction will depend on the nature of the ball and the surface, the *normal reaction, and the diameter of the ball. A surface which is heavily grassed, soft, and wet will have a much higher coefficient of rolling friction than one which is bare, hard, and dry. For any given surface, the coefficient of rolling friction will be less than the *coefficient of sliding friction. *See also* coefficient of friction.

coefficient of sliding friction (coefficient of kinetic friction) A measure of the roughness of two surfaces when at least one of the surfaces is sliding against the other. For any given surface the coefficient of sliding friction is always less than the *coefficient of static friction or the *coefficient of limiting friction. It is easier to keep a body sliding than it is to start it sliding in the first instance. *See also* coefficient of friction.

coefficient of stability The ratio of the *moment tending to maintain a body in equilibrium (M_m), and the moment tending to disrupt the body's equilibrium (M_o). That is: coefficicient of stability $= M_m/M_o$

coefficient of static friction The *coefficient of friction between two surfaces which have not yet begun to move. The coefficient of static friction equals maximum static friction force divided by the perpendicular force pressing the surfaces together (*see* normal reaction). For any given surface the coefficient of *sliding friction is always greater than the coefficient of static friction.

coeliac Pertaining to the abdomen.

coeliac disease (gluten intolerance; sprue) A condition due to a hypersensitivity to gluten, a mixture of two proteins found in wheat and rye. It is characterized by swelling of the intestinal wall and disappearance of the *microvilli in the presence of gluten. This results in impaired absorption of all nutrients (general malabsorption). Treatment is the avoidance of gluten in the diet. If adequately treated, coeliac disease does not prevent physical exertion.

coeliac trunk artery A principal *artery supplying the stomach region of the trunk including the spleen, liver, and gall bladder.

coenzyme An *organic, non-protein *cofactor which is needed for the normal functioning of an *enzyme. Many *vitamins function as coenzymes.

coercion The act of achieving a purpose through force or the threat of force.

cofactor A non-protein substance that is essential for the efficient functioning of an enzyme, binding with it during a reaction. Tightly-bound cofactors are called *prosthetic groups. *ATP and *NAD are examples of cofactors. *See also* activators; and coenzymes.

coffee *See* caffeine.

cognition The thinking processes such as *perception, *memory, language, and *problem-solving. A general term indicating knowledge and awareness; includes other means of knowing about oneself and the environment.

cognitive–affective stress management A form of *stress management which takes into consideration the aspects of the situation, the stressed person's cognitive appraisal (feelings and thoughts) of the situation, the physiological responses, and the overt behaviour of the stressed person. Cognitive–affective stress management is a technique used to reduce or eliminate negative thoughts or worry.

cognitive anxiety **1** *Anxiety as perceived by an individual in terms of how the individual feels about a situation. **2** The *anxiety a person is conscious of; actual worrying and anxious feelings (*compare* physiological arousal).

cognitive development Development of the thinking processes by which knowledge is acquired including perception, intuition, and reasoning. *Compare* physical development.

cognitive developmental approach A developmental view of how moral reasoning evolves from a low to a high level. This approach argues that persons with a low moral level are unable to conceive acts of *aggression as being immoral and are more likely to engage in such acts.

cognitive dissonance The experience of having competing, opposing, or contradictory thoughts, attitudes, or actions leading to a feeling of tension. Dissonance is removed by making a choice and looking favourably on the choice made. *See also* cognitive dissonance theory.

cognitive dissonance theory A theory which has the basic premise that people like to be consistent in their thoughts, opinions, attitudes, and behaviours. Therefore, if two cognitive elements conflict, dissonance is created and (according to the theory) people are motivated to reduce dissonance. Dissonant cognitions exist when belief A implies negation of belief B. For example, the belief that drugs can cause illness (belief A) is dissonant with the belief that drugs are necessary to win at sport (belief B). The dissonance can be reduced by adjusting belief A or B in a number of ways. Belief A could be adjusted by ignoring medical reports which support the belief and studying carefully the reports which state that drugs can be used safely; belief B could be adjusted by taking less drugs and converting to safer drugs. *See also* cognitive dissonance.

cognitive evaluation theory A theory which deals with the effect of *extrinsic rewards on *intrinsic motivation. Cognitive evaluation theory assumes that intrinsically motivated behaviour is affected by a person's innate need to feel competent and self-determining in dealing with the environment. The theory asserts that there are two main ways in which extrinsic rewards affect intrinsic motivation. First, the reward may have a controlling affect by being perceived as the primary reason for participating in an activity. Secondly, a reward may have an informational aspect which affects the recipient's opinion of his or her own competence. Most rewards have a controlling aspect and an informational aspect. The combined effects may either increase or decrease an individual's intrinsic motivation. Rewards which have mainly a controlling aspect tend to decrease intrinsic motivation.

cognitive learning A type of *learning which mainly uses cognitive processes, such as *perception and *reasoning, and in which the contribution of the learner is emphasized. *Compare* observational learning.

cognitive mediational model A model of anxiety reduction which is aimed at modifying affect-eliciting cognitions. It assumes that emotional arousal is mediated by cognition rather than environmental cues; therefore, it is possible to reduce anxiety by modifying thoughts that often elicit and reinforce emotionality.

cognitive processes Processes which include perceiving, remembering, and reasoning.

cognitive psychology The study, by indirect methods, of the nature of unobservable mental processes in human behaviour.

cognitive skills Techniques designed usually to change levels of *anxiety, *arousal, and *attention using processes such as *imagery and other thoughts.

cognitive somatic anxiety questionnaire A fourteen-item questionnaire designed to assess both *somatic and *cognitive modes of *trait anxiety, thereby taking into consideration the multidimensional nature of trait anxiety.

cognitive sport involvement Involvement in sport through the process of thinking and knowing about sport indirectly from information supplied by the mass media. Individuals who exhibit strong cognitive sport involvement may accumulate highly detailed information and statistics about their favourite sport. *See also* affective sport involvement; primary behavioural involvement; and secondary behavioural involvement.

cognitive state anxiety (TICA, task irrelevant cognitive anxiety) The aspect of *state anxiety which is concerned with thoughts and worry.

cognitive strategy (cognitive therapy) Any thought designed to produce an outcome, including those thoughts designed to control *anxiety and improve performance. Cognitive strategies are based on the belief that psychological problems, such as anxiety, are the product of faulty ways of thinking about the world. Cognitive strategies are used by sport psychologists to help athletes identify these false ways of thinking so as to avoid them and to prepare themselves mentally for competition.

cognitive stress management *See* cognitive affective stress.

cognitive theory A theory in which the behaviour of individuals is assumed to be directed not only by the occurrence of social events and the individual's own feelings, but also by the interpretation of those feelings and the individual's thoughts. Cognitive theory assumes that people think about the results and future consequences of their behaviour, and do not react mindlessly to other people, problems, or situations. *See also* attribution theory.

cognitive therapy *See* cognitive strategy.

coherence theory of truth Truth as social agreement conditioned by time and place. Within a coherence theory of truth a proposition is judged to be true if it coheres (is connected and consitent) with other propositions in a scheme or network that is in operation at a particular time. Therefore, coherence is a matter of internal relations as opposed to the degree of correspondence with some external reality.

cohesion The integration of the behaviour of different individuals as a result of social bonds, attractions, or other forces that hold the individuals together in interaction over a period of time. Cohesion is measured by the degree to which the combination of individuals produces and performs efficiently, regardless of interpersonal feelings and the emotions prevalent among the individuals, reflecting mutual attraction among them. Research shows that the performance of a sports team affects cohesion much more than cohesion affects performance. *See also* group cohesion; life cycle model of cohesion, linear model of cohesion; pendular model of cohesion; sociometric cohesion; task cohesion; and team cohesion.

cohort Group of persons possessing a common characteristic such as being born in the same year, or entering school on the same date.

coincidence-anticipation The ability to produce a response which accurately coincides with the arrival of a moving *stimulus. For example, being able to hit a moving ball accurately with a tennis racket.

cold therapy *See* cold treatment.

cold treatment (cold therapy) The treatment of a sports injury by the indirect application of ice or a cold compress. The cold reduces bleeding and inflammation, but only if applied quickly after injury since most bleeding occurs in the first few minutes. Direct application of ice may cause frostbite. Cold treatment may delay the healing of some conditions.

colinear force A *force which has its line of action along the same line as another force.

collagen A structural, fibrous *protein found in all *connective tissue, (*bones, *cartilage, *ligaments, and *tendons) and *skin. Collagen is the single most abundant protein in the body.

collagen fibre A fibre constructed mainly of the *protein *collagen. Collagen fibre is extremely tough with high tensile strength. When fresh it has a glistening white appearance and is called *white fibre. Collagen fibres occur in all *connective tissue.

collapse A condition of extreme prostration, causing a sudden loss of *consciousness, due to faulty circulation such as might occur from a defective heart, *shock, or haemorrhage.

collar-bone *See* clavicle.

collateral circulation Alternative routes in the circulatory system such as *blood vessels that may take over normal *coronary blood circulation after a coronary *thrombosis reduces the blood flow to *cardiac muscle.

collective aims Aims shared by all members of a *group of individuals working together.

collective behaviour Behaviour which occurs in response to events and by virtue of the fact that a group provides anonymity for, and affects the behaviour of, individuals within the group. Such behaviour is usually unstructured, disorganized, and transitory. *See also* contagion theory; convergence theory; crowd behaviour; emergent-norm theory of collective behaviour; and value-added theory of collective behaviour.

collective efficacy A group's confident expectation that it will successfully achieve its intended *goal. *Compare* efficacy; and self-efficacy.

collectivism Any social doctrine which advocates communal action; in political and economic doctrines, collectivism particularly relates to state ownership and control of the means of production and distribution. The term has been applied in sport to the role of 'domestiques' in professional cycling who sacrifice their individual chances of winning for that of the team. *Compare* individualism.

Colles' fracture *Fracture of the *radius, typically about 1 cm proximal to the wrist. It usually results from a forceful *trauma such as falling on outstretched hands. Because the *ulna plays no part in forming the wrist-joint, the radius receives the brunt of the force. Symptoms include local pain, numbness in fingers, and limited mobility.

colloid *Solute particles dispersed in a medium. The particles do not settle out readily and do not pass through natural membranes.

colloidal osmotic pressure The *osmotic pressure of blood *plasma and body fluids resulting from the presence of *protein.

colon The main part of the *large intestine. It has no digestive function but absorbs large amounts of water and *elecrolytes from undigested food as it passes through the colon from the *small intestine to the *rectum.

colour vision The ability to distinguish different wavelengths of light. Colour vision is conferred by the light-sensitive cells in the retina of the eye, called cones, which belong to three populations with maximum absorptions in the red, blue, and green regions of the spectrum. Some people are unable to distinguish colours but even those who are not colour-blind are responsive to some colours more than others. This can be important when considering the colour of team kit, when easy identification of fellow team-members is advantageous.

coma Condition of depressed consciousness in which, unlike sleep, oxygen use is below resting levels and the comatose person is totally unresponsive to sensory stimuli for an extended period.

combat An activity which involves defeating an opponent in a stylized way which has similarities to war or battle. Examples include chess and judo.

combined preparations Medications which contain more than one active ingredient.

comfort index An arbitrary index which has been used to indicate the suitability of environmental conditions fo physical activity.

$$\text{Comfort index} = T + \text{RH}/4$$

where T = temperature in °F and RH = *relative humidity. A comfort index above 95 during low windspeeds may require *acclimatization; the presence of wind allows higher values to be tolerated.

comfort zone A range of temperatures and humidity within which people feel comfortable under calm wind conditions. In general, as the temperature increases tolerance to humidity decreases, and vice versa. In temperate zones, *dry-bulb temperatures of 20–25 °C with the relative humidity between 25 and 75 per cent are regarded as the limits of the comfort zone. In Britain, optimum conditions for comfort are generally accepted as being 15 °C and 60 per cent *relative humidity. The *wind chill factor affects this. *See also* sensible temperature.

command style A coaching style in which the coach makes all the decisions while the athlete is expected to follow directions.

comminuted fracture Type of *fracture in which the bone fragments into many pieces. It is particularly common in elderly people with brittle bones.

common iliac artery A principal *artery which gives rise to the external and internal iliac arteries supplying blood to most of the lower limbs and the pelvic region.

common peroneal nerve *See* peroneal nerve.

communication Any imparting or exchange of information between two or more people. Communication may be verbal or non-verbal, and intentional or unintentional. *See also* interpersonal communication; intrapersonal communication; and non-verbal communication.

community 1 Set of social relationships existing within a geographically defined area, or the area itself. 2 Relationships which exist on an abstract ideological or social level; for example, a community of marathon runners.

compact bone (cortical bone) *Bone which consists of a central *Haversian canal surrounded by concentric rings of a hard, virtually solid mass of bony tissue intruded by minute canals called *canaliculi. Compact bone forms the dense outer shell of bones. It appears to be smooth and homogenous.

comparative method A method of testing hypotheses about causal relationships, or establishing social types and classes, by looking at the similarities and differences between phenomena, societies, or cultures. It could, for example, be used as a method for studying the role of sport in different countries.

compartment syndromes Painful conditions caused by increased pressure within the different muscle compartments. *Acute compartment syndromes can arise as a result of direct impact, muscle rupture, or over-use; *chronic compartment syndromes can arise as a result of increased muscle bulk following prolonged training. *See also* anterior compartment syndrome.

compensatory movement A reflex movement which is aimed at maintaining a particular body position.

competence Capacity to perform or teach a *skill. *See also* technical competence

competence motivation *See* Harter's competence motivation theory.

competing response *See* competing response theory.

competing response theory A theory proposed to explain the reduction of *intrinsic motivation when an *external reward is given. The theory suggests that the interjection of the external reward acts as a competing response which in turn acts as a potential distraction and so interferes with the responses which facilitate enjoyment of the task (e.g., prizes for children's races).

competition 1 Action in which one person or group vies with another or others to achieve a goal which may be to establish a position of superiority over others, or may be a goal in which defeating others in a personal sense may be a secondary consideration. Thus, competition is a strong motivating force which may be directed against a person's own standards or against the performance of others, or the two combined. Generally, performance improves with competition; however, there is some concern about the effects of subjecting young people to constant competitive situations since, although many situations in life foster competition, many others require *co-operation. 2 A contest in which a winner is selected from among two or more participants. In sport, competition is socially regulated and is generally direct.

competition period A period of *training in which *competition performance is stabilized as fully as possible so that the *athlete can produce optimal *performance in key competitions. *See also* peaking; and periodization.

competition-specific training *See* specific training.

competition training Form of *training in which a competitive environment is simulated over a number of *training sessions, usually by gradually introducing more and more aspects of the true competitive environment.

competitive ability The capacity to take part in situations in which a person's performance is judged in relation to that of others.

competitive A-state (competitive state anxiety) A feeling of heightened *anxiety in response to a specific *competitive situation which is perceived as threatening.

competitive A-trait (competitive trait anxiety) A relatively enduring personality characteristic predisposiing an individual to respond with elevated levels of *state anxiety before, during, or after any athletic competition.

competitive individualism In *sociology, a view which supports the proposition that achievement and non-achievement should be gained on the basis of merit. Effort and ability are regarded as prerequisites of success, and competition is seen as an acceptable means of distributing limited resources and rewards. Acceptance of this view of competitive individualism supports the cult of winning and the belief that competition brings out the best in people.

competitive process A process which sometimes occurs when the objective demands of *competition are perceived as threatening, resulting in an increase in *state anxiety.

competitive social situation Situation in which the goals of the separate participants are so linked that there is a negative correlation between their goal attainments. That is, individuals can only attain goals if other participants do not attain theirs. *Compare* co-operative social situation; and individualistic social situation.

competitive state anxiety *See* competitive A-state.

competitive state anxiety inventory *See* CSAI.

competitive stress The negative emotional reaction of an athlete when he or she feels threatened during *competition. The threat comes from an imbalance between the performance demands of a competition and the athlete's perception of his or her own ability to meet those demands successfully. The degree of *stress depends on how important the consequences of failure are perceived to be by the athlete.

competitive trait anxiety *See* competitive A-trait.

complete blood count A measure of the composition of *blood which includes *haemoglobin concentration and *white blood cell count.

complete ligament tear *See* ligament tear.

complete proteins Eggs, milk, and most proteins that meet all the body's *amino acid requirements for tissue maintenance and growth.

completion tendency In the *frustration–aggression hypothesis, the notion that the frustrated individual does not feel satisfied or fulfilled until the urge or drive for *aggression is completed.

complex carbohydrate (complex sugar) A *carbohydrate that is mainly in the *polysaccharide form. Complex carbohydrates are common in unrefined foods, such as wholemeal breads, and found in combination with *vitamins, *minerals, and *fibre. *Compare* simple carbohydrate.

complex sugar *See* complex carbohydrate.

compliance 1 A form of *direct motivation which relies on the use of *extrinsic rewards and *punishment. For example, compliance is used when a coach tells his or her team-members that they can have a day off training if they win (reward); or by telling team-members that if they do not listen to instructions they will have to do extra training (punishment). 2 The elastic resistance of a tissue to distension. 3 The volume changes in the lungs, measured in litres, produced by a unit of pressure, measured in centimetres of water. Lung compliance is measured using a balloon placed in the intrathoracic *oesophagus so that the pressure can be applied at the end of normal expiration and again after the subject has inhaled a known volume of gas. Compliance is reduced with some diseases.

component 1 A constituent part of something more complex (e.g., the separate factors which contribute to *displacement). 2 In *biomechanics, one of a set of two or more *vectors whose *resultant is a given vector.

component interaction A characteristic of some tasks in which the adjustment of one *component of the task requires an adjustment of some other component.

component vector Two or more *vector quantities, the sum of which produces a quantity which may be expressed in terms of a single vector known as a *resultant vector. If a runner on a cross-country course runs two miles east (vector AB), two miles north (vector BC), then two miles west (vector CD) then the resultant vector is vector AD, two miles due north of where the runner started: $AD = AB + BC + CD$.

compound A substance consisting of two or more different *elements, the atoms of which are chemically united.

compound fracture (open fracture) *Fracture in which broken ends of a bone protrude through soft tissues and the skin. It is more serious than a *simple fracture and may result in severe bone infections (*see* osteomyelitis) requiring massive doses of *antibiotics.

compress In medicine, a firm bandage that may hold an ice-pad or heat-pad onto an injured area.

compressed air illness *See* caisson disease.

compressibility The susceptibility of a material to change its volume and density when subjected to pressure due to loading.

compression Force applied per unit area on an object being squashed. Compression is a *stress caused by forces which are pushing down on an object and tending to reduce its volume. *Compare* tension.

compression modulus *See* modulus of compression.

compression neuropathy Condition in which the fibres of a *nerve become compressed, resulting in an inability to transmit impulses. In cycling, the *ulnar nerve in the palm of hand is commonly compressed onto the handlebars with a loss of sensation and weakening in the hand. It can result in permanent paralysis, but is easily treated in its early stages by frequently altering the hand position and protecting the hands with tape or gloves.

compression rupture A muscle-tear caused by a direct impact pushing the muscle against an underlying bone. Heavy bleeding may result. *Compare* distraction rupture.

compression syndrome A group of signs and symptoms, including pain and muscle stiffness, which occur in areas where the space available for muscles and other tissues becomes reduced. During exercise the muscle swells, fluid accumulates and cannot escape immediately, pressing on structures which become tense and painful. *See also* anterior tibial syndrome.

computerized tomography (CT) An application of computer technology to radiography which involves the making of X-ray images in layers or 'cuts' through the body. CT provides excellent visualization of the spatial relationship in the *transverse plane and is also used as a diagnostic tool.

conation Mental activities, such as will and drives, which lead to purposive action.

conative behaviour Behaviour dependent on effort of mind or willpower. It is the behaviour of a person who is striving for something.

concentration The ability to sustain *attention on selected stimuli for a period of time. Concentration can be learned and is therefore a *skill. It has been said that concentration is letting oneself become totally absorbed in the present moment of competition, and the ability to focus attention on the relevant stimuli to the total exclusion of all irrelevant stimuli. Concentration is important in all athletic performances and can be improved by specific concentration training, such as *distraction games.

concentration gradient The difference in the concentration of a particular substance between two different areas.

concentration training Training techniques, such as *distraction games, used to improve a performer's *concentration.

concentric contraction A form of *isotonic muscle contraction which occurs when the muscle develops sufficient tension to overcome a resistance, so that the muscle visibly shortens and moves a body-part. *Compare* eccentric contraction.

concentric force *See* direct force.

concept An abstract idea or conclusion based on a generalization from particular instances.

conceptual competency A managerial competency which refers to a *leader's ability to integrate information and make judgements using a number of relevant factors. The successful selection of a team, for example, depends on understanding the interactions between a number of factors including the interrelationships between players, their level of ability, the environmental conditions of the game, and the characteristics of the opposing team.

conceptual model of team cohesion A model which proposes that individuals are bound and attracted to a *group for two basic reasons: group task integration and *individual attraction.

conceptual schema A mode of thinking. According to Piaget's stage theory, there is a typical conceptual schema for each stage of a child's development.

concomitant variation An empirical relationship in which the magnitude of one variable varies with the magnitude of a second variable. This *correlation between variables may be used as a test of causal relationships but there are dangers of false conclusions since two variables may show concomitant variation without any *cause-and-effect relationship.

concurrent feedback *Feedback which is presented simultaneously with the action.

concurrent validity In *psychology, the extent to which a test is validated by achieving a relationship with a related and previously validated test.

concussion (knock-out) Sudden loss of *consciousness due to a blow to the head. It may last a few minutes or a few hours and is often accompanied by pallor, slowness, feebleness of heartbeat, shallow breathing, and abolition of reflex function. Athletes suffering from concussion are usually advised to avoid body-contact sport for three weeks.

In some sports, such as Rugby Union football, this lay-off is mandatory. Boxers suffering from concussion after being knocked out in the ring may also be required to avoid boxing. In Britain, amateur boxers are not allowed to box until 28 days after the first knock-out, 84 days after a second knock-out, and 1 year after a third knock-out.

conditional floater A person who has a body composition which enables that individual to float in water when the lungs are inflated but who sinks when the lungs are deflated.

conditioned reflex *See* conditioned response

conditioned response (conditioned reflex) A response which is trained or learned. In *classical conditioning, a conditioned response is aroused by some *stimulus other than that which normally produces the response. In *operant conditioning, a conditioned response is one which has become more frequent after being reinforced.

conditioned stimulus A previously neutral *stimulus which acquires the property of eliciting a particular response through pairing with an *unconditioned stimulus. *See also* classical conditioning.

conditioning 1 The process of training or changing behaviour by association and reinforcement. There are two main types: *classical conditioning and *operant conditioning. 2 The sum total of all physiological, anatomical, and psychological changes made by an individual in adaptating to the demands of a training programme. 3 General training of the whole body to establish *aerobic fitness as well as *muscle strength and *endurance. Conditioning is not primarily concerned with the acquisition of skills (*compare* training). *See also* preparation period.

conditioning exercise An activity which improves *cardiovascular endurance as well as *muscle strength and muscle endurance. Conditioning exercises result in an increase in the energy capacity of the muscle or muscles which are exercised. They are not primarily concerned with developing *skill. *Compare* training.

conductivity The ability of a conductor (including human tissue) to transmit an electrical impulse.

conduction 1 The transmission of a *nerve impulse along a *neurone. 2 The transfer of heat, electricty, or sound through a medium. *See also* heat conduction.

condyle A rounded, knuckle-like projection at the end of a bone which *articulates with another bone to form an efficient joint.

condyloid joint *Joint, such as the wrist-joint, formed when a convex surface of a bone fits a concave surface of another bone. It allows angular movement in two planes with slight circumduction.

confidence A belief and a self-assurance in one's own abilities. In sport, it is essentially a feeling of having an expectation of success. Very often, the most successful sportspeople have high *aspirations and high levels of confidence. Confidence is situation-specific so that, to take one example, a person may be highly confident when playing tennis but not when swimming. *Compare* self-efficacy.

conflict 1 An overt struggle between individuals or groups. Conflict occurs whenever the action of another person or group prevents, obstructs, or interferes with a goal or action. 2 A group motive whereby the group functions together to overcome natural obstacles or the opposition. The group motive will be to overcome the opposition or to struggle against opposing forces, whether those forces are from the natural environment or other people. 3 The *tension or *stress involved when the satisfaction of specific needs is thwarted by equally attractive or equally unattractive desires.

conflict perspective A view based on the premise that *conflict is generated in a *society by groups competing for economic and political resources which enable one group to acquire power. *Sport is believed by some to replace outright war as a way for one group demonstrating superiority over another group.

conflict perspective on social inequality A point of view which argues that inequality is unjust and that the existing social structure should be changed to eliminate or minimize inequality.

conflict theory Any theory which suggests that change and/or progress in human societies is made by one group, mainly at the expense of another. *Compare* balanced tension theory.

conformity A tendency of individual members of a *group to behave in a manner which agrees with the *norms of the group. Groups have norms which group-members are expected to abide by in order to maintain the integrity of the group. An individual feels the pressure of the group's expectations to conform to these norms. Conformity may involve compliance, in which the member outwardly agrees with the norms but inwardly rejects them; or internalization, in which the member adopts the norms of the group both overtly and internally.

confrontation Face-to-face discussion between individuals in *conflict. Confrontations can play a positive part in sport by bringing conflict into the open, enabling the conflict to be resolved; confrontations need not necessarily result in overt hostility.

congenital Applied to characteristics, such as certain heart defects, which have been present in a person since birth but which are not necessarily innate.

congestive heart failure The inability of the heart muscle to pump blood at a life-sustaining rate.

conjugated protein A *protein containing a non-protein group.

conjunctiva The thin, protective, *mucous membrane lining the eyelids and covering the *anterior surface of the *eye.

conjunctivitis *Inflammation of the *conjunctiva which may be due to a viral or bacterial infection, or chemical irritation. Bacterial infections can cause *pus formation. Such purulent infections can be exacerbated by exercise. Water in swimming pools commonly acts as a chemical irritant causing conjunctivitis similar to purulent infections. Wearing goggles offers protection against this condition.

connective neurone *See* interneurone.

connective tissue A *tissue found in all parts of the body. It has a number of functions including support, storage, and protection. All connective tissues are *vascularized and composed mainly of an *extracellular matrix. This enables the tissue to bear weight without great tension and endure abuses, such as physical trauma and *abrasion, that no other tissue could stand. *Bone, *cartilage, *tendons, and *ligaments are all forms of connective tissue. *See also* collagen.

conquest activity An activity which involves a person or group gaining a victory over another person or group.

conscience A person's sense of right and wrong which constrains behaviour and causes feelings of guilt if its demands are not met. These moral strictures are believed to be learnt through *socialization. It is generally agreed that sport can play an important part in the process.

conscious component In Freudian theory, the part of the mind consisting of events, and the contents of which the individual is unaware.

conscious experience Experience of which the individual is currently aware as distinguished from *past experience. Conscious experiences may be described as those which the individual can describe, such as sensory experience and feelings.

consciousness **1** The condition of a person who is awake rather than asleep so that he or she is able to respond to stimuli. **2** Clinically, different levels of behaviour which can be described on a continuum from a high state of consciousness (alertness and great awareness) to a depressed state of consciousness (coma). **3** The mechanism or process by which humans are aware of sensations, elements in memory, or internal events.

consensus A fundamental agreement within a society, community, or a group of basic values.

consensus theory of truth A philosophical viewpoint based on the assumption that truth is a matter of social agreements, including the agreements reached by the scientific community, of reality. *Compare* correspondence theory of truth.

consequences 1 The results or effects of an action. 2 In *Cartwright's model of team cohesion, consequences are the outcomes derived from *cohesion. These include team success, team performance, and *team satisfaction.

conservation of angular momentum The postulate, based on Newton's first law, that a rotating body will continue to turn about its *axis of rotation with constant *angular momentum unless an extended *couple or eccentric force is exerted on it. Consequently, given that the angular momentum is constant, the *moment of inertia and *angular velocity are inversely proportional. Thus, if a spinning person changes his or her moment of inertia by changing body shape, then the rate of rotation will also change.

conservation of energy (first law of thermodynamics) A law which states that in any system not involving nuclear reactions or velocities approaching the velocity of light, *energy cannot be created or destroyed.

conservation of linear momentum *See* conservation of momentum.

conservation of mechanical energy The principle which states that when *gravity is the only *external force acting on a body, the *mechanical energy of the body is constant. Therefore, when a trampolinist or other body is in flight, and the effect of air resistance is small enough to be ignored, the sum of the trampolinist's *kinetic energy and *potential energy is constant during ascent and descent.

conservation of momentum (conservation of linear momentum) The principle which states that in any system of bodies that exert *forces on each other, the total *momentum in any direction remains constant unless some external force acts on the system in that direction. Thus, the total momentum of two colliding bodies before impact is equal to the sum of their total momentum after impact. In most sport situations, the total momentum of bodies is only approximately constant because of the presence of external forces such as *friction, but usually the magnitude of these external forces is relatively small.

consideration A *leadership behaviour that utilizes friendship, mutual trust, respect, and warmth between coach and athlete. Leadership-styles which are at least partly dependent on consideration are those which are democratic, equalitarian, exhibit *employee-orientation, and use relationship motivation. *See also* intiating structure; and leader-behaviour description questionnaire.

consistency 1 In a *naturalistic approach to research, the dependability of the research method. 2 Applied to the performance of a skill which conforms to a previous performance or performances.

consolidation theory *See* continuity theory.

constant In science, a term or symbol whose value does not vary.

constant error The average error, with respect to sign, of a set of scores from a target value. It is a measure of *accuracy. *See also* absolute error; error measuremant; and variable error.

constipation Infrequent and difficult evacuation of faeces usually accompanied by abdominal discomfort. Constipation is generally deemed to occur if there is a failure to evacuate the bowels for three days in succession. Intermittent bouts of constipation may occur with changes in environment and diet. Constipation can adversely affect athletic performance. Stimulant laxatives are used in its treatment, but these may induce abdominal cramps which cause performances to deteriorate. Chronic constipation is often linked with low dietary fibre.

constitutional theory A theory based on *somatotyping which posits that each dimension of *somatotype is associated with a set of *personality characteristics: *endomorphy with affection and sociability; *ectomorphy with tenseness, introversion, and a preponderance of artistic and intellectual types; and *mesomorphy with athletic build, aggressiveness, dominance, and risk-taking. The constitutional theory is generally considered to be an oversimplistic view of personality.

constitutive rule An official rule of a sport.

constraint 1 A *limiting factor. 2 In *biomechanics, a restriction to the performance of free human movement patterns. 3 In *sociology, a restraining social influence which leads an individual to conform to social *norms or social expectations.

constriction A contraction or binding of a place or part.

construct An hypothesized relationship concerning structures or processes underlying observable events. *Motives and other theoretical terms such as *engrams, the *subconscious, and *insight are constructs. The term is often used in sociology to refer to any theoretical concept.

construct validity The extent to which specific situational or intervention conditions on the one hand, and outcome measures on the other, constitute adequate operational definitions of the concepts involved in the 'if—then' theoretical proposition.

consumer culture A *culture in which the marketing and consumption of goods and services has a dominant influence.

contact force A *force generated when different objects come into physical contact with one another. *See also* friction; and impact.

contact sport Any sport in which the impact of one person, or part of a person, against another is an inherent part of the sport (e.g., American football, boxing, and rugby).

contagion theory A theory of *collective behaviour which proposes that crowd behaviour depends on the emotional interaction which occurs when people are in close proximity one with another. Proponents of the contagion theory argue that the anonymity provided by the crowd, combined with high emotional arousal, compels different individuals to act as one body and adopt what has been called *herding behaviour.

content analysis A method of objectively and systematically analysing written documents and other forms of communication by creating categories to classify qualitative information. Content analysis has been used to analyse the behaviour of coaches during a game.

contest A formal game or match in which individuals or teams attempt to demonstrate physical superiority, or struggle to gain victory over opponents. *Compare* competition; and games.

contest mobility A process whereby higher social status is gained through the personal effort and ability of an individual competing openly against others. *Compare* sponsored mobility.

contextural interference The effect on performance of a *skill arising from the environment or context in which the skill is performed.

contextural template-matching An analytical technique for exploring and predicting how the characteristics of persons and situations interact to determine certain types of behaviour. Each behavioural pattern of interest is characterized by a number of templates which are based on the personality descriptions of hypothetical persons most likely to exhibit that behaviour in the situation of interest. An individual's behaviour is predicted by comparing his or her personality description to that of each template. For example, with respect to self-confidence, templates would be constructed for an optimally self-confident person, one who has low self-confidence, and one who is over-confident in the situation of interest.

contingency The relationship between a *behaviour and the consequences that are dependent on that behaviour.

contingency principle A coaching principle which states that *reinforcement should occur only after a desired action.

contingency theory Suggestion that the effectiveness of a leader (e.g., coach) and a particular *leadership style is dependent on the situation in which the leader is working. *See also* Fiedler's contingency theory

continuity theory (consolidation theory) A *gerontological theory of adjustment to old age which has been applied to the adjustment of athletes to retirement. The continuity theory states that satisfactory adjustment is associated with integration between stages of the *life cycle. It stresses the value of continuing activities in old age (or in retirement) which were of value in middle age (or before retirement). The theory maintains that the best adjusted individuals will replace lost roles with new ones.

continuous reinforcement A schedule of *reinforcement used in *learning, in which every correct response is reinforced.

continuous servo A control mechanism, either behavioural or physiological, consisting of a *closed-loop system in which there is a one-to-one relationship between the instruction from the *executive level and the state of the environment controlled. Therefore, every deviation in output from the controlled system results in a corresponding compensatory response. *Compare* discontinuous servo.

continuous skill *See* continuous task.

continuous task (continuous skill) A task or skill that appears to have no recognizable beginning or end. In theory, a continuous task, such as a gymnastics floor exercise, could be continued as long as the performer wished. The end of one cycle of the skill or task becomes the beginning of the next. *See also* discrete task; serial task; and task classification.

continuous training *See* continuous work.

continuous variable In statistics, a *variable, such as time or temperature, that has consecutive values which can take any value over a defined range.

continuous variation A collection of measurements which form a continuous spectrum of values. Examples are muscular strength and *aerobic endurance. *Compare* discontinous variation.

continuous work (continuous training) Exercise performed at a steady pace to completion without any periods of rest.

contraception The prevention of conception; birth control. *See also* contraceptive pill

contraceptive pill A pill which prevents conception. Contraceptive pills containing *steroids are sometimes taken by female athletes to control the *menstrual cycle so that *menses does not coincide with an important competition. However, such contraceptive steroid pills are not popular among endurance athletes because they are sometimes associated with a weight increase and a lowering of *maximum oxygen consumption.

contraceptive steroids *See* contraceptive pill.

contractile components *See* contractile elements.

contractile elements (contractile components) The contractile part of *skeletal muscles, consisting of *actin and *myosin filaments in the *sarcomere. *Compare* elastic components.

contractile time The time taken for a muscle to become fully contracted from a fully relaxed condition.

contractility The ability of a *muscle to shorten forcibly when an adequate *stimulus is received. It is this property which distinguishes muscle from other tissue.

contraction *See* muscle contraction.

contract–relax stretching A method of stretching that involves a reflex relaxation of the muscle. A muscle is contracted against a resistance, usually another person, then relaxed into a static extension while the partner pushes the muscle into a stretch that extends it farther than before. *See also* proprioceptive neuromuscular facilitation.

contracture A state of prolonged resistance in a muscle which does not involve an *action potential. Contracture may result from mechanical, physical, or chemical agents. It is commonly associated with a *fibrosis of muscle tissue which shrinks and shortens.

contra-indicated procedure A procedure or technique which is inadvisable or undesirable.

contra-indication Any factor that makes it unwise to use a particular treatment for a sports injury or to take a particular course of action.

contrast baths A common treatment for sports injuries, such as a sprained ankle. It involves the use of two baths or basins, one filled with water as hot as the subject can tolerate and the other filled with water as cold as the subject can tolerate. Alternate use of the baths stimulates the blood supply to the immersed part and helps reduce swelling.

contrast medium A substance, such as barium sulphate, which is used to improve the visibility of structures when using *radiography.

contrast X-ray *Radiography which uses a *contrast medium to highlight structures under investigation.

contritely-interdependent situation A social situation in which the achievement of a *goal by an individual in a team prevents the other team-members from reaching their respective goals (e.g., the attainment of a 'best player' award). *Compare* promotively-interdependent goals.

control *See* social control.

control dynamics The mechanical characteristics of levers, hand wheels, etc., in control systems affected by variables, such as spring tension and inertia, which change the 'feel' of the control.

control group In a trial of a drug or other procedure, a group matched with the experimental group in all respects except for the condition under investigation. A control group is an essential part of the scientific method since, unless a comparison is made between two groups, one subjected to the test variable and the other not, it is difficult to conclude that any change is due to the variable. *See also* double-blind trial; and placebo.

controllability A dimension of *attribution theory which refers to the extent to which the causes of events are perceived by an individual to be either within or beyond the individual's control. Controllability is sometimes confused with *locus of control, consequently Weiner renamed the dimension *locus of causality.

controlled factors Factors which are varied or held constant, according to certain specifications, by the investigator of an experiment.

controlled-interval method A form of *interval-training in which the intensity of exercise repetitions is controlled. A typical programme may consist of the athlete first raising the *pulse rate to about 120 per minute during a *warm-up. Then, each set of repetitions is run at a pace sufficient to raise the pulse to about 170–180 beats per minute. The *recovery between each set consists of a walk or jog which continues until the pulse is lowered to 120–140. The session is terminated when recovery takes longer than 90 seconds. The number of sets can be increased as the athlete becomes fitter.

controlled-variable velocity and resistance testing Measurement of *force and *velocity change during movements which contain both *isotonic contractions and *isokinetic contractions.

controlling aspect The extent to which *extrinsic rewards affect an athlete's perception of what controls his or her behaviour; it is an important component of *cognitive evaluation theory. Rewards which encourage athletes to attribute their participation to those rewards can reduce *internal motivation. *Compare* informational aspect.

control precision A skill-oriented ability which underlies the production of a response, the outcome of which is rapid and precise, but which is made with relatively large body-segments (e.g., the swing in a golf-drive).

contusion An injury which is usually the result of a direct blow to the surface of the body with a blunt object, such as the toe of a football boot, which does not break the skin. A contusion may result in a *bruise or *muscle haematoma if blood vessels are ruptured and blood escapes into the skin or muscle tissues.

convection The transfer of heat from one place to another by the motion of a *fluid. The rate of convection increases with the speed of relative movement of the body and the fluid. *See also* wind chill factor.

convergence The medial rotation of the eyeballs so that each eye is directed to the object being viewed. Convergence combines with *accommodation and *pupillary constriction in enabling a person to retain focus on an approaching projectile, such as a ball.

convergence theory A theory which proposes that *collective behaviour is the result of people with similar interests coming together and acting upon those interests. People at a sporting event, for example, often have similar class, racial, or residential backgrounds with which they strongly identify, and they are likely to respond in a similar way to *precipitating agents.

convergent muscle An essentially triangular muscle, such as the *trapezius or *pectoralis major, which has a broad *origin and whose *fasciculi converge towards a single *tendon.

conversational analysis A method of studying the social interactions within a group by analysing the naturally occurring forms of talk between members of the group. The group structure, such as dominant personalities and hierarchies, along with negotiated meanings, may be revealed by the manner in which conversation is managed by the participants.

conversational index A very approximate indicator of the *anaerobic threshold given by the pace at which a runner can no longer hold a conversation because the supply of oxygen is insufficient to meet the demands of the exercise.

conviction An *attitude dimension which is concerned mainly with how a person is predisposed to think about a situation.

cool-down exercise Light-to-moderate tapering-off activity after vigorous exercise. Cool-down exercises are performed to minimize the risk of injury and muscle soreness, and to restore the body as quickly as possible to the pre-exercise condition. *Compare* warm-up.

co-operation Behaviour which occurs when individuals work together towards goals which can be shared. There is much debate concerning the relative merits of co-operation and *competition in facilitating *learning. Many conditions contain both competitive and co-operative elements and it is not easy to decide which is more beneficial. In team-sports, each performer has to learn to play co-operatively as well as to express a desire for defeating opponents. Generally, co-operation requires a greater degree of maturation and intellectual development than competition. *See also* social interactive force.

co-operative social interaction Situation in which the *goals of separate individuals are so linked that there is a positive correlation between their goal attainments. That is, individuals can attain their goals only if other participants can attain theirs. *Compare* competitive social situation; and individualistic social situation.

Cooper twelve-minute test A test of *aerobic endurance in which the total distance a subject runs in twelve minutes is recorded. The Cooper twelve-minute test is a maximal test and requires total and exhaustive participation on the part of an athlete if results are to be comparable.

co-ordination The ability to integrate the *sensory system, *nervous system, and *skeletomuscular system in order to control the independent body parts involved in a complex movement pattern and to integrate these parts in a single, smooth, successful effort at achieving some goal.

co-ordinative structure Various *muscles or muscle groups which are functionally co-ordinated, enabling them to behave as a single unit.

coping A face-saving mechanism employed to meet perceived threats to prestige and *self-esteem (e.g., losing a competition, or retirement and *desocialization). Coping applies to teams and individuals, and is regarded as being positive if it enables the threat to be dealt with successfully.

coping-skills model Model based on the proposition that *cognition affects *anxiety. The coping-skills model underlies several approaches to reducing anxiety, such as *anxiety management training, *stress inoculation, and *cognitive–affective stress management training. *See also* *cognitive mediational model of anxiety

coplanar forces *Forces which act along the same *plane.

co-praxamol A *drug belonging to the *narcotic analgesics which are on the *IOC list of *banned substances.

coraco-acromial ligament A *ligament joining the *acromion process to the *coracoid process of the *shoulder.

coraco-brachialis A small cylindrical *muscle which crosses the shoulder-joint. The coraco-brachialis has its *origin on the *coracoid process of the *scapula and its *insertion on the inner surface of the *humerus. It contributes to *adduction and *flexion of the humerus, enabling the arm to swing forwards, and it is a *synergist of the *pectoralis major.

coraco-clavicular ligament Trapezoid and conoid *ligament which binds the lateral end of the *clavicle to the *coronoid process. Through this ligament, the weight of the *arm is transmitted to the *clavicle and thence to the *axial skeleton.

coracoid process (crow's beak projection) A beak-like projection of the *shoulder-blade which acts as an *origin for the *biceps brachii and the *coraco-brachialis, and as an *insertion for the *pectoralis minor.

core temerature Temperature in the part of the body which contains the vital organs (the brain, heart, lungs, and kidneys). The core temperature is taken internally (e.g., in the *rectum or *oesophagus) and it normally remains within a narrow range, usually 36.5–37.5 °C. This is the temperature at which the majority of *metabolic processes work most efficiently. The temperature of the rest of the body may differ from the core temperature. During exercise, heat is generated and the muscle temperature may rise to 39–40 °C. *Skeletal muscle functions best at 38.5 °C. *Compare* body temperature. *See also* warm-up.

cori cycle The reaction cycle in which *muscle *glycogen is broken down into *lactic acid, transported to the *liver, and converted to *glucose. The glucose is carried by the blood to the muscles where it is resynthesized into glycogen.

corn A hard pad of skin which develops on or between the toes as a result of friction or pressure. It is often caused by ill-fitting shoes. The corn has a small fluid sac below to allow the hard pad to slide back and forth without damaging underlying tissue. Pressure on top of the corn (e.g., from a shoe) pushes it downwards causing pain. Corns can be treated with warm water or other softening agents.

cornea Transparent *epithelium overlying the *iris and *pupil and through which light is refracted.

coronal plane *See* frontal plane.

coronary In anatomy, pertaining to the *heart.

coronary artery One of a pair of *arteries which branch off the *aorta to supply the heart wall muscle with blood.

coronary collateral circulation theory A theory which suggests that regular exercise can improve *coronary collateral vascularization and thus reduce the risk of *heart disease. There is some evidence gained from studies of dogs that coronary collateral circulation occurs and that the size of the *coronary arteries increases as a result of exercise, but the evidence for exercise-induced coronary collateral vascularization in humans is inconclusive.

coronary collateral vascularization Formation of new arteries in the heart. If a *coronary artery is blocked, the additional arterial network may form a natural by-pass from one side of the blocked artery to the other.

coronary heart disease Malfunction of the heart caused by blockage of an *artery supplying the *heart muscle. *See also* coronary occlusion.

coronary heart disease risk factor A factor which affects the chances of suffering *coronary heart disease. Risk tends to increase with age, tobacco-smoking, *obesity, high *blood pressure, high *blood cholesterol levels, and high *stress. Heredity is also important; those with a family history of heart disease being at a high risk. Males, particularly bald-headed males, are at greater risk than females. There is much inferred evidence that exercise reduces the risk of heart disease.

coronary ligament strain Damage to a *ligament binding the *cartilage of the knee onto the *tibia. The knee-joint becomes tender along the top of the tibia, just below the joint, but there is no locking (*compare* meniscus tear). Sufferers often have a history of rotational strain of the flexed, weight-bearing knee (e.g., through lateral tackles in rugby or soccer). The condition responds well to *ultrasound and *hydrocortisone treatment.

coronary occlusion The blocking of the *coronary blood vessels either through *vascosconstriction or a mechanical obstruction such as a blood *clot.

coronary-prone personality A person who exhibits *type A behaviour. It has been suggested that such a person tends to be prone to *coronary heart disease, though more recent evidence indicates that it might only be particular aspects of the type A constitution that are related to coronary heart disease.

coronary sinus Large vein of the *heart which deposits *venous blood from the *coronary veins directly into the right *atrium of the heart.

coronary thrombosis The formation of a *clot that blocks a *coronary artery.

coronary vein A *vein which collects deoxygenated *blood from the *heart muscle and transports the blood to the *coronorary sinus.

coronoid fossa Depression above the *trochlea on the *anterior surface of *humerus which, with the *olecranon fossa, allows free movement of the *ulna during *extension and *flexion of the elbow.

coronoid process A process on the *ulna which, with the *olecranon process, forms a stable *hinge-joint with the *humerus.

corpus Any clearly distinguishable body of *tissue.

corpus callosum The band of nervous tissue connecting the two hemispheres of the *brain. It is believed to enable the development of duplicate *memories in both *cerebral hemispheres by transmitting information gained in one hemisphere to the other.

corpuscle Any small cell or body of tissue. *See also* red blood cell.

corpus luteum An *endocrine gland formed in a ruptured *Graafian follicle after *ovulation. The corpus luteum secretes *progesterone preparing the womb for implantation of an embryo. The corpus luteum persists during pregnancy, but if implantation does not occur it degenerates.

corrective therapy Therapy, using physical exercise, designed to correct physical disabilities such as poor posture.

correlation An association between two *variables such that when one changes in magnitude the other changes also. A correlation may be positive or negative: if positive, as one variable increases so does the other; if negative, as one variable increases the other decreases. A statistically significant correlation does not necessarily imply a *cause-and-effect relationship. *See also* correlation coefficient.

correlation coefficient A statistical measure, referred to as r, of the degree of *linear association between two tests. A statistical measure of *association between two *variables. *See also* Spearman rank correlation coefficient

correspondence theory of truth A philosophical viewpoint which is based on the concept that truth corresponds to facts which have their existence in a reality that is external to individual cognition. Thus, truth has its own sense in this independently existing reality and can be known for what it is. *Compare* consensus theory of truth.

cortex The outer part of an *organ.

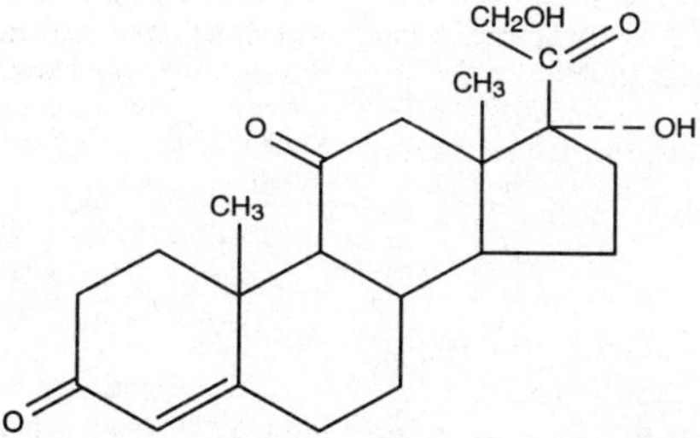

cortisone

cortical arousal Activation of the *reticular formation of the brain, with associated increases in wakefulness, vigilance, muscle tone, *heart rate, and *respiratory minute volume. *See also* arousal; and inverted-U hypothesis.

cortical bone *See* compact bone.

corticoid *See* corticosteroid.

corticospinal tracts *See* pyramidal tracts.

corticosteroids (corticoid) Naturally-occurring or synthetically-produced drugs which are related to the *adrenocorticosteroid hormones released from the *adrenal cortex. There are two main groups: the *glucocorticoids which are essential for carbohydrate, protein, and fat *metabolism and are involved in normal *stress reactions; and the *mineralcorticoids involved in salt and *water balance. The glucocorticoids are powerful anti-inflammatory drugs and *analgesics. They are administered in and around damaged muscles, tendons, or joints. They are not given directly into the structures because of the risk of weakening them and impairing healing. The corticosteroids are on the *IOC list of *banned substances. They can be used for certain *topical purposes, inhalation therapy, and local or intra-articular injections but the details of their use by a competitor must be submitted in writing to the *IOC Medical Commission. *Oral and *parenteral administration of corticosteroids are banned by the *IOC.

corticotropin (adrenocorticotropic hormone) A hormone belonging to the *peptide hormones and *analogues which are on the *IOC list of *banned substances. Corticotropin has been misused to increase the release into the blood of *corticosteroids and thereby to obtain a euphoric effect.

cortisol *See* hydrocortisone.

cortisone A *drug belonging to the *corticosteroids which are on the *IOC list of restricted drugs. Cortisone can have serious side-effects including muscle and bone damage. *See also* hydrocortisone.

coryza A cold in the head. It is generally regarded as safe to continue competition during a mild cold, but it is a golden rule that no athletic exertion should take place during a fever.

cosine A trigonometric function applied to an angle that in a right-angled triangle is the ratio of the length of the adjacent side to that of the hypotenuse.

costal In *anatomy, pertaining to the *rib.

costal cartilage *Cartilage which attaches the *ribs to the *sternum.

costal facet An *articulating surface on the *centrum of a *thoracic vertebra which receives the *head of a rib.

cost–benefit analysis A method by which the benefits of pursuing a particular action can be weighed against its costs. Cost–benefit analysis can be applied to a number of sports situations. For example, coaches have been urged to employ the notion that anticipating (*see* anticipation) has certain benefits and costs, and that whether or not to anticipate in a certain situation should be determined by weighing the probable gains against potential losses.

costochondritis Inflammation of the *cartilage which connects the ribs to the *sternum.

costo-clavicular ligament A short, flat, strong *ligament attached to the upper part of the *cartilage of the first *rib and to the undersurface of the *clavicle.

costo-vertebral joint *Gliding joint consisting of two sets of points of *articulation between the *thoracic vertebrae and the ribs. One set is between the head of the ribs and the bone of the *vertebrae; the other set is between the *tubercles of the ribs and the *transverse processes of the vertebrae. The joints enable *ribcage movements during *inspiration and *expiration.

counter-conditioning A method of *anxiety reduction which attempts to break the link between the stimuli which induce anxiety and the anxiety-provoked responses. This is achieved by *conditioning pleasant responses incompatible with anxiety to the anxiety-arousing stimuli. *See also* systematic desensitization.

counter-movement jump A jump which utilizes the *stretch-shortening cycle by the athlete bobbing down before jumping upwards.

couple *See* force couple.

coupled reactions Two chemical reactions in which the release of energy and/or the products of one reaction are used by the other. In the *ATP–PC system, the energy released from the breakdown of *phosphocreatine is functionally linked to the energy needs of resynthesizing *adenosine triphosphate from *adenosine diphosphate and inorganic phosphate.

covalent bond A bond created by electron-sharing between atoms.

covariation principle A principle which suggests that a person's attributions about a performance are influenced by the performance of others with whom the subject is comparing himself or herself. When the performances are similar, attributions tend to be external (*see* external locus of control); when the performances are dissimilar, attributions tend to be internal (*see* internal locus of control).

covert behaviour Behaviour that is secretive and generally hidden from others; non-observable behaviour.

coxal In *anatomy, pertaining to the *hip.

coxal bone (hip-bone; innominate bone; ossa coxae) One of a pair of coxal bones which forms the *pelvic girdle. Each unites with its partner anteriorly and with the *sacrum posteriorly. Each coxal bone is large and irregular. In *childhood, the coxal bones consist of three separate bones, the *ileum, *ischium, and *pubis which in adults are firmly fused and indistiguishable. The place where the three bones meet at the point of fusion is the *acetabulum.

coxalgia A pain in the *hip-joint.

coxal joint *See* hip-joint.

coxa plana Degeneration of the *head of the *femur accompanied by *inflammation.

coxa valga A deformity of the *hip-joint in which the angle between the *neck and *shaft of the *femur is greater than normal.

coxa vara A deformity of the *hip-joint in which the angle between the *neck and *shaft of the *femur is less than normal.

CP *See* phosphocreatine.

CPI (California psychological inventory) A questionnaire-type inventory designed to measure interpersonal behaviour in normal subjects. It has eighteen scales divided into four categories. Class 1 measures poise, ascendancy, self-assurance, and interpersonal adequacy. Class 2 measures *socialization, maturity, responsibility, and intrapersonal structuring values. Class 3 measures achievement potential and intellectual efficiency. Class 4 measures of intellectual and interest modes.

CP index *See* cardiopulmonary index.

CPR (cardiopulmonary resuscitation) A combination of chest compression (cardiac massage) and mouth-to-mouth resuscitation, used to help restore breathing and heartbeat until more sophisticated intensive care treatment can be used.

cramp A sudden, uncoordinated, prolonged spasm or tetanic contraction of a muscle, causing it to become taut and painful. As yet, there is no complete explanation for the development of cramp but several causes have been suggested including muscle damage, *dehydration, an imbalance of *electrolytes, low blood-sugar levels, irritability of spinal cord neurones, and *ischaemia of the muscle. Cramps commonly occur in the calf, thigh, and hip-muscles after or during strenuous exercise.

cranial In *anatomy belonging, or related to the *head.

cranial bones *See* cranium.

cranial nerve One of twelve pairs of *nerves originating directly from the *brain.

cranium Part of the *skull which consists of mainly *flat bones enclosing and protecting the fragile *brain, and organs of hearing and equilibrium.

creatine kinase (creatine phosphokinase) An *enzyme which catalyses the breakdown of *phosphocreatine, releasing energy and inorganic phosphate used to manufacture *ATP in the *phosphagen system.

creatine phosphokinase *See* creatine kinase.

creatine phosphate *See* phosphocreatine.

creative thinking Productive thinking which results in novel, rather than routine, outcomes.

creativity The aspect of *intelligence characterized by originality of thought and problem solving. Creativity involves divergent thinking; that is, thoughts directed widely towards a number of varied solutions.

credulous argument The proposal that athletic performance can be predicted from *personality traits. *Compare* sceptical argument.

creep effects A process which takes place in the *vertebrae when the compressive forces exceed the pressure within the *intervertebral disc, forcing tissue fluid to be expelled and the disc to narrow and stiffen. Creep effects are caused by excessive and, commonly, repetitive loading which causes vibrations.

crepitation *See* crepitus.

crepitus (crepitation) A crackling sound heard with or without a stethoscope over broken *bone, an inflamed *lung, or damaged joint. The *pressure-wave associated with crepitus may be felt as a grating sensation over a joint following inflammation of the *tendon sheath.

crest A narrow, usually prominent, ridge of *bone; a site of *muscle attachment.

crestload The highest workload at which all the energy can be supplied by the *aerobic system. *See also* anaerobic threshold.

crista Folds of the inner *membrane of a *mitochondrion. The folding increases the surface-area-to-volume ratio of the membrane. The surface of cristae contain *enzyme systems and *elementary particles involved in *aerobic respiration.

crista ampullaris A *sensory receptor of *dynamic equilibrium occurring in each *semicircular canal duct. The crista ampullaris consists of a tuft of hair-cells which respond to *angular or *rotary movements in one *plane.

criterion-referenced test A test in which an individual's score in a test or performance is compared with some previously established criterion, rather than with the performance of others.

criterion variable In studies of *prediction, the *variable or score that is predicted from predictor variables; the 'best' obtainable measure of the *constant that is to be predicted.

critical closing pressure The *blood pressure at which a *blood vessel closes completely and blood flow is stopped. When the pressure immediately outside the blood vessel exceeds the intravascular pressure, the blood vessel collapses. This happens during the measurement of blood pressure with a *sphygmomanometer.

critical learning period Refers to that crucial time in the development of an organism when the ideal intermix of sensory, motor, psychological, and motivational factors is present for learning a specified behaviour. Critical learning periods have been studied mainly on animals other than humans, but many coaches recognize that successful *skill attainment is dependent on the timeliness of instruction. In psychology, the critical learning period has special reference to *imprinting, and is the period when imprinting is most likely to occur.

critical mass The minimum number of a group which is needed for the group to be viable and for sufficient exchange of ideas.

critical Reynold's number A critical *velocity of a fluid in a tube, expressed by a *Reynold's number, at which *laminar flow becomes *turbulent.

criticism The analysis of a performance. The term is often used in the pejorative sense of making an unfavourable or severe comment, but criticism of athletes can be a useful *motivational strategy if used sensitively (e.g., when combined with *praise and followed with suggestions as to how to improve). It is generally agreed that criticisms consisting only of unspecifc exhortations to try harder are not very effective.

critique A perspective that attempts to problematize the everyday and familiar aspects of sport by questioning how practices in sport are constructed, why they have been constructed in certain ways, and who or what categories of individuals benefit from these decisions. A critique usually involves an analysis that relates individual events to wider social, political, and economic contexts.

Crohn's disease A localized inflammatory disease affecting the wall of the *alimentary canal, usually the terminal *ileum. *Acute inflammation may mirror *appendicitis. *Chronic inflammation causes abdominal pain, *diarrhoea, and malabsorption of nutrients. The disease is treated with medicines which reduce inflammation, or surgical removal of the offending portion of gut. Sufferers of the disease usually perform poorly in sport because of nutritional deficiencies associated with the malabsorption, but those who have been successfully treated may take part in sport at almost full capacity.

cross-adaptation The transfer of adaptation acquired from one *stressor to another stressor. Some argue that adaptations to hard, physical work carries over to improved adaptation to emotional stresses. The evidence is equivocal.

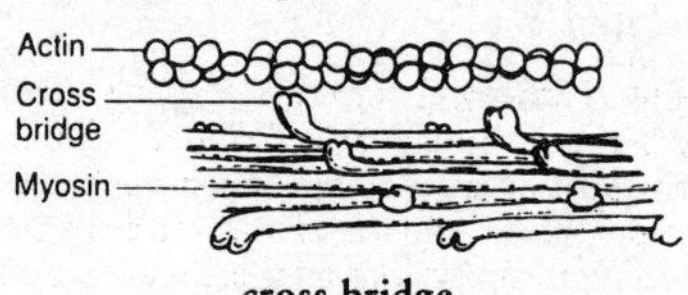

cross-bridge

cross-bridge (actin–myosin cross-bridge) An extension of *myosin which, according to the *sliding-filament theory, attaches onto *actin during muscle contraction.

cross-education *See* bilateral transfer.

cross-eyed patellae *See* femoral torsion.

cross-frictional massage A form of *massage in which the masseur rubs the body-part using small movements but firm pressure across the line of the muscle or tendon growth. Cross-frictional massage is thought to break down *scar tissue.

cross-lagged panel design A *correlation analysis that takes into consideration time factors in the measurement of performance and *cohesion.

Crossman–Goodeve theory A theory based on the observation that humans tend to trade-off speed of movements with their accuracy (*see* Fitt's law). The Crossman–Goodeve theory proposes that rapid movements are dependent on intermittent control, with the commands for action being produced alternately with the analysis of *feedback to determine movement corrections.

cross-preference The tendency not to prefer the eye, hand, and foot on the same side of the body to perform tasks. The preference is to use a combination such as the right eye, left hand, and right foot.

cross-sex effects The effects on an athlete's performance of having members of the opposite sex in the audience (*see* audience effect) or performing alongside the athlete. *See also* coaction.

cross-sex-typed Individuals having different sex- and gender-role orientation, such as an individual who is a sexual male with female gender-role orientation. *Compare* sex-typed.

cross-training A form of *training which involves performing more than one *aerobic activity to exercise different muscle groups and provide variety. A cyclist, for example, in addition to cycling may include jogging and swimming in a programme of cross-training.

crowd A relatively unstructured mass of people who group together in a given area in a more or less spontaneous way for a short time in response to an attraction, such as a sports event.

crowd behaviour The behaviour of people in large groups or a *crowd. The close physical proximity of large numbers of people provides relative anonymity and protection for individuals whose behaviour often departs from what would be expected when they are alone. The unruly behaviour of a few individuals may quickly spread so that crowd behaviour may be more than usually explosive and unpredictable. In a number of sociological studies it is seen as a potential threat to normal social order. *See also* collective behaviour; and hooliganism.

crow's beak projection *See* coracoid process.

cruciate ligaments *Intracapsular *ligaments of the *knee. The cruciate ligaments cross each other forming an X-shaped structure within the notch between the *femoral condyles. They help prevent displacement of the *articular surfaces and secure the *articulating bones together. *See also* anterior cruciate ligaments.

crural In *anatomy, pertaining to the leg.

crural index The ratio of thigh length to leg length. A high crural index is advantageous to long-jumpers since it enables the jumper to apply a *force against the ground for a longer time than someone with a low crural index.

cryogenic Pertaining to the production of low temperatures.

cryotherapy The use of ice or cold packs to treat injuries, reduce pain and swelling, decrease muscle spasms, and reduce metabolic and oxygen needs of injured tissue. *See also* cold therapy; compression; and RICE.

CSAI (competitive state anxiety inventory) A ten-item test of *competitive state anxiety; it is a shortened, situation-specific version of the *SAI.

CSAI—2 (competitive state anxiety inventory—2) A multidimensional test of *competitive state anxiety which is situation-specific and accurately assesses three different dimensions or manifestations of state anxiety: *cognitive state anxiety, *self-confidence state anxiety, and *somatic state anxiety. It has been adopted by many sport psychologists as an appropriate tool for measuring sport competition state anxiety.

CSAQ *See* cognitive somatic anxiety questionnaire.

CT *See* computerized tomography.

cubital vein A *vein in the forearm which crosses the *elbow-joint.

cubitus recurvatus *Hyperextension of the *elbow-joint which may occur in isolation or as part of *hypermobile joint disease.

cuboid In *anatomy, the *tarsal bone *articulating with the fourth and fifth digits of the feet.

cue A *signal for some particular action. The term is used in *performance models of behaviour to describe that to which a person reacts or that which precipitates behaviour in a particular situation. Cues may be verbal, visual, or *kinaesthetic. *See also* stimulus.

cue-utilization theory A theory which predicts that as an athlete's arousal increases, so his or her attention focus narrows, that the narrowing process tends to *gate out irrelevant environmental cues first, and then, if arousal is high enough, the relevant ones. This results in the reduction of the availability of important information to the overaroused performer, and the overwhelming influx of irrelevant information in the underaroused performer.

cue-words Words which have developed a special meaning through training and which are used to a evoke a particular behaviour. A coach may use special cue-words to remind a competitor to concentrate.

cuff technique A method of temporary *deafferentation in which blood flow to the arm is eliminated by a *blood-pressure cuff rendering the *afferent neurones *anoxic so that they cannot deliver sensory information.

cult of personality An intense interest in, and devotion to, a person, idea, or activity. The phrase was originally used to describe the practice of totalitarian regimes in which a leader such as Hitler was elevated to a position of total pre-eminence, and presented as a source of all political wisdom and the architect of all worthwhile political and social actions. The phrase has been applied to pre-eminent, famous sports personalities who have acquired a similar following, and to leaders of political organizations.

cult of slenderness An intense interest in, and devotion to, the development of a body that is not *obese but that is shapely and slender. The cult of slenderness is a manifestaton of the wider ideology of shapism in which definitions of the desirable body image are constructed by a range of groups who have a vested interest in promoting the ideal shape for women as slim, and that for men as slim muscularity. *See also* mesomorphism.

cultural assimilation The incorporation of a *culture into the general host society (*see* melting-pot theory). The acceptance of the host culture may result in the loss of cultural identity of an ethnic group. In reality, cultural assimilation can range along a continuum from complete isolation or segregation (*see* apartheid) to complete assimilation. *Compare* structural assimilation.

cultural diffusion A social process which results in the transfer of *beliefs, *values, and social activities (e.g., games or sports) from one society to another.

cultural-mosaic theory A theory which suggests that society should encourage ethnic groups to maintain their ethnic diversity and identity (*compare* melting pot theory). Participation in sports may strengthen ethnic identity such as when a team comprised of members from one ethnic background competes against another team comprised of members from a different ethnic background.

cultural norm The *norms of a *culture.

cultural norms theory A theory of *mass communication which suggests that the *mass media selectively presents and emphasizes certain contemporary ideas or values. According to this theory, the mass media influences *norms by reinforcing or changing them. For example, the cultural norm theorists argue that television programmes presenting an active lifestyle for older people can change the attitudes of viewers in that direction.

culture The ways of behaving of a society; the norms and values of a society. Culture has been taken as constituting the way of life of an entire society and includes the codes of manners, language, rituals, norms of behaviour, and systems of belief. Sociologists stress the importance of culture in determining human behaviour; thus the attitude of individuals to sport may be greatly influenced by their culture. In North America, for example, there is a very stong cultural influence to win at all costs. Sport has also been seen as an important means of encouraging people to conform to a particular culture. *See also* acculturation; high culture; idioculture; Lombardianism; and mass culture.

Cumming test A test of *alactacid anaerobic power. The subject pedals from a standing position on a cycle ergometer with known resistance for 30 s at maximum effort. The highest alactacid power is determined by the highest number of pushes on the pedal in a 5 s period. The force which the subject overcomes is usually proportional to his or her body-weight, and the distance the force moves is a product of the number of pedal pushes and the flywheel circumference.

cumulation The process by which blood levels of a drug build-up, thereby increasing its therapeutic and toxic effects. If the frequency of administration exceeds the elimination rate of the drug, it will cumulate. Cumulation may result from poor elimination due to slow *metabolism, binding of the drug to plasma proteins, or inhibition of excretion as occurs in sufferers of a kidney disease. *Compare* drug resistance.

cuneiform bones Three bones in the *tarsus which articulate with the *navicular behind and the first, second, and third metatarsals in front.

Cunningham and Faulkner treadmill test A long-term *anaerobic test consisting of a subject performing a maximal run on a treadmill at a 20 per cent gradient, at 8 miles per hour. The time to exhaustion in seconds is recorded.

Cureton's test for minimal levels of flexibility A series of indirect tests of flexibility which includes the *standing toe-touch. *See also* flexibility tests.

Cureton tables A set of tables based on over one hundred parameters which indicate *cardiorespiratory endurance. The parameters include pulmonary gas and blood examinations, *ECGs, and many other physiological data such as heart rate, blood pressure, and examination of respiratory gases. *See also* endurance test.

curl-up **1** A weight-training exercise which strengthens the anterior muscles of the upper arm. The subject stands with feet shoulder-width apart and a barbell or dumb-bells held with an underhand grip at thigh level. The weight is brought up to the chest and lowered again to the thigh. **2** Form of abdominal exercise, similar to a *sit-up but which involves curling the chin onto the chest.

current A flow of electrical charge from one point to another. The amount of current (I) moving between two points depends on voltage (V) and resistance (R) and is given by: $I = V/R$.

curriculum A list of all the courses of study offered by an educational establishment.

curvilinear motion **1** A motion in which the points of a body describe a curved line. **2** A motion which has both linear and angular components, such as that of a discus-thrower advancing and turning across the throwing circle.

curvilinear translation Curved-line-type of linear motion; that is, a *translation in which the parts of the body follow a curved line.

custom Any established pattern of behaviour within a *community or *society. A custom is an accepted rule of behaviour which is informally regulated. Shaking hands with the umpire is the custom after a tennis match, for example.

cutaneous Pertaining to the skin.

cyanocobalamin *See* vitamin B_{12}.

cyanosis Bluish discolouration of the skin and mucous membranes caused by lack of oxygen.

cyanotic Relating to *cyanosis.

cybernetics The scientific discipline which deals with control mechanisms and communication in humans, other living organisms, and machines.

cycle ergometer A stationary, one-wheeled bicycle with adjustable resistance used for estimating the *work output of an individual. *See also* ergometer.

cyclical involvement An involvement in sport characterized by sporadic participation, such as an individual who plays golf only during holidays.

cyclic AMP An important intracellular chemical that mediates intracellular responses to some hormones. Cyclic AMP is formed from *ATP by the action of adenylate cyclase, an *enzyme associated with the *plasma membrane.

cyclopenthiazide A *drug belonging to the *diuretics which are on the *IOC list of *banned substances.

cyproheptadine hydrochloride A *drug used to increase appetite and weight, possibly through its actions in affecting the appetite centre in the *hypothalmus. Drowsiness is a common side-effect.

cyst A cavity lined with *epithelium and filled with fluid or a semi-solid, usually formed as a result of a *pathological process in a tissue or organ.

cystitis Inflammation of the urinary bladder commonly caused by coliform bacteria. Treatment is usually with appropriate antibiotics. Athletes are advised to abstain from physical exertion until the infection has been completely cleared.

cytochrome A protein pigment containing *iron involved in *redox reactions in the electron-transport system of the *respiratory chain which takes place in *mitochondria.

cytochrome oxidase *Enzyme which catalyses the final stage of *aerobic respiration when oxygen combines with hydrogen ions to form water.

cytology The study of the structure and function of *cells.

cytoplasm The jelly-like part of a cell outside the *nucleus.

D

dactylion A *landmark located at the tip of the middle (third) finger, or the most *distal point of the middle finger when the arm is hanging and the fingers are stretched downward.

dactylion height A *body-height measurement made from *dactylion to *base.

Dal Monte five sprints-test A test devised to evaluate the ability of athletes to perform alternate *aerobic and *anaerobic activities. The subject performs five sprints at maximum effort from standing starts, over distances of 50 m for men and 40 m for women, at intervals of 1 min. The athlete's time to perform the five sprints is recorded to indicate the ability to repeat power performances. Heartrate is taken between the 40th and 55th second after each sprint, and between the 60th and 90th second after the fifth sprint, and finally at the end of the third minute to evaluate recovery capacity.

Dal Monte test A test of *alactacid power based on the estimation of the heaviest thrust applied by a subject against a dynamometric bar set at the level of the *centre of gravity, whilst running for 5 s up a 10 per cent gradient on a treadmill. The test is performed at three different speeds.

Dalton's law A law named after the English chemist John Dalton (1766–1844) which states that the total pressure of a mixture of two or more gases or vapours is equal to the sum of the pressures that each gas would exert if it were present alone and occupied the same volume as the whole mixture.

danozol An *anabolic steroid which has features similar to *stanazolol.

dark adaptation An increase in the sensitivity of the eye to light when a person remains in darkness or in low illumination.

dart thrower's elbow A tender swelling around the tip of an elbow due to a *bursitis at the *olecranon. It is caused by repeated physical flexing of the elbow, or rubbing the elbow.

data set In *sociology, a collection of information or observations made on a group of individuals relating to certain variables of interest to the investigator. The *data may be gathered in a number of ways including interviews, surveys, and experiments.

datum (pl. data) A single piece of information.

daydreaming A fantasy experienced in the waking state.

dead-lift A *weight-training exercise in which the lifter is in a standing position with the barbell held in the hands. The lifter bends over keeping the arms and legs straight, touches the floor with the barbell, and then lifts the barbell back to the standing position.

dead space The volume of gas taken into the *lungs which does not take part in *gaseous exchange. It consists of the *anatomical dead space, the volume of the *alveoli which are not perfused, and the volume of underperfused alveoli.

dead-space-to-tidal-volume ratio The proportion of *tidal volume taken up by the *dead space; the ratio gives a measure of the efficiency of pulmonary gas exchange.

deafferentation A technique for eliminating, usually by surgery, the sensory input to the spinal cord while leaving the *efferent output intact. *See also* cuff technique.

deamination Removal of an amine ($-NH_3$) group from an organic compound by reduction, *hydrolysis, or *oxidation. Deamination occurs especially in the liver where amino acids are converted into ammonia, which is ultimately converted into *urea and excreted.

de Bruyn–Prevost constant load test A *short-term anaerobic test performed to exhaustion on a bicycle ergometer with a constant workload of 400W and pedal speed of 124–8rpm for males, and work load of 350W and pedal speed of 104–8rpm for females. The time to reach the required pedal speed (known as the delay time) and the total time the subject can maintain the required pedal speed (known as total time) are used to compute an index of total time divided by delay time which is used to evaluate anaerobic tolerance and performance.

decalification Loss of calcium or salts from bone.

decarboxylation Removal of carbon dioxide from a molecule. For example, decarboxylation occurs in the *Krebs cycle and the carbon dioxide is eventually exhaled.

decay theory A theory of loss of *learning based on the premise that the *engram deteriorates during an interval when it is not activated.

deceleration A reduction in the *acceleration of a body; the non-technical term for negative acceleration.

decision-making An important *cognitive process by which individuals, or groups and organizations, decide actions and determine policies. Decision-making depends, among other things, on perceptual ability and neuronal integration. It covers a wide area of human behaviour and consists of the decision, which is the phase of volition following normally upon deliberation and preceding the action. Sport sociologists and sport psychologists are particularly interested in the decision-making strategies of individuals and teams in competitive situations (*see* game theory). Decision-making varies in sport. Some are very simple and similar to reflex actions, but other decision-making is very complex. Decision-making is usually adversely affected by *anxiety. *See also* response-selection stage.

decompensation Inability of the heart to maintain an adequate circulation (when confronted with increased workloads, for example).

decompression A reduction in gas pressure in the body, (e.g., during ascent to high altitudes or from deep to shallow water). *See also* surgical decompression.

decompression sickness *See* caisson disease.

dedication A strongly positive attitude that leads to intensive activity; it is often associated with self-sacrifice.

deduction A logical method of reasoning from generalizations to specific relations or facts. *Compare* induction.

deductive explanation An explanation in which a specific phenomenon is deduced from an established general law. *Compare* induction.

deep In *anatomy, away from the body surface; more internal, as in *deep muscles.

deep-body temperature *See* core temperature.

deep fascia *See* fascia.

deep friction massage A form of *massage in which a firm pressure is applied to treat *deep muscle injuries.

deep palmar branch An *artery deep in the palm of the hand.

deep stroking A form of *massage performed by moving the pads of the thumbs along the length of a muscle, starting from the point farthest from the *heart and moving towards it. Deep stroking moves much *blood and *lymph through the muscle thereby removing fluid build-up but it can be painful, causing athletes to tense up. Tension is relieved by *jostling.

defaecation Elimination of faeces from the bowels.

defence mechanism A behaviour pattern primarily concerned with protecting the *ego. *See also* ego defence; rationalization; and repression.

deferred gratification Behaviour in which sacrifices are made in the present in the hope of greater future reward.

deficiency disease A disease caused by the lack of *essential nutrients. *See also* vitamin-deficiency disease.

definition *See* muscle definition.

definition of situation Concerns the importance of the subjective perspectives of social *actors for the objective consequences of social interactions. Therefore, if a sportsperson defines a situation as real or existing, its consequences are real. As an example, if a sportsperson assumes that a coach does not like him or her, and acts accordingly, the assumption will have real consequences.

deformation An alteration in the size or shape of a *body.

deformative movement A movement which exerts a *force which changes the shape of an object.

degeneration The deterioration and loss of function in body organs and tissues. Degeneration is usually associated with the ageing process, but it can also result from disease and inactivity. *See also* atrophy.

degenerative disease A disease involving gradual deterioration and loss of function of a tissue or organ.

degenerative joint disease *See* osteoarthritis.

degree 1 A unit used in measurement of angular distance. One degree equals 1/360 revolutions of a circle. **2** The loft of a golf-club which is usually given as the number of degrees the club-face is set back from the vertical. **3** Unit of temperature *see* celsius and fahrenheit. **4** Extent of something, for example, sporting achievement.

dehydration A depletion of fluids from the body which can hinder *thermoregulation and cause an increase in *core temperature. The reduction in the body's fluid volume may result in a reduction in *blood pressure and *cardiac output. Mild dehydration may result in a general malaise and *insomnia. Dehydration occurs during exercise if the fluid lost through perspiration exceeds fluid replacement. It can cause poor performance even in temperate climates. A 2 per cent loss of body-weight due to water-loss, can lead to a 20 per cent drop in the working capacity of muscles. Training tends to increase tolerance to dehydration. *See also* heat-stroke; and water replacement.

dehydroepiandrosterone (DHEA) A *steroid produced in the *testis. It has relatively weak *anabolic and *androgenic activities.

dehydrogenase An *enzyme which catalyses the removal of hydrogen from a *substrate. *See also* succinic dehydrogenase.

delayed conditioning A method of *classical conditioning in which the *conditioned stimulus remains present until the appearance of the unconditioned stimulus.

delayed feedback Situation in which there is a time-lag between the performance of a *skill and the *feedback which is given to a subject about the performance.

delayed onset muscle soreness (DOMS) Muscular discomfort which develops one to two days after exercise has stopped. It may be due to torn muscle fibres or muscle spasms but its most likely cause is disruption of *connective tissue elements as DOMS is usually accompanied by increased levels of urinary *hydroxyproline. DOMS typically affects those who only exercise occasionally or who perform strenuous exercises to which they are unaccustomed. It is greatest following exercises which use mainly *eccentric contractions.

delegated performance Group performance in which various individual members are assigned specific functions. Delegated performance affects social interaction and social facilitation. Types of delegated performance are *sequentially-independent tasks and *sequentially-dependent tasks. *Compare* interdependent performance.

deliberation The initial phase of *decision-making when different choices are presented as possible courses of action.

delinquency Antisocial or illegal acts, commonly performed by young males. *See also* football hooliganism.

delinquency deterrence hypothesis A proposition that participation in sports reduces the tendency towards antisocial behaviour in young people.

delinquent subculture A *social group which is committed to values considered within the general society to be criminal or antisocial.

deltoideus *See* deltoid muscle.

deltoid ligament A *ligament connecting the *tibia to the *calcaneus in the *ankle.

deltoid muscle (deltoideus) A thick, *pennate muscle responsible for the roundness of the shoulder. Its *origin, on the lateral third of the *clavicle, and the *acromion and *spine of the *scapula, embraces the *insertion of the *trapezius. Its own insertion is on the *deltoid tuberosity of the *humerus. The deltoid muscle takes part in all movements of the upper arm. Its main action is as *prime mover of arm *abduction. It also acts as an *antago-

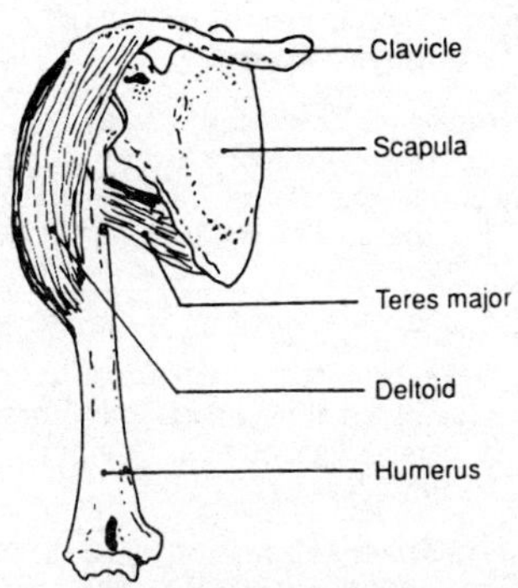

deltoid muscle

nist of the *pectoralis major and *latissimus dorsi which adduct (*see* adduction) the arm. Contraction of anterior fibres of the deltoid muscle results in powerful *flexion of the arm and *medial rotation of the humerus; contraction of the posterior fibres on their own, cause *extension and *lateral rotation of the arm. The deltoids are particularly active during rhythmic swinging movements of the arms during walking.

deltoid tuberosity An attachment site of the fleshy *deltoid muscle on the *shaft of the *humerus.

delusion A false judgement or conclusion; usually used in reference to a mentally ill person but it has also been applied to sports people, particularly when they act irrationally under the pressure of competiion.

democratic behaviour *Coaching behaviour which allows greater participation by athletes in decisions pertaining to group goals, practice methods, game tactics, and strategies.

democratic leadership A relationship-oriented form of leadership that encourages coach–athlete interaction. It is a leadership style which can best be explained in terms of *consideration.

democratization A process whereby a social activity such as sport becomes more accessible to, and popular among, different segments of society, such as different age groups, genders, races, social classes, and people of varying abilities.

demography The scientific study of populations; their age-structure, migrations, mortality rate, occupations, and other factors affecting the quality of life within populations.

demulcent An *antitussive drug which acts as a substitute for the natural function of mucus by creating a mechanical barrier which coats and protects the *epithelium of the *respiratory tract.

denaturation A disruption of the chemical bonds maintaining the three-dimensional structure of proteins. Denaturation may be caused by extremes of temperature, organic solvents, or ultrasonic vibrations. The activity of *enzymes depends on the enzymes' shape, thus denaturation results in a reduction or even loss of their activity.

dendrite A short branching process of a *neurone which serves as a receiver of information from neighbouring neurones, transmitting *nerve impulses towards the *cell body.

dendron Part of a *neurone carrying *nerve impulses towards a *cell body. *Compare* axon.

denial A mechanism of *ego defence in which an individual under threat, particularly if immature or emotionally disturbed, may deny the existence of an object, situation, person, or threat. Mild forms of denial can be seen in young athletes who, when facing formidable opponents, reject the obvious threat to their self-esteem and deny the abilities of their adversaries. As people mature and form more accurate perceptions of reality, this form of ego defence is less likely to occur.

dense fibrous connective tissue *See* dense regular connective tissue.

dense irregular connective tissue *Connective tissue consisting mainly of *collagen fibres interwoven and arranged irregularly in more than one plane to form sheets. It occurs particularly in areas where *tension is exerted in many different directions (e.g., in the *fascia surrounding muscle). *Compare* dense regular connective tissue.

dense regular connective tissue (dense fibrous connective tissue) A white, flexible *connective tissue comprised mainly of regularly arranged bundles of *collagen fibres running in the same direction. It has great *tensile strength where the tissue tends to be pulled along one *plane. It occurs in *tendons, *aponeuroses, and *ligaments. *Compare* dense irregular connective tissue.

densitometry Methods, based on *Archimedes' principle, for assessing total *body density, and from which fat and fat-free masses are sometimes estimated.

density Mass per unit volume of an object:

$$\text{density } (\text{g/cm}^3) = \text{mass}(\text{g})/\text{volume } (\text{cm}^3)$$

See also body density.

deoxyribonucleic acid (DNA) A chemical which carries hereditary information, found in the nucleus of all cells.

dependence *See* drug dependence.

dependent variable A *variable which is acted on or influenced by another variable. For example, in an investigation of the affects of age on running speed the *independent variable (the age of the athlete) is manipulated or otherwise controlled, and the affect of this manipulation can be seen in the change in the dependent variable (running speed). An aspect of behaviour or experience which goes with or depends on the changes in the independent variable.

depolarization The reversal of potential difference across a cell membrane (especially a *neurone or muscle cell) during an *action potential. The inside of the cell loses its negative charge and becomes positive relative to the outside due to an influx of sodium ions. *Compare* resting potential. *See also* hyperpolarization.

depot preparation A preparation of a medicine in which the active ingredients are only slowly released into the tissue.

depression 1 A melancholy mood; a feeling of hopelessness, or an attitude of dejection. Depression can seriously affect the motivation to train and compete. In serious cases, depression is a symptom of mental illness. 2 A linear movement of a body part (e.g., the shoulders) when dropping or moving inferiorly along the frontal plane. *Compare* elevation.

deprivation–satiation proposition A proposition that the more often in the recent past a person has received a particular reward, the less valuable any further unit of that reward becomes.

deprofessionalization The process by which members of a high-status occupation loses the facility to have autonomous control over its internal affairs and the behaviour of its membership. Deprofessionalization also results in a loss of the monopoly of the members of the profession to have exclusive rights to do certain kinds of work and a loss of control over the expert knowledge which, before deprofessionalization, was not available to the general public. It could be claimed that aerobic and diet clubs act to deprofessionalize sports scientists who are now not seen as having a monopoly of knowledge in these areas.

depth of processing The level to which information is processed after being introduced into the *memory. The concept is based on the rejection of the idea that information is stored in discrete memory stores. It adopts the view that an item enters the information-processing system and undergoes an increasing amount of processing thereby moving deeper into the system. It is postulated that the retention characteristics of information are determined by the depth of processing, with deeper levels being associated with more abstract coding and greater retention.

depth perception Three-dimensional perception which is essential to the ability of a person to judge quickly and accurately the speed and distance relationships between an object and the individual.

de Quervain's disease *Tendovaginitis of the base of the thumb. *See also* paddler's wrist.

derived unit Unit used to measure quantities, including *joule, *newton, and *watt, derived from the *basic units.

dermatitis Inflammation of the skin often accompanied by a rash.

dermatome An area of skin innervated by the branches of a single *spinal nerve. Dermatomes are represented as distinct areas on a dermatome map, but in reality their distribution is much more complex as there is considerable overlap (about 50 per cent) between dermatomes. *See also* TENS.

dermatome map A diagram of the body showing the main area covered by each *dermatome.

dermis Deep layer of the *skin which lies beneath the *epidermis. The dermis contains *blood vessels, *muscles, *dense irregular connective tissue, and *sensory nerve-endings.

descriptive statistics Statistics which summarize the characteristics of a particular sample. *Compare* inferential statistics.

desensitization *Stress-management technique, more accurately called systematic desensitization, which uses relaxation techniques. The subject compiles a hierarchial list of anxiety-inducing situations (such as those associated with a competition) with the one inducing the most *anxiety at the top. The subject then undergoes *progressive muscle relaxation. Once relaxation is achieved, each stress-provoking situation is visualized, starting with the one causing least anxiety. At the same time, the subject visualizes performing very well in the competition. Desensitization is a form of *counter-conditioning.

desire for group failure A group-member's expectations and hopes that the group will fail to achieve a goal. A substituted player, for example, may sit on the bench secretly hoping that his or her team will lose. Those with a desire for group failure have a sense of satisfaction when failure has been realized.

desire for group success A group-member's expectations and hopes that the group will succeed at a task. Desire for group success has been proposed as a key, situation specific element in group motivation which spurs group-members to set and strive for challenging goals. Those with a desire for group success generally have a sense of pride and satisfaction when a group goal has been achieved.

de-skilling A process by which individuals cease to plan and control large parts of their work. The skills essential for doing the tasks self-reflectively and well, waste away and are forgotten. In sport, the role of the coach in constructing a training programme can now be done by a computer program; therefore, the coach's skill in this area is not needed.

desocialization The process whereby an individual experiences role-loss and an accompanying loss of associated power or prestige (e.g., following retirement from a sport). The individual may experience a loss of *social identity resulting in an *identity crisis, loss of peer status, loss of self-image and self-esteem, and have difficulty finding a substitute activity or another peer group.

detached retina Separation of the whole or part of the *retina from the *choroid coat causing loss of vision in the region of separation. The actual separation may be due to extreme physical exertion, such as lifting a heavy weight, but the underlying causes of the detachment may be a hole or tear in the retina associated with degenerative changes. Treatment is by fixation of the retina. Sufferers of detached retinas are usually advised to avoid contact sports such as boxing.

detection *See* stimulus identification.

determinant Any factor which causes a particular phenomenon. For example, in *Cartwright's model of team cohesion, determinants are factors that lead to the development of *team cohesion and include co-operation, team stability, team homogeneity, and the size of the group.

detoxify To remove poisonous substances.

de-training effects The loss of *training effects following the cessation of *training. Most training effects are lost within eight weeks but some effects, such as an increased *aerobic capacity and decreased *lactic acid production during submaximal exercises, can be maintained for several months by continuing a light exercise programme for one or two days a week.

development The process of continuous change towards a condition of specialized function. Physical development usually results in an increase in complexity of anatomical structure. Intellectual development, resulting largely from *learning, is characterized by an increase in complexity of behaviour.

deviance Any social behaviour which departs from that regarded as normal or socially accepted within a society or social context.

deviance amplification Process, often performed by the *mass media, in which the extent and seriousness of deviant behaviour, such as *football hooliganism, is exaggerated. The affect is to create a greater awareness and interest in deviance which results in more deviance being uncovered, giving the impression that the initial exaggeration was actually a true representation.

deviant behaviour The conduct of individuals whose behaviour is contrary to the generally accepted *norms or values of a society. *See also* deviant sport acts.

deviant sport acts Actions, on or off the field of play, which involve violating the rules of the sport or contravening the commonly accepted definitions of fair play or sportsmanship.

deviant sport subculture A sport group whose members' behaviour is contrary to some of the *norms or values of the wider society. Some regard boxing as a deviant sport subculture, for example, because of the intent to inflict physical harm on the opponent. *Compare* avocational sport subculture; and occupational sport culture.

deviation In statistics, the difference between one value and the *mean of the set of values. Mean deviation is the mean of all the individual deviations of a set.

Dewey's theory of experiential continuum A theory which maintains that every experience takes up something from those experiences which have gone before and modifies in some way the quality of those experiences which occur later. Dewey argued that education should at each stage build on what has been learnt in the previous stage.

dexamethasone A *drug belonging to the *corticosteroids which are on the *IOC list of *banned substances. Dexamethasone is used to treat rheumatic and other inflammatory conditions.

dexamphetamine A *drug belonging to the *stimulants which are on the *IOC list of *banned substances. Its actions are similar to those of *amphetamine.

dexfenfluramine An *anorexiant drug.

dexterity Ability to manipulate fine objects with the hands.

dextrin A *carbohydrate formed as an intermediate breakdown product in the digestion of starch by *amylase.

dextroamphetamine *Drug belonging to *amphetamine group of *stimulants on the *IOC list of *banned substances.

dextromethorphan An *analgesic which was removed from the *IOC list of *banned substances in 1986. It is used as a cough suppressant in some cold and cough medicines. It sometimes causes dizziness and drowsiness which can affect performance in some sports.

dextromoramide A *drug belonging to the *narcotic analgesics which are on the *IOC list of *banned substances

dextropropoxyphene A *drug belonging to the *narcotic analgesics which are on the *IOC list of *banned substances.

dextrose A simple sugar containing one sugar unit; also another name for *glucose.

DHEA *See* dehydroepiandosterone.

dhobie itch (groin itch) Infection, particularly of the groin, caused by fungi belonging to the genera *Trichophyton* or *Epidermophyton* .

diabetes *See* diabetes mellitus.

diabetes insipidus Metabolic disorder caused by inadequate release of *antidiuretic hormone (ADH), characterized by the elimination of excessively large quantities of dilute *urine. It is accompanied by intense thirst and results in *dehydration.

diabetes mellitus (diabetes) A disorder of carbohydrate metabolism characterized by an increased blood sugar level due to the body's inability to produce enough *insulin or to use it properly. Physical activity has for a long time been recommended as an effective measure in modifying the course of the disease, helping to reduce the risk of vascular complications. However, it is important that the diabetic, coach, and friends are well acquainted with potential problems, such as *hypoglycaemia, if the subject over exerts himself or herself. There is some evidence that exercise also plays a role in the prevention of diabetes although it does not give absolute protection. Physical activity reduces the concentration of insulin in the *serum and trained people tend to have an enhanced sensitivity of body tissues to insulin.

diagonal plane *See* oblique plane.

dialysis Separation of small molecules from larger ones through a *differentially permeable membrane.

dianabol (methandrostenolone) An *anabolic steroid which, in *drug trials, has been claimed to cause an increase in muscle strength among athletes engaged in continuous hard training.

diapedesis Passage of cells through intact *vessel walls into tissue spaces.

diaphragm **1** Any partition or wall separating one body area from another. **2** A sheet of *muscle and *tendon between the *abdominal cavity and *thoracic cavity. The diaphragm is attached to the inferior border of the *ribcage at each side, the *sternum in the front, and the vertebrae at the back. Its *insertion consists of a boomerang-shaped central tendon. The diaphragm has an important role in *ventilation. During *inspiration, it contracts and flattens, thereby increasing the volume of the thoracic cavity. With each *expiration it relaxes and regains its dome shape by its inherent elasticity. When strongly contracted the diaphragm increases *intra-abdominal *pressure. This may help to support the backbone and reduce *flexion when lifting heavy weights.

diaphysis The elongated central part (shaft) of a long bone. The diaphysis consists of *compact bone surrounding a *medullary cavity.

diarrhoea Frequent evacuation of the bowels or the passage of soft, watery faeces. Diarrhoea may occur with intestinal infections or extreme exertion and exhaustion. The loss of fluid impairs physical performance and increases the risk of muscular cramps.

diarthordial joint *See* synovial joint.

diarthrosis *See* synovial joint.

diastase An *enzyme which accelerates the breakdown of *starch to *maltose; it is common in barley seeds. Diastase has been used to aid *digestion of starch in some sufferers of digestive disorders.

diastole Resting phase of the *cardiac cycle when all parts of the heart are relaxed. It lasts about 0.5 s and occurs immediately after *systole.

diastolic blood pressure The lowest pressure in the *arteries which occurs when the heart is relaxed and filling with blood between beats. A typical value is 80 mmHg. It is usually represented by the bottom number in the fraction of a *blood pressure reading.

diastolic volume The amount of blood which fills the *ventricle during *diastole.

diathermy A form of heat therapy in which a high frequency electric current produces heat and increases blood flow in the body tissues. It is used to relieve pain.

diazepam A 1,4 *benzodiazepine derivative used as a *tranquilizer; an example is the brand *drug Valium®.

dichloracetic acid A *drug that decreases *lactic acid production in rats. No beneficial effects have been demonstrated in humans.

diclofenac An *analgesic, which belongs to the non-steroidal anti-inflammatory drugs. It has relatively long-lasting effects and tends not to irritate the stomach.

diclorphenamide A *drug belonging to the *diuretics which are on the *IOC list of *banned substances.

diencephalon The central core of the *forebrain, between the *cerebral hemispheres. It includes among its structures the *thalamus and the *hypothalamus.

diet Pattern of eating. The quality, quantity, and times a person eats. *See also* balanced diet.

dietary fibre *See* roughage.

diethylypropion hydrochloride A *drug belonging to the *stimulants which are on the *IOC list of *banned substances.

diet-induced thermogenesis Heat production associated with the ingestion of food. It indicates that energy is needed in the process of *digestion, absorption, and storage of *nutrients. *See also* specific dynamic action.

difference threshold *See* differential threshold.

differential approach Approach to the study of behaviour that focuses on individual differences, abilities, and predictions.

differential diagnosis The recognition of one disorder from another or others which have similar signs and symptoms.

differential threshold 1 The smallest perceptible difference between two *stimuli. 2 The least amount of change in a stimulus in order for it to be recognized.

difficulty The state or quality of being not easy to perform. In some models of movement-behaviour, difficulty is jointly related to the distance the limb has to move and the narrowness of the target at which it is aimed. As the movement becomes more difficult, the time required to complete the movement accurately increases (*see* Fitt's Law).

diffidence Lack of *self-confidence. Diffident individuals typically respond to competitive situations with *fear of failure, are easily intimidated, and act with trepidation.

diffusing capacity of lung *See* pulmonary diffusion capacity.

diffusion 1 The spread of cultural traits such as language forms, technological ideas, or social practices from one society to another. 2 The net movement of molecules of a liquid or gas from a high concentration to a low concentration. Diffusion is a passive process resulting from the random movement of molecules due to their *kinetic energy. In organisms, diffusion is usually through a cell *membrane, with the rate of diffusion depending on the concentration gradient and diffusion distance, and the surface area and properties of the membrane. Diffusion through biological membranes is called permeation.

diflunisal A *NSAID which is closely related to acetylsalicylic acid (aspirin) and which has similar effects, but which may irritate the stomach-lining less.

digestion The process whereby complex food is broken into simple compounds by mechanical processes, such as chewing, or chemical processes using *hydrolytic enzymes. Digestion takes place in the alimentary canal so that food can be absorbed and assimilated into the body.

digestive system Body system concerned with the *digestion of food. *See also* alimentary canal.

digit One of the fingers which are numbered one to five starting at the thumb.

digital In *anatomy, pertaining to the toes or fingers.

digitalis A group of drugs derived from foxgloves (*Digitalis* species). They stimulate the contraction of cardiac muscle and slow the rate of conduction of impulses through the *atrioventricular node, thereby enabling the ventricles to beat more effectively. Digitalis preparations are used in the treatment of heart disorders but they frequently produce unwanted side-effects such as *nausea, vomiting, blurred vision, and irregular heartbeats.

dihydrocodeine A *drug belonging to the *narcotic analgesics which are on the *IOC list of *banned substances.

dihydrotestosterone A *steroid hormone produced in the testis which has *androgenic and *anabolic effects approximately equal to those of *testosterone.

dilation Widening.

dimetamfetamine A *drug belonging to the *stimulants which are on the *IOC list of *banned substances.

dimethyl sulphoxide (DMSO) An anti-inflammatory *drug rubbed into the affected area of skin.

dipeptide A compound consisting of two *amino acids joined by a *peptide bond.

dipheniramine An *antihistamine *drug commonly found in cough and cold medicines.

diphosphoglycerate (2,3-DPG) An organic phosphate bound to *haemoglobin in red blood cells. Diphosphoglycerate is a by-product of the breakdown of *glycogen to *glucose. It reduces the affinity of haemoglobin for oxygen, shifting the oxygen dissociation curve to the right and thereby assisting the unloading of oxygen to the tissues. Prolonged training increases the 2,3-DPG concentration in red blood cells. *See also* altitude acclimatization.

diphosphonate Any chemical which binds strongly to bone.

dipivefrine A *drug belonging to the *stimulants which are on the *IOC list of *banned substances.

diploë Layer of spongy bone sandwiched between the inner and outer layer of compact tissue in the *skull.

direct calorimetry The measurement of the heat production of a person in a *calorimeter to obtain a direct measurement of the person's energy output and an estimate of energy consumption. *Compare* indirect calorimetry.

direct competition *Competition involving persons in a clearly personal contest against each other. Opponents may confront one another as teams or as individuals.

direct descriptive feedback *Feedback, given to a performer by a coach or other observer, consisting of a description of the

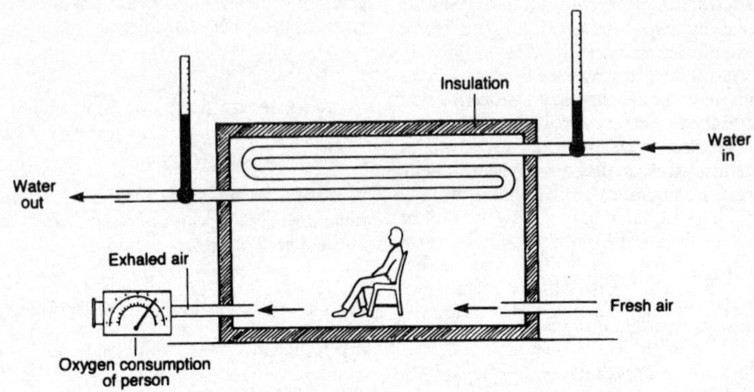

direct calorimetry

performance followed by a description of how the coach reacted to it.

direct evaluative feedback Form of *feedback, given to an athlete by a coach or other observer, in which the coach directly evaluates the athlete's behaviour without describing what led to that evaluation. Direct evaluative feedback may consist of statement such as 'you were terrible', or 'you were great'. *Compare* direct descriptive feedback.

direct force (concentric force) A *force which has its line of action passing through the *centre of gravity of the *body on which it acts. *Compare* eccentric force.

direct impact The collision of two objects moving along the same straight line before impact, or the collision of a stationary object with another object travelling at right angles to the surface where contact occurs. Direct impact occurs when a snooker cue strikes a ball, or when a footballer kicks a ball. *Compare* oblique impact.

directional terms Terms used by anatomists, physiologists, and medical personnel to describe precisely where one structure is in relation to another. *See also* anterior; caudal; cranial; deep; distal; dorsal; inferior; intermediate; lateral; medial; posterior; proximal; superficial; superior; and ventral.

direct measure In sport psychology, a measurement in which individuals are asked direct questions. In the assessment of team cohesion, for example, team-members might be asked direct questions about how well they work together in the pursuit of team goals.

direct motivation Motivation which is clear and unambiguous, such as when a coach makes a direct appeal to an athlete to try harder for the sake of the team. There are three main forms of direct motivation: *compliance, *identification, and *internalization. *Compare* indirect motivation.

directrix A fixed line used to describe and define a curve. It is a straight line, the distance of which from any point on the curve bears a constant ratio to the distance of the same point to the *focus. *See also* parabola.

direct trauma An injury caused by a direct impact.

DIRT Mnemonic used to remember the components of interval training.'D' represents the distance to be covered in each run, swim, cycle-ride, etc.; 'I' is the interval of rest between each run, etc.: 'R' is the number of repetitions in each *set of runs, etc.; and 'T' is the target time for each run, etc.

disability Any partial or total, mental or physical inability to perform any activity (sporting, social, or occupational) the affected person wishes to perform.

disaccharide (double sugar) Sugars formed by two *monosaccharides joined together by a reaction in which water is removed. For example, when *glucose and *fructose combine they form the disaccharide *sucrose. Other common disaccharides are *lactose (formed from glucose and *galactose) and *maltose (formed from two molecules of glusose).

disc *See* intervertebral disc.

disc displacement Removal of an *intervertebral disc from its normal position without herniating through the joint capsule. Some of the cushioning effects of the disc are lost as a result of displacement. Disc displacment is a common cause of low back-pain.

disease Any disorder with a characteristic set of signs and symptoms, except that resulting from physical trauma.

discontinuous servo A closed-loop control system in which the control actions of the effector are not continuously related to the state of the system being controlled. A simple home thermostat controlling room temperature is an example of a discontinuous servo: the room temperature continuously fluctuates but the heater (which acts as the effector) does not behave in the same way: it is either on or off with no one-to-one relationship between the changes in room temperature and the state of the heater. *Compare* continuous servo.

discontinuous variable *See* discrete variable.

discourse A formal treatment in speech or writing of a subject using specialist language. A discourse is a domain of language use, structured as a unity by common assumptions. There may be competing discourses, and discourses change with time. Attention has focused on the social functions of discourses, in particular with regard to their ability to close off possibilities. Within a discourse there are literally some things that cannot be said or thought. That is, any discourse contains implicit and explicit rules about what is said and left unsaid. For example, a dominant discourse in sports science is that of *positivism which focuses attention on one way of understanding sport and excludes others.

discovery learning Learning situation in which the learner must discover for himself or herself the chief contents or principles of the phenomenon to be learnt, and then incorporate them into his or her behaviour and thinking.

discrete skill (discrete task) A *skill which contains a single unit of activity with a definite beginning and end. A tennis-serve and golf-swing are examples of discrete skills. *Compare* continuous skill.

discrete task *See* discrete skill.

discrimination **1** Prejudicial and, therefore, unequal treatment of a group of persons. Discrimination can apply to race or ethnic group (*see* racism), gender (*see* sexism), or age (*see* ageism). **2** The ability to distinguish between different levels or types of stimulation when they are presented simultaneously. **3** The ability to make precise distinctions between different stimulus–response conditions, as when a person distinguishes between a reinforced *stimulus, to which a response is given, and an unreinforced stimulus, to which no response or a different response is given.

discrimination reaction-time The *reaction time for a task in which different combinations of a number of stimuli are presented, with a response being made only if the combination includes a given *stimulus.

disengagement The withdrawal from participation in an activity. In sport, disengagement tends to increase with age, and it is common during certain critical periods of the *life course such as during adolescence.

disengagement theory A theory which proposes that society and the ageing individual mutually withdraw from one another for the benefit and satisfaction of both. Thus, the theory states that as a person ages, he or she should withdraw from the roles adopted in middle age, allowing these roles to be filled by younger people and releasing the older person to pursue new leisure interests. The theory is not supported by many gerontologists.

disinhibition The suppression of *inhibition, such as might occur through the inhibitory action of one *neurone on another inhibitory neurone.

dislocation (luxation) Complete separation (displacement) of *articulating bones as a result of a *joint being forced beyond its *maximum passive range. The joint becomes immobile or unstable, but there is little pain unless the displaced bone presses on a nerve. Considerable care is required when putting a dislocated bone back in place as great damage can be done to surrounding blood vessels and nerves by an unskilled person. It is usually relatively easy for a skilled person to replace a dislocated bone (it may even realign automatically) within a few hours of the injury. If, however, treatment is delayed, the condition is as hard to correct as any *fracture because the *ligaments damaged during the injury tend to stick together. *Compare* subluxation.

displaced aggression Hostility directed against an inanimate object or a person, other than the source of the hostility, from which retaliation is unlikely. The person against whom the *aggression is displaced is usually weaker than the agressor.

displacement 1 A *vector quantity which refers to the distance which an object has moved in a given direction. It is measured as the length of a straight line between the initial and final positions of a body. In a race around one complete circuit of a 400m track, the displacement is 0m. *Compare* distance. 2 Volume of fluid displaced by a body completely or partially submerged in a fluid. 3 In psychology, applied to behaviours and emotions which are transferred from their original object to a more acceptable substitute. For example, a tennis player who feels aggrieved about an umpiring decision may throw a tennis racket at the ground rather than at the umpire.

displacement activity *See* displacement.

display A specific learning situation or task which confronts an individual. In sport, the display includes the equipment, cues, and environment in which an athlete acquires skills. One of the challenges of a coach is to be able to modify displays to make it easier for athletes to achieve desired learning outcomes.

dissociation An *attentional style characterized by *distraction. Dissociation is exhibited by athletes who are unaware of their surroundings because they are mentally absorbed thinking about other things while participating in their sport. *Compare* association.

dissociators Individuals who externalize or adopt an external *attentional focus. Those particpating in *contact sports are often dissociators as they attempt to focus on things unrelated to body sensations. *Compare* associators.

dissonance *See* cognitive dissonance.

distal A *directional term applied to a part of the body further from the centre of the body or trunk. *Compare* proximal.

distance A *scalar measurement of the extent of a body's motion, irrespective of the direction in which it has travelled. Thus, when a body moves from one location to another, the distance through which it moves is the length of the path it follows. In a race around one complete circuit of a 400m track, the distance travelled is 400m. *Compare* displacement.

distance acuity The ability to focus on, and distinguish, fine detail at 6m or more with each eye separately and together, under a variety of lighting conditions.

distance–time curve A smooth line or curve which best fits the points on a graph in which distance is plotted on the y-axis and time on the x-axis. The distance–time curve enables changes in *speed (e.g., during a 100m race) to be identified since the slope (gradient) at any point of time gives the speed of the body at that time. *See also* instantaneous speed.

distensibility The capacity to expand or stretch under pressure.

distorting force A *force which changes the dimensions of a body. *Compare* rotating force.

distractability The ease with which irrelevant thoughts and external stimuli interfere with *concentration on the task in hand. Distractability is affected by levels of *arousal: as arousal increases, an athlete's *attention narrows and distractability decreases. Eventually, with levels of arousal above an optimum, the athlete's attention shifts sporadically from one cue to another, increasing distractability and the chances of a poor performance.

distraction game A form of concentration-training in which one person deliberately tries to distract another or others by any means other than those which physically impede the subject. *See also* desensitization.

distraction rupture An intrinsic injury resulting in a muscle-tear caused by overstretching or overloading. Distraction ruptures commonly occur in *biarticulate muscles, such as the hamstrings, in performers of explosive events when demands on the muscles exceed their strength. *See also* distraction strain.

distraction strain A muscle strain which occurs when a muscle accidentally contracts when it is being stretched. Distraction strains often occur among athletes who do not *warm up or who are suffering from *fatigue and are not able to respond adequately to neuromuscular reflexes. There are three degrees of distration strain: first degree strain, where there is some swelling, inflammation and discomfort, but no appreciable tear; second degree strain, in which there is considerable pain, more damage to the muscle, but there is not a complete tear; and third degree strain, in which there is a complete tear of the muscle (a distraction rupture).

distress The negative, unpleasant, and harmful aspects of *stress. *Compare* eustress.

distributed practice A procedure for *learning a *skill in which small units of practice are interpolated with rest periods; usually the practice time is less than the rest time. *Compare* massed practice.

distributive-justice proposition The proposition that the perceived adequacy of a *reward depends not so much on a person's needs but on what rewards are available and how they are shared. Individuals may compare their own reward with those of teammates.

disuse atrophy A degeneration or loss of mass of muscle which results from inactivity. Paralysis can result in muscles being reduced to one quarter of their original size. *Fibrous connective tissue replaces the muscle making rehabilitation impossible. *See also* bilateral transfer.

diuresis The excretion of large volumes of *urine. An increase in urine output may be induced by disease or by drugs. *See also* diuretics

diuretic drugs **1** A pharmacological class of agents which are banned by the *International Olympic Committee. Their use results in an increase in urine flow which helps to eliminate tissue fluids. This has important therapeutic applications for certain pathological conditions such as *oedema, but diuretics have been misused in sports with strict weight-controls to reduce weight quickly. They have also been misused to flush out drugs and reduce the concentration of *banned substances in a sample of urine taken for dope tests. Diuretics may also cause the excretion of valuable water-soluble vitamins and minerals. **2** Any substance that increases the elimination of fluid from the body through urination. In addition to the pharmocological class of agents banned by the IOC (see above), diuretics also include *alcohol and *caffeine.

divergent involvement An involvement in sport which almost amounts to an obsession, with a disproportionate amount of time being devoted to the sport, often to the detriment of family and career. Primary divergent involvement in sport is exhibited by individuals who play sports to the exclusion of most other things; secondary divergent involvement refers to individuals who consume sport to excess and become sports addicts.

divergent sport involvement *See* divergent involvement.

divergent thinking A form of thinking in which a single idea or problem generates many other ideas or solutions.

diverticulitis Inflammation of the intestinal *diverticulum. Extensive inflammation may obstruct the bowel. The disease is linked with poor dietary habits. A balanced diet and physical activity can be beneficial to uncomplicated diverticulitis by improving the mobility of the gut and easing the passage of stools.

diverticulum A pouch or sac protruding from the walls of a hollow *organ or structure (e.g., in the *large intestine).

divided-target-type test A test of accuracy in which a target is divided up into several parts each of which receives a different point value.

divisible task A *task performed by members of a *group whose functions are differentiated but which results in the production of a final group effect.

division of labour The process whereby tasks become separated and more specialized. Division of labour is seen in American football teams which have highly specialized teams of offence and defence, and specialized kickers and punters.

dizziness A mental condition which results in unsteadiness when standing with a tendency to stagger and fall. *See also* vertigo.

DMSO *See* dimethyl sulphoxide.

DNA *See* deoxyribonucleic acid.

dobutamine A *drug belonging to the *stimulants which are on the *IOC list of *banned substances.

dominant response *See* reaction potential.

domination In general usage, the influence exerted by one person or group over another person or groups. In sociology, domination is indicated by the likelihood that a command will be obeyed, and is distinguished from *power which may be imposed despite resistance.

DOMS *See* delayed onset muscle soreness.

Donaggio test A qualitative test of urine mucoproteins used as an indicator of *stress. An increase in mucoproteins is associated with a *stress reaction induced in the cortex of the adrenal gland as a result of *metabolic fatigue. The test consists of taking a 2 ml sample of urine and adding 1 ml of 1 per cent thionin and 2 mls of a 4 per cent solution ammonium molybdate. A positive reaction is indicated by the urine turning violet; the intensity of colour indicates the degree of positive reaction, which may be represented as +, ++, or +++.

Donnan equilibrium An electrochemical equilibrium established when two solutions are separated by a membrane that is impermeable to some of the ions in solution.

dopamine A metabolic *neurotransmitter belonging to the *biogenic amines which is an intermediate in the synthesis of *noradrenaline. Dopamine is regarded by the *IOC as a *stimulant and is on their list of *banned substances. It is secreted by some sympathetic ganglia in the *hypothalamus, and by some neurones in the midbrain. It is the main neurotransmitter of the *extrapyramidal system. Its release is enhanced by amphetamines. High dopamine levels have been associated with aggression. Antipsychotic drugs, such as *thorazine, have been used to block dopamine receptors and reduce aggression, but prolonged use reduces dopamine levels in parts of the brain controlling skeletal muscles and motor problems may result.

dopaminergic system Part of the nervous sytem which uses *dopamine as a *neurotransmitter.

doping A term derved from the African Kaffirs who used a local liquor called 'dop' as a stimulant. Doping is generally regarded as the administering or use of substances which are alien to the body, or of physiological substances in abnormal amounts, or the use of abnormal procedures by persons with the exclusive intention of gaining an artificial and unfair improvement in performance in competitions. Doping includes the use of medicines if these raise the physical capacity above the normal level. Defining which *drugs and methods constitute doping is a major problem and there is no universally agreed definition for all sports. The *IOC has a list of *banned substances which is used by all sports during the Olympic Games, but governing bodies of individual sports have their own lists which may differ from that of the IOC.

doping classes A classification of substances banned by the *International Olympic Committee based on pharmacological classes of agents. The doping classes are *anabolic steroids, *beta blockers, *diuretics, *narcotics, *peptide hormones and *analogues, and *stimulants. *See also* banned substances.

doping methods Pharmacological, chemical, and physical manipulations which are banned by the *IOC. They include the use of substances and methods which alter the integrity of urine samples used in doping tests, (e.g., urine substitution and alteration of renal function). *See also* blood doping.

dorsal Towards the upper surface, the side closest to the spine; opposite of *ventral. *See also* directional terms.

dorsalis pedis artery An *artery running across the *dorsal surface of the foot and supplying *blood to the toes.

dorsal rhizotomy The cutting of the *dorsal roots of nerves at various segmental levels of the *spinal cord, resulting in *deafferentation from the associated area of the body.

dorsal root The collection of nerve fibres from the *peripheral nervous system which occurs as a bundle near the upper surface of the *spinal cord at each spinal level; the major sensory input to the cord.

dorsal venous arch An arch-like *anastomosis made up of branches of *veins on the *dorsal surface of the foot.

dorsiflexion *Flexion of the *ankle so that the *superior aspect of the foot approaches the *shin. This movement is brought about by the combined action of the *tibialis anterior, *peroneus tertius, *extensor hallucis longus, and *extensor digitorum longus. Although dorsiflexion is not a powerful movement, it is important in preventing the toes from dragging during walking.

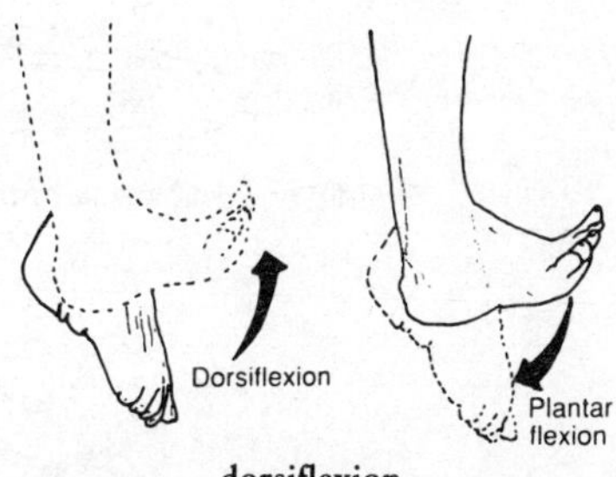

dorsiflexion

dorsum In *anatomy, pertaining to the *back.

dose The precise amount of a *drug prescribed by a doctor to be given to a patient at any one time.

dose regime The amount of *drug taken, expressed in terms of the quantity of the drug and the frequency at which it is taken.

double-blind procedure *See* double-blind study.

double-blind situation A situation in which contradictory demands or meanings are communicated in the same message or environment. The club coach, for example, may encourage a performer to be competitive and follow the 'law of the jungle', while family or teachers urge the individual to co-operate with other people or to turn the other cheek. The individual is then in a double-blind situation.

double-blind study (double-blind procedure; double-blind trial) An experimental protocol in which neither the investigator nor the subject knows which group is receiving a control treatment (e.g., a placebo) or the experimental treatment (e.g., a drug).

double-blind trial *See* double-blind study.

double circulation Circulation in which the *blood goes through the heart twice for each complete circuit of the body. It consists of a *systemic circulation and a *pulmonary circulation.

double-jointed *See* hypermobility joint disease.

Small drag in streamlined position

Large drag in unstreamlined position

drag force

double pendulum Two rigid bodies joined together, with one of the bodies supported at a fixed point in such a way that the whole assembly can swing smoothly about that point. In *biomechanics, the arm and the golf-club can be regarded as a double pendulum during a golf-swing.

double progressive system A system of *strength-training in which both the *resistance and number of *repetitions are adjusted.

double sugar *See* disaccharide.

Douglas bag A rubber-lined canvas bag used for the collection of gas expired from a person.

doxapram A *drug belonging to the *stimulants which are on the *IOC list of *banned substances.

DPG *See* diphosphoglycerates.

drag force Component of *force acting on a *body moving in a fluid. Drag force acts in the original direction of the fluid flow, tending to resist the progress of the body and reduce its *velocity. *See also* form drag; surface drag; and wave drag.

drain A medical procedure which allows the outflow of fluid from, for example, a wound.

drawer sign Sliding of the *tibia in respect to the *femur indicating severe strain or rupture of the *cruciate ligaments of the knee which cross each other in the *sagittal plane and provide *stability in both the sagittal and *coronal planes.

dressing Material applied to an injured part of the body to protect it and assist healing. The material may also act as a means of carrying or enclosing medicines.

drill **1** A precise, well-defined *motor skill practised repeatedly. **2** A pre-determined series of actions.

drive A physiological condition, involving sensitivity to certain types of stimulation, which activates behaviour. Drives are distinguished from *motives in being initially indiscriminate without an appropriate direction. Drives may be grouped into two main categories: primary, innate drives which include hunger, pain, thirst, and sex; and secondary drives including socially learned rewards not directly dependent on biological needs, and other rewards including verbal and monetary reinforcements.

drive theory Theory of *learning that predicts a linear relationship between drive (arousal) and learning. *See also* Hull's drive theory.

driving phase Part of the running action which commences when the foot first contacts the ground during the running stride. The body-weight is supported on the foot while the hips pass over the feet, and the

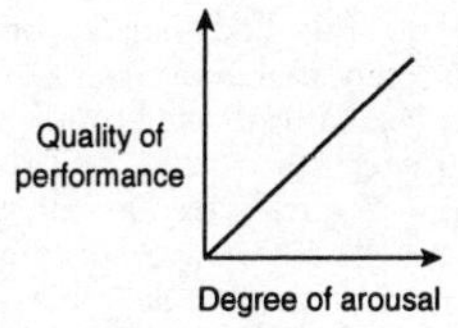

drive theory

hips, knee, and ankle extend to push the runner upwards and forwards.

drop-jump A jump in which the performer drops down from a specified height and then jumps upwards; the drop-jump uses the *stretch-shortening cycle.

dropping out Discontinuance of an activity or an assigned role. *See also* withdrawal.

drug Any substance which alters the body's actions and natural chemical environment. In sport, drugs are often misused to enhance physical or mental performance artificially. Drugs taken to prevent or cure a disease or other body disorder are often referred to as medicines to distinguish them from addictive substances, such as *narcotic analgesics taken illegally. *See also* doping.

drug addiction Chronic physical craving or compulsion to continue to take a *drug to avoid the unpleasant physical effects resulting from withdrawal of the drug. Many drugs are associated with addiction including *barbituates, opiates (e.g., heroin), morphine, and alcohol. The term is often used to include psychological dependence. *See also* drug dependence.

drug allergy An *antigen–*antibody reaction induced by a *drug. The drug or one of its products sensitizes the individual by combining with a *protein within the body to produce an antigen which, in its turn, leads to the formation of antibodies. Subsequent exposure to the drug initiates an antigen–antibody reaction which may manifest itself as anything from a mild skin irritation to a potentially fatal *anaphylaxis.

drug-control policy A policy of drug control in sports which includes a list of drugs and procedures banned by sporting bodies. The most quoted is that of the Medical Commission of the International Olympic Committee, but different sporting organizations may ban different drugs. *See also* banned substances.

drug dependence A compulsion to take drugs because of the physical and/or psychological effects produced by the habitual taking of the drug. Many drugs, such as *cannabis, are associated with psychological dependence only, when repeated use induces reliance on it for a state of well-being. Other drugs, such as *morphine, are associated with both psychological dependence and a physical need to take the drug to avoid unpleasant withdrawal symptoms.

drug detection *See* drug screening.

drug idiosyncracy An abnormal reaction to a drug which is genetically determined.

drug screening Methods carried out on a group of athletes to separate those who probably have used a *banned substance from those who have not. Screening is essentially a procedure to clear athletes of any possibility of having used drugs. If a test is positive then specific identification is needed. Techniques used in drug detection include *mass spectrometry and *radioimmunoassay.

drug tolerance An acquired resistance to the effects of a *drug which develops with repeated administration of the drug. When tolerance occurs, more drug is needed to produce the same pharmacological effects.

dry bulb thermometer A common thermometer used to record the temperature of air.

duct A canal or passageway, especially one for carrying secretions from an *exocrine gland.

dumb-bells A short bar with weights, sometimes adjustable, at each end. They are usually used in pairs during *weight-training, one for each hand.

duodenal ulcer An ulcer in the *duodenum. *See also* peptic ulcer.

duodenum The first part of the *small intestine connecting the *stomach to the *ileum. The walls of the duodenum are highly folded with *villi containing paneth cells (which are thought to remove heavy metals and to secrete amino acids), Brunners glands (which produce alkaline fluid and mucus), and narrow pits called crypts of Lieberkuhn. The duodenum receives *bile from the *gall bladder and *pancreatic juice from the *pancreas.

Dupuytren's contracture Permanent bending of one or more fingers due to fixation of the flexor tendon of the affected finger to the skin of the palm. Dupuytren's contracture is caused by fibrosis and contraction of the palmar fascia which become thickened and nodular.

dura mater The outermost and toughest of the three membranes (meninges) covering the *brain and *spinal cord.

duration Length of time of a training session. *See also* training duration.

dyad Social interaction or relationship comprising two elements. It may be between individuals, groups, or states. Certain properties of dyads pertain to whether the parties are individuals, groups, or states.

dynamic Pertaining to forces which produce motion.

dynamic balance *Balance maintained either on a moving surface or while the body is moving through space.

dynamic balance movements Movements which are made in order to maintain a balanced position. Such movements often take the form of irregular oscillations. *See also* balance.

dynamic contraction Muscle contraction in which the muscle changes length, producing forces which result in movement and a change in joint angle. *See also* isokinetic contraction; and isotonic contraction.

dynamic endurance The ability of a muscle to contract and relax repeatedly. *Compare* static endurance.

dynamic equilibrium State of an object which is moving with constant (uniform) *linear velocity and *angular velocity; that is, it is moving with zero *acceleration.

dynamic flexibility Ability to move a part or parts of the body quickly, or to make rapid and repeated movements. Dynamic flexibility is greatly affected by the ability of muscles to recover quickly and the forces which oppose or resist the movements. Tests of dynamic flexibility are concerned with how easily movements take place over any range, rather than the range itself (*compare* extent flexibility). It is a *gross motor ability which is important in speed and power events. *See also* flexibilty.

dynamic friction *See* sliding friction.

dynamics A branch of *mechanics concerned with the study of mathematical and physical properties of bodies in motion. It is especially concerned with the forces that produce or change the motions of bodies.

dynamic spirometry The determination of ventilatory capacity per unit time used to assess an individual's respiratory function. The subject breathes into a low-resistance *spirometer and its displacement is recorded with the aid of a *kymograph or a chart recorder to determine the volume of gases inspired and expired. *See also* spirometry.

dynamic strength (ballistic strength) The ability to exert muscular force repeatedly or over a period of time.

dynamic stretching *See* ballistic stretching.

dynamic visual acuity Ability of an observer to detect details of an object when there is movement between the observer and the object.

dynamogeny The concept that the presence of others moving alongside or faster than a performer stimulates the production of nervous energy which can be converted into increased *kinetic energy in the performer. Dynamogeny has been proposed to explain the improved performances of athletes in competition or when using a pacemaker.

dynamometer An instrument used to measure *torque or *force exerted by a muscle. In sport, dynamometers, such as the hand dynamometer, are specially designed to measure the force exerted by selected muscles.

dyne *Unit of force in the *metric system. One dyne is required to give a *mass of 1g an *acceleration of $1 cm s^{-2}$.

dysfunctional activity Any social activity seen as making a negative contribution to the maintenance, and effective working and functioning of a social system.

dysfunctional aggressive behaviour Aggressive or assertive behaviour that interferes with the attainment of a *goal. A footballer who intentionally fouls an opponent rather than intercept the ball exhibiting dysfunctional aggressive behaviour. *Compare* functional aggressive behaviour.

dysmenorrhoea Pain on menstruation. This often interferes with training and competition but it is sometimes possible to change the timing of the monthly cycle by using contraceptive pills. There is some evidence that dysmenorrhoea may be less common in physically active women. It is important that athletes who are taking medicines to treat dysmenorrhoea check that they do not contain *banned substances. *See also* menstrual cycle.

dyspnoea Laboured breathing which usually causes some distress to the subject because it seems inappropriate for the demands being placed on the body. Shortness of breath at the end of a race is not dyspnoea, because the effort of breathing is appropriate, passes quite quickly, and causes no real distress. Dyspnoea occurs when there is a malfunction in the airsupply to the lungs, as in *bronchitis and *asthma; when circulation to the lungs is impaired, as in *heart failure; or if the blood cannot carry enough oxygen, as in *anaemia.

dystonia 1 An impairment of tone in tissue, particularly muscle (*see* tonus). **2** A postural disorder affecting the muscles of the head, neck, and trunk due to disease of the basal ganglia.

E

ear The *sense-organ concerned with both hearing (*see* cochlea) and *balance (*see* labyrinth).

eardrum temperature The temperature of the outer ear taken with a thermocouple placed next to the eardrum. Eardrum temperature is used as an indicator of *core temperature, but it varies with the temperature within the ear-canal.

ear-lobe (pinna) The expanded, most external part of the external ear.

early recall Recall of information within two hours or so of its being stored. In most sports, this is the approximate time interval in which the performer must be able to retain information about the opponents' strengths and weaknesses. *See also* short-term memory.

early responding A situation which occurs prior to tests of *reaction times in which the subject anticipates the relevant *stimulus and processes all of the aspects of a movement so that the movement can occur at or before the stimulus. Early responding may also occur in anticipation of the signal to start a race.

eburnation The wearing away of *articular cartilage exposing underlying bone. Eburnation is the end-result of *osteoarthritis.

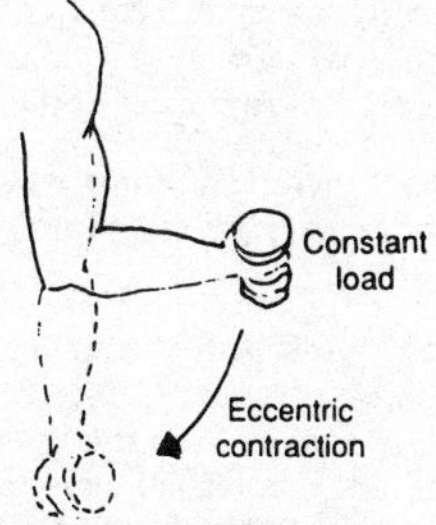

eccentric contraction

eccentric contraction An *isotonic contraction in which a muscle lengthens while developing tension. Such contractions are used to resist external forces such as *gravity. They also occur during the deceleration phases of locomotion. For example, the *quadriceps muscles undergo eccentric contractions when a person walks down a hill or down steps. During eccentric contractions, the muscle moves in the opposite direction to the change in joint angle and the mechanical work done is negative:

$$W = F(-D)$$

where W=work; F=force and D=distance. *Compare* concentric contraction.

eccentric force A *force which does not pass through the *centre of gravity of the body on which it acts or through a point at which the body is fixed. Such a force results in *translation and *rotation. *Compare* concentric force

eccrine gland A *gland which secretes externally. The term is applied especially to *sweat-glands which are distributed over most of the body surface, but occur in greatest density on the palms of the hands, the soles of the feet, in the *axillae, and on the forehead. Eccrine sweat-glands are involved in *thermoregulation. *Compare* apocrine glands.

ECG *See* electrocardiogram.

ecchmyosis A bruise, caused by injury or a spontaneous effusion of blood from blood vessesls, characterized by a bluish-black discolouration just under the skin.

echocardiography A technique by which ultrasound waves are used to map out and study the internal structures of the heart.

eclectism A method of study which selects theories and ideas from a variety of disparate sources.

ecological viewpoint A point of view emphasizing the study of movement in the natural environment, and the evolutionary, physical, and biological constraints of movement. *Compare* information-processing theory; and SR viewpoint.

ectoderm The outermost layer of tissue in an embryo from which nerves, epidermis, and related structures are derived.

ectomorph A dimension of *somatotype (body-build) characterized by a tall, thin, and linearly constructed body.

ectomorphy A body-type component characterized by linearity and delicacy of body. *See also* somatotype.

ectopic bone Bone which forms outside the area in which it is normally expected to occur. *See also* myositis ossificans.

ectopic heartbeat A *heartbeat which momentarily loses its rhythm. The heart may miss a beat which is then followed by a heavy jolt. It is not sinister as long as the individual concerned has an otherwise normal heart and as long as the ectopic beat occurs during rest. If it occurs during exercise and increases with the intensity of exercise, or if it combines with other abnormalities, the sufferer should seek medical advice.

eczema A non-infectious skin complaint characterized by itching and often accompanied by small blisters. One form may be induced by cold, windy conditions, or chemical irritants dissolved in water. Another form is caused by an *allergy to one of a wide range of substances. Flexural, or atopic eczema, primarily affects children at sites, such as the back of the knee, which are frequently involved in flexion. Although swimming is not generally suitable for eczema sufferers, irritant eczema has little affect on sport participation. Contact sports are generally not suitable for sufferers of flexural eczema because of the risk of bacterial infection of the eczematous blisters.

eddy currents Whirling currents of fluid formed during turbulent flow. Eddy currents double back on themselves and eventually become detached from the main body of water, thereby opposing the main current-flow.

eddy resistance (tail suction) *Drag force caused by *eddy currents. Eddy resistance is reduced by *streamlining and increased by certain positions and movements of the body in the water. Lateral movements of a swimmer, such as wriggling hips and legs, increase eddy resistance. *See also* form drag.

edema *See* oedema.

EEG *See* electroencephalogram.

effective anticipation An ability to predict the duration of internal processes and planned movements so that the response can be made coincident with some anticipated external event. Effective anticipation is needed when swinging a bat or racket to hit a moving ball.

effective behaviour *Behaviour which results in desirable outcomes.

effective force A *force producing the desired outcome. An effective force is produced by a limb when it accelerates sufficiently to overcome a resistance when a subject wishes to do so.

effectiveness The degree to which a purpose is achieved. In *biomechanics, effectiveness refers to how appropriate movements are in helping a performer accomplish the mechanical purposes of the movement. A technique may be effective in enabling a person achieve a desired goal, but inefficient in terms of energy expenditure.

effective synergy *See* synergy.

effector **1** Any body structure, such as a *muscle, *gland, or organ, that brings about an action (e.g., a muscular contraction or glandular secretion) as a result of a *stimulus it receives. The stimulus may be from a *nerve or from an *endocrine gland. **2** A structure which brings about an activity in a gland or muscle.

effeminacy The presence or manifestation of feminine characteristics, either physical or behavioural, in a male.

efferent **1** Applied especially to *nerve fibres which carry *impulses away from the *central nervous system. **2** Applied to *blood vessels or *lymph vessels which carry fluid away from a body-part.

efferent nerve A neurone that conveys motor impulses away from the *central nervous system to an effector organ such as *skeletal muscle or a *gland.

efficacy The ability to achieve an intended result. *See* collective efficacy; and self-efficacy.

efficiency In human movements, the relationship between the amount of *work done on a load and the energy expended in completing the work. It is usually expressed as a percentage of the ratio of work accomplished to energy expended:

efficiency = (work done/energy expended) ×100

An efficient movement is one in which a given amount of desired work (energy output) is achieved with the minimum amount of energy expenditure. A perfect, frictionless machine will have an efficiency of 100 per cent, but all machines in the real world have lower efficiencies because some of the useful energy expended is converted into *heat during the energy transformations. Until relatively recently it was assumed that muscle efficiency was quite low (about 20–25 per cent) but it is now believed that *elastic components may enable greater efficiencies to be achieved.

effleurage *See* effluage.

effluage (effleurage) A form of *massage consisting of superficial or deep stroking movements, administered with the flat of the hand and fingers, that stimulates venous and lymphatic circulation.

effort The *force applied to a *lever which is used to move a *load or resistance. In human locomotion, the effort is provided by muscle contractions at the point of muscle attachment to the part of the skeleton which moves.

effusion A form of *oedema in which there is an accumulation of fluid in a potential space, such as a *joint capsule.

egestion Evacuation of faeces or unused food from the body.

ego The individual's concept of himself or herself. Ego is a part of the mind which develops from the individual's experience of the outside world. It operates in direct contact with reality and is concerned with processing and evaluating information about the importance of, and relationships between, specific actions and behaviours of the individual. It is one of the three elements of Freudian theory. The ego, which is thought to have developed from the *id, attempts to reconcile the unconconscious primitive demands of the id with the constraints imposed by the *superego and with the individual's awareness of the real world.

ego defence mechanism Mechanism whereby the *ego reconciles the basic instincts of the *id with the more sedate cultural values of the *superego to make them acceptable to reality. Ego defences include *projection, *reaction formation, *denial, and *sublimation. *See also* intellectualization; and repression.

ego-enhancing strategy A psychological device by which a person attributes all success to internal causes.

ego-protecting strategy A psychological device by which a person attributes all failures to external causes.

ego threat Any factor which tends to diminish a person's opinion of himself or herself.

EIA *See* exercise-induced asthma.

eight-state questionnaire An *inventory designed to measure eight *affective states which are believed to be important in athletic performance. The questionnaire has been used successfully in measuring the psychological states of élite, world-class runners.

ejection fraction The difference between the left ventricular *end diastolic volume and the end systolic volume. It is a measure of the degree of emptying of the *ventricle during *systole.

elastic Material which regains its original shape on removal of a distorting force. *See also* plastic.

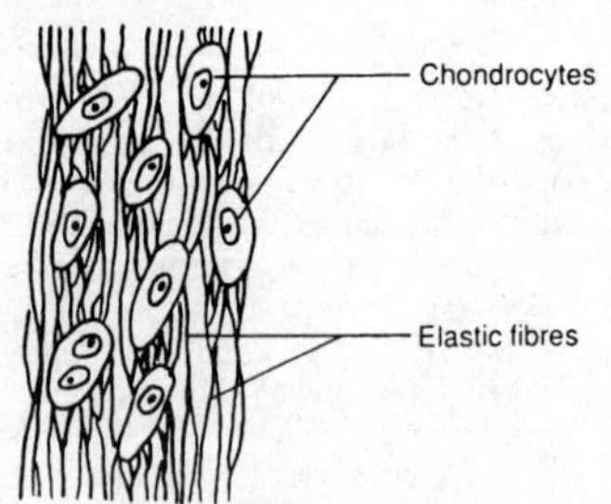

elastic cartilage

elastic cartilage *Cartilage with an amorphous, unstructured matrix containing *elastic fibres in addition to *chondrocytes. Elastic cartilage supports the *pinna and the *epiglottis, maintaining their structure while allowing the flexibility which is essential for their functions.

elastic components The viscoelastic structures associated with the *contractile elements of muscles. Elastic components include *parallel elastic components and *series elastic components.

elastic energy *See* strain energy.

elasticity (restitution) **1** Property of a body that causes it to tend to regain its original shape after any compression and deformation has occurred. **2** The ability of a *tissue to resume its resting length after it has contracted or has been stretched.

elastic limit The limit of *stress within which the *strain in a material completely disappears when the stress is removed. If a solid is stretched beyond its elastic limit, it will undergo permanent deformation.

elastic modulus Ratio of *stress to *strain in a given material. Strain may be a change in length, a twist, or a change in volume. *See also* flexural rigidity; modulus of compression; modulus of rigidity; torsional modulus; and Young's modulus.

elastic strength The ability of *muscles to exert *forces quickly and to overcome resistance with a high speed of contraction. Elastic strength requires a complex co-ordination of speed and strength of muscle contractions. It is important in explosive sports such as jumping and sprinting. In old textbooks, elastic strength was used synonymously with power. *Plyometric exercises are used to improve elastic strength.

elastin *Elastic fibrous *protein found in *connective tissue. *See* elastic fibre.

elbow The structures in and around the joint formed between the *humerus of the upper arm, and the *ulna and *radius of the lower forearm (*see* elbow-joint).

elbow dislocation Forceful displacement, anteriorly, laterally, or posteriorly, of the *ulna or *radius on the *humerus, with soft tissue injury. *See also* dislocation.

elbow extension Movement of the forearm which straightens the arm. The *prime mover is the *triceps brachii; the *anconeus pulls the capsule of the *elbow-joint out of the way of the advancing *olecarnon process during the extension.

elbow extensors Muscles which effect the *extension of the forearm. Only two muscles are involved: the *triceps brachii and the *anconeus.

elbow flexion Movement of the forearm towards the shoulder due to bending of the elbow. Elbow flexion is effected by the *biceps brachii, the *brachialis; and *brachioradialis muscles. They may be assisted by the *pronator teres.

elbow flexors The muscles which effect straightening of the forearm (*see* elbow flexion).The *biceps brachii, *brachialis, and *brachioradialis muscles serve as the main elbow flexor group.

elbow injury Physical damage to the elbow. Elbow injuries require skilled help, particularly in children, as they may be permanently disabling. Treatment after severe injury usually includes slow mobilization to reduce the risk of ectopic calcification (*see* ectopic bone). Many elbow injuries are named after the sport in which they most often occur (*see* boxer's arm; dart-thrower's elbow; golfer's elbow; judo elbow, pitcher's elbow; tennis elbow; and thrower's elbow).

elbow-joint A complex of three *synovial joints enclosed in a common *joint capsule: the humeroulnar joint, between the *trochlea of the humerus and the trochlear notch of the *ulna; the *humeroradial joint, between the head of the *radius and the *capitulum of the humerus; and the *radioulnar joint, between the radius and ulna. The elbow-joint functions as a *hinge-joint allowing *flexion and *extension; pronation and supination of the forearm is possible because of the radioulnar joint. The *articular surfaces of the elbow are highly complementary and are the most important factor contributing to its *joint stability.

elbow pronation Movement of the *radius on the *ulna which results in the hand changing from palm up to palm down position.

elbow pronators Muscles which effect *elbow pronation; the *pronator teres and the *pronator quadratus.

elbow supination Movement of the *radius on the *ulna which results in the hand changing from the palm down to the palm up position.

elbow supinators Muscles which effect *elbow supination; the *supinator assisted by the *biceps brachii.

electrical energy The *energy associated with electric charges and their movements. In the human body, electrical currents are generated as charged particles and the nervous system uses electrical currents called *nerve impulses.

electrical potential A measure in volts of the work required to bring a unit of positive electric charge from an infinite distance to a given point. Electrical potential is the capacity for producing electrical efforts, such as an electric current, between two bodies (e.g., between the inside and outside of a cell). *See also* action potential.

electrical synapse A *synapse which allows *ions to flow directly through protein channels from one *neurone to another. Electrical synapses provide low-resistance electrical pathways for rapid unidirectional or bidirectional transmission of information from one neurone to another. They are found in regions of the brain responsible for the normal, jerky movements of the eyes.

electric charge The basic units of electrically-charged matter are the *electron, which is negatively charged, and the *proton, which is positively charged. Matter containing an equal number of protons and electrons is electrically neutral; matter containing an excess of electrons is negatively charged; and matter containing an excess of protons is positively charged. A force of attraction exists between unlike charges. The attribution of these positive and negative conventions is purely arbitrary but the explanations for many phenomena, such as the formation of *nerve impulses, are based on them. Conduction of nerve impulses, contraction of muscles, and sense-organs are all dependent on these properties of charged matter.

electricity A general term used for all phenomena, such as a *nerve impulse, caused by an electric charge.

electric muscle stimulation The use of electricity (direct current, alternating current, or both) to treat muscle injuries. Electric muscle stimulation has been used to treat muscle atrophy which occurs when a limb is immobilized. *See also* Faradism.

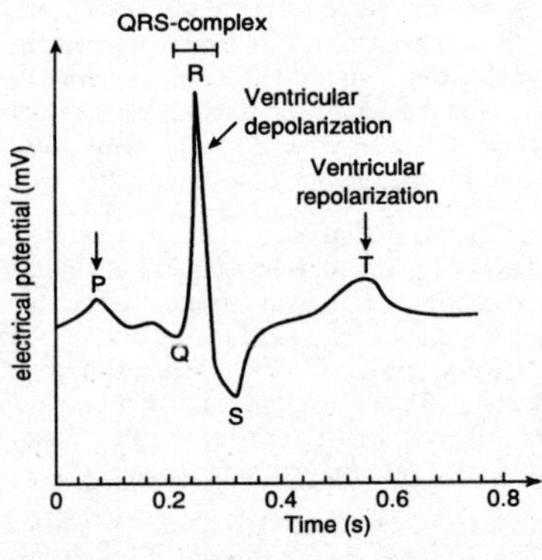

electrocardiogram

electrocardiogram (ECG) A graphical record of the electrical changes occurring during a heartbeat. The characteristic features on the recording are the *P wave, *QRS complex, and *T wave. An ECG is probably the most useful record of heart function. It can reveal the cause of irregular heartbeats and, at times, damage to the heart muscle. It can also show enlargement of the heart chambers, mineral imbalances in the blood, and whether someone has had or is having a *heart attack. ECGs are usually recorded while the individual is at rest, however an exercise ECG, also called a stress test, can provide information on how the heart responds to physical exertion.

electrocardiography The recording of electrical activity associated with the heart's action. Electrocardiography is a tool of the clinical and the exercise physiologist. *See also* electrocardiogram.

electrode A conductor of electrical activity. Electrodes are used to receive and transmit electrical activity from a cell or tissue to a recorder.

electroencephalogram (EEG) A graphical record of the electrical activity of the brain as recorded during *electroencephalography.

electroencephalography Measurement of the electrical activity of the cortex of the brain. Three types of brainwaves are associated with different arousal states: θ waves (sleep), α waves (wakefulness), and β waves (excitement). There is a close correlation between the record on the electroencephalogram and *fatigue or *over-training. Electroencephalography is also used in contact sports, particularly boxing, to assess possible damage to the *nervous system.

electrogoniometer (elgon) An electrical device for measuring *flexibility in which the protractor (used to measure joint angles) has been replaced by a *potentiometer. An electrogoniometer can record continuously, in degrees, the changes in the angles of joints during movement, but *goniometers measure angles of joints in stationary positions only.

electrolyte Any substance such as a *salt, *acid, or *base that ionizes and dissociates in water, and is capable of conducting an electric current. *See also* electrolyte drink.

electrolyte drink A drink which contains *electrolytes, such as sodium, potassium, and chloride, usually taken to replace salts lost during *sweating and to avoid *heat-cramps. Sodium is the most important electrolyte in these salt-replacement drinks. As exercise progresses, the salt content of sweat tends to decrease thus tending to increase the concentration of salt within the body. Therefore, electrolyte replacement without adequate replenishment of water will increase the state of *dehydration and may adversely affect performance. *See also* energy drink.

electromagnetic energy Energy that travels in waves which vary in length and which are part of the electromagnetic spectrum. Electromagnetic energy includes light, X-rays, and infra-red.

electromotive force (EMF) The source of *electrical energy needed to produce an electric current in a circuit. It is the rate at which electrical energy is drawn from the source and used up in the circuit. The *SI unit for EMF is the *volt.

electromyogram (EMG) A record of the electrical activity of muscle, as recorded during *electromyography.

electromyograph Machine able to make highly-sensitive recordings of electrical activity in muscles.

electromyography Measurement and recording of muscle excitability and electrical activity. Electromyography can be performed by *telemetry during exercise to indicate which muscle groups are active during different phases of a locomotory cycle.

electron A negatively-charged elementary particle which is a constituent of an *atom. A free electron is one that has been detached from its normal path around the *nucleus of an *atom.

electron acceptor A recipient of *electrons in *redox reactions. *See also* electron-transport system.

electron donor A substance which donates *electrons in *redox reactions.

electron microscope Microscope that produces high-resolution images (that is, it can produce highly-detailed images at high magnifications) by the interaction of electrons with the specimen. The electrons are focused by electromagnets. Transmission electron microscopes (TEMs) pass electrons through very thin sections of the specimen and give a resolution of 1 nm (×250 000). Scanning electron microscopes (SEMs) bombard the surface of specimens with electrons. Reflected electrons are gathered to form an image of the surface. Resolutions of 5 nm and magnification of more than 100 000 are possible with the SEM.

electron-transport system A series of biochemical reactions by which energy is transferred from a higher to a lower level. Electron-transport systems occur in the *mitochondria. Each step involves a specific electron-carrier molecule which has a particular affinity for the electrons which are derived from hydrogen released during the *Krebs cycle. The carriers are organized in a sequence of increasing affinity. The *free energy generated along the electron-transport system is used to synthesize *ATP during *aerobic respiration.

electrophoresis A method of separating particles of different electrical charge (e.g., proteins). The apparatus consists of a supporting medium (e.g., gel) soaked in a buffer at a suitable pH with an electrical field set up across it. The test substance is placed on the medium and the components with different charges separate from each other. Their eventual positions are compared with the positions of known standards.

electrophysiology The study of electrical activity in the human body.

element. One of a limited number of unique varieties of matter that composes every kind of substance. An element cannot be destroyed by normally available heat or *electrical energy and each element consists of atoms with the same number of *protons in their *nuclei. The most common elements in the human body are carbon, hydrogen, oxygen, and nitrogen.

elevation **1** A non-angular movement which occurs when a body-part is lifted superiorly along a *frontal plane. The *scapulae are elevated when the shoulders are shrugged. *Compare* depression. **2** The process of raising a limb after injury. The injury reduces the ability of *peripheral muscles to pump blood back to the heart (*see* muscle pump) resulting in pooling of blood. Elevation enables gravity to help the blood return to the heart and reduces the risk of swelling.

elgon *See* electrogoniometer.

Eliasian An approach to sociological analysis which follows that of Norbert Elias (1897–1990). He promoted a figurational developmental viewpoint to sociological analyses (*see* figurational sociology) in which social configurations rather than individuals or societies are analysed

élite 1 The best, or most talented individuals in society. 2 A minority group which has power or influence over others and which is recognized as being in some way superior.

élite athlete An *athlete who has reached the highest level of a particular sport.

élitism The restriction of an activity to a privileged group. Some sports clubs restrict access on the basis of social characteristics and not athletic ability. Such élitism has resulted in the sports being associated with certain social classes and social statuses.

emancipation The term is applied specifically to the freeing of slaves from bondage, but is used more generally in relation to the liberation of any person or group from social or legal restraint, and from forms of oppression.

Embden–Meyerhof pathway Sequence of chemical reactions which make up *anaerobic glycolysis discovered in the 1930s by the Germans, Otto Embden and Gustav Meyerhof.

embolism The condition in which an *embolus, such as fat, a blood clot, or an air bubble, obstructs a blood vessel.

embolus Material (solid or fluid) which is carried by the blood from one point in the body to lodge at another point. *See also* embolism.

embrocation A liquid rubbed onto the body to treat strains and sprains.

emergency muscle An *assistant mover that is brought into action only when an exceptional amount of total force is needed. The long head of the *biceps brachii, for example, contributes to the shoulder-joint *abduction only in times of great need.

EMF *See* electromotive force.

EMG *See* electromyogram.

emic perspective Applied to linguistic analyses and sociological accounts made from a perspective internal to a language or social situation. In sport, an emic perspective involves gaining an understanding of the sport situation from the participant's point of view. *Compare* etic perspective.

eminence A projection, usually rounded, on the surface of an *organ or *tissue, particularly bone.

emotion A complex state of *arousal which occurs as a reaction to a perceived situation. In its most obvious manifestation, an emotion is an acute condition characterized by disruption of routine experience and activities; as such, an emotion may provoke subjective feelings of pleasure or displeasure, physiological responses (such as changes in heart rate), and behavioural responses. There is much disagreement as to the exact nature of emotions and how they differ from motives and distractions, but there is no doubt that emotions may have an organizing or disorganizing effect on performance in sport.

emotional health *See* mental health.

empathy The ability to project oneself into the situation of another person and thereby understand the feelings and thoughts of that person. Empathy is an important characteristic of an effective coach–athlete relationship, since an athlete's problems can only be understood if the coach experiences the athlete's subjective perception of the problems. *Compare* sympathy.

emphysema A degenerative disease, fairly common in the elderly, in which living tissue loses its elasticity, and air tends to be trapped in the lungs. This effectively reduces breathing capacity. The physical capacity of sufferers can be improved by sensibly-graded exercises, although exercise will not cure the condition.

empirical Pertaining to *empiricism.

empirical method A method of scientific investigation which involves systematic observation or experiments rather than speculation or mere theorizing. Observations are made and facts gathered primarily for their own sake without regard to theories.

employee-enrichment model A model, adopted by some sport psychologists and coaches, which proposes that task enrichment increases employees' (or athletes') capacity for increased *motivation, success, and satisfaction.

employee orientation A *leadership style which may be considered as equivalent to *consideration.

empty calories Foods which are highly refined, such as sweets and soft drinks, which provide *energy but are very low in *nutrients such as *vitamins and *minerals.

emulsification A process in which a liquid, known as an emulsion, containing very small droplets of imiscible liquid, is formed. Fats are made into an emulsion in the *duodenum by *bile. The process increases the surface area of the fat making it easier to digest. Unemulsified fats usually pass down the intestine and are egested in the faeces.

enarthrosis A *ball-and-socket joint in which a *long bone is able to move freely in all planes.

encephalins (enkephalins) A group of *endogenous *analgesic substances which are secreted in many parts of the brain where their effects are mimicked by *morphine, *heroin, and *methadone. *See also* endorphins.

encephalopathy (chronic cerebral injury; punch-drunk; traumatic encaphalopathy) A neurological disorder commonly induced by repeated blows to the head, causing the victim to be unsteady when standing, fatuous, euphoric, voluble when speaking, and even aggressive. Memory and intellect may become impaired and, in advanced cases, encephalopathy results in coarse tremor, rigidity, and *ataxia.

encoding In psychology, the ability to perceive and understand the meaning of the important features of a situation, and to change this information into a form which can be stored in the memory.

encounter Any meeting between two or more people in face-to-face *interactions. Sporting competitions are made up of many such interactions.

enculturation The process of formally and informally learning and internalizing the prevailing values and accepted behavioural patterns of a culture. The term is sometimes used synonymously with *socialization.

end artery A terminal *artery which does not communicate with other arterial branches. An end artery is usually the only source of *blood for the *tissue it supplies.

end diastolic volume The volume of blood in the heart at the end of *diastole. Increases in end diastolic volumes are correlated with increases in *stroke volume (*see* Starling's law).

endemic A disease (or condition, such as famine) which is prevalent among the population of a certain area. *Compare* epidemic.

endergonic reaction (endothermic reaction) Reaction needing an external source of free energy (usually heat) to be activated.

endocarditis Inflammation and infection of the heart lining, especially of the heart valves. It is usually due to a bacteria (frequently originating from dental infections) or rheumatic fever and is accompanied by fever and heart murmurs. Strenuous exercise is very strongly contra-indicated until after full recovery and consultation with the treating physician.

endocardium The inner lining of the *heart, consisting of an *endothelium.

endochondral ossification A form of *indirect ossification in which *bone is formed by replacing *hyaline cartilage in a *foetus. *Long bones and *short bones develop by endochondral ossification. *Compare* intramembranous ossification.

endocrine gland Ductless *gland producing *hormones which are secreted directly into the *blood system.

endocrine system The body system consisting of *organs and *tissues which secrete *hormones.

endoderm The inner layer of *cells in an embryo which gives rise to the lining of the *alimentary canal, the *bronchi, *alveoli, and the urinary tract.

endogenous substance A substance such as a *hormone or *neurotransmitter produced naturally in the body.

endomorph Dimension of *somatotype (body build) characterized by a rounded body shape and predominance of fat, especially in the *abdominal and lower body region. It is sometimes known as a 'pear-shaped' form.

endomorphy A body-type component characterized by roundness and softness of body. In layman's terms it is the fatness component of a person's body build. *See also* somatotype.

endomysium The *connective tissue surrounding each individual *muscle fibre.

endoplasmic reticulum (ER) A series of interconnected, flattened, membrane-lined cavities in the *cytoplasm of cells. The endoplasmic reticulum may be covered with *ribosomes (rough endoplasmic reticulum) or be uncovered (smooth endoplasmic reticulum).

endorphins *Neuropeptides which function as *neurotransmitters through their *metabotropic effects. Endorphins are similar to *encephalins. They are secreted in many areas of the brain where their inhibitory effects are imitated by *morphine, *heroin, and *methadone. The release of endorphins is believed to increase when an athlete gets his or her *second wind and may be responsible for the phenomenon known as *runner's high.

endoscope An instrument used to view the inside of a hollow organ or cavity.

endoskeleton *Skeleton internal to the skin. In humans, it consists of *bone and *cartilage.

endosteum Thin membrane lining the *medullary cavity of bones; it contains *osteoblasts and *osteoclasts.

endothelium Simple sheet of *epithelial tissue composed of a single layer of cells which provide a friction-reducing lining in circulatory structures such as *lymph vessels, *blood vessels, and the *heart.

endothermic reaction *See* endergonic reaction.

endothermy Ability of an organism to producc sufficient metabolic heat to raise the *core temperature.

endplate A modified muscle fibre membrane occurring at the junction between *muscles and *nerves. *Acetylcholine acts as the *neurotransmitter released by the nerve-ending and attaches to *receptor sites on the endplate, which *depolarizes the muscle membrane. If the depolarization is sufficient, it will result in an *action potential and contraction of the muscle fibre.

end-position Limit of the *range of movement of a joint that the *skeleton can attain unaided. It is generally believed that improvement to *mobility is unlikely unless the joint is taken to this position during *stretching and *flexibility training.

end-tidal carbon dioxide partial pressure *Partial pressure of carbon dioxide at the end of exhalation.

end-tidal oxygen partial pressure The *partial pressure of oxygen at the end of exhalation.

endurance (staying power) The maximum duration an individual can maintain a specific activity. It has proven useful to sports scientists investigating functional systems to divide endurance into *short term endurance (35 s–2 min), *medium-term endurance (2–10 min) and *long-term endurance (longer than 10 min).

endurance capacity *See* maximal aerobic power.

endurance force A *force identified on the basis of the following formula: force = mass × acceleration, where neither the *mass nor *acceleration component prevails.

endurance training *Training of relatively long duration and moderate intensity which develops the *aerobic capacity.

energy The capacity for doing *work. The *SI unit for energy is the *joule, although the *calorie is still commonly used. There are many different interconvertible forms of energy (including *mechanical energy, *electrical energy, *heat energy, *nuclear energy, and radiant energy) but the only form which can be used directly by the body is *adenosine triphosphate, derived from food by *respiration.

energy balance The relationship between energy intake (input of food) and energy output (energy expenditure) for body maintenance and activity. A balance occurs when the energy input equals the energy expenditure. *See also* negative energy balance; and positive energy balance.

energy continuum A concept used to describe the type of respiration demanded by physical activities. Those activities demanding 100 per cent *anaerobic respiration are at one end of the continuum, those requiring 100 per cent aerobic respiration are at the other. In between these two extremes are activities which require various proportions of anaerobic and aerobic respiration.

energy coupling *See* coupled reactions.

energy drink Drink, usually containing glucose, especially designed to replace or supplement energy expended during exertion. Consumption of low concentrations of liquid glucose (less than 2.5g per 100ml) may prevent *hypoglycaemia and *dehydration, and delay *fatigue. An intake of large doses of energy drink can cause dehydration and *insulin rebound. *See also* electrolyte drink.

energy expenditure The energy cost of body activities. The most common expression of energy expenditure is the *kilocalorie, but in scientific work there is a movement to use the *joule. The daily energy expenditure of a person is dependent on sex, *basal metabolic rate, body-mass, body composition, and activity level. The approximate energy expenditure of a male lying in bed is 1.0kcal/h/kg body-mass; for slow walking (25min per mile), 3.0kcal/h/kg; and for fast, steady running (6min per mile), 16.3kcal/h/kg. Females have on average an energy expenditure 10per cent lower than males in a comparable activity.

energy nutrient A food which is a major source of energy. *Carbohydrates, *fats, and *proteins are the main sources of energy.

energy of rotation The *kinetic energy, associated with an axis rotation, of a mass about an axis. It is expressed by $E=Iw^2$ where E is the kinetic energy of the mass, I is the mass's *moment of inertia, and w is the *angular velocity of the mass.

energy potential The maximum capability of an *energy system to supply *ATP. Tests of energy potential are designed to create a situation in which ATP is supplied predominantly by a single energy system and either *capacity or *power is measured.

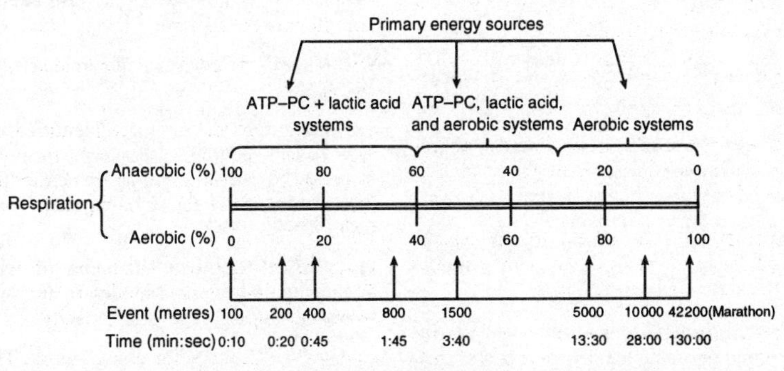

energy continuum

energy-rich bonds Chemical *bonds, such as those in *adenosine triphosphate and *creatine phosphate, which, when broken during *hydrolysis, yield a large amount of *free energy.

engine A device which converts other forms of energy into *mechanical energy. The human body can be viewed as an engine which converts chemical energy (food) into mechanical energy (movement).

engorgement Congestion with blood.

engram An altered state of living tissue which is believed to underlie *memory. An engram may occur as a permanent trace left by a *stimulus in *nervous tissue. A memorized motor pattern stored in the brain is an example of an engram. *See also* memory trace.

enkephalins *See* encephalins.

ensemble In psychology, the combination of various sources of sensory information that enable the accurate perception of movement and position.

enteric canal *See* gut.

enthesitis Inflammation at the junction between a tendon and bone. *See also* tennis elbow.

enthesopathy Any rheumatic condition characterized by persistent pain in which the *tendon of a *muscle inserts into a bone.

entramine *See* serotonin.

entrapment The trapping of a nerve between two other structures with subsequent mechanical irritation and usually some loss of function.

entropy The amount of disorder or the degree of randomness in a system. Heat is associated with a higher degree of disorder than other forms of energy. Therefore, since heat is always produced during energy transformations, entropy increases during these changes.

environment In a sporting context, the surroundings in which the sport takes place. It is the sum of the outside influences on the athletes including all the physical conditions, the surrounding buildings, weather, and the audiences. This external environment may also include the social or cultural conditions. Other types of environment include the intracellular environment, consisting of the conditions within a cell; the intercellular environment, composed of tissue fluid beween cells; and the prenatal environment, which is the immediate surroundings of an embryo or foetus.

enzyme A *protein that acts as a biological *catalyst. Enzymes regulate and accelerate the rate of specific biochemical reactions by lowering their *activation energy. They are not used up or changed in these reactions and they cannot force chemical reactions to occur between molecules that would not otherwise react. Enzymes can be *denatured by changes in *pH or temperature.

eosinophil Granular white blood cell whose cytoplasm is readily stained with a dye called eosin.

ephedrine A *sympathomimetic drug which is sometimes used in the treatment of *asthma and respiratory ailments. Ephedrine belongs to the *stimulants which are on the *IOC list of *banned substances. *See also* β_2 agonist.

epiandrosterone An *androgenic and *anabolic steroid. Epiandrosterone is an *isomer of *androsterone and a metabolic product of *testosterone, and is produced in the liver. It is naturally present in the *plasma and urine. Epiandrosterone has relatively weak anabolic and androgenic activity.

epicardium The outermost layer of the *heart wall which forms the innermost layer of the *pericardium.

epicondyle Protruberance of bone, on or above a *condyle, which forms part of a joint. The epicondyle provides an attachment site for muscles.

epicondylitis Inflammation of muscles and tendons which are attached to the *epicondyles of the *humerus. *See also* tennis elbow.

epidemic The sudden appearance in a population of an infectious disease which spreads quickly and affects a greater number of people than is usually expected. *Compare* endemic.

epidemiology The study of the incidence and distribution of epidemic diseases in order to identify the role of non-biological factors (for example, the relative importance of geographical location, occupation, gender, and lifestyle) in the occurrence of disease and health.

epidermis The outer layer of *skin made of stratified *epithelium covered by dead cells which have become impregnated with *keratin.

Epidermophyton A genus of fungi which grows on the skin and is responsible for *athlete's foot and *dhobie itch.

epidural anaesthesia A form of anaesthesia provided by injecting an anaesthetic into the *epidural space.

epidural space The space between the *dura mater and the wall of the *vertebral canal.

epigastrale A *landmark located on the anterior surface of the trunk at the intersection of the mid-*sagittal plane and the *transverse plane through the most inferior point on the tenth ribs.

epiglottis Flexible *cartilage guarding the entrance to the *larynx. The epiglottis prevents food from entering the *trachea.

epilepsy An established tendency to recurrent fits of varying degrees of seriousness, brought about by sudden abnormal discharges from brain cells. Epileptics can participate in many sports; the Bristol Epilepsy Association advises only against those sports in which a blow to the head is likely, and underwater sports or climbing where an epileptic fit could be fatal.

epimysium Layer of *connective tissue, consisting mainly of *collagen, surrounding an entire *muscle. The epimysium provides a smooth surface against which other muscles can glide.

epinephrine *See* adrenaline.

epiphyseal avulsion A dramatic injury resulting in partial or complete detachment of the *epiphysis from the rest of the bone.

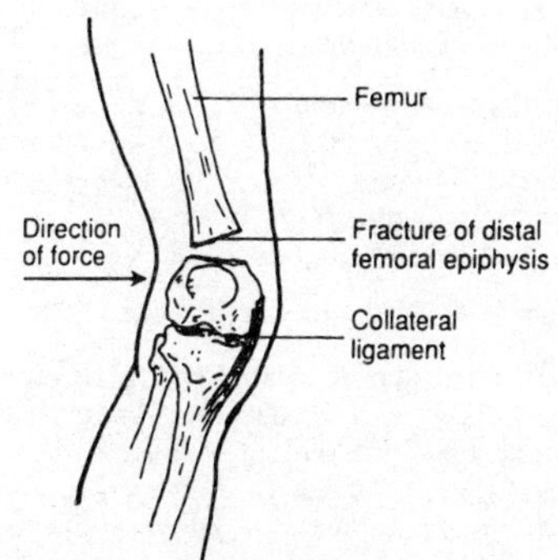

epiphyseal avulsion

A complete avulsion is most common in boys 12–14 years old (pre-adolescents and adolescents). It may occur during rapid deceleration, such as when a basketball player comes to a sudden stop or a long-jumper lands, causing the epiphysis to be pulled upward by the contracting *quadriceps. The resulting *fracture may extend right through the knee-joint.

epiphyseal disc (epiphyseal plate; growth disc) A plate of *hyaline cartilage at the junction between the *diaphysis and *epiphysis. It is the only region in a *long bone where an increase in the length can take place.

epiphyseal line An elevated ridge on the surface of mature bone which marks the point of fusion between the *epiphysis and *diaphysis.

epiphyseal plate *See* epiphyseal disc.

epiphysiolysis (slipped epiphyseal plate) An injury to the growth centre of a bone in which the growth zones or *epiphyses are displaced in relation to the bone. The most common site is a slipped femoral epiphysis when the ball of the joint slips. It is an over-training injury occurring in young athletes.

epiphysis (pl. epiphyses) A prominent process projecting from the end of a *long bone. It consists of a thin outer layer of *compact bone enclosing *spongy bone. The epiphysis develops separately from the *diaphysis to which it fuses when growth is complete. *Compare* apophysis.

epiphysitis Inflammation of the growth centre or *epiphysis of a bone. Epiphysitis commonly occurs in young people who over-train. It may result in extreme discomfort, retardation of growth, and disability.

epistaxis Bleeding from the nose.

epistemology A branch of philosophy which deals with the nature and validity of knowledge. Epistemology is concerned with establishing the kinds of things which exist and with how we can know about the world.

epitestosterone An *anabolic steroid on the *IOC list of *banned substances.

epithelial Pertaining to *epithelial tissue.

epithelial tissue Primary tissue, usually one-cell thick, which covers the body surface, lines its internal cavities, and forms glands. The cells are often secretory and have descriptive names such as cubical, ciliated, or columnar.

EPO *See* erythropoietin.

epoietin A *drug which is an *analogue of *erythropoietin which is on the *IOC list of *banned substances.

EPSP *See* excitatory postsynaptic potential.

equalitarian Leadership style which may be regarded as equivalent to *consideration.

equality The state of being equal in some respect. In *sociology, equality is viewed mainly in a social context and the lack of equality is regarded as being profoundly shaped by social structures.

equality of access The concept that all persons should have equal rights of *access; freedom from constraint. Equality of access does not necessarily lead to *equality of opportunity.

equality of opportunity A situation in which all persons, regardless of social *class, age, race, or *gender have equal rights to compete for, and attain, sought-after positions in society. *Compare* equality of access.

equilibrium The state of an object when the *resultant forces acting on it are zero; that is, when the object is at rest or moving with *uniform velocity and zero acceleration. The *stability of a person depends on whether he or she is in a state of *stable equilibrium, *neutral equilibrium, or *unstable equilibrium. *See also* dynamic equilibrium; and static equilibrium.

equilibrium point For a given level of *muscle innervation, the hypothetical *joint angle at which the *torque from the two opposing muscle groups are equal and opposite.

equilibrium principle A principle which states that the *line of gravity of a body must be located within its supporting base if the body is to be in a state of *equilibrium at rest.

equilibrium sense An ability to use sensory information from the *vestibular apparatus (the eyes and proprioceptors) to maintain balance and to know one's body position relative to *gravity.

ER *See* endoplasmic reticulum.

erector spinae *Prime mover of back *extension which consists of three columns of muscle: the *iliocostalis, *longissimus, and *spinalis muscles. These three provide resistance to bending forward at the waist, act as powerful extensors to promote return to the erect position, and help to hold the body upright. The erector spinae readily go into painful spasms following injury to back structures.

ERG A unit of work or energy; the work done by a *force of one *dyne acting through a distance of 1 cm.

ergogenic aid Any factor which improves athletic performance above normal expectation. Ergogenic aids are frequently thought of as drugs only, but they may also include psychological techniques (such as hypnosis), mental practice and suggestion, music, oxygen, and nutritional substances.

ergograph Device invented by Angelo Mosso (1848–1910) to study muscular function in the human body.

ergo-jump A mechanical powertest (*alactacid powertest) of the leg *extensor muscles which consists of the measurement of the off-the-ground time during a series of vertical jumps performed one after the other for 15 seconds. Standardized jumps are made on a plate which automatically records the off-the-ground time. The following formula is used to estimate power:

$$\text{power} = \frac{(g^2 \times T_v \times 15 \text{ seconds})}{4 \times n \times (15 - T_v)}$$

where the gravitational constant $g=9.81$, T_v=total off-the-ground time, $15\text{-}T_v$=total on-the-ground time, and n=number of jumps performed.

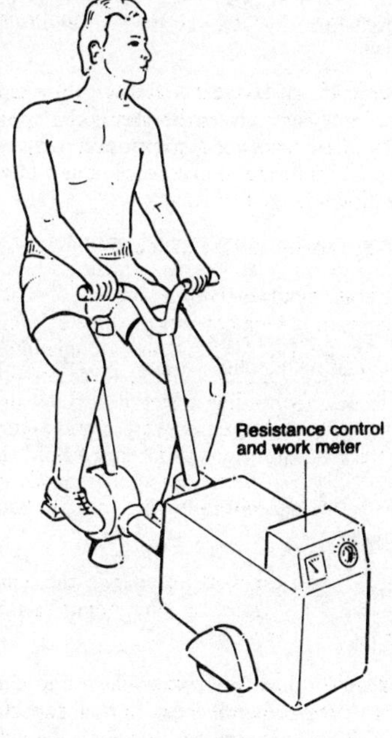

ergometer

ergometer An apparatus on which a workload can be adjusted and on which the rate of human energy expenditure can be measured. *See also* cycle ergometer.

ergonomics The study of the relationship between workers and their environment with particular emphasis on engineering aspects. In sport, ergonomics includes the study of designs which produce the most efficient bicycles, canoes, and other sports equipment.

ERGO sixty-second test A test of *lactacid *anaerobic power which consists of the measurement of the off-the-ground time during a series of vertical jumps performed one after the other for 60 s. *See also* ergo jump.

error A deviation from accuracy or correctness. *See also* absolute error; constant error; error of movement; and variable error.

error in execution A movement *error in which the planned movement, with respect to its timing and direction, is appropriate, but in which the movement deviates from the desired path because some unexpected event occurs that disrupts the movement. A gust of wind, for example, could slow an otherwise well-timed swing of the racket during a tennis-swing, resulting in an error of execution.

error in selection A movement *error in which the planned direction and/or timing of the movement is inappropriate. For example, a goalkeeper facing a penalty may move to the right when a movement to the left would have been appropriate; or the goalkeeper may move in the correct direction, but make the move slightly late. *Compare* error in execution.

error of knowledge An *error which occurs when an athlete does not understand what is demanded, or is unable to recall what is expected of him or her in a particular situation. The athlete may be capable of doing something but forgets what to do.

error of movement *Error in retrieval and/or execution of a *motor program. Errors which occur during the execution of a movement include two main types: *error in execution and *error in selection.

ERV *See* expiratory reserve volume.

erysipelas A severe, contagious, bacterial infection of the skin which can cause a diffuse, spreading inflammation, high fever, and sometimes complications such as *pneumonia or *nephritis. It is relatively common following elbow-blows during basketball. While infected, the athlete's vision and timing are impaired to some degree. Training and competition are strongly contra-indicated during the infective phase and a gradual return to physical activity after recovery is advised.

erythema Abnormal reddening of the skin due to dilation of blood capillaries. Erythema may be due to a number of conditions, but it is often a sign of inflammation and infection.

erythrocyte Biconcave, non-nucleated, red blood cell which contains *haemoglobin and transports oxygen.

erythrogenin An *enzyme released by the *kidney when exposed to low *partial pressures of oxygen. Erythrogenin transforms a plasma globulin into *erythropoietin which will enhance the production of red blood cells.

erythropoiesis The production of red blood cells regulated by *erythropoietin. Erythropoiesis normally occurs in the tissue of bone marrow.

erythropoietin A *hormone which stimulates the production of red blood cells in bone marrow. Erythropoietin is a protein produced in the blood through the action of an *enzyme released from the kidneys in response to *hypoxia. It is on the *IOC list of *banned substances. *See also* erythrogenin.

escape-training Training which enables a person to behave in such a way as to extricate himself or herself from an unpleasant situation.

essential amino acid An *amino acid that must be obtained from the diet so that the body can synthesize protein and carry out its functions. The nine essential amino acids are isoleucine, leucine, lysine, methionine, phenylalanine (tyrosine), threonine, tryptophan, valine, and histidine. (Histidine is required for infants, but it has not been fully established that it is essential for adults.) They must be available simultaneously in the correct proportions for protein synthesis to occur. *Compare* *non-essential amino acids.

essential element An *element without which neither growth nor reproduction can take place.

essential fat Fat which forms an essential part of the body storage. Fats needed for normal functioning of the body occur in bone marrow, heart, lungs, liver, spleen and kidney, muscles and CNS and, in women, the breasts.

essential fatty acid An *unsaturated fatty acid, such as *linoleic acid, that is needed for normal, healthy functioning of the body but which cannot be synthesized by the body. Lack of essential fatty acid may result in hyperactivity, reduced growth, and even death.

essential nutrient A *nutrient which cannot be synthesized by the body but is essential for normal activity and growth. Essential nutrients must be obtained from the diet.

esteem Refers to the evaluation of individual qualities and performances and may be negative or positive.

ester Compound formed from an organic acid and an alcohol by the elimination of water.

esterification Formation of an *ester; for example, in the synthesis of *fats.

estradiol *See* oestradiol.

estrogen *See* oestrogen.

ethacrynic acid A *drug belonging to the *diuretics which are on the *IOC list of *banned substances.

ethamivan An *analeptic *drug belonging to the *diuretics which are on the *IOC list of *banned substances.

ethanol *See* alcohol.

ethic A belief or attitude which contributes to the moral values of a society, culture, or organization.

ethics **1** The study of how people ought to act in order to be moral. **2** A moral code that guides the conduct of a group of professionals such as medical doctors. Medical ethics is particularly relevant to the application of *drugs and *ergogenic aids in sport.

ethmoid bone A plate-like *bone behind the nose.

ethnic group A group of individuals with a shared sense of belonging based on a common heritage and sociocultural background. The individuals within an ethnic group are often visibly different from other individuals by virtue of unique lifestyle or appearance, and they usually share a common culture, customs, and norms.

ethnicity A *social stratification system based on the *ethnic group to which individuals belong.

ethnic resistance Opposition of an *ethnic group to the dominant culture. An ethnic group may resist attempts to eliminate or discourage their traditional sporting activities, for example.

ethnocentrism The tendency of members of one social group to mistrust individuals belonging to another social group. Ethnocentrism involves the belief that one's own social group is culturally superior to another group. It also involves an inability to understand that cultural differences do not imply the inferiority of those groups distinct from one's own. *See also* racial discrimination.

ethnography A written description of an organization or small group based on direct observation or participant observation. The researcher usually gathers data by living and working in the social setting being researched.

ethnomethodology An approach to sociology which attempts to reveal the methods and social competencies used by members of social groups to establish their sense of social reality. It emphasizes the role of individuals in creating social reality.

ethophetazine A *drug belonging to the *narcotic analgesics which are on the *IOC list of *banned substances.

ethyl alcohol *See* alcohol.

etic perspective Applied to linguistic analyses and sociological accounts made from a perspective external to a language or social situation. In sport, the etic perspective attempts to understand sport from the detached stance of an outsider. *Compare* emic perspective.

etilamfetamine A *drug belonging to the *stimulants which are on the *IOC list of *banned substances.

etiocholanone An *isomer of *androsterone. Etiocholanone is a metabolic product of *testosterone formed in the liver. It has no *androgenic activity.

etiology *See* aetiology.

Eustachian tube The tube, sometimes called the auditory tube, which connects the middle ear to the *pharynx, and allows pressure to be equalized on either side of the *eardrum.

eustress The positive or pleasant aspect of *stress; such as the demands of competition which produce positive responses of excitement and happiness. *Compare* distress.

evaluation apprehension The idea that an *audience heightens the *arousal level of performers only if the audience is perceived as evaluating the performance. *See also* Zajonc's model.

evaporation The conversion of liquid into vapour. Evaporation of water from the body surface during *sweating is a very important source of heat loss. *See also* latent heat of vaporization.

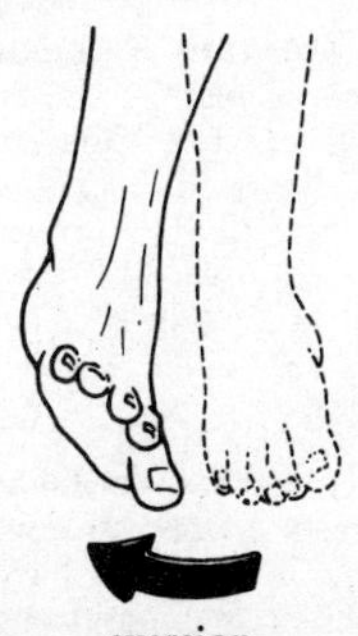

eversion

eversion of foot (plantar eversion) Sideways movement of the sole of the foot so that it faces laterally. It is effected mainly by the *peroneus longus and *peroneus brevis muscles. *Compare* inversion of foot.

excessive flexibility *See* hyperflexibility.

exchange theory (social exchange theory) A theoretical viewpoint of human social relationships based on the idea that individuals always seek to maximize the rewards they obtain from their interactions with others.

excitability The ability to receive and respond to a *stimulus.

excitation The act of stimulating a *neurone or muscle cell to conduct an impulse.

excitatory postsynaptic potential (EPSP) A transient, graded reduction in *resting potential of a *post-synaptic membrane of a *neurone of muscle fibre due to the release of a *neurotransmitter from a pre-synaptic neurone. If the EPSP exceeds a critical level an *action potential will form.

excretion The elimination of metabolic wastes (including *carbon dioxide and *urea) from the body.

excretory system The body system concerned with the elimination of *metabolic wastes, mainly through the action of the *kidneys.

executive level In *cybernetics, part of a control system which compares deviations of output from the norm and decides how to reduce the error toward zero.

executive program A *motor program for a *skill consisting of a number of movements. A skill such as a tennis-serve consists of a number of movements such as taking a stance, throwing the ball up, swinging the racket, transfer of weight from one foot to another, and striking the ball. The executive program for the whole action consists of subroutines for each component movement.

exercise 1 Human movements and physical activities which involve the use of large muscle groups rather than highly specific, relatively non-taxing movements of small muscle groups. Exercise includes dance, calisthenics, games, and more formal activities such as jogging, swimming, and running. 2 Any set of movements designed to train or improve a *skill.

exercise addiction *See* addiction to exercise.

exercise adherence Maintenance of an active involvement in physical exercise. Those with strong exercise adherence continue to participate in physical activity despite opportunities and pressures to withdraw.

exercise dependence *See* addiction to exercise.

exercise-induced asthma (EIA) A form of *asthma resulting from physical activity. Typically, *bronchioles in the airways are dilated during exercise but a few minutes after the cessation of activity the bronchioles constrict, making breathing difficult. The same level of exertion may produce diffent degrees of asthmatic attack depending on the nature of the activity. Running tends to provoke worse attacks than cycling, for example, and both provoke worse attacks than swimming which is among the best sports for asthmatics. Factors which increase the risk of an asthma attack include: activity performed in cold weather or a smoky environment; continous exercise; running; high intensity of activity; inferior physical fitness; cold, dry air; air pollutants; pollens and grass; recent respiratory infection; and taking beta blockers. Those which tend to decrease the risk include: intermittent exercise; swimming; low exercise intensity; enhanced aerobic fitness; and warm, moist air.

exercise-induced bronchospasm *See* exercise-induced asthma.

exercise machine A machine used in strength and general fitness training. Exercise machines may be multi-units or single units and there are a number of differences in the form of resistance and the way it is applied. Many machines support the body while particular muscle groups work against predetermined resistances. *See also* variable resistance exercise; and Zander apparatus.

exercise physiology A study of the functioning of the various organs of the human body during and after exercise, and the effects of exercise on physiological processes. Exercise physiology often has the objective of improving the exercise response. A knowledge of exercise physiology equips coaches and athletes to make sound judgements concerning the amount and type of training to prescribe in a given case.

exercise prescription A programme of exercise designed specifically for an individual, based on that individual's level of health and fitness, and his or her aspirations.

exercise psychology **1** The study of the psychological factors which affect participation in health-related *exercise, rather than competitive sport. *See also* sport psychology. **2** The study of the psychological outcomes (or 'mental health' aspects) of exercise.

exercise recovery (active recovery) Performance of light exercise during the recovery phase of *training. Exercise recovery often forms a part of *interval-training to enhance the removal of *lactic acid.

exercise science The study of the natural phenomena associated with physical activity and sport. *See also* sports science.

exercise stress *Stress associated with physical exertion.

exercise therapy Use of exercise as a mode of therapy for promoting psychological or physical well-being. Running is often used as an effective psychotherapeutic tool. In rehabilitation from illness and injury, controlled exercise is a key factor in returning the sportsperson to normal activity.

exergonic reaction A chemical reaction that releases *energy.

exhalation Breathing air from the lungs out through the nose and mouth.

exhaustion A condition of extreme *fatigue when a person can no longer continue a physical activity. *See also* heat exhaustion.

exocrine gland Glands with ducts through which their secretions are carried to a particular site.

exogenous Developing or originating outside an organ or part.

exophthalmic goitre A condition, characterized by protrusion of the eyeballs, hyperactivity, and weight-loss, resulting from over-production of *thyroxine from the *thyroid gland which becomes swollen (goitre).

exostosis A benign outgrowth of *cartilage from a bone which may occur spontaneously or as a result of the margins of joint surface knocking against each other. *See also* impingement exostosis.

expectancy The probability that a particular *reinforcer will be given to an individual who behaves in a specific manner in a particular situation.

expedition-type endurance A special type of *endurance engendered by expedition-training. It applies to a number of important and specialized aspects of fitness which are needed for the successful completion of a demanding expedition. These may include, in addition to *aerobic endurance, *acclimatization to altitude, the ability to judge the degree of exhaustion in a team, and the conscious marshalling of resources for a supreme effort.

experiential continuum *See* Dewey's theory of experiential continuum.

experiential learning Learning through experience.

experiment An observation made for scientific purposes under conditions which are controlled as far as possible by the experimenter. Experiments are conducted to formulate and test *hypotheses. In a classical experiment (sometimes called the single-factor experiment) only one condition, called the independent variable, is manipulated at any given time to determine its influence on a dependent variable. *See also* multifactor study.

experimental error A source of variations in experimental results due to the way a test has been conducted. Experimental error can be minimized by strict *standardization.

experimental group A group of subjects exposed to the *independent variable of an experiment (*compare* control group). Typically, the experimental group is treated with the independent variable to test an experimental hypothesis. The resultant effect, measured by the *dependent variable, is compared with any change observed in the control group. If a statistically significant difference (*see* statistical significance) is found between the dependent measures in the experimental and control groups, then the *experimental hypothesis is upheld. If there is no significant difference then the *null hypothesis is upheld.

experimental hypothesis The *hypothesis that there will be a statistically significant difference (*see* statistical significance) between an *experimental group and a *control group and that this difference will have been caused by the *independent variable under investigation in an experiment. *Compare* null hypothesis.

experimental method Scientific method used to test an *hypothesis by comparing an *experimental group with a *control group. *Sociology has developed other methodologies to cope with less controllable data. *See also* causal modelling; and comparative method.

experimenter effects The influence of the experimenter's behaviour, personality traits, or expectations on the outcome of research.

expiration Breathing out; exhalation.

expiratory reserve volume (ERV) Maximal volume of air expired from end expiration. Typical value at rest is 1200 ml.

explanation An account which attempts to identify the cause, nature, and interrelationships of a phenomenon. Scientific explanations, especially those of the physical sciences, often involve the use of scientific laws and theories. In the social sciences, explanations may also involve the reasons and meanings provided by *actors. *See also* causal explanation; deductive explanation; functionalist explanation; probablistic explanation; and teleological explanation.

explosive power *See* explosive strength.

explosive strength (explosive power) The ability to expend *energy in one explosive act or in a series of strong, sudden movements as in jumping, or projecting some object, as far as possible.

extensibility The ability to stretch a material beyond its resting length.

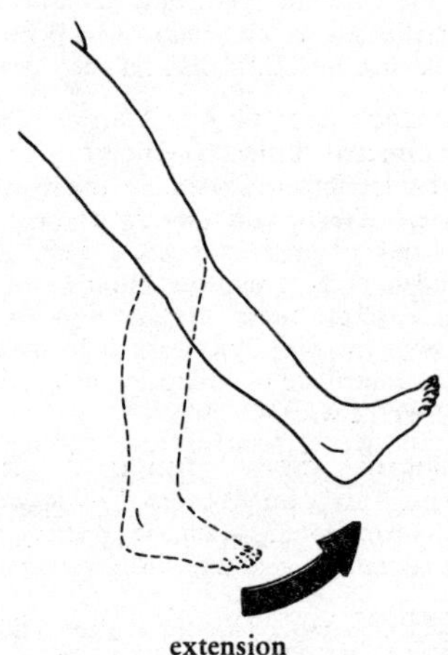

extension

extension A body movement that increases the angle between articulating bones. *Compare* flexion.

extensive interval work *Interval training for a long distance (typically 800–3000 m) or long duration (typically 1–5 min) with short recovery periods.

extensor A muscle which straightens a joint. *Compare* flexor.

extensor carpi radialis brevis One of a group of *superficial muscles lying in the posterior fascial compartment of the forearm acting on the wrist and fingers. It lies a little deeper than the *extensor carpi radialis longus. It has its *origin on the lateral *condyle of the *humerus and its *insertion on the base of the third *metacarpal. Its contractions contribute to the *extension and *abduction of the wrist and steadies the wrist during finger *flexion.

extensor carpi radialis longus One of a group of *superficial muscles lying in the posterior fascial compartment of the forearm acting on the wrist and fingers. It lies just above the *extensor carpi radialis brevis and it has its *origin on the lateral *supracondylar ridge of the *humerus and its *insertion at the base of the second *metacarpal. Contractions of this muscle contribute to the *extension and *abduction of the wrist and, with the extensor carpi radialis brevis, it acts as a *fixator, steadying the wrist during finger flexion.

extensor carpi ulnaris A slender *superficial muscle of the posterior compartment of the forearm which acts on the wrist and fingers. It is the most *medial of the group. It has its *origins on the *lateral *epicondyle of the *humerus and the posterior border of the *ulna. Its *insertion is at the base of the fifth *metacarpal. Its contractions contribute to *extension and *adduction of the wrist.

extensor digiti minimi A slender *muscle in the forarm which lies medially to the *extensor digitorum. It contributes to the straightening of the wrist and fingers.

extensor digitorum A slender *muscle that runs along the posterior fascial compartment of the forearm. It has its *origin on the lateral *epicondyle of the *humerus and its *insertion consists of four tendons which attach to the distal phalanges 2 to 5. Its contractions straighten the fingers, the wrist, and finally the elbow; it is also involved in *abduction of the fingers.

extensor digitorum longus A muscle of the anterior compartment of the lower leg which runs along the anterior and lateral surface. It is involved in *dorsiflexion and *eversion of the foot and is a *prime mover of toe extension acting mainly at the *metatarsophalangeal joint.

extensor hallucis longus A *muscle in the anterior compartment of the lower leg which is involved in *extension of the great toe, and *dorsiflexion and *inversion of the foot. It has its *origin on the *anteromedial surface of the *shaft of the *fibula and the *interosseus membrane between the fibula and *tibia. It has its *insertion on the *distal *phalanx of the great toe.

extensor indicis A small, *deep muscle arising close to the wrist in the *posterior compartment of the forearm. It is involved in *extension of the index finger. It has its *origin on the *posterior *distal surface of the *ulna and the *interosseus membrane between the ulna and *radius. It has its *insertion on the extensor expansion of the index finger where it joins with the *tendon of the *extensor digitorum.

extensor pollicis brevis A *deep muscle, in the *posterior compartment of the forearm, which extends the thumb. It has a common *origin with the *extensor pollicis longus on the *dorsal *shafts of the radius and *ulna, and on the *interosseus membrane between the *radius and ulna. Its insertion is on the base of the *proximal *phalanx of the thumb.

extensor pollicis longus A *muscle with similar features to the *extensor pollicis brevis, but with its *insertion on the *distal *phalanx of the thumb.

extensor tenosynovitis Inflammation of the tissue around the tendons that extend or straighten the wrist and fingers. In the past, the condition was treated with ointments, injections, and splints. A newer treatment uses a small operation which relieves symptoms and allows the resumption of activity within days.

extent flexibility The maximum *range of movement possible at a particular joint or series of joints in functional combination. Extent flexibility is largely joint-specific; that is, good flexibility at one joint does not guarantee flexibility elsewhere. Use of the term is sometimes restricted to the ability to flex and stretch the trunk and back muscles as far as possible in any direction. *See also* dynamic flexibility; and flexibility.

external axis An *axis which is outside the body. For example, the high-bar in gymnastics is the external axis around which the gymnast rotates.

external cardiac massage Rhythmic pressure exerted by the heel of the hand on the lower half of the *sternum in order to stimulate the heart to beat after a *cardiac arrest.

external control An individual's perception that external factors determine performance outcomes. *Compare* internal control. *See also* externals.

external controls *See* externals.

external force A *force outside the system under consideration. The classification of forces as external or internal is largely a matter of convenience and depends on how the system is defined. In *biomechanics, the human body is generally regarded as the system and any force acting on it from outside the body, such as air resistance and gravity, is regarded as an external force. *Compare* internal force.

external heel-counter support Part of a *training shoe which usually consists of a nylon collar supporting the *heel counter and helping to prevent excessive sideways movement of the foot inside the shoe.

external iliac artery An *artery which supplies blood to the lower leg.

external imagery A form of mental practice in which individuals imagine they are external observers watching themselves perform.

external intercostals Eleven pairs of muscles which lie between the *ribs. The fibres run downwards and forwards from each rib onto the rib below; therefore, the *origin is on the inferior border of the rib above, and the *insertion is on the superior surface of the rib below, each muscle. The external intercostals take part in *inspiration, elevating the ribcage, and act as *synergists of the *diaphragm.

external jugular vein A principal *vein in the neck.

external locus of causality A cause of an outcome perceived by an individual as being in the environemnet and beyond his or her control.

externally-paced skill A skill in which the timing and form are determined by factors outside the control of the performer; for example, a sailor adjusts sails according to wind direction and speed. *Compare* self-paced skill.

external oblique The largest and most superficial of the three pairs of *muscles which form the lateral abdominal wall (*see* abdomen). The external oblique has its *origin on the outer surfaces of the lower *ribs and most fibres are inserted (*see* insertion) via a broad *aponeurosis onto the *linea alba with other fibres inserting onto the pubic *tubercle or the *iliac crest. When the pair of external oblique muscles contract simultaneously, they aid the *rectus abdominis in flexing the *vertebral column, compressing the abdominal wall, and increasing abdominal pressure. When acting individually, they aid muscles of the back in the *rotation and lateral *flexion of the trunk.

external overload An *attentional style in which an individual has the tendency to become confused and overloaded with external stimuli. *Compare* broad external.

external reinforcement Reinforcement provided by another person (e.g., through praise) or an object (e.g., a trophy).

external rotation Movement of the limbs around their long axis, away from the midline of the body. *Compare* internal rotation.

externals (external controls) Individuals who tend to believe that events in their lives result from external factors beyond their control, such as luck and referees' decisions. Whether players are external controls or *internal controls may influence their performance and the method most appropriate to motivate them. External controls tend to fear failure and are chance-oriented.

external validity **1** The applicability of experimental results to real situations. **2** In *statistics, the extent to which the results of an investigation may be generalized to the population as a whole, and to other populations, settings, measurement devices, etc. External validity depends on the adequacy of the sample.

exteroceptor A *sensory receptor sensitive to stimuli which arise outside the body. They include *touch, *pressure, *pain, and *skin-temperature receptors, as well as the special receptors of the *eye and *ear concerned with sight and hearing. *Compare* interoceptors.

extinction The gradual elimination of a learned response due to lack of reinforcement. In *classical conditioning, extinction of the *conditioned response occurs when the *conditioned stimulus is repeatedly presented in the absence of the *unconditioned stimulus.

extinction model A model of *anxiety reduction which perceives *anxiety as an emotional response. The extinction model is based on the idea that anxiety is elicited by originally neutral stimuli through a process of *classical conditioning. Through pairing with painful or aversive stimuli (which thereby act as unconditioned stimuli), the neutral stimulus becomes a conditioned stimulus capable of eliciting a conditioned reflex. For example, a horse-rider thrown during a race who suffers painful fractures may later find that riding a horse elicits intense anxiety. The anxiety is reduced by exposing the sufferer to anxiety-arousing stimuli in the absence of the primary aversive stimuli in the expectation that the anxiety will be eliminated by extinction.

extracellular Outside the cell.

extracellular fluid A *body fluid located outside the cells. Extracellular fluids include *plasma and *interstitial fluid.

extracurricular activities Activities which are outside the normal curriculum of a school or other educational establishment. Much sport in schools is taken as an extracurricular activity after the normal hours of school.

extradural haemorrhage Bleeding into the *epidural space between the *vertebral canal and *spinal cord.

extrafusal fibre A typical, contractile *muscle cell or muscle fibre which lies outside *muscle spindles. *Compare* intrafusal fibre.

extrapolation The process of extending the values or terms of a series on either side of the known values (e.g., on a graph) thus increasing the range of values.

extrapyramidal system *See* extrapyramidal tracts.

extrapyramidal tracts (**extrapyramidal system**) A system of *nerve pathways occuring in the *brain between the *cerebral cortex, *basal ganglia, *thalamus, *cerebellum, *reticular formation, and spinal *motor neurones. The extrapyramidal tracts are mainly concerned with the co-ordination of stereotype reflex movements. *Compare* pyramidal system.

extrasensory perception (**ESP**) Perception which allegedly occurs without sensory awareness; for example, communication between two individuals when there appears to be no channels of information exchange.

extrasystole An extra heartbeat.

extraversion A *personality dimension characterized by orientation towards the outside world, sociability, and impulsiveness.

extravert A *personality-type characterized by individuals who are sociable, outgoing, and who like others. Extraverts are generally outwardly expressive, active, and readily engage in social activities. *Compare* introvert.

extremity The *distal part of the body, or of a limb.

extrinsic Outside an organ or body-part.

extrinsic factor A factor external to the human body, such as equipment and playing surfaces.

extrinsic feedback *See* augmented feedback.

extrinsic injury An injury which results from forces outside the body. The external force may be produced by another person, an implement, or some other environmental factor. Fractures, dislocations, head injuries, and severe injuries to ligaments tend to belong to this group. *Compare* intrinsic injury.

extrinsic motivation *Motivation derived from external rewards such as praise, money, and trophies. Extrinsic motivation may encourage a person with a low motivation for success, or one with a high motivation to avoid failure, to take part in an achievement situation contrary to what is expected from the *McClelland–Atkinson model. *Compare* cognitive evaluation theory.

extrinsic reward A *reinforcement which takes the form of a tangible item such as a trophy or money, or something intangible such as praise and public recognition. *See also* motivation.

extropunitive behaviour *See* aggression.

exudate Material including pus, fluid, and cells that has slowly escaped from intact blood vessels and has been deposited in tissues, usually as a result of inflammation.

eye Organ of sight. Each eye is a single organ possessing an *iris which controls the aperture (*see* pupil) through which light passes to a *lens, which in turn focuses the light on to a *retina.

eye injury Damage to the eye due to physical trauma. The eye is surprisingly tough, but any injury should be regarded as potentially dangerous and requiring expert attention. Direct blows to the eye should be regarded very seriously because of the risk of blindness from retinal detachment. Medical advice should be sought in all cases of eye injury, especially if signs of bleeding or impaired sight are present after a blow.

Eysenck personality inventory An inventory which is based on the assumption that personality can be best measured by studying two basic trait dimensions: the introversion–extraversion dimension and the neuroticism–stability dimension.

F

facet Smooth, nearly flat, articular surface of a bone.

facial bone Part of the *skull which forms the framework of the face and holds the eyes in the *anterior position. The facial bone provides cavities for the organs of taste and smell, and the openings for the entry of air and food; it also secures the teeth and anchors the facial muscles.

facial injury Physical damage to the structures in and around the face, for example, a fracture of a facial bone caused by impact with a squash racket. Facial injuries tend to heal very quickly but because there is a risk of deformity, serious facial injuries often require the urgent attention of a *maxillofacial surgeon.

facial nerve A mixed sensory and motor nerve supplying the lacrimal and salivary glands, and the muscles of facial expression; the seventh *cranial nerve.

facilitated diffusion A special case of *diffusion; passive transport through a membrane is facilitated by a carrier molecule (that is, one that is lipid-soluble) which increases the mobility of the diffusing substance (e.g., *glucose).

fact An event or thing which can be verified by experience, observation, or experiment.

factor A component, constituent part, or condition which contributes to a result.

factor analysis A complex statistical procedure in which the correlations between a large set of observed variables are explained in terms of a smaller number of new variables called factors. Factor analysis has been used especially in sociology and psychology. In the case of personality analysis, it has been used to discover the constituent, irreducible traits from a complex mass of data.

FAD (flavin adenine dinucleotide) An electron-carrier in the respiratory chain, important in *aerobic respiration. FAD is derived from *riboflavin.

faeces Bodily waste which contains a mixture of excretory material including undigested food, bile pigment, bacteria, and mucus.

Fåhraeus–Lindquist effect The effect of vessel dimension on blood flow. In very narrow vessels, blood behaves as if *viscosity were reduced. This contributes to reducing the demand on the heart to produce a driving force. The effect is very important during heavy muscular activity when the blood flow through muscle capillaries is very high.

fahrenheit Temperature scale based on the melting point of ice being 32° and the boiling point of water being 212° at standard atmospheric pressure (that is, 760 mmHg).

failure anxiety *Anxiety associated with an anticipation of failure prior to performing a feared task.

fainting *See* syncope.

fallen arches (flat feet) A loss of the arched shape of the foot with a flattening of the arch (*see* arches of foot) between the heelbone and the toes. Fallen arches usually result from excessive strain, and weakening of the tendons and ligaments supporting the arch. The condition may occur after an individual has stood immobilized for extended periods, or after running on hard surfaces without proper arch supports. Fallen arches may be treated with appropriate *orthotics or exercise.

false consciousness An individual or group's social perceptions which another individual or group define as not matching the objective features of a situation. It is applied especially to class consciousness and is often seen to act against the interests of oppressed groups or individuals.

false ribs Ribs which either attach to the *sternum indirectly or not at all. *Compare* true ribs.

falsification The process of using an empirical method to refute or disprove a scientific hypothesis.

family A group of people, who share a blood relationship or similar close ties, in which the adults provide care and socialization of their children or adopted children. *See also* nuclear family; and significant other.

fan An individual who is devoted to, and enthusiastic about, a given sport.

fanning A form of *massage in which the masseur begins with hands together and then spreads them out to cover a muscle by moving away from a central point and out to the edges. Fanning is applied to muscles, such as those of the chest and abdomen, which radiate from the body's centre. It provides equal pull and pressure over the whole muscle to improve circulation.

fantasy *Imagery that is more or less coherent, as in dreams or daydreams, yet without due regard to reality.

faradism The use of an electrical current to treat conditions such as muscle strain. The affected muscle is supported in the shortened position, and a rapidly alternating current used to produce alternate contractions and relaxations to discourage *adhesions and encourage drainage of *exudate. Differential faradism is the use of a selective machine which makes one muscle contract just ahead of another, so altering muscle balance.

far-sighted *See* hypermetropia.

fartlek training (speed play) A relatively unstructured form of training, originating in Scandanavia, over natural terrain. Typically, although the route may be predetermined, the pace is varied spontaneously from fast bursts to jogging according to the terrain and the disposition of the runner. Fartlek training is often done as an alternative to highly structured *interval training to provide variety. It is claimed that fartlek training improves both the *aerobic and *anaerobic capacity of the athlete.

fascia A tough *connective tissue which may be superficial or deep. The superficial fascia is fatty and underlies the skin, forming a lining separating the skin from the deep fascia. The deep fascia usually ensheaths muscles, blood vessels, nerves, and organs, and contains dense *elastic tissue.

fascia lata The deep *fascia that surrounds the muscles of the thigh. The fascia lata is particularly evident as a broad band, the iliotibial tract, that passes down the lateral aspect of the thigh.

fascial hernia (muscle hernia) The protrusion of muscle through the *fascia when increased pressure occurs, sometimes accompanied by pain. In a person with a fascial hernia a definite bulge can be felt through the defect during or immediately after exercise, and it is often possible to feel a hole in the fascia when the limb is in a relaxed state. A fascial hernia commonly involves the *anterior tibialis muscle which bulges through the anterior compartment of the lower leg and may be associated with *anterior compartment syndrome.

fascicle (fasciculum) 1 A portion of *muscle which consists of a discrete bundle of muscle cells, segregated from the rest of the muscle block by a sheath of connective tissue called the *perimysium. 2 A bundle of nerve fibres.

fasciculum (pl. fasciculi) *See* fascicle.

fast force A *force identified on the basis of the following formula: force = mass ×acceleration, in which the *acceleration component contributes more than the *mass. Fast force is important for the production of *explosive power. *Compare* endurance force.

fast glycolytic fibre (FG fibre) A *muscle fibre which is an extreme type of *fast twitch fibre. It has a low *aerobic capacity reflected by its white colour due to low levels of *myoglobin and its tendency to *fatigue quickly. However, it is rich in *phosphocreatine and enzymes which enable it to generate contractions very quickly for a short period of time. It is, therefore, best adapted to the contractions needed for power activities.

fast oxidative glycolytic fibre (FOG fibre) A type of *muscle fibre which, although it is classed as a *fast twitch fibre, shows some features, such as *myoglobin content, mitochondrial density (*see* mitochondrion), *phosphocreatine levels, and susceptibiltiy to *fatigue, intermediate between those of the *fast glycolyitic fibres and *slow twitch fibres. There is evidence which suggests that *endurance-training can cause fast glycolytic fibres to be converted to the FOG type, enabling speed to be sustained for longer periods.

fast strength *See* elastic strength.

fast twitch glycolytic fibres (white fibres) Muscle fibres characterized by their fast contraction time, high *anaerobic capacity and low *aerobic capacity. They *fatigue quickly but are used predominantly in activities which require high power, such as sprinting and jumping. There are two main types: *fast oxidative glycolytic fibres and *fast glycolytic fibres.

fat A *lipid extractable by a fat solvent. A true fat, or neutral fat, is a *triglyceride of *fatty acids and *glycerol, and provides energy, heat insulation, cushioning, and buoyancy. Fat also helps to create certain other chemicals in the body, such as *steroids. Fats are one of the basic *nutrients and are the body's most concentrated source of energy. Each gram produces about 9cal of energy at a cost of 2.031 of oxygen. (i.e., 0.2551 of oxygen cal^{-1}). Fat is preferentially metabolized during low intensity, long duration exercises. Because of the association of high fat diets with *obesity and *vascular diseases, it is generally recommended that fat should contribute less than 35 per cent of the total calorific intake in the diet (*see* essential fatty acid). *See also* balanced diet.

fat cells *See* adipocytes.

fatfold test *See* skinfold test.

fat-free body-mass *See* lean body-mass.

fat-free body-weight The weight of the body excluding *storage fat and *essential fat. *See also* lean body-mass.

fatigue Exhaustion of muscle resulting from prolonged exertion or overstimulation. *Endurance-training generally has the effect of delaying the onset of fatigue. *See also* muscle fatigue; physiological fatigue; and psychological fatigue.

fatigue fracture *See* stress fracture.

fatigue index A concept used in the study of *fatigue experienced in *anaerobic activities. The fatigue index is expressed as the power decline divided by the time interval in seconds between peak power and minimum power.

fatigue theory A theory concerning the origin of *stress fractures which states that during repeated protracted activity loads are not adequately supported by muscles, consequently they are transferred directly to the skeleton. When the tolerance of the skeleton is exceeded, a stress fracture occurs.

fat malabsorption A reduction in the ability to absorb *fat in the intestines, usually due to a deficiency of *bile salts. The body becomes deprived of *fat soluble vitamins, the stools become fatty, and the gut becomes bulky.

fat mobilization The breakdown of stored fat so that it can be transported to respiring tissue. The fat must be converted into small units by *β-oxidation before it can enter the *Krebs cycle.

fat pad Pad of fatty tissue which occurs between the fibrous capsule and *synovial membranes in and around bony joints. Fat pads help to cushion the *joint.

fat-soluble vitamins Vitamins A, D, E, and K, which bind to ingested *lipids and are absorbed along with the digested products. Anything interfering with fat absorption, such as a deficiency of bile, will interfere with the uptake of fat-soluble vitamins. All except vitamin K are stored in *adipose tissue in the body and can cause fat-soluble vitamin toxicity.

fatty acids Long linear chains of carbon, hydrogen, and oxygen atoms with an organic acid group (–COOH) at one end. They have the general formula $R–(CH_2)n–COOH$ where R represents a hydrocarbon group, e.g., $–CH_3$ or $–C_2H_5$. Fatty acids are components of *triglycerides and are classified as either *saturated fatty acids or *unsaturated fatty acids. *See also* essential fatty acid.

FDA (Food and Drug Administration) A government agency in the USA that regulates and monitors food and drug safety.

fear An *emotion characterized by unpleasant feelings of tension evoked by a specific situation or object. Physiological changes associated with fear include increases in heart rate, blood pressure, and sweating. Behavioural changes can include an overwhelming desire to avoid the fear-evoking situation.

fear of failure *See* motive to avoid failure.

fear of success *See* motive to avoid success.

feedback 1 In *cybernetics, feedback occurs when some of the output from a system is isolated and fed back as input (*see* feedback mechanism). 2 The information provided to a performer during or after an activity which enables the performer to assess the success or failure of his or her performance. Feedback is regarded by many as the single most important factor in the acquisition of skills. *See also* augmented feedback; intrinsic feedback; and knowledge of results.

feedback mechanism Mechanism by which the products or outcomes of a process are coupled to the input. Feedback mechanisms are important in regulating many physiological processes. *See also* negative feedback; and positive feedback.

feedforward control A mechanism within some control systems by which *information is sent ahead in time to prepare a part of a control system for future action, or to prepare the system to receive a particular kind of *feedback. Feedforward control mechanisms are important in the control of movement by the *central nervous system.

feeling An affective experience reported by the individual as pleasantness, unpleasantness, excitement, calmness, sadness, happiness, etc.

felon (whitlow) An abscess in the pulp of the fingertip.

femininity Physical and behavioural characteristics, such as tenderness and consideration, which tend to be perceived by society as being in greater abundance in women, but which many regard as qualities desirable in both sexes. *Compare* masculinity. *See also* BEM sex-role inventory.

feminism 1 An *ideology which opposes misogynous ideologies and practices. 2 A social movement which confronts the sex-class system. 3 A theory concerned with the nature of women's oppression and subordination to men. 4 A sociopolitical theory and practice which aims to free all women from male supremacy and exploitation, and which demands equal rights for women.

feminization 1 The social process which has resulted in certain occupations, such as nursing, being regarded as women's work. 2 Development of female secondary characteristics, such as breasts. Feminization in males is sometimes associated with taking anabolic steroids.

femoral In *anatomy, pertaining to the thigh.

femoral artery An *artery which runs down the front of the thigh from the *iliac artery in the *groin to the back of the knee.

femoral canal An opening just below the *inguinal ligament through which the femoral artery passes as it descends from the abdomen into the thigh.

femoral condyle A *condyle on the *femur which forms part of the knee-joint.

femoral nerve A mixed nerve in the thigh which receives sensory impulses from the foot and inner regions of the thigh, and supplies the *quadriceps muscle at the front of the thigh.

femoral torsion (cross-eyed patellae; squinting patellae) The non-alignment of the *femur and *tibia so that the *patellae face inward slightly instead of facing forward. Femoral torsion is thought to indicate an imbalance of strength among the different muscles of the *quadriceps. The condition is often relieved by strengthening the *lateral *rotators of the hip-joint and stretching the *medial *rotators.

femoral valgus A condition in which the *femur is curved outwards from its *proximal to *distal end, giving the appearance of bowed legs. It is an unusual condition usually caused by skeletal deformity rather than being mechanically induced. It results in extra tensile stress being exerted on the medial side of the hips and the lateral side of the knee. *Compare* femoral varus. *See also* valgus.

femoral varus A condition in which the *femur curves inwards from its *proximal to *distal end. It contributes to a knock-kneed posture. Femoral varus causes extra tensile stress to be exerted on the lateral side of the hip and the medial structure of the knee, and can contribute to injuries. The condition is relieved by strengthening the hip *adductors and the *quadriceps which stabilize the knee. Femoral varus is sometimes accompanied by a compensatory *tibial valgus, which puts added stress on the knee. *Compare* femoral valgus.

femoral vein A principal *vein in the thigh.

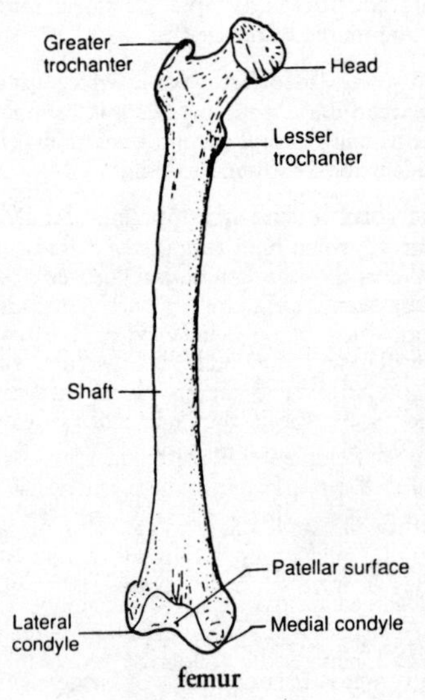

femur

femur The thigh-bone; the longest and strongest bone in the body. Stress on the femur during vigorous exercise can reach 2 tons per square inch. It articulates proximally with the *pelvic girdle at the hip and distally with the *tibia at the knee.

femur width In *anthropometry, the distance between the *medial and *lateral *epicondyles of the *femur when an individual is seated with the leg bent at the knee to form a 90° angle. *See also* body breadths.

fenbufen An effective, nonsteroid, anti-inflammatory *drug used in the treatment of *osteoarthritis.

fencamfamin A *drug belonging to the *stimulants which are on the *IOC list of *banned substances.

fenetylline A *drug belonging to the *stimulants which are on the *IOC list of *banned substances.

fenoterol A drug which, although it is an effective prophylactic for *exercise-induced asthma, belongs to the *stimulants which are on the *IOC list of *banned substances.

fenproporex A *drug belonging to the *stimulants which are on the *IOC list of *banned substances.

fentanyl A *drug belonging to the *narcotic analgesics which are on the *IOC list of *banned substances.

ferritin A conjugated protein containing *iron. Ferritin is found mainly in liver, spleen, and bone marrow where it acts as an iron store.

ferrodoxin Iron-containing protein acting as an *electron-carrier in the *electron-transport system in *mitochondria.

feud Relations of continuing mutual hostility between groups where one group has been wronged, or perceives itself to have been wronged, by another, and retribution is sought. Feuds are sociological phenomena observed in situations of kin solidarity. They are also seen in sports teams where there is an assumed kin solidarity; thus, if one member of the team has been abused by the opposition, he or she can rely on support from other team-members.

FEV *See* forced expiratory volume.

fever (pyrexia) A condition in which the *core temperature is higher than normal (oral temperature more than 37°C; rectal temperature more than 37.2°C). Fever is usually due to an *infection, but may sometimes be linked to an emotional condition. It is usually accompanied by headaches, shivering, and nausea. Fever is triggered by stimulation of the temperature control centre in the *hypothalamus of the brain. Fever can result in *dehydration. Physical exertion should be avoided during a fever.

FFA *See* free fatty acids.

FG fibre *See* fast glycolytic fibre.

fibre (roughage) **1** The indigestible part of plants. Nutritionists have divided fibre into two basic types—*insoluble fibre and *soluble fibre—and have identified five major forms of fibre: *cellulose, *hemi-cellulose, *lignin, *pectin, and *gums. They are found especially in cereals, vegetables, and fruit. Fibre is resistant to human digestive *enzymes and therefore passes through much of *digestive tract virtually unaltered, absorbing water, and helping to speed elimination. Some types of fibre are broken down by microorganisms in the *large intestine into substances that can be absorbed by the body. These substances produce various physiological effects. They regulate the transit time of the *faeces and reduce the risk of *constipation. It is thought that fibre may reduce blood *cholesterol levels. **2** A thread-like process such as a *muscle fibre, *collagen fibre, or *nerve fibre.

fibre splitting Longitudinal splitting of a *muscle fibre which increases the total number of muscle fibres and which may contribute to an increase in muscle bulk. Experimental evidence indicates that in a variety of animals, fibre-splitting is related to intensity of exercise and occurs only after a high resistance weight-training programme.

fibrillation Rapid and irregular beating of the heart, or quivering of *cardiac muscle fibres, causing inefficient emptying of the heart chambers. Fibrillation in the *ventricles causes *cardiac arrest.

fibrin A fibrous, insoluble *protein formed during blood-*clotting. Molecules of fibrin form a network, trapping cells and debris, which seals off a damaged blood vessel.

fibrin deposit theory A theory suggesting that regular exercise can reduce *fibrin deposits in the blood thereby lowering the risk of *atherosclerosis.

fibrinogen A relatively soluble blood *protein that is converted to *fibrin during blood *clotting.

fibrinolysis The process which removes blood clots from the circulation by digestion of the insoluble *fibrin.

fibroblast A young, actively dividing cell that forms the fibres of *connective tissue. Fibroblasts develop into *fibrocytes.

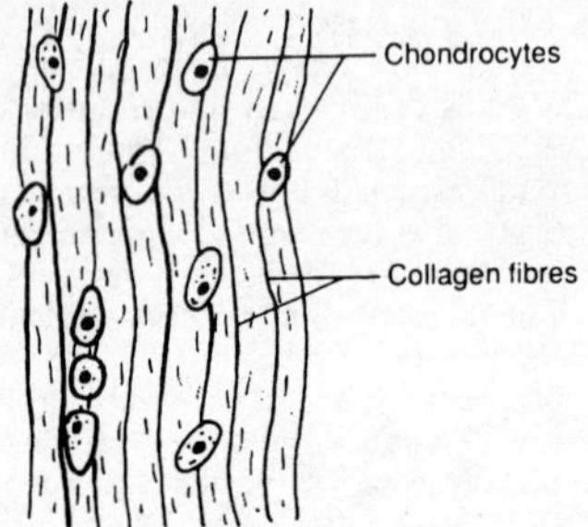

fibrocartilage

fibrocartilage (fibrous cartilage) A tough *cartilage with a matrix consisting of dense bundles of fibres. Fibrocartilage is located in intervertebral discs, pubic *symphysis, and the knee-joint. It has high tensile strength and is able to absorb considerable stress. *See also* cartilage.

fibrocyte Mature cell which forms the fibre of *connective tissue and maintains the matrix.

fibromyositis Combination of *strain and *inflammation of a muscle's *connective tissue coverings.

fibrosis Proliferation of fibrous *connective tissue; that is, scar tissue formation which is often the result of injury or inflammation.

fibrositis Inflammation of the fibrous connective tissue of muscles and tendon sheaths. The affected area is tender to the touch and painful. Although the condition is exacerbated by exercise, range of movement is not usually affected. The term is often applied rather loosely to any condition in the shoulder or upper back characterized by a dull ache. Fibrositis may result from chilling, toxic influences, chronic strain, or physical fatigue. It often responds well to heat and massage treatment. *See also* muscular rheumatism.

fibrous cartilage *See* fibrocartilage.

fibrous connective tissue *See* dense regular connective tissue.

fibrous joint A *joint which has no movement at all. The ends of the bones forming the joint are dovetailed together and connected by tough fibrous tissue.

fibrous protein An insoluble *protein which usually has an extended strand-like appearance. It is also called structural protein because it forms an integral part of body structures. *See also* collagen; elastin; and keratin.

fibrous tissue Component of a *fibrous joint.

fibula A stick-like long bone which articulates proximally and distally with the lateral ends of the *tibia. The lower end of the fibula forms the *lateral malleolus. The fibula stabilizes the ankle-joint but is non-weight-bearing.

Fick's principle A principle first proposed by the German physiologist Adolf Fick. He established that it is possible to calculate the lung blood flow from a knowledge of the oxygen absorbed by every 100 ml of blood during its passage through the lungs and the total oxygen uptake per minute. Since the lung blood flow is equal to the output from the left ventricle, this knowledge can be used to calculate cardiac output (Q), which is given by:

$$Q = (\text{oxygen uptake in ml min}^{-1}/A-V \text{ oxygen difference}) \times 100,$$

where A–V oxygen difference is the difference in the oxygen content betwen the blood leaving the lungs and blood arriving at the lungs expressed as ml per 100 ml of blood.

Fiedler's contingency model of leadership effectiveness *See* Fiedler's contingency theory.

Fiedler's contingency theory (Fiedler's contingency model of leadership effectiveness) A theory of *leadership which suggests that a particular personality disposition of a coach effective in one situation may not be effective in another. Coaches are viewed as being either task-centred and autocratic or athlete-centred and democratic. The task-centred coaches, high in *task motivation, are believed to be more effective in both the least and most favourable conditions. The athlete-centred coaches, high in *relationship motivation, are believed to be more effective in moderately favourable conditions. It is proposed that coach effectiveness can be improved by changing either personality or situational features, with the latter being easier to control.

field experiment An experiment conducted in a natural setting. The conditions of a field experiments are usually difficult to replicate.

field of vision The area that can be seen without moving the eyes or head. It is measured as degrees visible with both eyes while looking straight ahead. A wide field of vision reduces unnecessary head and eye movement.

field test In *sports science, this is usually a measurement of a *physiological function that is produced while the athlete is performing in a simulated or actual competitive situation. Usually such tests are not as reliable as *laboratory tests, but often have greater *validity because of their greater specificity.

field theory A theory, derived in part from *Gestalt psychology, in which *constructs from biology and physics have been borrowed to explain complex psychosocial behaviours and interactions. Field theory takes a holistic and dynamic view of psychological events as systems of psychological energy which can be represented mathematically; it holds that a person has personality and reacts from the very beginning as a whole. Psychosocial behaviour is seen as the outcome of interacting forces (psychological, intellectual, emotional, and social) similar to those operating within the field theory of physics.

figural after-effects A perceptual distortion that is produced after an extended period of exposure to a particular *stimulus or combination of stimuli. For example, after a person has concentrated on curved lines for a while, straight lines may be perceived as being slightly curved.

figuration The network of mobile links which occurs between people in any social context, but which is typified by those taking part in a sports game. The figuration indicates the interdependencies and interactions (including tensions) of the people involved which may result in both co-operation and conflict.

figurational sociology The sociological approach based on figuration of Norbert Elias (*see* Eliasian) and those influenced by his writing.

fine motor skill A *skill that requires delicate muscular control and in which certain parts of the body move within a limited area in order to produce accurate responses. Examples of fine motor skills are putting in golf, and rifle-shooting. *Compare* gross motor skill.

finger dexterity A skill-oriented ability underlying tasks in which small objects are manipulated primarily with the fingers; for example, spin bowling.

finger extensor A muscle which effects *extension of the fingers. Finger extensors include the *extensor digitorum, *extensor pollicis longus, *extensor pollicis brevis (thumb), and the *extensor indicis (little finger).

finger flexor A muscle which effects *flexion of the fingers. Finger flexors include the *flexor digitorum superficialis and *flexor digitorum profundus, with the thumb flexor being the *flexor pollicis longus.

finger-joint *See* interphalangeal joint.

first-class lever A *lever which has its *fulcrum between the *point of resistance and the *point of effort. In the human body, a first-class lever is activated when the head is raised off the chest.

first-degree strain *See* mild strain.

first law of thermodynamics *See* conservation of energy.

first-order traits (first-order factors; primary factors) *Innate *source traits of personality. *Compare* second-order traits.

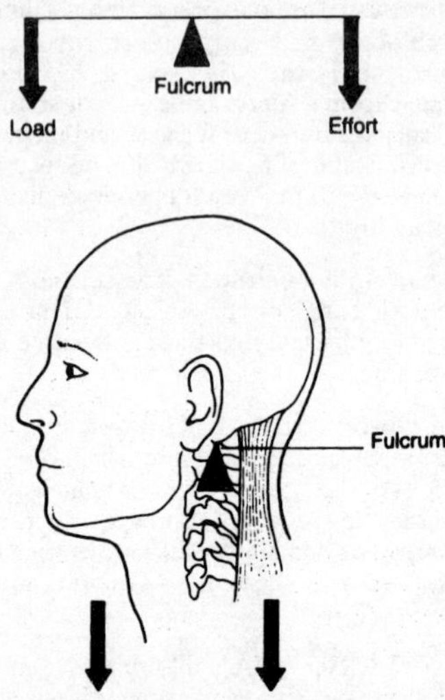

first-class lever

fissure 1 A groove or cleft-like defect in the skin or mucous membranes (*see* anal fissure). 2 A groove or cleft, such as a narrow, slit-like opening in bone through which blood vessels and nerves can pass. 3 Deep groove of tissue on the surface of the *cerebral hemispheres.

fistula An abnormal connection between a hollow organ and the exterior, or between two hollow organs.

fitness The ability of an individual to live a happy and well-balanced life. Fitness involves not only physical, but also intellectual, emotional, social, and spiritual aspects of an individual. These components of fitness interact and are interdependent so that if any component deviates from normal it affects the individual's overall fitness and ability to meet the demands placed on the individual by his or her way of life. Clearly, fitness is a relative term which must relate to each individual and has no absolute value. *Compare* unfitness. *See also* physical fitness.

fitness continuum A continuum used to describe a person's level of fitness. It extends from optimal capacity to accomplish a person's goals, through lack of disease, to severe disease and, finally, to death.

fitness target zone A range of levels of intensity of exercise from the minimum necessary to improve *physical fitness to a maximum amount above which exercise may be harmful.

fitness test A test usually conducted to assess an individual's *physical fitness level as an essential prerequisite before an injured sportsperson returns to competition. *See also* ECG.

Fitt's law A mathematical expression of the trade-off between the speed and accuracy of a movement. For a simple aiming movement, the average movement time (T) is linearly related to the $\log_2$ of the ratio of the movement amplitude (A) and target width (W), as follows:

$$T = a + b\log_2(2A/W)$$

The law indicates that as speed of movement increases, accuracy tends to decrease. The law holds for a wide variety of movements.

fixation A firm, stable, or inflexible aspect of behaviour. In childhood, fixation may result from traumatic events preventing the child from progressing to the next stage of mental development.

fixator (**stabilizer**) Muscle that immobilizes one or more bones, allowing other muscles to act from a stable base. Fixators stabilize joints, preventing undesirable movements.

fixed-action patterns (**fixed-pattern response**) Patterns of motor action which appear to be stereotyped, genetically-defined, and triggered as a single programmed action. Fixed-action patterns can be completed without the involvement of *feedback.

fixed-choice questionnaire Questionnaire in which the questions posed are accompanied by a range of answers from which the respondents are asked to indicate which, out of the fixed choices, best applies to themselves. Such questionnaires are useful in gathering data and standardizing responses but there is a danger that none of the fixed-choice responses really applies to the respondent or that the researcher's own meaning is imposed on the respondent.

fixed joint *See* fibrous joint.

fixed-pattern response *See* fixed-action pattern.

flaccid Flabby; lacking muscular *tone.

flat bone A *bone which is smooth, flattened, and usually slightly curved. Flat bones have two roughly parallel surfaces of *compact bone with a layer of *spongy bone between them. They have a protective function as with the *sternum and the bones forming the vault of the *cranium.

flat feet *See* fallen arches.

flavin adenine dinucleotide *See* FAD.

flaw A systematic *error in the performance of a *motor skill. Flaws occur because of faulty learning and, according to some theorists, result in ingrained mistakes in the motor programme. Usually, in order to eradicate the flaw, the whole skill has to be relearned.

flexed-and-tensed arm girth Maximum circumference of the arm (usually the right arm) in *supination when held at an angle of 45° with the *biceps fully tensed.

flexibility The range of motion of a joint. Flexibility is a measure of the ability of the muscle tendon units to elongate within the physical restrictions of the joint. Therefore, flexibility of a joint is affected by the nature of the joint structure, the condition of the *ligaments and *fascia that surrounds the joint, and muscle *extensibility. Flexibility may also be limited by the skin, *connective tissue, and *bones around the joint. High levels of flexibility are generally regarded as being important for good *health and *fitness as well as for specific sports. Flexibility exercises have been prescribed for the relief of *dysmenorrhoea, general neuromuscular tension, and low back-pains. However, an athlete who concentrates on flexibility exercises at the expense of strength-training may reduce joint stability (*see* benign hypermobility; and hypermobile joint disease). *See also* dynamic flexibility; and static flexibility.

flexibility test A method of measuring the *range of motion of a *joint or a series of joints. Tests include the direct measurement of the angular displacement of a joint using a *goniometer, *flexometer, still photography, or *X-rays. There are many indirect measurements of flexibility which involve taking linear measurements of the distances between two body-segments or between a part of the body and an external object. These tests include the *standing toe-touch test and the *sitting toe-touch test. Such indirect tests are quite easy to perform, but sometimes difficult to interpret because the movements are quite complex and there is uncertainty about which joints and muscles are involved.

flexion Bending movement that decreases the angle of the joint and brings two articulating bones closer together. *Compare* extension. *See also* dorsiflexion.

flexometer Instrument which uses a gravity needle and compass for the direct measurement of the range of motion about a joint (*see* static flexibility).

flexor A muscle which causes a *joint to bend.

flexor carpi radialis Muscle running diagonally across the forearm. Midway along its course its fleshy belly is replaced by a flat *tendon which becomes cord-like at the wrist. It has its *origin on the *medial *epicondyle of the humerus and its *insertions at the base of the second and third *metacarpals. It is a powerful *flexor of the wrist, and is involved in *abduction of the wrist. It also acts as a *synergist during elbow flexion.

flexor carpi ulnaris A two-headed *muscle which is the most *medial muscle of the *anterior forearm. It has its *origins on the medial *epicondyle of the *humerus and the *olecranon process of the ulna. Its insertions are on the *pisiform, the *hamate, and the fifth *metacarpal bones. It is a powerful wrist *flexor and hand *abductor working in concert with the *extensor carpi ulnaris. It stabilizes the wrist during finger extension.

flexor digitorum longus A long, narrow deep *muscle in the *posterior compartment of the leg. It has its *origin on the posterior surface of the *tibia and its *insertion tendon runs behind the *medial malleolus and splits into four parts to insert into the *distal *phalanges of the second to fifth toes. It bends the great toe and is involved in *plantar flexion and *inversion of the foot, and it helps the foot 'grip' the ground.

flexor digitorum superficialis A two-headed *superficial muscle at the *distal end of the forearm. It has its *origins on the *medial *epicondyle of the *humerus, the medial surface, and *coronoid process of the *ulna, and the shaft of the *radius. Its *insertion is by four tendons onto the middle *phalanges of the second to fifth fingers. Its actions include *flexion of the wrist and middle phalanges of the second to fifth fingers.

flexor hallucis longus A *bipennate muscle of the *posterior compartment of the leg with its *origins on the middle part of the shaft of the *fibula and the *interosseous membrane between the fibula and *tibia. Its *insertion is via a tendon which runs under the foot and *distal *phalanx of the great toe. Its actions include *plantar flexion, foot *inversion, and *flexion of the great toe. It is the muscle responsible for the 'push off' during walking.

flexor pollicis longus A deep muscle of the forearm, partly covered by the *flexor digitorum superficialis. It has its *origins on the *anterior surface of the *radius and the *interosseous membrane. Its insertion is on the *distal *phalanx of the thumb. Its actions include *flexion of the distal phalanx of the thumb and it also acts as a weak *flexor of the wrist.

flexor pollicis profundus A *deep muscle of the forearm, entirely covered by the *flexor digitalis superficialis. It has an extensive *origin on the anteromedial surface of the *ulna and the *interosseous membrane between the ulna and *radius. Its *insertion is via four tendons onto the *distal *phalanges of the second to fifth fingers. It is the only muscle which can flex the distal *interphalangeal joints. It is also a slow-acting finger *flexor and assists in wrist *flexion.

flexural rigidity The ratio of *stress to *strain in an *elastic material when that material is being bent. *See also* elastic modulus.

flight-path *See* trajectory.

flight-time *See* time of flight.

floating ribs The eleventh and twelfth ribs. They are *false ribs which have no anterior attachment; their *costal cartilage is embedded in muscle.

flooding A method of coping with *stress in which the subject is exposed to anxiety-provoking stimuli in the absence of the unpleasant experiences or feelings usually associated with those stimuli in the hope that the *anxiety will be eradicated by *extinction.

floor effects A restriction on performance imposed by the physiological or psychological limitations of the performer, or by a scoring system that places a minimum on the score that a performer can achieve in a task. For example, there must be a score of more than 0 s for a test of *reaction time. As a person approaches the floor, it becomes increasingly difficult to improve the performance. *Compare* ceiling effects.

flotation The ability of a body to float in a fluid. Flotation occurs if the body-weight is less than the maximum *buoyant force of the fluid. The *specific gravity is a measure of a body's capacity to float in water. Although flotation is a distinct advantage to a swimmer, there are many people who have learnt to swim without this ability, and some have broken world records.

flotation, principle of *See* Archimedes' principle.

flow A psychological state of extreme well-being which is sometimes experienced during the performance of an activity. A person experiencing flow has a feeling of great pleasure, satisfaction, and enjoyment in his or her actual performance. The subjective experience of doing the performance is the primary reward rather than the outcome. Flow is similar to *peak performance, but tends to be more voluntary in nature. Flow is thought to occur when there is a balance between the demands of the task and the skill one possesses.

flow-meter A device for measuring the rate of flow of a gas. Flow-meters are used to measure the rate of air movements in graded exercise tests.

fluctuation The characteristic feeling obtained by placing the fingers of one hand upon one side of a swelling containing fluid and, with the fingers of the other hand, tapping a distant point on the swelling. The sensation of a wave motion communicated from one hand to the other is an important *sign of the presence of an *abscess or the effusion of fluid into a joint.

fludrocortisone A synthetic *drug belonging to the *corticosteroids which are on the *IOC list of restricted substances. Side-effects of its use include muscle weakness and bone disorders.

fluid A substance which assumes the shape of the vessel in which it is contained. A fluid may be a gas or liquid.

fluid-flow *See* laminar flow.

fluid friction *See* fluid resistance.

fluidity Reciprocal *viscosity; the *SI unit for fluidity is the rhe, which is the reciprocal of the *poise.

fluid mechanics Study of the conditions which govern the movement of *fluids and the movement of objects through fluids, such as the study of the movement of the human body through air or water.

fluid resistance (fluid friction) Resistance to motion of a body in a *fluid, due to forces of *friction being exerted between the body and the fluid. Fluid resistance is directly proportional to the cross-sectional area of the body at right angles to the motion and directly proportional to the square of the *velocity of the body relative to the fluid. *See also* drag; form friction; and surface friction.

fluid retention (water retention) The retention of a fluid, mainly water, in the body. The amount of water within the human body is usually kept relatively constant by osmoregulation; excess water intake usually results in extra water being eliminated in the *urine (*see* water balance). However, water retention increases with increased storage of *carbohydrates as the water becomes bound to *glycogen molecules (*see* carbohydrate-loading).

fluoride A compound of *fluorine. Fluoride has been added artificially to water to harden teeth, but too much can cause discolouration and may increase the risk of *osteoporosis.

fluorine A chemical *element taking the form of a pale, yellow-green gas with similar properties to *chlorine. It is found in bones and teeth and contributes to their stability.

flurazepam A *benzodiazepine derivative used as a tranquilizer in some sleeping tablets. It has relatively low toxicity and few known side-effects, although it can cause dizziness and disturb muscular co-ordination.

flutter A disturbance of the normal rhythm of the heart in which the heart beats more rapidly than normal, but not so rapidly or chaotically as with *fibrillation.

flux 1 A flow or discharge of substances across a given area or in a given direction. **2** A state of continuous change or instability. **3** An excessive discharge of fluid from the body (e.g., watery faeces in diarrhoea).

FMN *See* vitamin B_2.

focal degeneration Deterioration in the function of a *tendon due to the formation of a tiny lesion with a microscopic loss in the continuity of *collagen, and the presence of blood vessels and granulation tissue. Healing is slow and disability may persist. It may require surgical decompression.

focus 1 In mathematics, one of the fixed points used to define a curve by a linear relationship with the distance of these fixed points to any point in the curve. *See also* parabola. **2** The degree to which an individual can integrate various factors and use them simultaneously to construct a more complete and balanced picture of his or her internal or external world. *See also* attentional style.

focused attention *See* narrowing.

focusing Concentrating on relevant *stimuli even when distracting stimuli are present.

FOG fibre *See* fast oxidative glycolytic fibre.

folic acid A bright yellow, crystalline, water-soluble substance which acts as a *coenzyme involved in the synthesis of *methionine and certain other *amino acids, *choline, and DNA. Folic acid is essential for the formation of red blood cells. Deficiency causes anaemia, *diarrhoea, and other gastrointestinal disturbances. It is stable to heat but easily oxidized. Little is known about the effect of folic acid on physical performance, but a deficiency is likely to affect endurance athletes due to anaemia.

follicle A small cavity or sac.

Food and Drug Administration *See* FDA.

foot 1 Part of the body which includes the *tarsus (ankle), *metatarsus (instep), and *phalanges (toes). The foot supports the body-weight and serves as a lever to propel the body forwards during walking and running. Its many bones give it a segmented, pliable structure which adapts well to uneven surfaces, unlike a single bone. 2 Imperial unit of length; equal to 0.3048 m.

footballer's ankle An impingement *exostosis around the ankle-joint which commonly occurs in footballers and others who repeatedly overstretch the *ligaments and *joint capsule of the ankle. Overstretching causes the edges of the bones which make up the ankle to knock against each other. This happens particularly to the front of the *tibia which knocks against the upper *talus causing spikes of bone to develop and, if large, break off. X-rays reveal the small fragments of bone which have broken off.

footballer's groin *See* groin pain.

football hooliganism Violent crowd disorder and associated soccer-related disturbance which first gained public attention in the 1960s. Attempts have been made to explain football violence in terms of the psychological characteristics of the hooligans, but more recent sociological explanations *see* it as a ritualized form of behaviour which is media-amplified. The *civilizing process has resulted in a decrease in its acceptance. *See also* deviance amplification; labelling theory; moral panic; and violence.

foot injury Physical damage to the foot. The foot is subject to many over-use injuries caused by the stress on small bones which have to take the whole weight of the body. Good *training shoes are essential for protection. Orthotics are often used in the treatment of foot injuries. *See also* March fracture; and runner's toe.

foot length In *anthropometry, the distance between the *acropodion and the *pternion. *See also* body breadths.

foot-pound Unit of *work representing the application of a one-pound *force through a distance of one foot.

foot-poundal Unit of *work. One foot-pound is the work done by a *force of one poundal acting through a distance of one foot.

foramen A round or oval hole or opening in a bone, or between body cavities through which *nerves and *blood vessels can pass.

force The effect one body has on another body so that it can cause or tend to cause a body at rest to move, or cause a moving body to slow down, stop, increase its speed, or change its direction. Forces can also result in *deformative movements, rotational movements, and translational movements. That is, they can change the shape of a body, cause a body to rotate, or move the body from one place to another. Therefore, forces include any agency which alters or tends to alter a body's state of rest or uniform motion. Force is measured in *newtons and is the product of the *mass of an object and its linear *acceleration; that is, force = mass × acceleration. On the basis of this formula, three different types of forces may be identified: *shear force, *fast force, and *endurance force.

force arm *See* lever arm.

force-couple

force couple (couple) Two equal *forces which are acting simultaneously and in parallel on an object but in opposite directions around the object's *centre of gravity. Since the translatory forces (forces which produce linear motion) cancel each other out, such a force couple can only produce *rotation. Couple = force×distance between forces. A force couple is produced when a person sits in a rubber tube floating in the sea and pushes forward with one hand on one side of the ring, and backward with an equal force on the other side. The force couple causes the tube to spin. In sport, perfect force couples are rarely established and both rotation and *translation usually occurs.

forced-choice scale A scale often used in questionnaires in which the respondent is instructed to pick the one response that best describes his or her reaction. *See also* frequency scale; and Likert scale.

forced expiratory volume (FEV) The percentage of the vital capacity that is expired in 45 s. It is used as a measure of the expiratory power of the lungs.

forced-pace task A task or *motor skill in which the timing and manner of performance is dictated by the environment rather than the performer.

force–length relationship The relationship between a muscle's length and the *force it can exert; the longer the distance between the *origin and the *insertion of a muscle, the higher the active force that can be obtained. The exact relationship varies for different muscles.

force moment *See* torque.

force platform An instrument which measures the magnitude and direction of a *force between a person and the ground.

force summation In the human body, the combination of a number of *forces produced by different body-parts. When a person is moving or attempting to move an object, several different parts act together to maximize the force. In theory, force summation occurs when all the body-parts act simutaneously. In practice, the strongest and slowest body-segments around the *centre of gravity, such as the trunk and thighs, move first, followed by the weaker, lighter, and faster extremities. This is known as *sequential acceleration of body-parts and results in successive force summation. To gain maximum force, summation also needs sequential stabilization of the body-parts, with some body-parts having to be fixed at stable points while other parts produce the effective forces. *See also* sequential force summation; and simultaneous force summation.

force vector A *vector quantity in which direction and the magnitude of *force is specified.

force–velocity curve A graph which shows the relationship between muscle tension and the velocity of the shortening or lengthening of the muscle. It is used to analyse the effects of training and to identify muscle fibre types used in exercises.

force–velocity principle A principle founded on application of the *force–velocity relationship. If training loads are selected from the force end of the curve so that loads are higher but movement velocity lower, the training effect is primarily in that part of the force velocity curve (that is, increased strength). If the training zone is close to the velocity end of the curve, then the training effect is also mainly in the velocity characteristics (that is, increased speed). The effects depend on the training status of the subject; if the subject is weak and slow, training will improve both strength and speed regardless of which part of the force–velocity curve is used.

force–velocity relationship The velocity at which a muscle shortens is inversely related to the load it must move; thus if a load is great, the velocity of shortening is slow; conversely, as the velocity of movement increases, the total tension produced by the muscle decreases.

forearm (antebrachium) Area of the arm extending from the fingertips to the elbow-point (*see* olecranon process).

forearm extension *See* elbow extension.

forearm extensor A muscle which effects *elbow extension.

forearm fexion *See* elbow flexion.

forearm flexor Muscle which effects *elbow flexion.

forearm girth In *anthropometry, the circumference of the right forearm when the hand is held palm up and relaxed. *See also* body girth.

forearm length In *anthropometry, the difference between the *radial height and the *stylion height.

forearm pronator *See* elbow pronator.

forearm supinator *See* elbow supinator.

forearm tenosynovitis An inflammation of a tendon sheath of any tendon in the hand or forearm. Forearm tenosynovitis affects the fingers and wrist, and is commonly caused by a direct blow but dietary imbalances and infections may also cause this problem.

forebrain The anterior part of *brain giving rise to *cerebral hemispheres, olfactory lobes (concerned with sense of smell), *pituitary gland, *pineal gland, and the *optic chiasma which carries nerve fibres from the eyes to the brain.

forefoot valgus Condition in which the first *metatarsals are in a more plantarflexed position (*see* plantar flexion) than the third to fifth metatarsals. Forefoot valgus can cause misalignment of articulations in the lower body, particularly *inversion of the subtalar joint (ankle) during weight-bearing. *Orthotics may be used to treat the condition. *Compare* forefoot varus.

forefoot varus A condition in which the first two *metatarsals are in a more dorsiflexed position (*see* dorsiflexion) than the third to fifth metatarsals. It causes *eversion of the ankle and misalignments of other articulations in the lower body during weight-bearing. Orthotics are used in the treatment of the condition. *Compare* forefoot valgus.

foreperiod In measurements of *reaction time, the interval between a warning signal and the presentation of a *stimulus to which the subject is expected to respond. It also refers to the period between a 'get set' command or signal and a 'go' at the start of a race. The duration and predictability of the foreperiod greatly influence reaction times.

form The manner of expressing a movement in time and space when performing a complex *gross motor skill. Form is unique from person to person, and though good form is usually associated with outstanding athletes, it is difficult to define exactly what constitutes good form. It is a factor taken into consideration in judging some sports, such as gymnastics, and relates to the aesthetic value of performance. Judges consider factors such as balance, symmetry, rhythm, and composition which contribute to the finished shape and action of the performance.

formal leadership theories Theories of *leadership behaviour which focus on the principles of good management and the formal aspects of organization. Formal leadership styles have strong similarities with *initiating structure. *Compare* human-relations theory.

form drag (frontal resistance, profile drag, pressure drag) The difference between the *resultant force acting on the front face of a body moving through a *fluid and the corresponding force on the rear face. The form drag of an asymmetrical body is a function of its orientation to the oncoming flow and is affected by the cross-sectional area of the body perpendicular to the flow, and the shape and smoothness of the body.

fossa A rounded basin-like depression in a bone which often provides a surface for articulation (e.g., the *acetabular fossa).

fossa suprasinatus A rounded depression on the upper surface of the spine of the shoulder-blade. It forms the *origin of the *supraspinatus muscle.

fovea In humans, a shallow pit about 1 mm in diameter in the centre of the *retina in which *cones are concentrated. There is no layer of nerve fibres over the fovea; it is an area of acute vision.

fovea capitis Small central pit in the *femur from which the *ligamentum teres runs to the *acetabulum in order to secure the *femur.

FR Respiratory frequency in breaths per minute.

fracture A break in bone resulting from more or less instantaneous application of excessive force. A suspected fracture requires proper medical diagnosis which includes X-radiography. *See also* comminuted fracture; compound fracture; compression fracture; depressed fracture; greenstick fracture; simple fracture; and spiral fracture.

frame of reference 1 In *sociology, a set of standards that determines and sanctions behaviour. **2** Any set of planes or curves, such as the co-ordinates and axes used to define a set of points.

Frankfort plane A plane which passes from the highest point of the ear-canal through to the lowest point of the eye-socket.

FRC *See* functional residual capacity.

free body diagram A sketch showing, in *vector form, all the *forces acting on a *body.

free energy Amount of *energy available to perform biological *work such as synthesis (*see* anabolism), *active transport, and the movement of thin filaments past thick filaments in muscle contraction (*see* sliding-filament theory). *Adenosine triphosphate is the most important source of free energy in the human body.

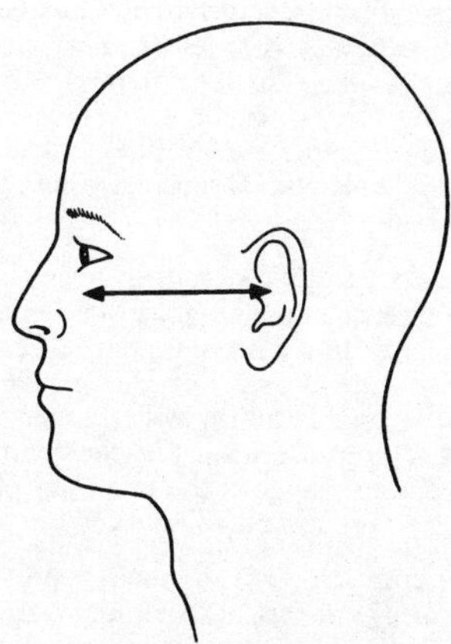

Frankfort plane

free fall The fall of an object which has only the gravitational pull of the earth acting on it. *See also* acceleration of free fall.

free fatty acid A *fatty acid that is only loosely bound to *plasma proteins in the *bloodstream. Free fatty acids are an important source of energy for exercises of long duration. High levels of free fatty acids in the bloodstream are considered by some as indicating high reserves of energy and a fitter metabolic state. Levels of free fatty acids decrease after endurance activity.

free phosphate Phosphate ions not bound tightly to an *atom, *molecule, or *ion.

free radical A chemical group that has unshared electrons available for a reaction.

free standing weight *See* free weight.

free weight (free-standing weight) A weight, such as a *barbell or *dumb-bell, not attached to a specialized weight machine or exercise device. Free weights allow movement in any direction and so lend themselves to a great variety of exercise routines for *weight-training. However, they do not isolate muscle action as clearly as weight-training machines.

freezing spray *See* aerosol administration.

Freiberg's disease An *osteochondritis affecting the heads of the *metatarsal bones.

frequency 1 In statistics, the number of members of a class or set (the absolute frequency), or the ratio of the number of members in a class to the total number of individuals under survey (the relative frequency). 2 Number of times an event occurs in a given period.

frequency code The code by which information concerning the nature of a *stimulus is conveyed in the nervous system. The frequency code consists of the number of *nerve impulses transmitted per unit time along a *neurone; changes in stimulus intensity cause a change in the frequency of the impulses. *See also* population code.

frequency curve A graphical representation of *frequency distribution, with the values a variable may take forming the *x*-axis and the number of times each value occurs (or percentage occurrence) forming the *y*-axis.

frequency distribution A way of representing observations in a table with at least two columns: the left-hand column contains the values which a variable may take, and the right-hand column contains the number of times each value occurs or its percentage occurrence.

frequency of training (training frequency) Number of days per week that an individual trains. Most fitness components require at least three days, and some up to six days of *training per week.

frequency scale A scale, often used in questionnaires, to measure *behaviours or *cognitions. The respondent circles the appropriate number indicating the frequency of a particular variable, and this number is used in the analysis of the results.

Freudian theory Theory concerning the structure and dynamics of *personality derived from the works of Sigmund Freud (1865–1939), one of the most important figures in psychoanalysis. Practitioners of Freudian theory divide mental experiences into the *conscious and the *unconscious; and the personality into *id, *ego, and *superego.

friction A *force offering resistance to the relative motion between surfaces in contact. Friction arises whenever one body moves or tends to move across the surface of another. Types of friction include moving friction; *rolling friction; and *sliding friction.

frictional bursitis *See* bursitis.

friction burn A burn caused by the skin rubbing against a surface such as synthetic turf. Friction-burns range from a superficial redness to deep abrasions. They should be treated as any other burn. *See also* mat burn

friction, first law of A scientific law which states that for two dry surfaces, the frictional force is proportional to the *normal reaction, and is dependent on the nature of the surfaces: friction=normal reaction×coefficient of friction.

friction sore A sore which develops from mechanical irritation of the skin, usually the hands and feet. *See also* friction burn.

frontal In anatomy, pertaining to the forehead.

frontal plane (coronal plane) An imaginary line which passes through the body from left to right, dividing body or body-part into an *anterior and a *posterior portion.

frontal resistance *See* form drag.

front region The public, open part of a social organization where its members may be viewed by non-members. *Compare* back region.

front thigh skinfold A *skinfold measurement of a vertical fold of tissue in the middle of the interior surface of the thigh, along the long axis of the femur, when the leg is flexed at a 90° angle at the knee.

frostbite A collective name for tissue damage resulting from exposure to very low temperatures. Affected parts should not be rubbed because there is no blood circulation in the tissues but should be gently warmed in tepid water. The extent of the frostbite depends on the temperature, the length of the exposure, and the wind chill factor. For temperatures above freezing, dampness is also an important factor.

frozen shoulder Chronic pain, inflammation and restricted movement in the shoulder-joint. A frozen shoulder is a common over-use injury in the 50+ age-group. It may be caused by wrenching the shoulder, resulting in a protective spasm of the subscapular muscle, but it may follow a *stroke or *myocardial infarction, or develop for no apparent reason. Treatment is by gentle massage and exercises, sometimes combined with *corticosteroid treatment.

fructose *Carbohydrate which is thought to be an atypical *ketose sugar because it acts as a reducing sugar. Fructose is a *monosaccharide sugar found in honey and sweet fruits. It is often added to drinks as a sweetener because it is much sweeter and more readily absorbed than *glucose. It can be quickly converted to fat.

fruitarian A vegetarian who has a diet of raw or dried fruit, nuts, seeds, honey, and vegetable oil. *See also* vegetarian diet.

frusemide A *drug belonging to the *diuretics which are on the *IOC list of *banned substances. Frusemide is used to treat kidney complaints and *high blood pressure. Side-effects include vomiting and nausea.

frustration A psychological state which results when the satisfaction of motivated behaviour is rendered difficult or impossible.

frustration–aggression hypothesis The hypothesis which posits that *frustration increases the likelihood of aggressive behaviour and that aggressive behaviour results from frustration which arises because the aggressor is unable to attain an instrumental goal. If the frustrated person cannot be aggressive towards the cause of the frustration, then he or she will attempt to displace the aggression onto another person or object. Some people have suggested that competitive sport, by its very nature, produces frustration because there are usually losers. Consequently they regard sport as being inherently aggressive. *See also* instinct theory of aggression; and social-learning theory.

frustration tolerance The ability to withstand *frustration without developing inadequate modes of response, such as 'going to pieces' emotionally or becoming neurotic.

FTG fibre *See* fast twitch glycolytic fibre.

fulcrum Fixed point of support of a *lever which acts as the pivot about which the lever turns. In *biomechanics, when viewing movement of the skeleton, the fulcrum is a fixed point, usually a joint, on which a bony lever moves.

function 1 A mathematical expression describing the relationship between *variables. In scientific literature, a *dependent variable may be expressed as a function of one or more *independent variables. 2 Applied to a group, the behaviour of the group and how it operates. 3 In *sociology, the contribution to the working and maintenance of a social system made by a particular social occurrence.

functional activities Activities which have beneficial influences on society. *See also* functionalism.

functional aggressive behaviour Aggressive or assertive behaviour, such as rebounding, stealing, or shot-blocking in basketball, that facilitates successful performance. *Compare* dysfunctional aggressive performance.

functional brain systems Networks of *neurones, not localized within one region of the brain. They include the *limbic system and *reticular formation.

functional capacity Maximal oxygen uptake expressed in *METs or millilitres of oxygen per kilogram of body-weight. *See also* aerobic capacity.

functionalism A major sociological perspective which views society as composed of parts or institutions. These parts include the family, the church, the military, the education system, and sports organizations. In a healthy society, all these parts work together to ensure that the society remains healthy. *Compare* dysfunctionalism

functionalist explanation Explanation of the persistence of any feature of society in which this feature makes an essential contribution to the maintenance of the society or social system. Sometimes biological analogies are made in functionalist explanations in which the society or system is regarded as being similar to a biological organism and its features as persisting merely to help that organism survive.

functionalist perspective of social inequality A viewpoint which argues that social inequality is necessary for the survival of any society or for any small or large organization. It is argued that without this inequality, division of labour would be difficult (not everyone can be team captain). It is also argued that to attract people to both the important and less important roles there must be variation in rewards which motivates individuals to make the effort needed to gain the top positions. *Compare* conflict perspective of social inequality.

functionalist perspective of sport A view of the relationship between sport and politics which suggests that sport is used to promote common values held essential to the integration and developmment of a society. Thus sport helps to maintain social order. *Compare* conflict perspective.

functional model of attribution A model used by sport psychologists to study *attributions. It assumes that the main function of an individual's attributions of the causes for a particular performance is to maintain *self-esteem. Thus athletes tend to attribute positive outcomes to personal controls, (e.g effort) and negative outcomes to external factors, such as luck. The model assumes that athletes adopt a *self-serving attributional bias.

functional model of leadership A *leadership theory which proposes that it is difficult for a single leader to display both high levels of task and relationship behaviour at the same time. Therefore, a single coach cannot satisfy the needs of all athletes and might require the assistance of other coaches to complement his or her behaviour. For example, if a head coach is very task-oriented, an athlete-oriented assistant coach might be selected to complement the head coach's behaviour.

functional overload Training that is closely related to the conditions which will be experienced in competition but with a greater workload than normal. For track events, for example, training might be carried out in heavy boots and harness. Functional overload ensures that the same muscle groups and patterns of movement are involved in both training and competition.

functional proteins *See* globular proteins.

functional residual capacity (FRC) The volume of air remaining in the lungs after resting expiration; typically about 2.4l, with a slight increase during exercise.

functional short leg A condition in which the anatomical leg lengths are equal, but the legs are functionally unequal because of differences in *pronation or *supination of one foot relative to the other. Functional short leg may cause complications and joint dysfunctions in the lower back. *Compare* anatomical short leg.

fundamental motor skill A *motor skill such as sprinting, jumping, or throwing which is a common element in many sports and games.

fundamental movement pattern A movement which forms part of a more complex skill. In some theories of motor control, fundamental movement patterns are represented in *motor programmes as subroutines. There are three main types: locomotor (e.g., walking and skipping), non-locomotor (e.g., balancing and stretching), and manipulation (e.g., kicking and throwing).

fundamental skills *See* basic movements.

fundamental units The physical quantities of matter, space, and time. *See also* base units.

fundus The part of an *organ farthest from its opening; the base of an organ.

fungal infections Diseases, such as *athlete's foot, which are caused by a *fungus.

fungus (pl. fungi) A plant-like organism which, lacking chlorophyll, is unable to photosynthesize and obtains nutrients by absorbing organic matter from its surroundings.

funiculus **1** A cord-like stucture, such as a bundle of *nerve fibres enclosed in a sheath.

2 A column of white matter in each lateral half of the *spinal cord.

furfendrex A *drug belonging to the *stimulants which are on the *IOC list of *banned substances.

furuncle *See* boil.

fusiform muscle A spindle-shaped *muscle, such as the *biceps brachii, with an expanded belly. The *fascicles are arranged more or less parallel to each other and the long axes of the fascicles run parallel to the long axis of the muscle to converge at each end. This strap-like arrangement provides the greatest degree of shortening and enables the muscle to perform a large range of movements quickly, but it is not a very powerful type of muscle. *Compare* pennate muscle.

G

GABA *See* γ-aminobutyric acid.

gain The relationship, usually expressed as a ratio, between the amount of input to a system and the output produced by it.

gait Style of walking or running. Gait is an important sign of health and disease. A person walking with toes turned out at right angles may be suffering from *flat feet, or the gait may be due to stiffness (following disease of the knee-joint, for example).

galactose A *simple sugar found mainly in yeast and liver. It is also a constituent of milk and *lactose.

gall-bladder A small sac lying beneath the right lobe of the liver; it stores *bile.

gallstones (cholelithiasis) Concretions of *bile, *cholesterol, and calcium salts which form in the gall-bladder where they may cause severe pain. They may pass into the bile duct where they form an obstruction. Pain is relieved with *analgesics which may contain *banned substances. Surgical removal of the gallstones is often necessary. Physical exertion during an acute attack of gallstones is strongly contra-indicated. Activity is usually possible during symptom-free periods.

galvanic skin response The ease with which a small electric current flows between two points on the skin. When the body is tense or the subject emotional, the sweat glands become more active increasing moisture on the skin which allows electric current to flow more readily. Thus galvanic skin responses are often used to indicate the affect of stressors on a person. They may also be used in relaxation training: information about the galvanic skin response is fed back aurally or visually to the subject who can, with practice, learn to increase or decrease sweating on the skin by learning to relax or tense muscles (*see* biofeedback).

game A contrived competitive experience existing in its own time and space.

gamesmanship (gamespersonship) The art of winning or defeating opponents by cunning practices without actually breaking the rules.

gamespersonship *See* gamesmanship.

game theory Mathematical theory concerned with the optimum choice of strategy in situations involving a conflict of interest. *See also* theory of games.

γ-aminobutyric acid (GABA) An *amino acid which functions as an *ionotropic neurotransmitter. It is secreted by some *neurones in the *cerebellum and *spinal cord where its effects are generally inhibitory. GABA acts as a muscle relaxant. Some anti-anxiety drugs, such as the *benzodiazepines, are thought to have their effects mediated by GABA. It is suspected that GABA has been used by some sports competitors to reduce *anxiety.

γ globulin A class of specialized plasma proteins. Nearly all γ globulins are *immunoglobulins which recognize and deactivate bacterial toxins and some viruses; they function in the immune response which helps protect the body from invasive foreign substances.

γ loop *See* γ system.

γ motor neurone A type of small *efferent nerve cell that innervates the ends of *intrafusal muscle fibre within a *muscle spindle.

γ system (γ loop) A nerve pathway by which the *central nervous system controls muscle contractions. It carries nerve impulses from the *motor cortex which stimulate *γ motor neurones in a *muscle, causing *muscle spindles to be stretched. Sensory impulses are sent from the spindles to the *spinal cord, stimulating the *α motor neurones and causing the muscle to contract. The sensory impulses also convey information to the central nervous system about the state of the muscle. This information is needed for the execution of smooth, co-ordinated, voluntary movements. *See also* stretch reflex.

ganglion 1 A cyst-like mass of fibrous tissue on a tendon or in an *aponeurosis. The ganglion is a fibrous sac which fills with fluid. It develops into a relatively painless swelling on the top of the wrist, on the inside of the hand, or on the outside of the knee. 2 A collection of *neurone cell bodies located outside the *central nervous system.

gangrene Local death of body tissue due to a deficient blood supply. The dead tissue may decay through putrefaction by bacteria. Gangrene can be caused by *disease, *injury, *frost-bite, or *burns.

garlic A herb containing active ingredients which may lower *cholesterol level.

gas chromatography An analytical technique used to detect *drugs and their *metabolites. The chemical constituents of the sample are absorbed onto a stationary phase of the apparatus. A gas then displaces these chemicals at different rates, under different physical conditions. The molecules leaving the apparatus are monitored and recorded on a chart. The peaks in the chart are compared with those of known standard drugs.

gaseous exchange The transfer of gases, especially oxygen and carbon dioxide, between a person and the environment, and between *tissues and the *blood. Gaseous exchange occurs between air in the *alveoli and blood in the *pulmonary *capillaries, and between respiring tissues and capillaries.

gas exchange ratio *See* respiratory exchange ratio.

gas laws Laws which govern the physical state of a gas (e.g., its temperature, pressure, and volume). *See* Boyles's law; Charles's law; and Henry's law.

gastric gland A *gland in the stomach wall contributing to *gastric juices.

gastric juice Fluid secreted into the stomach containing *pepsin, *renin, and *hydrochloric acid.

gastritis Inflammation of the lining of the stomach due to a stomach ulcer or some other gastrointestinal disorder. Symptoms include nausea, and pain in the pit of the stomach. Important factors affecting the disorder include regularity of meals, stress, and anxiety. Gastritis does not necessarily interfere with physical activity, but it may result in deteriorated performances. The condition may be a warning sign that all is not well.

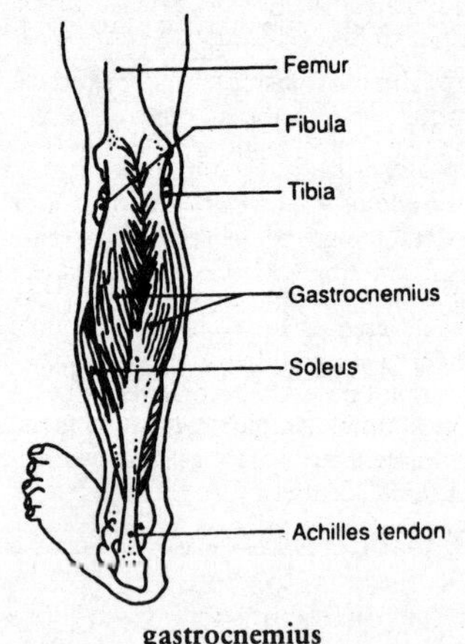

gastrocnemius

gastrocnemius A *superficial muscle with two prominent *bellies that form the *proximal curve of the posterior *calf. Its *origin consists of two heads which attach to the *medial and *lateral *condyles of *femur. Its *insertion is on the *calcaneous bone via the *Achilles tendon. Its actions include *plantar flexion of the foot when the knee is extended and *flexion of the knee when the foot is dorsiflexed.

gastroenteritis Inflammation of the stomach and intestines usually due to a bacterial or viral infection associated with food poisoning. Symptoms include *nausea, *vomiting, and *diarrhoea. Gastroenteritis can cause *dehydration which adversely affects physical activity. Training and competition should be avoided until the infection is cleared, and the salt and water balance have returned to normal.

gate out To exclude or ignore irrelevant sensory information.

gelatin A jelly-like substance produced when tissues such as *tendons and *ligaments, which contain *collagen, are boiled in water. Gelatin has been used as a source of dietary protein.

gemellus One of two small thigh muscles, the gemellus superior and the gemellus inferior, which have a common *insertion on the *greater trochanter of the *femur. The *origin of the gemellus superior is on the spine of the *ischium and that of the gemellus inferior on the *ischial tuberosity which are considered to extra-pelvic portions of the *obturator internus. The actions of the gemellus include lateral *rotation of the thigh and stabilization of the hip-joint.

gender In *sociology, the social and cultural differences between men and women. Gender is a social division frequently based on, but not necessarily coincident with, anatomical differences; it refers to attributes which are categorized as *masculine and *feminine. Gender is not biologically-determined but is socially and culturally determined. *Compare* sex.

gender differentiation The process of assigning social significance to biological differences between the sexes. Gender differentiation often results in gender inequality, with one gender being considered inferior to the other with regards to certain activities.

gender identity The subjective perception a person has of his or her own gender. Gender identity occurs as a result of a complex interaction between the individual and others, and results in the internalization of masculine and feminine traits.

gender inequality Social process by which people are treated differently and disadvantageously, under similar circumstances, on the basis of *gender. *See also* sex discrimination.

gender relations The social relations between males and females. In most social contexts, males have more power than females.

gender role conflict A conflict which may result from a male taking part in social activities which are ascribed as feminine, or a female taking part in activities ascribed as masculine.

gender role stereotyping The labelling of certain forms of behaviour and actions as being appropriate to one sex but not the other.

gender stratification *See* sex stratification.

gene A biological unit of heredity which transmits hereditary information. It is generally considered that one gene contains the information responsible for the synthesis of one *polypeptide chain.

genealogical method A method, based on the study of an individual's family history, of determining the effect of inheritance on any individual trait. It has been used to ascertain whether sporting proficiency runs in a family.

general adaptation syndrome A set of characteristics which are manifested in the body as a response to *stress. The syndrome typically has three stages. Initially, a stage called the alarm reaction occurs when there is an increase in heartrate and mobilization of glucose which occurs, for example, as an acute adaptation to exercise. During this stage, resistance is temporarily lowered and defence mechanisms activated. This is followed by a resistance stage where the body shows maximum adaptation to the stress which includes an increase in the activity of the *adrenal cortex, changes in muscle tone, and an increased heartrate. If stress persists, a third stage of exhaustion occurs during which the defences of the body begin to breakdown. Overstress causes changes such as gastrointestinal ulceration, enlargement and hyperactivity of the adrenal cortex, pathological heart conditions, and strains to the muscles, tendons, and joints.

general avoidance skill A general awareness of danger and the ability to take avoidance measures when confronted with high-risk situations. *See also* escape-training.

generalization (stimulus generalization) Tendency of a person to respond to an unfamiliar *stimulus or situation in a manner similar to a trained response to a familiar stimulus. Generalization is believed to be important in *transfer of training.

generalized motor program A *motor program consisting of a group of muscle commands, formed and stored in the *central nervous system, whose expression can be varied depending on the choice of certain *parameters. It is believed that a motor program for a particular kind of activity is stored in the *memory and that a unique pattern of activity will result if the program is executed. However, in order to execute the program, certain parameters must be applied to the program which define exactly how it is to be executed on that particular trial. Since the program's output, in terms of movement of the limbs, can be altered somewhat according to the parameters chosen on a particular trial, the program is said to be generalized.

general malabsorption *See* coeliac disease.

general motion A combination of *linear motions and *angular motions; the usual form of motion in sport. A racing cyclist, for example, uses a combination of several angular motions to produce the linear motion of the bicycle.

general motor ability An early concept about motor abilities in which a single ability was thought to account for major portions of the individual differences in motor behaviour. Thus, a person high in general motor ability would tend to learn a *motor skill more quickly than a person with low general motor ability. It is now thought that there are a large number of specific, independent motor abilities.

general physical capacity A measure of the ability of active muscle systems to deliver, by the *aerobic system or *anaerobic system, energy for mechanical work, and to continue working for as long as possible. This capacity increases through training. *See also* aerobic capacity; anaerobic capacity; and capacity.

general strength The strength of the whole muscular system. *See also* conditioning.

general trait anxiety *See* trait anxiety.

generation An age-based subgroup consisting of people in adjacent birth *cohorts, most members of which have shared a similar sociohistorical event in a similar manner (e.g., the baby boom generation). This event often influences *life chances and lifestyles throughout the *life cycle. Different generations may experience different processes of *socialization which may result in conflict due to what has been called the generation gap. A recent example in sport is the decline in popularity among young people of team-sports in favour of individual activities, while many older people retain their enthusiasm for team-sports.

generator potential *See* receptor potential.

genetic Pertaining to a *gene.

genetic endowment The *genes a person inherits from parents which affect characteristics such as cardiovascular traits, *muscle fibre-type proportions, and the capacity to improve physical fitness with training. It has been estimated that genetic factors account for 94 per cent of the *variance in physical factors and maximum *V_{O_2}.

genetic potential The limitations imposed by the genetic constitution (genotype) of a person. *See also* genetic endowment.

genital herpes (herpes genitalis) A form of *herpes caused by a type of sexually-transmitted *Herpes simplex* virus. It is characterized by painful lesions in the genital area and is very contagious. Genital herpes does not usually interfere with physical activity.

genome All the *genes in an individual.

genotype The genetic constitution of an individual. *Compare* phenotype.

genu The knee or any anatomical structure similar to the knee.

genu recurvatum Hyperextension of the knees.

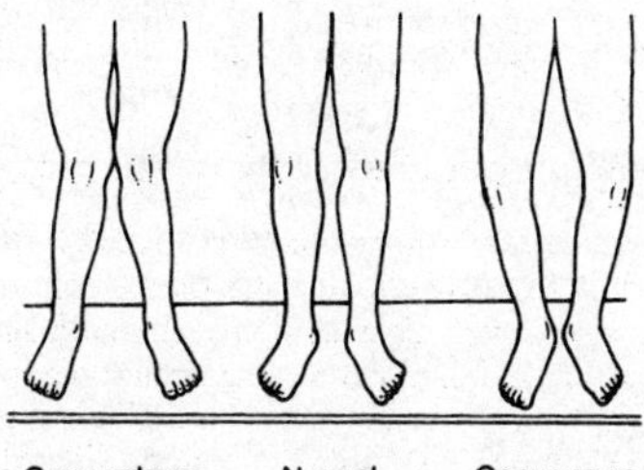

genu valgum

genu valgum Medical term for knock-knees. The condition is associated with lax *ligaments which predispose the sufferer to knee injuries. *See also* hyperflexibility.

genu varum Medical term for bow-legs. The condition is associated with lax *ligaments which predispose the sufferer to knee injuries. *See also* hyperflexibility.

geographical location In sport, the position and role of a player on a team which can be described in terms of *propinquity, *task dependence, and *centrality. Geographical location of the athlete seems to be correlated with leadership opportunities. Many of those players who are in highly visible, interactive, and interdependent positions (e.g., quaterback in American football) are often perceived to have leadership skills and go on to be coaches or managers.

germ Any microorganism, especially one causing disease.

German measles (rubella) A highly contagious viral disease marked by headaches, soreness in the neck, and mild fever accompanied by a pale rash of minute pink spots. Complications are uncommon except in pregnant women where there is a high risk of foetal damage. Physical exertion during the incubation period may lead to a more severe form of the disease.

gerontological theories *See* activity theory; and disengagement theory.

gerontology The study of ageing and of elderly people. Some gerontological studies, such as those concerned with adaptation to retirement, have had particular application to *sports sociology. *See also* ageing process; and ageism.

Gerschler interval work A form of *interval training consisting of a large number of *repetitions run at a short distance, typically 200–400 m, with a relatively long recovery period of 2–3 min. The training is designed mainly for middle-distance runners. Each repetition is run at or above race pace in order to develop a sense of race pace.

Gestalt psychology School of psychology which disparages the partist, reductionist approach to experience and behaviour, and argues for emphasis on the whole individual which, Gestalt psychologists say, is more than the sum of his or her parts. In learning, this school emphasizes the ability of a person to organize and interpret sensory experience; stimuli are not merely received by the sense-organs, but meaning is imposed on the sensory data during the process of *perception.

GH *See* growth hormone.

gigantism Abnormal growth of the body, usually due to an overactive *anterior pituitary gland during childhood.

gingivitis Inflammation of the gums which bleed easily.

ginglymus *See* hinge-joint.

ginseng A herbal root from the plant *Pinax ginseng* which is made into a tea-like drink. It is the best known of the traditional Chinese medicines, and is claimed to give the consumer a long and happy life. Pharmacological analysis has identified saponins (ginsenosides) as the active substances. There is no concrete, irrefutable evidence that ginseng improves athletic performance, but it has been taken by élite athletes before major competitions. Reported side-effects of chronic intake include *hypertension, *insomnia, and *depression.

girdle An arrangement of bones which form an arching and encircling structure. *See* pectoral girdle; and pelvic girdle.

girth In *arthropometry, the distance around a structure; its circumference.

glabella The elevated, smooth, rounded surface of the *frontal bone, just above the bridge of the nose, between the eyebrows.

gland One or more cells specialized to produce substances called secretions which are used by the body or eliminated. *See also* endocrine gland; and exocrine gland.

glandular fever A viral infection characterized by *fever, *fatigue, *nausea, and *inflammation of the *lymph nodes in different parts of the body. It is accompanied by an abnormally high *monocyte count (mononucleosis). Strenuous activity should be avoided during infection. The course of the illness may last several months.

glare recovery The ability to adapt the eyesight to varying light conditions.

glass arm A condition involving *inflammation of the muscles and tendons of the arm and shoulder which limits their function.

glass jaw A colloquial term used to describe the susceptibilty of an athlete, especially a boxer, to be knocked out or sustain a fracture of the *mandible from a blow to the jaw.

glenohumeral joint The shoulder-joint; a *synovial, multiaxial, *ball-and-socket joint in which the head of the *humerus articulates with the *glenoid cavity of the *scapula. Joint stability is sacrificed for flexibility and depends on the surrounding muscles; the ligaments contribute little to stability. The glenohumeral is a freely-moving joint allowing *flexion, *extension, *abduction, *adduction, *circumduction, and *rotation.

glenoid cavity A shallow *fossa in the *scapula into which the head of the *humerus is inserted.

glenoid labrum A rim of *fibrous cartilage on the edge of the *glenoid cavity. It slightly deepens the cavity, adding a little to the stability of the *glenohumeral joint.

glenoid labrum tear A rupture of the *glenoid labrum commonly associated with dislocation of the shoulder. The condition, which can be confirmed by *arthroscopy of the shoulder, is characterized by a deep pain and tenderness, a sensation of locking on motion, and a feeling of instability. Isolated tears, without instability, can occur in young athletes participating in throwing events, boxing, or racket sports.

glia *See* neuroglia.

gliding joint *See* arthrosis.

gliding movements A movement produced by one flat, or nearly flat, bone surface slipping over another similar surface. The bones are merely displaced in relation to one another. The movements are not angular or rotatory. Gliding movements occur at *intercarpal, *intertarsal, and *sternoclavicular joints.

global attribution A concept used in *attribution theory to describe attributions which are generalized and relate to many areas of sport. An individual who states that he or she is hopeless at sport, for example, is making a global attribution.

global self-esteem Generalized feelings of self-worth which are not specific to a particular situation but which apply to many activities or areas of life and predisposes the subject to view new activities in particular ways.

globular protein (functional protein) A member of a group of *proteins, including most *enzymes, with globular-shaped molecules. Most are water-soluble, mobile, and chemically active.

glomerular filtrate A filtrate that has passed through the *glomerulus of the kidney into the kidney tubule or nephron.

glomerulus The unit in the kidney through which ultrafiltration of the blood takes place. Each glomerulus consists of a knot of capillaries enclosed in a *Bowman's capsule. Substances of low molecular weight filter through the *endothelium of the glomeruli into the *nephron or kidney tubule.

glossopharyngeal nerve A mixed *nerve sending *motor impulses to the *pharynx and salivary glands, and transmitting *sensory impulses from the tongue to the soft palate; the ninth *cranial nerve.

glottis Elongated, narrow opening between the vocal cords and the *larynx.

glucagon A *polypeptide hormone secreted by the α cells of the *islets of Langerhans in the *pancreas. Glucagon has the opposite effect to *insulin, causing blood glucose levels to increase. Glucagon levels generally increase in response to exercise but this response is lessened by training.

glucocorticoids *Hormones belonging to the *corticosteroids produced by the *adrenal cortex that enable the body to resist stressors by increasing blood glucose, *fatty acid, and *amino acid levels, and by raising blood pressure. High levels of glucocorticoids depress the immune system and inflammatory response.

glucocorticosteroids *See* glucocorticoid.

gluconeogenesis *Synthesis of glucose from noncarbohydrate sources such as amino acids, *lactate, and *pyruvate. Gluconeogenesis occurs mainly in the *liver and *kidneys when *carbohydrate in the diet is not sufficient to meet the demands of the body for *glucose.

glucose A *monosaccharide sugar which is the main form of *carbohydrate used by the human body. Glucose serves as the primary fuel for the *brain, *red blood cells, and *muscles. Because the brain is very sensitive to shortages of glucose, the blood glucose level (commonly referred to as the blood sugar level) is kept constant (*see* diabetes mellitus). Excess glucose is either converted by the *liver to *glycogen or turned into body *fat. Glucose occurs naturally in many fruits. *See also* carbohydrate-loading; and glycogen overshoot.

glucose–alanine cycle Chemical reactions preceding *gluconeogenesis which may be important in enabling blood *glucose levels to be maintained during prolonged exercise. *Protein, including muscle protein, is broken down and some of the *amino acids transferred to *pyruvic acid to form another amino acid called alanine. Alanine is then transported to the *liver where it is converted back into pyruvic acid, and eventually changed to liver *glycogen and glucose.

glutamate *See* glutamic acid.

glutamic acid An amino acid, the salt (glutamate) of which functions as an *ionotropic neurotransmitter. Glutamate is secreted in many areas of the brain and by some *neurones in the *spinal cord where its effects are generally excitatory.

gluteal In *anatomy, pertaining to the buttocks.

gluteale A *landmark located in the mid-*sagittal plane where the *sacrum and the *coccyx fuse.

gluteal girth (hip girth) The circumference of the hips at the level of the greatest posterior protruberance.

gluteal muscle One of the muscles of the buttocks which have their *origin in the pelvis. The gluteal muscles are the *gluteus maximus, *gluteus medius, and *gluteus minimus.

gluten A combination of two proteins (glutenin and gliachin) present in wheat, barley, rye, and other grains. Hypersensitivity to gluten results in *coeliac disease.

gluten intolerance *See* coeliac disease.

gluteus maximus (large buttock muscle) A muscle which passes across the hip and forms the bulk of the buttocks. It extends and adducts the hip, rotating the thigh outwards. Its *origins are on the pelvic girdle, the posterior part of the *sacroiliac crest, the *sacrum, and the *coccyx. Its *insertions are on the outer surface of the *femur just below the *greater trochanter (gluteal tuberosity) and via a strong tendon band on its lateral surface (the iliotibial tract). The gluteus maximus is used to swing

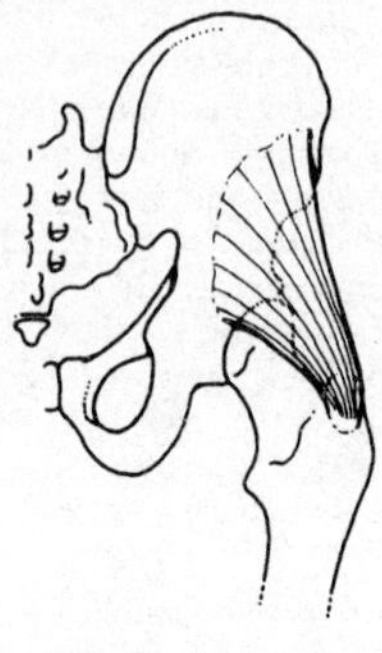
Gluteus minimus

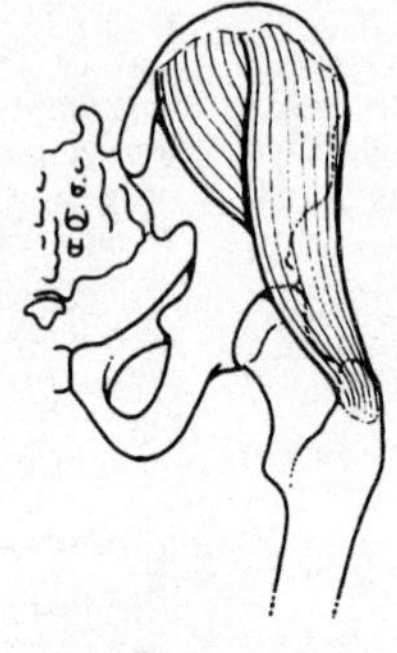
Gluteus medius

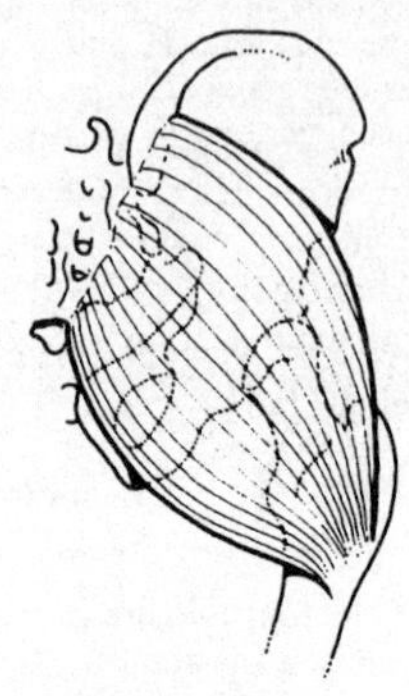
Gluteus maximus

gluteal muscles

the leg powerfully backwards. The muscle can work better if the body is bent forward at the hip (e.g., in a crouch start). It is generally inactive during walking.

gluteus medius A thick buttock muscle, largely covered by the *gluteus maximus. Its *origin is on the lateral surface of the *ilium and its *insertions by a short tendon into the lateral aspect of the *greater trochanter of the *femur. Its actions include *abduction and *medial *rotation of the thigh. It also steadies the pelvis during walking and running, preventing the upper body from falling to one side. It comes under great stress during downhill running.

gluteus minimus The smallest and deepest of the buttock muscles. It has its *origin on the external surface of the *ilium and its *insertion on the *anterior border of the *greater trochanter of the *femur. Its actions are similar to those of the *gluteus medius; it is particularly active during walking downhill.

glycerol An alcohol derived from sugar. Glycerol is a component of *triglycerides (neutral fats).

glycine A simple *amino acid which acts as an *ionotropic neurotransmitter. It is secreted by some *neurones in the *spinal cord and *retina. Glycine is believed to be the main inhibitory substance of motor neurones in the spinal cord. Blocking its action with *strychnine results in uncontrolled muscle spasms, convulsions, and respiratory arrest.

glycogen (animal starch) A highly-branched *polysaccharide. Liver glycogen is the main store of *carbohydrate in the body. Glycogen is derived from the condensation of α glucose molecules. It acts as an energy source for muscles. Glycogen is readily hydrolysed to *glucose in the *liver to maintain blood sugar. *See also* muscle glycogen.

glycogenesis The manufacture of *glycogen from *glucose. *See also* insulin.

glycogen-loading *See* carbohydrate-loading.

glycogenolysis The breakdown of *glycogen to form *glucose. *See also* glucogon.

glycogen overshoot *See* carbohydrate-loading.

glycogen sparing Diminished utilization of *glycogen that results when other substrates are available and are used as fuels for physical activity. If *fat or, less commonly, *protein is used more than usual as a fuel, glycogen will be spared and may be kept available for later use.

glycogen supercompensation The process of filling the *muscle glycogen stores which occurs during carbohydrate-loading.

glycolysis The first stage of *cellular respiration, occurring with or without oxygen in the *cytoplasm, in which one molecule of *glucose is broken down into two molecules of *pyruvic acid. During the process, *nicotinamide adenine dinucleotide (NAD) is reduced, generating energy which is used to produce *adenosine triphosphate from *ADP.

glyconeogenesis (neoglycogenesis) Manufacture of the *carbohydrate *glycogen from noncarbohydrate sources such as *fats and *proteins.

glycoprotein A conjugated *protein with a *sugar group.

glycosidic bond Bond formed in the polymerization (*see* polymer) of *monosaccharides into *disaccharide or *polysaccharide.

glycosuria Condition in which *glucose is excreted into the *urine; a symptom of *diabetes mellitus.

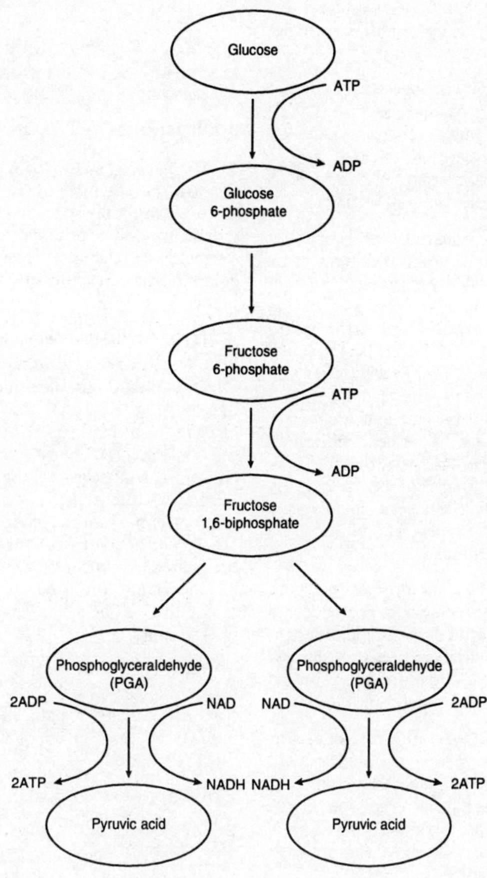

glycolysis

gnathion A *landmark located on the most inferior border of the *mandible in the midsagittal area.

goal The end towards which an action, physical or mental, is directed, and towards which an individual consciously or unconsciously strives. A goal is a specific target that is either achieved or not. Well-defined goals play an important part in *motivation, providing athletes with something concrete towards which to direct their energies. The setting of appropriate goals (*see* goal-setting) is regarded as critical for all performers in sport.

goal-acceptance The agreement by an athlete to attempt to achieve a defined goal. Goal-acceptance may change between training and competition: a goal set in training may well be regarded as too high for competition. *See also* goal-setting.

goal-difficulty A measure of the probability of a performer not achieving a goal. Goal difficulty is usually expressed as a percentage. Research indicates that as goal difficulty increases, so too does performance, up to a critical point, thereafter performance decreases. The critical point varies, but some evidence suggests that it lies around the 70 per cent difficulty level and that, therefore, goals which are only 30 per cent achievable should produce the best performance. It is generally agreed that competition goals should be set at a level the performer expects to achieve about 70 per cent of the time during normal training.

goal displacement The process by which means designed to achieve a goal become ends in themselves. For example, runners who perform time-trials in preparation for a competition may expend more energy on the trial than the actual competition.

goal orientation A motivational construct referring to personal definitions of success. Those defining success as winning or defeating others have an 'ego' goal orientation, whereas those viewing success as personal improvement and task-mastering have a 'task' or 'mastering' goal orientation.

goal-setting A motivational technique widely used in sport which involves the assigning and choosing of specific, objective, concrete targets or *goals which an athlete strives to achieve. It has been shown that a systematic programme of goal-setting and working to achieve these goals is highly effective in developing both physical and psychological skills: well-defined goals improve performance and quality of practice, clarify expectations, relieve boredom, and increase pride and self-confidence. Ideally, goals should be specific, realistic but challenging, and short-term. Generally, individual goals are more effective than team-goals.

goblet cell (goblet mucus cell) Wine-glass-shaped cell which produces *mucus in the respiratory and digestive tracts.

goblet mucus cell *See* goblet cell.

goitre Swelling of the front part of the neck due to an enlargement of the *thyroid gland. Goitre commonly results from a lack of iodine, essential for the synthesis of *thyroid hormone, in the diet. The thyroid gland enlarges in an attempt to produce the hormone.

golfer's elbow (javelin thrower's elbow; medial epicondylitis) An injury affecting the *origin of the common *flexor muscle on the *radial side of the elbow, causing an inflammation of the tendon on the *medial *epicondyle (*compare* tennis elbow). The muscles curl the wrist and close the fingers into a fist. Forceful curling and gripping can strain the tendon and even pull off a piece of bone or damage the *epiphyseal plate in youngsters. It commonly occurs on the right-hand side of golfers and is thought to be due to making too big a divot in chip shots.

golfer's toe An acute inflammation of the hallux (big toe) which may develop into an *arthritis causing a painfully rigid joint. It usually develops on a foot which has structural imbalances.

Golgi apparatus Series of cell *organelles consisting of a stack of membrane-lined *vesicles called *cisternae. The Golgi apparatus is often linked temporarily to the *endoplasmic reticulum. Secretory vesicles formed by the apparatus may be exported from the cell. The apparatus is thought to have a storage role as well as enabling the assembly of simple molecules into more complex ones.

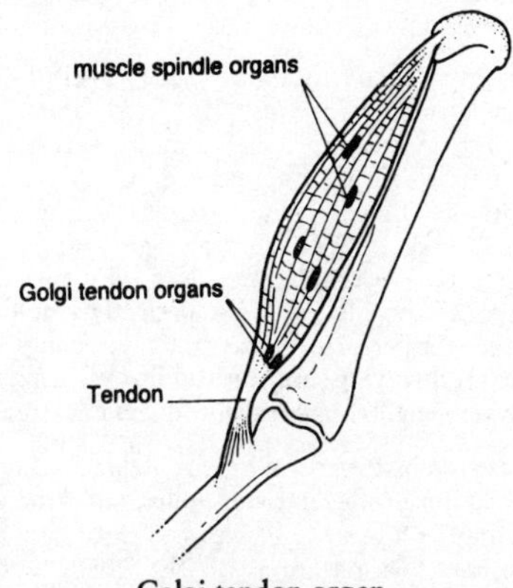

Golgi tendon organ

Golgi tendon organs (tendon organs) Small stretch receptors located at the junction between a *muscle and *tendon. The organs consist of small bundles of tendon fibres enclosed in a layered capsule, with *dendrites coiling between and around the fibres. Golgi tendon organs are activated by muscular contractions which stretch the tendons. This results in an inhibition of the activity of *α motor neurones which causes the muscle to relax, protecting the muscle and *connective tissue against excessive loading. It was once believed that the Golgi tendon organs were only stimulated by prolonged muscle stretches, but it is now known that they are very sensitive detectors of tension on localized portions of a particular muscle; they feed back information about force levels in the muscle to the *central nervous system.

gomphoses Fibrous joint represented solely by articulation of a tooth with its bony socket.

gonad Primary reproductive organ (i.e., the *testes of the male or the *ovary of the female) which produces the *gametes.

gonadotrophic hormone *See* gonadotropin.

gonadotrophin chorionic *See* human chorionic gonadotrophin.

gonadotropin (gonadotrophic hormone) A *hormone, such as *follicle-stimulating hormone or *luteinizing hormone, secreted by the *anterior *pituitary that acts on the *gonads (testes or ovaries) to stimulate production of the sex hormones.

goniometer A device which contains a 180° protractor for measuring *flexibility. The centre of the goniometer is positioned at the *axis of rotation of a *joint, and the arms of the goniometer are aligned with the *long axis of the two bones of the joint being measured. It measures the angle of the joint in stationary position only. *Compare* electrogoniometer.

gonorrhoea A sexually-transmitted disease caused by the bacterium *Neisseria gonorrhoea*. Gonorrhoea is characterized by purulent urethral discharges and pain when passing urine. It is treated with antibiotics. Serious complications can occur if it is untreated. Physical exertion should be avoided if a fever is present and should only recommence when the disease has been successfully treated.

Graafian follicle Structure in the *ovary consisting of granular *follicle cells which enclose a large fluid-filled cavity containing *oocyte.

gracilis A long, thin *superficial muscle of the *medial thigh. Its *origin is on the *pubis and *ischium, and its *insertion is just below the medial *condyle of the *tibia. Its actions include *adduction and *rotation of the *femur, and *flexion of the knee, especially during walking.

graded exercise test A test which evaluates an individual's physiological response to exercise, the intensity of which is increased in stages.

graded potential A transient local change in the potential difference across a *membrane which may result in either *hyperpolarization or *depolarization. The strength of the graded potential varies with the intensity of the *stimulus and causes local flows of current which decrease with the distance from the stimulus point. Graded potentials are given different names according to their function. *See also* generator potential.

gradient Degree of inclination of a slope, usually expressed as a unit rise in height per number of units covered along the slope. The gradient of a linear graph is the ratio of the vertical distance to horizontal distance.

graft A tissue or object used to replace a faulty body part by implantation or transplantation.

gram (gramme) Unit of *mass (symbol g) in the *CGS system which is equivalent to 1/1000 of a *kilogram. One *ounce is equal to 28.35 g. A paper-clip weighs about a gram.

gramme *See* gram.

gram weight Unit of *force; the pull of the Earth on a *gram *mass. A gram weight varies slightly according to the *acceleration of free fall at different localities, but a force of 1 gram weight equals approximately 981 *dynes. one gram = 0.0353 oz; 453.6 g = 1 lb.

granulation tissue Growth of new, florid, bright pink *connective tissue and blood vessels in a healing wound.

granulocyte White blood cell with granules in the *cytoplasm which forms 70 per cent of *leucocytes. There are three types: *eosinophils, *basophils, and *neutrophils.

graph A diagram, generally plotted on axes at right angles to each other, showing the relation of one variable quantity to another (e.g., the variation of oxygen consumption with time).

-graph Suffix denoting instruments that automatically record or write down observations, for example an *electrocardiograph.

grass burn A form of *friction burn due to abrasion of the skin on grass. Grass burns are notorious for the ease with which they can become infected.

gravitational field The region in which one body which has *mass exerts a *force of attraction on another body which has mass.

gravitational field strength *See* gravity.

gravitational movement A form of passive movement resulting from an accelerating *force which is relatively constant in direction and magnitude (*see* free fall). Gravitational movements include pendulum swings of the limbs or the whole body in gymnastics.

gravity (gravitational field strength) The attraction between the Earth and an object on its surface or within its *gravitational field. The *force exerted by the *gravitational field of the Earth's surface is $9.806\,\mathrm{N\,kg^{-1}}$. The Earth's gravitational force is very slightly less near the equator because the planet is not perfectly round, hence the performance of athletes in competitions involving jumping and throwing may be very slightly enhanced near the equator.

gravity line Vertical line, showing the line of action produced by an individual *force acting on a body, which passes through the point of application of the force and through the point on the *fulcrum upon which the force is balanced.

greater trochanter A large protruberance at the lateral junction between the shaft and neck of the *femur. It acts as an attachment point for the *gluteal muscles.

greater tuberosity A large rounded protruberance on the *humerus which is an attachment point for a number of muscles, including the *supraspinatus, *infraspinatus, and *teres minor.

great man theory of leadership *See* trait theory of leadership.

great saphenous vein *See* long saphenous vein.

great toe *See* hallux.

Greek ideal A philosophical ideal of ancient Greeks who believed that there should be a harmonious blend (sometimes called balance) of the physical, mental, and spiritual aspects of a person.

green stick fracture *Fracture in which bone breaks incompletely, in the same way that a green twig breaks. It is common in children whose bones have relatively more organic *matrix and are more flexible than adults' bones.

grey matter Region of the *central nervous system containing a large density of nerve *cell bodies and unmyelinated fibres of neurones. *Compare* white matter.

gripe A severe abdominal pain.

groin Region of the body which includes the upper part of the front of the thigh and lower part of the abdomen.

groin itch *See* dhobie itch.

groin muscle One of the *adductor muscles of the groin which include the *gracilis, *pectineus, and *adductor longus. All these muscles originate from the pubic bones and are inserted into the posterior surface of the *femur. The muscles work powerfully when, in a running action, the foot leaves the ground and begins to swing, and the leg rotates outward in relation to the hip. *See also* groin strain.

groin pain (inguinocrural pain; osteitis pubis) A pain in the *groin which is characterized by a particular tenderness in the region of the *pubic symphysis. The pain reduces the ability to spread the legs. It often occurs in football players and others who perform hip rotations or who overload one leg more than the other (by repeated kicking, for example) which loosens the ligament joining the pelvic bones. Groin pain responds well to rest and *anti-inflammatory drugs. Rehabilitation involves hip-mobilizing exercises to maximize the possible range.

groin strain An injury caused by overexertion of the *adductor muscles of the *groin, such as occurs in the forceful movements of broadside kicks in football, bringing the free leg forward in skating, or tough sprint-training. Groin strain can be avoided by developing muscular strength and flexibility of the adductor muscles. One such exercise comprises holding a football between the knees and compressing the ball with both knees.

groove A furrow in a bone which may act as a tract for *blood vessels, *nerves, and *tendons.

grooving The establishment of a behaviour as a *conditioned reflex by specific and repeated training.

gross anatomy The study of large body structures such as the heart or lungs which can be examined easily without any type of magnification. *Compare* microanatomy.

gross-body co-ordination The *co-ordination of the simultaneous movements of different body-parts which are involved in a whole body-action. Gross body co-ordination is believed to be one of the abilities underlying physical fitness.

gross-body equilibrium An ability to maintain balance when blindfolded which is regarded as one of the abilities underlying physical fitness.

gross-body movement Movement of the whole body or large segments of the body.

gross motor ability An ability, such as gross motor *co-ordination, which is believed to underlie physical fitness.

gross motor skill A *skill, such as running, that requires movement of the whole body involving the activity of many muscle groups. *Compare* fine motor skills.

gross strength *See* absolute strength.

grounded theory A sociological theory which is formulated after careful naturalistic observations of selected social phenomena. It is very important in qualitative analysis and allows categories to emerge from the data obtained, rather than imposing a theory upon data before research has begun.

ground reaction force A *force which is exerted by the ground in response to the forces a body exerts on it. If the body is pushing down and forwards, the ground reaction force is up and backward; if the body pushes down and backwards the ground reaction force is up and forwards.

ground substance A relatively unstructured material, usually containing fibres, that fills the space between cells of *connective tissue.

group Two or more persons interacting with one another in such a manner that each person influences and is influenced by each other person. Accordingly, some teams are types of groups. However, a group is sometimes distinguished from a *team by having

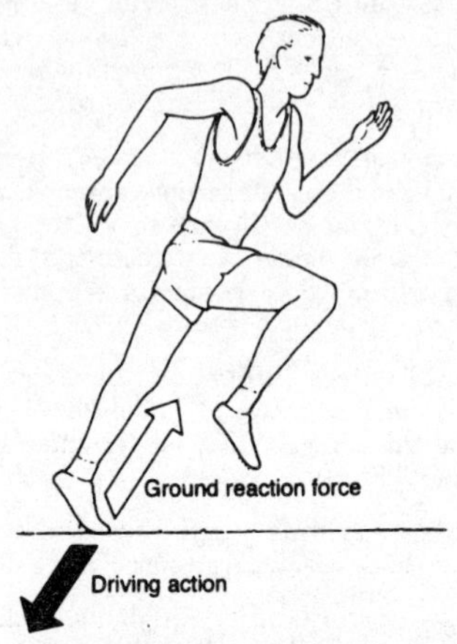

ground reaction force

an indefinite group structure, organization, and communication pattern; assignments that are assumed in the course of group interaction rather than designated beforehand; and yields which are products that can be a function of one or more of the group-members involved, depending on the quality and quantity of the member's participation. *Compare* aggregate.

group cohesion An adhesive property or force that binds group-members together. Group cohesion increases the significance of membership for those who belong to the group, motivates members to contribute to group welfare, and encourages a sense of loyalty and commitment. *See also* cohesion.

group dynamics 1 The interactive processes within groups. Sport sociologists tend to focus on the shifting patterns of tension, conflict, adjustment, and cohesion within groups as well as the effect of different styles of leadership. 2 The study of the underlying features of group behaviour such as group motives and attitudes. Group dynamics is concerned with the characteristics of groups which change rather than those which are stable.

group environment The physical, psychological, and social suroundings of a group. The group environment especially refers to the social relationships beteen the members of the group.

group environment questionnaire A multidimensional questionnaire which directly measures *team cohesion in terms of individual attraction and *group integration.

group integration The functioning of a *group as a unit. The opportunity to belong to a cohesive unit is, according to the *conceptual model of team cohesion, one reason why individuals are attracted to join groups. Measures of group integration take into consideration an individual's perception of closeness, similarity to other group-members, and bonding to the group as a whole. *See also* individual attraction.

group locomotion Motivational construct that represents the reason or purpose behind a *group's existence and symbolizes the activity of the group in relation to achieving group objectives.

group mentality Characteristic which reflects the unanimous will of a *group. Individuals may be unaware of the contributions they make to group mentality and they may influence other members negatively when they feel they are at variance with group principles, norms, and objectives.

group motives *Motives which contribute to the success of a *group. They include four which are very important: *conflict, *cohesion, *socialization, and expectation. Other group motives include achievement need, and need to avoid failure. Groups behave in much the same way as individuals when *goal-setting or reacting to failure and success. However, the group as a whole tends to be more resistant to negative criticism and is less likely than an individual to adjust goals downwards after failure. *See also* group personality.

group performance (group productivity) The actual productivity of a *group; that is, its achievements (such as scoring a goal or winning a game) or the potential productivity which consists of the group's best possible performance given its resources and task demands. Resources include all the relevant knowledge and skills of individual members. *See also* Ringelmann effect; and social loafing.

group personality Characteristic of a *group which is analagous to that of the *personality of an individual,in that the group behaves as a unit in certain circumstances; it possesses energy (*see* synergy), has drives and emotional states, and it engages in collective deliberations in much the same way as one person deliberates as an individual. The group personality is relatively independent of those apparently possessed by the group-members. *See also* synality.

group productivity *See* group performance.

group processes Everything a *group does while transforming its group resources into a product or a performance.

group resources The combined relevant knowledge and skills of individual members of a *group, including the level and distribution of talents.

growth Increase in size. The growth of human tissue, such as muscle, results in an increase in the quantity of *protoplasm due to *hypertrophy or *hyperplasia. *Compare* development; and maturation.

growth disc *See* epiphyseal disc.

growth hormone (GH; hGH; human growth hormone; somatotropin; STH) A hormone, secreted by the *anterior pituitary, that stimulates growth in general, and lengthening of *long bones in particular. Whereas *steroids act primarily on muscles, growth hormone is claimed to strengthen bones and tendons as well. Growth hormone belongs to the group of *banned substances classified as *peptide hormones and *analogues. Production of hGH increases during exercise, but the increase is not so fast in a trained as an untrained person.

growth spurt A period of accelerated physical development during which there is a rapid increase in height. Typically, there is a major growth spurt in males between the ages of 11 to 14 years, and in females between 9 and 11 years of age.

GSR *See* galvanic skin response.

guidance A series of techniques, used when practising a skill, in which the behaviour of the learner is limited or controlled by various means to prevent errors. The learner is in some way guided through the task that is to be learned; for example, gymnasts may have manual assistance and support-belts to ensure a mistake will not result in an injury.

guide movement (tracking) A gross-body movement requiring accuracy and steadiness, but not force or speed, in which both *agonist and *antagonist muscles contribute to the movement.

gum 1 A member of a large class of substances of vegetable origin which are usually exuded from plants. Gum is a source of dietary *fibre. **2** The layer of tissue that covers the necks of the teeth.

gumshield A protective device which fits around the teeth and gums to reduce the likelihood of *concussion during a contact sport.

gut *See* intestine,

gymnast's back A lower-back injury due to vertebrae rubbing against each other when the back is arched during *hyperextension.

gymnast's fracture A supracondylar *fracture of the elbow, common in children. It results from excessive *extension or *flexion causing an indirect trauma to be transmitted through the *radius and *ulna against the *distal *humerus. Gymnast's fracture is often accompanied by injuries to the *brachial artery and *ulnar nerve.

gynaecomastia Development of breasts in a man; due either to a hormone imbalance or the adminstration of *anabolic steroids.

gynoid fat distribution Distribution of *adipose tissue, predominantly on the hips, buttocks, and thighs. Often called 'pear-shaped' obesity, it is found more commonly among females than males. *Compare* android fat distribution.

gyroscopic stability The resistance of a rotating body to a change in its plane of rotation. The faster a body spins (the greater its *angular velocity) the greater the *stability of the body in its particular position or orientation. Gyroscopic stability accounts for the stability of a spinning discus, or a spinning football in American Football.

gyrus An elevated ridge of tissue on the surface of the *cerebral hemispheres. The most prominent gyri are similar in all people and are important anatomical *landmarks.

H

habit A learned, stereotyped response to a particular *stimulus or stimuli. A habit results in the formation in the nervous system of a path of preferred conduction between the stimulus and response.

habitual skill A form of *motor skill which requires a fixed response to a given situation. Such skills are usually performed in a relatively stable environment and are acquired only after much practice. *See also* closed skill; perceptual skill; and self-paced skill.

habituation A learning process which results in the diminution and eventual loss of a normal behavioural response or sensation. Habituation results from continuous stimulation with a constant stimulus. It explains how, for example, cricketers become accustomed to uncomfortable sports equipment, such as protective helmets, and swimmers become accustomed to cold water.

habitus The general, outward, physical appearance of a person especially when this is associated with a particular disorder of the body.

haem The ring-structured *porphyrin group containing ferrous iron, which is the *prosthetic group of *haemoglobin. Haem gives the blood its colour and its ability to transport oxygen. *See also* haem iron.

haemarthrosis Presence of blood or bleeding into a *joint which causes swelling and joint pain. It may be due to an injury or disease. Treatment is by immobilization, cold compresses, and withdrawal of the blood from the joint.

haematin An oxidized derivative of the iron-containing, nonprotein portion of *haemoglobin.

haematocrit The volume of red blood cells usually expressed as a percentage of total blood volume.

haematoma A swelling caused by the accumulation of clotted blood in tissues. There are two common types in sport: *intramuscular haematomas and *intermuscular haematomas; they sometimes occur together. A large haetamoma may never be reabsorbed; it undergoes reorganization into a *fibrosis and scar.

haematopoiesis *See* haemopoiesis.

haematopoietic tissue Tissues involved in the production of red blood cells. These include the *diploë of *flat bones and the marrow cavity of *long bones.

haematuria Discharge of *blood into the urine. The blood may come from the diseased or damaged *kidneys, *urethra, or bladder. *See also* runner's haematuria

haeme iron Iron incorporated in the blood pigment, *haemoglobin. It constitutes about 40 per cent of the iron in meats and is the type most easily absorbed by the body.

haemobursa A *bursa containing *blood. It often results from direct trauma of superficial bursae leading to *bursitis.

haemoconcentration An increase in the proportion of red blood cells in the *blood, usually due to reduction in the volume of *plasma. Haemoconcentration results in an increased viscosity of the blood. It occurs as a result of *dehydration and may be artificially induced by *blood doping.

haemocytoblast A cell in the bone marrow which gives rise to *blood cells and *platelets.

haemocytometer A glass chamber used for examining and counting the cellular components of a sample of *blood viewed with a microscope.

haemodilution A decrease in the proportion of red blood cells in the *blood due to a relative increase in the volume of *plasma. *Compare* haemoconcentration.

haemodynamics Study of the physical laws which control the behaviour of blood flow in the circulatory system. Haemodynamics uses and applies principles of fluid dynamics to the special conditions pertaining to a living circulatory system which contains a fluid, *blood, with unusual properties, and vessels which can change their shape.

haemoglobin A large *conjugated protein consisting of four *polypeptide chains, each with a prosthetic (nonprotein) haem group which contains ferrous iron, able to combine reversibly with oxygen. It is the oxygen-transporting component of red blood cells.

haemoglobinuria The presence of free haemoglobin in the urine. It sometimes occurs after strenuous exercise (*see* march haemoglobinuria) and after repeated hand trauma in karate. It is also associated with some infectious diseases.

haemolysis Disintegration of red blood cells. The cell membrane ruptures, releasing the contents. Premature haemolysis can lead to *anaemia.

haemophiliac A person suffering from an hereditary disease in which the blood clots slowly. Haemophiliacs are unable to take part in contact sports because of the danger of internal bleeding.

haemopoiesis (haematopoiesis) The process of *blood cell and *platelet formation. In healthy adults it takes place only in the *bone marrow.

haemorrhage Loss of *blood through the ruptured walls of blood vessels. Bleeding from a major artery can result in such blood loss that it leads to shock, collapse, and death, if untreated.

haemorrhoid A swollen blood vessel in the *anus. Cushions of blood vessels, muscle, and connective tissue are normally present in the anus. A haemorrhoid results from one of the veins becoming swollen and tender as a result of constipation, pregnancy, or *obesity. Haemorrhoids may adversely affect performances in sports such as horse-riding and cycling, but they do not usually interfere with other sporting activities, except when the symptoms are severe.

haemostasis Stoppage of bleeding or blood flow.

haemostatic A *drug or other agent which stops or prevents bleeding.

haemothorax A condition in which blood has passed from the lung into the *pleural cavity.

hair follicle The sheath in which a hair is formed by *epithelial cells.

half-reaction time The time it takes for a chemical reaction to be half completed. For example, a half-reaction time of thirty seconds for restoration of phosphagen stores following an *anaerobic activity, means that in thirty seconds half of the total *ATP and *PC stores are replenished.

hallux In *anatomy, pertaining to the great toe.

hallux rigidus Degenerative condition of a bone of the big toe causing stiffness and disability. It may occur after repeated minor injuries to the *metatarsophalangeal joint of the big toe.

hallux valgus Permanent lateral displacement of the great toe in which the *sesamoid bones under the head of the first *metatarsal bones are displaced so that they lie between the first and second metatarsal bones. Normally the big toe can be angled outwards by ten degrees, but in hallux valgus the displacement is greater. It is a common disorder in those who wear shoes with pointed toes or who exhibit excessive pronation.

hamate (unciform bone) A bone which forms part of the *carpus (wrist). It has a hooked-shaped projection, and articulates with the fourth and fifth *metacarpals distally, and the *triquetral behind.

hammer toe A deformity in which the *proximal *interphalangeal-joint of the first *phalanx is pointed upwards in a flexed position. It is commonly caused by an insufficiency of the anterior transverse arch (*see* arches of foot) or by wearing ill-fitting shoes. A painful *corn may develop over the affected area.

hamstring muscles Fleshy group of muscles of the posterior thigh, consisting of the *biceps femoris, *semitendinosus, and *semimembranosus. The hamstrings extend the hip and flex the knee.

hand dynamometer A *dynamometer which measures grip strength.

handedness A tendency for an individual to prefer the use of either the right or left hand. Humans are predominantly right-handed, but being left-handed can have the advantage of producing the novel and unexpected in sports such as tennis, fencing, and boxing. *See also* cerebral dominance.

handicapped Term used to describe individuals with some form of *disability. Use of the term is regarded by some as a form of negative stereotyping which often leads to those with physical disabilities or learning difficulties from achieving their full potential.

hand injuries The hands are sensitive parts of the body containing many *bones, *ligaments, *tendons, and *muscules which may suffer breaks, *sprains and *strains. Sometimes sprains and *fractures are difficult to distinguish. Injuries to the forearm may also affect the hands.

handlebar palsy A *neuropathy caused by repeated irritation of the deep *palmar branch of the *ulnar nerve, which results in motor weakness of the muscles innervated by the nerve. It is an over-use injury experienced by cyclists which can be prevented by protecting the hands with gloves and frequently changing the position of the hands on the handlebars.

hand length In *anthropometry, the difference between the *stylion height and the *dactylion height.

haptic perception Perception which pertains to the sense of touch provided by *cutaneous receptors and which combines with information from *proprioceptors to contribute to *kinaesthesis.

hard bone *See* compact bone.

hardening of arteries *See* arteriosclerosis.

harmonic motion A motion that repeats itself, usually in equal intervals of time, back and forth across the same path in a harmonic or vibratory motion. Harmonic motion is characterized by the continuous conversion of *kinetic energy into *potential energy and back. It occurs when a trampolinist stretches the bed of the trampoline imparting potential energy to it. This is then converted to kinetic energy that projects the trampolinist up into the air, and so on.

Harter's competence motivation theory A theory of *achievement motivation that is based on a person's feelings of personal competence. According to the theory, *competence motivation increases through elevated feelings of *intrinsic motivation and positive emotion when a person successfully masters a task. This encourages the person to master more tasks. *See also* perceived competence scale for children.

Harvard step test A test of physical fitness devised at Harvard University during World War II. It involves a subject stepping up onto, and then down from, a 20 inch (50.8 cm) stool or bench with both feet, repeating the sequence thirty times a minute at steady rhythm for up to 5 minutes or until exhausted. The pulse rate is taken a minute after exercise, then two and three minutes after exercise. Fitness levels are estimated from the rate at which the pulse rate returns to its resting level. The test is not used in medicine any more because it is not very reliable.

Haversian canal A central canal within the *lamellae of *compact bone and which forms part of the *Haversian system. The canal contains blood vessels, nerves, and lymphatics.

Haversian system A cylindrical unit of *compact bone which consists of a system of interconnecting channels (canaliculi) around a central *Haversian canal. The canalculi ramify through the concentric rings of bone matrix (*see* lamellae), supplying the bone cells with nutrients.

Hawthorne effect A general improvement in performance which occurs when an individual receives special attention. Successful coaches often show considerable respect for this effect, providing members of their group with as much support and sense of importance as possible.

hay fever (allergic rhinitis) A very common, allergic condition often triggered by pollen, characterized by symptoms which include nasal congestion, a thin watery discharge from the nose, and sneezing. Although there is no actual risk to hay fever sufferers taking part in sport, performance is usually adversely affected. Some *drugs used in hay fever treatment are on the *IOC list of *banned substances.

HCG *See* human chorionic gonadotrophin.

HDL *See* high-density lipoproteins.

head **1** Part of the body which contains the brain, and organs of sight, hearing, smell, and taste. **2** The rounded expansion of bone which fits into a cavity of another bone to form a *joint.

headache A pain felt deep within the skull. Headaches have a variety of causes; most are relatively trivial including those associated with fatigue, emotional stress, and poor posture. Some headaches, however, have more sinister implications and may be due to poisoning, very high blood pressure, or brain damage after a blow to the head. Those suffering from persistent headaches, or headaches following physical trauma, should seek medical advice.

head extension Movement of the head backwards, moving the chin away from the chest. Head extension is effected by the *splenius muscle and *erector spinae muscle. *Compare* head flexion.

head extensor Muscle which effects *head extension.

head flexion Movement of the head forwards with chin moving towards the chest. Head flexion usually results from the combined action of *gravity and relaxation of the *head extensors. It may also be caused by the active, simultaneous contraction of the two heads of the *sternocleidomastoid muscle. Excessive flexion is prevented by *ligamentum nuchae.

head flexor Muscle which effects *head flexion. Head flexors include the *sternocleidomastoid muscles and a number of deep muscles in the neck.

head girth The maximum circumference of the head at a level midpoint between the brow ridges. *See also* body girth.

head injury A number of sports, particularly body contact or vehicular sports such as boxing, horse-riding, and cycling, carry a high risk of injury to the head. A blow to the head can result in brain damage and should be treated with great caution. Other injuries, such as those to the face, may be potentially disfiguring or disabling. Some symptoms including numbness, an inability to move limbs, or a pins-and-needles sensation in the arms and legs should be treated very seriously and medical advice sought. *See also* concussion.

head-louse A parasite, *Pediculosis capitis* , which lives in the scalp causing irritation and itching. Lice may induce *eczema. They do not have a harmful affect on physical performance, but they are very contagious and can be spread in contact sports.

head rotation Lateral movement of the head around its axis. Head rotation is effected by the *sternocleidomastoids, a number of deeper neck muscles including the *scalenes, and by several straplike muscles of the *vertebral column at the back of the neck.

head rotator A muscle which effects *head rotation.

health Ability of an individual to mobilize his or her resources—physical, mental, and spiritual—to the preservation and advantage of him or herself, and the dependents and society to which the individual belongs. Health is a state of complete physical, mental, and social well-being. It is not merely freedom from disease and infirmity.

health history (medical history) Information about the health record of an individual.

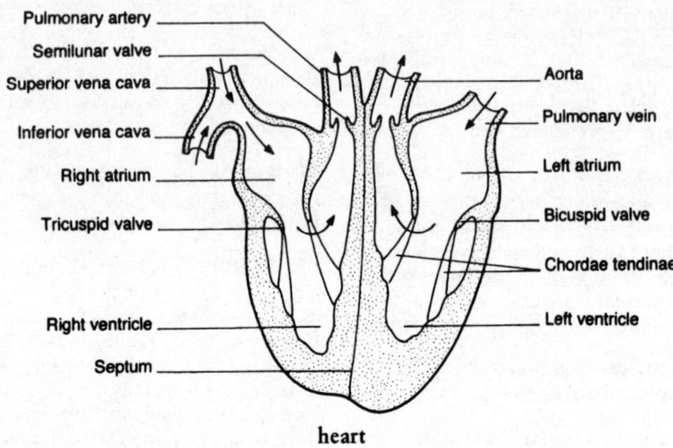

heart

health-related fitness Aspects of *physical fitness which are associated with improving *health. Emphasis is usually on *flexibility, *aerobic endurance, muscular condition, and body composition.

health-risk appraisal An assessment tool used by health promoters to evaluate how well or healthy an individual is. A health-risk appraisal usually takes the form of an extended questionnaire which enquires into personal lifestyle habits, and personal and family medical history, and which may be accompanied by laboratory tests for blood analysis, blood pressure, and *physical fitness levels. The outcome is a profile outlining areas of high risk, and this is usually accompanied by strategies and targets for lifestyle change.

healthy person A person who is not obviously ill, and whose physical and mental functions correspond to those of the average person in the same age group.

heart A hollow, four-chambered muscular organ lying in the *thoracic cavity between the *lungs. Its wall consists mainly of *cardiac muscle. The heart is divided by a *septum into a left side and a right side, each of which has two chambers: an *atrium and a *ventricle. Deoxygenated *blood from the *veins enters the right atrium and is passed into the right ventricle. This contracts and pumps the blood through the *pulmonary artery into the lungs. Oxygenated blood returns through the *pulmonary vein into the left atrium and then into the left ventricle. This contracts forcefully to pump the oxygenated blood to the rest of the body. The unidirectional flow of blood is maintained by the *heart valves.

heart attack Blocking of blood flow to a portion of the heart muscle. If the block is towards the end of a *coronary artery, the heart attack may not be severe since the amount of heart tissue deprived of oxygen would be minimal, but if the block is toward the beginning of the artery, the amount of tissue involved would be large and the heart attack severe. Much inferential evidence indicates that exercise, if properly prescribed and supervised, can reduce the risk of heart attack. *See also* anastomoses; and coronorary heart disease risk factors.

heartbeat The events of a single *cardiac cycle.

heart-block Impaired transmission of impulses from the pacemaker region in the *sinoatrial node to the rest of the *heart resulting in a slowing down of the *heart-rate. The condition may be congenital or caused by heart diseases such as *myocarditis.

heart failure A condition in which the pumping action of the heart is insufficient to meet the demands of the body. Heart failure may result from overload, damage, or disease of the heart. The sufferer experiences breathlessness.

heart hypertrophy An increase in the size of the heart. Heart hypertrophy may be a *pathological condition resulting from the need for the heart to pump more blood due to some defect in the circulatory or respiratory systems. In athletes, however, it can be a non-pathological training effect consisting of enlargement of the left *ventricle which increases *stroke volume and *cardiac output. *See also* athlete's heart.

heart murmur Abnormal heart sound which may be the result of defects of the *heart valves.

heart overload A condition which occurs when the demand for oxygenated blood exceeds the ability of the *heart to pump the blood around the body.

heart-rate Number of heart beats per minute. The heart-rate is commonly taken in four positions: sitting, supine, quick-standing, and after standing for one minute. The *resting heart-rate of the same individual in these positions may vary by as much as 10 beats per minute. The heart rate normally refers to the average of the four heart-rates, or the standing heart-rate. *See also* maximum heart-rate; and resting heart-rate.

heart-rate method A method used to determine optimal training intensity based on *heart-rate, so that the *overload principle can be applied. Generally, heart-rate increases with work rate. *See also* maximal heart-rate method; maximal heart-rate reserve method; and target heart-rate.

heart-rate reserve The difference between *maximal heart-rate and *resting heart-rate. *See also* maximal heart-rate reserve.

heart sounds Normally, during the cardiac cycle, two heart sounds (usually described as 'lub-dub' or 'lub-dup') can be heard over the chest through a stethoscope. The first is caused by closure of the *atrioventricular valve towards the beginning of *ventricular systole, and the other is caused by the closure of the *semilunar valves of the *aorta and *pulmonary artery at the beginning of *ventricular diastole. *Compare* heart murmurs. *See also* phonocardiogram.

heart valve A structure which restricts the flow of *blood through the *heart to one direction only. The heart valves are the *tricuspid valve between the right *atrium and right *ventricle, the *bicuspid (mitral) valve between the left atrium and left ventricle, and the *semilunar valves in the *pulmonary artery and *dorsal aorta.

heat Energy possessed by a substance in the form of atomic or molecular *kinetic energy. The heat contained in a body is the product of its *mass, its temperature, and its specific heat capacity. Heat is transmitted by *radiation, *conduction, and *convection. Changes in the heat content of a body may cause changes of state or changes in temperature. The *SI unit for heat is the *joule.

heat acclimatization Physiological adaptations that are associated with prolonged exposure to high environmental temperatures which result in an improved tolerance to high temperatures. Heat acclimatization results in a decrease in pulse rate, improved blood flow to the skin, an increase in the rate of sweating but a reduction in the salt content of sweat, and an increase in blood volume. Heat-acclimatized individuals tend to suffer less from nausea, dizziness, and discomfort in hot temperatures than those who are not acclimatized. *See also* acclimatization.

heat balance A condition reached when the heat gained by a body is equal to the heat lost from it. The amount of stored heat does not change and the body temperature remains constant. In humans, the heat is gained both by *metabolism (which increases dramatically during exercise) and the environment. Heat is exchanged with the environment by *radiation, *conduction, and *convection.

heat collapse Loss of consciousness associated with hot environmental conditions or exercising in clothing which restricts heat-loss and causes overheating. Excessive sweating, and *shunting blood to the skin and muscles reduces the blood flow to the brain causing fainting. Heat collapse is one of the commonest medical conditions on a hot day and is exacerbated by standing for long periods. It is a potentially dangerous condition which can lead to *heat exhaustion and *heat-stroke. Uncomplicated heat collapse, which often occurs when a person stands for long periods in a very hot environment, responds rapidly to adoption of a supine position, elevation of legs, tepid sponging, and administration of fluid. However, if loss of consciousness is combined with high rectal temperatures (41 °C or above) heat-stroke should be suspected until a medical diagnosis proves otherwise.

heat conduction The transfer of heat from the warmer to the cooler of two solid bodies that are in contact. In the human body, the rate of heat conduction depends upon the temperature gradient between the skin and the material with which the skin is in contact, and on the thermal properties of the materials.

heat-cramps Painful muscular contraction caused by prolonged exposure to environmental heat. It probably results from electrolyte imbalances. Adequate hydration and intake of electrolytes from the diet should prevent heat-cramps.

heat equivalence (calorific equivalence) The energy produced by the oxidation of food in one litre of oxygen. Heat equivalence varies according to the mixture of food types—*fat, *carbohydrate, or *protein—being oxidized. It is usually measured in *kilocalories. *See also* net oxygen cost of exercise; and respiratory quotient.

heat-exhaustion Condition of fatigue caused by prolonged exposure to environmental heat. Sufferers of heat-exhaustion usually have a normal body temperature but their pulse rate is accelerated, their skin is cold and sweaty, and they often experience drowsiness and vomiting. The condition can be prevented by regular water replacement. Heat-exhaustion usually responds to rest and cooling, but if the condition persists there is a risk of *heat-neurasthenia. *Compare* heat-stroke.

Heath–Carter somatotype Body-type rating based on a combination of anthropometric (*see* anthropometry) measures such as *skinfold measurements, and inspectional ratings of factors such as age, height, and weight. The *endomorphic and *mesomorphic components of the rating are based on skinfold measurements, and the *ectomorphic component is based mainly on the *ponderal index. *See also* somatotype.

heat-neurasthenia A progressive condition leading to chronic *neurosis brought about by prolonged *heat-exhaustion. The condition is characterized by apathy, hysteria, and aggression.

heat-stroke A potentially fatal condition caused by overexposure to heat. Heat-stroke is characterized by high body core temperatures, and hot, dry skin which is usually flushed. Sufferers show signs of mental confusion and loss of motor control, and may collapse into unconsciousness. There is an urgent need to reduce the core temperature rapidly by loosening clothing, fanning, and tepid sponging. However, iced fluids and iced baths should not be used because they may cause *vasoconstriction and reduce the elimination of heat. Medical attention is necessary and hospitalization may be required as there is a danger of renal failure.

heat-syncope Fainting or sudden loss of strength due to overheating. *See also* heat-collapse.

heat treatment The use of heat to treat injuries and accelerate recovery. The heat is usually applied superficially inducing feelings of relaxation and comfort, and increasing blood flow through the damaged tissue. *See also* diathermy.

heavy metals Metals, including arsenic, mercury, lead, and zinc, with toxic effects on the body. Iron, which is also a heavy metal, is toxic only in high concentrations.

heel Part of the foot formed by the heel-bone (*see* calcaneus) which extends behind the *ankle-joint.

heel-bone *See* calcaneus.

heel bursitis (retrocalcaneal bursitis) A chronic *over-use injury characterized by inflammation of the *retrocalcaneal bursa commonly produced by abnormally high pressures from the *heel-counter of the shoe creating shearing forces within the bursal sac. Athletes with high-arched feet are particularly prone to the condition because of the prominent heel-bone.

heel counter Rigid cup of material which wraps around the heel of a *training shoe to hold the *heel in place.

heel-raise An insertion, usually made of rubber, in a *training shoe which alters the angle of the foot as it strikes the ground during walking and running.

heel spur *See* plantar fasciitis.

heel tab Tab which protrudes from the top of the *heel counter of a training shoe. If it is hard and extends too far up the heel, it can damage the *Achilles tendon. There is no danger of this with low, flexible tabs.

height *See also* stature.

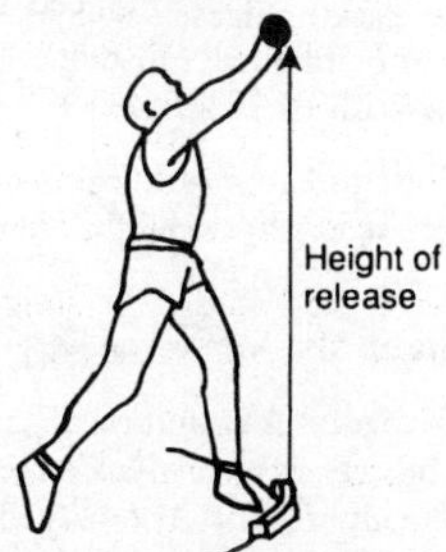

height of release

height of release The height above ground level, or the height above the point of landing, of the *centre of gravity of a projectile immediately before it leaves the ground. The height of release affects the *trajectory of the projectile and, for a given *speed of release and *angle of release, the horizontal displacement increases as the height of release increases.

Heimlich manoeuvre A technique to dislodge an obstruction from the *trachea of a choking person. The arms are wrapped around the person from behind. A tight fist is made with one hand which is grasped above the navel and just below the ribcage, by the other hand. The person hangs forwards and the fist is forcefully pressed upwards into the abdomen.

helper T-cell Type of T-lymphocyte (*see* T-cell) which releases chemicals called *lymphokines. Helper T-cells make direct contact with other immune cells in order to organize cellular immunity. They also help to bring about humoral responses by interacting with *B-cells.

hemiplegia Paralysis of one side of the body due to disease or injury of the opposite *cerebral hemisphere.

hemisphere *See* cerebral hemisphere.

Henry's law A gas law which states that the mass of a gas dissolved by a given volume of liquid at constant temperature is directly proportional to its pressure. Therefore, the volume of a gas absorbed by a given volume of liquid at constant temperature is independent of the pressure. The law holds only for sparingly-soluble gases at low pressures.

Henry's memory drum theory Theory concerned with memorization of *motor skills which postulates that neuromotor coordination patterns are stored in the higher centres of the *central nervous system on what is called a memory drum. The drum has been likened to a computer memory store which contains programs ready to function in a desired fashion upon the appropriate signal. Thus, in humans, whenever a specific movement pattern is needed, a *stimulus causes the memory drum to 'play back' the particular learned skill. The theory supports the idea that learning motor skills is specific rather than general and that there is little or no carry-over from one skill to another unless the skills are nearly identical.

heparin An *endogenous, complex organic acid which inhibits blood coagulation by interfering with the formation and action of *thrombin.

heparinoid Ointment containing an anticoagulant used to treat contusions.

hepatic artery An *artery carrying oxygenated blood to the *liver.

hepatic portal system A system of blood vessels consisting of hepatic portal veins which carry dissolved nutrients from the intestines to the liver tissues for processing.

hepatic vein A principal *vein carrying deoxygenated blood away from the liver.

hepatitis A highly infectious inflammatory disease of the liver commonly caused by viruses, but also by alcohol, drugs, and overexposure to toxic chemicals. Hepatitis comprises at least two very different illnesses. Hepatitis A (infectious hepatitis) is spread via viruses taken in with food and excreted in the faeces. Hepatitis B (serum hepatitis) is transmitted via infected blood or blood products and is a very serious illness. There is also a hepatitis C virus. Hepatitis has been spread in the past during orienteering events by runners brushing past undergrowth in a wood where an infected person has already been scratched. Rules specifying clothing to be worn in orienteering are aimed at minimizing this risk.

herbal preparations Substances extracted from naturally-occurring plants. These may include *banned substances. Ma Huang (Chinese ephedra), for example, contains *ephedrine and the use of *ginseng-based preparations has embarrassed some athletes because a preparation may also contain additional or substitute substances which are banned by the *IOC.

herding behaviour *See* contagion theory of collective behaviour.

hereditary Dependent on *genes.

heredity That which is passed on from parents to offspring biologically through the genes.

Hering–Breur reflex The reflexes involving *muscle spindles within the *intercostal muscles which prevent overinflation of the lungs and help maintain the normal rhythm of inspiration and expiration.

hermeneutics The science of interpretations. The word hermeneutics derives from a term for interpreting scriptural texts, but in sociology it refers to the theory and method of interpreting meaningful human action. Hermeneutic research on the behaviour of soccer fans, for example, includes the different interpretations of the fans themselves, and of other observers who may include the researcher.

hernia The protrusion of an organ through a weakness in its body cavity wall; commonly caused by heavy lifting, or obesity and muscle-weakening. Some hernias are quite easy to return to their normal site while others (irreducible hernia) may by impossible to replace. *See also* fascial hernia; and inguinal hernia.

herniated disc *See* prolapsed intervertebral disc.

herniated muscle (fascial hernia; muscle hernia) *See* fascial hernia.

herniography The use of X-radiography to investigate the presence of a *hernia.

heroin A white, crystalline *drug belonging to the *narcotic analgesics which are on the *IOC list of *banned substances. Its continued use leads to *dependence.

herpes Inflammation of the skin caused by viruses. *See also* genital herpes; herpes simplex; and herpes zostera.

herpes genitalis *See* genital herpes.

herpes simplex A condition characterized by small blisters or ulcers (cold sores) in and around the mouth. It is generally associated with overexertion and poor health, and may be viewed as a warning sign that all is not well. *See also* genital herpes.

herpes zoster (shingles) A disease caused by the same virus as *chicken pox. It is characterized by skin lesions on the face, and pain along the distribution of a nerve usually on the face, shoulders, or chest. Physical activity can be continued during shingles as long as there is no fever and the symptoms are not too troublesome.

heterotopia Displacement of an organ or part of the body, such as a bone, from its normal position.

heuristic device 1 In sociology, any general concept that is proposed merely as an aid to analysis. 2 A method of solving mathematical problems which cannot be solved in a finite number of steps. The method involves progressively limiting the field of search by inductive reasoning from past experience. 3 A method of teaching in which students are allowed to learn things for themselves.

hexose A *simple sugar, such as *glucose, containing six carbon atoms.

hexose monophosphate shunt (pentose–phosphate cycle) A metabolic pathway which provides an alternative system to the *tricarboxylic acid cycle for the interconversions of carbohydrate in which a six-carbon carbohydrate is converted into a five-carbon carbohydrate and carbon dioxide. The interconversions generate reducing power in the form NADPH (reduced nicotinamide adenine dinucleotide phosphate) for *fatty acid and *steroid synthesis. It is sometimes known as the direct oxidative pathway.

hiatus An opening or aperture such as those in the *diaphragm for the *oesophagus and *aorta.

hiatus hernia A protrusion of part of the stomach through the hole through which the *oesophagus enters the *thoracic cavity.

Hick's law Mathematical statement that the choice-reaction time is linearly related to $\log_2$ of the number (N) of stimulus–response alternatives, or to the amount of information that must be processed in order to respond. It is expressed as follows:

$$\text{choice-reaction time} = a + b(\log_2 N)$$

where a and b are constants. In simple experiments, reaction time increased by nearly a constant (150 ms) for every doubling of the stimulus–response alternatives.

hidden audience The *audience not actually present at an event. The hidden audience may include television viewers and others interested in the event, and those who study the results in the media. The hidden audience can be a source of *anxiety which can disrupt the performance of an athlete. *Compare* audience effect.

hidrosis Sweating; especially applied to excessive sweating.

hierarchy An organization of people habits, or concepts, in which simpler components are combined to form increasingly complex integrations.

high altitude pulmonary oedema A serious, potentially fatal condition in which fluid accumulates in the lungs of some individuals who ascend heights exceeding 2400 m.

high arches An exaggerated arching of the foot which can increase the risk of injury since the foot does not hit the ground properly. High arches (*see* arches of foot) may also result in problems on the top of the foot if a shoe is not cut high enough and constricts the foot when the laces are tightened.

high blood pressure *See* hypertension.

high culture The moral, social, and physical qualities which are perceived to be the most valuable to a *culture. High culture is thought by many to be developed and refined by training in the tastes and manners of society. In western societies, high culture includes classical music, ballet, poetry, and the fine arts which involve a relatively small segment of the population. These aspects of culture are usually the domain of the upper class or well-educated social élite. *Compare* mass culture; and taste culture.

high-density lipoproteins (HDL) A group of *proteins found in blood *plasma and *lymph that are combined with *lipids. High density lipoproteins transport *cholesterol from the tissues to the *liver to be broken down and excreted. Thus, HDL seems to accelerate the clearance of cholesterol from the blood, reducing the likelihood of cholesterol becoming deposited in arterial walls to cause *arteriosclerosis, and thereby reducing the risk of *coronary heart disease. Research has shown that regular *aerobic exercise results in an increase in high density lipoproteins. *Compare* low-density lipoproteins.

higher-order conditioning The use of previously *conditioned stimuli to condition further responses, in much the same way as unconditioned stimuli are used. *See also* conditioning.

high means interdependence Relationship exhibited by team-members in interactive sports that require the members to depend upon each other to achieve team goals. *Compare* low means interdependence.

hindbrain Part of the *brain consisting of the *medulla oblongata, the *pons, and the *cerebellum.

hinge-joint (ginglymus) A *synovial joint which allows motion along a single plane, permitting *flexion and *extension only.

hip Region on either side of the *pelvis where the *femur articulates with the *coxal bones.

hip-bones *See* coxal bones.

hip abduction Movement of the thigh to the side, away from the midline, or lifting the leg sidewards. Hip abduction involves the *concentric contraction of the *gluteus medius and *gluteus minimus.

hip abductor A muscle which effects *hip abduction.

hip adduction Movement of the *femur towards the midline or from a sidewards position. Hip adduction also involves *concentric contractions of the *adductors, the *pectineus, and *gracilis muscles.

hip adductor A muscle which effects *hip adduction.

hip extension Movement of the *femur backwards on the *pelvis. It involves *concentric contractions of the *biceps femoris, *semitendinosus, and *semimembranosus. Hip extension also involves the *gluteus maximus when the movement between the pelvis and the femur approaches and goes beyond 15° (mainly during running).

hip extensor A muscle which effects *hip extension.

hip flexion Movement of the *femur forwards from the *pelvis. It involves *concentric contractions of the *iliopsoas, *sartorius, *rectus femoris, *tensor fascia latae, and *pectineus muscles, with the *adductor longus assisting.

hip flexor A muscle which effects *hip flexion.

hip girdle *See* pelvic girdle.

hip girth *See* gluteal girth.

hip injuries The hips form strong joints with a wide range of movements but flexibility is usually sacrificed for stability, and *overextensions commonly cause injuries such as *adductor strains.

hip-joint (coxal joint) A multiaxial *synovial, *ball-and-socket joint between the *acetabulum of the *os coxa and the *head of the *femur. The hip-joint permits a wide range of movements in all planes including *flexion, *extension, *abduction, *adduction, *rotation, and *circumduction. The *articular surfaces of the hip-joint fit snugly together. The socket is deep and the *joint capsule is heavy and reinforced by strong ligaments. Consequently, dislocations are rare. The hip-joint is highly adapted for weight bearing.

hip lateral rotation Rotation of the *femur outwards, around its axis. Hip lateral rotation involves the *concentric contractions of the *gluteus maximus, *gluteus medius, *biceps femoris, and, during *adduction, the *adductor brevis.

hip lateral rotator A muscle which effects *hip lateral rotation.

hip medial rotation Rotation of the thigh inwards around its longitudinal axis, towards the midline of the body. This movement involves *concentric contraction of the *gluteus medius, *gracilis semitendinosus, and *semimembranosus muscles.

hip medial rotator A muscle which effects *hip medial rotation.

hip-movements Movements allowed by the *hip, described with respect to the *femur.

hip outward rotation Rotation of the femur around its longitudinal axis towards the midline of the body. The movement involves *concentric contractions of the *gluteus medius, *gracilis semitendinosus, and *semimembranosus muscles.

hippocampus A swelling in the *lateral *ventricle of the *brain that screens sensory data in order to discard or store the data. The hippocampus is involved in the functions of the *limbic system.

hip pointer Inflammation of the crest of the *ilium resulting from a physical blow.

His, bundle of Atrioventricular bundle of modified cardiac muscle fibres in the *heart that run from the *atrioventricular node down to the *septum. The fibres transmit the electrical stimulation which causes ventricular contraction over the ventricle wall.

histamine An endogenous substance which mediates allergic responses in the nose, eyes, and skin. Histamine is released by *mast cells in most tissues during inflammation. It acts as a powerful vasodilator and increases vascular permeability. It is also secreted from some areas of the *hypothalamus and functions as a *metabotropic neurotransmitter belonging to the *biogenic amines.

histidine An *amino acid from which *histamine is derived. Histidine is possibly essential in the diet of children, but its requirement in adult diets is not clearly established. *See also* essential amino acids.

histogram A graph used in statistics in which frequency distributions of interval-level data are represented by contiguous rectangles. In a histogram, the area of each rectangle is directly proportional to the frequency of each class interval represented. *Compare* bar chart.

HIV (human immunodeficiency virus) The virus that causes *AIDS.

holism The idea that the whole is greater than its parts. Thus a holistic view of behaviour is one in which a particular behaviour cannot be explained by reducing it to its simplest units. *See also* Gestalt psychology.

holistic Pertaining to holism.

hollow sprints A form of *training in which one sprint is separated from the next by a so-called hollow period involving either walking or jogging.

holocrine gland A gland that accumulates its secretions within its own cells. The secretions are released only upon the complete disintegration of the cells.

holoenzyme A conjugated *protein consisting of an *enzyme and its *cofactor.

home-court advantage (home-field advantage) The notion that playing at home is an advantage because of audience support. *See also* self-attention.

home-field advantage *See* home-court advantage.

homeostasis Compensatory mechanisms by which a constant physical or chemical state is maintained. Physiological homeostasis is illustrated by the maintenance of a constant body *core temperature and *blood sugar levels. Psychological homeostasis is illustrated by the maintenance of self-respect through such compensatory devices as rationalizing and blaming others for faults. In *sociology, homeostasis has been applied to the controversial suggestion that social systems tend to act in ways which are self-maintaining and self-equilibrating.

homeotherm An organism which maintains a constant body *core temperature.

homologous In anatomy, applied to body-parts or organs which have a similar embryological origin but which do not necessarily have similar functions.

homophobia An irrational fear or intolerance of homosexuality, or behaviour that is perceived to uphold and support traditional gender role expectations. The prevelant assumption in Western society is that heterosexuality is the only acceptable sexual orientation. In sport, homophobia can be expressed in ways ranging from the telling of jokes directed against homosexual activity through harassment to physical violence against homosexual sportspeople.

Hooke's law A law which states that within the *elastic limits of a material, a *strain is proportional to the *stress producing it. Therefore, the deformation imparted to a body is directly related to the magnitude of the *distorting force. *See also* elasticity; and elastic modulus.

hooliganism Rough, antisocial behaviour commonly associated with young people. Hooliganism has been used to describe the behaviour of lawless soccer fans who form a subcultural element of British soccer structure. The term is probably derived from an antisocial family named Houlighan who lived in the East End of London during the nineteenth century.

horizontal displacement The distance a projectile has moved between the point of release and the point of landing measured as a straight line parallel to the ground. *Compare* vertical displacement.

horizontal projection The horizontal path of a projectile.

horizontal status The different but equal positions in an organization among individuals who are on approximately the same levels within a *hierarchy. On a team, the horizontal status reflects comparisons of different team-members. *Compare* vertical status.

horizontal velocity Component of a projectile's *velocity which acts parallel to the ground and has no tendency to lift the projectile into the air.

hormone A chemical produced in one part of the body which has its effects in another part. Endocrine glands are the sites of production from which the hormones are carried away by the bloodstream. Hormones act as chemical messengers to regulate specific body functions.

horse-power A British unit of power; one horsepower is equal to the *work done at a rate of 550 foot-pounds per second and is equivalent to 745.7 watts.

hostile aggression (hostility) *Aggression against another person with intent to do physical or mental harm; the goal or reinforcement is to inflict pain or suffering on the victim. It is always accompanied by anger. *Compare* instrumental aggression.

hostility *See* hostile aggression.

housemaid's knee (prepatellar bursitis) An inflammation of the *prepatellar bursa. It is relatively harmless but can interfere with normal physical activity.

HR *See* heart-rate.

5HT *See* serotonin.

Hull's drive theory *See* drive theory.

human choriongonadotrophin *See* human chorionic gonadotrophin.

human chorionic gonadotrophin (chorionic gonadotrophin; HCG; human choriongonadotrophin) A *hormone produced by the *placenta during pregnancy which stimulates the production of *testosterone. *Exogenous sources of the hormone have been misused by athletes to increase testosterone levels artificially. Consequently, HCG is on the *IOC list of *banned substances.

human competency A component of managerial competency which refers to a leader's or coach's power of persuasion and ability to establish harmonious relationships within a team. It is a critical component of leadership.

human development model A framework around which the study of behaviour may take place. The model incorporates statements about desirable goals; focuses on sequential change; emphasizes techniques of optimization rather than remediation; considers the individual as an integrated biopsychosocial unit and therefore amenable to a multidisciplinary focus; and views individuals as developing in a biocultural context. There is, therefore, more concern with the development of an individual's potential than with the therapeutic or remedial handling of a person's social or emotional problems.

human immunodeficiency virus *See* HIV.

humanistic Applied to beliefs which emphasize *self and the power of individuals to realize their human potential.

human relations theory Theory of *leadership behaviour which focuses on the employee or, in a coach–athlete relationship, the athlete. It is consistent with the *consideration approach to leadership. *See also* McGregor's theory X; and McGregor's theory Y.

human science model A theoretical approach to psychology based on the view that human psychological processes are qualitatively distinct from those of other forms of life. *Compare* natural science model.

humeroulnar joint *See* elbow-joint.

humerus The *long bone in the upper arm. The humerus articulates with the *scapula in the shoulder and with the *radius and *ulna at the elbow.

humerus width The distance between the *medial and *lateral *epicondyles of the *humerus when the arm is bent at the elbow to form a 90° angle. *See also* body breadth.

humidity A measure of the content of water vapour in the atmosphere. *See also* absolute humidity; and relative humidity.

humoral immune response Immunity provided by *antibodies present in blood *plasma and other body fluids.

hunchback *See* kyphosis.

hunger Physiological need for food that is usually experienced as an unpleasant sensation. The desire for food may become so intense that it dominates thought and action. *Compare* appetite.

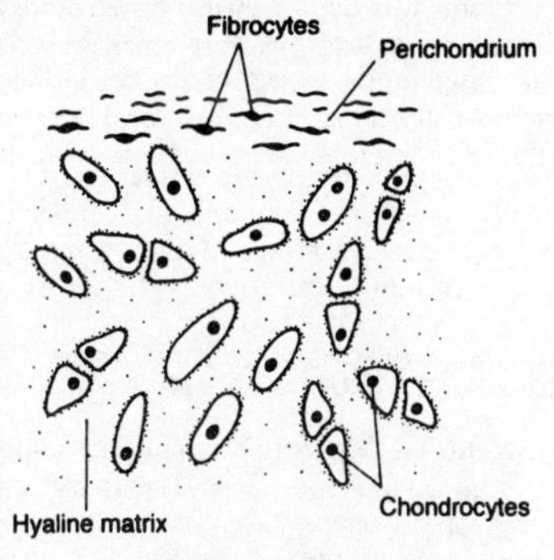

hyaline cartilage

hyaline cartilage A common type of *cartilage. It is a smooth, shiny cartilage which covers the *articular surfaces of *bones. Hyaline cartilage contains whitish-blue elastic material with *chondrocytes forming distinct *cell nests, and a fine network of *collagen fibre. Its smoothness reduces *friction between opposing bones in a *joint. *See also* McCutchen's weeping lubrication theory.

hyaluronic acid An acid *mucopolysaccharide found in *synovial fluid and nearly all types of *connective tissue. Hyaluronic acid acts as a binding agent and affects the viscosity of the *ground substance.

hyaluronidase An *enzyme formed in the *testes, *semen, and other tissues. Preparations of hyaluronidase have been used successfully to treat bruises (contusions).

hybrid system In *cybernetics, a large control system that consists of smaller systems of various types. Most cyberneticians regard humans as such a hybrid.

hydrarthrosis A swelling in a *joint, commonly the knee, caused by an accumulation of *synovial fluid.

hydrochlorothiazide A *drug belonging to the *diuretics which are on the *IOC list of *banned substances.

hydrocollator A hot, moist pack used as a *therapeutic aid in the treatment of *contusions, *muscle sprains, and *muscle spasms. A pack is heated to about 65 °C and applied to the injured region. Dry towels are placed between the athlete and the pack to prevent excessive heat reaching the skin. The pack has an *analgesic effect by increasing surface circulation.

hydrocortisone (cortisol) The main *glucocorticoid synthesized and released by the *adrenal cortex. Hydrocortisone is a *drug belonging to the *corticosteroids which are on the *IOC list of restricted drugs. It has a strong anti-inflammatory action. Its use in the treatment by injection of *Achilles tendinitis has sometimes resulted in complete rupture of the *Achilles tendon. There is an increased risk of *ligament rupture if training or competition is carried out within 48 hours of pain-killing injections or a *steroid injection. It is now universally agreed that to inject a tendon with a steroid injection is likely to cause rupture and the procedure should not be used.

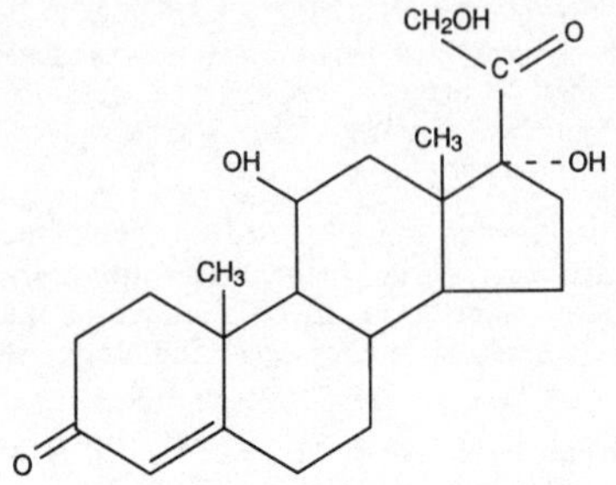

hydrocortisone

hydrodynamic drag force The *drag force of water which resists the movement of a body. *See also* profile drag; and wave drag.

hydrodynamic lift force A *lift force developed in a *fluid, especially water.

hydrodynamics The mathematical study of *forces, *energy, and *pressure of liquids in motion. *Compare* hydrostatics.

hydroflumethiazide A *drug belonging to the *diuretics which are on the *IOC list of *banned substances.

hydrogen acceptor Any substance that can become reduced by the addition of *hydrogen.

hydrogenation The process of adding *hydrogen atoms to *unsaturated fat to make it more *saturated, solid, and more resistant to chemical change. Food manufacturers often hydrogenate fats to enable them to be stored for longer periods.

hydrogen bond A weak *bond between the slightly positively-charged *hydrogen atom of one molecule and a slightly negatively-charged part of another molecule.

hydrolysis Chemical reaction in which large molecules are broken down by the addition of water.

hydrolytic enzyme An *enzyme which catalyses an *hydrolysis. Digestive enzymes are hydrolytic, breaking down food by the addition of water.

hydrophilic Applied to molecules, or portions of molecules, that interact with water and charged particles. Hydrophilic molecules have an affinity for water.

hydrophobic Applied to molecules,or portions of molecules, that interact only with nonpolar molecules. Hydrophobic molecules are repulsed by water.

hydrostatic pressure The *pressure exerted by a liquid.

hydrostatics The mathematical study of *forces and *pressures of liquids at rest. *Compare* hydrodynamics.

hydrostatic weighing Underwater weighing which, by an application of *Archimedes' principle, is used to determine body volume and as an indirect method of determining *body density (*see* body density) and *body composition.

hydrotherapy The use of water in the treatment of disorders. Hydrotherapy has been successfully used to treat *sprains, *strains, *contusions, *tendinitis and *tenosynovitis. Water is also often used as an exercise medium after surgery or immobilization to help regain range of motion. Usually low temperatures are used (8–12 °C) since hot water may exacerbate bleeding and swelling.

hydroxyproline A chemical similar to an *amino acid and found only in *connective tissue. An increase in urinary hydroxyproline is an indication of damage and breakdown of connective tissue.

hydroxytryptophon *See* serotonin.

hygiene 1 The science of preserving health. **2** Clean or healthy practices. Personal and corporate hygiene are of considerable importance in sport to prevent the occurrence and spread of contagious disorders such as *athlete's foot which can spread rapidly through communal changing facilities.

hygrometer An instrument for measuring the *relative humidity of the atmosphere.

hyoid bone A small U-shaped bone in the neck which supports the tongue.

hyperaemia The presence of excess blood in a vessel or body-part. Hyperaemia may be caused by an increased blood flow or blockage of the affected part.

hypercapnia An abnormally high carbon dioxide concentration in the blood causing an overstimulation of the respiratory centres.

hypercholesteraemia An abnormally high *cholesterol level in the blood.

hyperextension The *extension of a *joint beyond its normal range of extension.

hyperflexibility Excessive *flexibility, either of one or a number of joints, resulting in joint-looseness and an increased risk of dislocations. Hyperflexibility can cause bow-leggedness (*see* genu varum) or knock knees (*see* genu valgum), and a propensity to knee injuries. It can be caused by *osteogenesis imperfecta (abnormally brittle bones) or over-training when young, before completion of *epiphysial growth.

hyperglycaemia An abnormally high level of glucose in the blood. It may occur as a result of an excessive dietary intake of *carbohydrates or of diseases such as *diabetes mellitus.

hyperhidrosis Excessive sweating not related to exercise. It may be associated with a hot environment, wearing inappropriate warm clothing, fever, and certain hormonal conditions such as *hyperactivity of the *thyroid gland. Hyperhidrosis is not in itself a problem in sport as long as there is sufficient replacement of fluids. However, it can cause problems in gripping equipment.

hyperkinesis A condition characterized by excessive motor activity.

hyperlipaemia A condition in which there is excessive *lipid in the blood.

hyperlipoproteinaemia The presence of abnormally high levels of *lipoproteins in the blood .

hypermetropia (far sighted; hyperopia; long sightedness) An eye defect which results in light rays converging beyond the *retina and an inability to focus on close objects.

hypermobile joint disease (double-jointed; hypermobility syndrome) A condition in which the joints are excessively mobile ('double-jointed'). It occurs especially in young people who do too much *flexibility training. Some so-called double-jointed individuals may suffer growing pains as children. As they mature, they may develop *osteoarthritis, joint pains and degenerative joint changes, recurrent *dislocations, and other musculoskeletal injuries. *Compare* benign hypermobility.

hypermobility Excessive motion at a *joint which lacks *stability due to laxity of *ligaments, *muscles, or *joint capsule.

hypermobility syndrome *See* hypermobile joint disease.

hypernatraemia An abnormally high sodium ion concentration in the blood. It is usually diagnosed as being greater than 150 mmol l^{-1}. It may occur as a result of excessive sweating or inadequate fluid intake.

hypernoea A marked increase in *pulmonary ventilation with both increased rate and depth of breathing that is related to increased levels of exercise or *metabolism.

hyperopia *See* hypermetropia.

hyperostosis An excessive thickening of the outer layers of bone. *See also* exostosis.

hyperplasia An increase in the number of cells in a tissue or organ which increases in size as a consequence.

hyperpolarization The reduction of the potential difference across a membrane, especially that of a *neurone, to a value less than the normal *resting potential. *See also* after hyperpolarization.

hyperpronation Excessive or prolonged *pronation during the support phase of running. It can be diagnosed by an examination of the wear of a shoe: excessive wear of the *medial side of the heel suggests hyperpronation. Hyperpronation creates an increased or unusual *stress on the foot structure and extrinsic muscles. It often results in a compensatory increase in the internal rotation of the entire leg which exaggerates the twisting forces within the *Achilles tendon and places abnormal stress on the joint between the *patella and the *femur.

hyperreactivity A response, similar to an allergic reaction, to contact with an extremely small dose of an irritant substance.

hypersensitivity An abnormally high sensitivity, especially to a particular *antigen, which may result in conditions such as *hay fever, *asthma, or even *anaphylactic shock.

hypertension High blood pressure, both *systolic and *diastolic. In adults it is generally agreed that the blood pressure is abnormally high when the average of several resting supine blood pressures is equal to or more than 140 mmHg, and the average of several diastolic pressures is equal to, or more than, 90 mmHg. Hypertension increases the risk of *heart attack, *stroke, and kidney failure because it adds to the workload of the heart, causing it to enlarge and, over time, to weaken; in addition, it may damage the walls of the arteries. Arterial hypertension occurs in about 20 per cent of the population in western countries. The preventative and therapeutic values of a mild but extensive endurance exercise training programme with respect to most hypertensions is well established. In one study the systolic blood pressure of 62 males aged 35–58 averaged 188 mmHg before training; after a period of exercising for 30 minutes three times per week systolic pressure averaged 155 mmHg.

hyperthermia An abnormally high body *core temperature (more than 41 °C). *Compare* hypothermia. *See also* heat-stroke; and fever.

hypertonic Applied to a solution that tends to cause the volume of a cell to decrease. Thus the cell, when immersed in a hypertonic solution, tends to lose water and shrink. *Compare* isotonic solution.

hypertrophy An increase in tissue- or organ-size due to an increase in the size of functional cells without an increase in the number of cells. Muscles are believed to undergo this process although there is some evidence that the number of fibres may increase by longitudinal splitting as a result of chronic exercise such as weight-lifting.

hyperventilation Excessive *ventilation of the lungs caused by increased depth and frequency of breathing. It can occur voluntarily or as the result of impaired gas exchange in the lungs. It may be an important response to low *partial pressures of oxygen at high altitudes. Voluntary hyperventilation results in the elimination of carbon dioxide and a reduction in the stimulus to breathe. It may provide a small advantage where a short burst of activity is needed (e.g., during a sprint) as more carbon dioxide is removed from the *alveoli, possibly allowing more oxygen to combine with *haemoglobin (*see* Bohr effect). However, hyperventilation is dangerous prior to underwater swimming because it may result in fainting. *See* alkalosis; and Valsalva's manoeuvre.

hypervitaminosis A condition caused by the intake of excessive quantities of certain *vitamins, such as the fat-soluble vitamins A and D.

hypervolemia An increased volume of circulating blood.

hypnosis An artificially-induced, trance-like mental state in which the subject is more than usually receptive to suggestions. Hypnosis has been used in sport for a variety of reasons including as a relaxation strategy in stress management and in dealing with various psychological problems such as phobias. Hypnosis has also been used as an *intervention strategy to improve the *self-confidence of boxers.

hypnotic Applied to a sedative drug; a sleeping pill.

hypnotic induction The process used by a hypnotist to bring a subject into a hypnotic trance.

hypnotic trance The state of being hypnotized. *See* hypnosis.

hypocapnia A condition in which there is a deficiency of carbon dioxide in the blood. One cause of hypocapnia is *hyperventilation.

hypodermis (superficial fascia) Tissue lying immediately beneath the skin. The hypodermis, which is made of loose *connective tissue containing *areolar and *adipose tissues, anchors the skin to underlying organs.

hypoflexibility A condition in which *joint mobility is less than normal due to joint stiffness or tightness. Hypoflexibility may increase the risk of injuries such as *strains and *sprains.

hypoglycaemia An abnormally low concentration of *glucose in the blood. It causes loss of *co-ordination, muscular weakness, sweating, and mental confusion. Severe hypoglycaemia is rare and dangerous; it may lead to a *coma. It can be caused by severe physical exhaustion or an intake of medicines such as *insulin. Sufferers of *diabetes mellitus are particularly prone to hypoglycaemia which is rapidly relieved by the administration of glucose.

hypohidrosis *See* hypoidrosis.

hypoidrosis (hypohidrosis) The secretion of abnormally low amounts of sweat. *Compare* hyperidrosis.

hypokalaemia A condition characterized by a profound lowering of potassium levels in the blood and extracellular fluid. It may occur after repeated use of *diuretics or after *dehydration.

hypokinesis A condition characterized by the lack of, or insufficient, regular exercise and movement of the body. *See also* hypokinetic disease.

hypokinetic disease A disease brought on, at least in part, by insufficient movement and exercise. Hypokinesis has been identified as an independent risk factor for the origin and progression of several widespread, chronic diseases including *coronary heart diseases, *diabetes, *obesity, and lower back-pain.

hyponatraemia Abnormally low concentration of *sodium ions in the blood *plasma which may be caused by imbibing too much water, particularly after excessive sweating.

hypophysis An embryonic pouch in the buccal cavity which forms part of the *pituitary gland.

hypopnoea Condition in which the depth of breathing is shallow.

hyposensitization A method of reducing sensitivity to an allergen. *See also* desensitization.

hypotension An abnormally low *arterial *blood pressure. It occurs after excessive fluid losses and bleeding. *See also* orthostatic hypotension.

hypothalamus A small portion of the *diencephalon below the *thalamus of the *brain derived from the sides and floor of the *forebrain. The hypothalamus is the main *visceral control centre and is vitally important for *homeostasis. It regulates the activity of the *autonomic nervous system and controls the activity of a number of *endocrine glands. It also contains centres for *thermoregulation, *ionic regulation, and *osmoregulation. The hypothalamus is involved in many other autonomic functions including the control of thirst, sleep, and hunger. It plays a role in regulating the *metabolism of *fats, *carbohydrates, and *proteins and is also concerned with motivation and emotions.

hypothermia A condition characterized by an abnormally low body *core temperature resulting in a rapid, progressive mental and physical collapse. This is caused by exposure to cold, aggravated by wet and windy conditions, when a person is suffering from physical exhaustion and lack of food. Victims have a weak pulse, become irrational, slow to respond, are cold to touch, and have speech and visual difficulties. Application of external heat can be dangerous. Hypothermia may prove fatal if untreated.

hypothesis A conjectured statement which implies or states a relationship between two or more *variables. An hypothesis is usually formed from facts already known or research already carried out and is expressed in such a way that it can be tested or appraised as a generalization about a phenomenon. *See also* experimental hypothesis; and null hypothesis.

hypotonia A condition characterized by deficient *muscle tension.

hypotonic 1 Applied to an external solution which causes cells to increase in volume. 2 Term indicating conditions below normal *tension or *tone.

hypoventilation A reduced *ventilation of the lungs due to reduced breathing-rate and *tidal volume.

hypovitaminosis A deficiency of *vitamins which may result from lack of dietary vitamins or an inability to absorb vitamins in the *alimentary canal.

hypoxaemia A deficient oxygen-content of the blood.

hypoxia A condition in which there is an inadequate supply of oxygen to the tissues.

hysteria 1 A temporary state of tension or over-excitement in which there is loss of control over emotions. 2 A neurotic condition, marked by emotional instability, which may be converted into physical symptoms such as paralysis of an arm or leg.

H-zone The area in the middle of a muscle *sarcomere where *actin and *myosin filaments do not overlap; it contains myosin filaments only.

I

I Symbol for *iodine.

iatrogenic Applied to a disease or disorder caused by surgical or medical treatment, including the side-effects of a *drug which has been inappropriately prescribed or administered.

I-band A zone bisected by the *Z-line within a *sarcomere of a *muscle fibre which contains the contractile protein *actin.

ibuprofen An *analgesic *drug derived from propionic acid. Ibuprofen is commonly used in sport as a *nonsteroidal anti-inflammatory drug to reduce swelling and pain, and accelerate recovery of soft tissue injuries.

IC *See* inspiration capacity.

ICE *See* RICE

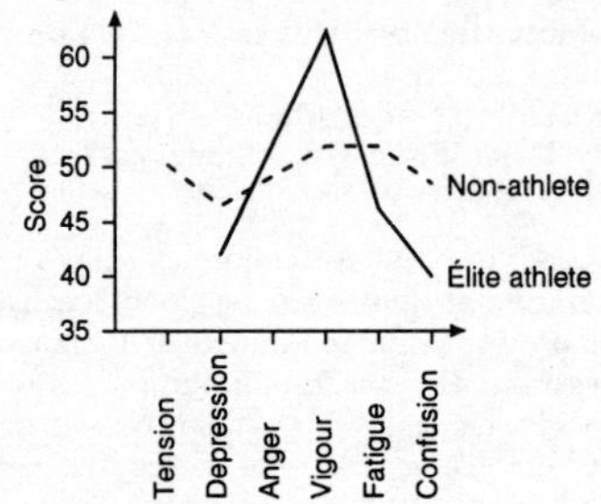

iceberg profile

iceberg profile The expected *psychological profile of an élite athlete incorporating the six factors measured by *POMS in which the élite athlete scores low on all negative mood states and high on vigour. *See also* mental health model.

ICSH *See* luteinizing hormone.

icterus *See* jaundice.

id One of the three elements of personality proposed by Freud (*see* Freudian theory). The id is the unconscious part of the mind and the basis of personality; it contains all the inherited resources, especially the instincts. It has been referred to as 'the deepest part of the *psyche'. It is from the id that the other two elements, the *ego and *superego develop.

ideal Pertaining to a highly desirable and possible state of affairs.

idealization The representation of a general or particular phenomenon by, or in accordance with, our desires or ideals.

ideal model A hypothetical description of how an ideal performance can be attained by a particular individual. An ideal model can be used as a standard against which the actual performance of an athlete can be compared. It is assumed that learning takes place as the performance of the skill more closely approximates that of the ideal model. It is generally agreed that, if there is to be effective communication and good interpersonal relations, the ideal model must be formulated by both coach and athlete.

ideal self A concept of self which refers to the person one would like to be. The ideal self is usually based on moral principles acquired from *significant others, especialy family.

ideal type A representation of a phenomenon in its abstract or pure form.

ideal weight A misnomer; the average, but not necessarily the most desirable, weight given in insurance tables for persons of a given height and sex.

identical elements theory Theory which posits that *transfer of learning between two tasks increases with the similarity between components of the tasks.

identification 1 The process of modelling one's behaviour after that of another individual, usually an older person. 2 A form of *direct motivation used by a coach. It involves disguised *compliance. For example, a coach using identification may say to the athlete 'If you care about the team, you will do this for me.' Successful use of identification depends on a positive relationship between a coach and athlete in which the athlete wishes to please the coach.

identity The perception of *self that develops as a child differentiates from parents and family, and takes a place in society. *Play is regarded as an important element in the formation of identity.

identity crisis A condition which occurs when a person experiences great difficulties in acquiring a clear perception of *self. It occurs especially with a young person who urgently seeks greater self-understanding, or when a person undergoes psychological turmoil in attempting to formulate a concept of self and decide upon future goals.

ideological Pertaining to an *ideology.

ideology 1 Rationalization or justification of an identifiable group. 2 A political programme or social movement. 3 Broad-reaching world-view or outlook, involving unconscious assumptions about the world and society, that influences the thoughts, and the political and social actions of people.

idioculture 1 A group, such as a sports team, that creates norms and behaviour patterns, such as nicknames and rituals, that are different from those in the *subculture of which it is a part. 2 The *culture of a small group, such as a sports team. The idioculture consists of a system of knowledge, beliefs, behaviours, and customs shared by members of the group.

idiogram *See* karyogram.

idiographic An orientation to social enquiry which focuses on unique persons, events and phenomena. Methods such as *ethnography and biography are used to study individual and unique experiences.

idiopathic Applied to a disease or condition whose cause is unknown.

idiosyncracy A condition in which a *drug produces an unusual reaction within an individual. The effect is normally genetically-determined and may be due to a biological deficiency (e.g., an inability to metabolize the drug) resulting in the subject over-reacting to the drug.

ileum Part of the *alimentary canal, where food is absorbed and digestion completed, between the *duodenum and *colon.

iliac artery One of several arteries which supply the lower limbs and pelvic region. *See also* common iliac artery.

iliac crest The thickened *superior margin of the *ilium which terminates posteriorly in the *iliac spine; it forms an attachment point for muscles of the *trunk, hip, and thigh.

iliac crest skinfold A *skinfold measurement of a vertical fold of tissue immediately *superior to the *iliac crest.

iliacitis An inflammation of the crest of the *ilium.

iliacus The large fan-shaped thigh muscle, starting on the *pelvis, crossing the hip, and inserting on the *femur. It works in close association with the *psoas major with which it has a common *tendon on the femur. The iliacus is the *prime mover of hip *flexion, flexing the thigh on the trunk when the pelvis is fixed. Its *origin is on the iliac fossa and its *insertion is on the *lesser trochanter of the femur via the *iliopsoas tendon.

iliocastrale A *landmark which is the most *lateral point of the *iliac crest.

iliocostalis (sarcospinalis) A *lateral member of the *erector spinae group of muscles. The iliocostalis extends from the *pelvis to the neck and divides into three regional parts: the iliocostalis lumborum, iliocostalis thoracis and iliocostalis cervicis. Its *origins are on the *iliac crest and the *thoracic ribs. The muscle *insertions are on the ribs. The iliocostalis extends the *vertebral column and helps to maintain an erect posture. When acting on one side, it bends the vertebral column.

iliolumbar ligament A *ligament connecting the last *lumbar vertebrae to the crest of the *ilium.

iliopsoas A composite of two closely-related thigh muscles, the *iliacus and *psoas major, which share a common insertion *tendon in the *femur. The iliopsoas lies in the *anterior, *medial part of the thigh.

iliospinale A *landmark which is the *inferior aspect of the tip of the anterior superior iliac spine. It is sometimes inexactly referred to as the spinale.

iliotibial band (iliotibial tract) A *tendon running along the outside of the thigh that helps to stabilize the *knee-joint. It is the thickened lateral portion of the *fascia lata extending from the *iliac crest to the *tibia.

iliotibial band syndrome *See* runner's knee.

iliotibial tract Thickened lateral portion of the *fascia lata. It extends on a tendinous band from the *iliac crest to the knee.

ilium A large, flaring bone which forms the upper part of each side of the hip-bone. The two ilium bones are separate in children but become fused in adulthood. It is sometimes called the haunch-bone.

illogical model A model used in *attribution theory which is based on evidence that people are not always logical in making causal attributions but often make blatantly self-serving ones which are ego-enhancing or ego-protecting. *Compare* logical model.

illusion 1 A sensory perception considered as mistaken because it does not conform to an objective representation of the physical form or pattern. **2** A subjective falsification of past experience.

imagery A technique used in the acquisition of skills and involving the production of vivid mental pictures of situations by the normal processes of thought.

imagery relaxation A relaxation procedure which involves athletes imagining themselves in some environment or place where they always feel relaxed and comfortable. For example, Jackie Stewart, ex-world champion racing driver, used to sit in his car for several moments before a race and imagine his body inflating like a balloon. Then he would let the air out and feel himself relax. This, he contended, helped him prepare physically and mentally for a race. It is a form of *somatic stress management.

imaging *See* visualization.

imbalance Lack of balance, for example, between antagonistic pairs of muscle, between water and an electrolyte, or between the limbs which make up a pair.

immobilization Fixation of the position of a body part to make movement impossible.

immune response A host reaction in response to foreign *antigens involving the formation of *antibodies by *B-cell lymphocytes, or a cell-mediated response from *T-cells.

immunity The ability of the body to resist many agents (both living and non-living) that can cause disease; resistance to disease. Immunity is provided by *antibodies and white blood cells (*see* leucocyte). *See also* active immunity; and passive immunity.

immunization The process of giving immunity by artificial means. Passive immunity may be conferred by the injection of an *antiserum. Active immunity is conferred by the administration, orally or by injection, of *antigens in the form of a *vaccine which promotes production of *antibodies. The vaccine may consist of dead or inactivated bacteria, or viruses or their toxins which trigger the production of antibodies to a specific disease so that the individual is then immune to it.

immunocompetence The ability of *lymphocytes to recognize (by binding) specific *antigens.

immunodeficiency disease Disease resulting from the deficient production or function of *lymphocytes or certain molecules required for normal immunity.

immunogen Foreign substance which stimulates an *immune response.

immunoglobulin A *protein in the blood, such as *γ globulin, made in *B-cells and which possesses *antibody activity. Immunoglobin is an important part of the immune defence system.

immunological status The condition of the immune system of an individual. Intense sports competition and psychological stress can have a depressive effect on the immune system which can favour the development of infections. However, biological resistance is stimulated through varying the workloads.

immunology The study of immunity and all the defence mechanisms of the body.

impact The collision of two bodies.

impacted fracture *Fracture in which the ends of the broken bone are forced into each other. It is a type of fracture commonly associated with hip-fractures and occurs when a person falls and attempts to break the fall with outstretched arms.

impact force A *force which reaches its maximum value earlier than 50 milliseconds after first contact. An impact force occurs during the take off and landing phases of jumps; for example, when a long-jumper strikes the take-off board, the contact time is about 100 ms with the first 20–30 ms being the duration of the impact force. *Compare* active force.

impact injury An injury resulting from a collision with another person or with an object.

impact, Newton's law of A law formulated by Sir Isaac Newton (1642–1727) after his studies of impacts between elastic bodies. He observed that if two bodies move toward each other along the same straight line, the difference between their velocities immediately after impact has a constant relationship with the difference between their velocities at the moment of impact: $(v_1-v_2)/(u_1-u_2) = -e$, where e is the *coefficient of restitution, v_1 and v_2 are the velocities of the two bodies immediately after impact, and u_1 and u_2 are the velocities of the two bodies immediately before impact.

imperial unit A British system of units based on the pound, yard, and gallon. It has been replaced by *SI units for scientific purposes.

impetigo A skin disorder caused by the bacterium *Staphylococcus aureus* , characterized by small pus-filled blisters and fever. It is extremely contagious and should preclude participation in all contact sports. If extensive, all activity should be avoided.

impingement Trapping of soft tissues leading to a painful inflammation. *See also* swimmer's shoulder.

impingement exostosis A benign bony outgrowth from a bone where the surfaces of two bones rub against each other in a joint.

impingement syndrome *See* swimmer's shoulder.

impression management A person's management of his or her own behaviour and social actions so that the impressions he or she conveys to others can be controlled. The aim of impression management is for the person to present himself or herself in a generally favourable way which is appropriate to the social setting, and it often involves the person adopting a particular *role.

imprinting A form of *learning which occurs in young animals, usually during a critical, sensitive period of their lives. During imprinting, a young animal learns to direct some of its social responses to a particular object, usually a parent.

impulse Impulse of force is the area under a force–time curve which represents the amount of *force applied to a bone at each moment of an action. For a constant force, impulse is the product of the force and the time for which it acts, impulse = force×time; for a variable force, the impulse is the *integral of the force with respect to time. In either case, the impulse of an object is equal to the change of *momentum that is produced by it, and the longer the time a force is applied to an object the greater the change in momentum of the object. Techniques have been developed in athletic throwing events to extend the length of time the thrower can apply a force to the projectile and thereby increase its change in momentum (*see* O'Brien technique). Athletic movements are often analysed in terms of two types of impulse: controlled impulse and transmitted impulse. A controlled impulse is due to direct muscular effort and joint leverage, as with the driving leg during a sprint start. A transmitted impulse occurs when, for example, a high-jumper is about to take off. The take-off leg braces itself against the ground, but the magnitude and direction of the impulse is determined by the free arms and legs, and not through the take-off leg.

impulse–momentum relationship An important relationship between impulse and momentum can be derived from *Newton's second law, and shows that the impulse of force (*see* impulse) is equal to the change of *momentum ($mv_f - mv_i$) that it produces. It is basic to an understanding of many sports techniques including starting in track and swimming events.

impulse-timing model A model of the control of limb movement which suggests that *motor programs time the onset, duration, and amount of electrical activity delivered to the muscle, thereby controlling the *impulse of forces from the muscles. Since the pattern of limb movement can be determined by the amount and duration of the forces applied to it, the impulse-timing model is viewed as one way in which the trajectory of the limb can be controlled.

impulse-variability theory A theory applied to simple, rapid aiming movements in which the variability of the *impulse of forces of muscles leads directly to variations in the movement end-point of a limb. The impulse-variability theory maintains that as the distance from a target increases, more *force must be exerted, leading to a greater variability in movement trajectory, decreasing the chances of hitting the target. To compensate for this, the movement time can be slowed down.

impulsion A motion produced by an *impulse.

inborn motivation (primary motivation) Motivation which is part of an individual's biological inheritance such as the need for food, drink, and rest. *See also* acquired motivation.

incentive A more or less extrinsic motive for acting in a certain way. Incentives often act in addition to other *motives. An incentive strengthens a *drive towards an end or objective (such as food, drink, or money) by attaching additional values to that objective.

inch An *imperial unit of length, equal to 0.0254 m.

incidental learning *Learning without making a direct attempt to learn. Sometimes referred to as *passive learning.

incommensurability A relationship between two characteristics or two phenomena which cannot be directly compared in terms of the same unit, standard, or scale. Incommensurability applies especially to the relationship between two competing scientific theories which cannot be compared directly because of the nature of their different propositions and content.

incomplete proteins Foods such as legumes, nuts, and cereals that may be protein-rich but are low in one or more of the *essential amino acids. Cereals, for example, are low in *lysine, and leafy vegetables are low in *methionine.

incontinence An inability to control the passage of urine and faeces.

incremental run Run which increases in intensity at predetermined fixed levels. Incremental runs are performed on treadmills as part of fitness tests and for determining maximum *aerobic capacity.

incubation period The time-lapse between *infection and manifestation of the symptoms of an infectious illness.

indapamide A *drug belonging to the *diuretics which are on the *IOC list of *banned substances. Side-effects include dizziness and fatigue.

independent variable *Variable which is controlled, sometimes experimentally, in order to observe its effects on a *dependent variable. In a study of the effects of age on sports participation, age is the independent variable and frequency of sporting participation the dependent variable.

indexicality The use of a word or expression which makes sense only from the immediate context of its use. Indexicality is an important feature of many explanations made by social *actors of social events.

index of difficulty A measurement of the theoretical difficulty of a movement task. It is based on *Fitt's law and is expressed as $\log_2(2A/W)$, where A is the amplitude of the movement required, and W is the width of the target. It indicates that the difficulty of a movement is jointly related to the distance a limb moves and the narrowness of the target at which it is aimed.

indication In medicine, a strong reason for believing that a particular course of treatment is desirable.

indigestion Dyspepsia; pain in the lower chest or abdomen after eating. Indigestion is often associated with *stress. Some sports, such as cycling, in which the athlete is in a crouched riding position, encourage the build-up of gas in the stomach which presses against the *diaphragm. *Antacids, such as a weak solution of sodium bicarbonate, may be used to bring up wind, and thus release the gas and relieve the symptoms.

indirect calorimetry The measurement of oxygen consumption using either *open-circuit spirometry or *closed-circuit spirometry to determine the energy consumption of a subject. When the oxygen consumed is expressed in *heat equivalents, it is found to be equal to the heat produced by the subject, as determined by *direct calorimetry.

indirect competition Competition against a standard rather than directly against other people. An individual strives to better an objective mark such as a record or a personal best, or gain a personal achievement such as climb a mountain. *See also* parallel competition.

indirect measure In sport psychology, a measurement in which individuals are asked indirect questions. For example, in the assessment of *team cohesion, team-members are asked questions about other team-members, but not specifically about *cohesion. *Compare* direct measure.

indirect motivation An alteration of the situation or the *environment, either psychological or physical, to enhance *motivation. Indirect motivation includes changing practice location or training partners.

indirect ossification Process of bone formation in which foetal cartilage is replaced by *bone. After birth, the growth areas of the bone are confined to *epiphyseal plates of cartilage which generate new cells. At maturity the plates themselves become ossified and the bone can no longer grow in length.

indirect trauma An injury which is not the result of a direct blow. *See also* over-use injury.

indisposition A manifestation of *run down. Indisposition is a deterioration in performance which may be caused by psychological factors, such as worry, or physiological factors in which the complaints are transitory, lasting a few hours to a few days. Indisposition may or may not be associated with over-training.

individual attractions Those factors which personally attract an individual to a group, team, or another individual. Analysis of individual attractions take into account how team-members feel about each other and the quality of team-mate interaction. *See also* conceptual model of team cohesion.

individual differences Stable deviations of individuals from the average or from each other on some task or behaviour. The study of individual differences examines the factors that make individuals different from each other. *Compare* personality.

individual differences principle of training The assertion that optimal benefits from training are achieved by devising training programmes which suit the specific needs of individuals since different people respond differently to the same programme.

individual differences scaling analysis (INDSCAL) A multidimensional form of *scaling analysis which allows the investigator to interpret how the characteristics of a person and situations interact to determine behaviour.

individual differences theory A theory of *mass communication which proposes that individuals respond differently to the *mass media according to each person's psychological needs, and that individuals consume the mass media to satisfy those needs. The need may be informational (e.g., providing statistics about players and teams), integrative (offering a sense of belonging to a group of similarly-interested people), affective (e.g., by providing excitement), or escapist (helping to release pent-up emotions). *Compare* social categories theory.

individual difference variable (organismic variable) A variable peculiar to an individual which can be studied to *see* if it affects the performance of the individual. Individual difference variables are usually definable traits that can be measured, such as age, height, weight, sex, or skin-type.

individualism Any social doctrine which advocates the autonomy of the individual in social actions and social affairs. Individualism also supports the view that individuals are responsible for their own actions and life-situations. Thus, it fails to recognize fully that different individuals have different *life chances because of their sex, class, racial background, or social and economic circumstances. Advocates of individualism in sport emphasize the importance of allowing the free expression of an individual's skills. In many sports, there is a tension between individualism and *collectivism.

individualistic social situation A situation in which there is no correlation between the *goal attainments of the participants. *Compare* competitive social situation; and co-operative social interaction.

individual motive *Motive which originates in unique individual experiences as contrasted with those that are inborn and those that are learned by most members of a particular culture.

indolamines A subclass of chemicals called *biogenic amines which can act as *neurotransmitters. They include *serotonin and *histamine.

indomethacin A very effective *non-steroidal anti-inflammatory drug, used to treat soft-tissue sports injuries. However, indomethacin can produce side-effects in the *central nervous system such as headaches and dizziness, as well as gastric irritation.

indoramin A selective *alpha blocker in current use for treatment of *hypertension.

INDSCAL *See* individual differences scaling analysis.

induction A process of reasoning in which a general statement suggesting a regular association beween two or more *variables is derived from a series of specific *empirical observations.

induction time The period of time between the administration of a *drug and the manifestation of its effects.

inert 1 Applied to an object which has an inherent inability to move or which resists movement. 2 Applied to a substance which has a very limited ability to react chemically.

inertia Tendency of a body to preserve its state of rest or uniform motion in a straight line. Inertia depends on *mass. The greater the mass of an object, the greater is its inertia and the larger the *force required to move it.

inertia, law of Newton's first law of motion which states that an object at rest tends to remain at rest unless acted upon by an external *force. Also, an object in motion tends to remain in motion and to travel in a straight line with uniform *velocity unless acted upon by an external force.

inertial movement (coasting movement) A form of *passive movement, such as sliding into a base during a baseball run, in which there is a continuatuon of a previous movement but there is no concurrent motive muscular contraction. Inertial movements are affected by decelerating forces, such as *air resistance and tissue viscosity.

infarct A small localized region of dead, deteriorating tissue resulting from a lack of blood supply.

infarction Formation of an *infarct. *See also* myocardial infarction.

infection 1 The process by which a *disease is communicated from one person to another. 2 A disease which can be communicated from one person to another. Such diseases always involve a microorganism, such as a *bacterium, *virus, or *fungus (*compare* infestation) which has a high capacity for reproduction. Sport offers many opportunities for the epidemic spread of infections due to the close contact of both spectators and performers. It is generally agreed that physical exertion should be avoided during some viral infections because good performance is unlikely and there is evidence that exercise may be very harmful during the *incubation period (*see* myocarditis).

infectious parotitis *See* mumps.

inference A guess or judgement derived by *deduction or *induction from certain data. *See also* hypothesis.

inferential statistics Complex statistical techniques used to infer cause and effect, and to determine the degree to which the findings of a sample can be generalized to a larger population. For example, in a study of the effect of a pre-match pep talk on performance, a researcher may design a study with appropriate *control groups and use an appropriate statistical analysis to see if a significant difference occurs between the test and control groups. If a significant difference exists, the researcher would infer that the pre-match talk caused the effect. *Compare* descriptive statistics.

inferior (caudal) A *directional term applied to the lower part of a structure or to a position near the tail end of the long axis of the human body.

inferior gemellus *See* gemellus.

inferior gluteal nerve A nerve which is closely connected to the *sciatic nerve at its origin; it supplies the *gluteus maximus muscle.

inferiority complex A psychological disorder resulting from a conflict between a desire to seek self-recognition and the desire to avoid feelings of humiliation frequently experienced in similar situations in the past. The disorder is charcterized by compensatory behaviour such as aggressiveness and withdrawal.

inferiority feelings Feelings of worthlessness and inability to cope with situations. The individual concerned usually has difficulty accepting the inferiority which may be real or implied.

inferior mesenteric artery An *artery supplying the upper part of the *abdomen.

inferior vena cava The lower large *vein which leads into the right *atrium of the *heart.

infestation The presence of animal parasites such as fleas, mites, and tapeworms on the skin or in the body, or in the clothing or the home. *Compare* infection.

inflammation (inflammatory response) Non-specific defensive response of tissues to a physical or chemical injury, or bacterial infection. The response includes dilation (widening) of blood vessels and an increase in vessel permeability, and is indicated by redness, heat, swelling, and pain. Inflammations function to destroy, dilute, or isolate the injurious agent and the injured tissue.

inflammatory response *See* inflammation.

influence system An approach to *leadership in which influence or power between coach and athlete flows both ways. Coaches adopting such a system recognize the importance of interaction between themselves, the team, and the specific situation they are in. *Compare* power system.

information 1 Any unit of data or knowledge. 2 The content of a message that serves to reduce uncertainty. 3 In the *information-processing model or theory of behaviour, the data to which a person reacts, and which precipitates behaviour in a particular situation. *See also* bit.

informational aspect In *cognitive evaluation theory, the extent to which *extrinsic rewards provide positive feedback about an outcome and thereby increases *intrinsic motivation by enhancing feelings of competence. According to the cognitive evaluation theory, people are intrinsically motivated to perform activities that make them feel competent. If a reward, such as a 'best player' award, makes an individual feel more competent, it will increase intrinsic motivation. *Compare* controlling aspect.

information dependence Social situation, occurring within a group, team, or *dyad, in which knowledge from another is needed by a performer to achieve some goal. *Compare* performance-dependence.

information-processing The storing and handling of information within a system as in a computer or a human being. In humans, the main processes involved include *perception, *memory, *reasoning, and other forms of thinking.

information-processing theory A theory which views humans as information-processing systems which take in information from the *environment, process it, and then output information to the environment in the form of movement. The theory is based on the proposition that humans process the information they receive rather than merely respond to stimuli. Many *cognitive processes are involved between the reception of a *stimulus and the response of an individual; these include sensory input, perception, and the storage and retrieval of information. *Compare* stimulus–response approach. *See also* black box model.

information theory A branch of *cybernetics that attempts to define the amount of information required to control a process of given complexity. The theory has been used in the study of learning processes and acquisition of skill. One of its most valuable contributions has been in the analysis of the processes associated with selection, *perception, *memory, and *decision-making in skilled performances.

infrared radiation Invisible heat radiation which is longer in wavelength than the red of the visible spectrum. *See also* infrared therapy.

infrared therapy The use of infrared radiation in *physiotherapy to warm tissues, ease pain, relieve muscle spasms, and increase circulation.

infrared thermography A method of measuring skin temperature by the amount of *infrared radiation emitted at the skin surface. It may be used clinically to locate inflamed areas which are warmer than surrounding tissues.

infraspinatus A *rotator cuff muscle of the shoulder which is partially covered by the *deltoid and *trapezius muscles. The infraspinatus has its *origin underneath the *shoulder-blade spine in the infraspinus *fossa, and its *insertion on the *greater tubercle of the *humerus. Its actions include helping to hold the head of the humerus in the *glenoid cavity, and lateral *rotation of the humerus.

ingestion The act of taking food in to the *alimentary canal. It includes chewing and swallowing.

inguinal In anatomy, pertaining to the groin.

inguinal canal One of a pair of openings connecting the abdominal cavity with the *scrotum, The spermatic cord and blood vessels pass through the inguinal canal to the *testes in males.

inguinal hernia (abdominal hernia) A *hernia which may occur during intense exertion due to the production of a very high abdominal pressure. A sac of *peritoneum is forced through the *inguinal canal, an anatomical opening in the region of the *groin. In men, the hernia tends to descend along the *spermatic cord into the *scrotum. Presence of a hernia in athletes is potentially dangerous because an increase in intra-abdominal pressure accompanying exertion can cause strangulation, stopping blood flow and resulting in *gangrene. Therefore, surgical repair is usually recommended.

inguinal ligament (Poupart's ligament) A *ligament connecting the *anterior *spines of the *ilium to the *pubis. The inguinal ligament is part of the *aponeurosis of the *external oblique muscles.

inguinocrural pain *See* groin pain.

inhalation 1 The process of breathing air into the *lungs through the mouth and nose. 2 Taking medication by breathing it in as a gas or vapour, or in aerosol form.

inheritance The acquisition of characteristics by the transfer of genetic material from ancestor to descendant.

inherited characteristics Characteristics which are passed from parent to offspring.

inhibition The complete or partial prevention of an activity or process. Muscle-actions are inhibited by certain nerve impulses. In psychoanalysis, specific commands may be given which prevent the subject from doing something forbidden. In psychology, inhibition may be a central, cortical, or subcortical process restraining an instinctual drive. The *extinction of conditioned reflexes may also be regarded as inhibition.

inhibitory postsynaptic potential (IPSP) A transient decrease in the electrical potential of a *postsynaptic membrane resulting in *hyperpolarization during which a stronger than normal excitatory *stimulus is necessary to initiate *depolarization and evoke the discharge of a *nerve impulse.

initiating structure A *leadership style in which patterns of organization, channels of communication, and procedures are well established. Other descriptions of leadership styles which are consistent with initiating structures include *autocratic leadership, *authoritarian leadership, *product-orientation leadership, and *task-motivation leadership. *See also* leader behaviour description questionnaire.

injection The introduction of fluid usually containing medicines into the body by means of a syringe.

injury A physical hurt or damage. Participation in some sports carries a high risk of specific injuries, to such an extent that the injury has acquired a sporting epithet. Examples are swimmer's shoulder, runner's knee, and tennis elbow. Surveys have shown that the region of the body at greatest risk to an injury in sport is the knee. Many sports injuries are not serious or life-threatening, but a variety of unpleasant and even potentially fatal conditions, including *multiple sclerosis, *osteomyelitis, and *bone cancer, may first appear in what seems at the outset to be a sports injury. For this reason, if for no other, sports injuries should be taken seriously and medical advice should be sought if symptoms persist or recur.

injury-prone *See* accident-prone.

innate ability An ability that is inborn or instinctive.

inner ear *See* labyrinth

inner range One of three parts to the *range of movement of a *joint during which the *muscle responsible for the movement is moving into full contraction. *See also* midrange; and outer range.

innervation The nerve supply to a bodily organ or part.

innominate bone *See* coxal bone.

inoculation Process by which infective material is introduced into a culture or the body system through a small wound in the skin or in a mucous membrane. Inoculations are used as preventative measures against infective disease. Many athletes have inoculations during the off-season when they will have their least effect on performance. *See also* vaccine.

inorganic Pertaining to chemical substances, such as water and salts, that do not belong to the large class of carbon compounds termed *organic.

inorganic salt A *salt, such as calcium phosphate and other calcium salts, which does not belong to the *organic compounds. *Bone contains large quantities of inorganic salt.

inositol A substance similar to *hexose sugar. Inositol is sometimes classified as a *vitamin but, although it is essential to the health of some animals, there is no evidence that it is essential to the health of humans.

input The information fed into a system. In the *systems theory of behaviour, the input is what a person reacts to; that which precipitates behaviour in a particular situation.

insert *See* insock.

insertion The point of attachment of a *muscle to a *bone or other structure and which is relatively movable during *concentric or eccentric muscle action. The insertion is usually *distal to the *origin.

insight 1 The phenomenon of gaining a sudden understanding of something in a way not readily apparent, as when one 'sees through' a situation. Insight may be inferred from a sudden improvement in *learning, or the solving of a problem. 2 In psychology, self-knowledge, particularly with regard to the recognition by a patient of psychological problems.

insock Insert of a *training shoe usually made of material which absorbs shock. The insock goes into the shoe and fills the gap between foot and shoe. It is the part of the shoe which is in direct contact with the sole of the foot.

insoluble fibre A type of dietary *fibre that absorbs many times its weight in water and swells up in the *intestine. By increasing the bulk of *faeces, it promotes efficient waste-elimination from the *colon and may help to prevent colon *cancer. Insoluble fibre is found in wholegrains as well as in vegetables; it includes *cellulose and *lignin.

insomnia Difficulty in falling asleep or inability to stay asleep. Nervous anticipation experienced before a major competition commonly causes insomnia. The use of *hypnotics, such as the *benzodiazepines, to induce sleep can be habit-forming over a long period. Also, they may have side-effects such as drowsiness which adversely affect physical performance.

inspiration The act of drawing air into the lungs through the mouth and nose. In this sense, it is synonymous with inhalation.

inspiratory capacity (IC) Maximum volume of air inspired from resting expiratory level. A typical resting value of IC is 3600 ml; this increases during exercise.

inspiratory mechanism Mechanism by which air is drawn into the *lungs. A combination of movements of the ribs upwards and outwards, and of the *diaphragm downwards results in a reduction of the intrapulmonary and intrapleural pressure which in turn results in a rush of air into the lungs. During resting inspiration, the ribs are fixed by the *scalene muscles and contraction of the external *intercostals elevates the ribcage while the diaphragm contracts and flattens downward. Additional muscles become active during exercise when inspiration is a much more dynamic process: the scalenes elevate the first and second ribs, the *sternocleidomastoid muscles elevate the *sternum, and the extensors of the back and *trapezius muscle may also play a role.

inspiratory muscles Muscles involved in the *inspiratory mechanism.

inspiratory reserve volume (IRV) Maximum volume of air inspired from the end of an unforced inspiration. The IRV decreases during exercise.

instability The lack of *stability in a joint, often through having lax ligaments which give a predisposition to dislocations.

instantaneous angular velocity The *angular velocity of a body in rotation at any one moment of time. *See also* average angular velocity.

instantaneous speed The *speed of a body at a given moment of time. It is estimated as the average speed of a body over such a short distance or short period of time (starting from the position occupied by the body at the instant in question) that the speed will not have time to change. It can be determined by the *gradient of a *distance–time curve. The concept of instantaneous speed is useful in comparing different periods of performance, such as the different stages of a sprint.

instantaneous velocity The *velocity of a body at a given instant in time.

instinct A complex, unlearned adaptive response; an unlearned, fixed pattern of reflexes. If the responses are learned, the behaviour pattern is called a *habit.

instinct theory of aggression A theory that human *aggression is an *innate biological drive similar to sex and hunger that cannot be eliminated but must be controlled through *catharsis for the good of society. The theory is based on observations of non-human species in which aggression is used to maintain territory, and fighting is necessary for survival. The theory supports the contentious notion that sport acts as a catharsis providing a safe and socially-acceptable outlet for aggression. *Compare* frustration–aggression hypothesis; and social learning theory.

institution An established entity or activity in society comprising rule-bound and standard behaviour patterns. Institutions include any enduring activity by groups or organizations (e.g., the family, education system, the law, polity, economy, and religion) which address some important and persistent societal problem. Many regard sport as a social institution because it has a distinctive kind of organization; it represents a unique form of social activity; it provides a basis for social identity; it serves as a link to other social structures; and it can act as an agent of social control.

institutional discrimination Control of social *institutions by one social group to the disadvantage of another; applies to race, gender, and age.

institutionalization The process by which social units and social activities become organized in a relatively permanent and enduring way. *See also* ludic institutionalization.

instructional goal A general statement given by a coach of what he or she expects of his or her athletes. The statement commonly incorporates the following three features: first, a description of the performance goal in observable, measurable terms; secondly, the conditions under which the performance is to occur; and thirdly, an indication of the standard upon which goal-attainment can be evaluated.

instrumental Applied to something which is, like an instrument, useful and can serve as a means to achieve a purpose.

instrumental aggression A form of *aggression against another person frequently found in sport, in which the aggression is used as a means of securing some reward or to achieve some external goal such as a victory. Unlike *hostile aggression, harm to others is incidental and is not the perceived goal.

instrumental conditioning *Conditioning in which the response is instrumental in achieving some end such as obtaining a tangible reward or escaping punishment. It is often used as synonym for *operant conditioning but some psychologists make a distinction in the usage of these two terms.

instrumental error A constant error due to a defect in an instrument.

insufficiency The inability of a *biarticulate muscle which spans two *joints to produce a full *range of movement in both joints at the same time. *See also* active insufficiency; and passive insufficiency.

insufficiency fracture *See* stress fracture.

insulin A *hormone secreted by the β cells of the *islets of Langerhans in the *pancreas in response to elevated blood glucose levels. Insulin stimulates the *liver, muscles, and fat cells to remove *glucose from the *blood for use or storage; stimulates absorption of glucose into muscle and adipose tissue by changing cell permeability; stimulates conversion of glucose into *glycogen in liver and muscle; promotes conversion of glucose into fats (*see* lipogenesis); and promotes *glycolysis in cells. Inhibition of its production results in high blood glucose levels. The secretion of insulin is reduced by *adrenergic impulses, and by *epinephrine. Although insulin secretion falls during exercise, sensitivity to insulin increases. In trained individuals, insulin does not fall as much during exercise as in the untrained. This allows more energy to be derived from *free fatty acids.

insulin rebound A physiological response induced by ingesting too much sugar. The high blood sugar causes an exaggerated *insulin response so that the blood glucose level, after initially rising, actually falls to a level lower than it was before the intake of glucose. Thus, less glucose than normal is available to respiring muscles.

integrating motor pneumatachygraph An instrument for measuring energy expenditure in *indirect calorimetry.

integrator Part of the *brain which controls the way an athlete integrates individual components of a skill into a complex whole. The integrator takes the *analyser's blueprint of step-by-step instructions and converts it into a single, complex image so that the brain need process only a single image rather than a series of complex verbal instructions. It is suggested that *imagery may guide the integrator in the same way as verbal instructions direct the analyser.

integumentary system *Skin and its derivatives which provide the external protective covering of the body.

intellectualization *Ego defence mechanism by which unacceptable emotions are transformed by explanations making excuses for the undesirable behaviour.

intelligence Although there is no universally-accepted definition of intelligence, it is generally regarded as an ability to act purposefully, to think rationally, and to deal effectively with the *environment; it is often measured by an *intelligence test. A person of high intelligence has the ability to adapt to new situations which often involves the ability to utilize *abstract concepts and to learn to grasp novel relationships. *See also* sport intelligence.

intelligence quotient (IQ) The ratio of mental age to chronological age expressed as a percentage. It is used as an index of intellectual development. *See also* intelligence test.

intelligence test A standardized procedure for measuring levels of *intelligence. The score is usually expressed as an *intelligence quotient. No completely satisfactory (that is, universally accepted) intelligence test has yet been devised.

intensity The quantitative as contrasted with qualitative aspect of stimulation or experience; for example, the magnitude or *amplitude of sound-waves as distinguished from their *frequency.

intensity of training The total training workload. According to the *overload principle, in order to improve *physical fitness, exercise must be hard enough to require more effort than usual. The method for estimating appropriate training intensity levels varies with each fitness component. *Flexibility, for example, requires that muscles be stretched beyond their normal length; *cardiovascular fitness requires elevating the heart-rate above normal (*see* target heart-rate); and strength-training requires increasing resistance above normal loads (*see* repetition maximum).

interaction **1** The combined effect of two or more *independent variables acting simultaneously on a *dependent variable. *Analysis of variance is used to assess the effect of the interaction between the variables as well as the specific effect of each. **2**

The interplay which occurs between two or more persons or groups. Sport psychologists are interested in the way members of teams interact and how that interaction can be made more productive. In some sports, such as basketball, the need for interaction is high and requires a lot of *co-operation, while in other sports, such as athletic field events, interaction is not important.

interactional model A model based on the proposition that an individual's behaviour is determined by the interaction between the individual's *personality traits and the environmental situation in which the behaviour is occurring.

interactionism A behavioural viewpoint which adopts the *interactional model.

interaction, law of Newton's third law of motion. *See* Newton's laws of motion.

interaction orientation A *psychological orientation in which an individual is concerned about forming and maintaining harmonious and happy relationships, at least superficially. If these needs interfere with performance, the individual often finds it difficult to contribute to the task at hand, or to be of real help to others. *See also* self-orientation; and task orientation.

interactive audience An *audience which interacts verbally and emotionally with performers.

interactive sports Sports such as soccer and volleyball in which team-mates must interact with each other to achieve success. *Compare* coactive sport; and low means interdependence.

interbrain A region of the *brain which includes the *thalamus, *hypothalamus, and *basal ganglia.

intercalated disc A junction interconnecting *cardiac muscle cells.

intercarpal joint A *synovial, *diarthrotic *joint between adjacent *carpals. Intercarpal joints are mainly *gliding joints.

intercellular Pertaining to the region between body cells.

intercellular matrix Material between adjacent cells. The intercellular matrix is an important feature determining the nature of *connective tissue such as *bone and *cartilage.

intercept The value (usually designated as '*a*') on the *y*-axis when *x* is zero; one of the constants for linear *empirical equations.

intercostal muscle Muscle lying between the ribs. The superficial *external intercostals contract to raise the *thorax and increase the volume of the *thoracic cavity during *inspiration.The deeper, *internal intercostals, draw the ribs together, lower the thorax, and decrease the volume of the cavity during *expiration.

intercostal space The space between two ribs. One of the positions for placing a stethoscope when examining a patient is the fifth intercostal space.

interdependent task Type of *interaction in which all members of a group simultaneously apply themselves to the same task. The group-members' contribution may be added together to produce the final outcome, known as summatory interdependence, or the group-members may constantly adjust their performance so that errors of others in the group are either corrected or reduced. *Compare* delegated performance.

interference **1** Conflict which occurs when two tasks are performed simultaneously, resulting in the quality of performance of the tasks decreasing. **2** Difficulty in *learning or remembering a task or event due to confusion between the material that needs to be remembered and another experience occurring before or after the task or event in question. *See also* capacity interference; proactive inhibition; retroactive inhibition; and structural interference.

interferential A medium-frequency electrical apparatus for heating muscles and joints in the treatment of soft tissue injuries. By the application of an adjustable current, circulation can be increased in the damaged tissue, which is particularly valuable in the treatment of certain *lesions. The improved circulation may also stimulate muscle recovery.

intermediate In *anatomy, between a more *medial or a more *lateral structure.

intermediate anaerobic performance Exercise lasting about 30s. *See also* intermediate anaerobic performance capacity.

intermediate anaerobic performance capacity The total work output during maximal exercise lasting about 30s. It is a measure of a performance which is primarily supported by the *anaerobic system with a small contribution from the *aerobic system.

intermediate cuneiform The middle of three *cuneiform bones in the *tarsus. The intermediate cuneiform articulates with the second *digit which lies in front of it and the *navicular bone which lies behind it.

intermediate-term anaerobic tests Tests of physical performance lasting 20–50s, primarily of *lactic anaerobic power and *anaerobic capacity. *See also* the de Bruyn–Prevost constant load test; and the Wingate test.

intermittent claudication A term derived from the latin word 'claudicare' meaning to limp. A patient suffering from this disorder experiences cramping in the legs due to a reduction in the arterial blood supply to the muscles, causing the patient to limp. Intermittent claudication is commonly associated with *arteriosclerosis. It is induced by exercise and relieved by rest. Controlled exercise programmes, such as walking, are often recommended to improve circulation.

intermittent training A form of training which incorporates periods of physical exertion interspersed with periods of rest. *See also* interval training.

intermittent reinforcement A schedule of discontinuous *reinforcement in which not all the correct responses of an individual are reinforced.

intermittent work Exercise interrupted by periods of relief. *Compare* continuous training.

intermuscular Applied to the region between muscles. *Compare* intramuscular

intermuscular haematoma Internal bleeding developed in between the *fascia and in the *interstitial spaces when the muscles and fascial vessels are injured. An intermuscular haematoma usually causes greater loss of function and more persistent swelling than an *intramuscular haematoma.

internal axis of rotation An *axis which passes through the human body, usually at a *joint. *Compare* external axis.

internal controls (internals) People who are likely to *see* events in their lives as being dependent on their own behaviour. Internals believe that if they perform well or poorly, appropriate consequences will follow. They do not consider luck as having much effect on the outcome of their performance, and do not see their fate as being always in the hands of other people. Good athletes tend to be internal controls because they have learned that their abilities and efforts bring them reward and success. *Compare* external control.

internal environment The medium in which all cells are bathed; tissue fluid.

internal feedback *See* intrinsic feedback.

internal fixation The rendering of structures such as a fractured bone immovable by implanting a support, such as a *Kuntscher nail, inside the body.

internal force A *force internal to the system under consideration. Whether a force is regarded as internal or external depends on how the system is defined and classified, and is largely a matter of convenience. In *biomechanics, the human body is generally regarded as the system and any force exerted by one part of the body on another is an internal force. Muscle contractions produce internal forces which move a joint. *Compare* external force.

internal imagery (kinaesthetic imagery) Form of *visualization in which subjects imagine what they would feel inside their own bodies by *kinaesthetic feedback if they performed a particular skill. *Compare* external imagery. *See also* mental practice.

internal intercostal One of eleven pairs of muscles lying between the ribs. The fibres run downward and posteriorly, and are deeper than the *external intercostals. Each internal intercostal muscle has its *origin on the *inferior border of the rib above and its *insertion on the superior border of the rib below. The internal intercostals take part in *expiration by drawing the ribs together and depressing the ribcage, and may work as *antagonists to the external intercostals, but opinion is divided on this.

internalization **1** The acceptance and incorporation of the beliefs or standards of others. Internalization occurs, for example, when individual team-members adopt the mores of the team for which they play. *Compare* conformity. **2** A form of *direct motivation in which a coach seeks to motivate players by appealing to the players' own beliefs and values, not by administering *rewards and *punishments. For example, a coach may praise an athlete for the preparation work the athlete has done, express confidence that the athlete will perform to the best of his or her ability, and assure the athlete of the coach's support whatever the outcome of the performance.

internal jugular vein A principal *vein in the neck which carries blood from the brain, face, and neck to the *subclavian vein.

internal locus of causality The attribution of performance outcomes to causes which are perceived as being inherent and under personal control, such as ability and effort, state of health, or fitness. *Compare* external locus of causality. *See also* internal control.

internal locus of control *See* internal control.

internal oblique muscle One of four pairs of *abdominal muscles which lie under the *external oblique muscles. They have their *origins on the lumbodorsal fascia, *iliac crest, and inguinal ligament; they have their *insertions on the *linea alba, pubic crest, and the lowest three ribs. They function with the external oblique muscles to help flex and rotate the trunk, and compress the abdomen.

internal overload An *attentional style in which an individual tends to become confused when having to deal with several ideas at the same time. *Compare* broad internal.

internal reinforcement *Reinforcement emanating from an increase in personal satisfaction and pride in an achievement.

internal respiration (cellular respiration; tissue respiration) The manufacture of high-energy *adenosine triphosphate from food by a series of metabolic reactions (*see* aerobic respiration; and anaerobic respiration). The term internal respiration has also been used to refer to the exchange of gases between blood and tissue fluid, and between tissue fluid and cells (*see* gaseous exchange). *Compare* external respiration.

internal rotation Movement around the long axis, toward the mid-line of the body. *Compare* external rotation.

internals *See* internal controls.

internal sprain of ankle Condition in which there is little outward indication of an *ankle injury except, possibly, a slight swelling, but the sufferer experiences great pain and limited movement. Internal bleeding in the damaged joint causes the blood-filled *joint capsules to bulge outwards on either side of the *Achilles tendon. The condition can lead to permanent stiffness if it is not treated quickly and properly (for example, by *aspiration).

International Olympic Committee (IOC) The governing body of the Olympic Games. The IOC is a permanent committee which is entrusted with the control and development of the modern Olympic Games. It is responsible for ensuring the Olympics are celebrated in the spirit that inspired their revival in 1894. The IOC elects its own members. Each member speaks either French or English and resides in a country which has a National Olympic Committee, accepted by the IOC, to promote the Olympic movement and amateur sport in that country.

International Olympic Committee Medical Commission (IOC Medical Commission) A body created in 1966 to combat *doping. It is now divided into four subcommissions with responsibilities which include, in addition to combating doping, helping athletes to improve their performances without contravening basic principles, enabling athletes to avoid injury, and disseminating information, such as a code of ethics, to doctors treating athletes and to other interested people.

interneurone (association neurone; connective neurone; internuncial neurone) A *neurone, originating and terminating wholly in the *spinal cord, that connects various segments of the spinal cord. Interneurones are located between afferent (sensory) and efferent (motor) nerve cells where they act as a link between incoming and outgoing impulses.

internuncial neurone *See* interneurone.

interoceptor (visceroceptor) An internal sense-organ composed of nerve-endings which respond to stimuli, such as changes in acidity in the blood, which arise inside the body. *See also* proprioceptor.

interosseus membrane A flexible *membrane connecting two bones (e.g., the *radius and *ulna).

interosseus muscle One of eight muscles in each hand that lie deep to the *lumbricals with which they work to flex the *metacarpophalangeal joints and help extend the fingers.

interparietal bone An occasional, isolated, sutural bone lying at the back of the *cranium, between the parietal bones and the *occiput.

interpersonal communication *Communication between a minimum of two parties in which meaningful exchange is intended with the sender trying to effect a response from a person or group. The message may be received by the person for whom it was intended or by people for whom it was not intended, or both. The message may be distorted during transmission so that the sender's intentions are not perceived by the recipient and the intended effect is not achieved. Effective interpersonal communication is essential for successful relationships between coach and athletes.

interpersonal relationship Interactions between one *group and another. *Compare* intrapersonal relationship.

interphalangeal joint A *synovial, *hinge-joint between adjacent *phalanges. It allows only *flexion and *extension.

interpolation The process of estimating intermediate values or terms between known values or terms. *Compare* extrapolation.

interpretation The process of giving an explanation.

interpretivism A sociological approach which emphasizes the need to understand or interpret the beliefs, motives, and reasons of social *actors from the perspective of the actors in order to understand social reality.

interquartile range In statistics, the *range obtained by subtracting the value for the first quartile (i.e., the value which lies at the boundary between the values in the first and second quarters of the range when the values are arranged in ascending order) from that of the third quartile (i.e., the value which lies at the boundary between the values in the third and fourth quarters of the range when the values are arranged in ascending order). The interquartile range gives a measure of the spread represented by half of the entire sample, and has the advantage of excluding extreme values.

interrater reliability Degree of similarity of results from different researchers using the same instrument to observe the same behaviour or events at the same time. If interrater reliability is high, results will be closely similar.

intersocietal systems Any social arrangement or social system which spans the dividing line between different societies. The intersocietal nature of sport is illustrated by the 1992 Olympic Games in which over 170 countries took part.

interstitial Pertaining to the area or space between cells.

interstitial cell-stimulating hormone *See* luteinizing hormone.

interstitial fluid The fluid bathing cells through which material is exchanged between the blood and the cells.

interstitial haematoma An accumulation of fluid and blood which has escaped into *interstitial spaces through a split in a muscle envelope. An interstitial haematoma is often accompanied by bruising which makes its way along tissue planes to the surface causing discolouration. This has sometimes beeen referred to as 'the bruise coming out'. Treatment is similar to that for an *intramuscular haematoma and rapid recovery is usual.

interstitial tear A rupture in the *fascial envelope of a *muscle, *muscle fibre, or *connective tissue.

intertarsal joint A *synovial, *gliding joint occurring between adjacent *tarsals. Of particular importance is the midtarsal joint, formed by the articulation of the *calcaneus with the *cuboid, and by the articulation of the *astragalus with the *navicular bone, which has greater mobility than the other tarsal joints, allowing foot *inversion and *eversion.

intertrigo *See* chafing.

intertubercular groove (biceps groove; bicipital groove) A deep groove in the upper part of the *humerus separating the *greater tubercle from the *lesser tubercle. The groove guides the tendon of the *biceps brachii to its point of attachment at the rim of the *glenoid cavity. It also receives the *insertion of the *latissimus dorsi.

inter-unit training ratio The ratio of the number of training units to *recovery units within a *microcycle.

interval goal-setting A form of *goal-setting in which past performances are used to compute target intervals of time or distance in which a future performance should be achieved. A performance falling within the interval is considered successful regardless of the outcome in terms of winning and losing. Interval goal-setting can provide incentives for accomplishing both short-term goals and long-term goals.

interval measurements Measurements which are based on placing *variables in rank order with the distances between categories fixed and equal. Interval measures are artificial and the zero point is arbitrarily determined; negative values may represent real values. The Celsius temperature scale is an example of an interval measurement.

interval scale A scale in which the distance or interval between any two numbers on the scale is of known size. *See also* interval measurements.

interval-sprinting A method of training whereby an athlete alternately sprints 50 m and jogs 50 m for a distance of up to 5000 m.

interval-training A system of *training that alternates spurts of intense exertion (the work interval) with periods of lower-intensity activity (the relief period) in one exercise session. By optimally spacing the periods of exertion and relief, the subject can accomplish more total work than would be possible in a continuous training session. *See also* controlled interval method; and interval-training prescription.

interval-training prescription Written instructions containing pertinent information for an *interval-training session. The prescription indicates the number of sets or repetitions, training distance, training time, and relief time. One set from a prescription for a running programme may be written as follows: SET1 6×200 at 0.30 (1:40), that is, one set, containing six repetitions of 200 m at a training time of 30 s and a relief interval of 1 min 40 s.

intervening variable A variable that brings about the effect of an *independent variable on a *dependent variable. As an example, a study may reveal that social class has an observed effect on the ability to play golf, but this effect may be mediated by an intervening variable such as income, or proximity of housing to a golf course.

intervention strategy (intervention technique) Various physiological and *cognitive strategies for altering existing levels of *anxiety, *arousal, and *self-confidence. Intervention strategies are used by sport psychologists to modify particular psychological *sets or thought-processes that may be inhibiting an athlete's performance. Through various techniques such as *biofeedback, *behaviour modification, anxiety management training, and attentional control training, an athlete can be trained to identify and modify undesirable psychological responses that may occur before and during competition.

intervention technique *See* intervention strategy.

intervertebral disc (disc) A cushion-like pad between adjacent vertebrae which is composed of an inner semifluid material (nucleus pulposus) and a strong outer ring of *fibrocartilage (annulus fibrosus). The intervertebral disc acts as a shock absorber during walking, jumping, and running, allowing the *spine to move. The discs are thickest between *lumbar and *cervical vertebrae, enhancing the flexibility of these regions.

intervertebral foramina Gaps between the *dorsal processes of adjacent *vertebrae through which the spinal nerves can pass.

intervertebral joint A cartilaginous, amphiarthrotic joint between adjacent vertebral bodies, showing *symphysis and allowing only slight movement.

interview Research technique involving face-to-face verbal interchange in which an interviewer or interviewers attempt to obtain information, opinions, or beliefs from another person or persons. Highly structured interviews, in which the interviewer poses set questions, are not so liable to interviewer-bias and are easier to analyse than unstructured interviews, but the latter often generate a greater depth of data.

intra-articular Pertaining to the inside of a joint.

intracapsular ligament A *ligament within a *joint capsule.

intracellular Pertaining to the inside of a cell or cells.

intracellular fluid Internal fluid located within cells.

intra-competition Competition against oneself by, for example, attempting to improve on one's own previous level or score, or particular standards. Intra-competition is used in training as part of *motivation strategy but it needs to be used wisely as it can have negative effects.

intrafusal fibre A small *muscle fibre lying inside a *muscle spindle. The middle portion of the intrafusal fibre is non-contractile. When it is stretched, sensory nerve-endings convey the information to the *central nervous system. The ends of the intrafusal fibres can contract when stimulated by their motor neurones, the *γ motor neurones. *See also* stretch reflex.

intramuscular Within a muscle. The term is also applied to a method of drug administration by injection into a muscle.

intramuscular haematoma An accumulation of blood that clots within a muscle. It may be caused by muscle strain (*see* distraction strain) intramuscular tear, or bruise. The muscle *fascia and the *epimysium remain intact, preventing blood and tissue fluid from escaping; therefore, these fluids gather at the site of the injury. The intramuscular haematoma results in pain and tenderness, and it limits the ability of the affected muscle to contract or to be passively stretched. It requires quick treatment by *RICE, or some other means, followed by methods to increase blood flow, such as *short-wave diathermy or *ultrasound, if long-term problems are to be avoided. *Compare* intermuscular haematoma.

intramembranous ossification Development of *flat bones and some *irregular bones (e.g., the skull and *clavicle) directly and in one stage from connective, fibrous tissue. *Compare* endochondral ossification.

intrapersonal communication Communication a person has with him or herself. In coaching, intrapersonal communication is generally less important than *interpersonal communication

intrapersonal relationship Interactions between members within a group and the resultant influence on individual members. *See also* interpersonal relationship.

intrapulmonary pressure The pressure within the *lungs. It is usually greater than the pressure within the *thoracic cage and explains why the lungs remain partly inflated after *expiration.

intra-task interference The mutually negative effects on performance of certain aspects of a task with other aspects of the same task.

intrathoracic pressure Pressure within the *thoracic cage. This is usually less than the pressure within the *lungs.

intra-training unit The ratio of exercise duration to recovery duration within a *training unit.

intravenous administration The introduction of medication directly into a vein.

intrinsic factor 1 A *glycoprotein substance produced by the stomach that is required for the absorption of vitamin B_{12} (known also as the extrinsic factor) across the *intestinal membrane into the bloodstream. A lack of intrinsic factor results in a deficiency of vitamin B_{12} and pernicious *anaemia. 2 An internal anatomical factor, such as misalignment of the legs or muscle imbalance, which may contribute to a sports injury. *Compare* extrinsic factor.

intrinsic feedback (internal feedback) The *feedback athletes receive as a natural consequence of their performance. For example, the *kinaesthetic feedback arising from sensory receptors in *muscles, *tendons, and *joints which provides performers with *information about their movements. *See also* augmented feedback.

intrinsic injury Damage deriving directly from some act or action of the victim; a form of primary, consequential injury. Intrinsic injuries are usually caused by relatively low forces (*compare* thrower's fracture). *Compare* extrinsic injury.

intrinsic motivation Motivation derived from engaging in an activity for its own sake, for the satisfaction and the sheer enjoyment that it brings, and for no other reason. Such intrinsic motivation is often associated with persistence, high levels of achievement, and feelings of self-determination or control. *Compare* extrinsic motivation.

intrinsic muscle Small, deep muscle found entirely within the body-part it acts on; for example, there are intrinsic muscles of the foot and hand.

intrinsic reward Reward derived from feeling competent and satisfied with a performance. When a person plays soccer for the sheer joy of playing the game, for example, and then experiences that joy, the motive to play soccer is reinforced. *Compare* extrinsic reward. *See also* intrinsic motivation.

intrinsic value The value of doing something for its own sake rather than for any external reward. *See also* intrinsic motivation.

intropunitive behaviour *Aggression which is directed against oneself.

introspection The process of looking inward and describing one's own experiences.

introversion A *personality trait characterized by a tendency to be preoccupied with oneself, to be shy, cautious, and to be inwardly reflective more than to be overtly expressive. *Compare* extraversion.

introvert A person who exhibits high levels of *introversion.

invariant features Applied to aspects of movement that appear to be fixed (or invariant) even though other, more superficial features can change. Invariant features are regarded as important features contained in *motor programs.

invasion games Games, such as American football, which involve the occupation and defence of territory.

inverse stretch reflex A *reflex action mediated by the *golgi tendon organs which, when stimulated by a prolonged stretch, causes a stretched muscle to relax. *Compare* stretch reflex.

inversion The turning of the sole of the foot inwards and sideways so that the sole turns medially. Inversion during running or walking results in the body-weight being

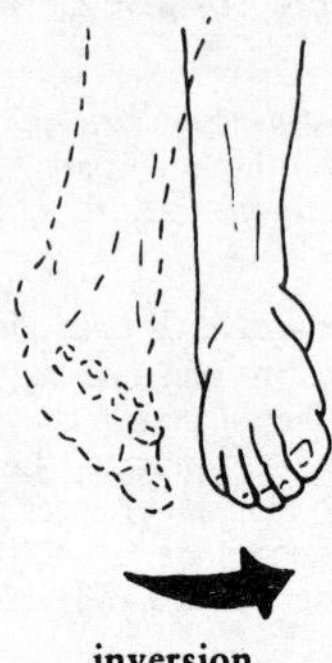

inversion

applied mainly onto the outer edge of foot. The muscles which effect inversion include the *tibialis posterior; *flexor digitorum longus, *flexor hallucis longus, and the *tibialis anterior. *Compare* eversion.

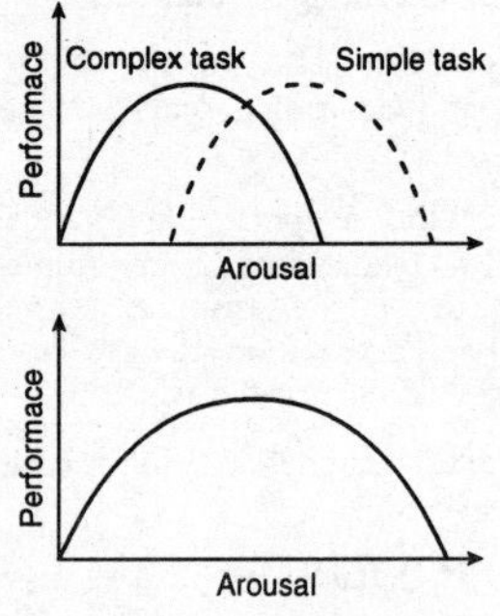

inverted-U hypothesis

inverted-U hypothesis Hypothesis which states that performance improves with increasing levels of *arousal up to some optimal point, whereupon further increases in arousal will produce a detrimental effect on performance. Therefore athletes may perform badly because they are over-aroused or under-aroused. The hypothesis is qualitative and does not attempt to quantify the relationship between arousal and performance. The optimal levels vary between people doing the same task and with one person doing different tasks. A basic assumption in the hypothesis is that arousal is unidimensional and that there is consequently a very close correlation between indicators of arousal; this is not the case.

inverted-V pattern The observed relationship between precompetitive *state anxiety and the amount of time before the event. The inverted-V pattern appears when *anxiety (*y*-axis) is plotted against time (*x*-axis) on a graph. It indicates that anxiety experienced prior to competition is typically more than that experienced during competition.

in vitro Applied to conditions outside the living body such as a test-tube or other artificial environment.

in vivo Applied to a biological process or experiment occurring in a living body.

involuntary muscle Muscle, such as *smooth muscle and *cardiac muscle, which is not normally under voluntary, conscious control.

involuntary nervous system *See* autonomic nervous system.

involvement Applied to different forms of participation in sport. *See also* patterns of sport involvement.

IOC *See* International Olympic Committee.

IOC Medical Commission *See* International Olympic Committee Medical Commission.

iodine Symbol: I. A trace element present in cod liver oil, iodized salt, and vegetables grown in iodine-rich soil. Iodine is an essential ingredient of *thyroid hormone. The recommended daily intake is 100–130 mg. An excess depresses synthesis of thyroid hormone. A deficit leads to an underactive thryroid gland.

ion An electrically charged atom or group of atoms. Those which are positively charged are known as cations and have fewer electrons than are needed to make the atom neutral. Those which are negatively charged are known as anions and have more electrons than needed to make the atom neutral.

ionic bond A chemical bond formed by an electron-transfer between atoms.

ionization The formation of *ions.

ionotropic neurotransmitter Chemical substance, such as *acetyl choline and *amino acid *neurotransmitters, which opens channels through which *ions can pass in a *postsynaptic membrane causing a change in the postsynaptic membrane potential. *Compare* metabotropic neurotransmitter.

iontophoresis A method by which ionized medication is driven through the skin, commonly by an electric current or *ultrasound, so that it reaches deep tissues.

ipsative data analysis The analysis of data so that *individual differences can be identified. In *sport psychology, such analysis may be used to recognize the idiosyncratic nature of a particular athlete's behavioural responses. It includes analysis of the variety of responses among individuals and how an individual's response varies in different situations.

ipsilateral In anatomy, situated on, or affecting the same side of the body.

IPSP *See* inhibitory postsynaptic potential.

IQ *See* intelligence quotient.

iris The coloured part of the eye made up of two layers of muscle which controls the entry of light through a central opening, the *pupil.

iritis Inflammation of the *iris.

iron A metal element essential to survival. It is a component of *haemoglobin, *cytochromes, and other chemicals involved in vital metabolic activities. Sources of iron in the diet include meat, liver, dried fruit, nuts, molasses, and legumes. The recommended daily intake is 10 mg for men and 18 mg for women. Excess intake of iron can damage the liver, heart, and pancreas, and cause gastric irritation. A deficiency of iron may lead to *anaemia. There is some evidence that heavy training loads can increase the risk of iron deficiency in athletes because of the increased demand for haemoglobin, *myoglobin, and cytochromes.

iron-deficiency anaemia A reduction in the quantity of *haemoglobin in the *blood due to the *iron supply not meeting the demands of the body. This may result from an iron-deficient diet, an inadequate absorption of iron through the intestinal wall, or an increased demand for iron (because of bleeding, for example).

irreducible hernia A *hernia that will not return to its normal position in the body cavity, even with gentle manipulation.

irregular bone Bone of irregular or no definite shape, consisting of mainly spongy, *cancellous bone sandwiched between two thin, outer layers of *compact bone. Examples of irregular bones are the facial skull bones, and vertebrae.

irritability The responsiveness of an organism to changes in its immediate *environment.

IRV *See* inspiratory reserve volume.

ischaemia Local and temporary deficiency of the *blood supply to tissues, chiefly due to constriction of *blood vessels.

ischaemic heart disease Myocardial *ischaemia in which there is an insufficient blood supply to the heart muscle. Endurance-training is an effective measure in primary and secondary prevention, and aids rehabilitation in cases of ischaemic heart diseases.

ischaemic pain Pain within a tissue induced by a deficient blood supply to that tissue.

ischial tuberosity A *tuberosity on the *ischium which forms the point of *origin of the long-head of the *biceps femoris, the *semimembranosus, and *semitendinosus muscles.

ischium One of the three bones which make up the *coxal bone of the *pelvic girdle. Each ischium forms the lower part of each side of the *hip-bone. During sitting, the body-weight is borne entirely by the *tuberosities of the ischium, which are the strongest parts of the hip-bone.

islets of Langerhans *Endocrine tissue in the *pancreas which secretes *insulin and *glucagon.

isoelectric point The *pH at which an *amino acid or *protein is electrically neutral and behaves as a *zwitterion. At the isoelectric point, *electrophoresis of a substance does not occur when an electric current is applied.

isoetharine A *drug belonging to the *stimulants which are on the *IOC list of *banned substances.

isokinetic contraction Contraction of *striated muscle, which is at a constant speed or at a constant *angular velocity, over the full *range of motion. The tension developed by the muscle is maximum over the full range of motion. To perform a controlled isokinetic contraction, special equipment is needed (e.g., an isokinetic dynamometer) which contains a speed governor so that the speed of movement is constant no matter how much tension is produced in the contracting muscle. Isokinetic training increases *capillarization of striated and *cardiac muscle, and thereby improves muscle strength, *endurance, and *cardiovascular fitness. It also has the advantage over *isotonic training of removing from the exercise, differences between forces exerted at different angles of limbs at a joint.

isokinetic dynamometer An apparatus for testing the *torque (and sometimes *work and *power) of *isokinetic muscle contractions at various velocities up to the limit of the *dynamometer.

isokinetic exercise An exercise performed using special apparatus that provides *maximal resistance through a full range of movement at a constant speed (*see* isokinetic contraction). Since the forces are moving at a constant speed, the *neuromuscular systems are able to work at a constant speed for each phase of movement. This allows the active muscles to apply large forces by releasing high tension over each movement phase. The effect is to develop uniform strengthening of active muscles, improving muscle strength, *endurance, and *cardiovascular fitness.

isolation stress A form of *stress modelling which has been used by coaches of international athletes especially in Eastern Europe. Isolation stress involves placing the competitor in a situation that requires self-coaching for a period. It is imposed when it is thought that a top competitor might be shifted to a new team and coach, unfamiliar with the athlete's unique characteristics, just before encountering international competition. It is hoped that voluntarily breaking away from an accustomed coach under controlled conditions may be less traumatic than would otherwise be the case.

isoleucine An *essential amino acid found in beans and other legumes but found only in small amounts in corn and other grains, indicating the need for vegetarians to include legumes in their diet.

isometheptene A *drug belonging to the *stimulants which are on the *IOC list of *banned substances.

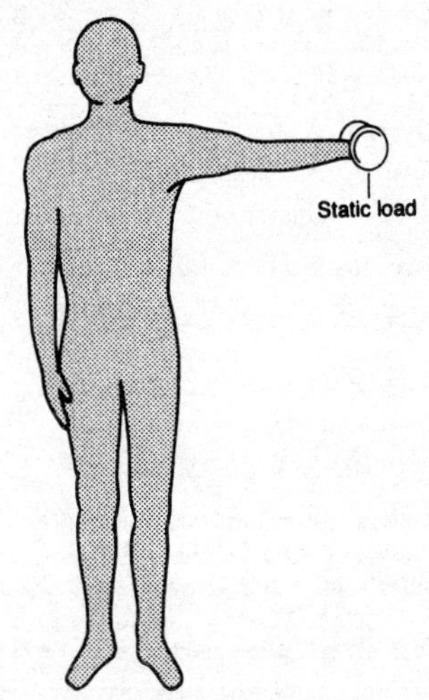

isometric contraction

isometric contraction (static contraction) The term, meaning equal in length, is conventionally used to describe a muscular contraction in which *tension is increased but the muscle does not change length and the external mechanical work done is zero. It is to some extent a misnomer because isometric contractions do involve a certain degree of initial shortening due to stretching of the tendon. Hence, some people prefer to use the term 'static contraction' rather than isometric contraction. The force of an isometric contraction is equal to the force expressed by the resistance. *Compare* concentric contraction; and eccentric contraction.

isometric dynamometry A procedure used to measure *shear force.

isometric exercise An exercise in which a *muscle group is contracted without moving the *joint to which the muscles are attached. Such exercises include pressing the hands together at the chest and pushing against an immoveable object. Isometric exercises produce good strength gains only at the specific angle of contraction. It has been recommended that for the best results, exercises should involve *maximal or near maximal contractions of the muscle statically against a resistance for at least 5 s. Isometric exercises can be performed almost anywhere and require no specialized equipment. However, they do little for *cardiovascular fitness. In fact, such exercises are *contra-indicated for individuals with cardiovascular disease because they can result in increases in intra-abdominal pressure, which can increase blood pressure and put a strain on the heart.

isometric strength The *force or *torque of reaction achieved when the greatest possible effort is brought to bear in a voluntary *isometric contraction for 2–6 s. Isometric strength is important in many activities including a rugby scrum, tug-of-war, and weight-lifting.

isometric-training *See* isometric exercises.

isoprenaline A *drug belonging to the *stimulants which are on the *IOC list of *banned substances.

isoprene A colourless liquid which can *polymerize to form *terpenoids. Natural rubber consists mainly of an isoprene polymer.

isosmotic Applied to two solutions having the same *osmotic pressure.

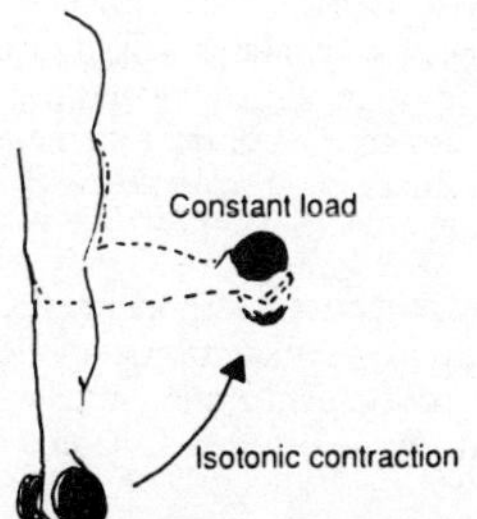

isotonic contraction

isotonic contraction (dynamic contraction) A muscular contraction in which muscle tension purportedly remains constant while the muscle changes its length as it overcomes a constant resistance. Isotonic means equal in *tone; however, the maintenance of tone is not normally achieved during isotonic contractions because of changing resistance and *mechanical advantage. *See also* concentric contraction; and eccentric contraction.

isotonic exercise An exercise which usually involves raising and lowering a weight. The muscles are used in a normal dynamic way, contracting at a speed controlled by the subject (*see* isotonic contraction). Isotonic exercises usually involve the movements and muscles used in the subject's chosen sport. Isotonic exercises are good for developing *strength and *cardiovascular fitness.

isotonic solution Applied to a solution which has no effect on the volume of a cell. Thus, a cell, when immersed in an isotonic solution, tends neither to gain nor to lose water.

isotonic testing Performance tests using *isotonic contractions. They usually involve *dynamometers which, in addition to measuring *absolute strength, may also measure *acceleration, peak *velocity, *work, and *power of isotonic contractions at various preset loads.

isotopes Different forms of the same *element which vary in the number of *neutrons they contain.

issueless riot A *collective behaviour which occurs spontaneously and does not appear to originate from a specific issue, as when a crowd celebrating a home team victory produces large scale property damage. *Compare* issue-oriented riot.

issue-oriented riot Spontaneous *collective behaviour initiated by a specific event, as in a sport-crowd rioting after a disputed decision by an official. *Compare* issueless riot.

IU (International Units) A standarized measure for comparing the biological activity in related forms of the same *fat-soluble vitamin. Although IUs are still used, it is becoming more common to relate each form of the vitamin to a pure standard form. For example, in the UK, vitamin A is now quoted in microgrammes of pure *retinol equivalent.

J

jaundice (icterus) A yellow discolouration of the skin and the *conjunctiva of the eyes due to an abnormally high level of bile pigments in the blood. It may occur when there is an excessive destruction of red blood cells (haemolytic jaundice) damage or disease of the liver cells (heptacellular jaundice), or failure of normal amounts of bile (*see* bile salts) to reach the intestines (obstructive jaundice or cholestasis).

javelin thrower's elbow *See* golfer's elbow.

jaw Bone of the face in which teeth are embedded. The jaw consists of the *maxilla of the upper jaw and the *mandible of the lower jaw.

jejenum Part of the *alimentary canal between the *duodenum and the *ileum.

jerk The sudden contraction of a muscle. Some jerks, such as the knee-jerk, are used to test nervous reflexes (*see* patellar reflex).

J-point The point on an *electrocardiogram at which the *S wave ends.

jogger's nipple Soreness of the nipple due to chafing by clothing, commonly experienced by male and female long-distance runners. The condition may be very painful and accompanied by bleeding. It can usually be avoided by the application of petroleum jelly to the nipples before running.

jogging A training technique involving slow, relaxed, continuous running. It cannot be defined in terms of minutes per mile but the running pace should enable the jogger to continue holding a conversation. People, particularly those over 35-years old, unused to exercise and considering jogging should check their fitness with their doctor. Jogging is regarded by some as the foremost *aerobic exercise. It requires no special skill, little expenditure, and can be done almost anywhere. In the 1970s, it caught the imagination of the public and made exercise generally acceptable. However, excessive jogging can result in musculoskeletal problems arising from *stress and the *shock of running on hard surfaces such as roads and pavements.

joint The junction of two or more bones; an articulation. The joint is an anatomical structure which constitutes a functional unit, biologically and biomechanically. It is comprised of the cartilage-lined extremities (*see* articular cartilage) of the articulating bones, the layer of bone (known as the subchondral layer) directly beneath the cartilage, the fibrous capsule with *ligaments, and the *synovial capsule and the appertaining musculature. These different parts are functionally interdependent; damage to one part usually affects all other parts. *See also* amphiarthrosis; ball-and-socket joint; condyloid joint; diarthrosis; fixed joint; gliding joint; hinge-joint; pivot-joint; saddle-joint; synarthrosis; and synovial joint.

joint capsule A double-layered sleeve of fibrous tissue surrounding the joints of the limbs and enclosing the *joint cavity of a *synovial joint.

joint cavity Area of *synovial joint filled with *synovial fluid. It is enclosed by the *joint capsule.

joint injury Physical damage (such as a sprain, dislocation, or stiffness) to a *joint. Joint injuiries, unlike many muscle injuries, may require absolute rest and *immobilization. In such cases, the damaged *ligament is kept unstressed while the joint is moved to keep the surrounding muscle fit.

joint laxity *See* hyperflexibility.

joint mice Loose bodies in the *joint of an elbow or ankle which may form as a result of an injury. They cause considerable *locking and necessitate surgery.

joint mobility (**mobility**) The ability to move a *joint indicated by the *range of movement in different *planes. Joint mobility is determined by the *ligaments, fibrous capsule, musculature, and the shape of the articular surfaces. *Compare* joint stability. *See also* hypermobility.

joint receptor A group of sense-organs located in *articular capsules that enclose *synovial joints; they are believed to be involved in *kinaesthesis providing information about joint position. *See also* Pacinian corpuscle; and Ruffini corpuscle.

joint stability (**stability**) The firmness and steadiness of a *joint. Low stability is associated with a tendency for the joint to become dislocated (*see* dislocation). Stability is provided by the support of the bones (osseous stability) and the soft tissues, including the *joint capsule, *ligaments, and *muscles. Stability varies according to whether the joint is moving (dynamic stability) or stationary (static stability). The bones contribute mainly to static stability; the ligaments and capsule to both dynamic and static stability; while the muscles contribute only to dynamic stability. Different joints vary greatly in their stability, and the different types of stability may vary within a single joint. For example, the hip has high osseous stability while the knee has low osseus stability but high ligamentous and muscular stability. Excessive flexibility may reduce stability and make an individual *accident-prone.

joint stiffness A condition, characterized by difficulty in moving a *joint, which is usually accompanied by discomfort and pain. Joint stiffness often follows a joint injury when muscles go into a *protective spasm which reduces movement. Joint stiffness should be treated cautiously and no attempt should be made to move the joint forcibly. Persistent, painful stiffness requires medical investigation and treatment.

jostling *Massage-stroke in which a *muscle is grasped at its point of *origin and shaken gently back and forth while the athlete relaxes. The stroke continues all the way down the muscle to the point of *insertion and then back again. Jostling is used mainly to relax muscle (for example, between *deep stroking) and is claimed to reduce the *stretch reflex.

joule The derived *SI unit of *work or *energy. One joule is the amount of work done when the point of application of a *force of one *newton is displaced through a distance of one metre in the direction of the force.

judgement The ability of an individual to assess a situation, consider the choices available for action, and to arrive at conclusions which best satisfy the needs of the situation. Sound judgement therefore involves making the most appropriate choice and is influenced by knowledge, experience, attitude, motivation, ability, and psychological and social factors such as *belief.

judo elbow A tearing of the *ligaments either side of the *elbow-joint. It is commonly caused in judo by a player resisting an armlock by clenching the fists extremely tightly.

jugular vein One of several large *veins in the neck which carry *blood from the head towards the *heart.

jumper's heel An injury to the heel region characterized by pain between the *Achilles tendon and the back of the ankle-bone. It is commonly associated with explosive jumping, stamping down, or the blocking of the foot as a ball is kicked which results in the compression of the *fat pad between heel-bone and shin-bone. Sometimes an *os trigonum is present, causing pain. *See also* retrocalcaneal bursitis.

jumper's knee Tendinitis involving either the *patellar tendon, the *quadriceps tendon, or both. It may be due to *focal degeneration or rupture of the tendon. This condition is peculiar to athletic activities, particularly those involving constant, repetitive jumping and landing such as basketball, long jump, high jump, and triple jump. Patellar tendinitis is the more common of the two conditions and presents itself as a localized pain. Treatment may include *surgical decompression.

jump height A measure of the difference between the standing height of an athlete and the height he or she attains in a jump. For jump heights to be comparable, the type of jump (e.g., *countermovement jump, *drop jump, or *squat jump) must be standardized.

junior leg *See* posterior tibial syndrome.

jury A group of people appointed to judge a competition and, sometimes, to award prizes.

just-noticeable difference The smallest difference between *stimuli which can be perceived.

juxta In *anatomy, prefix denoting near to.

juxtaglomerular apparatus Cells located near to the *glomerulus of the *kidney that play a role in *blood-pressure regulation by releasing the *enzyme *renin.

K

kallidin *See* kinins.

karyogram (idiogram) A photograph or diagram of the full complement of *chromosomes as seen during division of somatic cells (mitosis).

karyotype The appearance of the *chromosome complement of an individual or a cell. In humans, the chromosomes which genetically determine sex (*see* X-chromosome; and Y-chromosome) can be distinguished from the other twenty-two pairs of chromosomes enabling the karyotype to be used in determining a person's sex. The chromosomes are usually arranged in numbered pairs according to a standard classification. The female set differs only in the sex chromosomes XX instead of XY.

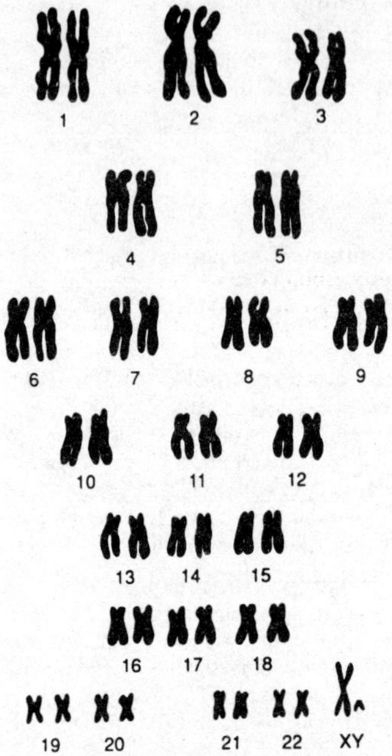

karyotype

karyotyping The determination of the *karyotype of an individual.

kcal *See* kilocalorie.

kelvin *SI unit of temperature which has the symbol K. The unit interval of kelvin temperature is the same as that for *Celsius temperature a temperature expressed in kelvins is the temperature in degrees Celsius plus 273.15. Thus absolute zero is equal to 0 degrees kelvin or –273.15 °C.

keratin Water-insoluble fibrous *protein found in the *epidermis. Keratin is the main constituent of hair and nails, and contributes to the waterproofing of skin.

keratitis Inflammation of the *cornea which may be caused by *trauma, exposure to dust or ultraviolet light, or extreme cold. Participants of winter sports such as skiing are particularly at risk. The treatment for keratitis consists of protecting the eyes by wearing dark glasses. *See also* snow-blindness.

keratoirits Inflammation of both the *cornea and the *iris.

ketone An organic compound containing a carbonyl group (C=O) having the general formula RR'C=O, where R and R' are hydrocarbon groups.

ketone bodies *Ketones formed as breakdown products of fat. They include *acetone, acetoacetic acid, and β-hydroxybutyrate.

ketonuria The presence of *ketone bodies in the *urea. Ketonuria may occur as a result of starvation or *diabetes mellitus.

ketosis Abnormally high levels of ketone bodies in the body tissue.

kg *See* kilogram.

kg-m *See* kilogram-metre.

kidney Excretory and osmoregulatory organ, found as a pair, dorsally, in the *abdomen.

kidney stones (nephrolithiasis; renal stone) Concretions of salt in the kidney which form irregularly-shaped stones. Kidney stones can cause excruciating pain and obstruct the passage of urine. They are usually removed to avoid the risk of complications, but they sometimes pass spontaneously. Athletes prone to developing kidney stones should ensure they have an adequate intake of water before, during, and after physical exertion.

kilocalorie (Cal; kcal) The amount of heat needed to raise the temperature of 1 l of water by 1 °C. Energy changes associated with biochemical reactions are often reported in kilocalories although the *SI unit is the *joule. Sometimes the term 'calorie', used to describe the energy content of foods, is really a kilocalorie; 1 kilocalorie equals 1000 calories.

kilocalorie/minute Unit of *power.

kilogram *SI *base unit of *mass, defined as the mass of the international prototype kilogram: a particular cylinder of platinum–iridium alloy kept at the International Bureau of Weights and Measures at Sävres, Paris. One kilogram is equivalent to 2.2 pounds.

kilogram-metre Unit of *work.

kilojoule (kJ) Unit of energy equal to 1000 *joules.

kinaesthesis The sense by which motion, weight, and position of various body-parts are perceived. Kinaesthesis depends on the sense-organs, especially *proprioceptors, skin receptors, and the *vestibular apparatus providing information about the state of contraction of muscles, and the position of the limbs and the body in space.

kinaesthetic Pertaining to *kinaesthesis.

kinaesthetic feedback *Feedback about the position and movement of the body, provided especially by *proprioceptors in muscles and joints.

kinaesthetic imagery *See* internal imagery.

kinaesthetic perception Awareness of body and limb position, and movements. Tests of kinaesthetic perception include asking a blind-folded subject to attempt to distinguish between objects according to their weight, or asking the blind-folded subject to maintain balance under controlled conditions.

kinaesthia An inability to perceive body positions and movements of the body, resulting in disrupted physical activity.

kinanaesthesia An inability to perceive body position and body movements, resulting in impaired physical activity.

kinanthrometrics *See* kinanthropometry.

kinanthropometry The study of human body-size and *somatotypes, and their quantitative relationship with exercise, sport performance, and nutrition.

kinematic chain *See* kinematic couple.

kinematic couple(kinematic chain) In the human body, a system involving the contact of two rigid body-segments which

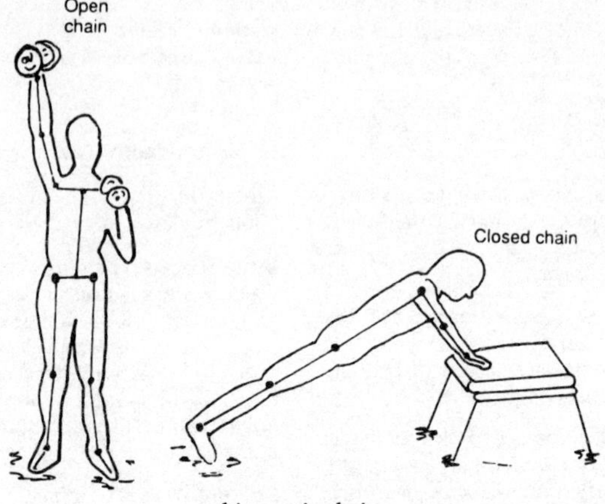

kinematic chains

transmit forces. Kinematic couples may connect successively or by branching to form chains of several kinetic links. If the final link in the chain is free, it is able to move independently of the other links and is known as an open link. If a link is not free, it is known as a closed link and it does not permit isolated movements but facilitates transmission of muscle action to adjacent or distant *articulations. *See also* kinetic link principle.

kinematic feedback *Feedback about a person's movement-pattern or movement-characteristics, without regard to the forces involved. *Compare* kinetic feedback.

kinematics A branch of mechanics concerned with the descriptive study of the motion of objects in terms of *distance, *speed, and *acceleration, without reference to *mass or *forces causing the motion. *Compare* kinetics.

kinesics Body language; a form of non-verbal communication by physical appearance (especially changes in facial and eye movements), posture, gestures, and touching behaviour.

kinesiology The study of the anatomical and mechanical basis of human movement. Kinesiology includes anatomy, mechanics, and physiology of the musculoskeletal system. There is considerable overlap between kinesiology and *biomechanics.

kinetic Pertaining to motion.

kinetic energy The *energy a body possesses by virtue of its motion. Kinetic energy is measured in *joules. A *mass (m) moving with *velocity (v), has a kinetic energy which is $1/2mv^2$, that is, its kinetic energy is half the product of the mass of an object by the square of its velocity, where energy is measured in J, mass in Kg, and velocity in ms^{-1}.

kinetic feedback *Feedback about the *force characteristics of a movement. *Compare* kinematic feedback.

kinetic link principle The general rule that body-segments can generate a high end-point velocity through accelerating and decelerating adjacent *links by the use of internal and external muscle *torques applied to body-segments in a sequential manner from *proximal to *distal, from most massive to least massive, and from most fixed to most free. The kinetic link principle is applied when different body-segments are rotated during throwing and kicking. These actions have been likened to the motion of a bullwhip. If segmental rotations are free to occur at the distal end, the body's base-segments in contact with the ground act like the handle of the bullwhip.

Just as the tip of the bullwhip can be made to travel at supersonic speed, the small distal segments of the hand and foot can be made to travel very fast by the sequential acceleration and deceleration of the body-segments.

kinetic mobility The ability to swing a limb into a desired position at speed, using its own momentum. *See also* ballistic movement.

kinetic mobility exercise *See* ballistic mobility exercise.

kinetics 1 The study of *forces acting on an object which are responsible for the object's movement. Kinetics is concerned with the causal analysis of motion. *Compare* kinematics. 2 Study of the rates at which chemical reactions proceed.

kinins A group of *endogenous *polypeptides, including kallidin, *bradykinin, *angiotensin, and *substance P, that cause *smooth muscle to contract and act as powerful *vasodilators which lower *blood pressure. They are not normally present in the blood but occur, for example, when tissue is damaged. Kinins are thought to play a role in the inflammatory response and may contribute to *ischaemic pain.

kiss of life Emergency mouth-to-mouth resuscitation in which the operator blows air into the victim's lungs to inflate them, allowing the air to be exhaled automatically.

kJ *See* kilojoule.

kneading A form of *massage similar to kneading dough. It involves gently grasping a group of muscles between the thumb and finger and, alternating hands, squeezing the thumb and fingers together while working the muscle up and down. Kneading is used to assess the state of muscle tension. It may also aid deep circulation and remove *metabolic wastes from muscles.

knee The complex *joint between the *femur and the *tibia. *See also* knee-joint.

kneecap *See* patella.

knee extension Straightening of the lower leg; an action used in climbing, running, and rising from a seated position. Knee extension is brought about by the *concentric contractions of the *quadriceps muscles. The *rectus femoris is an especially powerful knee extensor when the hip is extended but is weak when the hip is flexed.

knee extensor A muscle which effects straightening of the lower limb (*see* knee extension). All four muscles of the *quadriceps act as powerful knee extensors.

knee flexion Bending of the knee. The *prime movers are the *hamstrings but other muscles involved in knee flexion are the *gracilis, *popliteus, *plantaris and, especially when the foot is elevated, the *gastrocnemius.

knee flexor A muscle which effects the bending of the lower limb (*see* knee flexion).

knee injury Physical damage to the knee. The knee is a relatively unstable joint and vulnerable to injury in sport. Between one quarter to one third of all sports injuries involve the knee. It is a very complex structure and injuries often affect more than one component making diagnosis notoriously difficult. Many knee injuries are due to overuse (e.g., *chondromalacia patellae), but misalignments of muscles and bone in the lower leg may also increase the risk of knee injury (*see* unhappy triad).

knee instability A reduction in the *stability of the *knee-joint. It may be caused by a direct injury to the joint, or to a weakening of the muscles supporting the joint, particularly of the *quadriceps and *semimembranosus.

knee-jerk A reflex kick of the foot following a blow on the *tendon just below the *patella. *See also* patellar reflex.

knee-joint A *synovial joint where the *condyles of the *femur articulate with the upper *tibia. The knee-joint is the largest in the body and movements allowed are *extension, *flexion, and (to a lesser extent) *rotation. The articulating surfaces are shallow and condyle-like, but they are deepened by L-shaped *menisci. The *joint cavity is enclosed by a *joint capsule only on the *lateral and *posterior aspects. Several capsular *ligaments, the two collateral ligaments, and the intracapsular anterior and

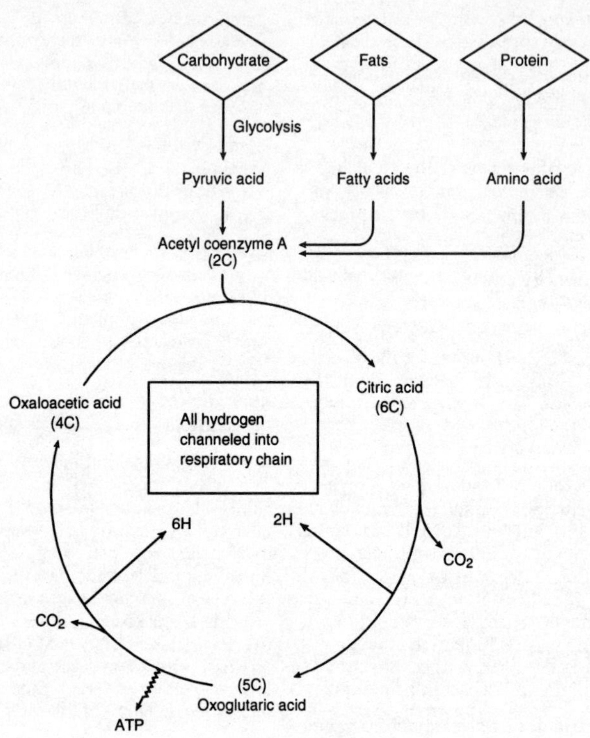

Krebs cycle

posterior *cruciate ligaments, help to prevent displacement of the joint surfaces. Muscle-tone of the quadriceps and hamstrings is important for maintaining knee stability.

knee rotation Movement of the knee around its *longitudinal axis. Although the knee behaves mainly as a *hinge-joint, some rotation is essential for locomotion.

knockout *See* concussion.

knot A unit of speed which equals one nautical mile per hour, or approximately 1.15 land miles per hour.

knowledge of activity The kind of knowledge about an activity that can be demonstrated in a paper and pencil test. Knowledge of activity may also include the ability to utilize information from various types of *feedback, including *knowledge of results and *knowledge of performance. Studies of the value of knowledge of activity on performance are equivocal, but it is generally agreed that to be fully physically educated a person should know, understand, and appreciate the factors that influence physical activity.

knowledge of performance (KP) A form of *augmented feedback given, for example, verbally by a coach at the end of a performance of a skill. The *feedback contains information about the nature of the movement-pattern produced during the performance, and may include identification of the parts of the skill which were performed correctly and the parts performed incorrectly. *Compare* knowledge of activity; and knowledge of results.

knowledge of results (KR) A form of *augmented feedback in which verbal (or verbalizable) information is given to a performer at the end of an action about the outcome of a movement rather than about the movement itself (*compare* knowledge of performance). Some authorities include both the *extrinsic and *intrinsic information a person may receive, but knowledge of results does not normally include intrinsic information. Research indicates that information about performance is one of the most important *variables for motor learning.

knuckle-joint *See* metacarpophalangeal joint.

KO Knockout. *See* concussion.

Kohler's disease An *osteochondritis affecting the *navicular bone in the *tarsus in children, causing pain and limping.

KP *See* knowledge of performance.

KR *See* knowledge of results.

Krause's end-bulbs Bulbous capsules in the skin containing sensory nerve-endings which may be mechanoreceptors, but which are also thought to be thermoreceptors sensitive to cold and activated by temperatures less than 20 °C. They are more superficial than the heat receptors.

KR delay The interval between the production of a movement and the presentation of *knowledge of results (KR). Evidence concerning KR delay on performance indicates that it has negligible effect on the performance of *motor tasks.

Krebs cycle (citric acid cycle; tricarboxylic acid cycle) A series of *aerobic chemical reactions, occurring in *mitochondria, in which *carbon dioxide is produced and *hydrogen and *electrons are removed from *carbon molecules; a process known as *oxidative decarboxylation. The cycle is named after Sir Hans Krebs, the Nobel prizewinner in Physiology and Medicine in 1953. The reactions are *exothermic enabling, during each cycle, one molecule of *adenosine triphosphate to be generated.

Kuntscher nail A long steel nail inserted down the cavity of a long bone to fix a fracture.

kurtosis In statistics, a measure of the extent to which the curve of a set of values is flatter or more peaked than a *normal distribution, which has a kurtosis value of 0. If the curve is more peaked it has a positive value, if flatter it has a negative value.

kwashiorkor A *protein-deficiency disease in children characterized by apathy, impaired growth, skin ulcers, an enlarged liver, and mental retardation. The level of *plasma proteins is inadequate to keep fluid in the bloodstream, resulting in *oedema and a bloated *abdomen.

kymograph A revolving drum which carries a piece of paper onto which a trace is produced by a lever connected to a physiological preparation, such as a nerve or muscle.

kyphosis (hunchback) Dorsally-exaggerated spinal curvature of the thoracic region. It is common in old people and those suffering from rickets or osteomalacia. It may also develop from poor posture or an unequal muscle-pull on the spine.

L

l *See* litre.

L- *See* laevoratatory.

labelling theory A theory applied to the social processes involved in attributing positive or (more commonly) negative characteristics to acts, individuals, or groups, and the effects such labelling has on behaviour. Labelling theory has been particularly influential in the study of *deviance.

labetolol A *drug which acts as both an *alpha blocker and *beta blocker, used in the treatment of *hypertension.

laboratory test In sport, usually a measure of a *physiological function that is conducted in a controlled environment and which uses *protocols and equipment that

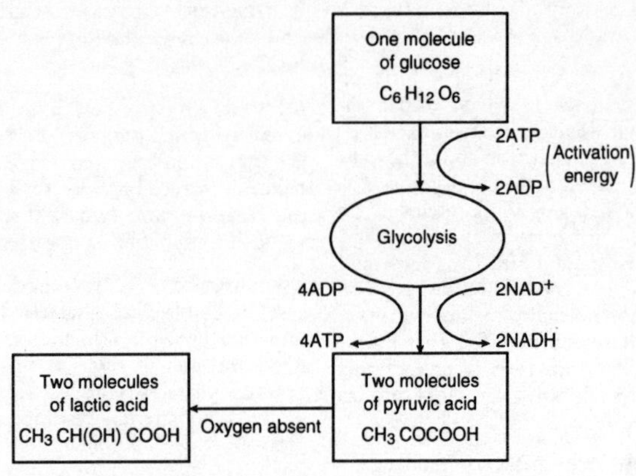

lactic acid system

simulate a sport or activity. *Compare* field test.

labrum A liplike structure, such as that around the margins of the *acetabulum.

labyrinth A system of interconnecting bony cavities and membranes of the *inner ear which comprise the organs of hearing and balance. The labyrinth includes the *cochlea and the *semicircular canals.

laceration Damage to the skin producing a wound; known colloquially as a cut. A laceration may be superficial or deep. Long, shallow lacerations may cause no great problems and require simple cleaning and closure. Sometimes scrubbing is required if the laceration is contaminated with gravel or some other substance. If an implement such as an arrow or javelin is involved, damage to deep structures may occur which require surgical exploration. There is a risk of *tetanus with any penetration of the skin by a foreign object.

lactacid oxygen debt The portion of oxygen consumed to remove accumulated *lactic acid from the blood following exercise. A negligible amount of the lactic acid is excreted in the *urine and sweat; a little contributes to the manufacture of protein; some is converted to *glucose or *glycogen in the *liver and *muscle; but, most lactic acid is fed back into the *aerobic system and is reconverted into *pyruvic acid to be finally metabolized to carbon dioxide and water. The maximum value of the lactacid oxygen debt is between five and ten litres; it is usually higher in athletes, especially sprinters. This component of the oxygen debt is repaid at a much slower rate than the *alactacid debt.

lactacid system *See* lactic acid system.

lactase An *enzyme produced in the *small intestine that helps to breakdown the *disaccharide, *lactose, into *galactose and *glucose.

lactate A *salt or *ester of *lactic acid in which a metal or organic *radical has replaced the hydrogen in the carboxyl group. Lactate is a dissociation product of lactic acid which occurs in the blood. Blood lactate levels vary but are usually 1–2 ml per litre of blood during low intensity exercise which may rise to 25 ml per litre during high intensity exercise (*see* lactate threshold).

lactate analyser An instrument used for the rapid, automatic analysis of *lactic acid levels using a blood sample from a single finger-prick. Although it is easy to use and reliable, it is expensive and can only be used by trained medical staff.

lactate dehydrogenase (LD; LDH) An *enzyme which catalyses the interconversion of *pyruvic acid and *lactic acid. It is found in many cells, but especially in muscle cells.

lactate threshold (OBLA; onset of blood lactate accumulation) The level of exercise at which the blood *lactate level begins to increase. Methods of identifying this level vary, but they include specifying a given concentration of blood lactate (usually between 2–4 mml^{-1}) and identifying graphically the onset of an exponential increase in concentration. The assumption that the lactate threshold represents the *anaerobic threshold has been challenged recently, but the lactate threshold is generally accepted as being useful in identifying a specific intensity of exercise below which *endurance is mainly a function of fuel supply, body temperature, or soft tissue trauma, and above which there is a significant reduction in endurance, probably due to metabolic disturbances such as *acidosis. Appropriate training can enable an athlete to postpone lactate accumulation until higher intensities of exercise are reached.

lacteal A central, blind-ended *lymph vessel in a *villus into which neutral fat is passed from the columnar epithelial tissue where it has been resynthesized from *fatty acid and *glycerol. The fat is in the form of a white, milky emulsion (hence the name lacteal) and is carried to all parts of the body.

lactic acid An organic acid, $CH_3CH(OH).COOH$ which is a *metabolite of the *lactic acid system resulting from the incomplete breakdown of *glucose. Lactic acid readily dissociates to *hydrogen and *lactate *ions. An excessive production of lactic acid is associated with *muscle fatigue and certain forms of muscle soreness.

lactic acid system (lactacid system; LA system;) An energy system in which *adenosine triphosphate (ATP) is manufactured from the breakdown of *glucose to *pyruvic acid, which is then converted to *lactic acid; it is a form of *anaerobic glycolysis. High-intensity activities lasting up to about two or three minutes use this energy system. The lactic acid system involves the reduction of *nicotinamide adenine dinucleotide which provides energy for a net production of two molecules of ATP for each molecule of glucose metabolized.

lactogenic hormone *See* prolactin.

lacto-ovo vegetarian A person who has a diet of plants supplemented with milk, milk products, and eggs. *See also* vegetarian diet.

lactose (milk sugar) A *disaccharide found in milk. It is made by the combination of *galactose and *glucose. Souring of milk is due to the conversion of lactose to *lactic acid by microorganisms. Lactose is an energy-rich food. Some individuals have an intolerance to high levels of lactose.

lacto-vegetarian A person who has a diet of plants supplemented with milk and milk products. *See also* vegetarian diet.

lacuna A small cavity or space, particularly one of many small spaces between the *lamellae of bone cells, or the space occupied by a *cartilage cell.

laddergraph A technique for displaying data in which two test scales are oriented vertically with an individual's scores joined by a line.

laevorotatory Applied to substances which rotate polarized light to the left of an observer looking against the oncoming light.

lambda In *anthropometry, the point on the cranium at the junction of the *sagittal and lamboid sutures.

lamella (pl. lamellae) A thin layer, membrane, or plate of tissue. The term applies especially to a concentric ring of hard bone in *compact bone.

lamellar bone *See* compact bone.

lamina 1 A thin layer or flat plate, especially of bone. 2 The part of a *vertebra which lies between the *transverse process and the *spinous process.

laminar flow (streamline flow) The smooth flow of a *fluid in which adjoining layers of the fluid flow parallel to one another. In laminar flow, all the fluid particles move in distinct and separate layers and

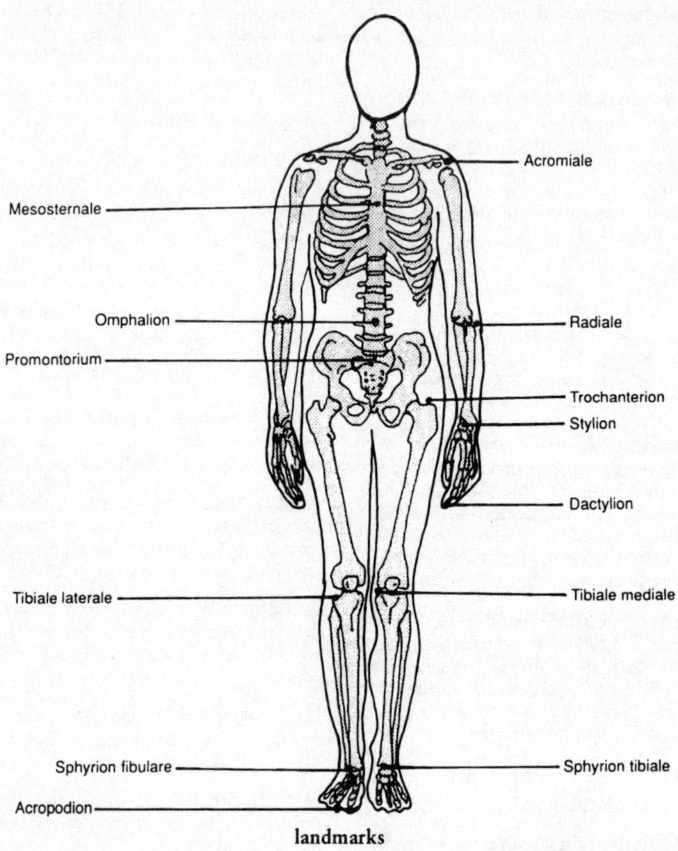

landmarks

there is no mixing between adjacent layers. *Compare* turbulent flow.

landmark (anatomical landmark) Specific point of the human body from which measurements are taken. *See also* *anthropometry.

large calorie *See* kilocalorie.

laryngeal prominence *See* Adam's apple.

laryngeal spasm Sudden closure of the *larynx which stops air flowing into the *lungs. It usually results from an *allergic reaction.

larynx (voice box) The muscular and cartilagenous organ, located between the *trachea and the *pharynx, which contains the vocal cords responsible for the sounds heard as speech.

laser An acronym for light amplification by stimulated emission of radiation. The laser is a device able to produce a very fine beam of highly concentrated light which can cut through strong materials. Lasers are used in surgery to operate on very small structures and now have many therapeutic uses.

LA system *See* lactic acid system.

latent function of sport A function of sport which is hidden, unintended, and unacknowledged by the participants.

latent learning Type of *learning which may not be immediately apparent. For example, a delay may occur between practising a *skill and improvements in the performance of the skill. The delay may be due to the integration of the different components of the skill.

latent period The period of time between the presentation of a *stimulus and the moment a response occurs. The latent period between stimulation and the onset of muscle contraction, for example, is about 0.001 s and is an irreducible component of *reaction time.

lateral In *anatomy, applied to structures away from the midline, or on the outer surface, of the body.

lateral axis (x-axis) In *anthropometry, the *axis formed by the intersection of a *frontal plane and a *transverse plane.

lateral compartment syndrome A pain in the lateral side of the lower leg caused by an increase in pressure in the lateral muscle compartment during exercise. *See also* compartment syndrome.

lateral cuneiform *Tarsal bone articulating with the third *digit.

lateral epicondylitis *See* tennis elbow.

lateral femoral circumflex A *principal artery in the *lateral outer part of the thigh.

lateral flexion Sideways bending of the trunk, involving the actions of the *iliocostalis and *quadratus lumborum on one side of the trunk. *Compare* abduction.

laterality A component of body awareness by which a person perceives that he or she has two distinct sides which are capable of independent movement.

lateral malleolus Lower end of the *fibula which forms the prominent lateral bulge of the ankle and articulates with the *talus. *See also* medial malleolus.

lateral rotation *See* rotation.

lateral rotator *See* thigh lateral rotator.

latissimus dorsi (lats) A broad, flat, triangular *muscle occurring on both sides of the lower back (*see* lumbar region), covered superiorly by the *trapezius and contributing to the *posterior wall of the *axilla. It has extensive superficial *origins on the *thoracic vertebrae and *lumbar vertebrae, the lower third and fourth ribs, and the *iliac crest. *Insertions are on the *intertubercular groove of the *humerus. The latissimus dorsi acts as a *prime mover of arm *extension and is a powerful arm *adductor. It also medially rotates the arm at the shoulder. (In 15 per cent of the population, there is a point of insertion into the inferior angle of the *scapula which enables the muscle to depress the scapula.) Because of its power in these movements, the latissimus dorsi plays an important part in bringing the arm down in a power stroke, as in striking a blow, swimming, or rowing. This is the broad-back muscle which swings the arm backward and rotates it inward.

lats *See* latissimus dorsi.

law 1 A *norm established by a legislative body and often sanctioned by punishments for violations. Generally, the governing body of each individual sport establishes its own laws. 2 In science, a statement which describes a stable dependency between an *independent variable and a *dependent variable.

law of acceleration *See* acceleration, law of.

law of conservation of mechanical energy *See* conservation of mechanical energy.

law of effect A law which states that rewarding a behaviour increases the probability that the behaviour will be repeated, and punishing a behaviour decreases the probability that the behaviour will be repeated. Thus, the law suggests that the effect of the act, whether it is pleasing or displeasing, influences the chances of its recurrence; acts resulting in pleasant sensations tend to be repeated, while those associated with unpleasant sensations tend to be avoided. *See also* law of exercise.

law of equal and opposite reaction *See* Newton's laws of motion.

law of exercise Law which states that, in *learning, the more frequently a *stimulus and response are associated with each other, the more likely the particular response is to follow the stimulus. The law implies that one learns by doing and one cannot learn a *skill, for instance, by watching others. It is necessary to practise the skill, because by doing so the bond between stimulus and response is strengthened. In applying this to *motor learning, the more often a given movement is repeated, the more firmly established it becomes. The performance of *drills attempts to utilize this law. *See also* law of effect; and Thorndike's stimulus–response theory of learning.

law of inertia *See* inertia, law of.

law of mass action Law which states that the rate of chemical reaction is directly proportional to the concentration of the reactants.

law of motion *See* Newton's laws of motion.

law of readiness A law which states that *learning is dependent upon the learner's readiness to act, which facilitates the strengthening of the bond between *stimulus and response. Thus an athlete who is highly motivated and eager to learn is more likely to be receptive to learning than one who is poorly motivated. *See also* Thorndike's stimulus–response theory of learning.

law of use and disuse A law which states that the size of a structure is modified by how much it is used. It applies especially to bones and muscles. Those which are used regularly are suitably stressed (*see* overload principle) and respond by *hypertrophy. Those which are not regularly used respond by *atrophy. *See also* Wolff's law.

laxity Looseness or slackness of the *muscles and soft tissue surrounding a *joint.

lazy eye *See* amblyopia.

LD *See* lactate dehydrogenase.

LDH *See* lactate dehydrogenase.

LDL *See* low-density lipoprotein.

leader 1 A role conferred on the basis of personal characteristics, experience, or through tradition by virtue of the position a person occupies in a group (e.g., team captain or coach). A leader generally takes a major role in making group decisions, motivating the group, and effecting group actions. *See also* leadership behaviour. **2** An individual or team occupying first position in a sports event.

leader behaviour description questionnaire A detailed *questionnaire designed to discover how leaders behave. Results of many questionnaires have shown that *consideration and *initiating structure were the two most important factors in *leadership-behaviour. They are independent and a leader can be high in both, low in both, or some other combination.

leadership The exercise of authority over another person or persons. Leadership implies that someone is willing to follow, and confer power and status on another person. *See also* leader.

leadership behaviour The *behaviour associated with the exercise of authority. Effective leadership behaviour is characterized by the ability of the leader to influence the activities of a group by *initiating structures (such as *goal-setting) which enable the group to overcome mutual problems successfully and to achieve their group goals. The leadership behaviour exhibited by leaders may or may not reflect their personalities. *Compare* situational behaviours; and universal behaviours. *See also* consideration.

leadership style The way a leader acts and the type of relationship he or she has with followers in particular situations.

leadership trait A relatively stable personality disposition, such as intelligence, aggressiveness, and independence, associated with a *leader.

lead-up A task or activity which is typically presented to prepare learners for an important goal response. Lead-up activities usually consist of simpler tasks which are thought to be fundamental to the learning of more complex tasks. For example, gymnasts are often taught a number of subroutines which eventually lead to a complex routine.

lean body-mass The mass of body tissue which does not contain fat; it is the total *body-mass minus the total body fat. Some authorities include *essential fat stores in the lean body-mass. *See also* body composition.

learned effectiveness A state of mind of individuals who feel that they can control their own successes or failures. Learned effectiveness often occurs in those who have been supported and encouraged during childhood, and who have a history of success at a sport. *Compare* learned helplessness.

learned helplessness A mental state in which people feel that they have no control over their failures, and that failure is inevitable. Such people suffer motivational losses and are very resistant to training.

learning An internal neural process associated with practice or experience, leading to relatively permanent changes in behaviour which are not due to growth or fatigue. Learning is often assumed to occur when relatively stable changes in performance occur.

learning curve A curve on a graph which shows performance changes against practice time or number of practice sessions. The term implies that changes in performance mirror changes in learning. Many scientists believe that this idea is an oversimplification (*see* latent learning). Learning curves (or, more correctly, performance curves) are used to depict the acquisition of *skill. For many sports, they are negatively accelerating; that is, the learning curve shows the fastest rate of improvement in the early stages of practice and the slowest rate as individuals approach the limits of their ability. However, accurate learning curves are difficult to obtain and are very variable since fluctuations are imposed by many factors, such as motivation, health, and concentration.

learning method A procedure used for *learning and teaching a *skill. No one method seems unequivocally the best for every skill. In fact, even the best method to learn a particular skill seems to be dependent on the individual learner. *Compare* training. *See* backward chaining; part method; part-whole method; progressive-part method; repetitive method; whole method; and whole-part-whole method.

learning objective An outcome a learner is expected to achieve at the end of a given unit of instruction. From the point of view of a coach, it is called an instructional objective. Learning objectives can be established at different levels of difficulty and in three domains: cognitive, usually concerned with verbal learning; motor, concerned with physical skills; and affective, concerned with attitudes, feelings, and values. Commonly, learning objectives in sport involve all three domains, although the motor domain may be the most obvious.

learning score A score computed as the difference between the initial and final levels of a *variable, sometimes used in estimating the changes in performance as a result of practice.

learning variable An *independent variable that affects both the performance of a *skill when it is present and the learning of the skill after it has been removed.

least preferred co-worker scale A scale which measures the *empathy of *leaders for their least preferred team-member. The scores are used to identify the type of *motivation a leader tends to use. A high score indicates that a leader has positive feelings towards a weak member of the group and thus has high *relationship motivation; a low score indicates the leader has high *task motivation. *Compare* Fiedler's contingency theory.

lecithin A *phospholipid present in egg yolk and soya beans. Lecithin is involved in *fat *metabolism and is a component of cell membranes and the *myelin sheath. It is claimed that inclusion of lecithin in a post-competition diet accelerates recovery.

left spin *See* side spin.

leg The lower limb, from the knee to the ankle, including the *tibia and *fibula.

legal system The social activities and organizations, including courts, lawyers, and police, charged with upholding and enforcing the *laws of a *society.

leger test *See* shuttle test.

leg-length discrepancy (anatomical short leg) An anatomical misalignment in which one leg is longer than the other. It rarely causes problems. Discrepancies of more than 6 mm have been recorded with no adverse effects in élite athletes, but the condition does increase the risk of *over-use injuries. Consequently, discrepancies of more than 10 mm may require *orthotics.

leg movements Movements of the lower limb which include those of the *ankle and the *knee.

leg-overuse compartment syndrome A condition characterized by a dull, generalized ache, associated with exercise, in the anterior, lateral, or posterior compartments of the leg (*see* muscle compartment). *See also* anterior compartment syndrome; lateral compartment syndrome; and posterior deep compartment syndrome.

leisure A time in which individuals are not compelled to do anything, and are free to choose to relax or to take part in a *leisure activity. Leisure has important social functions which include relief from the demands and restrictions of work. *See also* leisure activity.

leisure activity An activity, distinct from the routine obligations of work, family, and society, in which an individual voluntarily takes part. A leisure activity may or may not be physically demanding. Leisure activities include watching and taking part in sport. It is generally agreed that many leisure activities have strong socializing influences (*see* socialization).

length A linear measurement of an object, end to end; it is usually the longest dimension. The *SI unit of length is the *metre.

length–tension diagram A graph of the *tension produced by a contracting *muscle as a function of its *length. *See also* length–tension relatioship.

length–tension relationship The relationship between the length of a muscle and the contractile tension which it can exert. The contractile tension of a *muscle is generally *maximal when the muscle is at its resting length, but in normal muscle, a greater overall force is produced when the muscle is stretched, which seemingly contradicts the general length–tension relationship. However, the apparent increase is due to the contribution of the *elastic components of the joint tissues and not to an increased muscle tension.

lens Transparent crystalline body in the *eye. Its main function is in *accommodation. Although the lens contributes to *refraction, the *cornea is the most important refractive body in the eye.

lesion Any discontinuity in a tissue, or loss of function of a body-part, which is the result of damage by disease or wounding. Lesions range from *sores and *ulcers to *tumours.

lesser trochanter A bony protruberance on the inner side of the *neck of the *femur which acts as an attachment point for some muscles of the thigh and buttocks.

lesser tuberosity An elevation of the *humerus which acts as the insertion point for muscles such as the *subscapularis.

leucine An *essential amino acid found in corns and legumes. It is involved in *protein *metabolism and is vital for growth in infants.

leucocyte (leukocyte) A white blood cell. There are three main types: *granulocytes, *lymphocytes, and *monocytes. They are primarily involved in defence by *phagocytosis against *infection and *trauma and in the production of *antibodies, but they also take part in some other processes such as *bone-remodelling.

leukocyte *See* leucocyte

leukotrienes Endogenous chemicals derived from *arachidonic acid which play an active part in inflammatory reactions. One of their effects is to attract white blood cells (*see* leucocyte) to sites of tissue damage.

They may also have harmful effects, such as the triggering of *asthma attacks.

levelling effect The effect observed when highly skilled athletes compete with less skilled athletes. There is a tendency for the performance of the more skilled athletes to decline while the performance of the less skilled improves.

level of expectation The level of performance which an individual desires to reach or which an individual feels he or she can reach.

levels of processing framework A framework for memory research that views memory as continuous rather than discrete. The level of processing framework is a rival to the *black box model of memory which regards memory as consisting of three compartments: *short-term store, *short-term memory, and *long-term memory. The levels of processing framework attempts to explain the nature of processing which an item has received, without postulating discrete memory compartments. *See also* depth of processing.

lever A bar or some other rigid structure, hinged at one point and capable of rotating freely to do *work when an applied *force acts on it. In the human body, *bones, the axes of which pass through *joints, act as levers. Effort is provided by *muscle contraction at the point of muscle attachment to bone. The *load consists of any resistance to movement. Sports implements such as golf-clubs and rackets become levers when held in the hand. The usual function of a lever is to gain a *mechanical advantage whereby a small *force applied over a large distance at one end of the lever produces a greater force operating over a smaller distance at the other end of the lever, or whereby a given speed of movement at one end of the lever is greatly increased at the other. *See also* first-class lever; second-class lever; and third-class lever.

lever arm (force arm; momentum arm; torque arm) The shortest possible perpendicular distance between the *axis and the *line of action of a *force. *See also* torque.

levobunolol A *drug belonging to the *beta blockers which are on the *IOC list of *banned substances.

levorphanol A *narcotic analgesic similar to *morphine in its actions and addictive properties. It is used to relieve severe pain.

Leydig cell *Testosterone-secreting cell found in the *interstitial area of the *testis seminiferous tubules.

LH *See* luteinizing hormone.

lidocaine *See* lignocaine.

life chances The advantages and disadvantages, such as access to material objects and services, of an individual or group which determine opportunities in life for changing *status.

life course The sociohistorical process of change which occurs in a person, from infancy through to old age, brought about as a result of personal interactions with other people and societal events. The nature of a person's life course depends on his or her own personal experiences. It may or may not follow the same chronological pattern as that of another person, and it may have features which are quite distinct from those of another person. *Compare* life cycle.

life-cycle The process of change and development that a person, institution, or other entity undergoes in relation to chronological age. Use of the term implies that different people or institutions share common features, such as growth and decay, related to their age. *Compare* life course.

life-cycle model of cohesion A *model of *cohesion which suggests that teams and groups have a life cycle from creation or formation to dissolution, and that cohesion follows this same pattern. Five stages have been identified: encountering, boundary-testing, role creation, producing or constructing, and dissolution. Thus cohesion increases after the creation of the group, levels off when the group is well established, after which it decreases until the group finally separates.

life cycle theory of leadership A situational theory that proposes that preferred *leadership style depends on the maturity of the athlete. Proponents of the theory suggest that while it is difficult to predict exactly which sort of leadership behaviour is best for which maturity level, coaches and leaders must be sensitive to the maturity level of the athletes.

life events Any significant event in a person's life which may have beneficial or detrimental effects on a person's social relationships and *status. Disruptive events, such as loss of job, disability, and bereavement, are called life crises. However, both the apparently beneficial events (such as selection for an international team) and the detrimental events may increase *stress and *anxiety, and are implicated in the development of some diseases.

life space The psychological *environment as it exists for a person at any given moment in time. Life space may be divided into two dimensions, reality and unreality. The former refers to the objective aspects of life, the latter to fantasy and imagery.

lifestyle The set of values, beliefs, and practices by which an individual or group lives.

lift Component of *force which acts at right angles to the *drag component on an object moving through a *fluid. At any given *velocity of flow, the *lift and *drag depend in part on how the body is orientated. *See also* angle of attack.

lift–drag ratio The ratio of *lift to *drag of a projectile as it moves through the air. The lift–drag ratio is used to *analyse the effect of the *angle of attack on the *trajectory of a projectile, and to determine the best angle of attack to produce the maximum lift.

ligament Band of tough, fibrous *connective tissue joining two bones together. Ligaments may be capsular, extrinsic, or instrinsic. Capsular ligaments are thickenings within the fibrous *joint capsule. Extrinsic ligaments run between bony joints. Intrinsic ligaments occur within a *synovial cavity and are generally less common than the other types. Ligaments are relatively non-elastic, but flexible enough to allow freedom of movement. Their main tasks are to bind bones together, to strengthen and stabilize joints, and to limit their movement to certain directions. If a ligament is ruptured or subjected to prolonged tensile stresses (for example, through the over-enthusiastic performance of flexibility exercises) joint stability may be reduced.

ligament tear A tear in a *ligament which may be a partial or a complete tear. Partial tears involve only part of the ligament fibres and do not affect *joint stability. Complete tears involve most or all of the ligament fibres and the affected joint becomes unstable. *See also* avulsion fracture.

ligamentum nuchae A strong elastic *ligament extending from the *occipital bone of the *skull along the tips of the spinous processes of the *cervical vertebrae, inhibiting excessive head and neck *flexion thus preventing damage to the *spinal cord.

ligamentum teres A flat, *intracapsular *ligament that runs from the *femur head to the lower lip of the *acetabulum. It is not important in stabilizing the *joint since it is slack during most hip movements.

ligand An atom or *molecule (for example, of a *drug) that interacts with and attaches to a larger molecule at a specific receptor site.

light adaptation A term usually employed for the process which occurs when the eye is exposed to normal conditions for daylight vision, but it is used sometimes for the decreasing visual sensitivity which occurs when the eye remains in conditions of bright light.

light stroking Form of *massage, usually carried out with the palms of the hands, to apply oils and soothe muscles. The strokes are performed towards the heart to enhance blood circulation. Contact is maintained with the skin to maintain the subject's state of relaxation.

lignocaine (lidocaine) A *local anaesthetic commonly used in minor surgery including dental surgery. It is also prescribed for the treatment of conditions involving abnormal heart rhythms. *See also* banned substances.

Likert scale A measure of *attitude consisting of a series of attitude statements, such as 'jogging is a good activity for most people' or 'jogging is boring', each rated on a five-point scale (strongly agree, agree, undecided, disagree, strongly disagree).

Likert-type scale A scale used in many structured *questionnaires. As in a *Likert scale, an attitude statement is given such as 'during a football match I find mysef getting very tense and worried as the match progresses'; the respondent then marks a scale reflecting his or her attitude to the statement. The scale might be shown as follows:

definitely false 1 2 3 4 5 6 7 8 9 10 definitely true

limbic system Functional brain system which is mainly associated with the *forebrain and is concerned with emotional or affective behaviour, *learning, and *memory. Extensive connections with higher and lower centres of the brain allow the limbic system to respond to a wide range of environmental stimuli.

limiting factor Any factor that tends to inhibit growth or activity of an individual or a population, either by being below the level necessary for normal growth and activity or by exceeding the limits of tolerance.

limiting friction (static friction) The minimum *force needed to start one body sliding on top of another body. For two dry surfaces, the limiting friction is equal to the *normal reaction multiplied by a constant, the value of the constant depending on the nature of the surfaces.

line Narrow ridge, less prominent than a *crest, which runs along the *shaft of a *bone. It is a site of muscular attachment.

linea alba The narrow tendinous area (*see* tendon) extending from the xiphoid process to the pubic symphysis in the centre of the abdominal wall onto which the *transversalis and part of the external and internal oblique muscles insert.

linea aspera A rough ridge on the *posterior aspect of the *shaft of the *femur which acts as a site of muscle attachment.

linear Pertaining to a straight line.

linear equilibrium *See* equilibrium.

linear model of cohesion A model which originated in psychotherapy but has been applied to the development of *cohesion within a *group. The model suggests that cohesion develops through well-defined, progressive developmental stages. The stages have been referred to as forming, storming, norming, and performing. The forming stage occurs when the group-members first meet and is characterized by orientation problems; the storming stage follows and is characterized by conflict; during the norming stage the group comes together and cohesion is enhanced; and finally, the performing stage is characterized by the group working together to achieve its goals and directives.

linear momentum (quantity of motion) The product of the *mass and *velocity of an object. The greater the linear momentum of a moving object the greater the *force needed to stop it or alter its direction. Hence a rugby player or American footballer of large mass and velocity is harder to stop than one of less mass running more slowly.

linear motion Motion in which all parts of an object move the same distance, in the same direction, at the same time. Pure linear motion is unusual in human movement because of the limb movements that are necessary to produce movement of the whole body. To take the example of a sculler, the boat glides through the water, showing linear motion, but the sculler's body, as he or she pulls on the oars, does not. *See also* translation.

linear relationship Occurs when *variable quantities are directly proportional to one another. A linear relationship can be represented on a graph as a straight line.

linear velocity Rate at which a body moves in a straight line from one location to another. Average linear velocity = *displacement/(time taken). The linear velocity of a point on a turning body, such as a *lever, is directly proportional to its distance from the *axis. Therefore the maximum linear velocity of a moving lever occurs at its *distal end, and the longer the radius of the lever, the greater its linear velocity.

linear vibration Back and forth motion along a straight line. *See also* angular vibration.

line of action (line of force) The straight line extending indefinitely through the point of application of a *force and along the direction of the force. *See also* line of gravity.

line of force *See* line of action.

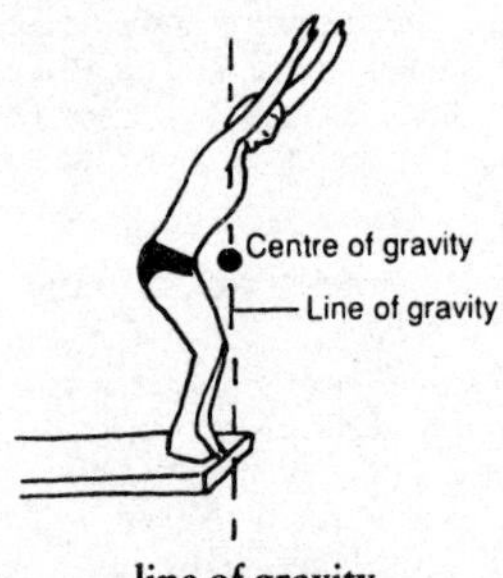

line of gravity

line of gravity An imaginary vertical line passing from the *centre of gravity of an object, down to the ground. It is also known as the line of action of the force of gravity.

liniment Preparation applied externally to the body in the belief that it warms and protects. A liniment, by providing a warm sensation, may have psychological benefits but it does not affect the *deep muscle (except, possibly by diverting blood from deep to *superficial muscles) and is no substitute for a proper *warm-up routine.

link In a biomechanical system, a straight line through a body-segment between adjacent hinge-joints.

linoleic acid A yellow, oily *polyunsaturated fatty acid ($C_{17}H_{31}COOH$). Linoleic acid is an *essential fatty acid which cannot be synthesized from other fatty acids. It is a component of *lecithin. Both *arachidonic acid and *linolenic acid may be synthesized from linoleic acid. It was once known as vitamin F but is no longer regarded as a *vitamin.

linolenic acid An *essential fatty acid ($C_{17}H_{29}COOH$) which can be synthesized from *linoleic acid.

lipase An *enzyme, secreted from the *pancreas, which *hydrolyses *fat into *fatty acids and *glycerol.

lipid Organic compound, insoluble in water, but which dissolves readily in other lipids and in organic solvents such as *alcohol, *chloroform, and *ether. Lipids contain *carbon, *hydrogen, *oxygen, and sometimes *phosphorus. They are classified according to their solubility and include *neutral fat (triglyceride), *phospholipid, and *steroid.

lipid deposit theory Theory which suggests that regular exercise can reduce *lipid deposits and *atherosclerosis, and thus reduce the risk of *coronary heart disease.

lipolysis The hydrolytic breakdown of *lipids into *fatty acids and *glycerol.

lipoprotein An organic compound formed from *lipid and *protein that transports *fats and *cholesterol through the *bloodstream and *lymph. *See also* high-density lipoprotein; low-density lipoprotein; and very low-density lipoprotein.

liposis The accumulation of abnormally large amounts of *fat in the body. Also known as adiposis. *See also* obesity.

liquid A *fluid in which the molecules are relatively free to move, but still maintain some cohesion. A liquid thus has a fixed volume but its shape assumes that of the vessel in which it is contained.

litre (l) A unit of volume formerly defined as the volume occupied by a *mass of 1 kg of pure water at its maximum density and under standard atmospheric pressure. It is equal to 1.000 028 decimetres cubed. It has subsequently been defined as a special name for a decimetre cubed. This has caused some confusion.

little league shoulder An injury which affects the growing ends of the *humerus due to excessive throwing. It tends to occur quite commonly in children in the USA because of the popularity in that country of baseball, the little league being a junior baseball league. *See also* golfer's elbow.

liver One of the largest *organs of the human body. The liver has many functions, including detoxification, *glucose *metabolism, *urea synthesis, *bile production, storage of *fat-soluble vitamins and some minerals (e.g., iron), and the manufacture of *prothrombin and *fibrinogen. The liver also plays a very important role in *thermoregulation; changes in the metabolism of its cells can vary heat production within the body.

load The sum of all the *forces and *moments acting on a body. In skeletal movement, the load is the bone itself along with overlying tissue and anything else that is resisting movement of that particular *lever.

loading The resistance or load which is used in strength *training. *See also* repetition maximum.

loading intensity The strength of a *stimulus, or the concentration of *work executed per unit time within a series of stimuli during a training session. Loading intensities for *endurance-training or speed-training are calculated from the speed in metres per second and the frequency of movement; for strength-training, loading intensity is reflected by the amount of resistance (*see* resistance maximum); for jumping or throwing, loading intensity depends on the heights or distances jumped.

loafer's heart theory The theory that the *heart of an inactive person is less able than that of an active person to cope with *stress and increases in demands, thereby making it more susceptible to a *heart attack.

local anaesthetic A *drug which temporarily blocks *nerve conductance, removing the sensation of pain when applied locally to nerve tissue. Although local anaesthetics do not damage the nerves, their use carries the risk of aggravating injuries, therefore the *IOC restricts their use. With the exception of *cocaine, local anaesthetics may be used by athletes as long as it is medically justified and the route of administration is either locally applied or by intra-articular injection. Where appropriate, details of diagnosis, dose, and route of administration of the local anaesthetic must be submitted, in writing, to the *IOC Medical Commission or a *Sports Federation. *Intravenous injections and the use of cocaine are always banned.

local cross-fibre stroke Gentle but deep *massage applied with thumb or fingertips across *muscles in which there are problem areas which feel hard. Used during *rehabilitation rather than on newly injured areas.

local muscular fatigue Reduction in the effectiveness of a *muscle or a muscle group reflected by a decline in peak tension. Local muscular fatigue may be due to one or more reasons, such as failure of a *motor nerve to transmit a *nerve impulse to the muscle; *fatigue at the neuromuscular junction; inability of the contractile mechanism itself to generate *force; accumulation of *lactic acid in the muscle; depletion of *adenosine triphosphate (ATP) and phosphocreatine (PC); and failure of the central nervous system (CNS) to initiate and relay nervous impulses to muscle. The most probable sites of local muscle fatigue are the neuromuscular junctions, the contractile mechanism of the muscle itself, and the CNS. Fatigue at the neuromuscular junction, which might be more common in *fast twitch fibres, is probably due to decreased release of *acetylcholine. Fatigue within the contractile mechanism may be caused by one of the following: accumulation of lactic acid; *depletion of ATP and PC; depletion of *muscle glycogen store; or lack of oxygen and inadequate blood flow.

locking Prohibiton of movement of a *joint through its full normal range due to a mechanical defect or obstruction within the joint. It may result in an inability to fully extend the joint or the fixation of a joint in one position. Locking or inability to move a joint can be caused by extreme *pain due to a *muscle spasm or by the interposition of a foreign body or torn *cartilage. Locking of the *knee-joint, for example, may be due to a spasm of *hamstring muscle, a tear of a *meniscus, or a loose body in front.

lockjaw *See* tetanus.

locomotion Movement of an organism from one place to another.

locomotives A form of *pyramid-training used especially in swimming. A typical session in a 25 m pool might consist of swimming four lengths hard, four lengths slowly; three hard, three slowly; two hard, two slowly; one hard, one slowly. Then back up the ladder starting with one hard, one slow; two hard, two slow, etc.

locomotor Pertaining to movement from one place to another.

locus of causality A dimension used in *attribution theory which relates to a competitor's perception of the cause of success or failure. The locus of causality may be internal (i.e., based on the competitor's own characteristics such as ability or effort) or external (i.e., due to factors outside the individual, such as luck).

locus of control A psychological construct that refers to whether individuals believe that their behaviour or, more correctly, the reinforcements from behaviour, is under their own control (internal locus of control: *see* internals) or not (external locus of control: *see* externals).

logical model The notion that people make logical *attributions about behavioural outcomes. *Compare* illogical model.

log-linear analysis Technique of statistical analysis used on cross-tabulations of data. It transforms nonlinear models into linear models by *log transformation. This is necessary because measurements from studies in sport sociology are often *nominal and *ordinal, and therefore do not meet the assumptions needed by many statistical techniques. It is a *causal modelling technique.

loin The area of the back between the *pelvis and *thorax.

Lombardianism View promoted by the American Football coach, Vince Lombardi, which endorses the statement that only winners matter in sport. He is reputed to have coined the phrase 'winning isn't the most important thing—it's the only thing.'

Lombard's paradox A situation which arises when a *muscle which spans two *joints contracts and affects the joints in two opposing ways. During running, for example, the *rectus femoris produces movements at two joints when contracting. While one movement, knee *extension, is required in a particular phase of the activity, the other, hip *flexion, is contrary to the desired action during that phase.

long biceps tendon A *tendon which runs from the *biceps brachii through the *intertubercular groove over the head of the *humerus to attach onto the *supraglenoid tuberosity of the *scapula. It is susceptible to degenerative changes and rupture in athletes over 40 years old.

long bone A *bone which consists of a long, hollow, cylindrical *shaft formed of *compact bone with *cancellous bone located at the ends of the *shaft. Examples include the *tibia, *humerus, and *femur. All the limb bones, except the *patella and those of the wrist and ankle, are long bones. The long bones are so named because of their elongated shape, not their size; the three bones in each finger are long bones even though small. Long bones are adapted for weight-bearing and can withstand considerable *stress; they also serve as levers for sweeping, speedy movements.

long head Refers to the longer of two heads of a muscle.

longissimus A three-part muscle of the *erector spinae group which extends from the *lumbar region to the *skull. The longissimus consists of the longissimus cervicis, longissimus thoracis, and the longissimus capitis. The longissimus has its *origins on the *transverse processes of the *vertebrae and its *insertions on the transverse processes of the thoracic or cervical vertebrae, and on ribs above the points of origin; the longissimus capitis inserts onto the *mastoid process of the *temporal bone. Thoracis and cervicis act together to extend the vertebral column and, acting on one side only, bend it laterally. The capitis extends the head and turns the face to one side.

longitudinal axis 1 An imaginary straight line that connects the centre of the *proximal joint of a *body-segment with the centre of the *distal joint. In the *anatomical position, it is the same as the body's vertical or *y*-axis. 2 In *anthropometry, the *axis formed by the intersection of a *frontal plane and a *sagittal plane.

longitudinal axis of foot In the *anatomical position, an imaginary horizontal line at right angles to the extended *longitudinal axis of the leg.

longitudinal design An investigational method that involves collecting data from the same sample of individuals at different times. *Compare* cross-sectional design.

longitudinal study An investigation which adopts the *longitudinal design.

long loop reflex A *stretch reflex with a *latency of 50–80 ms, modified by instruction and mediated by a higher centre of the *brain.

long saphenous vein (great saphenous) A principal *vein which runs from the foot to the groin; the longest vein in the body.

long, slow distance-training (LSD) A form of *aerobic training which consists of continuous low-intensity activity of extended duration which places emphasis on raising the heart-rate to levels of between 60–80 per cent maximal.

long-term anaerobic performance Exercise lasting about 90 s which is supported by both *aerobic and *anaerobic systems.

long-term anaerobic performance capacity The total work output of exercise lasting about 90 s.

long-term anaerobic test Test lasting from about 60–90 s which has been developed to evaluate total *anaerobic capacity and the ability to maintain a high-power output when a large *anaerobic energy component is present. Tests include the *Cunningham and *Faulkner treadmill test; the *Quebec ninety-second test; and the *sixty-second vertical jump test.

long-term endurance exercise An *endurance performance with a duration of more than 10 min. Such exercise is associated with recruitment mainly of *slow-twitch fibres, and the energy supplied mainly by the *aerobic system. The contribution of the aerobic system gets greater as the duration of the exercise increases, and becomes more reliant on *free fatty acids as a *substrate for *metabolism.

long-term memory According to the *black box model of memory, a relatively permanent memory compartment capable of storing very large amounts of information for long periods of time. The long-term memory is presumed to include a store of *movement programmes which are recalled during the execution of complex manoeuvres. It is believed that new information is added to the long-term memory from the *short-term memory, and that prior to the execution of movements, information from the long-term memory is processed together with that from the short-term sensory store in the short-term memory.

long-term motor memory A memory for relatively well-learned *motor skills with retention intervals of months or even years.

long thoracic artery A principal *artery in the chest.

long thoracic nerve A *nerve in the shoulder region which supplies the *serratus anterior muscle.

loose bodies Small pieces of *bone or *cartilage floating within a *joint capsule which may include bits of *articular cartilage. Their occurrence probably reflects a joint trauma or the wearing away of part of the articular cartilage which exposes the surface of the bone beneath, causing it to die and separate; symptoms are painful catching or *locking of the joint. Loose bodies may promote *osteoarthritis if not surgically removed.

lordosis (lumbar lordosis; sway back) An accentuated, convex, forward spinal curvature of the *lumbar region. Lordosis may result from *rickets but it is more commonly caused by poor posture or an unequal muscle-pull on the spine, as when carrying a large mass in front of the body in pregnant women or obese persons. There is also a tendency to develop lordosis or lumbar spine during a *growth spurt. There is wide ethnic variation in the shape of the back, and lordosis might be quite marked and normal in some people.

loudness The intensity aspect of auditory experience, scaled in decibels.

low back-pain A localized pain or discomfort in the *lumbar region of the back. It is often caused by postural defects when the normal relationship between muscles, bones, and other tissues is distorted. Low back-pain may also be caused by a shortening of the *hamstrings following vigorous exercise which puts a strain on the back. Sometimes, the origin of low back-pain may involve the vertebral column and its nerves, or it may be a *referred pain from organs in the pelvis and abdomen.

low-density lipoprotein (LDL) A specific kind of *lipoprotein that is the form in which *cholesterol is transported in the blood. High concentrations of LDL are associated with *atherosclerosis. *Compare* high-density lipoprotein.

lower leg flexion *See* knee flexion.

lower limb Region of the body which consists of three functional segments: the thigh, leg, and foot. The lower limb carries the entire weight of the erect body and is subject to exceptional forces during jumping and running. It contains thicker, stronger bones than the *upper limb, and is specialized for stability and weight-bearing.

lower means interdependence Relationships exhibited by *coactive sports that do not require team-mate interaction for success. *Compare* high means interdependence.

LSD 1 *See* long, slow distance-training. 2 *See* lysergic acid diethylamide.

LTH *See* prolactin.

LTM *See* long-term memory.

lub-dub Heart sounds as heard through a *stethoscope. The first sound, a lub, coincides with the beginning of *ventricular systole and the closure of the *atrioventricular valves. The second sound, dub, coincides with the beginning of *diastole and the closure of valves in the *aorta and *pulmonary artery.

luck An external *attribution, lack of which is often offered as an excuse for poor sports performance.

ludic activity Social interaction based on games or play. Ludic activities and *sport share at least two elements: uncertain outcomes and sanctioned displays. The uncertain outcomes provide suspense and excitement; sanctioned displays give participants a socially-acceptable opportunity to exhibit physical prowess.

ludic institutionalization The process by which simple, informal play and games have developed into formal, highly regulated sports.

lumbago Acute pain, resulting from inflammation of tissues in the lower back, which has many causes. The acute onset of lumbago may result from a *herniated disc, a strained muscle, or a sprained ligament. *See also* low back-pain.

lumbar In *anatomy, pertaining to the *loin.

lumbar curvature *See* spinal curvature.

lumbar lordosis *See* lordosis.

lumbar plexus A network of nerves in the lower back.

lumbar puncture The withdrawl of *cerebospinal fluid by inserting a hollow needle between the third and fourth *lumbar vertebrae.

lumbar region The region of the lower back defined by the five vertebrae situated between the *thoracic vertebrae and the *sacrum. The lumbar region forms the largest natural curve in the back and is sometimes referred to as the small of the back.

lumbar vertebra A *vertebra of the lower back between the *thoracic and *sacral vertebrae. There are five lumbar vertebrae, designated L1–L5. Each lumbar vertebra has a sturdy, large, kidney-shaped *centrum enabling it to carry out its important weight-bearing function; lumbar vertebrae take much of the strain during locomotion.

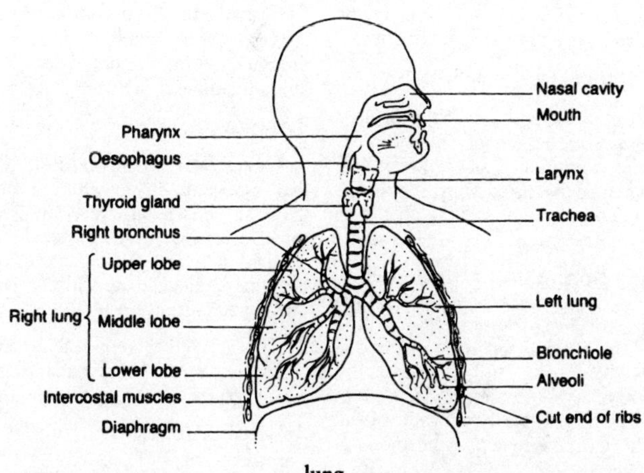

lung

lumbosacral joint The *articulation between the *lumbar and *sacral bones in the *spinal cord.

lumbrical One of four deep muscles, visible on the palm of the hand, that lie between the *metacarpals. Together with the *interosseal muscles they flex the *metacarpophalangeal joints (knuckles), and help extend the middle and *distal *phalanges of the fingers.

lumen Any cavity, such as a *blood vessel or the *alimentary canal, enclosed within a cell or structure.

lunate bone A bone in the wrist which articulates with the *triquetral and *scaphoid at the side, the *hamate and *capitate in front, and the *radius behind. *See also* carpus.

lung One of a pair of respiratory organs in the *thorax. The lungs consist of a system of air tubes terminating in *alveoli where *gaseous exchange takes place. The tubes are connected to the air by way of the *bronchi and *trachea. The lungs are fibrous elastic sacs which can be expanded and compressed by movements of the *diaphragm and *ribcage during *ventilation. The lungs are a site

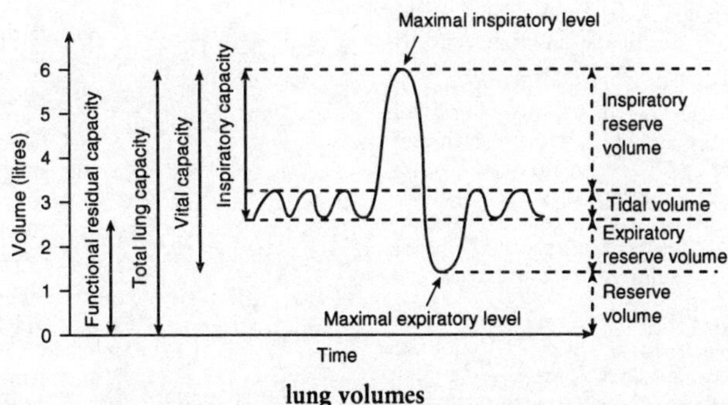

lung volumes

of water evaporation—an important factor in *water balance and *thermoregulation.

lung compliance *See* compliance.

lung volumes The volume of air inspired into, expired from, and contained within the lungs during breathing. Lung volumes and capacities can be measured using a *spirometer to produce a trace at body temperature and pressure saturation.

luteinizing hormone (LH) **1** An endogenous (*see* endogenous substance) *hormone secreted by the *anterior lobe of the *pituitary. In females, luteinizing hormone stimulates *ovulation and formation of *corpus luteum; in males, it stimulates secretion of *testosterone by the *interstitial cells in the testes. Luteinizing hormone is also known as interstitial-cell-stimulating hormone (ICSH). **2** A *drug belonging to the *peptide hormones which are on the *IOC list of *banned substances. Its use is considered to be equivalent to the administration of *testosterone.

luxation *See* dislocation.

lymph The *interstitial fluid within a *lymph vessel. It has a similar composition to blood *plasma, but is richer in *fat and white blood cells (*see* leucocyte).

lymphatics A vessel in the *lymphatic system.

lymphatic system A system of blind-ending vessels which drain excess tissue fluid from the *extracellular space. The lymphatic system contains *lymph nodes, which remove foreign bodies and produce antibodies, and other lymphoid organs and tissues.

lymph node One of a number of small lymphatic organs which filter foreign substances, such as *bacteria, from the *lymph, and produce *macrophages and *lymphocytes. Groups of nodes occur in most parts of the body, but particularly in the groin, armpits, and behind the ears and neck.

lymphocyte Type of *leucocyte formed in the *bone marrow which plays a vital part in the *immune defence system of the body. It forms *T-cells, which destroy *antigens, or *B-cells, which produce *antibodies.

lymphokine A substance, produced by *lymphocytes, involved in cell-mediated immune responses that enhances immune and inflammatory responses.

lymph vessel *See* lymphatic system.

lysergic acid diethylamide (LSD) An hallucinogenic *drug which is unlikely to have any beneficial effects on athletic performance. Side-effects include digestive upsets, muscle incoordination, dizziness, and psychological confusion (known as acute paranoid psychosis).

lysine *Essential amino acid found in all *complete proteins but which is low in certain vegetables, such as cereals.

lysis 1 The breakdown of the *plasma membrane of a cell usually by *hydrolytic enzymes, which results in the cell releasing its contents. **2** The gradual decline of a disease. *Compare* crisis.

lysosome *Cytoplasmic *organelle of *eucaryotes, bound by a single *membrane containing *hydrolytic enzymes.

M

machine A device which helps to perform *work. Machines take in some definite form of *energy, modify it, and deliver it in a form more suited to a desired purpose. The three simple machines found in the human body are the *lever, *pulley, and *wheel and axle.

macrocycle The sum of all *training units required to bring the status of training to level required to meet the macrocycle objectives. A macrocycle usually lasts about 4–weeks.

macromineral A mineral, such as *iron or *calcium, required by the body in relatively large amounts. *Compare* trace element.

macromolecule A very large molecule composed of many *atoms and having large *molecular weight.

macronutrient A category of *nutrients including *carbohydrates, *fats, and *pro

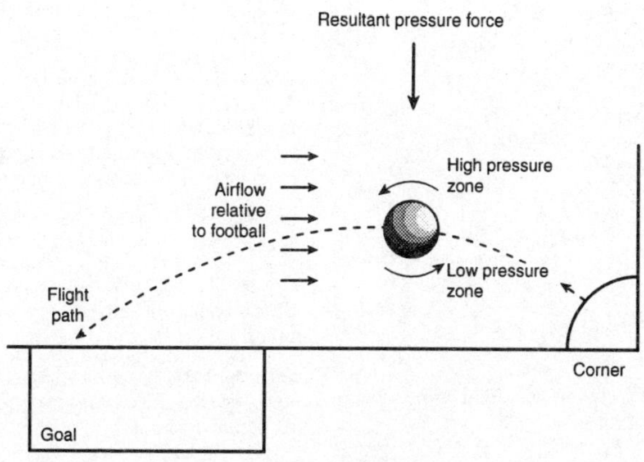

Magnus effect

teins, that are present in food in large quantities.

macrophage A cell-type which is closely related to *monocytes. Macrophages are common in *connective tissue and certain body organs where they act as scavenger cells, engulfing and destroying *bacteria, and other foreign debris. They also act as important *antigen presenters to *T-cells and *B-cells in the immune response.

macrosociology Sociological analysis concerned with whole societies, the totality of their social structures, and their social systems. *Compare* microsociology.

maculae Sensory receptors of *static equilibrium which occur in the *utricle and *saccule of the *inner ear. Each macula consists of hair cells sensitive to linear movements which initiate *action potentials in the *nerve fibres of the *vestibular apparatus.

magnesium A metallic element essential for life. Magnesium is a constituent of many *coenzymes that play a role in conversion of *ATP to *ADP. It is necessary for the efficient functioning of *muscles and *nerves. Magnesium is absorbed and stored in the *bones. Good sources of magnesium are milk, dairy products, wholegrain cereals, nuts, legumes, and, especially, leafy green vegetables. Excessive intakes may cause *diarrhoea, and deficiency can result in neuromuscular problems.

magnitude Term used in science to specify size or amount.

Magnus effect The effect of *fluid *forces that develop on a rotating body, causing the body to deviate from a straight-line path. The Magnus effect can be observed in the curved flight of a ball that has been sliced or hooked to impart sufficient spin before it is projected. The spin imparted to the ball causes an imbalance in the pressure exerted on it and a corresponding deviation from a straight line path. A football player can score direct from a corner by kicking the ball slightly off-centre, causing the ball to acquire a rotation about its vertical axis. *See also* side spin.

Magnus force A *lift force which acts on a rotating body in a fluid which is flowing perpendicular to the *axis of the body. The Magnus force is perpendicular to both the direction of flow and the *axis of rotation.

maintenance synergy *See* synergy.

making weight Quick loss or gain of weight so that an athlete (e.g., jockey, boxer, or wrestler) can compete in a given weight category.

malabsorption A condition in which the uptake of one or more substances from the *small intestine is reduced.

malacia Abnormal softening of tissue, such as bone (*see* osteomalacia) or cartilage (chondromalacia).

malalignment An abnormal position of a structure in relation to others. Malalignment of bones may be *congenital or caused by injury.

malate dehydrogenase A *Krebs cycle *enzyme.

malic acid An organic acid important in the *Krebs cycle.

malignant Any condition that is life-threatening. The term pertains especially to *neoplasms such as *cancers that spread and lead to death.

malleolus Either of two protruberances in the ankle. *See* lateral malleolus and medial malleolus.

mallet finger An injury resulting from a sudden forced *flexion of the terminal joint of a finger, resulting in the bony insertion of the *tendon being stripped off, leaving the person unable to extend the affected joint. The attachment of the tendon to *bone is so strong that damage may occur to the bone itself and a bony fragment may be torn away with the tendon. A mallet finger commonly occurs when a hand is slightly closed before a ball is caught. The ball therefore strikes the end of a finger forcing it into flexion and avulsing the tendon (*see* avulsion).

malleus Hammer-shaped bone in the middle ear. It is attached to the *eardrum and articulates with the *incus.

malnutrition Condition caused by an unbalanced diet with foodstuffs being deficient, in excess, or in the wrong proportions.

malphigian body Structure of ultra-filtration in the *kidney consisting of the *Bowman's capsule and its associated *glomerulus.

maltase An *enzyme which catalyses the following reaction: *maltose $\rightleftharpoons$ *glucose. Maltase is produced in the *crypt of Lieberkhun.

maltose A *disaccharide of two *glucose *molecules. During *digestion, maltose breaks down to *glucose molecules only. It occurs in malt extract, an energy-rich food used by some athletes.

mammary In anatomy, pertaining to the breast.

mammary gland Milk-producing *gland of the breast of females. *See also* bouncing breast syndrome.

management The members of an organization or business who are responsible for its administration.

manager A person who is responsible for the *leadership, co-ordination, and control of a sports team.

managerial competencies The personal characteristics or traits required by a manager or leader. Managerial competencies (also known as coaching cometencies) are required by coaches to manage athletes successfully). These competencies include *conceptual competency; *human competency; and *technical competency.

managerial grid A grid which shows how *leadership style is a function of both concern for production and concern for people. Managers are scored on two scales, one which relates to concern for production and the other which relates to concern for people. The managerial grid has been adapted to show leadership styles of coaches, where concern for the athlete is related to concern for performance.

mandible The lower jaw-bone.

mandibular Pertaining to the lower jaw.

manganese A metallic element which is required as an essential *trace element in the diet for the efficient functioning of a number of *enzyme systems. Good sources of manganese include nuts, legumes, wholegrains, leafy green vegetables, and fruit.

manipulation Any technique using the hands to produce a desired movement of a body-part, or to return bones, joints, and other body structures to their normal position after displacement. Manipulation may occasionally be used by *physiotherapists to relieve stiffness in joints. It is more vigorous than *mobilization and indiscriminate manipulation without prior knowledge and investigation can cause extensive damage to athletes.

manipulative skill A *gross motor skill involving the use of the hands in controlling the movement of other objects.

manometer A device for measuring the pressure of a fluid.

mantra A key phrase or mental device used in transcendental meditation and as an *intervention strategy by athletes to focus attention internally and to reduce *anxiety.

manual dexterity A skill-oriented ability which underlies tasks for which relatively large objects are manipulated, primarily with the hands and legs.

manual guidance A coaching technique exemplified by the coach standing behind the performer and helping him or her go though the motions of swinging a baseball bat, golf-club, tennis racket, etc.

manual resistive muscle testing A test of muscle function. A body-part is placed in the desired position and the athlete maintains the position while a firm constant resistance (not an overpowering force) is applied by the examiner in order to detect muscle dysfunction or weakness.

manubrium The upper part of the *sternum which articulates laterally with the *clavicular notches of the *clavicle and the first two pairs of ribs.

manumometer A grip *dynamometer which is placed in the hand and squeezed to measure strength of gripping muscles. *See also* muscle strength.

marasmus A form of *malnutrition, caused by deficiencies of protein and calorific intake, accompanied by progressive wasting.

march fracture *Stress fracture, typically of one of the long *metatarsal bones (usually the second, but sometimes the third, fourth, or fifth) of the *forefoot. March fractures were originally described as being found in military recruits who marched a lot; they often result from over-use in road-running. Pain is felt in the central bone in front of the foot when walking or running. Treatment consists of immobilization and rest.

march haemoglobinuria (runner's haemolysis) The presence of free *haemoglobin in the *urine associated with prolonged walking or running. March haemoglobinuria may be due to the breakdown of muscle *myoglobin in the legs or to mechanical trauma on the soles of the feet damaging red blood cells which release their contents of haemoglobin into the bloodstream. No treatment is needed but the complaint can be minimized by avoiding running on hard surfaces and wearing well-padded shoes.

margaria staircase test A short-term *anaerobic test in which the subject stands 2m from a staircase and then runs at top speed up the staircase, two steps at a time, each step being 175mm high. A *switch mat is placed on the eighth and twelfth step and *alactic power calculated as follows:

$$P=(W\times 9.8\times D)/t$$

where P = alactacid power, 9.8 = normal acceleration of gravity in ms^{-1}, W = weight of subject, D = vertical height in metres between the eigth and twelfth step; t = time from first to second switch mat.

marginal Applied to a role that is not considered important in the central functioning of a team or group. Those occupying such a role may be disadvantaged. An injured sportsperson, for example, may find themselves becoming marginalized if the team continues to be successful without the injured athlete, and the athlete's place in the team may be questioned.

margo lateralis Outer border of the *shoulder-blade which is the *insertion point for the *teres minor.

marijuana (cannabis; grass) A *drug obtained from the hemp plant *Cannabis sativa* which contains the active ingredient *tetrahydrocannabinol. The psychological effects of marijuana include sedation, euphoria, and relaxation. It may disturb the sense of balance and blunt aggression. It is generally agreed that persistent marijuana smoking is incompatible with serious training becaues it tends to demotivate athletes. Marijuana is not on the *IOC list of *banned substances, but it may be prohibited by the governing bodies of particular sports. Marijuana is also know as hashish or grass.

marrow cavity In adults, a *medullary cavity containing fat (yellow marrow). It is sometimes called the yellow bone marrow cavity.

masculinity Those qualities, such as physical strength, desirable in both sexes but found in greater abundance in men. *Compare* femininity. *See also* androgyny; BEM sex-role questionnaire; and personal attributes inventory.

masculinization (androgenital syndrome; virilization) Development of male secondary sexual characteristics, such as the growth of a beard. Masculinization in females and prepubertal males is associated with hypersecretion of *androgens, when the condition is known as androgenital syndrome.

mass The quantity of matter of which an object is composed. Mass depends on the *density and *volume of an object and is constant regardless of where it is. The *SI unit of mass in the *kilogram (kg). *Compare* weight.

massage The rubbing, kneading, and tapping of body-parts. Massage is used to treat sports injuries and prepare for competition. It requires experienced application because of the risk of damage; massage of recently traumatized muscle may disturb a clot and cause further haemorrhaging. Massage is not advised for those with circulatory, dermatological, and cardiac problems.

mass culture Aspects of culture, including sports products and services, which are transmitted to many in society through the *mass media, and which are designed to appeal to the mass of the population. An important aspect of services and goods produced for the mass market is that they are often standardized, homogenous, and associated with inferior experiences. *Compare* high culture; *see also* popular culture.

massed practice A sequence of practice and rest periods in which there is relatively little or no rest between repetitions. Some refer to massed practice as any practice session in which the amount of practice time is greater than the amount of rest time between repetitions. Massed practice tends to have less positive influence on performance than *distributed practice.

masseter Thick cheek muscle attached to the *mandible and the *zygomatic arch; it closes the jaw during mastication (chewing).

mass media Techniques and institutions including television, radio, and newspapers which can distribute information and other forms of symbolic communication simultaneously and rapidly to large geographically remote and socially distinct audiences. The mass media have great economic, political and social influences and have made significant contributions to sport.

mass spectrometer An apparatus used in exercise physiology to measure the *oxygen, *nitrogen, and *carbon dioxide fractions of respired gases. In the fixed collector type of mass spectrometer, samples of gases are ionized, accelerated by an electrical field, subjected to a magnetic field, and, because the directions taken in this field by different *ions depends on their mass, the fraction of a gas can be measured. The technique known as mass spectrometry is also used to analyse chemicals in dope tests.

mass spectrometry *See* mass spectrometer.

mast cells Large cells containing substances such as *histamines which are released during allergic reactions.

mastication Chewing.

mat burn A *friction burn or an *abrasion which often occurs in wrestlers when the skin over bony points rubs against the unyielding surface of a canvas mat. Mat burns are notorious for getting infected.

match analysis system An objectively compiled record of events in a match which can be subsequently analysed (usually statistically) to evaluate individual and team performance. Methods employed range from the very simple paper and pencil analysis to highly complex event recorders, video recordings, and computerized analysis. Paper and pencil records typically involve identifying key features of play which are recorded by the use of frequency tallies.

mathematical sociology The use of mathematical procedures, such as the *theory of games, and mathematical models in *sociology. In addition to the usual range of statistical techniques, mathematical sociology includes the use of a wide array of mathematical procedures to construct mathematical models which may be used to study real social situations.

mathematics A group of related sciences concerned with the study of number, quantity, shape, and space, and their interrelationships expressed in a language of symbols. Applied mathematics involves the use of mathematical language to discuss real problems. The areas of mathematics used in sports science include mechanics, statistics, and probability theory. A wide array of mathematical procedures are also used to construct and analyse mathematical models of, for example, motor behaviour.

matter Any substance composing physical objects which occupies space and has a *mass. Matter exists as *gas, *liquid, and *solid.

matrix 1 A substance, situation, or environment which encloses something or from which something originates. 2 In *connective tissue, the *extracellular substance secreted by cells that determines the specialized function of each connective tissue-type. The matrix typically includes ground substance, which ranges in consistency from fluid to solid, and may be fibrous (*see* collagen; elastin; and reticular) or nonfibrous. 3 In mathematics, a rectangular array of elements presented in rows and columns, used to facilitate the solution of problems.

maturation 1 The physiological ripening of an organism or organ. Maturation refers to the development towards mature size. It results from causes other than specific activity, such as exercise, or functioning. Upon maturation, the organism approaches a stable structure. 2 In psychology, the developmental and growth processes towards mature behaviour which depend almost solely upon biological conditions characterizing the species, as distinguished from *learning. *Compare* development; and growth.

Matveyev's six phases A system of training for athletes which is based on six periods. Periods one and two are preparatory, consisting of general body conditioning and some specific training elements; periods three and four involve more competition-specific training during which athletes take part in some early competitions and prepare for a peak performance; period five is the major competitive period during which athletes achieve their goals; and period six is a transition period in which the athletes recuperate from a competition season before preparing for the next.

max HR *See* maximal heart-rate.

maxilla (pl. maxillae) One of the pair of upper jaw-bones in which the upper set of teeth are embedded. The maxillae also contribute to the *orbits, the nasal cavity, and the roof of the buccal cavity (palate).

maxillary Pertaining to the upper jaw-bones.

maxillary bone One of the bones forming the upper jaw.

maxillofacial Pertaining to the upper jaw, face, and associated structures.

maximal The highest level possible.

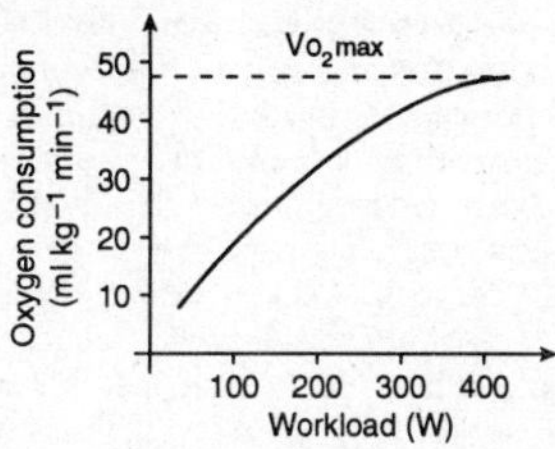

maximal aerobic power

maximal aerobic power (aerobic work capacity; endurance capacity; MAP; maximal oxygen consumption; maximum voluntary oxygen consumption; peak aerobic power; and Vo_2max) The maximum amount of oxygen that a person can extract from the atmosphere and then transport and use in the tissues. Maximal aerobic power is quantitatively equivalent to the maximum amount of oxygen that can be consumed per unit time by an individual during large muscle group activity of progressively increasing intensity that is continued until exhaustion. It is usually expressed as the Vo_2max: the maximum volume per minute of oxygen consumed. It may also be expressed as the absolute volume of oxygen consumed per minute (l/min) to indicate total work capacity, or volume per minute relative to body-weight (ml/(kg min)). The average MAP for a 20-year-old female is about 32–38 ml/(kg min); for 20-year-old male it is 36–44 ml/(kg min). Endurance athletes tend to have a higher MAP than do those involved in shorter duration sports. Training may improve MAP by 15–20 per cent or more. Such increases are due to changes within the *cardiopulmonary transport system and tissue chemistry.

maximal heart-rate (max HR) The highest heart-rate that can be achieved during a *maximal exercise. Maximal heart-rate is often used to compute *training heart-rates. It can be determined directly using maximal workloads but this is not always a safe or practical procedure. Therfore it is generally estimated using the formula (220−age) (in years), since maximal heart-rate decreases with age. This is only an approximation and may be subject to errors of 10 per cent or more. For example, maximal heart-rates of 250 beats per minute have been recorded for brief intervals in skiers subject to stress and intense *isometric control. Also maximal heart-rate varies according to the type of exercise; for example, it is about 13 beats per minute less in an upper-body exercise such as swimming, than in a lower-body exercises such as cycling. The lower max HR is probably due to the relatively smaller amount of muscle mass involved in the exercise.

maximal heart-rate method A method of calculating *training heart-rate as a percentage of capacity is given by: training heart-rate = $(x/100)\times200$ where x represents a percentage of maximal intensity of exercise, and 200 beats per minute is assumed to be the *maximal heart rate

maximal heart-rate reserve (HRR) The differences between the resting heart-rate and the maximal heart-rate. HRR = HR max−HR rest.

maximal heart-rate reserve method A method used to determine *training heart-rate. For example, at a 100 per cent training intensity:

training heart-rate = 100/100(heart-rate reserve) + resting heart-rate;

at 50 per cent training intensity:

training heart-rate = 50/100(heart-rate reserve) + resting heart-rate.

maximal oxygen comsumption *See* maximal aerobic power.

maximum active range *Range of movement through which any *joint can go under the direct pull of the muscles. It is always greater than the normal active range. In some sports, such as gymnastics, range of movement is kept as great as possible but the joints may become less stable and less powerful unless adequate strength-training is combined with flexibility training. *See also* hypermobile joint disease.

maximizing tasks Tasks, such as a tug-of-war, using speed, strength, etc., and which require an all-out effort.

maximum breath holding (maximum inspiratory breath-holding) An old physiological test of physical endurance, used in many modern formulae such as the *cardiopulmonary index. The subject takes a deep breath, exhales completely, and then takes another deep *inspiration which is held as long as possible.

maximum expiratory pressure A test of cardiorespiratory function in which the subject takes a deep breath and blows into a *manometer as forcibly as possible; the highest pressure maintained for at least three seconds is used in the *cardiopulmonary index and some other tests of cardiorespiratory endurance. Since expiratory pressure is more or less equal to *intrathoracic pressure at some instant of time, when maximum expiratory pressure exceeds *systolic pressure no blood leaves the heart which results in relative *hypoxia and may cause fainting.

maximum heart-rate The highest heart-rate reached during a specified period of time. *Compare* maximal heart-rate.

maximum inspiratory breath-holding *See* maximum breath-holding.

maximum passive range The greatest degree of movement which can be produced in a *joint by any means before significant joint damage occurs. The maximum passive range is greater than the *maximum active range. *See also* range of movement.

maximum strength The greatest force that the *neuromuscular system can exert in a single maximum voluntary contraction. *Compare* absolute strength.

maximum Vo_2 *See* maximal aerobic power.

maximum voluntary ventilation The maximum volume of air that can be breathed by an individual in one minute, estimated from an extrapolation of the volume breathed in 15 s of rapid and deep breathing.

mazindol A *drug belonging to the *stimulants which are on the *IOC list of *banned substances. Mazindol is used as an appetite supressant in the treatment of *obesity.

M-band *See* M-line.

McClelland–Atkinson model A mathematical model which proposes that peoples' motives to achieve and their fear of failure are the primary factors determining whether they will approach or avoid an achievement situation. The model proposes that: need to achieve = (motive to achieve success + incentive value of success + probability of success) – motive to avoid failure. That is, if the motivation to achieve success is stronger than the motive to avoid failure, the athlete will enter into the achievement situation, otherwise he or she may withdraw. *See also* extrinsic motivation.

McCutchen's weeping lubrication theory A theory which proposes that when a *joint is exercised, *synovial fluid is squeezed in and out of the *articular cartilage at the points of contact.

McGregor's theory X A management theory, consistent with an *initiating structure approach to *leadership behaviour, in which the workers are regarded as being lazy and irresponsible and therefore need motivation and direction. The theory can be applied to a coach–athlete relationship. *Compare* McGregor's theory Y

McGregor's theory Y A management theory, consistent with the *consideration approach to *leadership behaviour, in which workers are regarded as being naturally self-motivated and responsible, and therefore need only encouragement. The theory can be applied to a coach–athlete relationship. *Compare* McGregor's theory X.

mean Statistical value computed from the sum of a set of numbers divided by the number of terms. *See also* descriptive statistics.

mean arterial pressure Average of *systolic blood pressure and *diastolic blood pressure during a complete *cardiac cycle. The mean arterial pressure determines the rate of blood flow through the circulatory system. It is difficult to measure but is approximated using the following equation: mean arterial pressure = diastolic pressure + $^1/_3$ (systolic pressure–diastolic pressure).

meaningful action Any conscious course of action in which the *actor's meanings (motives, purposes, or reasons) guide the action and where this action is directed towards others.

meaningfulness Often used with reference to the value of tests of physical performance and to experimental designs. For a test to be meaningful to a particular athlete competing in a particular sport it must be *relevant, *valid, *reliable, *standardized, and repeated sufficiently to minimize the effect of chance factors. *See also* effective testing.

measles A highly infectious viral disease which mainly affects children. Symptoms include high *fever, runny nose, sore throat, and red or pink oval spots which quickly coalesce. Measles may be a very unpleasant illness with secondary complications in the form of ear and chest infections. All forms of physical exertion should be avoided during infection as participation in sport during the incubation period can provoke the illness. In the UK, children can now be immunized against measles.

measure of association Type of *descriptive statistic used to determine the degree to which one *variable changes in relation to changes in another variable. *See also* correlation coefficient.

measure of central tendency Type of *descriptive statistic which is used to conceptualize average values from a series of observations, numbers, etc. *See also* mean; median; and mode.

measure of dispersion A statistical measure of the extent to which a set of observations, numbers, etc., cluster round a central value. *See also* kurtosis; range; skew; standard deviation; standard error; and variance.

measure of relationship *See* measure of association.

measure of variability A type of *descriptive statistic which describes the spread or dispersion of data. *See also* range; standard deviation; and variance.

meatus A canal-like passageway such as the external opening leading from the *pinna to the eardrum, or an opening in bone which allows blood vessels and nerves to pass through.

mechanical advantage In a *lever, the ratio of the perpendicular distance of the *line of action of the effort from the *fulcrum to the perpendicular distances of the line of action of the resistance or *load from the fulcrum. The ratio of the actual forces involved is known as the actual mechanical advantage. The mechanical advantage (MA) of a *machine is the ratio of the output *force (i.e., resistance moved) delivered by the machine to the amount of input force applied by the mover. The mechanical advantage of a lever or any other machine is a measure of its efficiency in terms of the amount of effort required to move a particular resistance, and is given by the following equation: Actual MA = magnitude of resistance moved/magnitude of effort. Most skeletal bones act as *third-class levers which always have a mechanical advantage of less than one. Theoretical mechanical advantage is the ratio of the force arm to the resistance arm (or input distance to output distance): theoretical MA = length of effort arm/length of resistance arm. Because of the formation of heat in energy transformations, a machine never achieves its full theoretical mechanical advantage, and the theoretical mechanical advantage is always greater than actual mechanical advantage. *See also* mechanical efficiency.

mechanical efficiency The ratio of the actual mechanical advantage to the theoretical mechanical advantage (*see* mechanical advantage). Mechanical efficiency is often described as a comparison of the work output to the work input. For human movements, it is the ratio of external work performed to the extra energy consumed to perform the work. Mechanical efficiency for muscular movements is generally low because of the loss of free energy as heat. Values vary for different muscles and for different types of muscle contraction. The general opinion that mechanical efficiency of muscular work is around 20 per cent has been challenged in recent years and a mechanical efficiency of up to 40 per cent has been claimed for some runners. This level of efficiency was very unexpected and is thought to be due to part of the energy of descent being absorbed by the stretching of elastic tissues, providing a store that can be used in the next stride (*see* stretch-shortening cycle).

mechanical energy Type of *energy which a body has by virtue of its motion (*see* kinetic energy), position (*see* potential energy) or state of deformation.

mechanical kinesiology The study of the mechanical factors affecting the human body at rest or in motion.

mechanical stress *See* stress.

mechanics of human movement The study of the *internal forces and *external forces acting on the human body during movement and rest. *See also* biomechanics.

mechanics of material Study of conditions which determine the strength and deformation characteristics of materials, such as the various tissues which make up the human body.

mechanoreceptor A *receptor sensitive to mechanical pressures such as touch, sound, or muscle contractions.

medial A *directional term used to describe a position or structure toward or at the midline, or on the inner side of the body.

medial calcaneal nerve A *nerve which passes from a layer of deep *connective tissue to superficial layers at the inner edge of the heel. It can be trapped by overpronation.

medial calf skinfold A *skinfold measurement of a vertical fold of tissue on the *medial right calf at the greatest circumference.

medial cuneiform Bone of the *tarsus immediately behind the *hallux.

medial epicondylitis *See* golfer's elbow.

medial malleolus Inferior projection of the *tibia; it forms the inner, *medial bulge of the ankle. *Compare* lateral malleolus.

medial rotation *See* rotation.

medial tibial stress syndrome A *periostitis of the *medial margin of the *tibia. The main cause seems to be repeated loading of the leg on hard surfaces. *See also* shin splints.

median 1 Statistical term derived from the middle value in a *frequency distribution, on either side of which lie values with equal total frequency. It is the middlemost score in a series arranged in rank order. 2 In *anatomy, describes a structure placed in a central position, or situated towards or in the plane that divides the body into right and left halves.

median cubital vein A principal *vein in the elbow region of the arm.

median nerve The central of the three *nerves supplying the lower arm and hand. The median nerve runs in front of the elbow joint and passes the *pronator teres muscle.

median plane The *plane which runs vertically, dividing the body into right and left halves.

mediastinum Region of the *thoracic cavity between the *lungs.

medical history *See* health history.

medicalization in sport The extension of medical expertise, such as nutrition, training, and rehabilitation, which was once the domain of a lay person with a commonsense understanding, into areas of sport.

medical screening A procedure used to examine an individual for the presence of a disease. In sport, a medical screening is usually done to establish a person's ability to undertake strenuous exercise, particularly in competition. Its prime objective is usually to find abnormalities likely to present a risk of sudden death or injury to the individual, or to detect any condition that would be seriously aggravated by exercise. Routine screening of athletes is not common in the UK (except for boxing) but in the USA, there is an increasing demand for medical certificates for many sports and recreations.

medicine 1 The discipline concerned with the prevention, cure, and alleviation of *disease, and with the restoration and maintenance of *health. 2 A product which can be applied internally or externally to demonstrate, relieve, or cure disease, or the symptoms of disease.

medicine ball A large, heavy ball used for physical training.

medicine ball exercises Strength-training exercises involving lifting or throwing a *medicine ball. The exercises often include movements of the trunk, sup-

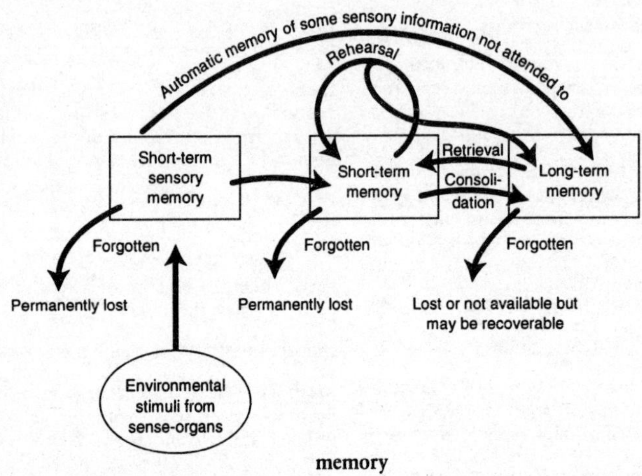

memory

ported by those of the shoulders, arms, hips, and legs.

mediolateral axis (frontal axis; transverse axis) An *axis of the body which runs in a side-to-side direction.

medium-term endurance The ability to perform activities which have a duration of two to ten minutes. *Electroencephalographs and *electromyographs indicate that medium-term endurance results in high activation of the *central nervous system and the recruitment of fast and slow twitch *muscle fibres. The energy for the activities is supplied by both *anaerobic and *aerobic energy systems.

medulla 1 The central part of an *organ. 2 The *myelin portion of some nerve fibres. Such a nerve fibre is called medullated.

medulla oblongata Part of the *brainstem which joins onto the *spinal cord below and the *pons above. The medulla oblongata contains several important centres, including the *cardiac centre, *respiratory centres, and *vasomotor centre, which control autonomic *reflexes involved in *homeostasis. The medulla oblongata also has nuclei which regulate vomiting, hicupping, swallowing, coughing, and sneezing.

medullary artery *See* nutrient artery.

medullary canal *See* medullary cavity.

medullary cavity Central cavity of a *long bone containing *yellow bone marrow and *spongy bone through which medullary canals allow blood vessels to pass. In adults, the cavity is filled with fat.

medullated nerve fibre A *nerve fibre containing a *myelin sheath.

mefendrex A *drug belonging to the *stimulants which are on the *IOC list of *banned substances.

mefruside A *drug belonging to the *diuretics which are on the *IOC list of *banned substances.

mega- 1 Prefix denoting large size or an enlargement. 2 In scientific measurements using metric units, denotes one million. 3 In computing, denotes 2^{20} (1 048 576), as in one megabyte of information units.

megadose A quantity of vitamin or mineral that far exceeds the *recommended daily allowance. In some cases megadoses can have serious toxic side-effects.

megakaryocytes Large cells formed in the *bone marrow which develop into *platelets.

meiosis 1 A division of the nucleus of cells in the reproductive organs that reduces the chromosomal number by half and results in the formation of four haploid cells. 2 An alternative spelling of miosis, denoting a contraction of the pupils.

Meissner's corpuscles *Mechanoreceptors sensitive to light pressure in the dermis of the skin particularly on the lips, nipples, external genitalia, eyelids, and fingertips.

melaena *Faeces which appear black and tarry because of the presence of blood.

melanin A dark pigment which imparts colour to skin and hair. Melanin is produced by cells called melanocytes, and its production increases in response to sunlight, causing the skin to become darker.

melanocyte *See* melanin.

melting-pot theory A theory which suggests that it is socially beneficial to encourage ethnic groups to assimilate into a host society. Sporting contacts between different ethnic groups may facilitate this assimilation when members of a team come from different backgrounds, but if a team is comprised of members from the same background, assimilation is less likely. *Compare* cultural mosaic theory.

membership group The group to which an individual is assigned by others on the basis of education, age, sex, place of residence, etc. Teams consisting of a relatively homogenous membership group include school and college teams. The membership group may or may not be the same as the *reference group, that is the group with whom the individual actually identifies. *See also* role theory.

memory The mental faculty which facilitates storage and retrieval of information that has been learned, such as sporting knowledge or a *motor programme. According to the *black box model, memory has been viewed as consisting of three compartments: *short-term sensory storage, *short-term memory, and *long-term memory. The *hippocampus of the *limbic system plays an important part in memory. The exact way in which the brain stores information is unknown, but it may involve chemical or structural changes. *See also* engrams; memory-drum theory; and sensory memory.

memory-drum theory (**Henry's memory-drum theory**) A theory which proposes that unconscious neural patterns acquired from past experience are stored in the *central nervous system as a memory-storage drum, analogous to the drum which is used to store music in old-fashioned roll-pianos.

memory storage Retention of information in a place so that the information can be recalled for later use. *See also* memory.

memory trace A modification of neural pathways in the *central nervous system which, it is hypothesized, underlies *memory. *See also* engram.

menarche The onset of *menstruation defined by the appearance of the first menstrual flow. Female athletes with long, lithe bodies and involved in regular heavy exercise may have their menarche delayed until their late teens. It is not known whether this has beneficial or deleterious effects. *See also* amenorrhoea.

meninges The *membranes covering the *central nervous system. There are three which are, from the most external to the most internal: the dura mater, arachnoid, and pia mater.

meningitis Inflammation of the two innermost layers of the *meninges surrounding the *central nervous system. Meningitis may be of bacterial or viral origin. Symptoms include headache, fever, and neck stiffness. Meningitis precludes participation in training and competition until after complete convalescence, and even then should be resumed only after proper medical consultation. Meningitis is a notifiable disease.

meningococcus A round bacterium, *Neisseria meningitidis*, which can cause *meningitis and other conditions.

meniscal injury An injury affecting the *meniscus within a *joint.

meniscus (pl. menisci) A semi-lunar disc or wedge of *fibrocartilage separating the *articular surface of *bones of certain *joints, including the knee. The function of menisci is not clear, but they are thought to modify the shape of the *articular cartilage to improve the fit of the bones of the joint and increase stability during compound movements. Menisci may also act as shock absorbers in the joints.

meniscus tear (torn cartilage) Usually refers to damage of the inner or *medial *meniscus of the knee. The *cartilage may not be torn in its mid-substance but may be detached along its outer border, from the capsule of the knee-joint, by rotatory stress. The injury may result in the development of *cysts which do not heal. If the menisci are torn, there is a choice of inactivity or surgical removal of the detached fragments. Once removed, the space occupied by the meniscus is filled by a replacement material, but not of the same type or quality as the original meniscus. Consequently, joint mobility becomes marginally worse and the likelihood of *arthritis at a later stage is significantly increased.

menopause The period during which *ovulation and *menstruation ceases. It usually occurs in women between 45 and 55 years. Menopause is associated with changes in the balance of sex hormones which can lead to emotional, and some physical, changes.

menorrhagia (menorrhoea) Abnormally heavy bleeding during menstruation.

menorrhoea *See* menorrhagia.

menses The blood and other material flowing from the genital tract of women during *menstruation.

menstrual adjustment The use of hormones, such as *oestrogen, progesterones, or progestogens, to adjust the time of *menstruation in a female athlete so that competition dates coincide with the time of maximum efficiency. Optimal performance varies between individuals; it is frequently in the pre-ovulation phase of the *menstrual cycle (days 9–12) or post-ovulation phase (days 17–20), but some women perform best during menstruation.

menstrual cycle The cycle of events in sexually mature, non-pregnant females, characterized by *ovulation followed by a breakdown of the wall of the *uterus at approximately monthly intervals.

menstruation The process or the instance of discharging the blood and fragments of the uterine wall. Some sportswomen may be particularly susceptible to iron-deficiency *anaemia during menstruation because of heavy blood losses combined with a demanding physical training programme. Menstruation does not necessarily preclude exceptional performances. World and Olympic titles have been won during all stages of the *menstrual cycle. *See also* menstrual adjustment.

mental 1 Pertaining to the mind. 2 Applied to the adjustments of individuals to the environment which involve symbolic functions of which the individuals are aware.

mental age A measure of an individual's level of intellectual development: for example, a person with a mental age of five years will function intellectually at the same level as an average five-year-old child.

mental device A word, phrase, object, or process used to help a person relax. Two commonly-used mental devices are a *mantra and the process of taking deep breaths and exhaling slowly.

mental health A mental state marked by the absence of personal discomfort and socially disruptive behaviour. Those in good mental health have the capacity to adapt to environmental stresses and to work productively with others or alone. They are usually able and willing to attempt to improve society's condition as well as their own personal condition.

mental health model A model which proposes that successful élite athletes enjoy greater *mental health than unsuccessful performers. The model implies that élite athletes share similar *personality profiles. *See also* iceberg profile.

mental illness A disorder of one or more functions of the mind resulting in the patient or others suffering. It does not include those conditions in which the only problem is that the individual does not conform to the behavioural norms of society, nor does it include conditions of subnormality, where the individual has a general failure of normal intellectual development.

mental practice (mental rehearsal) A form of practice in which subjects produce a vivid mental image of actually performing a technique; that is, they do not imagine that they are watching themselves perform, but they actually carry out the activity in a mental sense without overt physical movement. *See also* imagery.

mental preparation strategies Procedures, such as *psyching-up, *self-talk, and relaxation methods, which deal with psychological factors that can affect a performance.

mental rehearsal *See* mental practice.

mental well-being *See* psychological well-being

menthol crystals A naturally-occurring, white crystalline organic substance of the camphor group ($C_{10}H_{20}O$). Their vapours are inhaled to clear sinuses and nasal passages. Menthol crystals are particularly useful to athletes because they are not on the *IOC list of *banned substances.

meprobamate A mild, but highly addictive *tranquilizer administered by mouth or injection to relieve *anxiety.

meptazinol A *drug belonging to the *narcotic analgesics which are on the *IOC list of *banned substances.

meralgia paraesthetica Condition caused by trapping the *lateral *cutaneous *nerve which supplies the outer part of the thigh. Symptoms include a burning sensation and numbness felt over the skin supplied by the nerve in the upper outer thigh.

mere presence Used in *social facilitation theory to describe the facilitative effect of a *non-interactive audience or coactors on performers.

meritocracy A set of beliefs that lead adherents to argue that success is the result of ability and individual effort, encouraged by competition. In a meritocracy, it is assumed that a hierarchial position in society will be achieved on merit rather than on the basis of ascribed criteria such as age, gender, or social background. The term has also been applied to social institutions, such as sports. Competition is seen as a good means of enabling the fair distribution of limited resources and rewards.

merocrine gland A *gland which secretes substances intermittently and does not accumulate the secretions. *Compare* apocrine gland.

meromyosin segments The globular head of a *myosin molecule which contains the sites responsible for the affinity of myosin for *actin (*see* cross-bridge).

mesencephalic preparation A surgical procedure in which the *spinal cord is cut at the *midbrain, effectively separating the higher centres of the *brain from the spinal cord.

mesencephalon The middle brain. *See also* midbrain.

mesenchyme Embryonic tissue from which all *connective tissues arise.

mesentery Double-layered extensions of the *peritoneum that supports most organs of the abdominal cavity (including the stomach, small intestine, pancreas, and spleen) and by which these organs are attached to the posterior abdominal wall.

mesial Pertaining to the *median line or median plane.

mesocycle A sequence of training units lasting about 3–5 weeks, intermediate in duration between a *microcycle and a *macrocycle.

mesoderm Embryonic tissue that forms the skeleton, muscle, and connective tissues of the body.

mesomorph An individual who tends to be stocky, of medium height with well-developed muscles. *See also* somatotype.

mesomorphism The pattern of beliefs and values that defines preferred body shape as being of the mesomorphic type with little body fat. Mesomorphism defines musculinity and slimness as 'good' and assumes that the shape represents control, efficiency, discipline, health, and beauty.

mesomorphy A *somatotype dimension characterized by well-defined skeletal and muscular development, and a rugged, stocky appearance. Many sportspeople have a large element of this component

mesosternale A *landmark located on the *sternum.

mesterolone A *drug belonging to the *anabolic steroids which are on the *IOC list of *banned substances.

MET *See* metabolic equivalent.

meta-analysis A statistical summary and comparison of independent samples.

metabolic acidosis Abnormally high acidity of body fluids caused by a loss of *base, or an excessive production or ingestion of *acid other than carbonic acid. One of the main causes of metabolic acidosis is the accumulation of organic acids, especially *lactic acid, as a result of heavy exercise. *Compare* respiratory acidosis.

metabolic alkalosis Abnormally high alkalinity of the body fluids caused by ingesting excess *alkalis or loss of large amounts of acid (for example, by vomiting stomach contents). *Compare* respiratory alkalosis.

metabolic equivalent (MET) A measure of the amount of *energy required at rest, expressed as the required volume of oxygen in ml min^{-1} under quiet, resting conditions. For many purposes, one MET is assumed to be equal to 3.5 ml of oxygen per kg of body-weight per minute. METs are used to *compare* energy costs of different exercises. Therefore, an exercise requiring 10 METs would require 35 ml of oxygen per kg per min.

metabolic load The amount of *energy required to complete a given task.

metabolic rate *Energy expended by a person usually expressed in units of energy per unit *body-mass. *See also* basal metabolic rate.

metabolism The sum total of all the chemical reactions which take place in the body to sustain life. Metabolism includes *anabolism and *catabolism.

metabolite Any substance produced by a metabolic reaction (that is, a chemical reaction which takes place within the body), including chemicals formed by the metabolic transformation of a *drug.

metabotropic neurotransmitter A *neurotransmitter, such as a *biogenic amine or a *neuropeptide, which affects the *postsynaptic membrane potential indirectly and in a complex manner through a second intracellular chemical messenger in the postsynaptic membrane.

metacarpal **1** One of five small, *long bones forming the *metacarpus of the hand which join the fingers to the wrist. The metacarpals radiate from the wrist like spokes, forming the palm of the hand. **2** An adjective pertaining to the metacarpus.

metacarpale radialis A *landmark which is the most *lateral point on the *distal head of the second *metacarpal of the outstretched hand (i.e., on the *radial side of the body).

metacarpale ulnare A *landmark which is the most *medial point on the *distal head of the fifth *metacarpal of the outstretched hand (i.e., on the *ulnar side of the body).

metacarpophalangeal joint The *synovial, *condyloid joint formed by the rounded head of a *metacarpal bone articulating with a *phalanx. The movements normally executed by this joint are *extension, *flexion, *adduction, and *abduction.

metaphor A descriptive phrase or term applied to an object or to a phenomenon which it does not literally denote. Metaphors are used extensively in science and are of great value in suggesting new relationships or new explanatory mechanisms, but there are problems when they are interpreted too literally or when they are not supported by objective evidence. *See also* analogy; and model.

metaphysis The most recent-growing portion of *bone between the *epiphysis and *diaphysis of a *long bone.

metaraminol A *drug belonging to the *stimulants which are on the *IOC list of *banned substances.

metatarsal One of five arching bones joining the *tarsus to the *phalanges of the toes of each foot.

metatarsalgia An aching pain in the *metatarsal bones of the foot, often caused by over-use or by poorly-fitting shoes. *See also* Morton's syndrome.

metatarsal fibulare A *landmark which is the most *lateral point on the head of the fifth *metatarsal of a standing subject.

metatarsal tibiale A *landmark which is the most *medial point on the head of the first *metatarsal of a standing subject.

metatarsophalangeal joint A *synovial, *condyloid joint formed by the rounded head of a *metatarsal bone and the cavity of the *proximal end of a *phalanx. Movements which the joint normally allows are *abduction, *adduction, *extension, and *flexion.

metatarsus The five bones which form the instep of the foot, uniting the *tarsus with the *phalanges of the toes. The metatarsals are relatively large and strong foot-bones which play an important part in supporting body-weight. Distally, where they articulate with the phalanges, they form the ball of the foot.

methadone A powerful *drug belonging to the *narcotic analgesics which are on the *IOC list of *banned substances. Methadone is used to relieve severe pain and as a linctus to suppress coughs.

methamphetamine A drug belonging to the *stimulants which are on the *IOC list of *banned substances. Its use by athletes has been implicated in a number of fatalities.

methandienone An *anabolic steroid used to build up tissue in wasting diseases, but also misused by athletes to increase muscle bulk artificially. Tests show that withdrawal of the *drug results in loss of weight but little or no loss in strength gained.

methandrostenolone A synthetic *anabolic steroid, similar in structure to *testosterone, which has enhanced tissue-building properties and less *androgenic effects than testosterone. Methandrostenolone, a *banned substance, was administered as *dianabol to the disqualified 1988 Olympic 100 m champion, Ben Johnson. Johnson's coach, Charlie Francis, claimed that dianabol could allay fatigue, increase muscularity, and enhance self-image and confidence.

methenolone A synthetic *anabolic steroid with body-building actions, administered by mouth or injection.

methionine A sulphur-containing *essential amino acid found in corns and other grains, but only in small quantities in legumes.

methoxamine A *sympathomimetic drug belonging to the *stimulants which are on the *IOC list of *banned substances. Methoxamine is used to maintain *blood pressure during surgical operations.

methoxyphenamine A *sympathomimetic drug belonging to the *stimulants which are on the *IOC list of *banned substances. Methoxyphenamine is used to treat *asthma and may be added to cough mixtures to reduce *rhinitis.

methyclothiazide A *drug administered for the treatment of *high blood pressure and *oedema. Methyclothiazide belongs to the *diuretics which are on the *IOC list of *banned substances.

methylamphetamine A *drug with actions similar to those of *amphetamine which is a *stimulant on the *IOC list of *banned substances.

methylephedrine A *drug belonging to the *stimulants on the *IOC list of *banned substances.

methylphenidate A *drug belonging to the *amphetamines which are *stimulants on the *IOC list of *banned substances.

methylprednisolone A *glucocorticoid *drug belonging to the *corticosteroids which are on the *IOC list of *banned substances. Methylprednisolone is used to treat inflammatory conditions such as *rheumatoid arthritis and *rheumatic fever.

methyltestosterone A synthetic form of *testosterone which is an *anabolic steroid on the *IOC list of *banned substances. Methyltestosterone is an *androgen used to treat sexual underdevelopment in men, and to treat menstrual and menopausal disorders in women.

methylxanthines *Drugs related to *caffeine and which include *theophylline and *aminophylline. They are bronchodilators which have side-effects on the cardiovascular and central nervous systems but, although the use of caffeine is restricted, methylxanthines are not banned by the *IOC.

metipranolol A *drug belonging to the *beta blockers which are on the *IOC list of *banned substances.

metolazone A *drug belonging to the *diuretics which are on the *IOC list of *banned substances.

metoprolol A *drug belonging to the *beta blockers which are on the *IOC list of *banned substances. Metoprolol is used to treat high *blood pressure and *angina, and is *cardioselective, having a greater effect on the *adrenergic receptors of the heart than the *receptors of the *bronchi and *blood vessels.

metre The *base unit of length of the *SI system.

metric system A decimal system of measurements based on the metre which was intended to be 1/10 000 000 of a quadrant of the Earth through Paris. For scientific purposes, it has been superceded by the *SI system.

metrorrhagia Irregular bleeding from the *uterus, not associated with *menstruation.

Michigan studies Studies which identified two main kinds of orientation in *leadership behaviour: *employee orientation and *production orientation.

microanatomy The study of structures too small to be seen without the aid of a microscope. *Compare* gross anatomy.

microbe Often used synomymously with *microorganism, but sometimes limited to *pathogenic *bacteria and *viruses.

microcirculation The flow of *blood through the *arterioles, *capillaries, and *venules of an organ or a body-part.

microcycle The daily, weekly, or monthly cycles of training units that include the day-to-day training sessions. Microcycles contain *training units and *recovery units combined in such a way that their training-effects are optimized. *See also* inter-unit training ratio.

micrometre (micron) A unit of length equal to 1/1 000 000 of a metre (10^{-6}m)

micromineral A mineral present in the body in small amounts (usually less than five grams). Microminerals are also known as trace minerals; they include *chromium, *cobalt, *copper, *fluorine, *iodine, *iron, *manganese, molybdenum, nickel, selenium, silicon, tin, vanadium, and *zinc.

micron *See* micrometre.

micronutrient A component of a *balanced diet which is required only in small quantities. *See also* minerals; and vitamin.

microorganism An organism which cannot be seen with the naked eye; microorganisms include *bacteria, some *fungi, protozoa, and *viruses.

microsociology A branch of sociology which focuses on interpersonal interactions, and on behaviours of groups. *Compare* macrosociology.

microtrauma An injury at the microscopic level. For example, microscopic *fractures caused by repeated submaximal mechanical stress on a bone. *See also* stress fracture.

microvilli Microscopic projections on the free surfaces of some *epithelial tissue.

Microvilli increase the surface area to volume ratio for absorption.

microwave diathermy A form of *diathermy in which a very high oscillating current, up to 25 000 cycles per second, is used to produce very short wavelengths of electromagnetic radiation.

micturition (urination) The act of emptying the bladder and passing urine.

midbrain (mesencephalon) A short region of the *brain between the *diencephalon and the *pons. The midbrain carries a number of tracts of nerve fibres, including the *pyramidal tract.

middle ear Part of the ear through which sound vibrations are transmitted from the eardrum to the inner ear via three small bones. The middle ear is air-filled and connected to the *pharynx via the *Eustachian tube through which air pressure can be equalized.

midrange That third of the *range of movement of a joint in which the muscle is around the midpoint of contraction. The midrange separates the *inner range from the *outer range.

midsole A shock-absorbing layer of a training shoe, between the outsole and the insole.

migraine A severely painful type of headache believed to be caused by the constriction of blood vessels in the head. A migraine is often accompanied by visual disturbance, nausea, and numbness or tingling of the limbs.

mild strain Overstretching of a *muscle resulting in the rupture of less than 5 per cent of the *muscle fibres with no great loss of strength or deleterious effect on movement.

mile (statute mile) A unit of length equal to 1760 yards and equivalent to 1609.34 m. Although the use of miles has been replaced by metres for most purposes, the mile is still retained for certain sporting events, particularly in running.

miliaria rubra *See* prickly heat.

milk sugar *See* lactose.

milligram A unit of weight measurement that is equivalent to 1/1000 of a *gram. Abbreviated to mg.

millilitre A unit of volume, equivalent to 1/1000 of a *litre. Abbreviated to ml.

millimetre Unit of length, equal to 1/1000 of a metre. Abbreviated to mm.

millimole A measurement of the amount of a substance, equivalent to 1/1000 of a *mole. Abbreviated to mmol.

mind A hypothetical term representing the mental faculties in an individual, responsible for intelligent behaviour including memory, thought, and perception. There is much debate, particularly in philosophy and psychology, concerning the relationship between mind and *matter in human functions.

mineralcorticoid A class of *steroid *hormones, secreted by the *cortex of the *adrenal gland, that regulate salt and water balance. The most important mineralcorticoid is *aldosterone.

minerals Natural inorganic substances that are basic components of the earth's crust. They also occur in the human body where they play a vital role in a number of activities including *enzyme synthesis; regulation of *heart-rate, *nerve, and *muscle activity; bone-formation; and *digestion. The seven major minerals which are needed to form a balanced diet are *calcium, *chlorine, *magnesium, *phosphorus, *potassium, *sodium, and *sulphur. In addition, other minerals are needed in very small quantities (*see* microminerals).

mineral supplements *Minerals usually taken in tablet-form to boost the dietary intake of minerals. They are commonly taken by athletes who fear mineral deficiencies, but there is little scientific evidence to support the value of such supplements, with the possible exception of *iron supplements, since the minimum daily requirements are usually easily met through a normal *balanced diet. *See also* vitamin supplements.

Minnesota multiphasic personality inventory (MMPI) An inventory which includes twelve scales designed to measure the personality of abnormal subjects, but which has also been used successfully on normal subjects. The twelve scales are: hypochondriasis (Hs); depression (D); hysteria (Hy); psychopathic deviate (Pd); masculinity–femininity (Mf); paranoia (Pa); psychasthenia (Pt); schizophrenia (Sc); hypomania (Ma); lie (L); validity (F); and correction (K).

minor league Any non-professional baseball league in the USA.

minute **1** Unit of time. **2** Unit of angular measurement equivalent to 1/60 of a degree.

minute ventilation The volume of air inspired or expired in one minute. It usually refers to the expired amount and can be measured using the following equation:

$$VE = V_T \times f$$

where VE represents minute ventilation in $l\,min^{-1}$, V_T represents tidal volume (l) and f represents respiratory frequency in breaths per min. A typical resting value of minute ventilation is $6\,l\,min^{-1}$, but it may rise to as high as $180\,l\,min^{-1}$ in a very active person. The change in the minute ventilation has been used to identify the anaerobic threshold (*see* minute ventilation method).

minute ventilation method A method for estimating the *anaerobic threshold in which the *minute ventilation of a subject is monitored during a progressive exercise test on a *treadmill or *bicycle ergometer. The running or cycling speed at which ventilation increases abruptly is taken to represent the exercise intensity at, or slightly above, the anaerobic threshold.

miosis (meiosis) Contraction of the pupils which normally occurs in response to bright light.

miserable malalignment syndrome A condition characterized by a high *Q-angle at the knee, and disorders of the *patellofemoral joint. The syndrome results from excessive internal rotation of the *femur, excessive *tibial torsion, and hyperpronation of the feet.

mistake An occasional error that can occur in almost any performance of a skill, no matter how experienced or expert the performer. *See also* error; and flaw.

mitochondrion (pl. mitochondria) A double-membraned *organelle concerned with *aerobic respiration in cells. Mitochondria are sometimes referred to as the 'powerhouses' of the cell because they are the sites in which the *Krebs cycle and the *respiratory chain produce large amounts of *ATP. The muscle fibres of endurance-athletes have a higher density of mitochondria than those of non-athletes.

mitosis Process during which the nucleus divides to form two, genetically-identical daughter cells. Mitosis is the form of nuclear division used in the growth and repair of tissue. *Compare* meiosis.

mitral valve The bicuspid valve between the left *atrium and the left *ventricle in the *heart. The valve prevents backflow of blood from the ventricle to the atrium during ventricular *systole.

mixed nerve A *nerve containing sensory and motor fibres which carry impulses to and from the *central nervous system.

mixed pace Training consisting of continuous work performed at varying pace.

mixed venous blood *Blood, usually extracted from the *pulmonary artery, which has returned from all the body tissues and been mixed together in the right *atrium of the heart.

mixture A substance consisting of particles dispersed together and in which the particles retain their unique properties. *Solutions, *suspensions, and *colloids are all mixtures.

M-line (M-band) A line in the centre of the *H-zone of a *muscle *sarcomere. It is named after *mitteline*, meaning midline, in German.

MMPI *See* Minnesota multiphasic personality inventory.

mobility **1** The ease with which an articulation, or series of articulations, is able to move before being restricted by the surrounding structures. Mobility is very difficult to measure. Sometimes measurements of the end-position achieved by the extremity of a limb or limb-segment are used to reflect mobility, but these measurements are dependent on the positional relationships of other segments of the body. *See also* active mobility; flexibility; joint mobility; and passive mobility. 2 *See* social mobility.

mobilization The return of a limb to full *mobility by carefully applied pressure to a *joint or *muscle so that it will move through its normal *range of movement. Mobilization is used to move tissues more gently than through *manipulation, which is vigorous.

mode In statistics, the most frequent scores of a series; the peak in a frequency distribution.

model A mathematical, physical, pictorial, or computer representation of one phenomenon by another. Models are often used to simplify complex phenomena for analytical purposes. *See also* metaphor.

modelling A technique used in *behaviour modification and the acquisition of a *skill, whereby a person learns a behaviour or skill by observing and imitating someone else.

moderate strain (second-degree strain) A partial *muscle-tear involving a significant number of *muscle fibres (more than 5 per cent), but not all of them. Pain may be aggravated by muscle contractions.

modulus of compression The ratio of *stress to *strain in an *elastic material when that material is being compressed; it is the *modulus of elasticty applied to a material under a compression force. The modulus of compression = compressive force per unit area/change in volume per unit volume.

modulus of elasticity The ratio of *stress to *strain for a body obeying *Hooke's law. There are several moduli corresponding to different types of strain. *See* modulus of compression; modulus of rigidity; and Young's modulus.

modulus of rigidity The ratio of *stress to *strain in an *elastic material when that material is subjected to *shear forces; it is the *modulus of elasicity of a body under a shearing strain. The modulus of rigidity = tangential force per unit area/angular deformation.

molar 1 A back tooth used for grinding and mechanical *digestion of food. 2 Applied to a solution in which one litre of the solution contains an amount of solute equal to its molecular weight in grams.

molarity A measurement of the strength of a solution expressed as *moles per *litre; that is, the weight of dissolved substance in grams per litre divided by its molecular weight.

mole The *SI unit of amount of substance expressed as the molecular weight or formula weight of a substance in grams. Thus one mole of glucose which has a formula $C_6H_{12}O_6$ weighs 180g, where the atomic weight of carbon is 12, hydrogen 1, and oxygen 16.

molecule The smallest portion of a substance consisting of two or more atoms combined together, capable of existing independently, and retaining the properties of the original substance.

moment arm The shortest or perpendicular distance between the lines of action of the two *forces in a *couple. *See also* lever arm; and torque.

moment of force *See* torque.

moment of inertia A physical property, measured in kg m^{-2}, defining a body's resistance to rotational forces. For the human body, made of many segments, the moment of inertia of each body-segment is the product of the *mass of the segment and the square of the radius of gyration of the segment. The moment of inertia of the whole body is the sum of the moments of inertia of all its segments.

moment of couple *See* torque.

momentum The amount of motion possessed by a moving object. The linear momentum of the body is a product of its *mass and its *velocity: $p = m \times v$ Thus, an object's momentum can be changed by altering either its mass or its velocity. Linear momentum is a vector quantity directed through the body in the direction of motion. *See also* angular momentum.

momentum arm *See* lever arm.

momentum, law of *See* Newton's laws of motion.

monoamine oxidase (MAO) An important *endogenous *enzyme responsible for the metabolic breakdown of *monoamines such as *serotonin, *adrenaline, and *noradrenaline. Monoamine oxidase is found in many tissues but especially in the liver and nervous system.

monoamine oxidase inhibitor (MAOI) A *drug that blocks the action of *monoamine oxidase and results in an increase in *serotonin, *adrenaline, and *noradrenaline, which leads to an increase in mental and physical activity. MAOI is sometimes used to treat affective disorders such as *depression.

monoamines A group of organic, nitrogen-containing compounds to which *adrenaline, *noradrenaline, and *serotonin belong.

monoclonal antibodies Pure preparations of identical *antibodies derived from a single clone of cells. All the antibodies exhibit the same specificity for a single *antigen.

monocyte A large, white blood cell with a single nucleus. Monocytes engulf foreign substances, such as *bacteria, by *phagocytosis.

mononucleosis An abnormally high number of *monocytes in the blood. Mononucleosis may indicate an *infection such as *glandular fever.

monosaccharide (simple sugar) A crystalline, sweet-tasting, very soluble *carbohydrate which consists of a single chain or a single ring structure having the general formula $C_x(H_2O)_y$. Examples are *fructose, *galactose, and *glucose. They are very rich sources of *energy in the diet.

monosynaptic stretch reflex A reflex contraction of *striated muscle produced by stretching a muscle and its *muscle spindle organ which connect via a single *synapse to an *α motor neurone in the same muscle. *See also* stretch reflex.

Monteggia's fracture A *fracture of the *ulna combined with a *dislocation of its *articulation at the *elbow.

mood An emotional condition of an individual which persists for some time, such as an irritable or cheerful mood.

moral Pertaining to human behaviour, especially the distinction between what is right and wrong.

moral development The development of the capacity to distinguish between behaviour which society generally regards as right and wrong. Some claim that sport and physical education promote moral development, but the evidence is mixed.

morale The degree of mental confidence, self-control, and discipline of a person or group.

moral panic A social reaction to relatively minor acts of social deviance which have been exaggerated and amplified by the media. It is sometimes claimed that moral panic has resulted in an exacerbation of some deviances such as *football hooliganism. *See also* deviance amplification; and labelling theory.

moral reasoning A cognitive process by which an individual comes to distinguish between right and wrong.

morals Principles of behaviour based on the concepts of right and wrong.

morazone A *drug belonging to the *stimulants which are on the *IOC list of *banned substances.

morbid Applied to an abnormal, diseased, or disordered condition

morbidity rate The incidence of a particular disease or disorder in a population, usually expressed as cases per 100 000 or per million in one year.

mores The socially-approved forms of behaviour, promoted by laws and customs, which are generally regarded as essential for the maintenance of a *society or a *group.

morphine An alkaloid *drug obtained from *opium and belonging to the *narcotic analgesics which are on the *IOC list of *banned substances. Morphine is used to relieve severe pain but it is very addictive and *tolerance develops rapidly.

morphology The study of shape, general appearance, or form of an organism as distinct from *anatomy which requires dissection to reveal structure.

mortality (mortality rate) The death-rate in a population expressed as the percentage dying in a year, or the number of human deaths per 1000 population.

Morton's foot A condition in which the foot consists of an abnormally-short first *metatarsal bone and an abnormally-long second metatarsal bone. It is not normally disabling, but it can result in mechanical problems, particularly for middle- and long-distance runners, with the foot tending to over-pronate because of lack of stability.

Morton's metatarsalgia *See* Morton's syndrome.

Morton's syndrome (Morton's metatarsalgia) A painful condition of the *metatarsal area of the foot. Morton's syndrome is usually caused by a *neuroma of the interdigital nerve situated in the web between two toes, giving rise to pain and tingling in two adjacent toes. The condition may then require surgery. It may also arise from lateral pressure on the external *plantar nerve due to a short and hypermobile metatarsal. It may also be caused by ill-fitting shoes pressing against the nerve. The condition is accentuated in athletes who spin on the ball of the foot (e.g., golfers, bowlers, and tennis players). It is relieved by removal of shoes and rest.

motile The condition of a body which is capable of spontaneous, independent movement without external aid.

motility The state of being motile.

motion The continual change of relative position of an object in space. An accurate analysis of the motion of a body requires a description of its successive positions and the time between its successive positions. *See also* Newton's laws of motion.

motion, laws of *See* Newton's laws of motion.

motivation **1** The internal state which tends to direct a person's behaviour towards a *goal. The person may or may not be conscious of the motivation which can occur independently of any external *stimulus and is not due to *fatigue, *learning, or *maturation. Many psychologists consider that motivation has two dimensions: intensity and direction. Intensity is concerned with the amount of *activation and *arousal the person has; that is, how much effort is being given to reach a certain goal. Direction is concerned with movement towards a particular goal. Psychologists talk about people approaching or avoiding a task, and seek to understand why they do so. In sport, coaches are frequently interested in knowing why a talented youngster will not play a particular sport, or why someone quits a team. Others want to know why some players are so doggedly persistent in playing a sport when they apparently would be better doing something else. The study of motivation covers these issues. **2** The willingness to carry through a long and arduous training programme, a desire to excel in competition, and persistence in the face of discomfort and discouragement. *See also* extrinsic motivation; and intrinsic motivation.

motivational hierarchy A hierarchy of human needs attributable to the theorizing of Abraham Maslow (1908–70) which are, in ascending order from basic to higher needs: physiological needs; need for safety; need for love and belonging; need for *self-esteem and recognition; and the need for *self-actualization. Coaches are mainly concerned with enabling their athletes to fulfil the higher needs, but the concept implies that these can only be achieved when the lower needs, such as the fundamental physiological need for food and shelter, have been met in part or in full.

motivational sequence A series of related events involved in *motivation: *need, *drive, *incentive, and *reinforcement.

motivational strategy Technique used to improve or maintain the motivation of a sportsperson or team. Motivational strategies include providing appropriate *goals

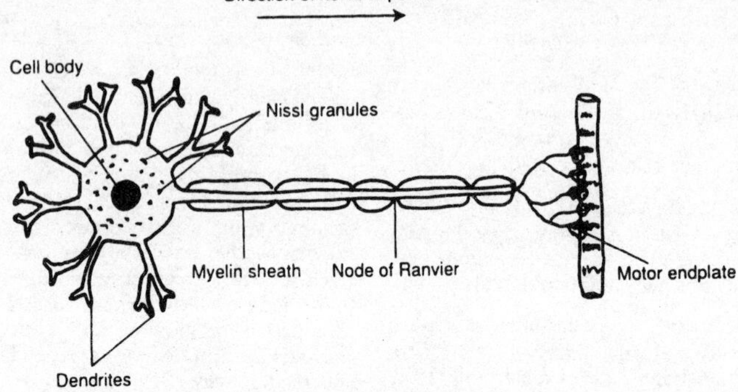

motor neurone

and *competition, and giving *pep talks, *praise, or constructive *criticism.

motivation principle The motivational acceptance that a certain amount of fatigue, effort of expenditure, boredom, and discomfort need to be endured if training is to be successful.

motive A latent, relatively persistent cause which determines a particular course of action.

motive force *See* propulsion.

motive to achieve success A relatively stable disposition which underlies a person's desire to to be successful. Those with a high motive to achieve success usually have high *self-esteem and a keen desire to take part in competition. *See also* McClelland–Atkinson theory.

motive to avoid failure (fear of failure) A relatively stable disposition which causes a person to tend to avoid competition because of a fear of failure. It is related to a person's *anxiety. A highly-anxious person is more likely to avoid competition than one who is low in this construct. *See also* McClelland–Atkinson theory.

motive to avoid success (fear of success) A *motive which results in a self-inflicted decrement in performance because of a fear of loss of status if a person succeeds. For example, an otherwise highly-motivated and highly-competent woman performer may purposely perform badly against men because she fears that success will result in a perceived loss of her femininity or social rejection by members of both sexes. There is little contemporary evidence to support the proposition that many are motivated to avoid success.

motoneurone *See* motor neurone.

motor Pertaining to muscular movements.

motor ability A genetically-defined personal characteristic or trait, such as *manual dexterity or fast *reaction time, which contributes to proficency in a number of *motor skills. Unlike motor skills, motor abilities cannot be easily modified by practice or experience. *See also* ability; and general motor ability.

motor area Region of the *cerebral cortex which controls voluntary movements. *See also* motor cortex.

motor behaviour An area of study concerned mainly with the behavioural analysis of human skilled movement. It is similar to the study of *motor control and *motor learning.

motor capacity The genetically-determined maximum potential of an individual to succeed in a *motor skill performance. Motor capacity is believed to be little influenced by the *environment or *learning. *See also* motor ability; motor educability; motor fitness; and physical fitness.

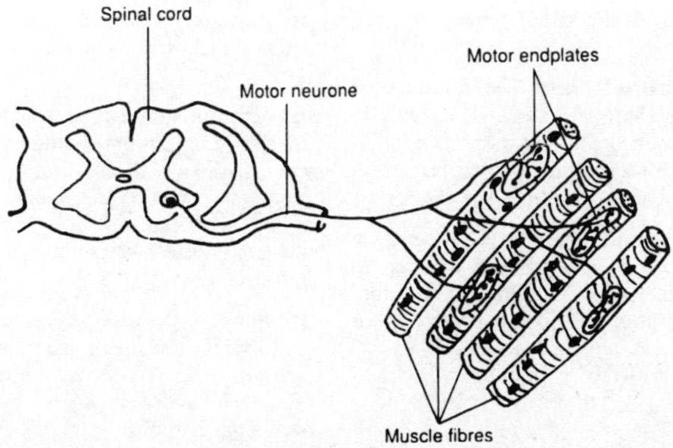

motor unit

motor control The study of the *neural, physical, and behavioural aspects of the control of movement. Motor control is often used alongside the terms *motor behaviour and *motor learning, but is not synonymous with them.

motor co-ordination *See* co-ordination.

motor cortex The region of the *cerebral cortex which controls the action of *voluntary muscle. Different regions of the motor cortex are responsible for controlling different muscles of different parts of the body.

motor development 1 The changes in skilled movement associated with growth, *maturation, and experience. 2 An area of study concerned with the changes in human skilled movements associated with growth, *maturation, and experience.

motor educability The inherent ability to learn new *motor skills easily and well. Tests of motor educability incorporate novel stunts which have not been previously practised or learned by the performer. *See also* motor ability; motor capacity; motor fitness; and physical fitness.

motor endplate The junction between a *motor nerve and a *muscle cell. *See also* *neuromuscular junction.

motor engrams Memorized *motor patterns that are stored in the *motor area of the brain. *See also* engrams.

motor fitness The *neuromuscular components of fitness which enable a person to perform successfully at a particular *motor skill, game, or activity. Specific motor fitness components include *agility, *balance, *co-ordination, *power, *reaction time, and *speed. Motor fitness is sometimes referred to as skill-related fitness. *See also* physical fitness.

motor imagery *Imagery which involves body movements such as imagining hitting a golf ball or kicking a football.

motor learning 1 The acquisition of *skills or skilled movements as a result of practice. Motor learning involves a set of internal processes associated with practice or experience leading to relatively permanent changes in a *motor skill. 2 The study of the acquisition of skills. *See also* learning.

motor maze An apparatus used in the research of *social facilitation to discriminate between dominant responses and non-dominant responses (*see* reaction potential).

motor nerve *See* nerve.

motor neurone *Nerve cell which conveys *nerve impulses from the *central nervous system to an effector organ, such as a *skeletal muscle.

motor neurone pool Collection of *α motor neurone cell bodies in the *grey matter of the spinal cord which serve *motor units in the same, or related, muscles.

motor outflow time The time period between the change in electrical activity in the *motor cortex and the start of electrical activity in *muscles prior to a movement. It is a component of *reaction time.

motor pattern A particular sequence of muscle movements which are directed to accomplishing an external purpose. It is similar to a *motor skill, but the term motor pattern is usually used to describe acts which are performed with a lesser degree of skill, and in which movement is stressed.

motor program An abstract code or structure that represents one or more skilled movements stored in the *central nervous system. It is believed that the motor programme resembles a computer program and consists of a series of *neural commands which when initiated results in the production of a particular co-ordinated movement sequence.

motor reaction time The interval from the first change in electical activity in a *muscle to the movement's initiation. It is a component of *reaction time.

motor skill A *skill associated with muscle activity. Sports form a continuum from *fine motor skills to *gross motor skills. Some people object to the prefix motor' being used on its own because it implies the skill is largely a motor reflex. They prefer to use terms such as perceptual motor skill, psychomotor skill, or sensorimotor skill because such terms emphasize the mental components of movement skills.

motor unit A *motor neurone and all the *muscle fibres it stimulates. Each motor neurone supplies between four and several hundred muscle fibres, with the average being one hundred and fifty. The motor neurone affects all its muscle fibres in the same way (*see* all-or-none law).

mountain sickness *See* altitude sickness.

mouthpiece *See* gum-shield.

movement The change in position of a whole body, body-part, or *centre of mass in relation to a reference system.

movement form A type of physical activity such as an exercise, a game, or a sport.

movement generator A component of the *information-processing model which, when loaded with the appropriate motor programmes by the *decision-making mechanism, is responsible for organizing and inititating these programmes to bring about particular movements.

movement pattern A general series of anatomical movements that have common elements of spatial and temporal configuration, such as movements of body-segments occurring in the same plane. Examples of motor patterns are walking, jumping, and kicking.

movement time The time that it takes to complete movements of a particular action, from its initiation to its termination. *See also* response time.

mucopolysaccharides A group of *polysaccharides which are a constituent of *bone and other *connective tissue. Mucopolysaccharides consist of repeating units of *disaccharides, one of which is derived from an amino sugar such as glucosamine. Mucopolysaccharides include *heparin and *hyaluronic acid.

mucous membrane A membrane which secretes mucus. Mucous membranes form the *epithelial lining of body cavities such as the *respiratory tract, *urinogenital tract, and the *alimentary tract which are open to the exterior.

mucus The slimy, viscous liquid secreted by mucous membranes that lubricates and protects the external surface of *membranes.

multiaxial movement Movement of a joint in three planes: *transverse, *frontal, and *sagittal.

multicellular Applied to structures composed of many cells.

multidimensional model of leadership A model of *leadership which views athlete satisfaction and performance as the product of three components of behaviour: *actual leader behaviour, *preferred leader behaviour, and *prescribed leader behaviour. Discrepancies between an athlete's preferred coaching behaviour and the actual or prescribed behaviour has a measurable effect on an athlete's performance and satisfaction.

multidimensional model of self-esteem A model in which *self-esteem is seen as a global construct underpinned by increasingly differentiated aspects of the *self including physical, social, and academic *self-perceptions

multidisciplinary study A study carried out by a team composed of members from various study areas for example, a study of running-efficiency carried out jointly by a team of physiologists, psychologists, and biomechanics.

multifactorial study Experimental investigation of the simultaneous influence of several *variables. These variables may be summative, with their total influence equal to the sum of the separate influences; or interactive, in which case the influence of any one variable depends on the presence, absence, or level of another variable. Multifactorial studies are usually more complex than traditional single-factor studies.

multi-joint muscles *Muscles which pass over, and affect the action of, more than one *joint.

multi-limb co-ordination An ability which underlies tasks for which the movements of a number of limb segments must be co-ordinated simultaneously. The simultaneous use of both hands and feet in a gymnastics floor exercise is one example.

multinucleated Applied to a cell, such as a muscle cell, with many nuclei.

multipennate muscle *See* pennate muscle.

multiple motor unit summation The combination of a number of *motor units contracting within a muscle at any given time. *See also* recruitment; and spatial summation

multiple regression analysis A form of *regression analysis used to explain the variations in one variable as being due to the variation in two or more *independent variables. *See also* multivariate analysis.

multiple sclerosis A condition in which the *myelin sheath gradually disappears from nerve cells, impairing the transmission of *nerve impulses and resulting in sufferers gradually losing control over their muscles. Multiple sclerosis is recognized as being patchy in its distribution and development.

multiplicative principle The notion that *intrinsic motivation and *extrinsic motivation are interactive and not additive. The principle is based on the observation that extrinsic motivation in the form of awards and trophies may enhance *achievement motivation, but that such rewards may also diminish it. *Compare* additive principle.

multi-poundage system *Strength-training schedule in which the *repetition maximum (usually 10RM) is established for each exercise and the first *set is worked with the full number of repetitions. Then, 5kg is removed from the bar and, after a rest, the weight-lifter attempts as many repetitions as possible. The procedure is repeated by removing 5kg each time for as many sets as possible.

multi-set system *Strength-training schedule in which several different exercises, with slightly different effects, are used to develop the same *muscle group.

multivariate analysis A statistical technique in which several *dependent variables are analysed simultaneously. For example, in a study of muscular strength, data may be collected on the age, type of training, and sex of the population being studied. In a multivariate analysis the effect of each of these variables can be examined, and also the interaction between them.

multivariate approach A statistical technique in which several *dependent variables are analysed simultaneously. *See also* multivariate analysis.

mumps (infectious parotitis) A viral disease affecting particularly the salivary glands in front of the ears (the parotid glands). Symptoms include fever, vomiting, and swelling of the glands which may spread to the tonsils. Physical activity during the

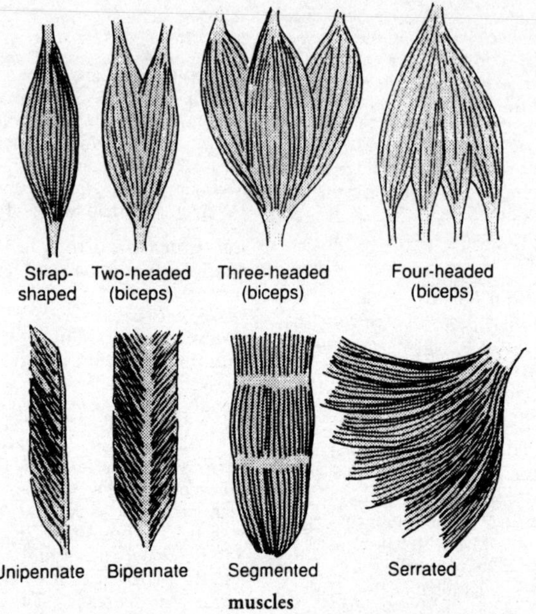

muscles

infection can cause a more severe attack of the illness.

murmur An uneven rustling sound heard through a stethoscope applied over the *heart and various *blood vessels. Murmurs are heard in nearly every athlete after severe exercise. In most cases they are not *pathological, but they may need to be evaluated by a cardiologist to exclude serious conditions, such as defective valves, which might preclude athletic involvement.

muscle 1 Fleshy *contractile tissue which serves to move parts of the body relative to each other. The three main types of muscle are *cardiac muscle, *smooth muscle, and *striated muscle. **2** A body structure composed of numerous *striated muscle cells wrapped in *connective tissue, and supplied with *blood vessels and *nerve fibres. There are approximately 600 muscles in the human body.

muscle action The effect produced by the development of tension in a *muscle. *See also* muscle contraction

muscle atrophy A wasting-away of *muscle tissue due to lack of stimulation or normal nutrition resulting in a diminution in the ability of the affected muscle to function. Muscle atrophy begins immediately after any muscle injury and occurs progressively as a result of disuse.

muscle belly The fleshy central part of a *muscle.

muscle biopsy The removal for examination of a small sliver of *muscle tissue by a needle, forceps, or a surgical method. *See also* biopsy.

muscle-bound A common colloquial term used to describe the condition of a person with well-developed *muscles that limit the *range of movement of a *joint. The *ligaments, *tendons, and muscles touch the joint and restrict its movement. The idea that weight-training always results in a person becoming muscle-bound is a myth. There is a risk of *muscle-bulk developing at the expense of joint mobility only with a high-resistance, low-repetition exercise programme that does not incorporate stretching.

muscle-bulk The absolute volume of *muscle in a human body. A large muscle-bulk is advantageous in contact sports both to give protection against opponents and to provide momentum to dislodge opponents

muscle bundle *See* fasciculus.

muscle cell *See* muscle fibre.

muscle compartment A well-defined region which contains groups of *muscles within a particular segment of the body. For example, the lower leg contains four muscle compartments: the *anterior compartment, lateral compartment, *posterior deep compartment, and the *posterior superficial compartment. *See also* compartment syndrome.

muscle contraction The generation of *tension within a *muscle which usually produces movement. In *striated muscle, a muscle contraction occurs when tension is exerted across a number of *actin and *myosin muscle filaments (*see* sliding-filament theory). Such muscle contractions can result in shortening (*see* concentric contraction), lengthening (*see* eccentric contraction), or no change in length of the muscle (*see* isometric contraction). Consequently, the term 'contraction', which implies shortening, is sometimes confusing, and it has been suggested that the term muscle action should replace it.

muscle-cramp *See* cramp.

muscle endurance *See* muscular endurance.

muscle enzymes *Enzymes such as *SDH and *LDH present in the *cytoplasm of a *muscle.

muscle fatigue A decreased physiological capacity to perform a maximum voluntary contraction or a series of repetitive contractions of a *muscle. *Compare* mental fatigue. *See also* fatigue.

muscle fibre In skeletal muscle, a single, multinucleated muscle cell which, under a light microscope, has a banded or striated appearance. Each *muscle comprises between 10 000 and 450 000 fibres. The two main types of muscle fibre are *slow-twitch fibres and *fast-twitch fibres. *See also* motor unit.

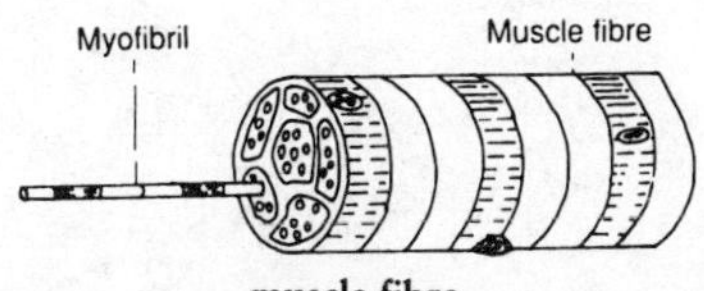

muscle fibre

muscle fibre recruitment *See* recruitment.

muscle force The *force exerted by a *muscle contraction. It is affected by the number, type, and size of the *muscle fibres, the *series-elastic elements, and the degree of muscle stretch.

muscle glycogen Muscular stores of the *polysaccharide, *glycogen, which do not contribute to blood *glucose concentration; glycogen is used only in the muscle in which it is stored. It is a vital *metabolic fuel during heavy and prolonged exercise. *Fatigue is associated with depletion of muscle glycogen, even when *fats may still be available as a fuel. Typically, a person has about 1.5g of glycogen per 100g of wet muscle providing enough fuel for approximately 80min activity.

muscle glycogen-loading *See* carbohydrate-loading.

muscle growth An increase in muscle volume which may occur by *hypertrophy or *hyperplasia.

muscle group Different muscles which contribute to the same action at a particular *joint.

muscle hernia *See* fascial hernia.

muscle hypertrophy An increase in the size of a *muscle which usually follows exercise. It is due to an incease in the size of individual *muscle fibres and an increase in capillary density in the muscle. *See also* hypertrophy.

muscle imbalance A condition resulting from the unequal development of the individual members of an antagonistic pair of

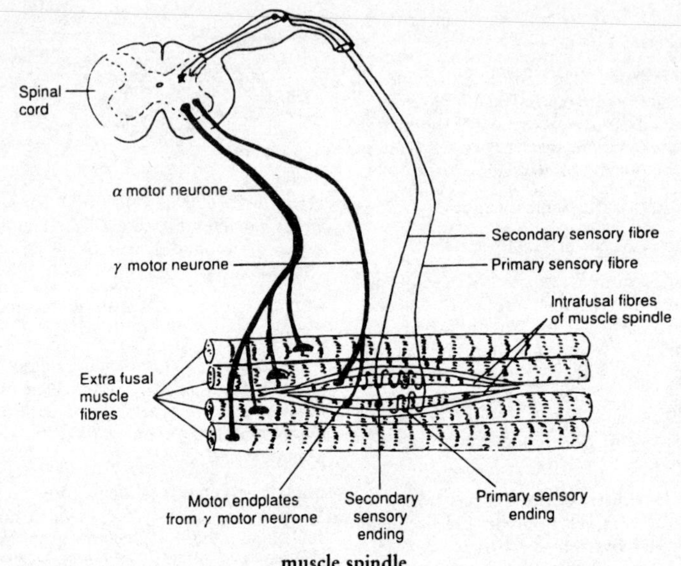

muscle spindle

muscles (*see* antagonist) with one being very much stronger than the other. Muscle imbalances sometimes result from enthusiatic but poorly scheduled weight-training programmes, and can increase the risk of such injuries as *muscle strains.

muscle jerk *See* myoclonus.

muscle poops A *fascial hernia in which a *muscle passes through the *fascia creating a bump in the skin, with no breakage or tearing in the muscle.

muscle-pull *See* partial muscle-strain; and muscle-tear.

muscle pump A mechanism for returning *venous blood towards the *heart. Due to alternate contraction and relaxation of *skeletal muscles, blood is squeezed through the veins towards the heart. Valves prevent backflow.

muscle rehabilitation Treatment of a *muscle following an injury which enables the muscle to regain its normal functionability. Promotion of extensibility is generally regarded as the most important single factor influencing muscle rehabilitation. It is generally agreed that, for muscle rehabilitation to be effective, muscle strengthening regimes should go hand in hand with muscle flexibility exercises. *See also* muscle-scarring.

muscle relaxant A *drug which reduces *tension within a muscle.

muscle-rupture *See* muscle-tear.

muscle-scarring The replacement by repair cells of damaged tissue with *collagen tissue. The scar may result in pain which leads to immobility and loss of extensibility of *muscle fibres. Scarring tends to cause the *muscle to become shorter as it heals and if this is not corrected by progressive mobilization of the damaged tissue, the muscle will tend to be susceptible to recurrence of the tear.

muscle selection A component of the *motor programme concerned with selecting which muscles will be used to perform a certain movement.

muscle soreness Pain and tenderness which typically occurs in a *muscle after strenuous exercise particularly if the exercise involved *eccentric contractions. The underlying cause of muscle soreness is thought to be a change occurring in the *ultrastructure of the muscle cells with a rupture of the *Z-lines. *Metabolic waste products, such as *lactic acid, have also been implicated because they can stimulate *pain receptors in the muscle. *See also* acute muscular soreness; and delayed onset of muscle soreness.

muscle spasm *See* spasm.

muscle spindle A small, complex spindle-shaped *proprioceptor, found within skeletal muscle, that is sensitive to muscle-stretch. The muscle spindle consists of several modified muscle fibres, called *intrafusal fibres. The ends are contractile but the central portion is non-contractile and innervated by *γ efferent fibres. Muscle spindles are sensitive to both the rate of change (*see* phasic stretch) and the extent of a muscle-stretch (*see* tonic stretch). *See also* muscle tone; and stretch reflex.

muscle stiffness *See* compression syndrome; and muscle soreness.

muscle-strain (muscle-pull) An injury which may involve the rupture or tearing of muscles, their *fascia, *ligaments, or the junction of the *muscle with its *tendon. Muscle-strains are usually due to a lack of co-ordination in a muscle or *muscle group, as when a person attempts rigorous exercise without a sufficient *warm-up, or when in poor physical condition. *See also* muscle-tear.

muscle strength The *force or *tension that a *muscle or, more correctly, a *muscle group can exert against a resistance in one maximal effort. Muscle strength can be measured using a *dynamometer or a *manumometer. *See also* absolute strength; and relative strength.

muscle system *See* muscular system.

muscle-tear An *intrinsic injury, sometimes called a muscle-pull, resulting in the rupture of *muscle tissue. Muscle-tears most commonly affect those muscles, such as the hamstrings, which span two joints (*see* Lombard's paradox). *See also* compression rupture; distraction rupture; interstitial tear; muscle-strain; and partial muscle-tear.

muscle tension *See* tension.

muscle tissue *See* muscle.

muscle tone (tone; tonus) The normal state of partial contraction in a relaxed *muscle which keeps the muscle ready to react to a *stimulus.

muscle tremor (tremor) An involuntary quivering of a *muscle. The tremor may be due to disease, or it may be an expression of the normal mechanism for maintaining posture, known as physiological tremor, which becomes exaggerated by *fatigue or *emotion. *Compare* steadiness.

muscle-twitch *See* twitch.

muscular 1 Pertaining to muscle. 2 Applied to a person with well-developed muscles.

muscular dystrophy A disease in which there is a progressive wasting of *muscle.

muscular endurance The ability of a *muscle or *muscle group to perform repeated *isotonic or *isokinetic contractions, or to sustain an *isometric contraction against a moderate resistance for an extended period of time.

muscular function test A test which evaluates the strength and stretching capacities of *muscles that co-operate functionally, thus assessing the developmental level and the training state of intermuscular co-ordination.

muscular haematoma Bleeding caused by damage to *muscle. The extent of the bleeding is directly proportional to the muscle blood flow and is inversely proportional to muscle *tension at the time of the damage to the muscle. *See also* intermuscular haematoma; and intramuscular haematoma.

muscular power The ability of a *muscle or *muscle group to exert a maximum *force in the shortest period of time. *See also* power; and sargent jump.

muscular strength *See* muscle strength.

muscular system (muscle system) The organ system consisting of the *skeletal muscles of the body and their *connective tissue attachments.

musculocutaneous nerve 1 A *nerve that arise from the *brachial plexus and supplies the skin of the lateral forearm and some muscles of the arm, including the *coracobrachialis and the *biceps brachii. 2 A nerve which supplies the muscle on the fibular side of the leg, the dorsum (back) of the foot, and some *integumentary areas of the lower leg.

musculoskeletal attachments Structures which attach *muscle to *bone, and bone to bone. *See also* ligament; and tendon.

musculoskeletal system The body systems comprising both the *muscular system and the *skeletal system.

musculotendinous junction The connection between a *muscle and a *tendon.

MVV *See* maximum voluntary ventilation.

myalgia A general term to describe a shifting pain or ache in a *muscle resulting from any disorder which inhibits normal muscle action.

myalgic encephalomyelitis (ME) A disorder characterized by lassitude, *muscle fatigue and pain, lack of concentration, and tiredness. Its cause is not established with certainty, but the condition often occurs after a viral infection.

myasthenia gravis A relatively rare chronic condition characterized by abnormal *fatigue, but not weakness, of *skeletal muscle. It is thought to be due to a disturbance of the transmission of *nerve impulses and the impairment of the ability of *acetylcholine to induce muscular contractions. Sufferers of myasthenia gravis find it difficult to take part in prolonged, continuous exertion, but fine motor control and co-ordination remain intact enabling participation in certain areas of sport, even at the highest levels.

myelencephalon The lower part of the *hindbrain. *See also* medulla oblongata.

myelinated fibres *See* myelin sheath.

myelin sheath A whitish sheath covering many *nerve fibres, known as myelinated fibres. The sheath is produced by *Schwann cells and the myelin consists mainly of fatty *phospholipids and *protein which protect and electrically insulate the fibres. Myelinated fibres transmit *nerve impulses faster than those fibres lacking the sheath (unmyelinated fibres). *See also* saltatory conduction.

myelography A specialized *X-ray technique used to examine the spinal canal and involving the injection of a radio-opaque *contrast medium.

Myers–Briggs-type indicator A personality inventory that indicates an individual's preferences for different kinds of activities. It consists of four basic dichotomous indices: extraversion/introversion; sensing/intuitive; thinking/feeling; and judgement/perception.

myocardial contractility The strength of *ventricular contraction.

myocardial infarction A condition characterized by the formation of a dense, wedge-shaped block of dead tissue in the *myocardium following an interruption of the blood supply to the area (*see* coronary thrombosis).

myocarditis Inflammation of the muscular wall of the *heart caused by a viral or bacterial infection. The risk of suffering myocarditis increases if the body is subjected to physical exertion when a viral infection is present. The myocarditis should have healed completely before the sufferer commences any form of physical activity, and even then exercise should be gradual and under medical supervision.

myocardium The middle region of the wall of the *heart composed mainly of *cardiac muscle. *Compare* endocarium; and epicardium.

myoclonus (jerk; muscle-jerk) A sudden, vigorous contraction of *muscle, usually of the limbs. A myoclonus sometimes occurs in normal individuals as they are falling asleep and is thought to be caused by temporary reactivation of the *reticular-activating system. It is also a feature of some neurological diseases.

myofibril A rod-like bundle of contractile *myofilaments found in muscle cells. A myofobril consists of a series of *sarcomeres made of *actin and *myosin. Its banded appearance results from a regular alternation of dark *A-bands and light *I-bands.

myofibrosis A condition characterized by replacement of *muscle tissue by fibrous tissue with a consequent reduction in muscle function.

myofilament A contractile *protein filament, made of either *actin or *myosin, that constitutes myofibrils.

myogenic Originating in muscle; the term is usually applied to the ability of a *muscle to contract automatically without neural stimulation. *See also* myogenic contraction.

myogenic contraction A contraction initiated in the muscle itself and independent of neural stimulation. The rhythmic contractions of *cardiac muscle are myogenic.

myogenic factors Factors inherent in, or derived from the activity of, muscle. *Muscle hypertrophy, which contributes to muscle strength, is an example. *Compare* neurogenic factor.

myoglobin An iron-containing pigment, present in *muscle, which acts as a store for *oxygen and plays an important role in oxygen *metabolism within the *muscle fibres. Each molecule consists of a single *polypeptide chain with a *haem group which has a stronger affinity for oxygen than for *haemoglobin.

myoglobinuria The presence of *myoglobin in the *urine. It sometimes occurs following very heavy exercise, and it occasionally follows *carbohydrate-loading. Myoglobinuria can lead to acute kidney failure if it persists.

myogram *See* electromyogram.

myography *See* electromyography.

myopia Short-sightedness due to an image being focused in front of the *retina.

myosin A *protein found in the thick filaments of a *sarcomere.

myosin cross-bridge A distinctive structure consisting of two globular heads on each *myosin molecule which interact in the presence of *calcium ions with specific sites on a thin *actin filament. The cross-bridges generate the tension developed by a *muscle fibre when it contracts, and contain *ATPase. *See also* sliding-filament theory.

myositis An inflammation of a *muscle.

myositis ossificans A condition in which calcium, and eventually bone, become deposited in muscle after severe bruising or a *fracture. Although the deposits are often reabsorbed, the condition can cause severe disability and necessitate surgical removal. *See also* rider's bone.

myotactic reflex *See* stretch reflex.

myotonia The lack of normal *muscle tone.

myotonometer An instrument designed to measure *muscle tone.

myotonometry A measurement of *muscle tone in which the state of the muscle in contraction and relaxation is examined; the greater the difference between the two states, the better the muscle tone.

myxoedema A condition characterized by swelling of the face and dry rough skin; it is associated with an underactive *thyroid gland which may result from *iodine-deficiency.

N

N *See* newton.

NAD *See* nicotinamide adenine dinucleotide.

nadolol A *drug which belongs to the *beta blockers which are on the *IOC list of *banned substances. Nadolol is used for the treatment of *angina and *high blood pressure. It is not *cardioselective.

nail *Epidermis on the end of each toe and finger which has become hardened with *keratin.

nalbuphine A *drug belonging to the *narcotic analgesics which are on the *IOC list of *banned substances.

naïve falsification The notion that a theory or hypothesis can be decisively rejected on the basis of a single non-supporting occurrence (the classical example is that the occurrence of one black swan would refute the hypothesis that all swans are white).

nandrolene A synthetic *drug belonging to the *anabolic steroids which are on the *IOC list of *banned substances. Nandrolene has effects and uses similar to *methandienone in promoting *protein *metabolism and skeletal growth.

nanometer A unit of measurement equal to one thousandth of a *micrometre.

naproxen A *non-steroidal anti-inflammatory *drug commonly used for the treatment of chronic inflammatory conditions such as *arthritis. There are generally good reports of the efficacy of naproxen and its use for treating soft-tissue sports injuries has been advocated.

narcissism Self-love; an excessive preoccupation with oneself and one's self-importance. It is a normal stage of infant development and common in small degrees in sportspeople, but extreme narcissism may be a symptom of a mental disorder in adults.

narcolepsy A condition characterized by an overwhelming desire to sleep. It was once treated with *amphetamines, but because of the rapid development of tolerance and dependence, the use of these *drugs has been withdrawn except in controlled circumstances.

narcosis An unconscious state induced by a *narcotic analgesic.

narcotic A substance which when swallowed, inhaled, or injected induces stupor, sleep, and insensibility (*see* narcotic analgesics). Substances classified legally into narcotics are divided into five groups: group I consists of substances such as *cannabis, *heroin, *LSD, and mescaline which have no medical application; group II includes habit-forming drugs with some medical applications, such as *amphetamines, *cocaine, and the *morphine group; and groups III, IV, and V include substances such as *codeine and *barbiturates which have greater medical use and less addictive properties.

narcotic analgesics A pharmacological class of agents, represented by *morphine and its pharmacological *analogues, which are banned by the *IOC (*see* doping classes). Narcotic analgesics induce a state of reversible depression in the *central nervous system (narcosis) and are administered to relieve pain, but their use carries a high risk of physical and psychological dependence.

nares The openings of the nose.

narrow focus An *attentional style in which an individual has the ability to concentrate on relevant *stimuli and ignore other stimuli when appropriate. *Compare* reduced focus. *See also* attention.

narrowing (attentional narrowing; focal narrowing; perceptual narrowing) The process whereby *attention is focused on a small area of interest so that specific sources of information are more likely to be perceived and rare events are more likely to be missed. It is sometimes referred to as tunnel vision because of its tendency to cause peripheral *stimuli to be ignored. Narrowing tends to increase under *stress. *Compare* scanning. *See* selective attention.

nasal Pertaining to the nose.

nasal bone One of a pair of bones that form the bridge and base of the nose.

nasion The point on the bridge of the nose at the centre of the joint between the *frontal bone and *nasal bone.

nativism A theoretical perspective which emphasizes the importance of *natural endowments as forming the basis of human *behaviour, rather than the effect of *environment.

natural athlete *See* born athlete.

natural endowment A person's qualities and talents which are dependent on genetic factors. Natural endowment plays a major part in determining performance. It has been calculated that about 70 per cent of an individual's *maximal *force, *power, and *aerobic capacity is established by genetic factors.

natural frequency The *frequency of free oscillations of any body or system. *See also* resonance.

naturalism In *sociology, a theoretical stance which adopts the *naturalistic approach.

naturalistic approach A form of sociological research which assumes that there are multiple views of reality influenced by the social context and environment in which a situation is viewed. Therefore a question concerning a situation may have a number of valid answers dependent on the perspective of the viewers. *See also* naturalistic research method.

naturalistic research method In *sports sociology, a method of conducting research which emphasizes the importance of studying social interactions within a sport in naturally-occurring settings.

natural science model An approach to *psychology based on the view that psychological events are physically based, observable processes. *Compare* human science model.

nature–nurture issue An issue concerned with the relative importance of heredity (nature) and environment (nurture) in various aspects of an individual's development and behaviour, including the ability to perform at sport. At one time, there were two diametrically opposed viewpoints, but now it is generally accepted that a person's behaviour and ability are determined by a variable mixture of the two factors. *See also* natural endowment.

nausea A feeling of impending vomiting due to a change in the tone of muscles in the *stomach or intestinal wall. The *autonomic nervous system controls the vomiting response and nausea can be brought about by some irritant or a heightened emotional state, such as that of an athlete prior to competition. As nausea can also be an early symptom of some acute illness, it is generally advisable to seek medical advice if it persists and the cause is unknown.

navicular bone The boat-shaped bone of the *tarsus between the three *cuneiform bones in front and the *talus behind.

N-band A region which may be a site of *intracellular *calcium concentration in the *sarcomere of a *muscle fibre.

nearpoint vision The ability to focus and see clearly objects which are close to the eye.

near-sightedness *See* myopia.

nebulizer therapy A method of administering a *drug in which the drug is dissolved in a solution, vaporized, and the vapour inhaled. It is used commonly for the application of *bronchodilator drugs in the treatment of *asthma.

neck **1** region of the body connecting the head to the trunk. **2** Any narrow region of an organ or body-part. For example, the neck of the *femur is a short bony connection between the *head and the *shaft, and is the weakest part of the *bone.

neck girth In *anthropometry, the circumference of the neck taken immediately above the *larynx.

neck injuries Damage to the tissues and structure of the neck. All the vital connections between the head and the body pass through this region, and injuries to the neck can lead to permanent damage. *See also* torticollis; and whiplash injury.

necrosis Death or disintegration of a cell or tissue due to a disease, or a physical or chemical injury.

need A basic requirement for survival, or a higher requirement for optimal adjustment to the environment. Basic needs include the need for food or water; and higher needs include the need for *self-actualization. Often the term is not applied with precision. *See also* motivational hierarchy.

need for achievement *See* achievement motivation.

need to avoid failure A personality factor which contributes to *achievement motivation. Those with a high need to avoid failure tend to avoid situations where they might be seen to fail and they tend to have a low need to achieve success.

negative acceleration (deceleration) The decrease of *velocity over a given period of time.

negative energy balance A condition in which less energy (food) is taken in than is expended in *metabolism, resulting in a decrease in *body-weight.

negative feedback A term used in *cybernetics to describe the compensatory effects a change of output of a system has on subsequent input. Thus, negative feedback tends to reduce deviations and maintain the output at a relatively constant level. It is the basis of the *homeostasis of many physiological systems.

negative nitrogen balance A condition in which *protein *catabolism exceeds protein *anabolism resulting in tissues losing protein faster than it can be replaced. A negative nitrogen balance may occur during physical or emotional *stress, *starvation, when an individual is on a *very low calorie diet, or when the quality of the protein is poor (e.g., when the diet is lacking in *essential amino acids). *Adrenal cortical hormones, such as *cortisone, released during stress enhance protein-breakdown and the conversion of *amino acids to *glucose.

negative reinforcement A form of *reinforcement in which the removal of a negative or aversive *stimulus, such as a loud noise or an unpleasant event, results in an increased probability that a particular behavioural response will occur in the future. *Compare* positive reinforcement; and punishment.

negative transfer A term applied to *transfer of training when a previously-learned task makes it more difficult to learn or perform a new task. *Compare* positive transfer.

negative work The *work done by an external *force on a muscle during an *eccentric contraction. When a muscle lengthens a distance (D) by an external force (F), it absorbs mechanical work and is said to do an amount FD of negative work. Lowering a weight, bending down, and walking down stairs are all examples of negative work.

neoglycogenesis *See* glyconeogenesis.

neopallium Part of the *cerebral cortex of the *brain associated with intelligence and muscular co-ordination.

nephritis Inflammation of the *kidney, which may result from taking too much *protein in the diet in an attempt to increase *muscle-bulk. Athletes need no more than about 0.8 g of protein per kilogram body-weight per day.

nephrolithiasis *See* kidney stones.

nephron The functional unit of *ultrafiltration and excretion in the *kidney. The nephron consists of the *Malphigian body and its associated tubule.

nerve A bundle of *nerve fibres together with associated *connective tissue and *blood vessels. When a nerve contains both sensory (afferent) and motor (efferent) neurones, it is known as a mixed nerve.

nerve axon conduction velocity The *velocity at which a *nerve impulse is propagated along a *neurone. It is affected by the diameter of the neurone, temperature, and the presence or absence of a *myelin sheath. Myelinated fibres have a conduction velocity of $12–120\,\mathrm{m\,s^{-1}}$, while unmyelinated fibres conduct impulses at between $0.2–2\,\mathrm{m\,s^{-1}}$.

nerve block A method of producing *anaesthesia in a region of the body by blocking the passage of pain impulses along *sensory neurones using a *local anaesthetic.

nerve cell *See* neurone.

nerve fibre A long, slender process which extends from a cell body and conveys *nerve impulses. *See also* axon; dendrite; and nerve.

nerve impulse A wave of *depolarization which passes along a *nerve fibre and is the means by which information is transmitted in the *nervous system. During the conduction of a nerve impulse, the *resting potential across the *membrane of a *neurone is reversed and becomes an *action potential. It is an all-or-none response (*see* all-or-none law).

nerve plexus *See* plexus.

nervous system The complex network of *neurones which carry information in the form of *nerve impulses to and from different parts of the body in order to co-ordinate body activity. *See also* autonomic nervous system; central nervous system; and peripheral nervous system.

net cost of exercise *See* net oxygen cost.

net oxygen cost (net cost of exercise) The amount of *oxygen, above resting values, required to perform a given amount of *work. It includes both the extra oxygen consumed during the exercise and during the recovery period. The net oxygen cost can be used to estimate the *energy required for the exercise.

neuralgia An acute pain experienced along the course of a *sensory nerve without the presence of inflammation. In sport, it is often the result of pressure from wearing ill-fitting kit but it may also be due to fatigue or an illness.

neural pathway The route, such as in a *reflex arc, along which a connected sequence of *nerve impulses is conveyed from one *neurone to another.

neural processing The treatment of information, conveyed in the *nervous system as *nerve impulses, in order to obtain the required responses. *See also* parallel-processing; and serial-processing.

neural spine The bony, *dorsal extension of a *vertebra which forms part of the neural arch protecting the *spinal cord, and to which some back muscles are attached.

neurilemma A thin membrane surrounding the *myelin sheath of myelinated nerve fibres. It is part of the *Schwann cell and lies close to the *axon, but is not part of the axon. *Compare* axolemma.

neuritis An inflammation of a nerve marked by pain, tenderness, and loss of function. It is not common in athletes but it can occur as a result of a physical injury to a nerve. This is known as traumatic neuritis, and may result from a blow, or pressure from ill-fitting sports gear or a bony *exostosis.

neurogenic Derived from, or produced by, nerve stimulation. *Compare* myogenic.

neurogenic factor A factor related to the activity of *nerves. For example, *muscle strength may be improved after a period of training because of an improvement in the nervous control of the muscle which acts as a neurogenic factor.

neuroglia (glia) Cells in the *nervous system which are non-conducting, and that support and protect the delicate *neurones.

neurohypophysis The posterior portion of the pituitary gland.

neuroma A *benign *tumour growing from the fibrous tissue around a *peripheral nerve.

neuromuscular electrodiagnosis An examination of the *excitability of a nerve or muscle which involves measuring the chronaxie, the time taken for a muscle or nerve to respond to a stimulus. Its use to monitor the recovery of a muscle after injury has been largely superseded by *electromyography.

neuromuscular feedback theory *See* psychoneuromuscular feedback theory.

neuromuscular functional test An evaluation of the co-ordinated functioning of nerves and muscles.

neuromuscular hypertension A condition characterized by an exaggerated *muscle tone and the production of excess *tension during *muscle contractions far beyond that needed to perform a given task.

neuromuscular junction The area of close contact between a *motor neurone and a muscle fibre. A neuromuscular junction consists of a small gap which is bridged by the release of a *neurotransmitter, such as *acetylcholine

neuromuscular spindle *See* muscle spindle.

neuromuscular system The system in the human body which depends on the co-ordinated activities of nerves and muscles.

neuron *See* neurone.

neuronal pools Functional groups of *neurones occurring in the *grey matter of the *brain and *spinal cord which process and integrate incoming information received from other sources, such as the *sense-organs, and transmit the processed information to other destinations.

neurone (nerve cell; neuron) A highly specialized cell that generates and conducts a *nerve impulse. Typically, a neurone is very long and branching and consists of a *cell body, *dendrites, and an *axon.

neuropathy A disorder of the *peripheral nervous system, usually marked by weakness and numbness of the muscles supplied by the affected nerve or nerves.

neuropeptides Chains of *amino acids which can function as *neurotransmitters. They include β *endorphins and *encephalins.

neurophysiology The study of the chemical and physical changes which take place in the *nervous system.

neuroprobe An instrument for locating and stimulating *trigger points to relieve pain. *See also* transcutaneous electrical nerve stimulation.

neurosis A functional behaviour disorder with no apparent underlying physical cause for the feelings of ill-health it engenders. Neuroses include a number of *affective disorders, such as *anxiety, *depression, and obsessive states.

neurotic A loosely-applied term to describe a person who suffers from a *neurosis or who has a *personality trait tending towards the unstable (anxious) end of the neuroticism–stability continuum. *See also* neuroticism.

neuroticism A *personality trait which is usually described by a continuum from complete stability to complete instability (the neuroticism–stability continuum). Generally, neurotics tend to be more easily aroused than stable individuals and may become overaroused in stressful situations such as a competition. The degree of neuroticism a person exhibits is complex and is dependent on factors peculiar to each situation.

neuroticism–stability continuum *See* neuroticism.

neurotransmitter A chemical released across a *synapse of a *neurone to affect the activity of another neurone or a *muscle fibre. Neurotransmitters may be excitatory or inhibitory and include *adrenaline, *acetylcholine, and *dopamine.

neutral equilibrium Position of a body which, when subjected to a slight displacement, has no tendency either to return to its original position or to move still further away from its original position. *Compare* stable equilibrium; and unstable equilibrium.

neutral fat *See* triglycerides.

neutral hypnosis A state of *hypnosis in which the subject's physiological responses are the same as the *relaxation response.

neutralizer A muscle which contracts in order to neutralize an undesired action of another contracting muscle.

neutral position The *anatomical position, when describing *rotation round a *joint.

neutral stimulus A *stimulus which does not elicit a response.

neutron An uncharged particle found in the nucleus of an atom.

neutropenia A decrease in the number of *neutrophils in the *blood associated with an increased risk of infection and caused by a number of diseases.

neutrophil A white blood cell (*see* leucocyte) which has a neutral reaction to acid and alkaline dyes. It is the most abundant type of white blood cell, and can kill and ingest *bacteria.

newton (N) The *SI unit of *force. One newton is equal to the force required to give a *mass of 1 kg an acceleration of $1\,ms^{-2}$.

Newton's first law of motion *see* Newton's laws of motion.

Newton's law of gravitation (attraction, law of) A law which states that any two particles of matter attract one another with a *force directly proportional to the product of their masses and inversely proportional to the square of the distance between them. In sport, the forces between bodies are usually imperceptibly small, except for the force known as *gravity produced by the Earth.

Newton's law of impact *See* impact, Newton's law of.

Newton's laws of motion Three fundamental laws of motion which form the basis of classical mechanics. The first law, sometimes known as the law of inertia, states that every object will remain at rest or continue with uniform *velocity unless acted on by a *force. The second law, also known as the law of momentum, proposes that when a force acts on an object, the rate of change of *momentum experienced by the object is proportional to the size of the force, and takes place in the direction of the force. The third law states that to every action there is an equal and opposite reaction. Therefore, when one object exerts a force on another, there will be an equal and opposite force exerted by the second object on the first.

Newton's second law of motion *See* Newton's laws of motion.

Newton's third law of motion *See* Newton's laws of motion.

new vegetarian An individual who has a diet of plants supplemented by animal products, but who places the emphasis on natural, unprocessed foods. *See also* vegetarian diet.

niacin (nicotinamide; nicotinic acid) A water-soluble *vitamin belonging to the *vitamin B complex, which is used to form the *coenzymes, such as *nicotinamide adenine dinucleotide, which play an important part in *glycolysis, *oxidative phosphorylation, and *fat *metabolism, inhibiting *cholesterol synthesis. Only a little niacin is stored in the body. The human body can synthesize niacin from the *amino acid tryptophan, but this rarely meets the total daily requirement and the balance is obtained from foods such as meat and yeast. Deficiency can result in *pellagra, symptoms of which include muscle weakness. Excessive intakes may cause irreversible liver damage. The recommended intake in the United Kingdom is 11.3 mg per 1000 kcal of resting metabolism, and in the USA, 6.6 mg niacin equivalent per 1000 kcal of total energy utilization.

nicotinamide *See* niacin.

nicotinamide adenine dinucleotide (NAD) A *coenzyme which readily accepts or gives up *hydrogen. It acts as a hydrogen carrier in cells and plays an important role in *glycolysis, when its reduction is coupled with the formation of *ATP.

nicotine A poisonous alkaloid obtained from the leaf of the tobacco plant, *Nicotiana tobacum* . The psychological and addictive effects of smoking cigarettes are attributed to nicotine. It is a *cholinergic agonist which has a stimulatory effect on the *central nervous system, enhancing *arousal. Smokers claim that it has relaxing effects.

nicotinic acid *See* niacin.

Nideffer's attentional model A model which proposes that *attentional style exists along two dimensions: width and direction. Width ranges from broad to narrow. Those with broad attention can focus on a large range of things, while those with narrow attention tend to focus on a limited range of cues. The direction of attentional style varies on a continuum from an *internal focus to an *external focus.

nikethamide A *drug belonging to the *stimulants which are on the *IOC list of *banned substances.

Nissl's granules Granules of *nucleoprotein combined with iron, concerned with *protein *synthesis and occuring in the cell bodies of *neurones.

nitrogen Colourless, odourless gas which makes up about 79 per cent of the atmosphere. Nitrogen is an essential component of *proteins and *nucleic acids.

nitrogen balance A condition which occurs when a person's *nitrogen intake, in the form of *protein ingested, is equal to the nitrogen utilized in protein synthesis and excreted in the *urine and *faeces. Estimates are based on the assumption that the nitrogen content of protein averages 16 per cent.

nitrogen narcosis (raptures of the deep) A condition affecting the *central nervous system due to pressure forcing *nitrogen into solution within the body; symptoms include dizziness, slowing of mental processes, euphoria, and fixation of ideas. *See also* caisson disease.

nitrogen waste The by-product of *nitrogen *metabolism in the body involving *amino acids and *protein. Nitrogen waste is eliminated mainly in *urea.

nitroglycerin A *vasodilator *drug used to treat *angina pectoris.

NMR *See* nuclear magnetic resonance.

nociceptors Sensory receptors which respond selectively to potentially damaging stimuli. Their stimulation results in *pain. Nearly every type of sensory receptor can function as a nociceptor if the *stimulus strength is high enough.

node A swelling or protruberance.

nodes of Ranvier Regularly repeated constrictions of the sheath of a *medullated nerve fibre which allow *saltatory conduction to take place and *axon collaterals to emerge from an *axon.

nodule A small swelling of specific *connective tissue structures.

noise 1 A term used in *information theory to indicate a disturbance that does not represent any part of a message from a specified source. 2 Background stimuli (or information) which a person might or might not be aware of, but which is not directly relevant to the task in hand. 3 In *signal detection theory, the random firing of the *nervous system; that is, background neural activity.

nominal analysis The identification and naming of components of a system. Nominal analysis forms one of the first stages in the development of any scientific study.

nominal measurement The designation of an observation with a value which represents a distinct category; the value is merely a name or label such as red, green, big, or small. Sometimes numerical values are given to the categories, but these nominal numerical values are without reference to the ordering or distance between categories. Consequently, many statistical applications are not valid with nominal measurements. *Compare* ordinal measurements.

nominal variable A *variable for which values represent the names of things, with no order implied.

nomogram (nomograph) A chart so aligned that the value of a *variable can be found without calculation. A straight line is drawn to intersect the known values of one or two variables to give the related value of another variable.

nomograph *See* nomogram.

nonaxial joints *Joints, such as *intertarsal joints, which allow only a very limited movement (e.g., side to side or back and forth).

nonaxial movement A slipping or sliding movement around a *non-axial joint that has no axis around which other movement can occur.

nonconscious motor control The control of *muscle movements of which the subject is unaware such as the peripheral corrections which occur in ballistic responses via the *muscle spindle reflex and which take only 20–30 ms to complete.

nonconsequential injuries Injuries which are not caused by sport but which interfere with athletic performance.

nonhaem iron *Iron not contained within the *prosthetic *haem group of respiratory pigments. Nonhaem iron makes up all of the iron in eggs, plant, and dairy products, and up to 60 per cent of the iron in animal tissue. Nonhaem iron is not as well absorbed as haem iron.

noninteractive audience A passive audience that does not interact verbally or emotionally with performers.

noninvolvement A lack of involvement in sport as performer, *producer, or spectator exhibited by individuals who have never been involved in sport or who abhor any association with sport. Noninvolvement also applies to those who have been active participants but who have lost interest in sport.

nonmedullated nerve fibre A *nerve fibre entirely devoid of a *myelin sheath.

non-narcotic analgesic A *drug, such as *aspirin, which relieves *pain but which does not have *narcotic effects. *Compare* narcotic analgesic.

non-parametric statistics Methods of statistical analysis which can be applied to both *ordinal and *nominal measurements. Non-parametric statistics are sometimes referred to as distribution-free statistics because they can be applied to samples from populations without regard to the shapes of their population distribution. Although the tests are robust, they are not as powerful as *parametric statistics.

non-rem sleep The deepest phase of *sleep, marked by a general absence of body movement and, in particular, absence of rapid eye movements.

nonresponse The incompletion of *questionnaires. Nonresponse may produce a bias in a sample.

nonscreeners Individuals with low *selective attention who have difficulty shifting attention from one *stimulus to another. Nonscreeners are generally more anxious (*see* anxiety) and show higher *empathy than *screeners.

nonsteroidal anti-inflammatory drug (NSAID) A *drug with anti-inflammatory and pain-reducing properties which is not related to the *corticosteroids. Commonly used NSAIDs include *naproxen and *acetylsalicylic acid (aspirin).

nonuniform speed The *speed of an object which varies over a certain period of time.

nonverbal communication Forms of communication (such as smiling and frowning, patting on the back, and blowing on a whistle) which convey ideas, feelings, and attitudes without using words. Experimental evidence shows that nonverbal communication can be a very important source of *motivation. *See also* kinesics; and paralanguage.

nonzero-sum competition *Competition in which all the participants may enjoy some degree of winning, or lose only partially. For example, an individual may achieve a *goal while opponents are also still able to achieve all or some of their goals.

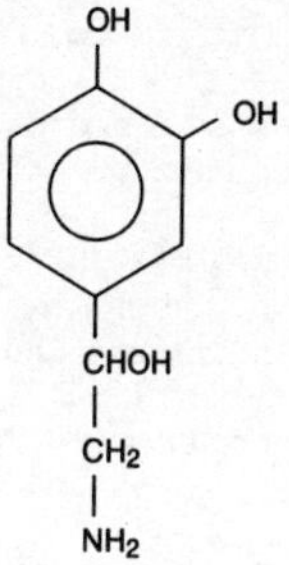

noradrenaline

noradrenaline (norepinephrine) A *drug belonging to the *stimulants which are on the *IOC list of *banned substances. Noradrenaline is an *endogenous *hormone secreted by the *medulla of the *adrenal gland, and released as a *metabotropic *neurotransmitter (*see also* biogenic amine) from nerve-endings in the *sympathetic nervous system and some areas of the *cerebral cortex. Its effects may be excitatory or inhibitory. A low level of noradrenaline is associated with *depression. Its release is enhanced by *amphetamines and its removal from the synapse is blocked by *cocaine. Noradrenaline is closely related to *adrenaline and has similar actions.

norepinephrine *See* noradrenaline.

norm 1 The set point, reference point, or system goal in a control system (*see* open-control system). For example, the norm for the *core temperature in humans is approximately 37°C. 2 An empirically-established standard. Sometimes the norm refers to the normal or average value. 3 A social rule, regulation, law, or informal agreement which prescribes and regulates behaviour in a particular situation; violations of norms are subject to sanction. Many sports sociologists consider that harmonious social interactions within teams are dependent on these shared expectations and obligations. *Compare* values.

normal A line perpendicular to the surface at the point of contact of a body.

normal active range The *range of movements of a *joint during activities which are a normal part of everyday life. *Compare* maximum active range.

normal distribution In statistics, a continuous distribution of a random *variable with its *mean, *median, and *mode equal. The normal distribution is depicted graphically by a symmetrical, bell-shaped curve.

normal force

normal force The *force between two bodies in contact with each other; it acts in a direction perpendicular to the point of contact.

normal involvement A pattern of sports involvement in which individuals participate regularly in sport and the participation has become integrated into their lifestyles.

normal reaction The *force produced when a body lies or moves on the surface of another and its weight acts on the second body in a direction at right angles to the surface of contact. The second body exerts an equal force on the first body, in the opposite direction, called the normal direction.

normative Pertaining to a *norm or norms.

normative approach A theoretical, prescriptive approach to sociological studies which has the aim of appraising or establishing the *values and *norms which best fit the overall needs and expectations of *society. *Compare* value-free approach.

normative theory Any theory which adopts a *normative approach.

normotensive Applied to a condition in which *blood pressure is within the normal range.

norm-referenced test A test in which an individual's scores are evaluated in the context of the performance of others. In sport, such norm-referencing is often used for purposes of team selection and for identifying individual differences. *Compare* criterion-referenced tests.

norms *See* norm.

nose The organ of smell which filters, warms, and moistens air on its way to the lungs.

nosebleed (epistaxis) Loss of *blood through the *nose due to changes in the continuity of the *blood vessels of the *nasal septum and surrounding *mucosa. A nosebleed may have a number of causes, including physical injury, fever, high blood pressure, or blood disorders. Most nosebleeds observed in sport are caused by physical trauma.

notch A depression in a bone.

novelty problem A problem encountered with early definitions of *motor program as structures that carry out movements in the absence of *feedback. Such programs would prevent the generation of movements that had not been produced previously.

NSAID *See* nonsteroidal anti-inflammatory drug.

nuclear magnetic imaging (NMI) *See* nuclear magnetic resonance.

nuclear magnetic resonance (NMR) A technique used both for analysis of *drugs (nuclear magnetic spectroscopy) and for producing images of internal structures (nuclear magnetic imaging). NMR can produce images which are far clearer than those produced by *X-radiography or even *computerized tomography, and without known risk to the patient. It has been used to diagnose joint injuries, *prolapsed intervertebral discs, and muscle injuries. The technique depends on atomic nuclei behaving like small magnets. When in a magnetic field these nuclei arrange themselves nonrandomly, producing signals which can be analysed and used in chemical analysis or to produce an image.

nuclear magnetic spectroscopy *See* nuclear magnetic resonance.

nuclei *See* nucleus.

nucleic acid A type of organic acid; *DNA and *RNA are both nucleic acids.

nucleoli Small spherical bodies in a cell nucleus that contains *RNA for the *synthesis of *ribosomes.

nucleotide A complex, organic molecule which is the basic unit of *nucleic acid. Nucleotides consist of an organic *base, a pentose (five-carbon) sugar, and a *peptide linked together.

nucleus 1 A cell *organelle which is bounded by a nuclear membrane and contains genetic material and *nucleoli. Red blood cells lose their nuclei when they mature. 2 A group of nerve cells in the *brain and *spinal cord which share a similar structure and function. 3 The positively-charged central part of an atom.

nucleus pulposus Spongy, semifluid, inner contents of an intervertebral disc.

null hypothesis A hypothesis used in experimental analysis which postulates that there will be no statistical difference between two or more sets of results. For example, if two groups of people are tested for physical fitness, the null hypothesis would state there is no difference between the two groups' and it would be assumed that any differences that did occur were due to random chance. A significance test, such as the t-test, would then confirm whether the null hypothesis should be accepted or rejected.

nutation 1 Wobbling; the tilting of a body's principal *axis of rotation from its original position. *See also* twisting. 2 The act of uncontrollably nodding the head.

nutrient A substance present in food that is used by the body to promote normal growth, maintenance, and repair. The major nutrients needed to maintain health are *carbohydrates, *lipids, *minerals, *proteins, *vitamins, and water. *Roughage, although never assimilated into the body and therefore not a nutrient, is also regarded as an essential component of a *balanced diet.

nutrient artery (medullary artery) A large *artery which supplies the central *medullary cavity of a *long bone with *nutrients and *oxygen.

nutrition 1 The process of taking in and assimilating *nutrients. 2 The study of food in relation to the physiological processes used to acquire sufficient *nutrients to maintain good health.

nystagmus Rapid involuntary eye movements commonly associated with eye defects.

O

obesity The storage of excess fat in the body, particularly under the skin and around certain internal organs. Obesity usually results from a *positive energy balance and not having a *balanced diet. Obesity is a well-recognized predisposing cause for a number of diseases, such as *diabetes mellitus, high *blood pressure, and *cardiovascular diseases (*see* risk factors). Obesity is difficult to define quantitatively without knowing how much fat is normal for a given person. Many authorities use body-weight as an indicator but obesity is not quite the same as being *overweight. It is generally agreed that the proportion of fat in the body should not exceed 25 per cent in men and 30 per cent in women. Medical authorities generally use a *body-mass index of more than 30 as the definition of obesity. By this definition it is possible to be obese without being overweight. Conversely, athletes may be overweight for their height because of muscular development, without being obese. *See also* adipocytes; and heart overload.

object In biomechanics, anything which has *mass and occupies space.

objective **1** Applied to a material *object or *phenomenon which exists independently of perception. **2** Applied to studies and opinions which are free from distorting, subjective, personal, or emotional bias. *See* objectivity. **3** In medicine, applied to symptoms of a disease which can be perceived by persons other than the sufferer. **4** The object of one's efforts; sometimes used synonymously with *goal.

objective competitive situation A competitive situation that an athlete is placed in. It usually incorporates the following: a standard evaluation of the quality of performance; an evaluator who is familiar with the standard; and a comparison of the performance outcome against the standard.

objective danger A risk, such as an avalanche, flood, or storm, over which a person has little or no control and which is not merely a figment of his or her imagination. *Compare* subjective danger.

objective demand An environmental situation or *stimulus which contributes to *stress.

objective descriptive feedback A nonjudgemental type of *augmented feedback which describes as clearly as possible the behaviour observed. A coach, for example, might inform an athlete that the athlete's knees were bent as he or she was performing a movement with no judgement on that situation being given or implied.

objectivism The view that it is possible to describe the real physical and social world in purely objective terms, free from personal bias. *See also* objectivity.

objectivity The quality of being free from personal bias. Objectivity is the aspect of measurement related to the extent to which two observers achieve the same score. An experimental procedure is said to have objectivity if it is not influenced by the views and perceptions of the experimenter, and is a true reflection of reality. Knowledge gained from such procedures should have *validity, *reliability, and be free from bias. The subdisciplines of sports science all have working criteria of objectivity which they aim to fulfil. Many philosophers, however, maintain that strict objectivity is an unattainable goal and that all views of reality are to some extent influenced by the perceptions of the observer.

OBLA Onset of blood lactate accumulation (*see* lactate threshold).

obligatory activities Physiological activities, such as eating and sleeping, which a person is compelled to perform by the demands of the body.

oblique impact The collision of two objects not moving along the same straight line before *impact, or the collision of a stationary object with another object travelling at an angle other than 90° to the surface on which the impact occurs. *Compare* direct impact.

O'Brien technique Technique, demonstrated in the 1952 Olympic Games by Parry O'Brien of the USA, for putting the shot. Movement across the circle was used in order to apply *force to the shot for a longer period than was possible from a standing putt, thereby increasing the *impulse.

observation The deliberate act of an observer who studies events using his or her sensory processes.

observational learning Form of *learning which is dependent on observing the behaviour of a *model rather than by direct experience. Observational learning may involve learning about the consequences of another individual's actions with or without copying the actions.

obsession A thought which persistently recurs despite attempts to resist it. An obsession provokes *anxiety and dominates a person even though the individual concerned regards it as being senseless.

obturator externus A flat triangular *muscle deep in the upper *medial aspect of the *thigh. The obturator externus has its *origins on the outer surface of the obturator membrane, on the external surface of the *pubis and *ischium, and the margins of the *obturator foramen; its *insertion is by a *tendon into the *trochanteric fossa on the *posterior aspect of the *femur. It rotates the thigh laterally and stabilizes the hips.

obturator foramen An opening through which *blood vessels and *nerves pass in the *hip-bone, slightly in front of and below the *acetabulum. The obturator foramen is formed from fusion of the *pubic bone and the *ischium, and is nearly closed by a fibrous *membrane.

obturator internus A *muscle which surrounds the *obturator foramen in the *pelvis. It has its *origins on the inner surface of the *membrane around the *obturator foramen, on the greater *sciatic notch and the margins of the obturator foramen. It leaves the pelvis via the sciatic notch and then turns acutely forward to insert (*see* insertion) on the *greater trochanter of the *femur, in front of the *piriformis muscle. It acts with other *hip lateral rotators to rotate the thigh laterally and stabilize the hip-joint.

obturator muscle Either of two muscles covering the outer *anterior wall of the *pelvis. *See also* obturator externus; and obturator internis.

obturator nerve A *nerve originating in the *lumbar region which supplies the *obturator externus, the *adductor muscles of the thigh, the *articulations of the hip and knee, and the *integument of the thigh.

occipital Pertaining to the area at the back of the head or at the base of the *skull.

occipital bone Bone which forms part of the back and base of the *cranium, and encloses the *foramen magnum.

occipito-atlantal joint The *joint between the two *condyles at the base of the *occipital bone and the *atlas vertebra.

occipito-axial joint The *joint formed between the *occipital bone of the *cranium and the *axis.

occluded circulation The closure or obstruction of a *blood vessel.

occlusion A closure or obstruction of a hollow body structure.

occupational sport subculture A group of people, including athletes and all types of producers, who earn a livelihood from a particular sport. *Compare* avocational sport subculture; and deviant sport subculture.

octacosanol A 28-carbon alcohol found in wheatgerm oil. It has been taken as an *ergogenic aid in the belief that it enhances *endurance. There is no unequivocal, scientific evidence that octacosanol provides significant beneficial effects. It is likely that where it may have been beneficial, the results of endurance-training far outweighed the claimed effects of octacosanol.

ocular Pertaining to the eye.

oculomotor Pertaining to movements of the eye.

oculomotor nerve A *nerve supplying muscles in and around the eye, including those of the *iris which alter the *pupil aperture; the third *cranial nerve.

odontoid process (dens) Toothlike process on the superior surface of the *axis which acts as a pivot for rotation of the *atlas.

oedema (edema) An atypical accumulation of fluid in the *interstitial space leading to a swelling. The oedema may be caused by any event that increases fluid flow out of the bloodstream or hinders its return.

oesophagitis Inflammation of the oesophagus (gullet). Symptoms include irritation at the back of the throat; a pain may occur behind the *sternum (usually described as heartburn) similar to that associated with some heart complaints. Oesophagitis is a relatively common complaint often caused by the reflux of acidic stomach contents. Antacids are used to relieve the symptoms but the most important part of treatment is finding and resolving the underlying cause (e.g., a *hiatus hernia). Oesophagitis need not interfere with physical activity although the symptoms can be exacerbated by activities which increase abdominal pressure or involve bending forward.

oesophagus (gullet) Part of the *alimentary canal between the *pharynx and the *stomach. No *enzymes are produced in the oesophagus, but *peristalsis helps to move food from the pharynx to the stomach.

oestradiol One of a group of steroid hormones (*see* oestrogen). Synthetic oestradiol is used to treat amenorrhoea.

oestriol *See* oestrogen.

oestrogen (estrogen) A group of *steroid hormones (including *oestradiol, oestriol, and oestrone) produced by the ovary, the *placenta and, in small amounts, from the male *testis and *adrenal cortex. In females, it maintains the *secondary sexual characteristics and is involved in the repair of the uterine wall. Synthetic oestrogens are a major consitituent of many contraceptives. Side-effects of oestrogen use include *nausea and vomiting, irregular vaginal bleeding in women, and *feminization in men.

oestrone *See* oestrogen.

ointment An external application which is greasy and usually incorporates a *medicine.

old age The final stage in the *life course of an individual. Old age is usually associated with declining faculties, both mental and physical, and a reduction in social commitments. The precise onset of old age varies culturally and historically. It is a social construct rather than a biological stage.

olecranal Pertaining to the back of the elbow.

olecranon bursa A superficial *bursa at the back of the elbow which, because of its position, is particularly vulnerable to a direct trauma and *bursitis.

olecranon fossa Depression on the posterior surface of the *humerus which alows free movement of the *ulna during *flexion and *extension.

olecranon process Prominent projection at the *proximal end of the *elbow, forming the attachment point for the *triceps brachii and other muscles.

olfactory nerve The special *sensory nerve concerned with smell which runs upwards to the brain from the nose; the first *cranial nerve.

oligarchy A state or social organization governed by a small group of people.

oligomenorrhoea An infrequent occurrence of *menses. There is some confusion in the classification of menstrual frequency. A woman who has not experienced menses for five months might be classified as oligomenorrhoeic in one study and amenorrhoeic in another study. *See also* athletic amenorrhoea.

omega-3 fatty acids A group of *unsaturated fatty acids found in some fish oils and linseed oil. They are claimed to reduce blood *clotting thus lessening the risk of a *heart attack.

omnidirectional information cues *Learning or performance situations arranged so that each member of a group can use and benefit from information provided by any other member of the group, and can in turn ask questions or engage in two-way conversations with others. *Compare* unidirectional information transmission. *See also* social facilitation.

omphalion A *landmark which is the mid-point of the navel or umbilicus.

one-area-target-type procedures A test of accuracy in which an individual has a number of attempts to hit a single target. The successful attempts gain points and the misses count as errors. There are a number of variations. In basketball, for example, a basket made can score one point and a basket missed no points; or a clean shot may score four points, a rim shot that goes in scores three points, a rim shot that goes out scores two points, a shot that touches the basket scores one point, and a complete miss scores no points.

onset of blood lactate accumulation (OBLA) *See* lactate threshold.

ontogenesis The development of a particular individual.

ontogeny The general development of a race or other group of people.

ontology A branch of philosophy which deals with the nature of the fundamental things which exist in society.

onychia Inflammation of the bed of a nail in which pus forms. This is followed by the loosening of the nail which eventually falls off. *See also* runner's toe.

open-circuit spirometry A method of *indirect calorimetry in which the subject breathes air from the atmosphere. The composition of the air flowing in and out of the lungs is measured to estimate oxygen consumption. *Compare* direct calorimetry.

open-closed continuum A continuum, extending from an *open situation to a *closed situation, which describes the extent to which environmental conditions affect performance.

open-ended attribution An *attribution freely made by an athlete who can identify his or her own cause for a particular outcome without any suggestions or constraints from a questioner. Sometimes open-ended attributions are difficult to categorize. *See also* structural rating scale.

open-ended question A question, for instance, in a questionnaire, in which the respondent does not have to choose from a number of pre-structured answers but is left to answer entirely free from any constraints. *Compare* fixed-choice question.

open fracture *See* compound fracture.

open-loop system A control system with a preprogrammed set of instructions to an *effector which has no feedback or error-detection process; consequently, the system is unable to make compensatory adjustments. It has been suggested that open-loop systems control certain movements which are executed without any alterations due to sensory feedback. However, the performance of complex, skilled movements probably involves the use of many mechanisms, including both open-loop systems and *closed-loop systems.

open skill A *motor skill performed in an unpredictable, changing *environment which dictates how and when the skill is performed. *Compare* closed skill.

open situation An environmental situation which is unpredictable and changing.

operant conditioning (instrumental conditioning) A form of *learning in which an individual forms an association between a particular behavioural response and a particular *reinforcement. The process may be positive, such as when a player learns to associate a particular activity with a pleasant result; or negative, such as when a player associates an activity with an unpleasant result. *Compare* classical conditioning.

operant techniques Methods for learning in which certain behaviours are reinforced or rewarded, leading to an increase in the probability that the behaviours will be repeated. *See also* operant conditioning.

operational hypothesis *See* working hypothesis.

ophthalmic Pertaining to the eye.

opiate Any *drug containing or derived from *opium. Opiates include *codeine and *morphine. All opiates are *narcotic analgesics on the *IOC list of *banned substances.

opinion An attitude that is expressed in words.

opium The dried latex from unripe seedheads of the oriental poppy *Papaver somniferum*, from which *morphine is extracted. Opium is a highly addictive *drug belonging to the *narcotic analgesics which are on the *IOC list of *banned substances. *See also* opiate.

opponens digiti minimi An *intrinsic muscle in the hand acting only on the little finger and enabling *opposition with the thumb.

opponens pollicis A *muscle in the hand which facilitates *opposition of the thumb with other fingers on the same hand.

opportunity cost The cost of taking part in one activity in terms of the lost opportunities which could have been pursued using the same resources of time and money. Opportunity cost is mainly an economic concept, but it is applied to sport since success commonly depends on the athlete devoting his or her youth to the sport, often at the expense of career opportunities.

opposition The muscle action which enables the pad of the thumb to make contact with the pad of the other fingers, and so provide a firm and sensitive grip. It is a unique action involving the combination of *abduction, *circumduction, and *rotation.

optic Pertaining to the eye.

optic chiasma (**optic commissure**) The X-shaped structure formed by the crossing of fibres of the *optic nerve; some fibres on the *medial side of the *retina of each eye cross over to join fibres from the *lateral side of the retina of the other eye.

optic commissure *See* optic chiasma.

optic nerve Special *sensory nerve of vision carrying visual information from the eye to the *occipital lobe of the *brain; the second *cranial nerve.

optimal angle of release The angle at which a *projectile leaves the ground and gains maximum *horizontal displacement. When the height of release and landing are the same, assuming no *air resistance, the theoretical optimal angle of release is 45°. However, the actual optimal angle is usually 35–45° to compensate for the effects of air resistance. When the height of release is greater than the height of landing, as in shot-putting, the optimum angle is always less than 45°. When the height of release is less than the height of landing, for example when playing a bunker shot in golf, the optimal angle is more than 45°.

optimal arousal The notion that for every *skill there exists a specific level of *arousal which is conducive to a best-possible performance. The optimal arousal level varies as a function of the complexity of the task and the experience of the performer with the level for beginners tending to be lower than that for experienced performers of the same skill. The optimal level of arousal also tends to decrease as the complexity of the task increases. *See also* inverted-U hypothesis.

oral Pertaining to the mouth region.

orbit 1 The bony cavity containing the *eye. 2 The curved path of a body moving around another body.

orchitis Inflammation of the *testes from any cause including a blow or a disease such as *mumps.

orciprenaline A *drug belonging to the *sympathomimetic amines but which is permitted, according to the IOC 1988 Medical Controls Brochure, for the treatment via inhalation of *asthma and *bronchitis subject to written notification. Its use is not permitted in oral form.

ordinal measurement The designation of values into rank order so that if 'A' is greater than 'B', then 'B' is greater than 'C'. Often, numbers are used to identify the position of a value in the rank order, but the number does not indicate relative distances between the categories. Thus, a group of footballers may be arranged in rank order of aggressiveness, and although it might be possible to say that one player is more aggressive than another, it is not possible to state precisely by how much the relationship differs. *Compare* interval measurement; nominal measurement; and ratio.

ordinal variable A *variable for which values have rank-order relations implied only. *See also* ordinal measurements.

organ A *mutlicellular structure containing different types of *tissue and which carries out a specific role.

organelle A small part of a *cell that has a particular functional or structural role (e.g., *mitochondrion or *nucleus).

organic 1 Pertaining to carbon-containing substances. 2 Pertaining to an *organ or organs of the body.

organic development Development of the body-structures of a person.

organic fitness The fitness of the body and its physiological systems in terms of functional efficiency and state of repair. Organic fitness is regarded as an integral component of *health.

organismic theories of personality Clinically-oriented theories which view *personality as being shaped by the overall field of forces acting on the individual, and posit self-change or growth as central features of personality.

organismic variable *See* individual differences variable.

organization A social, administrative structure formed to pursue certain goals. An organization is characterized by having a formal set of rules and a limited membership (which is often hierarchial) with a well-defined division of labour.

organization theory Knowledge concerned with the structure and functioning of an *organization, particularly regarding the dynamics of its social relationships. Organization theory includes topics such as rewards and *motivation, *decision-making, and *leadership, all of which have particular relevance to sports organizations.

organ system A group of *organs in the human body that work together to carry out a vital body-function.

orientation The ability of a person to be aware of his or her position with respect to both time, place, and circumstances.

orienting response An *autonomic mechanism which directs *attention to anything unusual or different. Its function is to alert a person to potential danger. It is possible, with training, to override this response. It is often useful for athletes to be able to override the orienting response during a competition.

origin 1 The attachment point of a *muscle that remains relatively fixed during the action of the muscle; it is usually *proximal to the *insertion. 2 A point at which a *blood vessel or *nerve branches from a main vessel or nerve.

origin–pawn relationship A term based on the observation that some people think they control their own destiny, while others feel powerless to do so; the former have been called origins and the latter pawns. *See also* locus of control.

origins *See* origin–pawn relationship.

ornithine An *amino acid produced in the *liver during the formation of *urea from *ammonia.

ornithine cycle A series of reactions which take place in the *liver to convert *ammonia to *urea.

orthopaedics A branch of medicine dealing with skeletal deformities caused by disease or injury.

orthoses (orthotics) Foot-supports (usually custom-designed insoles) that fit in a shoe to make foot motion more efficient, reduce the risk of foot injury, and to correct certain structural imbalances that may lead to pain in the back, hips, knees, or feet. Some élite athletes, including runners, cyclists, and skiers, have been shown to benefit substantially from the use of orthoses.

orthostatic Pertaining to, or caused by, standing erect.

orthostatic hypotension (postural hypotension) A fall in *blood pressure that occurs on standing.

orthostatic proteinuria (postural proteinuria) Occurrence of *proteins in the *urine as a result of prolonged standing, particularly in young adults. It disappears after bed-rest. Orthostatic proteinuria has been linked to the *peripheral sequestration of blood during exercise.

orthotics *See* orthoses.

os (pl. ossa) A bone.

os (pl. ora) The mouth or any mouth-like opening.

os calcis apophysitis *See* Sever's disease.

O-scale A system of assessing *physique based on a scale constructed from *anthropometric data, including measurements of *skinfold, *body-height, *body-girth, and body-weight. The measurements are scaled to a common stature and then plotted relative to age and sex norms to provide a proportionality profile. The system is named after its computer anagram for obesity scaling, although it does not measure the fat content of the body. The O-scale is used to assist the management of health, fitness, and lifestyle, and to monitor the effects of training.

oscillation A vibration.

oscillatory motion A motion which recurs back and forth over the same pattern. An example of an oscillatory motion is that of the legs during running when the same cycle of movements is repeated.

Osgood's semantic differential scales Measures of *attitude which require that an individual rates an attitude on a set of semantic scales which are bipolar adjectives generally seven steps apart. For example, a scale for rating how a person feels about doing aerobics may include the following:

FOOLISH: –3 –2 –1 0 +1 +2 +3 :WISE

UNPLEASANT: :PLEASANT
–3 –2 –1 0 +1 +2 +3

Osgood–Schlatter disease An injury in which the attachment of the *patellar tendon on the tubercle at the top of the *tibia is damaged through over-use. Osgood–Schlatter disease is a form of *apophysitis in which the tibial apophysis and the growth-centres of the bones of the tubercle of the tibia become inflamed. It commonly occurs in children who take part in sports such as skating, gymnastics, and football. These sports include much knee-bending and jumping which exposes the apophyses to great tensile stress; this may cause an epiphyseal separation. The condition usually heals spontaneously but it may lead to permanent distortion and long-term functional disability if not treated properly. Usually, treatment consists of the restriction of activity for some months.

osmolality A measurement of *osmotic pressure in terms of *osmoles of substance per kilogram of water.

osmole A unit of *osmotic pressure equal to the molecular weight of the substance in grams divided by the number of *ions or other particles the substance dissociates into when in solution.

osmoreceptor A cell which is sensitive to changes in *osmotic pressure. A group of osmoreceptors occur in the *hypothalamus and monitor changes in the osmotic pressure of the *blood.

osmoregulation The homeostatic control (*see* homeostasis) of *osmotic potential or *water potential resulting in the maintenance of a constant volume of body fluids.

osmosis The net movement of water (or another solvent), from a high *water potential (or low solute concentration) to a low water potential (or high solute concentration) through a *semi-permeable membrane.

osmotic potential A measure of the tendency of a solution, by virtue of the solutes it contains, to withdraw water from pure water by *osmosis through a *semipermeable membrane. By convention, pure water has an osmotic potential of zero and all solutions have a negative osmotic potential.

osmotic pressure The pressure needed to prevent the osmotic movement of water or another solvent through a *semi-permeable membrane (*see* osmosis).

os pubis *See* pubis.

ossa coxae *See* coxal bone.

osseous Applied to tissue which is bony.

osseous tissue *See* bone.

ossicle A small bone, such as the auditory ossicles in the middle ear.

ossification (osteogenesis) The conversion of *fibrous tissue or *cartilage into *bone. The process is carried out in three stages by special bone cells called *osteoblasts: first, *collagen fibres are laid down to provide a framework; then, a cementing *polysaccharide is produced; finally, *calcium salts are deposited in the cement. *See also* endochondral ossification; and intramembranous ossification.

osteitis Inflammation of *bone due to disease or injury.

osteitis pubis *See* groin pain.

osteoarthritis (osteoarthrosis) A degenerative disease of joint *cartilage which may progress to affect the underlying *bone. The condition may result from *trauma, incorrect loading of the *joint, *ligament injuries, or *dislocation of the joint. Although it may affect any joint, it most commonly affects the joints of the hips, knees, and thumbs of those who have passed middle age. Athletes with osteoarthritis are often advised to participate in sports that put little stress on the affected joint, since the development of this condition is accelerated if an effected joint is subsequently subjected to damaging stresses or repeated injury.

osteoarthrosis *See* osteoarthritis.

osteoblasts A cell responsible for *ossification; it develops into a bone cell or *osteocyte.

osteochondritis (osteochondrosis) Inflammation of *bone and *cartilage causing *pain. Osteochondritis often occurs in young athletes who subject their growing *epiphyses and *apophyses to repeated stress. The condition is often marked by fragmentation of the affected cartilage and bone, distortion and collapse, and, after some time, *ossification of the bone into an irregular form. *See also* Freiberg's disease; Kohler's disease; Osgood-Schlatter's disease; Perthes' disease; and Sever's disease.

osteochondritis dissecans A form of *osteochondritis in which a fragment of *bone separates and lies freely in the *joint. It may result in *locking of the joint and require surgery.

osteoclast A large multinucleated cell of uncertain origin which destroys *bone cells and reabsorbs *calcium. Osteoclasts play a key role in *bone-remodelling.

osteocyte A spider-shaped, mature *bone cell, derived from an *osteoblast, which lies in a small cavity in the bone called a *lacuna.

osteogenesis *See* ossification.

osteogenesis imperfecta A *congenital condition, characterized by the formation of abnormally fragile *bones, which may result in *hyperflexibility.

osteolysis The breakdown of *bone through disease commonly due to restriction or loss of the *blood supply to the bone.

osteomalacia A term applied to a number of conditions in which *bones are inadequately mineralized and are abnormally soft. It may occur as a result of *vitamin D deficiency.

osteomyelitis Inflammation of *bone which results from an infection of *bone marrow.

osteon The structural and functional unit of *compact bone, also called an *Haversian system.

osteoperiostitis Inflammation of *bone and *periosteum.

osteophyte A bony deposit or outgrowth which often develops at the site of *cartilage degeneration near a *joint.

osteoporosis A group of diseases typified by the reduction in bone-mass due to bone resorption outpacing bone deposition. The bone becomes porous, brittle, and inclined to fracture. Osteoporosis is an age-related disease which primarily affects postmenopausal women. There is always some osteoporosis that occurs with ageing, but insufficient exercise may contribute to the development of the disease. Other causes include *calcium and *vitamin D deficiency. There is also some evidence of a link between *athletic amenorrhoea and osteoporosis. To help prevent the condition from developing, women are advised to exercise regularly before *menopause.

osteosclerosis An increase in the density of *bone.

osteotomy The surgical bisection of *bone. The operation may be performed so that the two parts can be realigned to facilitate healing, or to reduce pain and disability in an arthritic *joint.

os trigonum A small accessory bone behind the ankle-joint present in about 7 per cent of the population. The os trigonum is derived from a prominent *tubercle which

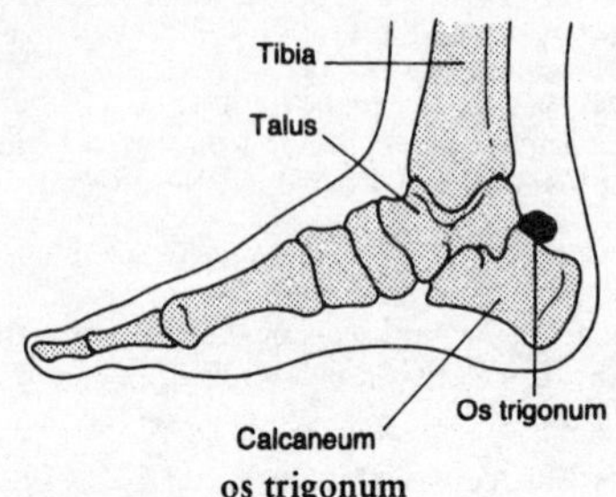

os trigonum

has separated from the *talus bone. It is generally of no significance, but it can be damaged by repeated *en point* positions in ballet or energetic bounding movements, such as jumping, when the bone may be squeezed between the *calcaneus and the *tibia causing pain and damaging tissue.

otitis externa Inflammation of the *outer ear characterized by an itchy irritation and watery discharge. It is usually associated with *eczema. Otitis externa need not interfere with physical activity except in the acute infective stage, as long as appropriate precautions are taken (for example, swimmers may use alcohol drops to help dry the ear and restore the correct pH).

otitis interna Inflammation of the inner ear (labyrinthitis) causing vomiting, vertigo, and loss of balance.

otitis media Infection of the *middle ear usually resulting from blockage of the *Eustachian tube and subsequent invasion by bacteria. Pus accumulates in the middle ear creating pressure against the eardrum which causes pain and impairment of hearing. Physical exertion should be avoided during the infection. This applies especially to swimmers since water entering the middle ear may seriously damage the *auditory ossicles.

otolith 1 A calcareous granule of which there are several in the inner ear. An otolith is attached to sensitive cells which enable body position to be assessed. **2** A stony secretion in the middle ear.

outcome The result or consequence of a performance in terms of success and failure. The outcome may be absolute, as with a team winning by scoring more goals than opponents, or dependent on the perceptions of particular individuals (*see* perceived outcome).

outcome goal A *goal which depends on the result or *outcome of a competition. Such goals are only partly under the control of any one individual and are partly dependent on others including team-mates, opponents, and officials. *See also* goal-setting; and performance goal.

outdoor education Education which takes place in the natural environment. It includes conventional field studies, outdoor pursuits, and any other educational activities which take place in the open air.

outdoor pursuits Physical activies, such as sailing, canoeing, and rock-climbing, which take place in a natural setting where part of the activity involves the challenge of coping with the natural elements.

outdoor recreation Leisure activities, such as hill-walking, which take place in the open air, usually in the natural environment, and are more obviously recreative than competitive.

outer ear *See* pinna.

outer range That third of the *range of movement of a *joint at which the muscle is at its most elongated and the joint surface is at its greatest angle. *See also* inner range; and midrange.

output A term used in *systems theory and systems models to describe the product of a particular device or physiological process, or the motor response of a person to a particular situation.

outsole Part of a *training shoe that comes into contact with the ground.

ovarian cycle An approximately monthly cycle of the development of an *ovarian follicle and the *ovulation of an *oocyte in women. *See also* menstrual cycle.

ovarian follicle Group of cells enveloping and nourishing a developing *oocyte in the *ovary.

ovary Female reproductive organ which produces *ova and *steroid hormones in a regular cycle.

overall duration parameter A parameter of a generalized *motor programme that helps to specify how a movement is to be expressed. The overall duration parameter defines the overall duration of the movement; it is sometimes called a 'speed' parameter.

overall force parameter A parameter of a generalized *motor program that defines the overall *force of the combined contractions of the participating muscles in an action.

over-compensation 1 A *mental process by which a person tries to overcome a disability by making greater efforts than are necessary. For example, a person may compensate for feelings of emotional insecurity by being over-aggressive or by showing off. 2 *See* over-correction.

over-correction An over-compensation of a mechanical fault during the performance of a *motor skill. For example, a canoeist falling over towards the water on one side may adjust by going over too far on the other side. Over-correction often occurs during the early stages of *skill-*learning.

over-determination In *psychology, a process in which several factors act simultaneously to produce a single mental phenomenon, such as an image in a dream or a neurotic symptom, but in which any one of the several factors on its own can produce the same phenomenon.

over-distance training Training over a distance which is greater than the competitive distance, but at a slower pace than race pace.

overfat *See* obesity.

over-justification hypothesis An hypothesis which posits that an individual's intrinsic interest in an activity may be decreased by inducing him or her with *extrinsic rewards to take part in the activity. If the reward is perceived to be the reason for participation, the individual infers that the behaviour is motivated by extrinsic rewards rather than *intrinsic motivation. Consequently, the individual tends to become less interested in the activity.

over-learning Repeating a technique or *skill after it has been learnt sufficiently well to be performed in training, so that it can be reliably performed under the stress of competition. It is generally assumed that it takes longer to learn a skill for a competition than for a noncompetitive situtation.

overload To impose demands on the body or body-parts which are greater than usual.

overload principle A basic physiological principle which specifies that the strength, endurance, and *hypertrophy of a *muscle, *bone, *connective tissue, *ligaments, etc., will increase only when they perform for a given period of time against workloads that are above those normally encountered. The workload can be quantified in terms of training intensity (rate of doing work) or training volume (amount of work done). The best training results occur when, for example, a muscle performs at the maximal limits of its strength and endurance. *See also* principle of progression.

overload theory A theory that certain *muscle groups contract in such a way as to bend the bones to which they are attached. Repeated bending causes a *stress fracture (*compare* fatigue theory).

over-practice Practising a *skill which has already been learned. *See also* over-learning.

overstrain A form of *run-down which develops in those training beyond the adaptation capacity of the body. Overstrain is found in those taking part in sports which require excessive energy outputs such as long-distance running and cross-country skiing. Unlike *over-training, it includes physiological fatigue which causes both nervous and hormonal disturbances. This is indicated by a decrease in sympathetic activity with a reduction in adrenal function and greater activity of the *parasympathetic nervous system.

overt behaviour Behaviour which can be observed by others.

over-training Training beyond the physiological and psychological capacities of the body to recover during the rest periods. Over-training is associated with *run-down and *burnout, and commonly causes physical and mental fatigue resulting a decrease in the quality of performance. The athlete typically complains of feeling tired and having difficulty sleeping. *See also* over-training syndrome; over-use injury; and over-use syndrome.

over-training syndrome A combination of signs and symptoms of *over-training which typically causes the sufferer to feel mentally fatigued without being physically fatigued and causes performance to deteriorate. The sufferer's *basal metabolic rate is elevated, there is usually a loss of body-weight associated with a negative nitrogen balance, and the rate of return of exercise pulse-rate to resting pulse-rate is delayed. The over-training syndrome is thought to involve changes in both the neurone and endocrine systems, particularly the *hypothalamus.

over-use injury An injury caused by over-exerting the body with excessive loads at a normal frequency of movement, or with a normal load at an increased frequency of movement, or with low loads at an excessively rapid frequency of movement. Over-use injuries often occur at the microscopic level and are caused by repeated microtrauma.

over-use syndrome The pathological signs and symptoms created by repeated use of the body in physically stressful conditions. *See also* overstrain; and over-training syndrome.

overweight An excessive *body-weight. There is no universally agreed quantitative definition. However, a person is usually considered as overweight when his or her weight is 15–20 per cent greater than the appropriate weight as determined by conventional tables. These take into account height, build, and sex. Excess weight can overload the locomotor apparatus, particularly the joints and back. Muscle weighs more per unit volume than fat, consequently muscular athletes may well be overweight although they are not obese since they do not suffer from excess fat storage (*see* obesity).

ovulation The release of an egg from the *ovary which occurs about once a month during the *menstrual cycle.

ovum The female gamete; egg cell.

oxalic acid A chemical found in vegetables such as spinach and rhubarb that combines with *calcium in the body to form insoluble salts which impede the absorption of food.

oxaloacetic acid A four-carbon organic acid involved in the *Krebs cycle where it combines with *acetylcoenzyme A to form *citric acid.

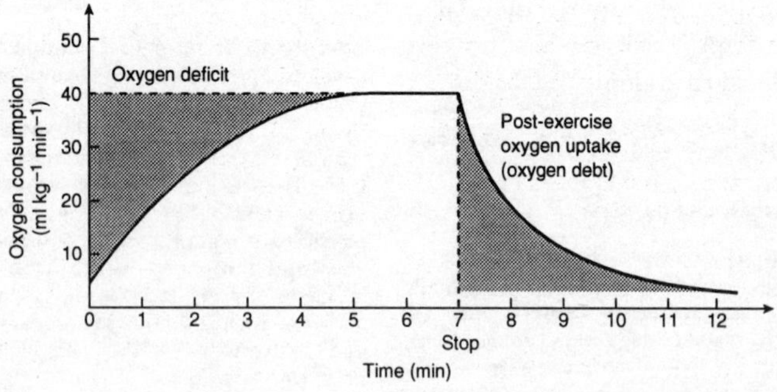

oxygen debt

oxazepam A *benzodiazepine tranquillizing *drug administered orally to reduce *anxiety. It is not on the *IOC list of *banned substances.

oxidase Any *enzyme, such as *cytochrome oxidase, involved in *oxidation reactions. These enzymes are now known as *oxidoreductases.

oxidation A chemical reaction involving the addition of *oxygen, the removal of *hydrogen, or the loss of an *electron from a substance.

oxidative decarboxylation The *catabolic process which takes place in the *Krebs cycle, where both *hydrogen and *carbon dioxide are lost during the conversion of *citric acid to *oxaloacetic acid. The hydrogen is passed on to the *respiratory chain and the carbon dioxide is eventually excreted from the lungs.

oxidative phosphorylation The process by which *adenosine triphosphate is synthesized during *aerobic respiration in the *mitochondria.

oxidoreductase One of a group of *enzymes involved in *redox reactions. These enzymes were formerly known as oxidases or dehydrogenases.

oximeter An instrument which measures the percentage saturation of *haemoglobin with *oxygen.

oxprenolol A *drug belonging to the *beta blockers which are on the *IOC list of *banned substances. It is used in the treatment of *angina, abnormal heart rhythms, and *hypertension. The drug has been misused in sports where physical activity is of little or no importance. Studies have shown an improved performance in ski-jumpers, bowlers, and pistol-shooters after the administration of oxprenolol.

oxygen An odourless, colourless gas that makes up about one-fifth of the atmosphere. It is essential for human survival. Attempts have been made to use oxygen as an *ergogenic aid, but there is little evidence of benefit before or following exercise. There may be some value in taking oxygen during exercise, but this is of little practical use because of the problems of administering the gas to an active athlete.

oxygenation The addition of molecules of *oxygen to another chemical. The term is used in particular to describe the process whereby *haemoglobin becomes saturated with oxygen to become *oxyhaemoglobin. Molecules of oxygen are carried by the haem group but the iron of this group remains in the ferrous form and does not become oxidized.

oxygen capacity The maximum volume of *oxygen which can be carried by *haemoglobin in the *blood. It is usually expressed as ml of oxygen per 100 ml of blood. Since each g of haemoglobin can carry 1.3 ml of oxygen, the total oxygen capacity of haemoglobin equals the haemoglobin concentratiion (in g of haemoglobin per 100 ml of blood) multiplied by 1.3.

oxygen consumption The volume of *oxygen used for *metabolism by the human body in a given period of time. It is usually expressed in l min^{-1}.

oxygen cost The amount of *oxygen used by the body tissues during an activity. It is directly related to the energy demands of the activity, but it is also affected by the nature of the substrate being respired.

oxygen debt (oxygen recovery) The amount of oxygen consumed during recovery from exercise above that which would be consumed at rest in the same period. There is a rapid component (*see* alactacid oxygen debt) and a slow component (*see* lactacid oxygen debt). The extra oxygen consumption is used in aerobic repiration to provide energy for restoring the body to its pre-exercise condition, including replenishing energy stores that were depleted, and removing any *lactic acid that accumulated during the exercise. The oxygen debt is incurred by active muscles during exercise when there is insufficient oxygen to satisfy their energy requirements. The muscle has to respire anaerobically. In trained athletes, the oxygen debt may be as high as 18 l. *See also* oxygen deficit.

oxygen deficit The difference between the theoretical *oxygen requirement and the volume of oxygen actually used during a period of exercise in which the level of oxygen consumption is insufficient to supply all the *adenosine triphosphate required.

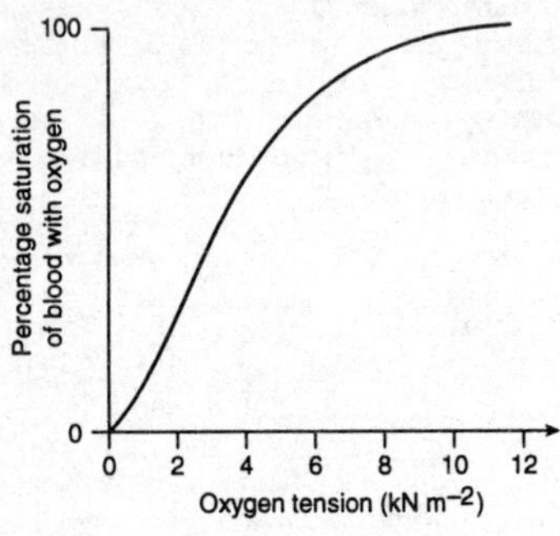

oxygen dissociation

oxygen dissociation curve (oxyhaemoglobin dissociation curve) A graph of the relationship between the percentage saturation of *blood with *oxygen and the *partial pressure (or tension) of oxygen. The curve is s-shaped indicating that *haemoglobin has a high affinity for oxygen. The blood becomes relatively highly saturated at low oxygen partial pressures (e.g., as occurs in respiring tissues) but a small drop in oxygen partial pressure results in a big fall in saturation of the blood. *See also* Bohr effect.

oxygen plateau A condition reached during exercise in a person subjected to successively increasing workloads when the *oxygen consumption no longer increases with further increments of workload. The oxygen plateau is most easily studied under controlled conditions using a *treadmill, *bicycle ergometer, etc. Results vary according to the type of test equipment and the type of workload increment (for example, increases in speed or gradient).

oxygen poisoning Condition caused by breathing pure *oxygen under high pressure. Symptoms include tingling of the fingers and toes, visual disturbances, auditory hallucinations, confusion, muscle-twitching, nausea, vertigo, and convulsions.

oxygen pulse The *oxygen uptake per heartbeat. The oxygen pulse can be used as an indirect measure of *stroke volume, and is closely correlated with body-weight.

oxygen pump theory The proposition that regular exercise increases the ability of the heart muscle to pump blood and thereby improve *oxygen transport.

oxygen recovery *See* oxygen debt.

oxygen requirement A measure of the *oxygen needed to produce the energy to complete an activity. It is usually expressed as litres of oxygen required per minute of activity. *See also* metabolic eqivalent.

oxygen system *See* aerobic system.

oxygen transport The carriage of *oxygen in the blood. More than 98 per cent is transported as *oxyhaemoglobin with the rest carried in solution in the *plasma.

oxygen transport system A concept used to describe the processes by which *oxygen is transported from the *lungs to the *tissue. It depends on the ability of the heart to pump the blood around the body and the ability of the tissues to extract oxygen from the blood. Thus the efficiency of the oxygen transport system is estimated as the product of *stroke volume, *heart-rate, and the *arterial-mixed venous oxygen difference.

oxygen uptake The volume of *oxygen extracted from inspired air at *STPD in a given time. If the oxygen content of the body remains constant during the period of determination, the oxygen uptake equals the volume of oxygen utilized in the *metabolic oxidation of foodstuffs, with 1l of oxygen corresponding to 19.7–21.2kJ (4.7–5.9 kcal). The oxygen uptake reflects the ability of the heart to pump oxygenated blood to the tissues, and the ability of the tissues to extract oxygen from the blood. Therefore the oxygen uptake of a particular tissue is a product of *cardiac output and *arterial—venous oxygen difference. The oxygen uptake for the whole body is a product of the cardiac output and the *arterial mixed-venous oxygen difference.

oxyhaemoglobin *Haemoglobin which has reversibly combined with *oxygen. Oxyhaemoglobin is a relatively unstable bright red substance and is the means by which most of the oxygen is transported in the bloodstream from the lungs to tissues. Each molecule of haemoglobin can carry four molecules of oxygen.

oxyhaemoglobin dissociation curve *See* oxygen dissociation curve.

oxymetazoline A sympathomimetic *drug belonging to the *stimulants, most of which are on the *IOC list of *banned substances; but since 1988 use of oxymetazoline in spray form has been permitted by the IOC. It is an *α agonist and is used as a decongestant in some cough and cold medicines.

oxymethalone A *drug belonging to the *anabolic steroids which are on the *IOC list of *banned substances.

oxymyoglobin A combination of *oxygen with *myoglobin. Each molecule of myoglobin can carry one molecule of oxygen. Oxymyoglobin acts as a store of oxygen in *muscles (with an average of 11.2 ml of oxygen per kg of muscle mass) and is important during intermittent exercise. Oxygen is released during the work intervals and oxymyoglobin restored during the recovery periods. It is also thought to be functionally important in transporting oxygen from the blood to muscle *mitochondria.

oxyphenylbutazone A *drug, belonging to the *nonsteroidal analgesic drugs, which is closely related to *phenylbutazone.

oxytocin *Hormone released by the *posterior pituitary that stimulates contraction of the *uterus during childbirth and stimulates milkflow.

ozone A gas containing three atoms of oxygen per molecule. Ozone occurs naturally at about 0.01 parts per million (ppm). When it occurs in concentrations above 0.1 ppm, it is regarded as toxic and can be a potent airway stimulant causing increases in *ventilation rate and decreases in *tidal volume for a given workload. High ozone levels in cities hosting marathon races have been the cause of respiratory distress in some athletes.

P

Pa *See* Pascal.

PABA (*p*-aminobenzoic acid) A member of the vitamin B group of chemicals, PABA is one of the most commonly-used ingredients in lotions and creams that are used to prevent sunburn. The derivatives made from it effectively screen out the *ultraviolet rays responsible for *sunburn, but do not offer protection against the full spectrum of ultraviolet rays, including those linked with skin *cancer.

pace The rate of movement, especially of walking, running, and swimming.

pace clock Clock used in swimming pool training so that swimmers can learn *pace judgement by self-timing. The clock is positioned at the side of the pool where the swimmer can easily observe it at the end of a length; ideally two clocks are used, one at each end of the pool.

pace judgement An inherent awareness of rate of movement without using external timing devices. Pace judgement is an important ability for racing and can be learned .

pacemaker 1 A small region of cardiac tissue in the right atrium of the heart (*see* sinoatrial node) which controls the rate of contraction for the heart as a whole. 2 A device used to control the *heart-rate of a patient who has *heart block.

pacing continuum A continuum, extending from *self-paced to *externally paced, concerned with the extent to which a performer has control over his or her actions.

Pacinian corpuscle A specialized *sense receptor in the skin which responds to firm pressure; named after F. Pacini (1812–83), an Italian anatomist.

pack A pad of folded material moistened, or containing hot or cold material, which can be applied to the surface of the body.

paddler's wrist Pain in the lower end of the *forearm due to an *inflammation of the long *tendon sheath of the thumb. Also known as de Quervain's thumb. *See also* tendovaginitis.

paediatrics Branch of medicine dealing with the treatment of children.

pain A feeling of distress, suffering, or agony caused by the stimulation of specialized nerve-endings. Pain has a protective function in acting as a warning, preventing further injury. Pain can be relieved by *cold therapy, *anaesthetics, anti-inflammatory *analgesics, *NSAIDS, morphine-related *drugs and *transcutaneous nerve stimulation therapy (TNS). Substances which increase sensitivity to pain include *bradykinin, *free radicals, *histamine, *potassium, and *serotonin. Some of these substances evoke pain by directly affecting nerve receptors (*see* nociceptor), others cause an inflammatory reaction. Excessive pain has detrimental effects on performance. *Pain thresholds may be influenced by genetic factors beyond an individual's control, but previous experience also influences a person's *pain tolerance. There is some evidence to suggest that training in painful, but not damaging circumstances, improves the ability of some athletes to withstand pain.

pain cycle A cycle involving recurrence of *pain associated with over-use. Pain may disappear during *warm-ups allowing the athlete to continue training which may damage tissue further. The pain cycle should be interrupted by rest and the injury treated.

painful heel cushion (bruised heel) An injury resulting from repeated compression of the fat compartments in the heel which may be ruptured and forced towards the side of the heel. This reduces the cushioning effects of the fat with the skin lying closer to bones, causing tenderness and pain when the heel is loaded.

painful shoulder A condition characterized by immobilization of the shoulder and pain around the *insertions of the *supraspinatous and *deltoid muscles which may, if severe, radiate to the elbow and hands. In a sportsperson, a painful shoulder is often due to over-use of *tendons, or partial tear of a tendon, around the shoulder. Another condition, affecting mainly the middle and older age groups, is *frozen shoulder the exact cause of which is unknown and which may restrict movement for 1 to 2 years.

pain-killer *See* analgesic.

pain receptor *See* nociceptor.

pain threshold The lowest *stimulus intensity which results in the perception of *pain. *Compare* pain tolerance.

pain tolerance An individual's reaction to *pain. The ability to continue an activity despite the perception of pain indicates a high pain tolerance. Pain tolerance varies widely and is strongly affected by genetic, psychological, and cultural influences.

palliative A *medicine which provides temporary relief, alleviating symptoms, but which does not provide a cure for a disease.

pallor Abnormal paleness of the skin, particularly the face, due to lack of pigment or reduced blood flow. It may indicate shock, faintness, or a number of other conditions.

palmar Pertaining to the palm of the hand.

palpation The examination of an area of the body by the sense of touch. Palpation is often used by *physiotherapists to examine the condition of *superficial muscles.

palpitation A condition in which the heart beats forcibly or irregularly, and an individual becomes conscious of its action. The condition may be brought on by a number of causes including undue excitement, *dyspepsia, drinking alcohol, frequent coffee- or tea-drinking, or smoking. Although unpleasant and worrying, it is not usually caused by *heart disease. Moderate exercise is often useful in alleviating palpitations not associated with *organic disease.

pancreas A mixed *gland producing *endocrine secretions (from the *Islets of Langerhans) and *exocrine secretions (the

parabola

*pancreatic juice) from small sacs known as acini.

pancreatic juice Secretion from the pancreas which is released into the duodenum. Pancreatic juice contains a mixture of digestive enzymes including *amylase, *lipase, nucleases, *peptidases, and other *proteases such as *trypsin. Production of pancreatic juice is stimulated by hormones secreted by the duodenum (*see* cholesystokinin; and secretin).

pancreatitis Inflammation of the *pancreas which may be *acute or *chronic. Symptoms include abdominal pain, fever, and vomiting. Acute pancreatitis can be dangerous if accompanied by bleeding. Chronic pancreatitis gives rise to tiredness and loss of weight because of maladsorption. Physical activity should be avoided during acute attacks. Those with chronic pancreatitis should participate in sport only with medical guidance.

panel study A form of *longitudinal study used in sociology which involves the questioning of the same sample at regular intervals to observe trends of opinion. It is usually of shorter duration and more focused than other forms of longitudinal studies.

pangamic acid (vitamin B_{15}) A substance marketed as a *vitamin, and claimed to improve physical performance. There is little scientific evidence to support the claim that pangamic acid is a vitamin.

panic A sudden unreasoning and overwhelming fear or terror, often affecting a *group. It may occur in a state of high *anxiety.

pannus 1 The growth of *vascular tissue in the *cornea of the eye which may occur after inflammation of the cornea; it impairs vision. 2 Extension of thickened *synovial membrane onto the *cartilage of a *joint surface.

panting Breathing with noisy, deep gasps, as occurs during or after strenuous exercise. The uncontrollable desire to pant indicates that insufficient *oxygen is reaching the tissues and *anerobic respiration is taking place. *See also* anaerobic threshold; and hyperventilation.

pantothenic acid A water-soluble *vitamin which is a constituent of *coenzyme A. It plays a part in *carbohydrate and *fat *metabolism. Some studies have indicated a beneficial effect of pantothenic acid supplements on physical activity, but it is generally believed that more detailed experimentation is needed to confirm these effects. Pantothenic acid is found in liver, yeast, and peas and other legumes.

papillary muscle A nipple-shaped projection of the *ventricular muscle to which the tendinous cords (*see* chordae tenineae) of the *atrioventricular valves are attached. Contractions of the papillary muscles assist the tendinous cords in preventing the valves from being thrust out into the *atrial cavity during ventricular *systole.

papular Applied to a rash which appears as small raised spots on the skin.

papaveretum A derivative of *opium belonging to the *narcotic analgesics and on the *IOC list of *banned substances.

***p*-aminobenzoic acid** *See* PABA.

parabola A curve traced out by a point which moves so that its distance from a fixed point, the focus, is equal to its distance from a fixed straight line, the directrix. In the absence of *air resistance the *flight path of a projectile, such as a long-jumper's body, is parabolic.

paracetamol (acetaminophen) An *analgesic which has very little *anti-inflammatory effects and, unlike *acetylsalicylic acid (aspirin), it does not increase the tendency to bleed. The use of paracetamol in sport is permitted by the *IOC.

paradigm Any generalized perspective or world-view which provides a means by which the real world can be studied by breaking down complexities. Paradigms are belief-systems about the world which shape the way research in sports science is carried out. *See also* scientific paradigm.

paradox A person or thing exhibiting apparently contradictory features, as in *Lombard's paradox; or a phenomenon, such as a medical symptom, in conflict with what is expected.

paraffin A *hydrocarbon derived from petroleum.

paraffin bath A treatment for *joint injuries, particularly of the hand or foot. The limb is dipped into warm paraffin (52–58 °C) or the warm paraffin is applied with a paintbrush to the injured part.

paralanguage Communication conveyed by the intonation of the voice and other vocal components of speech which do not depend on the actual words spoken. Paralanguage refers not to what people say, but to how they say it. Many sportspeople are unaware of the powerful effects, beneficial or detrimental, of paralanguage on the behaviour of their team-mates and officials.

parallax An optical effect which contributes to the perception of relative distances. Parallax occurs when movement at right angles to the line of vision alters the relative position of two unequally distant objects. The same effect is achieved by the difference in viewpoint of the two eyes when the distance between the eyes relative to the distance of the objects is significant.

parallel axes theorem A theorem which relates the *moment of inertia about an *axis through a *body-segment's *centre of

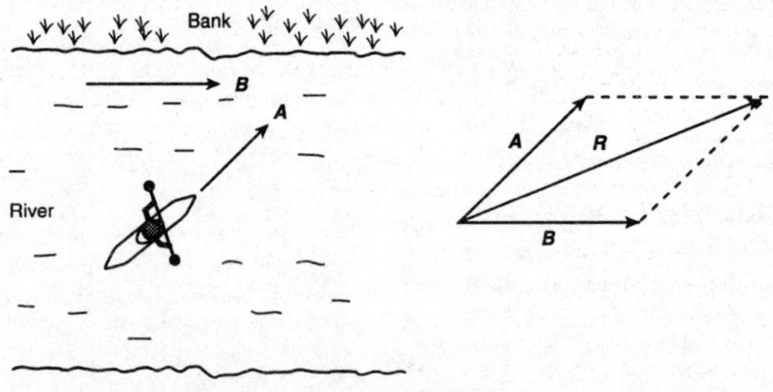

A is the velocity of the canoe with respect to the water;
B is the velocity of the water with respect to the bank;
R is the resultant velocity of the canoe with respect to the bank.

parallelogram of vectors

gravity to the body's movement about any other parallel axis. The theorem is stated in algebraic form in the folowing equation:

$$I_a = I_{cg} + md^2$$

where I_a = the moment of the body about an axis through the point a, I_{cg} = the moment of inertia of the body about a parallel axis through its centre of gravity, m = mass of the body, d = the distance between the parallel axes.

parallel competition A competition in which contestants compete with each other indirectly, by taking turns contesting in separate areas. *See also* indirect competition.

parallel elastic components Elements of the body which are in parallel with the *contractile elements of *muscle. Parallel elastic components are probably composed of the *sarcolemma and the *connective tissue of the muscle (*endomysium, *perimysium, and *epimysium). They are thought to enhance the *elasticity of stretched muscles or to contribute to muscle action by giving resistive tension to a passive muscle when stretched. *Compare* series elastic components.

parallelogram A plane four-sided rectilinear figure which has its opposite sides parallel. The opposite sides and angles of a parallelogram are equal; the diagonals bisect each other and the parallelogram itself.

parallelogram of forces A method of calculating the *resultant of two *forces acting on a body. The two forces are represented in *direction and *magnitude by the two sides of a *parallelogram drawn from a point, and the resultant of the two forces is represented by the diagonal of the parallelogram drawn from that point.

parallelogram of vectors A method of obtaining a *resultant vector from two or more *component vectors. The two component vectors form the adjacent sides of a *parallelogram drawn to scale. The resultant vector is given by the direction and length of the diagonal of the parallelogram. If necessary, this resultant vector can be used as a component vector in another parallelogram. The process is then repeated until one resultant vector remains.

parallelogram of velocities A method of calculating the *resultant of two *velocities acting on a body. The two component velocities are represented in *magnitude and *direction by two adjacent sides of a *parallelogram drawn from a point, and the resultant velocity of the body is represented by the diagonal of the parallelogram drawn from that point.

parallel-processing A type of *information-processing in which at least two processes can occur simultaneously. In the human body, parallel-processing is a form of *neural integration which underlies complex mental processes. *Nerve impulses are conveyed simultaneously along several pathways to different centres of integration. *Compare* serial-processing.

paralysis A loss or impairment of motor function due to a disorder in some part of the neuromuscular system. The extent of the paralysis will vary according to the location and extent of the disorder. The term is also applied to any concomitant loss of sensory function. Paralysis is a symptom rather than a disease.

paramedical 1 Pertaining to a person, such as a physiotherapist, associated with the medical profession in providing health care. 2 Refers to a person known as a paramedic, usually an ambulance crew member, who has advanced training in resuscitation.

parameter 1 An arbitrary *constant or *variable in a mathematical expression which gives rise to various cases of a particular phenomenon. 2 A quantity which is constant under a particular set of conditions but which differs with changing conditions.

parametric statistic Statistic which assumes that the sample has been drawn from a population which has a particular distribution (for example a normal distribution) and shares certain parameters (for example, equal *variances).

paranoia A mental disorder characterized by persistent delusions. The sufferer may show no symptoms of mental illness and apparently have an intact personality. The term is commonly applied more loosely to a person who feels unduly persecuted.

parasympathetic nervous system Part of the *autonomic nervous system which has *cholinergic nerve-endings. The parasympathetic system typically brings about opposite effects on the activity of *viscera to the *sympathetic nervous system. Most internal *organs are supplied with *nerves from the two systems. Whereas the parasympathetic nervous system helps to create the internal conditions found during rest, sleep, and digestion, the sympathetic nervous system prepares the body for physical activity.

paratenon Tissue between a *tendon sheath and its *tendon; the paratenon surrounds and nourishes the tendon.

parathormone (parathyroid hormone; PTH) A *hormone secreted by the *parathyroid gland that causes an increase in blood *calcium levels. Parathormone is needed to establish proper bone development.

parathyroid gland One of four small *endocrine glands, located on the posterior aspect of the *thyroid gland, which secrete parathormone.

parathyroid hormone *See* parathormone.

parenteral administration The application of a medicine or other substance by routes other than the mouth or rectum. The medicine is usually injected directly into a blood vessel.

parietal Pertaining to the walls of a cavity.

parietal pleura Thin *membrane lining the inner surface of the *thoracic wall; it secretes *serous fluid. *See also* pleura.

Parkinsonism *See* Parkinson's disease.

Parkinson's disease (Parkinsonism) A disease, usually of the middle-aged and elderly, affecting the *basal ganglia of the *brain. The disease is characterized by tremor, muscle rigidity, an expressionless face, and disturbance of gait, with a tendency to stoop. Parkinson's disease involves damage to the nerve pathway which uses *dopamine as a *neurotransmitter. Treatment aims to restore the balance between dopamine and acetylcholine pathways. Physical activity is an important element in treatment.

paronychia Inflammation and swelling of the tissue and skinfolds around a fingernail or toenail.

pars A specific part of an organ or structure.

partial dislocation *See* subluxation.

partial muscle-tear (muscle-pull; partial muscle-strain; pulled muscle) An injury of a *muscle in which only part of the muscle is damaged. Partial muscle-tear may occur deep in the *belly of the muscle itself (*see* intramuscular tear) or it may involve the *fascia (*see* interstitial tear). Bleeding tends to be slight but unless the blood can escape there is a build-up causing an *intramuscular haematoma.

partial pressure The pressure exerted by a single gas in a mixture of gases. It can be calculated by multiplying the total pressure of the mixture of gases within which the particular gas occurs, by the percentage of the total volume the gas occupies. Thus, if the normal pressure of the atmospheric gases is 760 mmHg and there is 21 per cent oxygen, the partial pressure of oxygen is $760 \times 0.21 =$ 160 mmHg.

participant observation A method of research in which the researcher becomes a participant in the social activity being investigated and adopts the role of a member of the group.

participatory-modelling A coaching technique in which a *model helps an athlete to achieve success. The subject first observes a model perform the task, then the model assists the subject to perform the task successfully; the subject is not permitted to fail. Participatory-modelling is used to promote strong feelings of *self-efficacy or confidence. *See also* Bandura's self-efficacy theory.

part-method of learning A method of *learning a *skill which can be subdivided into parts forming a natural and meaningful sequence. Each part is learned separately to a criterion and then an attempt made to join the parts together sequentially until they are combined to form the whole skill. The order in which they are learned and combined together usually follows the natural order in which they occur in the skill. *Compare* part-whole method of learning.

parturition The act of giving birth to an offspring.

part-whole method of learning *Learning technique in which the task to be learned is broken down into its parts for separate practices. The part-whole method is commonly used when parts do not form a natural and meaningful sequence of actions, and do not need to be practised together. They can be learned in any order, practised separately, and, once mastered, can be incorporated together in, for example, a game. *Compare* part-method of learning.

Pascal (Pa) The *SI unit of *pressure which is equivalent to 1 $\mathrm{N\,m^{-2}}$.

passive exercise (passive mobility exercise) An exercise performed on a subject by a partner who exerts an *external force not only to produce a *passive movement, but also to attempt to increase the *range of movement of a *joint. The partner presses the joint into its end-position (i.e., end of range) while the subject's muscles which normally carry out the movement are completely relaxed. There is a danger of over-extension beyond the range of movement and damage to the joint if the exercise is not carried out carefully. *See also* passive movement.

passive immunity A short-lived immunity resulting from the introduction of *antibodies obtained from an immune animal or a human donor.

passive insufficiency The inability of a *biarticulate muscle to be stretched enough to allow a full *range of movement in both *joints at the same time.

passive learning *See* incidental learning.

passive mobility exercise *See* passive exercise.

passive movement Any movement produced by a *force which is external to the *muscle or *muscle group normally responsible for the movement. Passive movements are used in the diagnosis of some sports injuries to distinguish between injuries of the muscle and the *ligaments of a joint.

passive PNF *See* proprioceptive neuromuscular facilitation.

passive smoking The inhalation of air containing tobacco smoke. Prolonged and frequent exposure to a smoke-filled room can have the same deleterious effects on physical performance as smoking cigarettes.

passive stability *Joint stability provided by passive forces, mainly from the *ligaments. *Compare* active stability.

passive transport The transport of substances across a cell membrane by processes that do not require cellular energy in the form of *adenosine triphosphate; examples of passive transport are *facilitated diffusion and *osmosis.

patella (kneecap) A small, lens-shaped *sesamoid bone situated in front of the knee in the *tendon of the *quadriceps muscle which is attached to the *tibia. The patella guards the *knee-joint anteriorly and improves the leverage of the thigh muscles acting at the joint. The patella is inadequately nourished and poorly protected, consequently it is very susceptible to injury.

patellar Pertaining to the front of the knee. *Compare* popliteal.

patellar ligament *See* patellar tendon.

patellar tendon (patellar ligament) A strong, flat ligamentous band which connects the apex of the *patella to the *tibia. Its central, superficial fibres, continuous with the *quadriceps tendon, cross the patella to insert the quadriceps onto the *tibial tuberosity.

patellitis A little-used term for patellar *tendinitis or jumper's knee; patellitis is an inflammation of the *patella commonly caused by a strain on its inferior border causing tenderness and swelling.

patellofemoral Pertaining to the area of the *femur adjacent to the *patella.

patellofemoral pain syndrome *See* chondromalacia patellae.

paternalism A system by which an organization deals with its members in a manner similar to that of a benevolent father dealing with a child. Paternalism is used widely in personal relationships including those between a coach and athletes.

path analysis A method of quantifying the relationship between *variables. A diagram, called a path diagram, is constructed using *regression analysis to show how the variables are assumed to affect each other. The assumptions can be tested by seeing if the relationships depicted on the diagram are compatible with observed data.

path–goal theory of leadership A theory of *leadership which can be applied to the coach–athlete relationship. The basic proposition of path–goal theory is that the function of the leader is to assist the follower to achieve his or her own goals. It hypothesizes an interaction between *leader or *coach and any situation (including both the personality characteristics of the subordinate and the environmental demands of a task), in which the emphasis is on the needs and goals of the *athlete. The coach is viewed as a facilitator helping the athlete to select worthwhile goals, and pointing out the 'path' to follow in order to reach the goals successfully. To be successful, the coach's behaviour must vary according to the situation.

pathogenic Applied to a microorganism which is capable of producing illness.

pathognomonic Applied to a *symptom or *sign which is characteristic of a specific *disease.

pathological condition A condition associated with *disease.

pathology A study of the nature of *diseases, especially how they affect the human body and what causes them.

pattern generator *See* central pattern generator.

Pavlovian conditioning *See* classical conditioning.

PC *See* phosphocreatine.

peak aerobic power *See* maximal aerobic power.

peak experience Rare moments of high happiness and fulfillment which are accompanied by loss of fears, inhibitions, and insecurities. Peak experiences occur during optimal performances and are marked by a heightened sense of awareness. Athletes generally report the experience as temporary, unique, and beyond one's control, and that it stands apart from normal happenings and experiences. The physiological basis of peak experience has not been analysed. *See also* flow; and runner's high.

peak force (peak torque) The maximum *force (in *newtons) or *torque (newton metres) developed during a muscular *contraction.

peak heart-rate The highest heart-rate during a specific activity.

peaking The process of achieving an optimal performance on a specific occasion. Ideally, peaking will occur on the very day, even the very minute, of an important competition. Peaking requires a thorough knowledge of *training and its effects on an individual athlete so that the training programme will produce the required response.

peak torque *See* peak force.

Pearson product moment correlation coefficient A *correlation coefficient (r) for use with *continuous variables with a normal distribution.

pectineus A short, flat *muscle of the medial compartment of the thigh. The pectineus has its *origin on the *pubic bone and its *insertion high on the *posterior surface of the *femur. It is one of the *adductor muscles. Its action causes *adduction, *flexion, and *lateral rotation of the thigh.

pectoral Pertaining to the chest.

pectoral girdle (shoulder-girdle) Bony structure which attaches the upper limbs to the *axial skeleton. The pectoral girdle consists of the right and left shoulder-blades (*see* scapula) and collar-bones (*see* clavicle).

pectoralis major Large, fan-shaped *muscle covering the upper portion of the chest and forming the anterior axillary fold. The *origins of the pectoralis major are on the *clavicle, *sternum, cartilage of ribs 1–6, and the *aponeurosis of the *external oblique muscles. Fibres from the muscle converge to insert by a short *tendon into the intertubercular *sulcus of the *humerus. The pectoralis major draws the arm forward and across the chest, and rotates the arm medially, movements which play an important part in climbing and throwing. When the *scapula and arm are fixed, the pectoralis major pulls the ribcage upwards, thereby contributing to inspiratory movements.

pectoralis minor A flat, thin *muscle of the *anterior *thorax which has its *origin on the anterior surface of ribs 3–5 and its *insertion on the *coracoid process of the *scapula. When the ribs are fixed, the pectoralis minor draws the scapula forward and downward. With the scapula fixed, the muscle draws the *ribcage superiorly.

pectoral muscles Two pairs of muscles which control the movements of the upper arm and shoulder. *See also* pectoralis major; and pectoralis minor.

pectorals *See* pectoralis major; and pectoralis minor.

peer group A group of individuals sharing the same *status.

peer group interaction The social exchanges which occur between individuals with the same status. Peer group interaction usually refers to the interactions of children and adolescents within groups of their own age.

pellagra A disease due to a deficiency of *niacin. Early signs of the disease include listlessness, headache, and weight loss, which progresses to soreness of the tongue, nausea, vomiting, and photosensitive dermatitis. These ulcerated skin and neurological symptoms are sometimes referred to as the 'four Ds'—dermatitis, dementia, diarrhoea, and death.

pelvic girdle Bony structure which consists of the paired *coxal bones that attach the lower limbs by very strong ligaments to the *axial skeleton. There are male and female differences in the structure of the pelvic girdle related to child-bearing.

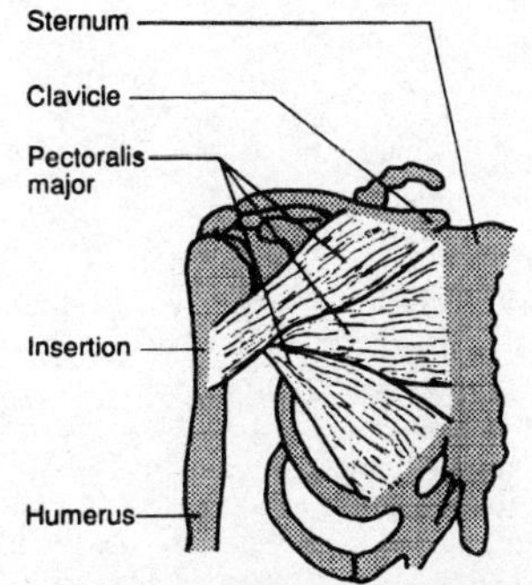

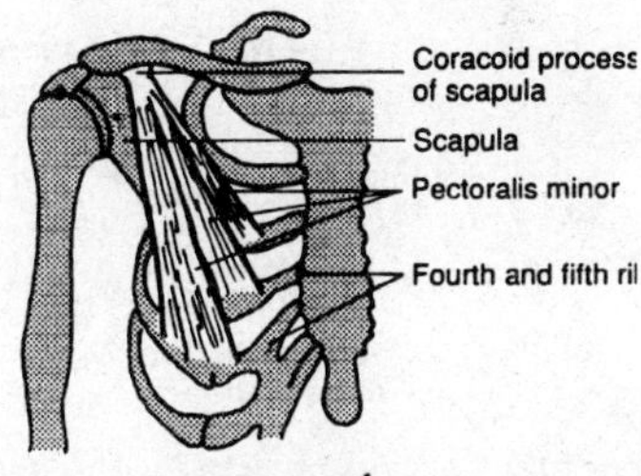

pectorals

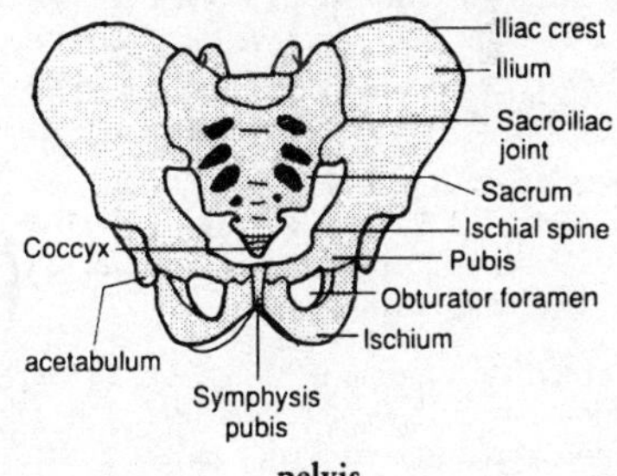

pelvis

pelvis A deep, basin-like bony structure formed by the two *coxal bones together with the *sacrum and *coccyx. The pelvis forms the lower portion of the trunk. A male pelvis (ventral view) is illustrated above.

pemoline A *drug belonging to the *stimulants which are on the *IOC list of *banned substances.

penbutolol A *drug belonging to the *beta blockers which are on the *IOC list of *banned substances.

pendular model. A model of *group cohesion which suggests that the amount of cohesion oscillates in a pendular fashion throughout a group's existence. For example, an American football team may have high cohesion when it first meets; the cohesion is reduced due to competition among players for selection to the final cut; and then cohesion rises again after the selection has been made prior to the first match.

pendular motion The regular swinging or oscillating movements of a body suspended from a fixed point. A form of pendular motion is exhibited in running. It is very complex, not only because it consists of three links in simultaneous rotation and translation, but also because it depends on the speed of other links in the *kinetic chain, and on *external forces and their *torques.

pendular period (period) The time taken for one complete to and fro movement of a vibration or oscillation.

pendulous abdomen The hanging downwards of the abdomen over the pelvis, usually due to weakness and lack of firmness of the abdominal muscles.

pendulum A body suspended from a fixed point so that it is free to swing or oscillate with a known *pendular period. *See also* double pendulum.

penicillin *Antibiotic formed by the fungi belonging to the genus *Penicillium* . Penicillin is used to treat a wide range of bacterial infections. Some people are allergic to penicillin and may develop painful rashes, swelling of the throat, and fever.

penicillinase An *enzyme produced by penicillin-resistant bacteria that breaks down *penicillin.

penis Male organ of reproduction and urination through which semen and urine pass.

pennate muscle (penniform muscle) Flat muscle with fibres arranged around a central *tendon, like the barbs of a feather. Pennate muscles have a very limited range of movement but they are very strong and powerful. Pennate muscle may be unipennate, when the *fascicles insert into only one side of the tendon (e.g., *extensor digitorum longus); bipennate, if the fascicles insert into the tendon from opposite sides so that the muscle appears externally to ressemble a feather (e.g., *rectus femoris); or multipennate, where muscle fibres converge onto several tendons, giving a herringbone appearance (e.g., the *deltoid muscle).

penniform muscle *See* pennate muscle.

pentazocine A *drug belonging to the *narcotic analgesics which are on the *IOC list of *banned substances. It is similar to *morphine and used for the treatment of moderate to severe pain.

pentetrazol A *drug belonging to the *stimulants which are on the *IOC list of *banned substances.

pentose–phosphate cycle *See* hexose monophosphate shunt.

pep pills Artificial *stimulants taken orally in order to improve physical and mental performance. *Drugs used as pep pills include *amphetamines, *caffeine, and *epinephrin.

pepsin An *enzyme present in *gastric juice which catalyses the breakdown of *protein in an *acid medium.

pep talk A *motivational strategy aimed at heightening *arousal. Pep talks are usually given prior to *competition or during an interval in play. They are a characteristic feature of managerial talks to soccer teams before a game and at half-time. Exhortations to try harder may help some athletes to reach an *optimal level of arousal, but may cause others to become overaroused.

peptic ulcer An *ulcer located in the *stomach or in the first part of the *duodenum. The ulcer is caused by digestion of the lining of the digestive tract by *pepsin and acids. Athletes with peptic ulcers, or other gastrointestinal ulcers, should be cautious about taking physical exercise until the ulcers have healed completely. *Anticholinergics, used to treat ulcers, may adversely effect vision and the ability to judge distances which may effect an athlete's performance.

peptide A chemical compound formed by the union of two or more *amino acids.

peptide bond Bond (O=C–NH–) joining the amine group of one *amino acid to the acid *carboxyl group of a second amino acid with the loss of a water molecule. *See also* protein.

peptide hormones and analogues A pharmacological class of agents which are banned by the *IOC (*see* doping class). The class includes *chorionic gonadotrophin, *corticotrophin, *erythropoietin, and *growth hormone. All the respective *releasing factors of these *hormones are also banned.

perceived ability An individual's assessment of his or her own ability. In sport, perceived ability is regarded as a major construct of *achievement behaviour and an important mediator of *motivation. Individuals who perceive themselves as having high ability tend to be more motivated towards that area of activity than those who perceive themselves as having low ability.

perceived competence scale for children (PCSC) A scale developed by Susan Harter which assesses a child's perceived competence in three domains: cognitive (school competence), social (peer-related competence), and physical (skill at sport). Results from several sport-related studies using the scale have provided support for this scale and for *Harter's competence motivation theory.

perceived contingency Situation in which a person feels that a future behaviour depends on current behaviours and rewards.

perceived exertion An individual's subjective assessment of how hard he or she has worked during exercise. Ratings have been devised by the Swedish physiologist, Gunnar Borg, to quantify the perceived exertions. One such rating consists of 15 grades from very, very light exertion to very, very hard exertion. In many situations, the rating mirror's the individual's heart-rate.

perceived importance The importance an athlete assigns to the *outcome of a performance. The perceived importance is strongly affected by the presence of *significant others and their perception of the importance of the event. Perceived importance has an important affect on *anxiety levels. Several *stress management techniques are aimed at reducing the perceived importance of an event.

perceived success A performer's own assessment of whether he or she has achieved *goals. *See also* perceived ability.

percentage saturation of haemoglobin The amount of oxygen combined with *haemoglobin, divided by the oxygen capacity of haemoglobin, expressed as a percentage. *See also* oxygen dissociation curve.

perception The mental process by which the *brain interprets and gives meaning to the information which it receives from the *sense-organs. Perception depends on both the psychological and physiological characteristics of the perceiver, in addition to the nature of the *stimuli.

perceptual ability The ability to be able to deal with, and give meaning to, sensory *stimuli.

perceptual anticipation A form of anticipation in which temporal predictions are made when a subject cannot measure the true passage of time. Perceptual anticipation is thought to depend on an internal biological clock. An athlete able to run at a regular pace may use internal feedback from his or her limbs to keep track of the time (*see* pace judgement).

perceptual motor *See* motor.

perceptual motor skill learning Acquisition of *skill in which movement is an important part. The term emphasizes that the process depends on the perceptual mechanisms which deal with the sensory input, the mental processes which select and control the movement, and the muscle effectors which carry out the movements.

perceptual narrowing *See* narrowing.

perceptual skill A *motor skill which is dependent on high *perceptual ability. Perceptual skills are particularly important in sports, such as basketball and tennis, in which the performer has to be able to adapt his or her skills to a changing environment. There are close similarities between a perceptual skill, an *externally paced skill, and an *open skill. *See also* habitual skill.

percussion The tapping of a body-part with a hammer or the fingers to gain information about the condition of underlying structures.

perforation The formation of a hole in an organ or tissue, as in a burst eardrum. Causes include disease and physical trauma, such as a deep penetrating wound.

performance **1** The observable act of carrying out a process, such as a *motor skill, which may vary according to circumstances, motivation, mood, etc. (*See* performance model.) **2** The manner or quality of carrying out an activity, including sporting activity. *Compare* learning. *See also* performance curve.

performance curve A plot of the average level of *performance of a group of subjects for each of a number of practice trials or blocks of trials. Graphs of changes in peformance plotted against time are often used to estimate changes in *learning but the level of performance will fluctuate from time to time due to *performance variables such as *fatigue, *motivation, and *boredom, even when no changes in learning have taken place. *See also* learning curve.

performance dependence A situation in which a person is dependent on the *performance of another person to reach a particular *goal. In netball, for example, a shooter relies on team-mates to provide a pass before being able to score a net.

performance goal A desire or objective to improve the level of personal performance at a task (as opposed to an outcome relative to others) which is observable, measurable, and relatively independendent of the actions of others. *See also* goal; goal-setting; and outcome.

performance plateau *See* arrested progress; and plateau.

performance ratio The level of a *performance of one group expressed as a the ratio of the level of performance of another group for the same observable, measurable activity. Such performance ratios have been used to examine the effect of gender on performances in each event of athletics, by dividing the women's world record by the men's world record.

performance variable An *independent variable that affects performance only temporarily and does not affect *learning of the task.

perfusion The flow of fluid, usually blood, through the vessel of an organ.

pericardial fluid A thin film of fluid contained within the *pericardium which prevents friction between the inner and outer surfaces of the pericardium as the heart beats.

pericardium A double-layered envelope surrounding the *heart which prevents overextension during heart beats.

pericarditis Inflammation of the membranes surrounding the heart usually caused by bacteria or viruses, but which may be linked with *rheumatic fever. The pericardial cavity swells with fluid, constricting the heart. Symptoms include pain in the chest, anxiety, and fear. Physical activity should be avoided until the inflammation is completely resolved, and then activity should be resumed only with medical guidance. *See also* myocarditis.

perichondrium Dense, fibrous, *connective tissue *membrane covering the external surface of cartilaginous structures.

perimysium A *connective tissue *sheath surrounding a bundle of *muscle fibres in a *fasciculum and segregating it from the rest of a *muscle.

perineal In anatomy, pertaining to the region between the *anus and the external genitalia.

perineum Region of the body between the muscular floor of the pelvis and the thighs, containing the *anal canal and external genitalia.

period *See* pendular period.

periodic motion A motion that repeats itself. *See also* harmonic motion; and oscillation.

periodization The organization of the training year into different periods to attain different objectives. There are a number of different schemes of periodization, but one commonly used divides the year into three periods: *preparation period, *competition period, and *transition period. Each period may be subdivided into three phases. Some training programmes adopt a double periodization involving two cycles of the periods in one year, and in others one cycle lasts 2 to 4 years (for example, when preparing for the Olympic Games) or even longer.

periosteal Pertaining to the periosteum.

periosteal ossification The growth of *bone by proliferation of *osteocytes from *osteoblasts in the inner layer of the *periosteum.

periosteum A glistening-white, double-layered *membrane of *connective tissue covering the outer surface of *bone. It is composed of an outer fibrous layer containing dense, irregular connective tissue and an inner layer of bone-forming cells called *osteoblasts. The periosteum is richly supplied with *nerve fibres, *lymph vessels, and *blood vessels. It is secured to the underlying bone by *Sharpey's fibres which are exceptionally dense where the peristoeum provides anchoring points for *tendons and *ligaments.

periostitis *Inflammation of the *periosteum covering any *bone. It is usually due to severe *strain at the *tendon *insertions where the *muscle fibres or muscle tendons either pull, stretch, or tear. Periostitis of the lower leg is particularly common in athletes who change from one playing surface to another, or who change techniques or equipment. *See also* shin splints.

peripheral nervous system (PNS) That part of the nervous system derived from the *cranial nerves, the *spinal nerves, and the *autonomic nervous system. *Compare* central nervous system.

peripheral resistance A measure of the amount of opposition encountered by *blood as it flows through the *blood vessels. It is the sum of all the regional individual resistances to arterial blood as it passes through the many and varied circuits on its way to the body organs and tissues. Peripheral resistance is caused by *friction between the blood and the walls of the blood vessels. It varies inversely to the fourth power of the radius of a vessel. Thus, if the radius is halved, resistance increases sixteenfold enabling substantial bloodflow changes to be effected by relatively small adjustments in the radius of the vessels (*see* shunting). It is an important indicator of *cardiovascular fitness. Experimental evidence indicates that physical training can favourably and significantly lower the total peripheral resistance, reducing the load on the heart.

peristalsis Progressive, rhythmic, wave-like contractions of *smooth muscle that move food through the *alimentary canal, or that move other substances through other hollow body organs.

peritendinitis *Inflammation of the soft *paratenon which causes *pain and swelling around a *tendon, such as the *Achilles tendon. Peritendinitis is a very disabling condition commonly associated with over-use. It is important for the injury to heal completely before training is resumed. If an athlete continues to train while suffering from peritendinitis, *acute peritendinitis can develop into *chronic peritendinitis. The injury may result in *scarring which increases the thickness of the paratenon, reduces *mobility, and may require surgery to correct. *See also* tenosynovitis.

peritendinitis crepitans Inflammation of the sheath around the tendon which has not been caused by *trauma (that is, it has been caused by *friction or over-use).

peritoneum A *membrane lining the interior of the *abdominal cavity and surrounding its organs.

pernicious anaemia A progressive decrease in the number, but an increase in the size, of red blood cells. Pernicious anaemia is due to a lack of vitamin B_{12} . In addition to the symptoms of other forms of *anaemia, sufferers of pernicious anaemia often have a sore tongue, fever, and abdominal pain.

peroneal Pertaining to the outer (fibular) side of the leg.

peroneal nerve (common peroneal nerve) A *nerve derived from the *sciatic nerve. The peroneal nerve divides into the superficial and deep peroneal nerves which supply the *muscles in the lateral anterior compartment of the lower leg, and some of the skin in the lower leg and foot.

peroneal tendinitis A form of *shin splint and a cause of *pain in front of the leg. Peroneal tendinitis is an *inflammation of the *sheath of the *peroneal tendons below the *ankle-bone on the outer side of ankle.

peroneal tendon A *tendon of the *peroneus brevis muscle.

peroneus brevis Muscle of the lateral compartment of the leg, lying deep to *peroneus longus. It has its *origin on the *distal fibula shaft and its *insertion by a *tendon (the peroneal tendon) running behind the *lateral malleolus to insert on the *proximal end of the fifth *metatarsal. The peroneus brevis acts as a *plantar flexor and foot *evertor.

peroneus longus A *superficial muscle of the lateral compartment of the leg which overlies the *fibula. The peroneus longus has its *origin on the head and upper portion of the fibula, and its *insertion by a long *tendon that curves under the foot to the first *metatarsal. Its actions include *plantar flexion and foot *eversion, and it helps to keep the foot flat on the ground.

peroneus tertius A small muscle, not always present, of the anterior compartment of the leg. The muscle is usually fused and continuous with the *distal part of the *extensor digitorum longus. It has its *origin on the *distal anterior surface of the *fibula and *interosseus membrane, and its *insertion on the *dorsum of the fifth *metatarsal. It dorsiflexes and everts the foot (*see* dorsiflexion; and eversion).

peroral By mouth.

personal attribute Physical and psychological characteristics of an individual.

Personal attribute questionnaire (PAQ) A *questionnaire used to measure a person's perceived sex-role; that is, the person's perception of his or her *masculinity or *femininity. The results of the questionnaire suggest that athletes differ in *achievement motivation consistent with differences in perceived sex-role.

personality The sum total of an individual's characteristic patterns of *behaviour, and the relatively stable and enduring organization of character, temperament, intellect, and physique that contribute to that person's uniqueness. Personality is sometimes viewed as consisting of three levels: the *psychological core, *typical responses, and *role-related behaviour. *See also* personality trait; and personality structure.

personality development An area of *sport psychology which includes the study of the genetic and environmental processes that influence *personality.

personality dynamics The study of the ways in which an individual's various characteristics interact and operate to influence behaviour. *Sports psychologists have been particularly interested in how *anxiety levels interact with *achievement motivation to influence behaviour or performance.

personality profile *See* psychological profile.

personality structure The basic psychological components or traits of an individual's *personality and the way in which they combine together to produce that individual's particular behavioural tendencies in certain situations. *See also* personality traits.

personality trait Relatively general and enduring personal characteristics which predispose a person to think and behave in certain ways in given situations.

personology The study of *personality.

perspiration *See* sweating.

Perthes' disease (pseudocoxalgia) Deformity of the hip in which the head of the *femur is deformed causing aching and a limp. The condition is named after G. C. Perthes (1869–1927), a German orthopaedic surgeon. It may be caused by an injury disturbing the blood supply. Perthes' disease occurs mostly in children between the ages of 3 and 10 years with a peak between 6 and 8; it is more common in boys than girls. *See also* osteochondritis.

pertinence model A model of *selective attention which suggests that all *stimuli are analysed but only the most relevant are attended to. *Compare* Triesman model.

pertussis *See* whooping cough.

pes The foot or a structure ressembling the foot.

pes anserine A division of the facial nerve which has the appearance of a bird's claw.

pes cavus A high-arched or 'supinated' foot. *See also* claw foot.

pes malleus valgus *See* hammer toe.

pes planus (flat foot) A physical defect of the foot characterized by a lowering of the longitudinal arch (*see* arch) so that the sole lies flat upon the ground and the foot becomes elongated. The gripping action of the toes is reduced or lost causing mechanical problems during walking and running.

pethidine A synthetic *drug belonging to the *narcotic analgesics which are on the *IOC list of *banned substances.

petrissage A form of *massage in which the masseur kneads muscles by applying pressure into a *muscle rather than along it. The massage is applied by grasping or picking up the muscle tissue then compressing, pinching, and rolling it.

PFK *See* phosphofructokinase.

pH A measure of the relative acidity or alkalinity of a solution expressed in terms of the *reciprocal of its *hydrogen ion concentration ($pH = \log_{10}(1/H)$ where H is the hydrogen ion concentration in $mol\,l^{-1}$). A pH of 7 indicates neutrality, values above 7 indicate alkalinity, and those below 7 indicate acidity.

phagocyte A cell capable of engulfing and digesting particles or other cells.

phagocytosis The act of engulfing foreign solids by cells.

phalanges (sing. phalanx) The bones of the fingers and toes. Each toe and finger contains three bones except the big toe (the hallux) and the thumb (the pollex) which have two bones each. The phalanges of the toes are smaller than those of the fingers and are consequently less nimble.

phantom (reference human; unisex reference human) A hypothetical human which is used as a model for assessing human proportionality, particularly in *élite athletes. The unisex phantom is defined by designated *body length, *body girth, *body breadth and *skinfold measurements, and has an arbitrary *stature of 1.7018 m and a *body-mass of 64.58 *kg.

pharmacokinetics The mathematical study of the time courses of *absorption, distribution, and *excretion of *drugs in the human body.

pharmacology The study of the properties of *drugs and their modes of action, uses, and side-effects on the human body.

pharmocopoeia A book containing an official list of the *drugs used in *medicine, together with information about their purity, and physical and chemical properties.

pharyngitis (sore throat) Inflammation of the throat. Pharyngitis is often caused by a virus infection. Symptoms include pain, fever, and difficulty in swallowing. Physical exertion should be avoided while symptoms persist to avoid delaying the healing process and avoid the risk of complications.

pharynx Muscular tube lined with *mucus membrane extending from the region *posterior to the nasal cavities to the *oesophagus. The pharynx acts as an airway, a conduit for food, and a resonating chamber for the sounds generated by the *larynx.

phase Period of the year during which there is a particular training emphasis dependent on the specific requirements of the sport. Commonly-used phases include *preparatory phase; *competition phase; and the *transition phase. *See also* periodization; and training.

phasic stretch A type of stretch imposed on a *muscle by a *load which affects the rate or *velocity of change in *muscle fibre length. *Compare* tonic stretch.

phasing The temporal structure of a sequence of *muscle contractions needed to perform a *skill; phasing is usually measured by the ratios of the duration of the component elements of a movement and the overall duration of the movement.

phenazocine A *drug belonging to the *narcotic analgesics which are on the *IOC list of *banned substances. It is an addictive.

phendimetrazine A *drug belonging to the *stimulants which are on the *IOC list of *banned substances.

phenmetrazine A *drug belonging to the *stimulants which are on the *IOC list of *banned substances.

phenomenon Anything capable of being perceived by human senses.

phenomenology A philosophical approach which concentrates on the detailed description of conscious experiences. Supporters of this approach do not deny objective reality but emphasize the importance of each person's unique subjective experience of events on the way he or she reacts to those events.

phenoperidine A *drug belonging to the *narcotic analgesics which are on the *IOC list of *banned substances.

phenotype The observable characteristics of an individual, determined by both the *genotype and *environment.

phentermine A *drug belonging to the *stimulants which are on the *IOC list of *banned substances.

phenylalenine An *essential amino acid found in beans and other legumes, and in corn and other grains. *Tyrosine may substitute for phenylalenine.

phenylbutazone A *nonsteroidal anti-inflammatory *drug introduced in 1949 for the treatment of *arthritis. Phenylbutazone is an *analgesic used to relieve pain in rheumatic and related conditions. It is a powerful drug but it has a number of side-effects. Some fatalities have been associated with its use, as a result of which its use has been restricted. Many physicians believe it is a very useful drug, and it has been used to treat a number of conditions including *ankylosing spondylitis. Other physicians think that it is too dangerous for use on humans although it has been used considerably in a form known as 'bute' for the treatment of soft tissue injuries of horses in equestrian sports. The governing bodies of these sports exclude its use on or immediately before competition days.

phenylephrine A *drug belonging to the *stimulants which are on the *IOC list of *banned substances.

phenylpropanolamine A *drug belonging to the *stimulants which are on the *IOC list of *banned substances. It has actions similar to those of *ephedrine.

phlebitis Inflammation of the wall of a *vein marked by pain and tenderness. It commonly occurs in the legs as a complication of *varicose veins. *Thromboses sometimes develop.

phobia A strong but apparently irrational fear, such as a fear of open spaces or a fear of standing in a high place even though there is no danger of falling.

pholcodine A *drug which is a common ingredient of cough medicines. It belongs to the *narcotic analgesics which are on the *IOC list of *banned substances.

phonocardiogram Recording of the sounds made by the heart during a *cardiac cycle. The sounds are thought to result from vibrations created by closure of the *heart valves. There are at least two: the first when the *atrioventricular valves close at the beginning of *systole, and the second when the *aortic valve closes at the end of systole.

phonophoresis A technique whereby whole molecules of *medication are driven through the skin into underlying tissues by *ultrasound.

phosphagen A group of energy-rich *phosphate *compounds; collectively refers to *adenosine triphosphate and *creatine phosphate.

phosphagen system *See* ATP–PC system.

phosphatidyl choline A *phospholipid found in the *membrane of cells.

phosphocreatine An energy-rich compound used in the production of *ATP from *ADP in muscle. The breakdown of creatine phosphate to creatine and inorganic phosphate is an *exergonic reaction coupled to the synthesis of ATP. *See also* ATP–PC system.

phosphoenolypyruvic acid An *organic acid which plays an important role in *glycolysis.

phosphofructokinase (PFK) An *enzyme which plays a key part in *glycolysis when a *phosphate of glucose is converted to a phosphate of *fructose. Phosphofructokinase activity is particularly important in power events, such as sprinting, where glycolysis must take place several hundred times faster than at rest. The concentration of the enzyme is higher in the muscle cells of sprinters than endurance athletes. *See also* fast twitch fibres.

phospholipid An organic *compound consisting of a *hydrophobic tail of two chains of *fatty acid, and a *hydrophilic head of *glycerol and *phosphate. Phospholipid is a major component of all cell *membranes, and is involved in *fat transport in *blood and *lymph. Phospholipids are also involved in many *metabolic reactions. Examples include *cephalins and *lecithins.

phosphorous A nonmetallic element which is an essential component of the diet. Phosphorous is a constituent of many vital compounds including *adenosine triphosphate, *deoxyribonucleic acid, and *phospholipids but it is mainly concentrated in the *bones. *Vitamin D and *calcium regulate the availability of phosphorous for bone formation. The *RDA for phosphorus is 800 mg. Most foods which are rich in *protein such as meat, fish, and legumes are usually also rich in phosphorous. Phosphorous deficiencies lead to *rickets and poor growth.

phosphorylase An *enzyme which plays a key part in regulating *glycolysis in *muscle cells. It catalyses the conversion of *glycogen to a *phosphate of *glucose. Phosphorylase is activated during exercise by increased amounts of *AMP, *calcium, and *epinephrine from the *adrenal glands.

phosphorylation Addition of one or more *phosphate groups to a molecule.

photophobia An intolerance of the eye to light due to systemic or environmental causes. An athlete suffering from photophobia is often helpless under stadium lights or in bright sunlight. *See also* photosensitivity; and snow-blindness.

photoreceptor A specialized *receptor that responds to light energy (e.g., a *rod or *cone in the *retina of the eye).

photosensitivity A heightened sensitivity to light which can be caused by certain *medications or chemicals. *See also* photophobia.

phototoxicity *Toxic reaction, provoked by light.

phrenic 1 Pertaining to the mind. 2 Pertaining to the diaphragm.

phrenic nerve One of a pair of *nerves which supply the muscles of the *diaphragm.

physical Pertaining to the body rather than the mind.

physical conditioning *See* conditioning.

physical culture The sum total of a *society's activities and attitudes connected with physical development and education.

physical dependence A state in which an abrupt termination of the administration of a *drug produces a series of unpleasant symptoms known as the *abstinence syndrome. The symptoms are rapidly reversed after readministration of the drug. *See also* dependence.

physical education 1 Any planned programme of motor activities that help individuals to develop and control their bodies. Physical education is a process through which favourable adaptation and learning (organic, neuromuscular, intellectual, social, cultural, emotional, and aesthetic) result from and proceed through, fairly vigorous physical activity. 2 A formal area of educational activity in which the main concern is with bodily movements and which takes place in an eductional establishment. *See also* physical recreation; play; and sport.

physical fitness The ability of a person to function efficiently and effectively, to enjoy *leisure, to be *healthy, to resist *hypokinetic disease, and to cope with emergency situations. The health-related components of physical fitness include *body composition, *cardiovascular fitness, *flexibility, *muscular endurance, and *strength. *Skill-related components include *agility, *balance, *co-ordination, *power, *reaction time, and *speed.

physical recreation Physical activity which is pursued for enjoyment and in order to refresh health or spirits. Physical recreation is usually more purposeful and planned than *play, but it tends to have a limited organizational structure. Some highly-competitive and organized sports are pursued as physical recreation, but the main purpose of the person taking part is to gain refreshment and not to compete. *See also* leisure; and sport.

physical sign A *sign that can be detected by a physician during observation or examination of an individual.

physical work capacity The maximum amount of *work a person can perform. Physical work capacity is usually related to a specific *heart-rate and it is used as a measure of *aerobic fitness.

physician A registered practicioner of medicine who diagnoses and treats physical diseases and injuries.

physics The study of the properties of *matter and *energy.

physiological Pertaining to *physiology.

physiological age *See* age.

physiological arousal (anatomical arousal) *Anxiety or *arousal which manifests itself in physiological changes such as an increased *heart-rate and *sweating. *See also* cognitive anxiety.

physiological cross-section The area of a *transverse section of *muscle. There is a direct correlation between physiological cross-section and the number of *muscle fibres contained within a muscle. Muscle force is dependent on its physiological cross-section, with maximum force being approximately $80\,N\,cm^{-2}$.

physiological dead space The volume of *alveolar space which is underventilated. *Compare* anatomical dead space.

physiological drive A state of *arousal which stems from biological needs such as the need for food and the need for sleep. *See also* primary drive.

physiological fatigue Reduction in the capacity of the *neuromuscular system to carry out its functions as the result of physical overwork and strain. *Compare* psychological fatigue. *See also* fatigue.

physiological functions Processes which are carried out by the *organs, *tissues, and *cells to maintain health. Major physiological functions include *respiration, *co-ordination, *excretion, *circulation, and *reproduction.

physiological limit Level of performance beyond which, by reason of physical limitation, an individual cannot go. In ordinary circumstances individuals do not reach their physiological limit although it might be approached in the heat of competition when *motivation is very high. Often, *arrested progress occurs when people believe they have reached their physiological limit.

physiological response The reaction of the physiological system to a *stressor.

physiological testing Tests designed to measure a specific *physiological function that is thought to be a primary determinant in the performance outcome of a sport. Physiological testing is used to monitor progress of an athlete and provide *feedback; to *compare* different groups of individuals; and to *compare* different training procedures. Physiological testing is generally a poor predictor of future performance since this will be determined by a complex of factors of which physiological function is only one.

physiology The study of the functioning of normal, healthy organisms and their body-structures. *Compare* pathology.

physiotherapy Use of physical methods (such as heat massage, exercise, and electricity) to assist recovery of damaged tissue.

physique The characteristic appearance or physical power of an individual. *See also* somatotype.

pi Symbol of the ratio of the circumference of any circle to its diameter; its approximate value is 3.142.

Piagetian Applied to theories, particularly of cognitive development, proposed by the psychologist Jean Piaget (1896–1980). Although he did not deny the effects of environment on the cognitive development of a child, Piaget emphasized the role of innate mechanisms. He suggested that development took place in a series of stages with each stage being the foundation of the next.

pia mater A thin *membrane or *meninge containing *blood vessels and surrounding the *brain and *spinal cord.

pica Craving for substances not normally considered *nutrients.

pie chart (pie graph) A diagrammatic representation of the proportions of an identifiable whole in which a circle is divided into sections proportional to the magnitude of the quantities represented.

pie graph *See* pie chart.

pigeon-toed An abnormal inward turning of the feet so that the toes of one foot point toward the toes of the other foot. It is often asociated with *genu valgum (or knock knees), and causes biomechanical inefficiencies during walking and running.

pill A tablet or capsule containing one or more *drugs and sometimes coated with sugar. Pills are taken orally.

pilot-study A small-scale version of a planned investigation used to test its feasibility and design, and to identify problems.

pindolol A *drug belonging to the *beta blockers which are on the *IOC list of *banned substances.

pinna (auricle) The flap of tissue projecting from the *external ear.

pinocytosis A method of transporting extracellular fluid through cell *membranes by active engulfment into the *cytoplasm.

pipradol A *drug belonging to the *stimulants which are on the *IOC list of *banned substances.

pirbuterol A *drug belonging to the *stimulants which are on the *IOC list of *banned substances.

pirertenide A *drug belonging to the *diuretics which are on the *IOC list of *banned substances.

piriformis A pear-shaped *muscle located on the *posterior aspect of the hip, *inferior to the *gluteus minimus. The *origin of the piriformis goes through the greater *sciatic notch to attach onto the anterolateral surface of the *sacrum; its *insertion is on the *superior border of *greater trochanter of the *femur. The actions of the piriformis muscle include lateral rotation of the thigh; it also assists in thigh *abduction when the hip is flexed, and helps to stabilize the hip-joint.

piroxicam An anti-inflammatory drug or *NSAID which is used in the treatment of *musculoskeletal injuries. In the past there was some concern that piroxicam might cause *ulcers to develop more than aspirin-like drugs. However, the Committee on Safety of Medicine, and the Drug Surveillance Unit in Britain concluded that large and chemically-important differences in the rate of gastrointestinal bleeding, perforation, and ulceration between piroxicam and aspirin-like drugs probably do not exist.

pisiform bone A small pea-shaped *bone in the wrist which articulates directly with the *triquetral bone and indirectly via *cartilage with the *ulna.

pitcher's elbow *See* thrower's elbow.

pitching moment *See* centre of pressure.

pituitary gland *Endocrine gland which co-ordinates the activities of many other endocrine glands. The pituitary gland is derived from, and attached to, the base of the *brain. *Hormones produced by the pituitary include *ACTH, *FSH, *thyrotropin, and *growth hormone from the anterior lobes, and *ADH and *oxytocin from the posterior lobes.

pivot A short shaft or pin supporting something that turns a *fulcrum.

pivot-joint (trochoides; trochoid joint) A ring-shaped joint which allows only *uniaxial *rotation of one bone around or against another (e.g., the *atlantoaxial joint and the *radioulnar joint).

placebo Substance or situation that should not have a beneficial effect on performance but that may do so, possibly as a result of

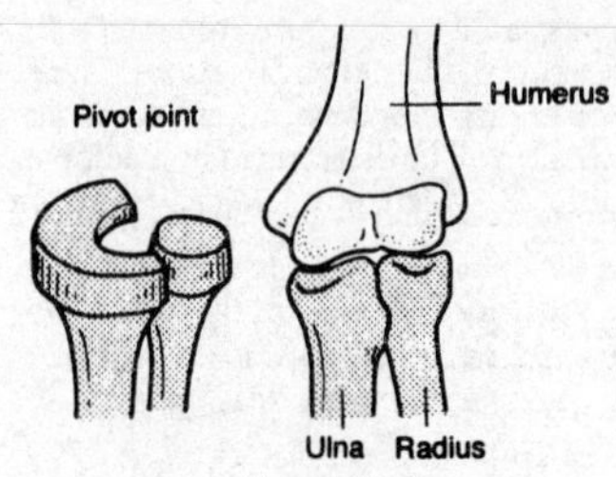

pivot joint

suggestion, but for no other known biochemical or physical explanation. Placebos are used in *drug experiments to prevent subjects knowing whether they have been given a drug or a *control substance and thereby distributing evenly the suggestive effect of taking the drug. Neither the investigator nor subject knows which is the placebo and which the genuine drug (*see* double-blind).

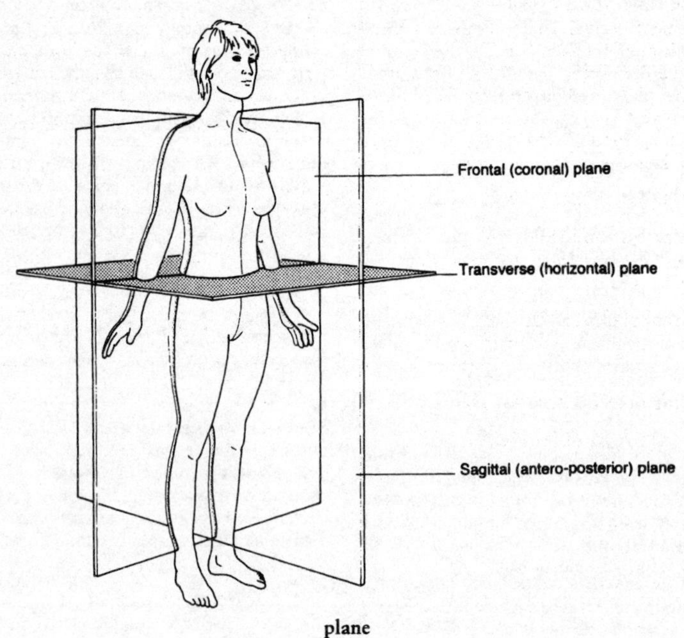

plane

placebo effect A response to a *placebo as if it were an active substance. The placebo effect is well established and is used as an *ergogenic aid. Placebo salves with no pharmacologically-active ingredients have been used to relieve *muscle fatigue, for example.

plane A level surface in which a straight line joining any two of its points lies entirely on that surface. It is applied especially to any of the hypothetical flat surfaces used to divide the human body (e.g., *frontal plane, the *sagittal plane, and the *transverse plane).

plane-joint A *non-axial joint in which the *articular surface is flat or only slightly curved. A plane-joint theoretically allows slipping or gliding movements of one bone on another in all directions, including twisting. However, because such joints are bound tightly in a *ligament, movement is limited (e.g., to back and forth or sliding movements). *See also* intercarpal joint; intertarsal joint; and sternoclavicular joint.

plane of motion A body *plane in which movement occurs. Three planes of motion pass through the human body: the *sagittal or anteroposterior plane, the *frontal or coronal plane, and the horizontal or *transverse plane. They are the basic references for describing motion. However, motion may also take place through an *oblique plane.

plantar Pertaining to the sole of the foot.

plantar aponeurosis A thin, strong fibrous sheet running forward from the *calcaneus to the toes.

plantar arch The arch-shaped arrangement of the interconnecting branches of the plantar arteries on the sole of the foot.

plantar arterial arch *See* plantar arch.

plantar eversion *See* eversion of foot.

plantar fascia A thick, band of tissue along the sole of the foot. Undue stress to this area from running or jumping can cause *plantar fasciitis.

plantar fasciitis An inflammation of the *plantar fascia at its attachment to the heel-bone. Plantar fasciitis is characterized by a gnawing pain or discomfort in the heel that radiates along the sole of the foot. It may also be caused by a partial tear of the fascia in the arch of the foot. Plantar fasciitis is most commonly associated with the pes-planus-type of foot.

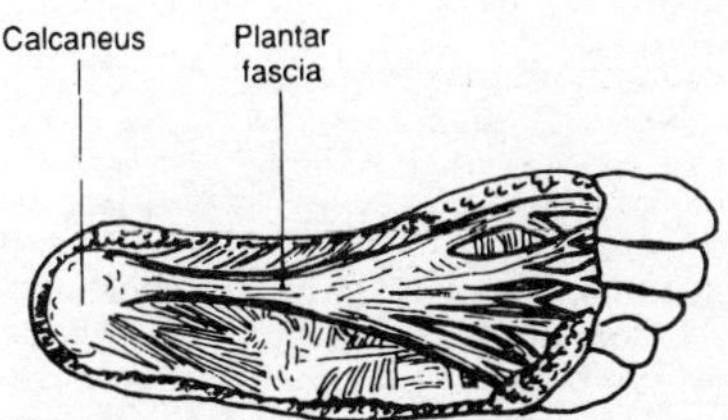

plantar fascia

plantar flexion A movement which results in the toes being pointed downwards by *extension or straightening of the ankle. Plantar flexion is accomplished by *plantar flexor muscles. *Compare* dorsiflexion.

plantar flexors Muscles of the posterior and lateral compartment of the leg which act in concert to flex the ankle and point the toes downwards. The following muscles can all act as plantar flexors; the *gastrocnemius, *soleus, *tibialis posterior, *flexor digitorum longus, *flexor hallucis longus, *peroneus longus, and *peroneus brevis.

plantaris A small and feeble muscle of the posterior compartment of the leg which varies in size and extent; it may even be absent. The plantaris has its *origin on the posterior *femur above lateral *condyle; its *insertion is via a long thin *tendon into the *calcaneus. The plantaris assists in *knee flexion and *plantar flexion.

plantaris lateralis nerve A *nerve on the outer side of the sole of the foot.

plantaris medialis nerve A *nerve on the inner side of the sole of the foot.

plantar reflex A *reflex induced by running a blunt object along the sole of the foot. The normal response is for the toes to curl downwards and bunch together. *Compare* Babinski reflex.

plantar wart (verruca plantaris) A *wart on the sole of the foot which may be contracted by walking barefoot. *See also* verruca.

plaque 1 Strands of fibrous tissue that attach to the inside of blood vessels. 2 Bacteria-containing encrustations on teeth.

plasma (blood plasma) The fluid, noncellular component of the *blood within which formed elements and various solutes are suspended and circulated. *Compare* serum.

plasma cell A member of a clone of *B cells which are specialized to produce and release *antibodies.

plasma membrane A boundary membrane enclosing the *cytoplasm of a cell.

plasma protein *Proteins, such as *albumins and *globulins, which circulate in the *plasma of blood. Levels of plasma proteins tend to increase during training in relation to the strength and endurance effort.

plasmin An *enzyme found in the *blood which catalyses the breakdown of *fibrin clots.

plasmolysis The shrinking of a cell, such as a red blood cell.

plaster An adhesive material which can be applied as a simple dressing to treat superficial skin-wounds.

plastic A material which can be permanently distorted when a *force is applied to it. *Compare* elastic.

plastic behaviour *See* plasticity.

plasticity 1 Property of a body that causes it to be permanently deformed when a *force is applied. *Compare* elasticity. 2 In *sociology and *psychology, the term is usually applied to the modifiability of human behaviour; plastic behaviour.

plastic surgery (reconstructive surgery) Surgery undertaken to revise or reconstruct tissue of superficial organs (i.e., those which can be observed) in a damaged area. *See also* reconstruction surgery.

plateau *See* arrested progress.

platelet *See* blood platelets.

play Spontaneous, childlike physical activity from which the individual derives immediate pleasure. Play is a voluntary activity which has no *goal other than enjoyment. It is an activity which proceeds within certain limits of time and space, in a visible order according to rules freely accepted, and outside the sphere of necessity or material utility. The play mood is one of rapture and enthusiasm, and is sacred or festive according to the occasion. A feeling of exhilaration and tension often accompanies the action, with mirth and relaxation following. Play is believed to be a necessary part of physical development, learning, social behaviour, and personality development.

plethysmography The process of recording changes in the volume of a limb which reflect changes in *blood pressure.

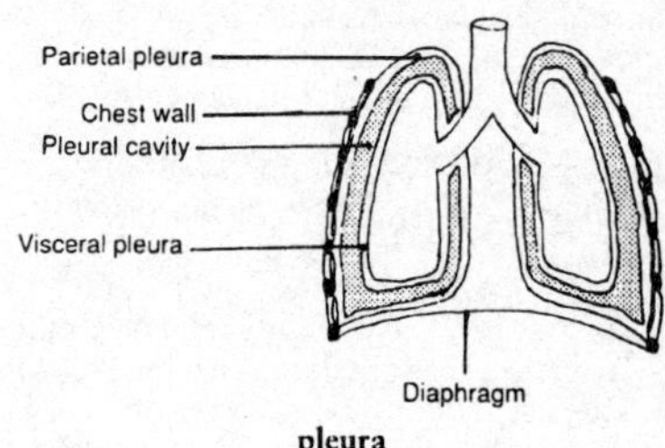

pleura

pleura A thin two-layered *membrane that secretes fluid and lines the *thoracic wall (*see* parietal pleura), the *diaphragm (*see* diaphragmatic pleura), and the *lungs (*see* visceral pleura).

pleural cavity A fluid-filled cavity between the *parietal and *visceral pleura surrounding the lungs.

pleurisy Inflammation of the *pleura which become sticky causing pain on deep breathing. It is always associated with some other disease, such as pneumonia.

pleuritis *Inflammation of the *pleura.

plexus A network of *blood vessels or *nerve fibres. There are five major nerve plexuses: the *brachial, *cervical, *coccygeal, *lumbar, and *sacral. Some of their fibres carry sensory messages to the *central nervous system, and others carry *motor impulses away from the central nervous system to the *effector organs, such as *muscles.

plica A fold of tissue.

plyometrics

plyometrics Bounding exercises in which maximum effort is expended while a *muscle group is lengthening during *eccentric contractions and doing *negative work. Examples of plyometric exercises include any jumping exercise in which a landing followed by a jump occurs.

PMS *See* premenstrual syndrome.

pneumonia Inflammation of a large part of the lung, usually caused by bacteria. Pneumonia and other lung infections generally preclude physical exertion. It can take several months for an athlete to return to the same level of fitness that had been attained before infection.

pneumotachograph A meter for measuring gas flow rates during breathing by recording pressure differences across a device of fixed-flow resistance that has known pressure-flow characteristics. Pneumotachographs are often used in conjunction with computers to give *minute ventilation, and breath-by-breath measurements of ventilation.

pneumotaxic centre One of the *respiratory centres in the upper part of the *pons of the *brain; it controls the frequency and rhythm of breathing.

pneumothorax The entrance of air into the *pleural cavity which causes the *lung to collapse. A pneumothorax results from a perforation in the chest wall or surface of the lung.

p_{O_2} Partial pressure of oxygen.

pocket valve *See* semi-lunar valve.

podiatry A branch of the paramedical profession dealing with biomechanical disorders of the feet and their relationship with the legs.

point of application The precise point at which a *force is applied on the body or system receiving the force.

point of release *See* release-point.

point of resistance In a *lever, the point at which the *load is said to act; it is the *centre of gravity of the segment of the body being moved plus the centre of gravity of the external resistance or load. *See also* moment arm.

poise The *CGS unit of *viscosity; it is the *tangential force per unit area (measured in *dynes per square centimetre) required to maintain unit difference in velocity between two parallel planes separated by one centimetre of fluid.

Poiseuille flow *Laminar flow of a fluid, such as *blood, through a long circular tube.

polar In chemistry, applied to a *molecule which has an uneven distribution of *electrons. Therefore, at least one part of the molecule has a slight positive charge while the another part has a slight negative charge.

polar co-ordinates A pair of co-ordinates (usually written r, θ) which give the location of any point lying in a plane with reference to the length of the radius vector (r), which pivots about any selected point in the plane (termed the origin) to make the angle (θ), that the position of the point makes with a coplanar reference line passing through the origin. *Compare* rectangular co-ordinates.

policy A plan of action adopted or pursued by an individual, organization, or government because of its advantages or expediency; as in a sport's policy.

political resistance A form of political behaviour, such as a boycott or riot within sport, which may be used to express opposition to situations and policies which a group finds intolerable. Political resistance may also be used to express dissatisfaction with an existing culture.

politics 1 The processes by which power and authority are exercised in directing and administering the goals and policies of states and other political units. Despite the wishes of many, international politics often intrudes into sport. Sport has been used as a symbolic representation of the image and strength of a nation; it has been used to convey the beliefs and values of a nation; and sport has been used as an effective channel for opposing policies such as *apartheid (*see also* political resistance). 2 The study of politics in the above sense.

pollex (thumb) The thumb, the first digit of the hand, which consists of two *phalanges.

polycythaemia (erythrocytaemia) An abnormal increase in the number of *red blood cells per mm^{-3} of *blood. The number of these cells varies considerably among healthy people, but there are normally about 5 million per mm^{-3} of blood. A figure above 6 million per mm^{-3} indicates polycythaemia. Relative polycythaemia occurs when the total number of red blood cells in the circulation is normal but the volume of circulating fluids has decreased due to dehydration, injury, or disease. Absolute polycythaemia, an increase in the total number of red blood cells, occurs in response to oxygen deficiency in those living at high altitudes and in those suffering from cardiorespiratory diseases. *Compare* anaemia.

polymer A *molecule formed from the linkage between a large number of smaller molecules. *Protein is a polymer formed by *amino acids linking together, and *glycogen is a polymer made from the linkage of *glucose molecules.

polyneuritis Simultaneous inflammation of *nerves in many parts of the body.

polyneuropathy A disease affecting many *peripheral nerves.

polyp A growth, usually benign, on a stalk from the skin or a mucous membrane.

polypeptide chain A chain of three or more *amino acids, linked together by *peptide bonds.

polysaccharide Long chains of *simple sugar molecules joined together. Polysaccharides are relatively insoluble, unsweet, and have a low *osmotic effect; they include *starch, *glycogen, and *cellulose.

polythiazide A *drug belonging to the *diuretics which are on the *IOC list of *banned substances.

polyunsaturated fat A *fat, usually a long chain *triglyceride of plant origin, containing at least one double bond between constituent *carbon atoms. Polyunsaturated fats are liquid at room temperature and metabolized along different pathways from those for *saturated fats.

POMS *See* profile of mood states.

ponderal index An indicator of body-size and shape used in *somatotyping. The ponderal index is equal to the *body height divided by the cube root of *body-weight.

pons Any bridge-like structure that joins two parts of an organ.

pons Varolii A short segment of the *brainstem connecting the *medulla with the *midbrain, and composed of conduction tracts of nerve fibres linking the upper and lower levels of the *central nervous system. It also contains the *respiratory centres which help maintain the normal rhythm of breathing.

pooling The accumulation of blood in the lower limbs due to gravity. *See also* postural hypotension.

popliteal Pertaining to the back of the knee.

popliteal vein A principal *vein which ascends through the popliteal space at the back of the knee to become the *femoral vein.

popliteus A thin, triangular, *deep muscle in the back of the knee. The popliteus has its *origin on the *lateral *condyle of the *femur and its *insertion on the *proximal part of the *tibia. Its actions include *flexion of the knee, and *medial rotation to unlock the knee when it is in the fully extended position.

Poppelreuter's law A law which states that when teaching a *skill where both speed and accuracy are required, it is better to retard the speed of movement in the early stages of practice until a high degree of accuracy is reached, and then gradually to increase the speed. The law is based on the assumption that it is easier to increase the speed of accurate movements than to correct fast, inaccurate ones. However, it has also been argued that the law does not have universal application and that, where it is a vital component of the performance and influences technique, speed should be emphasized from the beginning.

popular culture Cultural and recreational activities, including many sports, shared by many people in a *society. Popular culture originates and evolves from the general population itself in contrast to activities which have been created by the *mass media. *Compare* high culture; mass culture. *See also* taste culture.

population 1 All the people living in a particular locality. 2 In statistics, the aggregate of individuals or items from which a sample is taken.

population code A means of conveying information in the *nervous system by the number of nerve cells involved in transmitting *nerve impulses. *Compare* frequency code.

porphyrin A class of naturally-occurring pigments containing *pyrolle rings and a metal. The porphyrins include the iron-containing *haemoglobin, *myoglobin, and *cytochromes, and the magnesium-containing *chlorophyll.

position The attitude of a body or the posture of a person.

positional segregation *See* stacking.

positive acceleration An increase in the *velocity of an object during a given period of time.

positive energy balance A condition in which more *energy is taken in as food than is expended during *metabolism; *bodyweight increases as a result.

positive feedback A form of *feedback in a *closed-loop system in which small changes in the level of output tend to be exaggerated so that deviations from the *norm are increased. *Compare* negative feedback.

positive nitrogen balance A condition in the human body in which the rate of *protein synthesis is greater than the rate of protein breakdown and loss, resulting in tissue growth. A positive nitrogen balance is the normal situation in growing children and pregnant women. *Anabolic steroids accelerate protein synthesis and tend to create a positive nitrogen balance.

positive reinforcement The presentation of a desirable *stimulus. A positive reinforcement has pleasant properties which an athlete will pursue if at all possible. If such a reinforcement is to be effective it must follow the response, preferably immediately, and increase the likelihood that the response will occur in the future under the same or similar conditions.

positive transfer *Transfer of training is positive when previous learning aids the learning of a new task. There is positive transfer, for example, when an individual who has learned to roller-skate can acquire ice-skating skills more quickly than he or she would otherwise have done. *Compare* negative transfer.

positive work *Work done by *muscles against a resistance. *Compare* negative work.

post-concussional Applied to behaviour following injury to the *brain. *See also* concussion.

post-concussional syndrome A combination of *signs and *symptoms which follow *concussion; they include headaches, giddiness, and mental fatigue.

posterior (dorsal) The back of an organism, *organ, or part. *See also* directional terms.

posterior cruciate ligament A *ligament attached to the posterior *intercondyle region of the *tibia which passes anteriorly, medially, and upward to attach to the *anterolateral surface of the *medial femoral condyle. The posterior cruciate ligament is a strong ligament which prevents the *femur from sliding anteriorly, the tibia from backward *displacement, and the knee from overflexion.

posterior deep compartment syndrome An *over-use injury affecting the posterior *deep compartment, containing the tibialis posterior, the *flexor hallucis longus, and flexor digitorum longus muscles. The condition may be either *acute or *chronic. *See also* compartment syndrome.

posterior pituitary *See* neurohypophysis

posterior superficial compartment syndrome *Signs and *symptoms, including pain in the back of the lower leg, resulting from an increase of pressure in the posterior superficial muscle compartment affecting the *gastrocnemius or *soleus muscles. *See also* compartment syndromes.

posterior tibial nerve *See* tibial nerve.

postganglionic neurone A *motor neurone of the *autonomic nervous system; it has its cell body in a peripheral *ganglion and projects its *axon to an *effector.

posthypnotic suggestion A suggestion given during an alert *hypnotic trance that is to be carried out when the subject is awake.

post-knowledge of results delay Interval of time from the delivery of *knowledge of results to the production of the next response. If the interval is too short, performers have difficulty generating a new and different movement at the next response.

postsynaptic membrane A *cell membrane of a *neurone or *muscle fibre which conducts *impulses away from a *synapse. *Compare* presynaptic membrane.

postsynaptic neurone A *neurone carrying *impulses away from a *synapse.

postsynaptic potential A *graded potential in a *postsynaptic membrane resulting from the release of a *neurotransmitter across a *synapse.

postulate A statement in a theory that describes the relationship of the hypothetical constructs.

postulate of adequacy The sociological doctrine that descriptions or explanations of social situations must be comprehensible to those involved.

postulate of functional indispensibility (universal functionalism) The sociological doctrine that every aspect of *culture fulfils an important function for the society in which it occurs.

postulate of functional indispensibility (universal functionalism) The sociological doctrine that every aspect of *culture fulfils an important function for the society in which it occurs.

postural discrimination A skill-oriented ability which underlies tasks for which subjects must respond to changes in postural cues from *proprioceptors in the absence of vision when making precise bodily adjustments (e.g., when walking in the dark).

postural hypotension A condition, common in athletes, which manifests itself when a person changes position from sitting or lying to standing. When sitting, blood pools in the lower *abdomen and legs. Upon standing, because there is a temporary shortage of blood to the brain, a person feels dizzy for one or two seconds. After a long run, an athlete generally has wide-open *vascular channels which allow pooling until the vessels contract. Consequently, if a well-trained athlete is immobilized after running he or she may faint due to lack of blood returning to the heart. Adoption of a supine or prone position enables the heart to receive blood once again and to perfuse the brain. Walking or mild exercise during *cooling down prevents *pooling.

postural hypotension drop The amount by which *blood pressure is reduced when a person moves from a lying position to a standing position. The postural hypotension drop is employed as a test of physical fitness.

postural muscle A *muscle or group of muscles which play an important part in maintaining body *posture.

posture The position or attitude of the body as a whole.

posture plate (arch support) An *orthotic used to treat a number of foot defects by rebalancing the foot and providing a complete weight-bearing surface on which to stand.

posturography A technique for assessing body balance by measuring deviations from an erect posture of an athlete attempting to balance on a platform. The test is carried out once with open eyes and once with closed eyes while making movements in the *vertical, *frontal and *transverse axes. Movements of the platform are recorded on a computer and may be converted into graphs for analysis.

pot *See* marijuana.

potassium A mineral element which is an important constituent of the human body and forms the main cations in the intracellular fluid. Potassium is widely distributed in foods (including apricots, meat, fish, and poultry) and deficiencies are rare though they may result from severe diarrhoea or vomiting. Low concentrations of potassium can lead to muscular weakness, paralysis, *nausea, *tachycardia, and *heart failure. High concentrations of potassium can also lead to muscular weakness and *cardiac abnormalities and may accompany kidney disease.

potential difference The unit of potential difference is the joule per coulomb (JC^{-1}) or volt (V), 1 C being the equivalent to the electrical charge on 1.6×10^{-19} electrons; 1 V is the potential difference between two points in which 1 J of energy is converted when 1 C passes from one point to the other.

potential energy The energy an object has because of its position (or internal structure) in relation to other objects. It is stored energy that is able to do *work but which is not at present doing so. A stretched elastic band and a bicycle at the top of the hill both have potential energy. Potential energy is measured by the amount of work the body performs in passing from its position to a standard position in which the potential energy is considered to be zero. A *mass (m) raised through a height (h) has a potential energy (U) given by: $U = mgh$ where g is the *acceleration of free fall.

pound British unit of *weight which is equivalent to 0.45359237kg; it is also used as a unit of *force and *mass.

poundal A unit of *force. One poundal acting on a *mass of one pound will accelerate the body one foot per second per second. One poundal = 0.138 255 N.

Poupart's ligament *See* inguinal ligament.

power 1 The ability of a person or a group to control the behaviour of others even when actively opposed. This form of power may stem from a legal right to make decisions governing others where this authority is underlaid by the ability to enforce such decisions, or may be derived from the capacity to shape decisions by informal, nonauthoritarian means. **2** The capacity to intervene in a given set of events so as in some way to alter them. **3** The rate at which *energy is expended or *work is done. Power is measured in *watts (W) of work per unit time (power = work done/time taken). In sport, power is the ability to transform physical energy into *force at a fast rate and depends on the amount of *ATP produced per unit time. Sprinting, jumping, and throwing events are activities requiring great power and very high rates of ATP production. *Compare* capacity.

power system A *leadership approach in which influence and power tends to flow from the *coach to the *athlete in one direction only. The source of power in such systems includes *coercion, *reward, authority, expertise, and affection. *Compare* influence system.

practical knowledge Those things a person knows in relation to his or her behaviour and situation but cannot necessarily express.

practical reasoning Thought which is directed to a practical outcome.

practice The repetition of techniques and *skills, often taken out of the context of a whole game or event, so that they may be improved. As practice sessions increase, there is generally an improvement in performance (*see* learning curves). However, at high levels of performance, much of the time spent in practice is used to maintain the level of performance. Practice conditions which are most effective are those which are similar to those during actual competition. Practice which is staggered over several short sessions is more effective than one long session.

praise *Motivational strategy in which a coach or some other person commends a good performance of an athlete. To be effective, the praise must be warranted and not be excessive. Too much unwarranted praise can be counter-productive. The praise should be given either during the performance or immediately following it. If applied properly, praise can encourage athletes to persist with their training and performing despite difficulties. *Compare* criticism.

prandial Pertaining to a meal.

prazosin A selective *alpha blocker with reduced affinity for *α_2 receptors. Prazosin is administered to reduce the incidence of *tachycardia and to treat *hypertension.

PRE *See* progressive resistance exercise.

pre-adolescence The time from *childhood to the onset of *secondary sexual characteristics.

precession *See* twisting.

precision The number of significant figures to which data or readings are taken. The higher the number of significant figures, the greater the precision. *Compare* accuracy.

predictive value **1** The extent to which a test is useful for estimating future performance. **2** The ability of a test to measure what it claims to measure.

predictor variable A *causal variable which when changed, produces an effect on an event, and which can be used to predict the event. Usually a number of causal variables contribute to an event. For example, an athlete who is very nervous before competition may have many predictors of his or her *anxiety response. The athlete may have a high *trait anxiety, bad experiences at other high-level competition, or may be focusing upon negative thoughts. These predictors must be accurately identified before a sport psychologist can help the athlete control his or her anxiety.

predisposition A tendency to be affected by a particular disease or injury. The predisposition may be inherited or acquired. Athletes who do not warm up prior to training have a predisposition to *joint and *muscle injuries.

prednisolone A synthetic *drug belonging to the *corticosteroids which are on the *IOC list of *banned substances. Prednisolone is used to treat *asthma, *rheumatism, and allergic skin diseases.

prednisone A *drug belonging to the *corticosteroids which are on the *IOC list of *banned substances. Prednisone has actions and uses similar to *prednisolone.

preferred leader behaviour The style of *leadership behaviour preferred by members of a group.

prefrontal cortex Part of the *brain located in the *anterior of the *cerebral cortex and concerned with thought, *intelligence, *motivation, and *personality.

preganglionic neurone A *motor neurone of the *autonomic nervous system with its cell body in the *central nervous system and its *axon extending to a peripheral *ganglion.

pregnancy The period of time (about 280 days) between conception and birth. Although women with a history of poor health may be prescribed rest at various stages of pregnancy many women, including élite athletes, take part in highly-competitive sport during the early stages of pregnancy with no ill effects; participation in contact sports is not appropriate. During the later stages of pregnancy, usually after the fifth month, maximal physical exertion is not recommended.

prejudice Any attitude held towards a person or group which is not justified by the facts. Prejudice includes negative and positive attitudes towards people solely on the basis of their race, ethnicity, gender, or sex.

premenstrual stress *See* premenstrual syndrome.

premenstrual syndrome (PMS; premenstrual stress; premenstrual tension) Disruptive emotional and physical symptoms, including irritability and headaches, that appear to precede *menstruation and may last two weeks or more. The symptoms tend to disappear with the onset of menstruation. Premenstrual syndrome can adversely affect the performance of some female athletes (*see* menstrual adjustment). It is generally recognized that the cause of PMS is an altered balance of *sex hormones, *progesterone becoming relatively dominant in the premenstrual phase of the menstrual cycle. PMS may be treated by hormonal adjustment (*see* menstrual adjustment) or by *diuretics.

premenstrual tension *See* premenstrual syndrome.

premotor area *See* premotor cortex.

premotor cortex (premotor area) Part of the *brain, *anterior to the *primary motor cortex, which controls *motor skills of a repetitious or patterned nature. The premotor cortex contains *neurones which co-ordinate the movements of several *muscles by sending impulses to the primary motor cortex and other motor centres in the brain, such as the *basal nuclei.

premotor reaction time The interval from the presentation of a *stimulus to the initial changes in the electrical activity of a *muscle.

preparation The process which occurs prior to the reception of an expected *stimulus to which a subject has to respond quickly. The subject prepares for the stimulus arrival by a reorganization of *attention and initiates in advance the relevant *information-processing so that the stimulus can be received and responded to quickly.

preparation period A period of *training which is concerned with preparing an athlete for competition. The preparation period includes *conditioning, *special training, and *specific training. *See also* periodization.

preparatory arousal Mental techniques used to get excited, charged-up, *psyched-up, and *aroused just prior to performance. There is some evidence that preparatory arousal is beneficial for power events, such as jumping or sprinting, but is not necessarily very good for the execution of more complex *motor skills. *See also* optimal arousal.

prepatellar bursa A superficial *bursa at the front of the knee, between the skin and the *patella.

prepatellar bursitis *See* housemaid's knee.

pre-pubescence Applied to the period before *puberty.

presbyopia A diminished ability to *see* at close range due to an age-related loss of elasticity in the lens of the eye.

prescribed leadership behaviour A style of *leadership that conforms to the established norms of an organization (e.g., the teaching behaviour expected by a school of its physical education teachers). *See also* multidimensional model of leadership.

press Weight-training exercise using a barbell. The subject stands resting the barbell on the front of the shoulders with the palms of the hands facing upwards, feet comfortably spread, with the back and legs straight, and the arms flexed. From this position the barbell is pushed upward until the arms are fully extended upwards above the head, then it is returned to the starting position.

pressoreceptor A *nerve-ending in the wall of the *carotid sinus and *aortic arch sensitive to vessel-stretching. *See also* baroreceptor.

press-up *See* push-up.

pressure The *force transmitted per unit area of a surface, measured in Nm^{-2}. The average pressure on a supporting surface varies with the area of the surface involved. The ability to spread forces over a wide area and thereby reduce pressure has important applications in sport, particularly with regard to safety. High-jumpers, for example, spread their body forces by landing flat on their backs. In other sports, the use of protective equipment such as helmets also tends to spread forces and reduce pressure. Failure to minimize the pressure that any one part of the body must withstand can lead to serious injuries.

pressure bandage Bandage used for the compression of tissues.

pressure drag *See* form drag.

pressure point The point at which an *artery is adjacent to a *bone on which it can be compressed to stop blood flow.

pressure receptor *See* baroreceptor.

pressure-training A training system much used in team-sports which consists of deliberately creating intensive conditions for skill practice, much more difficult than those required by the game itself. In soccer, for example, a player may be put under pressure by being made to deal in a particular way with a much more rapid sequence of balls than would normally occur in the game itself. Pressure-training may improve the speed of executing skilled movements and it may impress upon performers that they can retain skills under the duress of competition. If pressure-training continues after the *skill breaks down, learners may have their confidence destroyed.

priapism A persistent, painful erection. Priapism occurs among racing cyclists due to pressure on the *pudendal nerve from a badly-fitting saddle pushing up against the *perineum. Treatment may include sedation to reduce the erection and the acquisition of a better fitting saddle.

prickly heat (miliaria) A condition, associated with exposure to the sun in a hot environment, in which the sweat glands are blocked so that efficient sweating is prevented. Prickly heat is accompanied by intolerable itching. Individuals travelling from a temperate to tropical climates are particularly vulnerable to prickly heat. Withdrawal from sun and avoidance of conditions causing perspiration are helpful. Rubbing the body over with the juice of a lemon after taking a bath has been recommended as a preventative.

primary behavioural involvement (primary sport involvement) The direct participation in a sport as a competitor or performer. *Compare* affective sport involvement; cognitive sport involvement; and secondary behavioural involvement.

primary consequential injuries In sport, injuries which occur directly as a result of a sporting activity.

primary deviance An initial act of *deviance. *Compare* secondary deviance.

primary factors *See* first-order traits.

primary group A small group, such as a sports team, family, or band of professional colleagues, which has its own *norms and in which there is much face-to-face interpersonal interaction.

primary immune response Initial response of the *immune system to an *antigen; it involves *clonal selection and the establishment of *immunological memory.

primary mechanical purpose A statement of the main objective of an activity, movement, or skill which can be expressed in mechanical terms. For example, the primary mechanical purpose in the long jump is to project the body for the maximum horizontal length. Skills that have the same mechanical purpose will share some of the mechanical principles which govern their effectiveness.

primary motivation *See* inborn motivation.

primary motor cortex Part of the *brain concerned with the conscious control of skeletal movements. The primary motor cortex is located in the precentral *gyrus of the *cerebral cortex and contains *pyramidal tracts of *axons connecting the brain and *spinal cord. Specific areas of cortical tissue control particular muscles.

primary ossification centre An area of *hyaline cartilage in the centre of the *shaft of a *long bone where *ossification typically begins.

primary reinforcement Satisfaction of physiological needs such as that supplied by food or sleep.

primary sport involvement *See* primary behavioural involvement.

prime mover (agonist) *Muscle that has the major responsibility for effecting a particular movement.

principal artery A major *artery in the circulatory system.

principal axes (cardinal axes) Three axes which pass through the *centre of gravity of a human body and which are used to describe the rotation of the body. For a person in an erect standing position, the principal axes are closely approximated by lines drawn through the centre of gravity and passing from the top of the head to the feet (longitudinal axis), from left to right (transverse axis) and from front to rear (frontal or anteroposterior axis).

principal plane *See* cardinal reference plane.

principle of contiguity A principle which posits that *classical conditioning is effective only when the *conditioned stimulus and *unconditioned stimulus are contiguous. *See also* classical conditioning.

principle of developmental direction A principle of development which states that *neuromotor organization proceeds from head to foot in the direction of the *longitudinal axis and from central to peripheral body-segments. Thus, there is a progressive advance of *motor control from larger, fundamental muscles to smaller muscles which execute more refined movements.

principle of functional asymmetry A principle of development based on studies of infant behaviour which recognizes that the infant is equipped for, and capable of facing, the world on a *frontal plane of symmetry and could become perfectly *ambidextrous. It suggests that a person comes to prefer the use of one hand, foot, or eye mainly because of the preference for the right hand in our culture, and not because the individual is incapable of learning with the left. Neurologically speaking, there is equal facility for developing either side of the body (e.g., right or left *handedness). This is demonstrated where an injury forces a person who is normally right-handed to use the left hand, and also by people who are right-handed for one skill and left-handed for another.

principle of individual maturation A principle which suggests that children achieve their individuality by becoming progressively differentiated from their fellows with every new maturational change and accompanying environmental experiences.

principle of levers (principle of moments) A principle which applies to a system of balanced forces about a *fulcrum or pivot, in which the total anticlockwise *moment is equal to the total clockwise moment. Therefore, a *lever will balance or turn uniformly about the point of support when the product of the *force and *force arm equals the product of the *resistance and *resistance arm.

principle of moments *See* principle of levers.

principle of overload *See* overload principle.

principle of progression A basic principle of *training which states that improved fitness will only result if there is a steady increase in the workload. The minimal level of training which satisfies the *overload principle tends to change regularly as progress is made, therefore the load should be increased gradually and persistently over a long period of training. If the workload is too high, there is a risk of *over-training and of *over-use injuries.

principle of reciprocal interweaving A principle of development, based on studies of infant behaviour, which refers to the intimate relationship that exists between the growth of an individual's body structures and the behaviour of an individual. Interweaving applies to the development of *neural pathways between *antagonistic pairs of muscles so that *reciprocal innervation occurs. The development of the neural network results in a progressive spiral of more advanced forms of *behaviour.

principle of specificity *See* specificity principle.

proactive assertion Forceful behaviour which is permitted by the rules of a sport (e.g., tackling in American football). It is sometimes difficult to distinguish between proactive assertion and *aggression; a player may tackle an opponent legitimately, but with the intent of injuring the person.

proactive inhibition The negative effect one learned task has on the retention of a newer task; a type of interference or *negative transfer observed in memory experiments and other learning situations. *Compare* retroactive inhibition.

probability The likelihood that a given event will occur. Probability is expressed as a value between 0 (complete certainty that an event will not occur) and 1 (complete certainty that an event will occur), or a percentage value between 0 per cent and 100 per cent.

probability of success The perceived *probability of succeeding at a task. *See also* risk-taking behaviour.

probablistic explanation An explanation in which a specifiable probability (a chance of less than 100 per cent and more than 0 per cent, or, in probability theory, less than 1 and more than 0) is taken as explaining the occurrence of an event.

probe A thin, pliable instrument with a blunt, swollen end; used to investigate, or introduce things into, body-spaces.

probenecid A *drug used in the treatment of *gout by reducing the level of *uric acid in the *blood. Probenecid inhibits the transport of *organic acids and *antibodies across some tissue barriers, such as the barrier between the blood and the *kidney tubule. It has two very important effects on other drugs: first, it can increase the concentration of another drug or antibody within the blood; secondly, it can reduce the amount of drug released into the urine, making it much more difficult to detect. Because probenecid may be used to alter the integrity of a urine sample and avoid detection in dope tests, its use by sports competitors is banned by the *IOC.

probe technique (reaction time probe technique) A technique used in studying the role of the amount of *attention required for movements in which the subject performs a primary task while presented with an occasional *stimulus (usually auditory) to which the subject must respond. The *reaction time to the stimulus is used as a measure of the attention demands of the primary task: low reaction times are assumed to indicate that the amount of attention required for the primary task is relatively small. The probe technique assumes that there is a fixed capacity for attention.

problem-solving The ability to adjust to a situation by acquiring new modes of response. Problem-solving applies especially to *learning in which a certain amount of *insight or reasoning may be displayed.

procedural skill A *skill which involves a series of discrete responses each of which must be performed at the appropriate time and in the appropriate sequence.

process In *anatomy, a prominence, projection, or outgrowth of a body-part.

processing capacity The amount of space a person has available in the *central nervous system for processing *information. The use of the term implies that individuals have a limited capacity for such processing. Processing-capacity has been used to explain a person's limited ability to do several things at the same time.

process-orientation An approach to the study of movement which emphasises the study of the mental processes underlying *movement and motor skills. The researcher using process-orientation is interested in the underlying mechanisms that contribute to the performance of a *motor skill rather than the outcome of the performance. *Compare* task-orientation

product In mathematics, the result of multiplying two or more quantities together.

product orientation A *leadership style which is best explained in terms of *initiating structure where the emphasis is on task-fulfillment.

profession 1 Any occupation requiring special technical and intellectual knowledge, for which education and training is received. Competency to carry out the profession is confirmed through examinations, and professional integrity is maintained through a code of conduct. Professions have a commitment to public service. 2 A high-status occupation which is self-regulating and controls entry into its membership. It is applied especially to the three learned professions: law, medicine, and theology.

professional 1 A person, such as a medical doctor, having an occupation which requires special training. 2 An expert player who gives instruction in a game; for example, a golf professional. 3 Applied to any person, such as a professional cricketer, who engages in an activity, generally followed as a pastime, as his or her means of livelihood, and who has access to expert knowledge.

professionalism An approach to an activity typified by a competent and dedicated *professional.

professionalization The process of gaining the status of a *profession for a particular occupational group. *Compare* deprofessionalization.

profile drag *See* form drag.

profile of mood states (POMS) A test designed to measure a person's *affective states which include *tension, *depression, anger, vigour, *fatigue, and confusion. Unlike *personality traits, mood states are thought to be transitory and specific to a given situation, although moods can also be measured for recent prolonged time periods, such as the past several months. POMS is a popular research tool among *sports psychologists.

profunda femoris A *principal artery which runs deep in the thigh. It supplies the *flexor muscles at the back of the thigh.

progesterone Female sex hormone, produced from the *corpus luteum and *placenta, which is concerned with preparing the *uterus to receive a fertilized *ovum.

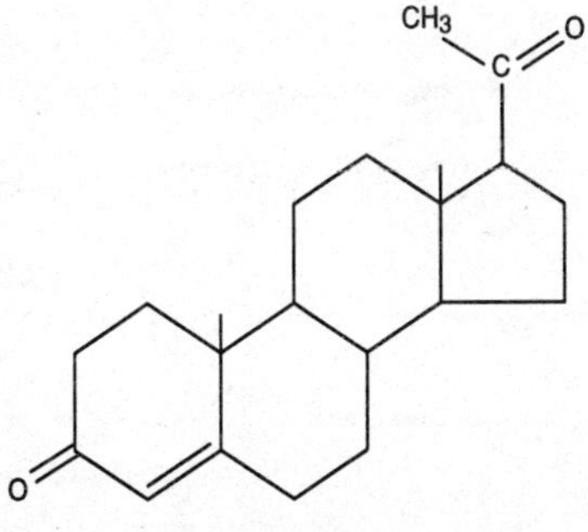

progesterone

prognosis Forecast of the course and outcome of a disease.

progression *See* progressive resistance exercise.

progression principle *See* principle of progression.

progressive muscle relaxation (progressive relaxation; PMR) A highly effective technique for managing *stress, *tension, *anxiety, and worry. *Muscle groups from head to toe are tensed for a few seconds and then relaxed in sequence. Tensing the muscles really hard produces a high level of relaxation to the muscle when it is subsequently relaxed. With practice, it becomes possible to relax in seconds. The technique is very important in reducing *arousal to optimal levels prior to competition.

progressive-part method A method of learning a multi-part task, in which the parts are learned and combined sequentially. After the first two parts are mastered, they are combined and practised together until learned. Then the third part is taught by itself. After it has been acquired, the three parts are combined and practised together until learned. This procedure is followed for each part until all of them can be practised as a whole. The technique is most appropriate when the parts form a natural and

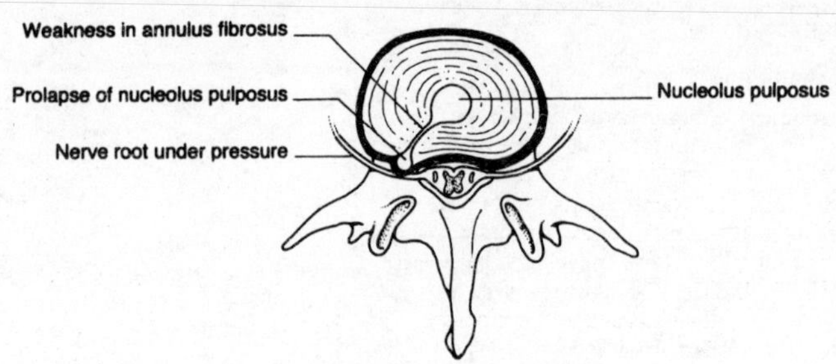

prolapsed intervertebral disc

meaningful sequence of actions, and they need to be practised together (e.g., a gymnast's floor sequence). *See also* learning method.

progressive relaxation *See* progressive muscle relaxation.

progressive resistance *Training in which the workload is gradually increased, as in *progressive resistance exercise.

progressive resistance exercise (progression) Exercise in which a *load is increased in predetermined steps. Ideally, the increments will be sufficient to apply the *overload principle but not great enough to cause damage. Progressive resistance exercises used in *weight-training are generally based on the *repetition maximum (RM). In one session, several sets of exercises are performed, each at a higher intensity than the preceding one. The following example consists of three sets of repetitions with a short rest of 1 to 2 minutes between each: set 1 at 50 per cent 10-RM; set 2 at 75 per cent 10-RM; set 3 at 100 per cent 10-RM. Between sessions, the 10-RM is re-evaluated to ensure that the training conforms to the overload principle. *See also* principle of progression.

progressive resistance system A system of *training based on *progressive resistance exercise.

projectile Any object, such as a human body, football, or javelin, that is released into the air.

projection A mechanism of *ego defense by which an individual transfers personally-unacceptable wishes or actions to another person or external object. For example, an athlete who dislikes himself or herself may transfer those feelings to the coach who he or she then perceives as disliking or even hating the athlete.

projective procedure (projective test) Psychological test that uses relatively-unstructured and open-ended tasks. The assumption is that such a test, in which there are no clear correct or incorrect responses, encourages open and honest responses. *See also* thematic apperception test.

projective test *See* projective procedure.

prolactin (lactogenic hormone; LTH; luteotrophic hormone; luteotrophin) A *hormone secreted by the *anterior lobe of the *pituitary. Prolactin stimulates the secretion of milk after pregnancy. Its secretion increases during exercise.

prolapse The displacement of an *organ or organ-part such as an *intervertebral disc.

prolapsed intervertebral disc (herniated disc; slipped disc) Displacement of part of the gelatinous interior of an *intervertebral disc so that it protrudes through the fibrous outer coat pressing on adjacent nerves. So-called slipped discs preclude physical activity but, once the patient has recovered, exercises are often used to strengthen abdominal and back muscles in order to reduce the risk of a recurrence of the prolapse. *See also* sciatica.

prolintane A *drug belonging to the *stimulants which are on the *IOC list of *banned substances.

promethazine A powerful and long-lasting *antihistamine *drug used to treat allergic conditions.

promotively-interdependent goal A social situation in which everyone in a team can achieve their goals; the achievement of a *goal by one individual does not preclude others from achieving their goals. *Compare* contritely-interdependent goal.

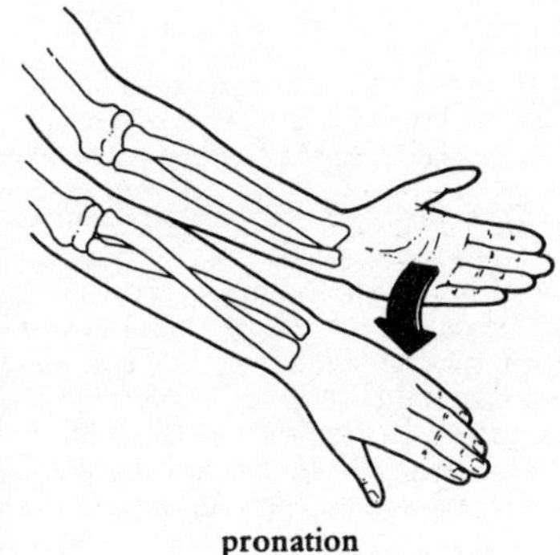

pronation

pronation 1 Movement of the *forearm so that the palm is facing downward. During this movement the *distal end of the *radius moves across the *ulna toward the body midline. Pronation is the natural position of the forearm when a person is in a relaxed, standing position. **2** During running and walking, the inward rotation of the foot associated with depression of the medial longitudinal arch (*see* arches of foot) that occurs during the weight-bearing phase of walking or running. Pronation serves as a shock-absorbing and an energy-return mechanism. *Compare* supination.

pronator 1 A person who exhibits *pronation during walking and running. **2** One of the muscles of the anterior fascial compartment of the *forearm involved in *pronation of the forearm and hand.

pronator quadratus The deepest *muscle of the *anterior fascial compartment of the *forearm. It has its *origin only on the *ulna and inserts only into the *radius. The pronator quadratus acts, with the *pronator teres, on the wrist and fingers during *pronation. It also helps to hold the ulna and radius together.

pronator teres A two-headed *superficial muscle of the *anterior *forearm which lies between the *brachioradialis and *flexor carpi radialis. It has its *origins on the *medial epicondyle of the *humerus and *coronoid process of the *ulna, and its *insertion by a common *tendon into the lateral surface of the *radius midshaft. The pronator teres is involved in *pronation and is also a weak flexor of the forearm.

pronator teres syndrome A *syndrome consisting of pain and tenderness in the middle anterior part of the elbow, numbness in the second, third and radial half of the fourth finger, pain during *pronation, and weakness during *palmar flexion. It is caused by entrapment of the *median nerve.

prone 1 Applied to the body position when lying horizontally, face down. **2** Appled to the forearm when the palm is facing down. *Compare* supine.

propaganda Information, or the dissemination of information, used to promote or undermine a government or other social organization. Sport has often been used as a means of propaganda. Success in sport has been used to promote the superiority of one nation over another, for example, with the intention of showing the strength of national character and the viability of a given political system.

propanolol A *drug belonging to the *beta blockers which are on the *IOC list of *banned substances. Propanolol is used in the treatment of angina, *cardiac arrhythmias, high *blood pressure, and to relieve high-*anxiety states.

prophylaxis Any preventative treatment of a disease.

propinquity Nearness; used, for example, of the nearness of an athlete to his or her team-mates. Propinquity is used in particular to denote the location of an athlete in terms of his or her visibility to and observability by team-mates.

proportionality In *anthropometry, the relationship of body-parts one to another or to the whole body.

proportionality, law of *See* Newton's laws of motion.

proprioception The awareness of body position in space. *See also* kinaesthesis.

proprioceptive neuromuscular facilitation (PNF) A technique in which a maximum *static stretch is performed in order to promote relaxation in the same *muscle and to enhance its *range of movement. There is some dispute about the effectiveness of the technique. Many coaches believe that it is a good method of improving *flexibility, but scientific evidence is contradictory.

proprioreceptor An internal sensory receptor, located in the *muscles, *tendons, and *joints, which conveys information about the physical state and position of *skeletal muscles to the *brain. Proprioceptors provide essential information for smooth, co-ordinated movement and the maintenance of body posture. *See also* golgi tendon organs; kinaesthesis; and muscle spindle organs.

propulsion (motive force, propulsive force) The *force that causes motion. In swimming the front crawl, for example, the propulsive force is provided by the combined actions of the feet and the hands pushing the water backward, resulting in forward motion of the swimmer.

propulsive drag force A *drag force which acts in the desired direction of body travel. In swimming, for example, a propulsive drag force results from paddling or pushing movements of the hand through the water and acts in a forward direction to resist the backward hand motion.

propulsive force *See* propulsion.

propylhexedrine A *drug belonging to the *stimulants which are on the *IOC list of *banned substances.

prosocial behaviour Behaviour in which one individual helps another. *See also* sporting behaviour.

prostaglandin A member of a group of *fatty acids derived from *arachidonic acid and found in cell *membranes. Prostaglandins have many effects including stimulating uterine contractions, regulating *blood pressure, and the control of *gastrointestinal tract mobility. They are involved in inflammation: they dilate blood vessels and make them more permeable to fluid and proteins, resulting in a rise in temperature and *oedema. Prostaglandins also increase the sensitivity of nerve-endings to *pain.

prostate gland A *gland, surrounding the neck of the bladder in men, that produces substances added to the *semen.

prostatic hypertrophy Enlargement of the *prostate gland which may constrict the flow of urine. The condition occurs in a large percentage of elderly men and may require surgical treatment. Exercise may exacerbate the problem of difficult urination. Those suffering from the complaint are advised to empty the bladder before physical exertion and not to suppress the urge to pass urine during exercise.

prostatitis Inflammation of the prostate gland, usually caused by bacteria though it may result from mechanical irritation (e.g., in cyclists). Exercise should be avoided during acute attacks.

prosthesis An artificial device (e.g., an artificial leg or a surgically-reconstructed hip-joint) which is attached to the body as a substitute for an absent part.

protective muscle spasm A sustained involuntary muscle contraction which occurs after injury to the muscle as a protective mechanism to prevent further movement. Such spasms commonly result in *muscle stiffness.

protective protein theory A theory which suggests that regular exercise increases the level of fat-carrying *high-density *lipoproteins in the *blood thereby reducing the risk of *heart disease.

protein One of a group of organic *polymers which contain chains of *amino acids linked together by *peptide bonds. Proteins play a vital part in the structure and function of all cells, comprising 10–30 per cent of the cell mass. Structurally, they are divided into two groups: fibrous proteins and globular proteins. Functionally they have many varied roles and act as *enzymes, *hormones, respiratory pigments, and *antibodies. The two main contractile elements in muscle cells, *actin and *myosin, are proteins. Excess protein cannot be stored in the body and is excreted, mainly as urea in the urine. The approximate daily requirement of protein is 0.8 $g kg^{-1}$ bodyweight, the figure rising for children, pregnant women, and nursing mothers. Contrary to what many coaches believe, the protein requirement during heavy exercise is not significantly increased in adults. Consumption of excess protein may cause *dehydration and *constipation, and can lead to *obesity. Protein deficiency causes profound weight-loss; retardation in children; *oedema, and *anaemia. Protein-rich foods include animal products, grains, legumes, and vegetables. *See also* essential amino acids.

proteinuria An abnormal concentration of *serum *proteins in the urine. Proteinuria is a constant feature of renal impairment. Its occurrence after exercise was at one time thought to indicate a serious disturbance of renal function but it is now recognized that moderate proteinuria is common in healthy young adults after heavy exercise. This condition, unlike pathological conditions, is quickly reversed when the athlete rests in a recumbent posture. *See also* athletic pseudonephritis; and orthostatic proteinuria.

proteolytic enzyme An *enzyme which catalyses the breakdown of *proteins. *Hylaluronidase is a proteolytic enzyme that has been used in the treatment of soft tissue injuries.

protocol The formal procedure for conducting an investigation, such as *physiological testing or *drugs-testing.

proton Positively-charged particle located in the nucleus of an atom.

protoplasm The living contents of a cell consisting of *cytoplasm and *nucleoplasm.

protraction Nonangular forward (anterior) movements of a body-part in a *transverse plane, such as the forward projection of a *mandible when the jaw is jutted out. *Compare* retraction.

proxemics The study of how people communicate nonverbally by the way they use the space between themselves and other people.

proximal In *anatomy, situated toward the centre, median line, or the attached end of a limb, or toward the origin of a structure, such as a bone. *See also* directional terms.

proximal convoluted tubule The part of a *kidney nephron nearest to the *glomerulus; it is mainly concerned with obligatory reabsorption of water, reabsorption of essential substances (particularly *glucose), and excretion of *urea.

PRP *See* psychological refractory period.

pruritis Itching caused by irritation of the skin or sometimes by nervous disorders.

pruritis ani Intense irritation and discomfort in the *anal region which may be exacerbated by scratching and secondary infections. Pruritis ani is commonly due to wearing tight clothes and often associated with increased sweating. Treatment consists of scrupulous toilet hygiene, careful washing and drying, followed by the application of *hydrocortisone cream.

pseudoarthrosis A false *joint formed after *dislocation around a displaced bone-end.

pseudocoxalgia *See* Perthes' disease.

pseudoephedrine A *drug belonging to the *stimulants which are on the *IOC list of *banned substances.

psoas *See* psoas major.

psoas major (psoas) A long, thick, thigh *muscle, just *medial to the *iliacus. Its *origin is on the *transverse processes and discs of *lumbar vertebrae. It shares a *tendon of *insertion with the iliacus with which it is the *prime mover of *hip flexion. The psoas major also effects *lateral flexion of the *vertebral column and is an important postural muscle (*see* posture).

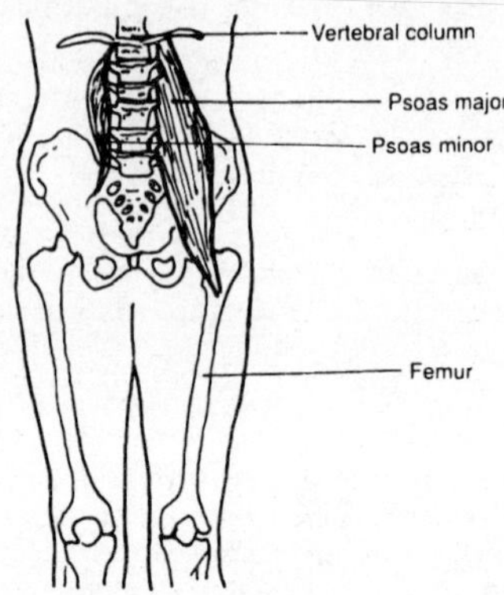

psoas muscles

psoas minor A small thigh *muscle which shares the same actions as the *psoas major. The psoas minor is often absent.

psoriasis A *chronic, noninfectious genetic skin disorder which is characterized by a recurring scaly rash. Although heavy sweating can cause discomfort in psoriasis sufferers, it does not usually stop participation in sport except where the condition is linked with the development of *arthritis.

psyche An ancient Greek word meaning soul or mind; it often refers to the mental as opposed to the physical aspects of an individual.

psyched-out A colloquial term indicating a disruption of *flow and a disturbance of mental balance.

psyched-up A colloquial term describing an increased state of *arousal and confidence of an athlete prior to competition.

psychiatrist A medical doctor who specializes in the treatment of mental of behavioural disorders. *Compare* psychologist.

psychiatry A banch of *medicine concerned with the study, prevention, and treatment of mental illness.

psychic energy A term sometimes used synonymosly with *arousal. It refers to the vigour, vitality, and intensity with which the mind functions. It can be either positive or negative. When performers go from low to high levels of psychic energy they are said to become *psyched-up; while those who go from high to low levels are *psyched-out. As in arousal, there is an optimal level of psychic energy. *See also* inverted-U principle.

psyching-up Colloquial term used by athletes and coaches to refer to *motivational strategy processes aimed at enhancing performance by raising *arousal and increasing the *activation level. Psyching-up often consists of a coach exhorting athletes to make greater efforts (*see* pep talk). Sometimes the process results in heightened levels of *anxiety and poorer performances (*see* inverted-U principle).

psychoactivator *See* psychomotor stimulant drug.

psychoanaleptic *See* psychomotor stimulant drug.

psychoanalysis A method of treating mental disorders, pioneered by Sigmund Freud (1856–1939), which employs the techniques of free association, interpretation, and dream analysis to reveal and release repressed fears so that they can be dealt with effectively.

psychoanalytically based theory Theory of psychosocial behaviour based on the assumption that the current behaviour of a person has developed as a result of past experiences, especially those of early childhood. *See also* psychoanalysis.

psychobiological model A model of behaviour which includes biological and psychological factors. A psychobiological model of *adherence may include body composition (biological factor) and self-motivation (psychological factor).

psychodynamic theory A major theoretical approach to the study of *personality based mainly on in-depth examination of the whole person and his or her unconscious motives. The most influential proponent was Sigmund Freud (1856–1939) who believed that the personality resulted from a dynamic interaction between its three components: the *id, the *ego, and the *superego.

psychogenic Originating from the *psyche rather than the body, such as an illness which has a psychological basis rather than an organic basis. *See also* psychosomatic.

psychogenic dependence A condition in which a *drug-taker experiences an irresistible craving or compulsion to take a drug for pleasure or for relief from discomfort.

psychological core The central, internal, and consistent part of an individual's *personality which includes an individual's self-concept, basic values, attitudes, and motives; a person's true self.

psychological fatigue *See* subjective fatigue.

psychological fitness Mental fitness; such as the fitness of an athlete to cope with the stresses of competition.

psychological measuring instrument A technique, usually with proven *reliability and *validity, for measuring a psychological phenomenon. An example is the *competitive state anxiety inventory for measuring *competitive stress.

psychological orientation The mental attitude which a person has towards the value of his or her work and workmates. The psychological orientation includes *self-orientation, and *task-orientation.

psychological preparation Mental preparation in which competitors learn how to deal with *psychological stresses and achieve optimal levels of *arousal so that they will be able to perform to the best of their ability.

psychological presence The degree to which a performer feels the presence of an audience. *See also* evaluation apprehension.

psychological profile (personality profile) A distinct pattern of behavioural responses that an individual or group displays. The profile is usually based on the results of several *inventories which are displayed on a graph or in a table. *See also* iceberg profile.

psychological refractoriness *See* psychological refractory period.

psychological refractory period (PRP; psychological refractoriness) The delay in the response to the second of two closely-spaced *stimuli. Ball-players often attempt to induce PRP in their opponents by disguising a shot or 'selling a dummy' (i.e., feinting to go one way and then going another).

psychological well-being (mental well-being) A mental condition characterized by pleasant feelings of good health, exhilaration, high *self-esteem and confidence, often associated with regular physical activity.

psychologist An individual who has completed a programme of study in psychology and is engaged in research, clinical treatment, teaching, or other applications of *psychology.

psychology A branch of science which studies the mind, mental activities, and behaviour.

psychometrics **1** Measurement of mental factors. **2** Investigation of the time factor in mental processes.

psychomotor (psychomotoric) Pertaining to both mental activity and muscular movement. *See also* motor.

psychomotoric *See* psychomotor.

psychomotor stimulant drug (psychoactivator; psychoanaleptic; psychostimulant) A *drug, such as *caffeine or *cocaine, which can reduce *fatigue and elevate mood so that a person feels capable of achieving greater muscular efforts. *See also* stimulant.

psychomotor test Psychological *questionnaires and tests which assess *psychomotor *reaction time and other psychomotor functions.

psychoneuromuscular theory A theory postulated to explain the positive effects of *motor imagery. The theory suggests that vivid, imagined events produce *neuromuscular responses similar to those of an actual experience. That is, the images produced in the *brain transmit impulses to the *muscles for the execution of the imagined skill, although these impulses may be so minor that they do not actually produce movement, or the movement may be undetectable. Support for this theory comes from a number of sources. *Electromyograph patterns of the muscle activity of skiers who imagine that they are performing a downhill run closely approximate the electrical patterns of the skiers' muscles when they have actually been skiing. *See also* imagery; and symbolic-learning theory.

psychophysiology The study of the relationships between psychological states and physiological measurements; for example, that between *anxiety and *heart-rate.

psychosis A severe mental illness characterized by a distorted perception of reality often resulting in delusions and hallucinations. The condition may be due to physical damage to the *brain (organic psychosis) or it may have no apparent physical cause (functional psychosis).

psychosocial behaviour The behaviour and mental activities of individuals and groups which influence and determine their relationships, their ability to work together, and their attitudes towards each other.

psychostimulant *See* psychomotor stimulant drug.

psychotherapy The treatment of emotional and personality problems, and mental illness by the use of psychological methods.

psychotonic A *stimulant, such as *amphetamine, which has its primary effect on the *brain and the *central nervous system. A psychotonic increases psychological tone and delays the subjective feeling of fatigue without actually improving muscular performance.

psychotrophic drug *See* psychotropic drug.

psychotropic drug (psychotrophic drug) A *drug which affects emotional state. Psychotropics include *antidepressants, *sedatives, *stimulants, and *tranquillizers.

psychrometer An instrument used to measure *relative humidity.

pternion A *landmark which is the most posterior point of the heel of the foot when the subject is standing.

pteroylglutamic acid An alternative name for *folic acid.

PTH *See* parathormone.

ptyalin An *enzyme (an *amylase) secreted by the *salivary glands to start the digestion of *starch.

puberty (pubescence) A period in the *life course between the appearance of pubic hair and (in females) the first *menarche, or (in males) the first development of sperm. Puberty varies but in females it usually occurs between 9 and 15 years, while in males it usually occurs between 11 and 14 years.

pubes Pubic hair or the region of the body on which it grows.

pubescence *See* puberty.

pubic bone *See* pubis.

pubic lice Small, wingless, blood-sucking insects which infect the hair around the genitalia and cause itching. They are sexually transmitted but do not usually interfere with physical activity.

pubic symphysis A fibrocartilaginous disc joining the two *pubic bones of the *pelvic girdle. The pubic symphysis is an *amphiarthrotic joint capable of slight movement which becomes more mobile during pregnancy.

pubis The two bones which make up the *anterior, *ventral part of the *pelvis. In adults the bones fuse at the *pubic symphysis. *See also* coxal bones.

pudendal nerve Nerve supplying the external genitalia.

pulled elbow A *subluxation of the head of the *radius in children, accompanied by paralytic pain and disability of the forearm and the hand.

pulled heel cord *See* Achilles tendon strain.

pulled muscle A common term for a *partial muscle-tear or a *muscle-strain.

pulley A wheel-like device for changing the direction of the application of a *force. A pulley usually has a groove on which a cord can run in order to change the direction of the force applied to the cord. A pulley-like action is represented in the human body by *tendons which wrap around parts of bones and thereby change the line of pull of a *muscle, resulting in a line of movement which might otherwise not have occurred. The *patellar tendon, for example, passes over the *patella and inserts on the tibia at a greater angle than would otherwise have occurred. This change in angle increases the rotary component of the force of the *quadriceps muscle and decreases the stabilizing component, thereby achieving a more effective force in movement.

pulmonary Pertaining to the lungs.

pulmonary artery A *blood vessel carrying deoxygenated *blood from the right *ventricle to the *lungs.

pulmonary blood pressure The *blood pressure within the *blood vessels supplying the *lungs.

pulmonary capillary blood volume The volume of *blood that is in contact with the gas within the *alveoli of the *lungs at any instant.

pulmonary circuit *See* pulmonary circulation.

pulmonary circulation (pulmonary circuit) The flow of *blood from the right *ventricle of the *heart through the *blood vessels of the *lungs and back to the left *atrium of the heart.

pulmonary diffusion capacity The volume of a gas that diffuses across the *membranes between the *alveoli and lung *capillaries per minute per *torr mean pressure difference. The pulmonary diffusion capacity represents the rate of *diffusion of the gas between the alveoli and the blood of the lung capillaries. It varies with many factors, but the surface area of contact between the alveoli and the blood in the pulmonary capillary is especially important. The pulmonary diffusion capacity for oxygen increases in an approximately linear manner with increasing workloads. It levels off at near maximum loads when it is up to three times more than at resting levels. Trained athletes tend to have larger diffusion capacities at rest and during exercise than non-athletes.

pulmonary edema *See* pulmonary oedema.

pulmonary function The role of the *lungs in meeting the demands imposed by muscular activity to deliver oxygen and to eliminate carbon dioxide from the *pulmonary circulation. Pulmonary function is accomplished by the flow of *blood through the lung *capillaries, by *ventilation, and by the diffusion of *oxygen from the lungs into the blood and of *carbon dioxide from the blood to the air in the lungs.

pulmonary function test A test of the ability of the lungs to carry out their function of supplying the *blood with *oxygen and eliminating *carbon dioxide. *See also* forced expiratory volume; and minute ventilation volume.

pulmonary oedema An accumulation of fluid in the *alveoli and tissue of the *lungs.

pulmonary perfusion The volume of *blood flowing through the *lungs.

pulmonary valve A *semi-lunar valve which prevents backflow of *blood from the *pulmonary artery to the right *ventricle.

pulmonary vein A *vein carrying oxygenated *blood from the *lungs to the left *atrium of the *heart.

pulmonary ventilation (breathing; external respiration) The movement of air in and out of the *lungs during *inspiration and *expiration respectively. *See also* minute ventilation.

pulse The rhythmic expansion and recoil of the arteries resulting from a wave of pressure produced by contraction of the left *ventricle of the *heart. The pulse can be felt in any *artery sufficiently close to the body surface which passes over a bone. *See also* pulse rate.

pulse pressure The difference between *systolic blood pressure and *diastolic blood pressure.

pulse rate The frequency per minute of pressure waves propagated along the superficial, peripheral arteries, such as the carotid and radial arteries (*see* pulse). In normal, healthy individuals, the pulse rate and *heart rate are identical, but this is not so in patients suffering from some *cardiovascular diseases such as *arrythmias.

pumping-up A body-builder's term for increasing the apparent size of *muscle by lifting comparatively light weights many times in quick succession. The contraction of muscles compresses *veins so that less blood leaves the *capillaries than enters through the *arteries. The pressure within the capillaries is raised, forcing some fluid out into the tissue spaces and thus increasing the size of the muscles. Shortly after exercise, the pressure is reduced as the excess fluid in the tissue spaces returns to the blood and the size of the muscle returns to normal.

punch drunk *See* encephalopathy, traumatic.

punishment An unpleasant *stimulus presented immediately following a particular behaviour. Punishment is applied to weaken the response. *Compare* negative reinforcement; and reward.

pupil Central opening of the *iris of the eye through which light enters the eye. The diameter of the pupil is controlled by contraction or expansion of the iris.

pupillary constriction Reduction in the size of the *pupil of the eye. Pupillary constriction functions with *accommodation and *convergence to enable a person, such as a batsman, to retain focus on a fast approaching projectile, such as a cricket ball.

Purkinje fibres Modified *cardiac muscle fibres consisting of *conduction myofibrils which act as a fast conduction system (known as the Purkinje system) from the right and left branches of an *atrioventricular bundle to all parts of the *ventricles of the heart.

purpose An intention, expressed as a conscious thought in the present, to realize a future goal or aim.

purposive explanation An explanation of behaviour in terms of the *purposes or the conscious intentions of the *actors.

purposive sampling A form of sampling in which the selection of the sample is based on the judgement of the researcher as to which subjects best fit the criteria of the study. *Compare* random sampling.

purposivism Any approach in *psychology which claims that, in addition to *stimuli, *purposes are effective determinants of *behaviour.

purulent Resembling, consisting of, or containing *pus.

pus A thick, yellow product of *inflammation consisting of dead *leucocytes and *bacteria, cell debris, and tissue fluid.

push-up An upper-body exercise. The subject lies in a prone position on the floor with legs together, palms of the hand flat on the floor, and hands pointed forward and approximately under the shoulders. The legs and back are kept straight while the subject pushes up with the arms to a raised position with the arms fully extended. The subject then returns to the starting position.

P wave A component of the *electrocardiograph which appears as a small positive deflection prior to the *QRS complex. It normally lasts less than 0.12 s and has an amplitude of 0.25 mV or less. It represents *atrial depolarization.

pyelonephritis An inflammation of the *kidney. Acute pyelonephritis is usually caused by bacterial infection. Symptoms include a frequent desire to pass water, pain in the loins, fever, and shivering. Untreated, it can cause permanent kidney damage. Treatment includes identification and elimination of the bacteria responsible. Physical exertion during attacks of pyelonephritis is strongly advised against and should not be resumed until all the symptoms have disappeared.

pylorus The lower region of the *stomach leading into the *duodenum.

pyragallol A soluble *phenol which in an *alkaline solution absorbs *oxygen and is used to estimate the volume of oxygen in a sample.

pyramid 1 A conical mass of cells in the *medulla of the *kidney. 2 A pyramid-shaped area in the *medulla oblongata of the *brain.

pyramidal cells Pyramid-shaped cells in the *motor cortex which send *nerve impulses to *voluntary muscle.

pyramidal system A collection of nerve tracts (*see* pyramidal tract) within the *pyramid of the *medulla oblongata.

pyramidal tract (corticospinal tract) A tract of *nerve fibres which transmit *nerve impulses from *pyramidal cells in the *motor cortex through the *medulla oblongata to the anterior *motor neurones of the *spinal cord. *See also* primary cortex.

pyramid system A type of *strength-training in which loads are increased successively in each set while the number of repetitions in a set is reduced. Assuming a 2-RM (*see* repetition maximum) of 45 kg, a typical session might consist of seven repetitions at 20 kg; six repetitions at 25 kg; five repetitions at 30 kg; four repetitions at 35 kg; three repetitions at 40 kg; two repetitions at 45 kg.

pyramid-training A formal method of varying the duration and intensity of work and *recovery intervals in running, swimming, and canoeing. *See also* locomotives.

pyrexia *See* fever.

pyridene A colourless organic liquid with a very unpleasant smell and taste, which is used to make methylated spirits unpalatable. Some medicines are derived from pyridene. Pyridoxine (*see* vitamin B_6) consists of the combination of three pyridene groups.

pyridoxene *See* vitamin B_6 .

pyrovalerone A *drug belonging to the *stimulants which are on the *IOC list of *banned substances.

pyrrole A five-membered ring structure which contains nitrogen. *See also* porphyrin.

pyruvic acid An important three-carbon molecule formed as an end-product of *glycolysis. In the *lactacid system, pyruvic acid is converted into *lactic acid, but if *oxygen is available it is converted to *acetylcoenzyme A which enters the *Krebs cycle.

pyruvate A salt or *ester of *pyruvic acid.

Pythagorean theorem A theorem which states that for any right-angled triangle, the square of the hypotenuse is equal to the sum of the squares of the opposite two sides. Pythagorean theorem is used in *biomechanics to solve problems dealing with the *vector quantities.

Q

Q An abbreviation used in physiology to denote cardiac output.

Q_{10} (temperature coefficient) A measure of the effect of a 10 °C rise in temperature on the velocity of a chemical reaction. The Q_{10} is expressed as the ratio of the velocity of a chemical reaction at a given temperature to that of the same reaction at a temperature 10 °C lower.

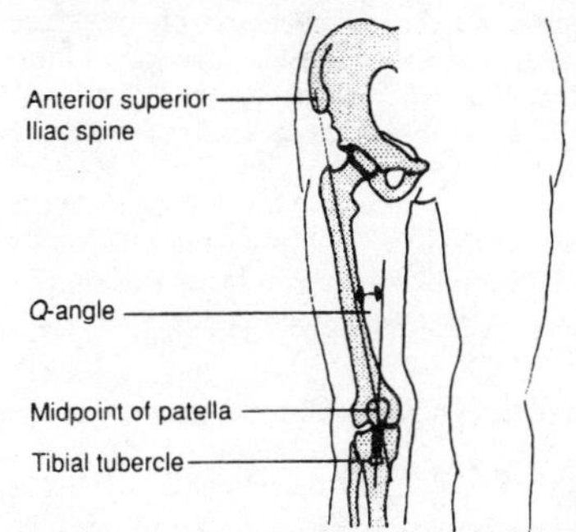

Q-angle

Q-angle (quadriceps angle) The angle formed between the longitudinal axis of the *femur, representing the pull of the *quadriceps muscle, and a line that represents the pull of the *patellar tendon. A clinical measure of the *Q*-angle is obtained by connecting the central point of the *patella with the anterior *iliac spine above and the *tibial tuberosity below. The *Q*-angle is normally less than 15° for men and less than 20° for women when the quadriceps are relaxed. The angle becomes smaller if the quadriceps are contracted.

QRS complex The largest component of an *electrocardiograph which corresponds to *ventricular depolarization; it normally lasts less than 0.1 s.

Q–T interval The time interval from the start of the *QRS complex to the end of the *T wave. It reflects the electrical *systole of the *cardiac cycle.

quackery The activities or methods of an unqualified person who claims to have medical knowledge.

quadratus In *anatomy, a four-sided *muscle.

quadratus femoris A short, thick four-sided thigh *muscle. The quadratus femoris has its *origin on the *ischial tuberosity and extends laterally from the *pelvis to have its insertion on the *greater trochanter of the *femur. Its actions include lateral rotation of the thigh; it also stabilizes the hip-joint.

quadratus lumborum One of a pair of fleshy *muscles forming part of the posterior abdominal wall. The quadratus lumborum has its *origins on the *iliac crest and the *iliotibial fascia. Its *insertions are in the *transverse processes of the upper *lumbar vertebrae and lower margin of the twelfth rib. The actions of the quadriceps lumborum include lateral trunk *flexion. It is also involved in maintaining an upright posture.

quadriceps *See* quadriceps femoris.

quadriceps angle *See Q*-angle.

quadriceps femoris (quadriceps; quads) A *muscle of the anterior aspect of the thigh which has four distinct portions: the *rectus femoris, *vastus intermedius, *vastus lateralis, and *vastus medialis. The four muscle heads join in a single *tendon which crosses the *patella to insert onto the *tibial tuberosity. The quadriceps femoris is the main extensor muscle of the knee-joint and is important in weight-bearing and locomotion.

quadriceps insertion strain An *overuse injury which is marked by pain in the tendon of the *quadriceps muscle, just above and on top of the knee-cap. Quadriceps insertion strain is commonly caused by excessive hill-running or squats.

quadriceps muscle-pull A relatively common injury, due either to overextension (e.g., when kicking) or to those in poor condition taking part in sports such as badminton, cycling, squash, soccer, and weight-lifting. The leg hurts when touched and feels sore when the *quadriceps contracts during the performance of activities such as going up stairs, going uphill, or doing squats. *See also* muscle-pull.

quads *See* quadriceps.

qualitative Applied to certain subjective aspects of experience, such as blue and sour, which cannot be defined by a single measurement. These are called qualitative aspects of experience or merely qualities. *Compare* quantitative.

qualitative analysis Identification of the components of a system and the evaluation of those components in non-numerical terms.

quality 1 A fundamental aspect or attribute of sensory experience which is distinguishable in non-quantitative terms from others in the same sensory field. **2** The value, grade, or standard of excellence of a performance. *Compare* quantity.

quantification The process of expressing observations in numerical terms to aid analysis and comparison.

quantitative Pertaining to considerations of measurable intensity, amount, or size.

quantitative analysis Description of the components of a phenomenon, such as movement, or a chemical substance in numerical terms. *Compare* qualititative analysis.

quantity The degree, amount, or size of a particular thing. *Compare* quality.

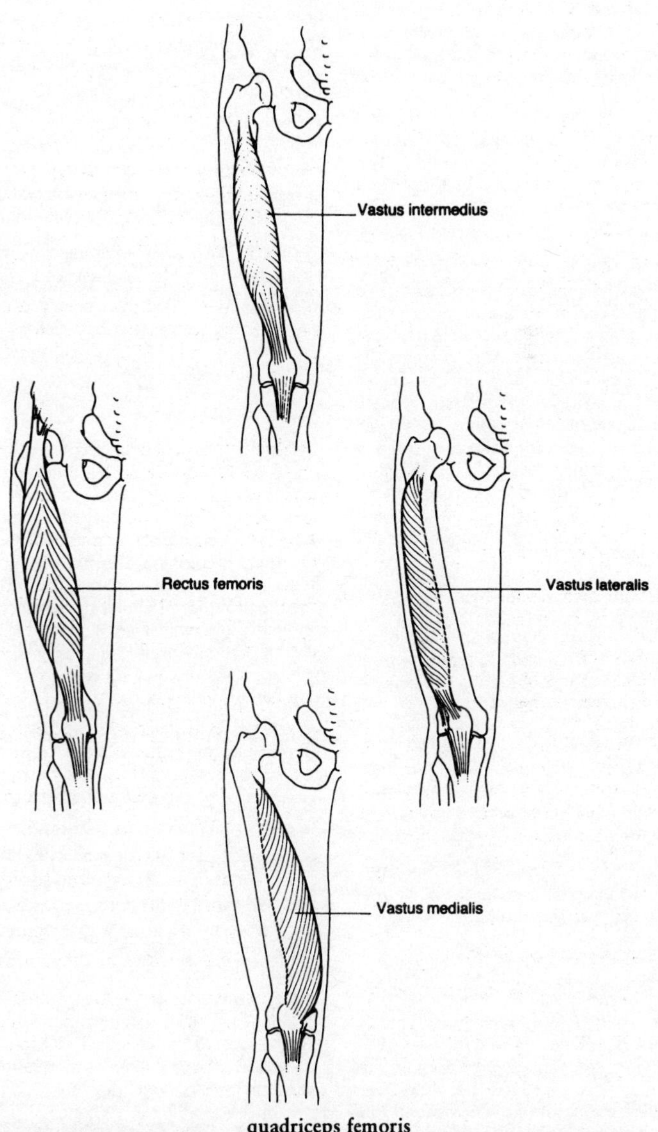

quadriceps femoris

quantity of motion *See* linear motion.

Quebec ten-second test A short-term *anaerobic test consisting of a ten-second maximal effort on a *bicycle ergometer with a microprocessor to record the total work performed each second.

Quebec ninety-second test A long-term *anaerobic test consisting of a ninety-second maximal effort performed on a *bicycle ergometer during which the total work performed is computed by a microprocessor.

questionnaire A form containing questions to which a number of people are asked to respond. The information gained from the questionnaire is often subjected to statistical analysis. It can be used to examine the general characteristics of a population, to compare the attitudes of different groups, and to test theories. Questionnaires appear simple, but they are very difficult to compile in a manner which establishes *reliability and *validity. A question worded in one way, for example, may obtain different responses from the same question worded slightly differently.

Quetelet index *See* body-mass index.

quiet breathing A form of *breathing which is relatively noiseless, typically by a person who is at rest or who is not making forced ventilatory movements.

quinine An alkaloid *drug obtained from the bark of the Cinchona tree. It has been used in the treatment of *malaria but has been largely replaced by more effective, less toxic drugs.

quinone A *benzene derivative. Many quinones act as electron-carriers in the *mitochondria. *See also* vitamin K.

quota sample A type of sampling, commonly used to study human populations, in which a sample is selected from a population as a proportion of each defined part of the parent population. The parent population is divided into a number of parts on the basis of some relevant factor, such as size, age, sex, or ethnic origin. The sample-size for each part reflects the parent population structure. During sampling, the selection of individuals within a category continues until the quota has been filled. Quota sampling does not conform to the requirements of *random sampling.

quota system Restriction of the number of a particlar group in a sports team. In English cricket, for example, each county team is allowed to have only a limited number of overseas players. The quota system is alleged to occur in the USA with the number of black players on a team (e.g., a basketball or American football team) being limited.

quotient The result of dividing one number by another. *See also* intelligence quotient; and respiratory quotient.

R

r *See* correlation coefficient.

R *See* respiratory quotient.

race (**racial group**) A group of people who share a common ancestry. The use of the term in everyday language often implies that the group are biologically distinct and share qualities which are unalterable; this view of race has been biologically discredited and many sociologists prefer to use the term *ethnic group.

racial discrimination (**racism**) A prejudicial or unequal treatment of an individual or a group on the basis of their supposed membership of a racial or *ethnic group. *See also* race; and racial stratification

racial group *See* race.

racial stratification Process by which the supposed membership of a race of an individual or group becomes the basis for *social stratification.

racism *See* racial discrimination

rad *See* radian.

radial 1 Pertaining to the *radius of the forearm. **2** Pertaining to a *radius of a circle or a ray. **3** Applied to lines which radiate from a central point, like spokes on a wheel.

radial artery A branch of the *brachial artery leading down the forearm from the elbow, across the wrist, and into the palm of the hand.

radial component The component of a given *vector (for example, a *force) acting at right angles to the curved path followed by a body. *Compare* tangential component.

radiale A *landmark located at the upper and *lateral border of the *head of the *radius.

radial fossa A depression on the *humerus which receives the head of the *radius when the elbow is flexed.

radial groove A groove which runs obliquely down the *posterior aspect of the *humerus *shaft and is the course of the *radial nerve.

radial height A *body height measurement made from *radiale to *base.

radial nerve An important mixed nerve (i.e., carrying both *sensory neurones and *motor neurones) which is a branch of the *brachial plexus in the arm. It is one of three nerves which supply the forearm and hand.

radial pulse The *pulse taken by *palpation at the wrist where the *radial artery runs alongside the *radius.

radial reflex A *reflex action which is induced by tapping the lower end of the *radius causing the forearm, and sometimes the fingers, to flex.

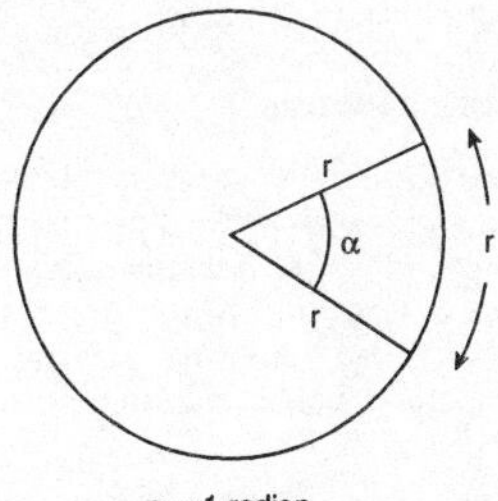

radian

radian (rad) A unit of *angular measure. The radian is the angle subtended at the centre of a circle by an arc equal in length to the *radius of the circle. 2π rad = 360°, 1 rad = 57.296°.

radiant energy *See* electromagnetic energy.

radiation The emission or transfer of *radiant energy as rays, waves, or particles. *See also* solar radiation.

Radin's rule A rule which states that structures will tear at their weakest point. For example, a *muscle-tear occurs most commonly at the *muscle–*tendon junction.

radioactivity The spontaneous disintegration of the atomic nuclei of the heavier *isotopes of certain *elements, during which energy or particles are emitted resulting in the atoms becoming more stable.

radiocarpal joint The *synovial, *condyloid *joint between the *radius and *proximal carpals which allows *abduction, *adduction, *circumduction, *extension, and *flexion of the wrist.

radiography *See* X-ray.

radiohumeral joint *See* elbow-joint

radioimmunoassay (RIA) A very sensitive technique which is widely used to measure a range of biological substances, and to detect *drugs such as *peptide hormones and *anabolic steroids during dope testing. The technique is based on the ability of an *unlabelled form of the substance to inhibit competitively the binding of a radioactively-*labelled substance by specific *antibodies. The concentration of the unknown sample is determined by comparing the degree of inhibition with that produced by a series of standards containing known amounts of the substance. The reliability of the test depends on the precise specification of the conditions under which the tests are made.

radioisotope An *isotope that exhibits *radioactivity and emits particles or energy during its decay into another element.

radionuclide scan *See* scintigraphy.

radioulnar joint A *synovial, *pivot joint between the *radius and *ulna. The head of the radius rotates within a ring-like *ligament secured to the ulna permitting *pronation and *supination of the hand.

radius 1 A *bone of the forearm. The radius is shorter than the *ulna and, in the *anatomical position, lies laterally, on the thumb side. **2** A line extending from centre to the circumference of a circle.

radius of gyration In a rotating system, a length representing the distance between the point about which rotation of a body occurs (the *axis of rotation) and the point at which the body's *mass is distributed and has the maximum effect. It is the horizontal distance between the axis of rotation and a point which represents the sum of all the separate *moments of inertia of the parts of the body. It is given by $k = 1/2(I/m)$, where k = the radius of gyration, I = moment of inertia, and m = mass of the body.

radius of rotation For a rotating body, the linear distance from any point on its path of rotation to the *axis of rotation.

ramus 1 A thin bar projecting from a *bone that usually helps to form a *joint. **2** A branch, especially of a *nerve, *artery, or *vein.

random Lacking any pre-arranged order, as if due to pure chance.

random sample A sample from a *population selected in a manner which ensures that each member of the population has an equal chance of being selected.

random sampling A procedure for selecting subjects or items for research on the basis of chance. The subjects or items are chosen from the *population in such a way that all of them have the same chance of being selected. *Compare* quota sampling.

range The spread of values of a set of data. The range is the difference between the maximum and minimum values and is a measure of the dispersion of a set of values. *See also* descriptive statistics.

range of joint movement *See* range of movement.

range of motion *See* range of movement.

range of movement The ability to move *bones about a *joint through an arc of a circle. For example, if the knee joint can be extended from 30° at full *flexion to 165° at full *extension, the range of movement is 165–30 = 135°. The complete range of movement of a joint is divided into three equal parts (*see* inner range; middle range; and outer range) in which the degree of muscle *contraction varies. *See also* maximum active range; *maximum passive range; and *normal active range.

range of projectile Total horizontal distance a projectile travels while it is in the air. In the absence of *air resistance, it is equal to the product of the *horizontal velocity at release and the time of flight.

ranked list (ranked response) A technique, often used in questionnaires, in which the respondent places items in order of importance.

ranked response *See* ranked list.

ranking structure A system used to assign a player to a hierarchial position of excellence based on ability in a particular sport.

raphe A line, ridge, or furrow in a tissue or organ.

raptures of the deep *See* nitrogen narcosis.

ratchet mechanism The mechanism by which a muscle fibre contracts. The ratchet mechanism consists of the attachment, detachment, and reattachment of *cross-bridges from *myosin onto *actin. *See also* sliding-filament theory.

rate control An ability which is thought to underlie tasks for which speed of movement of the body or a body-segment must be adjusted to movements within the environment; for example, shooting at a moving target, or kicking a ball to a moving team-mate. *See also* timing.

rate of force development (RFD) A measure of the rate at which a *force is developed. Rate of force development (RFD) is measured in Ns^{-1} or Nms^{-1}. The average RFD is sometimes calculated as the *peak force divided by the time taken to reach peak force.

rate of relaxation A measure of the rate at which a *force or *torque is reduced when a *muscle relaxes. It is important in sports which require a rapid cessation of contraction.

rating scale A technique used to measure, among other things, *personality. Characteristically, an independent judge or judges observe an individual in specific situations and use a checklist or scale to record behaviour.

ratio **1** The numerical comparison of one class of objects with another (e.g., the ratio of men to women). **2** In mathematics, the numerical relationship between two quantities of the same type. The ratio of 30g to 10g, and 60g to 20g, is 2:1 in both cases.

ratio level measurement *See* ratio measurement.

ratio measurement (ratio level measurement) Measurement of values or observations using real numbers where distances between categories are fixed, equal, and proportionate. Zero is naturally defined. A man two metres tall, for example, is two times the height of a boy one metre tall.

rational choice theory An approach to sociological theorizing which assumes that social life can be explained in terms of the rational choices of individual *actors. That is, social life is the result of individuals choosing options which they believe likely to have the best overall outcome.

rationality The process of using reason or logic to solve a problem.

rationalization **1** The conscious or unconscious explanation of events or *behaviour which avoids giving the true reasons for the events or behaviour because they would be disadvantageous to the subject, or would be socially unacceptable. **2** The process whereby social organizations increasingly emphasize efficient means and planning in order to achieve their goals. *See also* ludic institutionalization.

raw score Score obtained directly from the measuring instrument, and which has not yet been tested by statistical methods.

ray A straight beam of electromagnetic radiation, such as light.

RBC An abbreviation sometimes used for *red blood cell.

RDA *See* recommended daily allowance.

reaction board A device used to estimate the *centre of gravity of a person. It consists of a board supported horizontally on two very thin edges, one of which rests on a block of wood while the other rests on the platform of a set of scales. The subject's weight is recorded in different positions on the board and the figures used to estimate the centre of gravity.

reaction board method *See* board-and-scales method.

reaction force A counterforce; an equal and opposite *force exerted by a second body on a first in response to a force applied by the first body on the second. *See also* ground reaction force.

reaction formation The repression of an unacceptable feeling or condition by reversing it to a directly opposite emotion or condition. For example, an athlete may deny his or her real feelings about a coach and instead reverse the personally less-acceptable dislike or even hate, into the personally more-acceptable emotion of liking or even love. Reaction formation is regarded by some as a mechanism of *ego defense where the energies of the *id are redirected in the opposite direction.

reaction potential The level in an athlete of potential excitement associated with a particular response. Reaction potential is a construct of *drive theory. In any condition of competing responses (where one is correct and the other incorrect, for example), the selected response is the one associated with the highest reaction potential. This is called the dominant response and may or may not be the correct response.

reaction time **1** The interval from the presentation of a *stimulus to the initiation of the response. Reaction time is a very simple measure to collect and it is used extensively in the *chronometric approach to *information-processing to study the different stages of information-processing. It is a sum of all the event-durations that occur between the presentation of a stimulus and the evocation of response; it depends on the length of the *neural pathway between the *receptor organ (e.g., eye or ear) and the responding *muscles (e.g., in the leg of a runner) together with delays incurred in the central processing of information. Reaction times of 14–16 hundredths of a second for acoustic stimuli and 16–18 hundredths of a second for optical stimuli are generally regarded as good. 2 A skill-oriented ability which underlies tasks for which there is one stimulus and one response, and for which the subject must react as quickly as possible after a stimulus in single reaction time situation; for example, a sprint-start in swimming. *See also* choice reaction time; response time; and simple reaction time.

reaction time probe technique *See* probe technique.

reactive aggression A form of *hostile aggression in which there is a conscious attempt to injure another person, as in a retaliation. *See also* aggression.

reactive behaviour In studies of coaching behaviour, the responses or reactions of a coach to player or team behaviour. An example of reactive behaviour is a coach verbally correcting an athlete after the athlete has made a mistake. *Compare* spontaneous behaviour.

reactive inhibition A term used in *drive theory to describe a depressant variable that is built up during non-reinforced trials and that reduces the quality of a performance. Reactive inhibition has ben used to explain why a basketball player, attempting a hundred foul shots, performs better in the middle of the session than at the end, and generally performs better at the beginning of a session the next day than at the end of the previous session.

readiness The time, resulting largely from maturational factors, when somebody is first capable of correctly completing a task.

readying mechanism A mechanism that predisposes a person for *hostile aggression, but which is not the cause of the *aggression. For example, hostile aggression is more likely to occur in the presence of a readying mechanism such as high levels of *physiological arousal.

rear foot valgus A condition in which the rear of the foot tends to curve outwards; that is, it tends to be everted (*see* eversion) at the ankle-joint. Sufferers usually need to strengthen the *muscles which effect *inversion of the foot, and may need instep supports or *orthoses if participating in running sports.

rear foot varus A condition in which the rear of the foot tends to curve inwards due to *inversion of the ankle-joint. Sufferers have an increased susceptibility to ankle sprains upon landing after a jump. They usually need to strengthen the muscles which effect *eversion of the foot, to help pull the foot back to its neutral position.

reason A faculty of the human mind which enables logical inferences to be made and rational arguments to be undertaken to understand the world and solve problems.

reasoning Solving a problem implicitly, using symbols to represent objects or situations. Reasoning involves thinking through a problem rather than engaging in overt trial and error.

rebound The springing back of an object when it meets a resistance greater than its own. *See also* angle of rebound.

rebound angle *See* angle of rebound.

recall Retrieval of past experience; remembering a past event with minimal cues. In free recall, a series of events is recalled in any order; in serial recall, a specific order is required as well.

reception time The period of time between the beginning of a *stimulus and the first change in electrical activity in the *cerebral cortex of the *brain. It is a component of *reaction time.

receptor A cell or group of cells specialized for response to particular types of *stimuli. Receptors enable the body to detect changes in the external or internal *environment. All sensory nerve-endings function as receptors. *See also* exteroceptor; interoceptor; and proprioceptor.

receptor anticipation A situation in which an individual anticipates the arrival of an event by watching or listening to relevant parts of the *environment; the individual learns to associate critical events with the appropriate environmental stimuli. Receptor anticipation is very common and provides the basis for many motor tasks, enabling individuals to respond to signals at appropriate times. In cricket, for example, a fielder anticipates the time of arrival of the ball and makes preparatory movements to catch it by listening to how the ball was struck and watching its progress.

receptor potential *See* generator potential.

receptor site A molecular site on the surface of, or within, a cell that recognizes and binds with specific molecules, and which results in a specific change in the cell.

reciprocal inhibition A process which occurs in an *antagonistic pair of muscles to inhibit the *stretch reflex; when an *agonist muscle contracts, it sends inhibitory nerve impulses to its opposing muscle (antagonist) causing it to relax as a result of a reflex action.

reciprocal innervation An alternative term for *reciprocal inhibition which emphasizes that each member of an *antagonistic pair of muscles can transmit information to its opposing member, inhibiting its contraction. During *flexion of the elbow, for example, the *biceps brachii inhibits contraction of the *triceps brachii, while during *extension of the elbow, the triceps inhibits the biceps.

reciprocity An interaction between two parties (for example, a coach and an athlete) in which there is give and take on both sides, and the two parties are working to their mutual advantage.

recognition Perceiving something as having been experienced before, as being familiar; a method of measuring *memory.

recommended daily allowance (RDA; recommended dietary allowance) Recommended daily intake of *essential nutrients. The RDA refers to the estimated amount of nutrients needed to meet the needs of almost all healthy people so that they can maintain good health. The estimates are applied to population groups and are not aimed at meeting the requirements of a specific individual. These estimates differ for various conditions and ages, among women, men, children, the elderly, and pregnant and lactating women. RDAs are usually given as daily allowances; they are not minimum amounts required, but amounts recommended for optimal *health.

recommended dietary allowance *See* recommended daily allowance.

recovery The physiological processes taking place especially in the period following an acute bout of exercise when the body is restored to its pre-exercise condition. Recovery processes include replenishment of *muscle glycogen and *phosphagen stores, removal of *lactic acid and other *metabolites, reoxygenation of *myoglobin, and *protein replacement.

recovery period Period following exercise, when the body is restored to its pre-exercise condition. *See also* recovery.

recovery phase Part of the running action which starts when the feet leave the ground. The heel is pulled towards the buttocks and the thigh is swung through an arc, bringing it parallel to the ground. The lower leg reaches forward with the foot dorsiflexed (*see* dorsiflexion) as the thigh starts to move downwards. Then the lower leg and thigh are swept backwards and downwards. The outside edge of the ball of the foot strikes the ground lightly. The foot then rolls towards the inside, bringing the whole of the ball of the foot into contact with the ground.

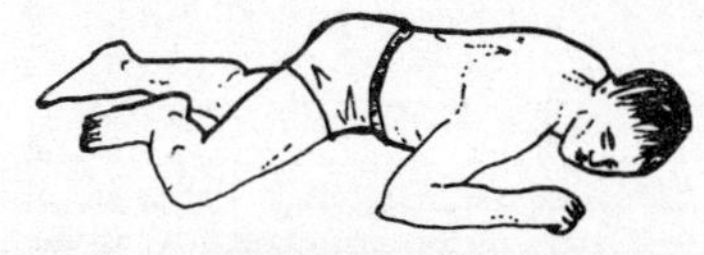

recovery position

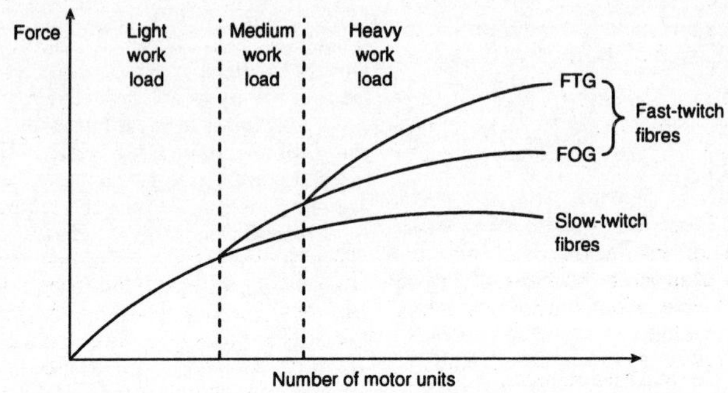

recruitment

recovery position A position in which an unconscious but breathing person is placed in order to ensure that the airways are kept open.

recovery principle A major training principle which posits that adaptation takes place during the *recovery period after training is completed.

recovery unit A period of time specified in a training schedule for rest and recovery within a *microcycle. Recovery is often accelerated if the athlete exercises lightly rather than rests completely.

recreation A term which is sometimes used synonymously with leisure. However, recreation is usually used to describe active leisure. Sometimes its use implies that the activities have positive value in terms of mental and physical therapy. *See also* physical recreation.

recruitment The enlistment of different numbers and types of *muscle fibre during the *contraction of a whole *muscle. Recruitment follows a set pattern. *Slow twitch fibres are brought into action first, then *fast oxidative glycolytic (FOG) fibres, and finally *fast twitch glycolytic (FTG) fibres. The level of recruitment is generally determined by the speed of movement and the *force exerted. Only very high levels of activity result in the recruitment of all the muscle fibres.

rectal Pertaining to the *rectum.

rectangular co-ordinates Reference projections that determine the position of a point in a plane relative to the *x-axis, *y-axis, and *z-axis. *Compare* polar co-ordinates.

rectangular motion *See* linear motion

rectangular plane A *plane of motion which is parallel to the front, side, or top of the body. *Compare* oblique plane.

rectangular reference plane *See* cardinal reference plane.

rectilinear motion Motion in a straight line (*see* linear motion).

rectum Terminal part of *alimentary canal which, in humans, stores the *faeces.

rectus abdominis One of a pair of *medial, *superficial, *abdominal muscles which extend from their *origin on the *pubis to insertion on the ribcage. The recti abdominis flex and rotate the *lumbar region of the *vertebral column; fix and depress the ribs, stabilize the pelvis during walking, and increase intra-abdominal pressure.

rectus femoris A *superficial muscle at the front (anterior) of the thigh. The rectus femoris is part of the *quadriceps femoris. It has its *origins on the anterior inferior *iliac spine and the superior margin of the *acetabulum, and its *insertion at the base of the *patella and *tibia via the *patellar ligament. Its actions include *extension of the knee and *flexion of the thigh at the hip.

reconstruction surgery Surgery undertaken to reconstruct damaged tissue in deep structures, such as the *cruciate ligament of the knee.

recurrent 1 Applied to an injury or illness that is likely to occur again. 2 In *anatomy, applied to a structure such as a *blood vessel or *nerve which turns back upon itself to form a loop.

recurrent dislocation Repeated *dislocations, particularly of the shoulders or patellofemoral joint (kneecap). Recurrent dislocations in athletes often result from too energetic early mobilization following an *acute dislocation. Once a recurrent dislocation pattern is established, surgical treatment may be necessary, but an alternative for non-contact athletes, such as jockeys or motor-cyclists, might be *harnessing.

red blood cell (red blood corpuscle) A cell, normally confined to the blood vessels, which is specialized to transport *oxygen. When mature, red blood cells are biconcave discs which lack a nucleus and contain *haemoglobin.

red blood corpuscle *See* red blood cell.

red bone marrow The blood-forming tissue found within the internal cavities of *bones. *See also* yellow bone marrow.

red fibre *See* slow twitch muscle fibre.

red muscle *See* slow twitch muscle fibre.

redox A chemical reaction in which there is a simultaneous *oxidation and *reduction.

reduced focus An *attentional style in which an individual has a tendency to concentrate on a few *stimuli and ignore other stimuli, even when this is not appropriate. *Compare* narrow focus.

reducible hernia An uncomplicated *hernia which returns, either spontaneously or after manipulation, to its original site.

reduction 1 Addition of *hydrogen or an *electron, or removal of *oxygen from an *atom or *molecule. 2 The restoration of a displaced part, such as a dislocated bone, to its orginal position (*see* reducible hernia).

reductionism The analysis of complex things into their simpler parts. The term is sometimes used disparagingly of the notion that all complex things can be completely understood in terms of their component parts.

reference group A group which is used as a basis for self-appraisal or comparison. The use of the term implies that the action and behaviour of people within various social contexts are to some degree influenced by the group with which the individual primarily identifies. *Compare* membership group. *See also* role theory.

reference human *See* phantom.

reference man and woman A theoretical model man and woman, based upon the average physical dimensions from detailed measurements of thousands of subjects of *anthropometric studies. Reference man has the following characteristics: age 20–24; height 68.5 in; weight 154 pounds; total fat 23.1 lb (15 per cent) of which storage fat is 18.5 lb (12 per cent) and essential fat is 4.6 lb (3 per cent); muscle 69 lb (44.8 per cent) bone 23 lb (14.9 per cent) remainder 38.9 lb (25.3 per cent). Reference woman has the following characteristics: age 20–24; height 64.5 inches; weight 125 lb; total fat 33.8 lb (27 per cent) of which storage fat is 18.5 lb (15 per cent) and essential fat is 15 lb (12 per cent); muscle 45 lb (36 per cent); bone 15 lb (12 per cent) remainder 31.2 lb (25 per cent).

reference point *See* norm.

referred pain (synalgia) *Pain felt in an undamaged area of the body away from the actual point of *injury. It may be a *visceral pain which is perceived as being *somatic in origin due to the impulses from visceral pain receptors travelling along the same pathways as those for somatic pain impulses, or the pain may arise in somatic structures and be referred distally.

reflection thesis The proposition that sport mirrors the beliefs, values, and norms that exist elsewhere in the wider society. Sport is therefore viewed, as in the *reinforcement theory, as maintaining the status quo. *Compare* resistance thesis.

reflex A rapid, involuntary, unlearned *motor response to a *stimulus which has predictable characteristics. *See also* reflex arc.

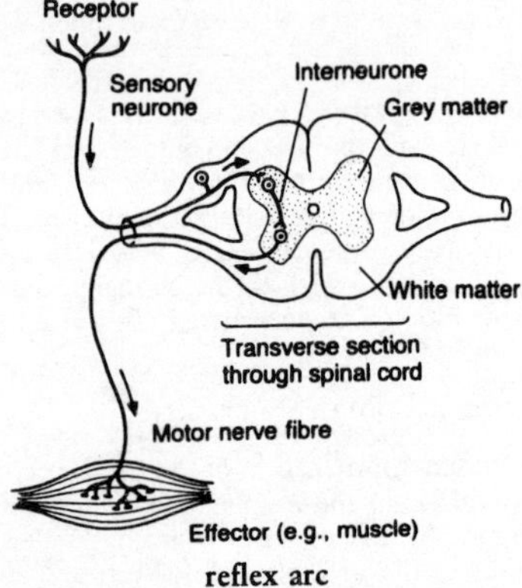

reflex arc

reflex arc The essential neural pathway involved in a *reflex which links the *stimulus, the activated *receptor, and the response. Reflex arcs usually consists of five elements: receptor, *sensory neurone, *integration centre (e.g., association neurone, which may be absent in some reflex arcs), *motor neurone, and *effector.

reflex-reversal phenomenon The phenomenon, observed in studies of locomotion, by which a given *stimulus can produce two different reflexive responses depending on the location of the limb in a movement. Usually, a *reflex action is thought of as a single stereotyped response to a stimulus.

refocusing The return of *attention to relevant *stimuli after it has been distracted.

refractory Applied to a medical condition which does not respond to treatment.

refractory period Period of total inexcitability of a *nerve or a *muscle cell immediately following stimulation. Following this *absolute refractory period there is a *relative refractory period during which only a stronger than normal *stimulus can excite the nerve or muscle.

regeneration Replacement of destroyed tissue by proliferation of the same kinds of cell. *Compare* fibrosis.

region A defined part of the body.

regional enteritis *See* Crohn's disease.

regional ileitis *See* Crohn's disease.

regression *See* regression analysis.

regression analysis A statistical technique for analysing the relationship between two or more *variables and which may be used to predict the value of one variable from the other or others.

regression line The 'line of best fit' between two *variables, whose slope and intercept are determined by *regression analysis.

rehabilitation The restoration of an injured person to the level of physical fitness he or she had before the injury. In the past, rehabilitation often followed the treatment of the injury, but now it more commonly begins at the same time as treatment. The aim of rehabilitation in sport is to facilitate the return of the athlete to *training and *competition at as high a standard and in as short a time as the specific priorities of each athlete determines.

rehearsal The repeated mental or physical practice of a *motor skill which is to be used by an athlete in competition.

reification The interpretation of an abstract idea or concept, such as the state, as real or concrete.

reinforcement (reinforcer) Anything following an action which tends to increase the probability of that behaviour occurring again. Some authorities include only rewards involving the satisfying of basic physiological needs. Others include social approval and similar psychosocial constructs. *See also* external reinforcement; internal reinforcement; negative reinforcement; and positive reinforcement.

reinforcement thesis The proposition that sport strengthens social inequalities experienced in the wider society and thereby maintains the status quo. It is argued, for example, that sport involvement is perceived by the socially disadvantaged as a means of *social mobility, thus reducing their frustration and imposing an element of *social control. *Compare* resistance theory.

reinforcement theory *See* social reinforcement theory.

reinforcer *See* reinforcement.

Reissner's membrane *Membrane in the *cochlea which separates the *middle ear from the *vestibular canal.

Reiter's syndrome A triad of *arthritis, *urethritis, and *conjunctivits, commonly associated with infection of the *urinary tract. Reiter's syndrome can cause restriction of movement, typically affecting the joints of the ankle, knee, or elbow. Treatment includes long-term *antibiotic therapy. Stress of the affected joints should be avoided but active exercise, under the direction of the treating doctor, is important to maintain *joint mobility.

relapse Recurrence of an illness.

relationship **1** The tendency for variations in one *variable to be associated with variations in some other variable. **2** The mutual dealings between two people or between groups of people. *See also* interpersonal relationship; and intrapersonal relationship.

relationship motivation A *leadership style which emphasizes concern with *interpersonal relationships. Relationship motivation is regarded as equivalent to *consideration. A *coach adopting this style gives *athletes' needs a high priority.

relative density The ratio of the density of a solid or liquid at a specified temperature (often 20 °C) to the density of water at the temperature of its maximum density (4 °C). Relative density is generally used in preference to *specific gravity.

relative force An hypothesized feature of a *motor programme that defines the relationships between the *forces produced in the various actions of a movement.

relative frequency *See* frequency.

relative frequency of knowledge of results The percentage trials when *knowledge of results are given; it is the *absolute frequency divided by the number of trials.

relative humidity Ratio of water-vapour content in the atmosphere to the water vapour required to saturate the same volume of atmosphere at the same temperature. Relative humidity is usually expressed as a percentage.

relative load In *strength tests, a *load which is a proportion of the weight of the lifter. *Compare* absolute load.

relative motion The motion of one body relative to another. For a body moving in a fluid, it is the difference between the speed of the body and the speed of the fluid. When considering the influence of a fluid on the motions of bodies, the relative motion is more important than the absolute speed of either one. Most studies find it convenient to consider the body to be at rest and the fluid to be moving past it.

relative refractory period A period following stimulation during which only a stronger than normal *stimulus can evoke an *action potential. *Compare* absolute refractory period.

relative strength The maximum *force that an individual can exercise in relation to his or her body-weight. *Compare* absolute strength. *See also* strength.

relative velocity The rate at which the one body is changing its position with respect to another body. If the velocities of the two bodies are represented by two sides of a triangle taken in order, the relative velocity is represented by the third side.

relaxation A controlled and relatively-stable level of *arousal which is lower than the normal waking state. Relaxation is incompatible with feelings of *tension, worry, and *anxiety. Techniques such as *progressive muscle relaxation can be used to induce relaxation and obtain levels of *optimal arousal before *competition.

relaxation procedure Technique, such as an *intervention strategy or the use of *drugs, employed to reduce *tension and *anxiety in sport. *See also* behaviour therapy; biofeedback training; desensitization; and progressive relaxation.

relaxation response A set of changes in bodily functions such as slowing of the *heart-rate and *respiration, and an increase in the brainwaves associated with relaxation, that take place as a result of meditating or practising other relaxation techniques.

relaxation therapy The use of muscle relaxation to treat high levels of *anxiety. The relaxation therapist may use a number of techniques, including *progressive muscle relaxation, to encourage the subject to reduce his or her *muscle tone.

relaxation time The time it takes for a contracted muscle to revert to its resting, relaxed state.

relaxed-arm girth The circumference of the right arm at the midpoint between the *acromiale and the *radiale, when the subject is standing erect and the relaxed arm is hanging by the side. *See also* body girth.

relearning Regaining a *skill that has been partially or wholly lost. The savings involved in relearning compared with original *learning gives an index of the degree of retention.

release angle *See* angle of release.

release height *See* height of release.

release point (point of release) The point at which a projectile, such as a javelin, is released from the hand as the hand moves in an arc. The projectile moves in a line which is tangential to the arc at the point of release.

releaser A *stimulus which serves to elicit instructive behaviour.

release velocity The *velocity of a projectile at the release point. *See also* speed of release.

reliability (reproducibility) A characteristic of a measurement or experimental procedure which produces similar results on two or more separate occasions. A typical way of testing reliability is to compare the results of two independent recorders. This is termed *interrater reliability. High correlations between results (for example 0.80 or better) indicate reliability. Several statistics, such as *standard deviation of repeated tests, can give a measure of reliability. *See also* objectivity; sensitivity; and validity.

relief interval In *interval training, the time between work intervals as well as between sets.

reminiscence An improvement in later performance due to a rest or nonpractice. The period of rest is called the retention interval. Thus far, studies yield inconsistent results as to the optimal retention interval for reminiscence. *See also* inhibition.

REM sleep A phase of sleep during which dreaming takes place. REM is an abbreviation for 'rapid eye' movement and during this phase the sleeper's eyes move quickly, heartbeat and *metabolism speed up, and toes and fingers twitch. Disturbance of REM sleep may result in fatigue and irritability, leaving the individual less able to cope with physical exertion. *See also* sleep.

renal Pertaining to the kidney.

renal artery A *principal artery supplying the *kidneys.

renal buffering A *homeostatic mechanism in which the *kidney helps to maintain the *acid–base balance by excreting either *acid or *alkaline *urine in response to changes in *hydrogen ion concentration. Renal buffering involves a complex series of reactions in the kidney tubules.

renal stone *See* kidney stones.

renin An enzyme released by the *kidneys in response to exercise and stress. Renin increases *sodium retention and helps to maintain the *plasma volume. It reacts with a substance in the *liver to produce *angiotensin which increases *blood pressure. Overproduction of renin causes *hypertension.

Renshaw cells *Interneurones located in the medial region of the *ventral horn of the *spinal cord which make connections with *motor neurones. Renshaw cells act as a link between motor neurones and sensory neurones from *muscles and the *skin.

repetition 1 In *interval-training, the number of work intervals in one set. For example, an interval training presciption of 6×200 m would constitute one set of six repetitions. 2 In *strength-training the number of times an exercise is performed without stopping. *See also* repetition maximum.

repetition maximum (RM) The maximum *load that a *muscle group can lift over a given number of *repetitions before fatiguing (*see* fatigue). For example, a 10RM load is the maximum load that can be lifted over 10 repetitions.

repetition running A form of training similar to *interval-training but differing in the length of the work interval and the degree of *recovery between repetitions. Repetition running consists of running a given distance at a predetermined speed a specific number of times with complete rest and recovery (walking) after each run. It is usually performed at, or near, race pace to develop the *anaerobic system.

repetition-training A form of training which follows the same pattern as *repetition running, but which may be adapted for swimming, cycling, and other sports.

repetitive method A method of *learning a *skill in which the subject learns a part, then combines it with a new part and practises them together until learned. These two are then combined with a third part and practised together until mastered. The procedure is followed for each remaining part until all are practised as a whole. It is a variant of the *progressive part method.

repetitive strain injury An injury to soft tissues, especially *tendons, due to repeated use of a *muscle or *muscle group. *See also* over-use injury.

replacement drink A drink specifically designed to replace energy and electrolytes, and to assist recovery after exertion. *See also* electrolyte drink; and energy drink.

replication The folding back of a tissue on itself.

repolarization The process by which a *neurone or *muscle fibre regains its *resting potential after it has discharged an *action potential.

representative sample In research, a small group which reflects accurately the characteristics of the total population.

repression An *ego defence mechanism whereby an unacceptable wish or idea is excluded from the conscious mind.

reproducibility *See* reliability.

reproduction *See* social reproduction.

reproterol A *drug belonging to the *stimulants which are on the *IOC list of *banned substances.

research method The techniques of investigation used by a particular academic discipline.

research question A question posed by a *scientist about a previously unknown area of a subject and which requires a systematic, scientific investigation to answer.

reserpine An *antihypertensive *drug which has been used to treat high *blood pressure. Reserpine is associated with reduced levels of *norepinephrine production and the development of severe *depression.

residual volume (RV) Volume of air remaining in the lungs at the end of maximal *expiration; a typical value is 1200 ml. RV = total lung capacity – *vital capacity

resilience A measure of a body's resistance to deformation. Resilience is usually defined as the *work required to deform an *elastic body to its *elastic limit divided by the volume of the body.

resistance (resistive force) The amount of *force which opposes a movement.

resistance arm The perpendicular distance from the *axis of a *lever to the *point of resistance in the lever.

resistance-runs Repeated runs against an added resistance such as a hill, a weight carried by person, a drag which has to be pulled, or a soft, uneven surface (often sand). *See also* functional overload.

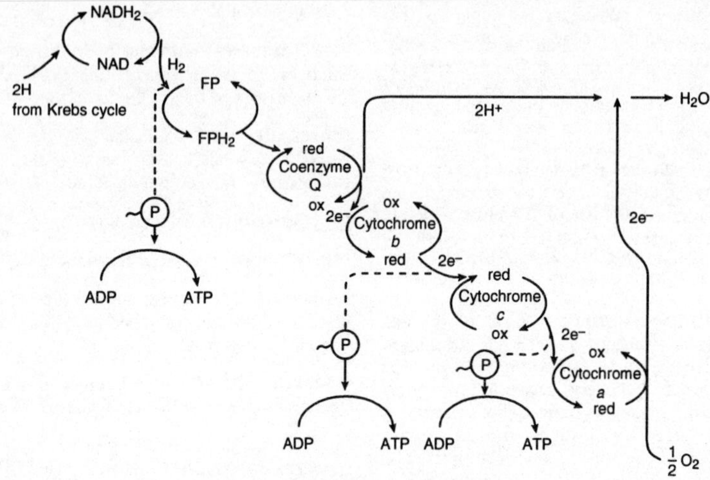

respiratory chain

resistance thesis The proposition that sport provides an arena for opposing and challenging the interests, values, and norms of the wider *society. *Compare* reflection thesis; and reinforcement thesis.

resistance vessel Vessel which regulates *blood pressure.

resisted movement Movement which makes a *muscle work but does not let the *joint move. Resistance movements are accomplished by attempting to make a particular movement and then blocking it. They are used in the diagnosis of *sports injuries to test for muscle and *tendon damage.

resistive force *See* resistance.

resocialization A process of *socialization which involves an individual taking up a new social identity and making a sharp break with a prior socialization. Resocialization applies to the socialization of an individual who adjusts to retirement from professional sport by taking up another sport (or the same sport at a lower level), and placing sport at a lower priority than work, family, or education.

resolution (resolving power) The minimum distance between two objects at which they can be seen as two distinct items (using, for example, the naked eye, or a microscope) rather than as a single item.

resolution of forces The mathematical process of dividing *forces into components that act in specified directions.

resolving power *See* resolution.

resonance The condition of a body when it is subjected to a periodic series of disturbances having a *frequency equal to one of the natural frequencies of vibration of the body. The body is set into vibrations which have a maximum amplitude. A trampolinist who moves in phase with the trampoline will be projected higher than one who is not.

respiration The breakdown of food materials to produce *metabolic energy in the form of *adenosine triphosphate. *See also* cellular respiration; and external respiration.

respiratory acidosis An increase in the *hydrogen ion concentration of the blood (*see* acidosis) caused by failure to expire *carbon dioxide from the lungs as quickly as it forms in the *tissues. Carbon dioxide accumulates in the blood where it forms *carbonic acid which dissociates to increase the hydrogen ion concentration. *Compare* metabolic acidosis.

respiratory alkalosis A decrease in *hydrogen ion concentration caused by *hyperventilation and a reduction in *carbon dioxide levels in the body fluids. It may occur where *partial pressures of *oxygen are low (e.g., at altitude). *Compare* metabolic alkalosis.

respiratory centre An area of the *medulla oblongata and *pons which controls the rate and depth of breathing in order to maintain respiratory rhythm.

respiratory chain A chain of organic molecules present on the inner surface of *mitochondria that is capable of accepting *hydrogen atoms and *electrons derived from the *Krebs cycle during *aerobic respiration. The hydrogen atoms, and then the electrons, are transferred in an ordered sequence along the chain by a series of *redox reactions; the final reaction involves the reduction of *oxygen to form water. The redox reactions are *exergonic and the *free energy generated is used to manufacture *ATP by *oxidative phosphorylation.

respiratory dead space *See* anatomical dead space.

respiratory frequency The number of breaths an individual takes per minute. Values vary, but an average figure for a healthy, resting, recumbent young male, breathing air at sea level is 12 breaths per minute. The value may change with position, age, size, sex, and altitude.

respiratory exchange ratio (gas exchange ratio; R) The ratio of the volume of *carbon dioxide expired per minute to the volume of *oxygen consumed during the same time in the *lungs. In a resting, steady state the respiratory exchange ratio equals the respiratory quotient (RQ), but during exercise an unstable state arises due to the expired air containing carbon dioxide and oxygen derived from stores within the body, and the R value is not the same as the RQ value.

respiratory insufficiency A condition in which the *respiratory system is unable to meet fully the demands of the body for the supply of extra oxygen and the removal of carbon dioxide during exercise.

respiratory minute volume *See* minute ventilation.

respiratory pump A mechanism which helps pump *blood back to the *heart during *inspiration. *Intrathoracic pressure decreases during inspiration, causing the pressure in the *atria of the heart to drop to around 2.1 kPa, aspirating blood in the *thoracic vein toward the right atrium.

respiratory quotient (RQ) The ratio of the amount of carbon dioxide produced to the amount of oxygen consumed in *tissues of the body (*compare* respiratory exchange ratio). RQ = volume of CO_2 expired/volume O_2 consumed. The RQ can be used to determine which food is being metabolized during *cellular respiration. The RQ for *fat metabolism is 0.7; for *protein metabolism is 0.9; and for *carbohydrate metabolism is 1.0. An RQ of more than 1.0 indicates that *anaerobic respiration is occurring.

respiratory rhythm The rhythm of alternating inspiratory and expiratory movements which take place during breathing. There are believed to be four *respiratory centres which control respiratory rhythm: the inspiratory centre, and expiratory centre in the *medulla; and an *apneustic and *pneumotaxic centre in the *pons.

respiratory surface A special area that is developed in order to satisfy the requirements of *gaseous exchange between an organism and the external environment. *See also* alveolus.

respiratory system The *organs and *tissues involved in the process of breathing and *gaseous exchange between a person and the environment. The system includes the nose, nasal passages, *nasopharynx, *larynx, *trachea, *bronchi, and *lungs.

respiratory threshold A critical level of exercise above which there is a nonlinear increase in *pulmonary ventilation. The respiratory threshold is sometimes taken as being equivalent to the *lactate threshold and to indicate the point at which there is a substantial switch from *aerobic respiration to *anaerobic respiration (*see* anaerobic threshold). The basis of this assumption is that increases in lactate levels in the *blood should reduce *pH, stimulating *chemoreceptors which effect an increase in pulmonary ventilation through the action of the *respiratory centres. However, this assumption has been seriously questioned because factors other than pH can contribute to the nonlinear increase in pulmonary ventilation.

respiratory tree (bronchial tree) The principal airway from the nose or mouth, through the *pharynx, *larynx, and *trachea into the *bronchi, which branches and terminates in the *alveoli.

respiratory work The *work done by the respiratory muscles during *inspiration and *expiration. Respiratory work consists mainly of overcoming *elastic resistance and flow-resistive forces of the *thorax and *lungs. At rest, the respiratory muscles require about 0.5–1.0ml of *oxygen per litre of *ventilation. With increasing ventilation, the oxygen cost per unit becomes progressively greater. It has been estimated that respiratory work uses as much as 10 per cent or more of total oxygen uptake during heavy exercise. However, under normal conditions, respiratory work is not a limiting factor unless the oxygen delivered to the circulation by the additional ventilation is less than the corresponding increment in oxygen consumption by respiratory muscle. Under most conditions ventilation is well adapted to ensure maximum uptake.

respondent A person who completes a questionnaire.

response The way a person, an organ, or a cell, reacts to a *stimulus. In the *social reinforcement theory, the response is not separated from the stimulus and is an alteration of behaviour occurring as the result of the presence of a stimulus.

response-chaining hypothesis An early explanation of movement control which posits that each action is triggered by feedback from the immediately previous action. A movement is initiated by an *external stimulus which causes a *muscle or *muscle group to contract. The muscle contraction generates sensory information called response-produced feedback. This feedback serves as a trigger for the next contraction and so on until the movement sequence is completed. Research has shown that feedback is not essential for all motor actions; therefore, the response-chaining hypothesis cannot be universally applicable.

response delay The period of time between a *stimulus and the reaction or *response of an individual. The response delay is a function of the amount of information which needs to be processed.

response integration An ability underlying tasks for which the utilization and application of sensory cues from several sources must be integrated into a single response.

response orientation An ability underlying tasks for which rapid directional discrimination among alternative movement patterns must be made. Response orientation is apparently related to the ability to select a correct movement under choice reaction time situations.

response-programming stage In *information-processing, a stage in which the previously chosen response is transformed into overt muscular action. The duration of this stage is affected by the response complexity.

response rate The percentage of the total number of subjects sampled who respond to a survey or *questionnaire.

response selection stage In *information-processing, a stage concerned with the translation of the decision mechanism which leads to the choice of response associated with the presented *stimulus. The duration of this stage is sensitive to variables such as the number of stimulus–response alternatives and *stimulus–response compatability.

response time The time interval from the presentation of a *stimulus to the completion of a movement; it is the sum of *reaction time and *movement time.

rest 1 In *biomechanics, the state of a body with a speed of zero which does not change position; a state of no motion. 2 A state of physical inactivity.

resting heart-rate (RHR) The number of heartbeats per minute while the body is at rest.

resting metabolic rate The metabolic rate of a person at rest. The term is often used to approximate to the *basal metabolic rate, but the resting metabolic rate is usually higher.

resting potential The electrical *potential difference between the inside and outside of a cell (that is, across the cell membrane) when the cell is in a resting state. In a *motor neurone, the inside is negatively charged (-60mv) relative to the positively-charged outside.

restitution *See* elasticity.

restorative drug A *drug used to restore, at least partly, a person's physiological condition after injury or illness. *Compare* additive drug. *See also* *anti-inflammatory drugs; *barbiturates; *enzymes; *muscle relaxant; *pain-killers; and *tranquilizers.

restoring force A *force which has a tendency to maintain the dimensions of a body and to restore the original dimensions of a body once a *distorting force is removed. *See also* elasticity.

rest recovery A form of *recovery used especially in *interval-training in which an athlete rests between work periods. *Compare* exercise recovery.

rest-relief In *interval training, a type of relief interval involving moderate moving about, such as walking and flexing of an arm or leg.

resultant (vector sum) A single *vector, such as a *force or *velocity, that produces the same effect as that of two or more vectors of the same type acting together.

resultant displacement The position from a starting point, expressed in terms of distance, when there have been two or move specified changes of direction.

resultant moment The sum of *moments about the point at which a body, acted on by a number of *forces, is tending to rotate.

resultant vector The net result of two or more *component vectors. *See also* resultant.

resuscitation The process of restoring to consciousness someone who appears to be dead. *See also* cardiopulmonary resuscitation.

retaliation hypothesis The supposition that an athlete will not participate in acts of *aggression if he or she fears counteraggression from a potential victim.

retardation 1 Negative acceleration or deceleration; the rate of decrease of *velocity. 2 The slowing up or delayed development of a process. Mental retardation, for example, refers to a delay in intellectual development.

retention The maintenance of *learning so that it can be utilized later, as in recall, recognition, or relearning.

reticular Resembling a network.

reticular activating system One of two parts of the *reticular formation in the brainstem, which maintains the alert state of the *cerebral cortex and is concerned with *arousal. The reticular activating system filters out repetitive *stimuli, preventing sensory overload.

reticular fibres A network of *connective tissue fibres. Reticular fibres support many structures including *muscles, *nerves, and *blood vessels.

reticular formation A functional brain system that spans the central core of the *medulla oblongata, *pons, and *midbrain. The reticular formation includes the two *reticular activating systems which are involved in regulating sensory input to the *cerebral cortex and in *cortical arousal, and contains *motor nuclei which help to regulate *skeletal muscle activity.

reticular tissue Tissue which consists of a network of *reticular fibres, typically in a loose ground matrix. Reticular tissue forms a soft internal skeleton supporting other cells; for example, in *bone marrow.

reticulin *Collagen-like *protein fibres found in the *reticular tissue.

retina Lining of the interior of the *eye containing the *photoreceptor cells, *rods, and *cones that are connected to the *optic nerve. The retina lies below the vascular *choroid which nourishes it.

retinaculum A band of thick tissue which supports and maintains the position of other tissues.

retinol *See* vitamin A.

retraction Nonangular backward movement in a *transverse plane that returns a protracted *bone or body-part to its original position. An example of retraction is squaring the shoulders in a military stance. *Compare* protraction.

retraining The recommencement of *training after a period of no training. There is no unequivocal, clear physiological evidence that prior training hastens the rate or increases the magnitude of training benefits gained from the subsequent training.

retrieval The mental process of recalling information from the *long-term memory.

retroactive inhibition The partial or complete obliteration of *memory by a more recent event, particularly new learning. *Compare* proactive inhibition.

retrocalcaneal bursa *Bursa between the *calcaneus and the *Achilles tendon. The *anterior aspect of the retrocalcaneal bursa consists of a thin layer of *cartilage covering a part of the *tuberosity onto which the Achilles tendon inserts.

retrocalcaneal bursitis (heel bursitis) An *inflammation of either the deep *retrocalcaneal bursa lying between the *Achilles tendon and the *calcaneus, or the superficial bursa, lying between the Achilles tendon and skin, in which case it is often referred to as postcalcaneal bursitis. Retrocalcaneal bursitis is characterized by tenderness and redness involving the posterior, superior aspect of the heel and calcaneus. The symptoms are usually absent if the individual goes barefoot. Heel bursitis is often caused by excessive compensatory *pronation.

retrograde amnesia A form of *amnesia in which there is a loss of memory of events occurring before a trauma.

retrospection A systematic recall of what has been experienced in the past.

retrovirus An *RNA-containing *virus that has the ability to take over certain cells and interrupt their normal genetic function. Retroviruses have been implicated in the development of certain *cancers.

rev *See* revolution.

reversibility principle A basic principle of *training which refers to the gradual loss of *training effects when the intensity, duration, or frequency of training is reduced. Training effects produced over a short term are usually lost quicker than those produced over a longer term, and strength losses tend to be faster than mobility losses.

revolution (rev) Unit used in the measurement of *angular distance. In some sports, such as diving, the unit is not stated but implied; for example, a twist is one revolution about the *long axis of the body and a somersault is one revolution about the *horizontal axis parallel to the end of the diving-board. One complete revolution would be an angular displacement of 360°. Use of the term is related to a particular axis of the body.

revolve The behaviour of a body which has a circular motion around an axis which is outside the body.

reward A term generally applied to a *positive reinforcement in which the consequences of a particular action have incentive value to the *actor.

rewarding behaviour *Coaching behaviour which reinforces an athlete by recognizing and rewarding good performance. *See also* positive feedback

Reynold's number A dimensionless quantity, named after Osborne Reynolds (1842–1912), applied to a *fluid flowing through a cylindrical tube. The Reynolds number is expressed by the equation $Re = vpl/n$, where v = velocity of flow, p = density of the liquid, l = diameter of the tube, and n = the coefficient of viscosity of the liquid. When the Reynolds number exceeds a critical value, the streamline or *laminar flow of the fluid becomes turbulent.

RFD *See* rate of force development.

rhe *SI unit of fluidity; it is the reciprocal of *poise.

rheography A *cardiovascular functional test which gives a graphical record of the flow of blood through blood vessels.

rheumatic fever An *autoimmune response to the *toxins produced by a *streptococcUus infection which can result in damage to the heart valves. The condition is characterized by pain, swelling, and stiffness in one or more joints.

rheumatoid arthritis A chronic inflammatory disorder which primarily affects the joints but may also affect *tendons, *tendon sheaths, *muscles, and *bursae. The main symptoms are stiffness, pain, and swelling of the affected joints. Although sufferers may find competitive sport difficult, physical exercise, particularly active mobility training, has been shown to be of benefit. *See also* arthritis.

rheumatism Any disorder in which aches and pains affect the *joints and *muscles. Rheumatism is marked by inflammation, stiffness, and pain in and around the joints.

rhinencephalon Part of the *cerebrum concerned with reception and integration of *olfactory impulses.

rhinitis Inflammation of the nose. Acute rhinitis is a symptom of a cold.

rhinovirus Any one of a group of *viruses that cause respiratory infections such as the common cold.

rhizopathy An intense, sharp pain which has clearly defined limits following the distribution of an affected *nerve.

rhizotomy A surgical procedure which involves cutting *nerve roots at selected points as they emerge from the *spinal cord to relieve pain (*see* dorsal rhizotomy). Motor nerve roots are sometimes cut to relieve *muscle spasms.

rhomboideus muscles *See* rhomboids.

rhomboid minor *See* rhomboids.

rhomboid major *See* rhomboids.

rhomboids Two rectangular *muscles, the rhomboid major and rhomboid minor, situated in the upper part of the back between the backbone and the shoulder-blade. The rhomboids have their *origins on the sixth and seventh *cervical vertebrae and their *insertions on the inner border of the *shoulder-blade. They act together and with the *trapezius to 'square' the shoulders; they rotate the *scapula so that the *glenoid cavity rotates downwards, as when the arm is lowered against resistance (for example, when paddling a canoe); and they also stabilize the scapula.

rhythm Any sequence of regularly-recurring functions or events such as certain physiological processes. Locomotory movements may also have a rhythm as in the regular repetition of a stride sequence in running or the stroke action in swimming. A sense of rhythm and an ability to maintain a regular recurrence of such functions is an important skill in sport. *See also* timing.

rib One of twelve pairs of long, flat, curved bones forming part of the *thoracic cage attached at one end to a *thoracic vertebra. *See also* false rib; floating rib; and true rib.

riboflavin *See* vitamin B_2.

ribonucleic acid (RNA) A *nucleic acid concerned with *protein synthesis. In some viruses RNA is responsible for carrying and passing on hereditary characteristics.

ribosomes *Organelles within the *cytoplasm which function as the site for *protein synthesis.

RICE An acronym for a simple and efficient treatment for many sports injuries: rest the injured body-part (R), apply ice (I), apply compression (C), and elevate the injured extremity above the heart level (E). This treatment helps reduce swelling and restricts the spread of bruising thereby accelerating the healing process.

rickets Deficiency disease of children in which the bones do not harden and are deformed due to a lack of *vitamin D.

rider's bone A condition resulting from *calcification in the thigh following inflammation of the thigh adductors (*see* adduction); a *myositis ossificans.

rider's strain (adductor strain) A strain of the adductor muscle, a thick band of muscle on the inner side of the thigh. It is a relatively common injury of fast bowlers, and footballers who make lunge tackles. *Compare* groin pain.

ridge A long, narrow protruberance on a *bone which runs along the *shaft as a crest.

right-hand thumb rule Convention for determining the direction of a *vector for *angular motion. The angular motion vector is represented by an arrow drawn so that if the curled fingers of a person's right hand points in the direction of *rotation, the direction of the arrow coincides with the direction indicated by the extended thumb. The *magnitude of the vector is indicated by the length of the arrow. Any angular motion vector can be represented in this way and can be either added to a corresponding vector to obtain a *resultant or can be resolved into components using a *parallelogram of vectors.

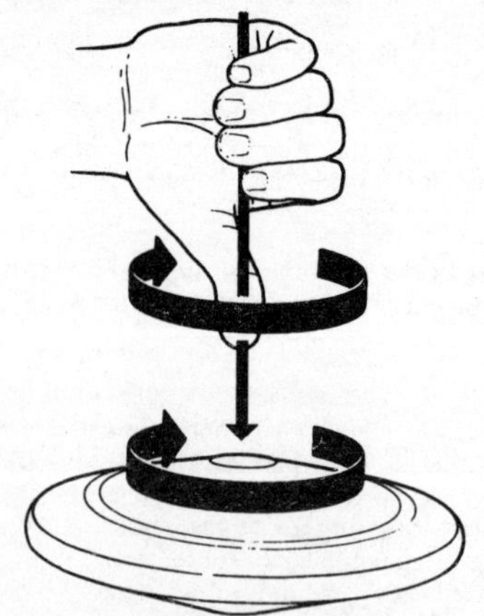

right-hand thumb rule

right spin *See* side spin.

righting reflex A *reflex which results in the human body or body-segment tending to regain its former body position when it is displaced. Righting reflexes are very strong in performers of physical activities, such as gymnastics, in which the head position is quickly altered. Gymnasts may need to learn to modify and overcome these response to perform certain routines.

rigid body A solid object which tends not to change shape when *forces are applied to it.

rigidity In the context of *learning, an inability to change *behaviour patterns, *attitudes or body *postures.

rimiterol A *sympathomimetic drug, belonging to the *β_2 stimulants, permitted by the *IOC for the treatment of *asthma in aerosol form only, subject to written notification. Rimiterol has been shown to be an effective *prophylactic treatment for *exercise-induced asthma.

Ringelmann effect The decrease in average individual performance with increases in group-size. The Ringelmann effect was named after a German *psychologist who studied groups pulling on a rope. The average *force for two people was 93 per cent of average individual force; the average force for three people was 85 per cent of average individual force, and the average force for eight people was only 49 per cent of the average individual force. *See also* social loafing.

ringworm (*Tinea*) An infection of the skin, hair, or nails by a microscopic fungus. The infection usually develops as a dry, scaly, circular area on the skin. *See also* athlete's foot; and dhobie itch.

risk factor Any factor, environmental or organic, which has a strong association with the onset and progress of a disease or injury. Risk factors for *hypokinetic diseases include poor *diet, heavy *smoking, an inactive lifestyle, and *stress. *See also* cardiac risk factor.

risk-taking behaviour Behaviour of a person who tends to choose challenging tasks with relatively low probabilities of success. It has been hypothesized that athletes with high achievement orientation tend to seek out relatively-challenging situations (such as those with a 50 per cent chance of failure) while those with low achievement orientation tend to choose very easy or very difficult tasks. The highly-motivated athletes tend to perform much better in challenging situations than in situations where there is a high probability of success.

rite of passage A ceremony or ritual which may take place when a person changes social status and social identity. One instance is the presentation of a county cap to a cricketer who has become a regular first-team player.

ritrodine A *drug belonging to the *stimulants which are on the *IOC list of *banned substances.

rivalry Behaviour in which defeating opponents has a high priority. *Compare* competition.

RM *See* repetition maximum.

robust statistic A statistic which gives valid results in spite of some of the assumptions for its use being violated.

roentgen ray *See* X-ray.

role The behaviour expected of a particular person by *society. Examples of those society expects to fill a role are teachers, coaches, team-captains, and referees.

role conflict (role strain; role stress) A situation which arises as the result of performing two or more inconsistent *roles. For example, a coach may have to perform the conflicting roles of teacher, friend, and team-selector. *See also* cognitive dissonance.

role differentiation The degree to which different members of a *group have specialized functions. *See also* division of labour.

role model A person whose behaviour and attitude conforms with that which society or other social group expects of a person in his or her position, and who has become an example for others to copy.

role-modelling hypothesis The hypothesis that young people from particular minority or ethnic groups take up specific roles and positions in sports teams because they wish to copy highly-successful players from the same group. For example, it is argued that many black youths in North America tend to compete in noncentral positions in sports teams because they are trying to emulate black élite athletes whom they previously saw performing successfully in those positions.

role-related behaviour An individual's behaviour which is determined by the person's *role and the perception of how he or she should behave in particular situations. Role-related behaviour is rarely a valid indicator of the *psychological core of an individual's personality. An athlete may play the role of a braggart but in truth be rather insecure, for example.

role strain *See* role conflict

role stress *See* role conflict

role theory A theory which suggests that a person's behaviour results from the individual conforming, or failing to conform, to various *roles defined by the social context in which the person finds himself or herself. *See also* action theory.

rolling friction A form of *friction that opposes the motion of a ball when it rolls across a surface. Rolling friction occurs because the ball and the surface upon which it sits are deformed sufficiently to impede the motion of the ball. The magnitude of the *rolling force depends upon a number of factors including the nature of the ball and of the surface. A soft, wet surface has a higher rolling friction than a hard, dry one. Awareness of this phenomenon is of particular importance to golfers.

Rorschach test A *projective procedure in which a subject describes an ink blot. The subject's responses are analysed by the tester in order to measure *personality. Although the test has had much clinical use, recent research suggests that it is not a reliable, objective, or valid measure of an athlete's personality.

rotary motion *See* angular motion.

rotation 1 Angular or circular motion of a body around an *axis that is located within the turning object. *See also* revolution. 2 A turning movement around the *long axis of a *bone. Rotation towards the midline is

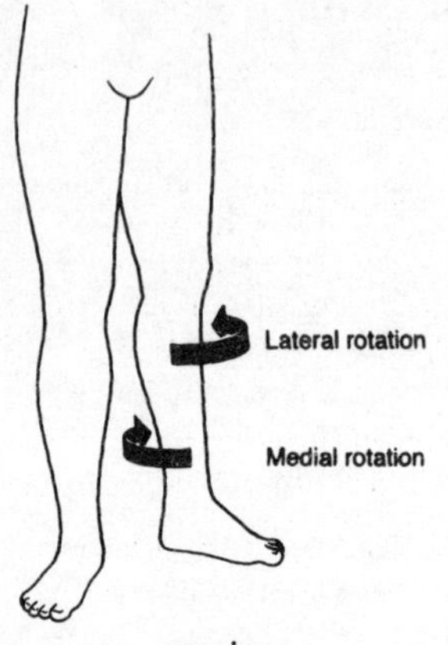

rotation

called medial rotation, and rotation away from the midline is called lateral rotation.

rotational energy The *energy stored in a spinning system. Rotational energy depends on both the *moment of inertia and the *angular velocity, and is given by: rotational energy = $1/2Iw^2$ where I = the moment of inertia of the object about an axis through the centre of gravity of the system, and w = the angular velocity of the system about an axis through the centre of gravity of the system.

rotational equilibrium The state of a body in which the sum of all the external *torques acting on the body is equal to zero.

rotational inertia A body's resistance to change in its state of rotary motion. It is also called the *moment of inertia.

rotational movement *See* rotation.

rotator A *muscle which effects *rotation of a body part.

rotator cuff Four small *muscles which bind the *ball-and-socket joint of the shoulder. These muscles are the *subscapularis, *supraspinatus, *infraspinatus, and *teres minor of the *shoulder-joint. The cuff gives stability to movements of the shoulder by synergistically steadying the head of the *humerus in the *glenoid cavity, thus preventing slipping and skidding.

rotatory motion *See* angular motion.

roughage *See* fibre.

RQ *See* respiratory quotient.

rubella *See* German measles.

Ruffini's corpuscle A flattened capsule containing nerve-endings which are thought by some to be heat receptors, sensitive to temperature increases in the range 25–45 °C. Ruffini's corpuscles are deeper than cold receptors (*see* Krause's end-bulbs) and occur in *joints which has led some to believe that they may function as *mechanoreceptors.

rule A regulation governing conduct or procedure.

ruler-drop test A simple test of *response time in which the subject attempts to stop a falling ruler. The distance the ruler drops is converted into response time using the formula:

$$d = ut + 1/2gt^2$$

where d is the distance the ruler falls in centimetres, u is the initial *velocity of the ruler (if static at the start time, this will be zero), t is the response time in seconds, and g is the acceleration of the ruler due to gravity constant (i.e., $9.801\,\mathrm{m\,s^{-2}}$).

run-down A condition of decreased sporting performance which may comprise at least four distinct causal and modal entities: physical fitness and form affected by factors, such as lack of adequate sleep, outside the sport; *over-training; overstraining which may result in *over-use injuries; and indisposition. *See also* over-training syndrome; and stress.

runner's haematuria A condition in which *blood is passed in the *urine after running a long distance. *See also* march haemoglobinuria.

runner's haemolysis *See* march haemoglobinuria.

runner's high A feeling, usually unexpected, of exhilaration and well-being directly associated with vigorous physical activity. Runner's high is thought to be related to the secretion of *endorphins. *See also* flow.

runner's knee Definitions for runner's knee vary, but include iliotibial band syndrome, a pain syndrome on the lateral side of the knee resulting from an irritation between the *iliotibial band and the lateral *femoral condyle. Running on cambered roads and excessive *pronation increase the risk of suffering from this condition. Treatment includes static stretching exercises involving the iliotibial band. Runner's knee may also include patellofemoral pain.

runner's toe *See* black nail.

running action The action of the *muscles and the *joints during running. Most long-distance runners strike the ground with the heel first and roll off with the toes while sprinters tend to run on the ball of the feet. *See also* driving phase; pronator; recovery phase; and supinator.

rupture 1 Tearing or bursting apart of an organ or tissue; a tear. **2** A term commonly applied to a *hernia.

ruptured disc *See* herniated disc.

RV *See* residual volume.

S

s *See* second.

sac A pouch or sac-like structure

sacral 1 Pertaining to the lower portion of the back, just above the buttocks. **2** Pertaining to the *sacrum.

sacral curvature *See* spinal curvature.

sacral nerves Five pairs of *nerves emerging from the *sacrum which supply *motor neurones and *sensory neurones to the *anal and *genital regions, and to the upper and lower leg.

sacral promontory Bulge of the anterosuperior margin of the first *vertebra of the *sacrum. The body's *centre of gravity lies about 1 cm behind this *landmark.

sacroiliac crest A ridge on the bony junction, between the *sacrum and *ilium, which is an attachment point for muscles including the *gluteus maximus.

sacroiliac joint The *synovial, *plane joint, consisting of *fibrocartilage, between the *sacrum of the *vertebral column and the *ilium of the *pelvic girdle. The sacroiliac joint is usually capable of only very slight gliding movements, except during pregnancy when the joint is more mobile.

sacrum Five fused *vertebrae forming a triangular-shaped, structure *posterior to the *pelvis. The sacrum articulates superiorly with a *lumbar vertebra and inferiorly with the *coccyx. It strengthens and stabilizes the *pelvis.

saddle-joint A *synovial joint in which each *articular surface has both concave and convex areas; that is, it is shaped like a saddle. Articular surfaces then fit together, convex surface to concave surface and allow movement in two planes. The *carpometacarpal joint of the thumb is a saddle-joint.

sagittal axis (*z*-axis) In *anthropometry, the *axis formed by the intersection of a *sagittal plane and a *transverse plane.

sagittal plane (anteroposterior plane) The *dorsoventral *plane which runs longitudinally and divides the body or organ into right and left halves.

SAI *See* state anxiety inventory.

SAID principle (Specific Adaptations to Imposed Demands principle) A principle which proposes that if a human body is placed under *stress of varying intensities and duration, it attempts to overcome the stress by adapting specifically to the imposed demands.

salbutamol A *drug belonging to the *β_2 stimulants. Salbutamol is used for the effective treatment of *exercise-induced asthma and some other forms of respiratory distress. Although stimulants are on the *IOC list of *banned substances the use of salbutamol, in aerosol form only, is permitted (subject to written notification) by the *IOC Medical Commission for the treatment of

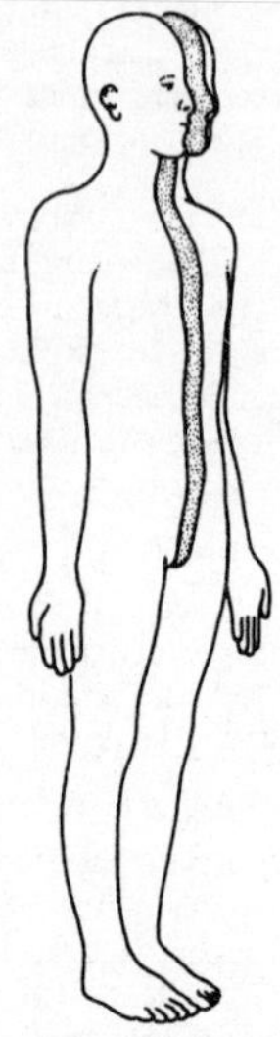

sagittal plane

*asthma and other respiratory conditions. It may not be taken orally.

salicylates *Drugs which are salts of *salicylic acid. Many have *anti-inflammatory, *antipyretic, and *analgesic effects similar to aspirin (*see* acetylsalicylic acid), and are used in the treatment of painful *muscle and *joint conditions.

salicylic acid A *drug which has bactericidal and fungicidal properties. Salicylic acid causes the skin to peel and is used in concentrated forms to remove warts and corns. A number of *analgesic, *anti-inflammatory drugs, such as *acetylsalicylic acid, are prepared from it.

salicylism Poisoning caused by high doses of *salicylates such as aspirin (*see* acetylsalicylic acid). Salicylism is characterized by dizziness, impaired hearing, drowsiness, sweating and, in very high doses, delirium and collapse.

saline A 0.9 per cent *sodium chloride solution which is *isotonic with *blood.

saliva A viscous, transparent liquid containing water, salts, mucin (a *glycoprotein), and sometimes salivary *amylase (*ptylalin). Saliva acts as a lubricant and starts the *digestion of *starch.

salivary glands The *glands which secrete *saliva: the parotid, submaxillary, and sublingual glands in the *buccal cavity.

salmonella A group of *bacteria that cause intestinal infection. A frequent contaminator of foods, salmonella is probably the most common cause of food poisoning which has resulted in the withdrawal of teams from major sporting competition.

salpingitis Inflammation of the uterine tubes commonly caused by bacterial infection. It is characterized by fever and pain in the lower abdomen. Treatment is with antibiotics and rest. Physical exertion should be avoided during the acute stage of infection when *fever is present.

salt A chemical compound formed when the *hydrogen of an *acid has been replaced by a *metal. A salt is produced, together with water, when acid reacts with a *base. Salts such as *sodium chloride, *calcium carbonate, and *potassium chloride are common in the body and play vital roles in body functions such as the conduction of *nerve impulses and the production of *muscle contractions.

saltatory conduction The propagation of a *nerve impulse in which the wave of depolarization appears to jump from one *node of Ranvier to the next along a *medullated fibre. Saltatory conduction increases the speed at which nerve impulses can be conducted.

salt depletion The loss of salt from the body, either by sweating, persistent vomiting, or diarrhoea. Salt depletion is common after heavy physical exertion and in hot environments, and can lead to muscular weakness and cramps. *See also* salt replacement.

salt replacement Replacement of *salt which has been lost from the body (*see* salt depletion). The best replacement fluid is one that contains as much salt and water as is lost through secretion (i.e., about 1–2g of salt per litre of water). As *sweat contains less *sodium chloride than blood *plasma

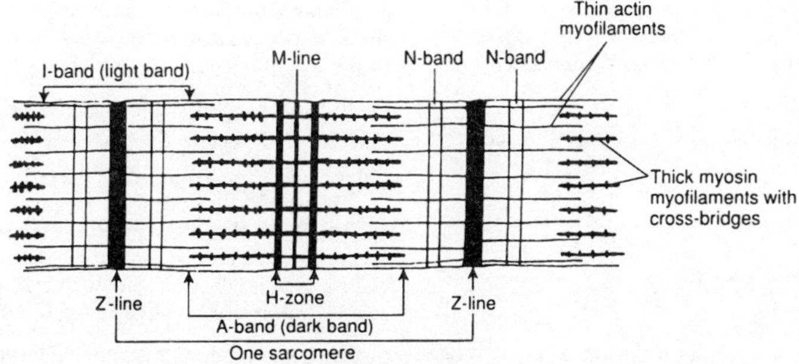

sarcomere

(0.9 per cent), unless *water replacement is large, the concentration of plasma tends to increase during competition. Consequently, salt replacment without adequate water replacement can disrupt the salt and fluid balance.

salt tablet Tablet containing sodium chloride which is used to replace *salt lost in sweating. If the tablets are taken without water, there is a danger of a salt imbalance occurring. *See also* salt replacement.

saluretic A *drug belonging to the *diuretics which are on the *IOC list of *banned substances. Saluretics act on the *kidney to increase the excretion of both *salts and water.

sample A portion of a given *population of people, objects, or events which accurately reflects all the significant features of that population.

sampling error Differences which occur between the true value of a characteristic of a population and the value estimated from a *sample. To reduce the error as far possible *random sampling is used.

sampling frame The full list of members of the *population to be studied from which a *sample can be drawn.

sanction A means by which a moral or social standard is enforced. Sanctions can be either positive (through *rewards) or negative, (through punishments). They may also be either formal, such as the imposition of a sporting boycott on a country whose policies are disapproved of by other governments; or informal, such as the refusal by one athlete to compete with another who has been found to have taken *banned substances.

SA node *See* sinoatrial node.

saphenous vein A *superficial *vein in the leg, receiving *blood from the foot. *See also* long saphenous vein; and short saphenous vein.

sarco- Prefix pertaining to *muscle.

sarcolemma The *cell membrane surrounding a *muscle fibre.

sarcomere Part of a *striated *muscle fibre that is contained between two *Z-membranes. The sarcomere is the functional unit of the muscle fibre, composed mainly of the *contractile proteins *actin and *myosin.

sarcoplasm *Cytoplasm of a *muscle cell.

sarcoplasmic reticulum System of membranous tubules surrounding each *muscle fibre. The function of the sarcoplasmic reticulum is to transmit the contractile impulse to all parts of the muscle fibres. It does this by releasing and then sequestering *calcium ions which are essential for *muscle contraction. *See also* sliding-filament theory.

sargent jump test A test of muscular *power which is often used in fitness-testing. The test consists of measuring the difference between the subject's maximum vertical reach and maximum reach after jumping. Typically, the subject swings his or her arms downwards and backwards, takes a crouch position, pauses momentarily to get balance, and then leaps upward as high as possible, swinging the arms forcefully forwards and upwards.

sartorius (tailor's muscle) A straplike *superficial muscle running obliquely across the *anterior surface of the thigh to the knee. It is the longest muscle in the body, crossing both hip- and knee-joints. Its *origin is on the *iliac spine and its *insertion is on the *medial aspect of the upper part of the tibia. It flexes and laterally rotates the thigh on the abdomen, and acts as a weak flexor of the knee.

satiation The fulfilment beyond capacity of a desire. Satiation may occur as the result of an excessive use of a *reinforcer which leads to a loss in the effectiveness of the reinforcer.

satisfaction The sense of achievement and the fulfilment of a need. It is generally accepted that sport can satisfy many desires, among them the desire for *recreation, social contact, *aggression, *play, and self-assuredness.

saturated fat (saturated fatty acid) *Carbon-containing *compound with only a single *covalent bond. Saturated fats are usually solid at room temperature. They are metabolized along different pathways from *polyunsaturated fats. Along with *cholesterol, saturated fats are implicated in the deposition of fatty substances on *artery walls which may eventually lead to *atherosclerosis. Saturated fats come chiefly from animal sources (such as beef, butter, whole-milk dairy products, the dark meat of poultry, and poultry skin) as well as tropical vegetable oils (coconut, palm, and palm kernel).

saturated fatty acid *See* saturated fat.

Saturday-night arm A condition in which the arm and hand lose sensitivity due to being kept for prolonged periods in a cramped position. It was named Saturday-night arm because it commonly occurs in athletes who make long weekend trips to sports venues, confined in a coach seat.

scabies A skin infection caused by the mite *Sarcoptes scabei*. The female burrows under the skin, particularly around the fingers and genitalia, and lays eggs. Scabies is transmitted by close body contact, especially in overcrowded and unhygienic places, but the mite is no respecter of social class. It does not interfere with physical activity, although it can be transmitted in close contact sports such as wrestling.

scala One of three chambers in the *cochlea. The superior chamber is called the scala vestibuli, the middle is the scala media (cochlear duct), and the inferior is the scala tympani.

scalar quantity (scalar) A *variable, such as time, which can be defined solely in terms of *magnitude. *Compare* vector.

scaled response (scaling) A method of measurement in the social sciences which uses a scaled continuum of responses for a particular dimension extending from one extreme, through neutral, to the other extreme. Scaling is commonly used in questionnaires for the measurement of *personality traits (for example, the *introvert–extravert dimension) and *attitudes. The respondent chooses one point along the continuum which applies to him or her.

scalene *See* scalenus.

scalenus (scalene) One of four *muscles (scalenus anterior, scalenus medius, scalenus minimus, and scalenus posterior) located anterolaterally on each side of the neck, deep to the *sternocleidomastoid muscle. They have their *origins on the *transverse process of the *cervical vertebrae, and their *insertions posteriolaterally on the first two ribs. They flex and rotate the neck, and elevate the first two ribs during *inspiration.

scaling *See* scaled response.

scalogram Scale for measuring *attitude which assumes that if a subject agrees with one statement, then the subject will also agree with all statements of a lower intensity.

scan 1 An examination of a human body or body-part using a moving detector or a sweeping beam of radiation as in computerized *tomography, *nuclear magnetic resonance, *scintigraphy, or *ultrasonography. The term also applies to an image formed from such an examination. 2 *See* scanning.

scanning Form of visual *perception in which a person attends to many aspects of the *stimulus field. Scanning tends to increase under great *stress. *See also* focusing; narrowing; and selective attention.

scaphoid A boat-shaped *bone of the wrist which articulates with the *radius behind, the *trapezium and *trapezoid bones in front, and with the *capitate and *lunate medially.

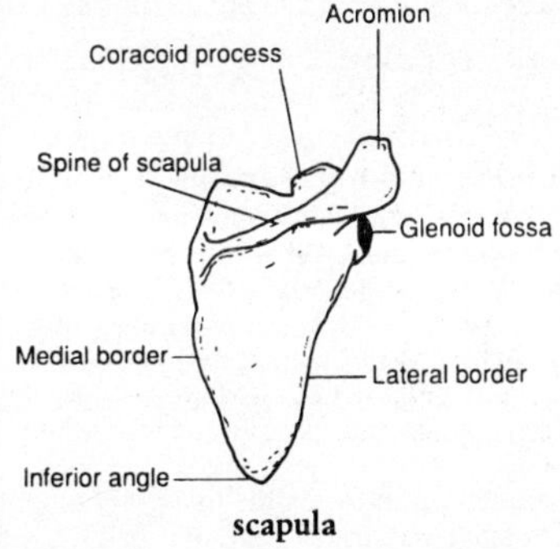

scapula

scapula (shoulder-blade) A flat, triangular *bone, on the upper and *posterior part of the *thorax, which forms the *pectoral girdle with the *clavicle. Many of the large muscles that move the arm are attached to it. The spine of the scapula arises from its surface and arches upwards and forwards into the *acromion process. The dorsal view of a right scapula is illustrated above.

SCAT *See* sport competition anxiety test.

scattergram A *graph on which a subject's scores in two tests can be jointly represented as a single datum point.

sceptical argument The proposal that athletic performance cannot be predicted from *personality traits. *Compare* credulous argument.

SCG *See* sodium cromoglycate.

schema 1 A mental framework or outline which functions as a kind of vague standard that arises out of past experience, growing and differentiating throughout childhood, and places new experiences in their appropriate context and relation. 2 In the schema theory of *motor control, a set of operational rules or algorithms, that have been acquired from practice or experience, which determine the motor responses in a given situation. It is proposed that there is a separate schema for each class of movement and that skill proficiency is determined by the efficiency of the schema. The use of schema implies there are generalized *motor programs for a given class of movement. It is proposed that the schema would not take up much storage space (storage is a problem with theories positing a one-to-one relationship between stored programs and generated movements) and would help to explain the ability to perform relatively novel tasks.

schema theory *See* schema.

Scheurmann's disease An *osteochondritis causing irregularities in the *epiphysis of *vertebrae. Scheurmann's disease results in vertebral wedging often characterized by back-pain during and after physical activity. Scheurmann's disease mostly affects young men between 15 and 20 years old. Treatment includes active back exercises. The condition does not usually preclude participation in sport, though it often results in reduction in the level of strenuous activity during the painful phase.

Schwann cell A *cell, named after the German anatomist T. Schwann (1837–1910), producing a *myelin sheath which covers some *nerve fibres.

sciatica A severe pain radiating down the *sciatic nerve, from the lower back into the leg. The onset of sciatica may be sudden and brought on by strain to the lower back or a slipped disc, though sometimes no cause can be identified, and tests need to be performed to search for other causes of buttock and leg pain.

sciatic nerve The largest and longest nerve in the body. The sciatic nerve leaves the pelvis via the greater *sciatic notch, descends deep to the *gluteus maximus muscle, and continues down the posterior aspect of the thigh. There it supplies the hamstring muscles and part of the adductor magnus. The sciatic nerve divides immediately above the knee to give rise to the peroneal nerve and tibial nerve.

sciatic notch A notch above the triangular spine of the *ischium which is converted into a *foramen for the passage of nerves, *blood vessels, and *tendons into the thigh region.

science A systematic study, using observation, experiment, and measurement, of physical and social phenomena, or any specific area of knowledge involving such a study.

scientific approach Set of systematic procedures which enable a problem to be approached or a question answered in a methodical and logical way. Typically, the stages of a scientific approach to the solution of a problem include posing a research question and making a plan, gathering information, analysing the information, interpreting the findings and results, formulating a *hypothesis, and testing the hypothesis.

scientific law Statement which connects phenomena in such a way that it can be said that if one phenomenon (A) occurs then another (B) will, or is likely to, occur also.

scientific management A theory of management which focuses on the efficiency of the management process; improved efficiency is assumed to increase production. Scientific management is a formal style of *leadership behaviour which is closely related to the *initiating structure.

scientific method *See* scientific approach.

scientific paradigm A scientific model, universally accepted and used, even if temporarily.

scientific realism An assumption that a physical world exists independently of human senses.

scientism Term, often used pejoratively, to describe a doctrine which oversimplifies scientific concepts or has an unrealistic expectation of science.

scintigram *See* scintigraphy.

scintigraphy A technique used to diagnose sports injuries. A radioactive tracer is used in conjunction with a scintillation counter for producing pictures. A diagram, called a scintigram, shows the internal distribution of a radioactive tracer in internal parts of the body. In sports medicine, scintigraphy is particularly useful in the detection of *stress fractures in bones. *See also* bone scan.

sclera Outer coat of the eye to which muscles are attached.

sclerosis Hardening of organs and tissues, usually due to excessive production of *connective tissue after inflammation. *See also* arteriosclerosis.

scoliosis (thoracolumbar scoliosis) Abnormal lateral curvature of the *spine that occurs most often in the *thoracic region. It may be *congenital or acquired (from poor posture, for example, or an unequal pull on the spine) when it is known as AIS or acquired idiopathic scoliosis. *See also* tennis shoulder.

screener An individual with a good ability to filter out various *stimuli from their *environment. Screeners are selective in the stimuli to which they respond and tend not to be easily distracted or upset. *Compare* non-screener. *See also* selective attention.

screening The testing or checking of an individual so as to determine his or her suitability to take part in a particular sport, or ability to undertake strenuous exercise. *See also* medical screening.

scrotum Paired pouch holding the *testes outside the *abdominal cavity.

scurvy A deficiency disease due to lack of *vitamin C. Initial signs of of the disease include bleeding gums. This may be followed by *anaemia, *cutaneous haemorrhage, degeneration of *muscle and *cartilage, and weight-loss. The effects are reversed by treatment with vitamin C.

SDH *See* succinic dehydrogenase.

sebaceous gland A *gland in the *epidermis that produces an oily secretion call *sebum.

sebum Oily secretion of *sebaceous gland. The sebum forms a thin layer over the skin reducing evaporation of water; it also has antibacterial effects.

second (s) **1** Base unit of time for the *SI system; symbol s. It was formerly defined as 1/86400 of the mean solar day, but it is now defined in terms of the periods of radiation from a caesium-133 atom. **2** A unit of *angle equal to 1/60 of a minute of an arc, or 1/3600 of a degree.

secondary analysis An inquiry based on data, such as census returns, which have already been collected and analysed.

secondary behavioural involvement The indirect participation in a sport as a *sport producer or *sport consumer. *Compare* primary behavioural involvement. *See also* cognitive sport involvement; effective sport involvement; and secondary behavioural involvement.

secondary deviance The process by which an individual, having once broken a rule, comes to change his or her attitudes and affiliations, and begins to associate himself or herself with being outside the normal or socially acceptable. That is, his or her *self-image is changed to one of *deviance.

secondary drive An acquired *drive which is not directly related to satisfying *physiological requirements; an example of a secondary drive is the drive to win a medal at the Olympics.

secondary infection A new *infection superimposed upon a pre-existing infection.

secondary immune response Second and subsequent responses of the *immune system to a previously met *antigen. The secondary immune response is more rapid and more effective than the *primary immune response.

secondary injury An *injury which follows a *primary injury but which is not a complication of the primary injury.

secondary ossification centre An area of *bone growth which appears at the junction between the *shaft and one or both *epiphyses of a *long bone; an area from which *ossification of the epiphyses occurs. *See also* epiphyseal plate.

secondary plane A *plane that passes through the *centre of gravity of a *body-segment, or through the centre of a *joint or through some other point of reference. *Compare* cardinal plane.

secondary reinforcement A learned *reinforcement. Secondary reinforcement occurs when something which does not satisfy a need directly has been paired with a *primary reinforcement which does satisfy a need. For example, a sound paired with the presentation of food (primary reinforcement) may come to have a reward value itself and serve as a secondary reinforcer.

secondary sexual characteristic Any of the several features of a male or female, produced when sexually mature, but not concerned directly with *gamete production.

secondary sport involvement *See* secondary behavioural involvement.

secondary task method A collection of experimental methods used in the study of *skill-learning in which a secondary task is performed simultaneously with the main task. Secondary task methods have been used especially to study the attentional demands of the main task. *See also* probe technique.

second-class lever A *lever in which the *point of resistance (or load) lies between the *fulcrum and *point of effort. In the human body, second-class levers are uncommon but second-class leverage is exerted when a person stands on tip-toe.

second-degree strain *See* moderate strain.

second messenger A molecule inside a cell which mediates *intracellular responses to *extracellular *chemical messengers. The second messenger is generated by the binding of the extracellular chemical (a *hormone or *neurotransmitter) to a

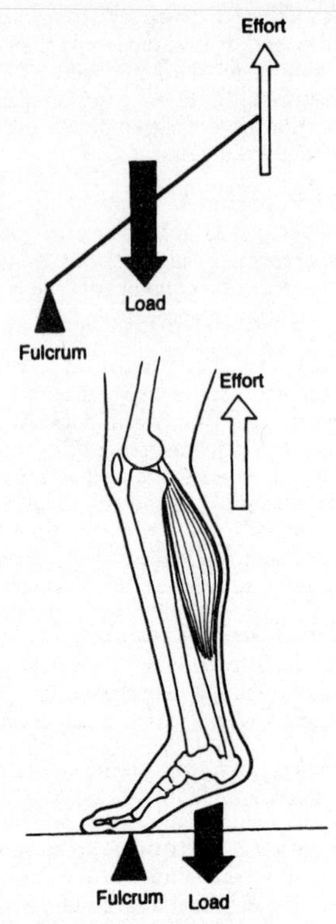

second-class lever

*receptor site on the outer surface of the *plasma *membrane.

second-order conditioning In *classical conditioning, the use of a *conditioned stimulus as the basis for further conditioning.

second-order trait *Personality trait used to describe a large number of similar, clustered traits. In Catell's 16 PF personality inventory, for example, six of the sixteen first-order traits cluster to form the second-order trait of *anxiety.

second wind A phenomenon characterized by a sudden transition from an ill-defined feeling of distress and difficulty in breathing during the early stages of prolonged exercise to a more comfortable, less stressful feeling later in the exercise. There is some debate about the physiological reality of second wind, but it may be due to an initial increase in *lactate levels at the beginning of the exercise, followed by recovery as a steady rate is established.

secretin An intestinal *hormone secreted by the *duodenum in response to acid chyme (partly-digested food) passing from the stomach. Secretin passes into the blood and promotes the flow of bile and pancreatic juices into the intestine, and inhibits gastric gland secretion.

secretion 1 Process by which a useful substance produced in a *cell is passed through the *plasma membrane to the outside. 2 A cell product that is transported to the exterior of the cell.

section 1 A cut made along a particular plane through the human body or through an organ. 2 A thin slice of *tissue prepared for microscopic study.

sedative A *drug, such as *alcohol, which can calm an individual without inducing sleep. Sedatives have been used by marksmen to improve their precision. *See also* anxiolytic.

sedentary Applied to a person who is relatively inactive and has a lifestyle characterized by a lot of sitting.

sedimentation rate Time taken for solids to settle out of a suspension under the influence of gravity. In medicine, the term is applied particularly to the time it takes for cells (mainly red blood cells) to settle out under standardized conditions in a *blood sample; this is known as the erythrocyte sedimentation rate.

segmental bond A social link which tends to divide a society into blocks or segments that internally are relatively homogenous and that maintain sharp bonds *vis-à-vis* outsiders.

segmental method (segmentation method) A method of estimating the *centre of gravity of the whole human body from the centres of gravity and weights of individual body-segments in the head, trunk, and limbs. The estimate involves quite complex computations and large amounts of measuring, but it hinges on the fact that the sum of the *moments of the weight-forces of the separate segments is equal to the moment of their *resultant.

segmentation method *See* segmental method.

selective attention (selectivity) The ability of a person to attend to specific *stimuli and exclude other, competing stimuli. Selective attention is regarded by many as the single most important *cognitive characteristic of the successful athlete. However, this apparently useful mechanism can also have unfortunate consequences. A footballer, for example, may perceive the ball as the only important aspect of the game and ignore all other sources of information. This ball-watching may allow an opponent to move undetected and unmarked into a scoring position.

selective filter A filter, found in most models of *selective attention, that either eliminates or attenuates information of minor importance.

selective malabsorption A disorder, usually of the *small intestine, which affects the ability of the body to absorb certain *nutrients. *Compare* coeliac disease. *See* fat malabsorption; and sugar malabsorption.

selectivity **1** *See* selective attention. **2** Referred to as the property of a *drug which, due to its chemical structure, tends to exert its greatest effect on particular *receptor sites, thus reducing the incidence of side-effects.

selenium A *trace element found in meat, seafood, and cereals. Selenium acts as an *antioxidant and is a constituent of some *enzymes. Its functions are closely related to those of *vitamin E with which it acts synergistically (*see* synergy).

self A person as perceived by the individual concerned in the context of *society and his or her relationships with others. Self is an important determinant of *motivation and interaction with other people.

self-actualization (self-realization) The realization of a person's full potential, whatever it may be and regardless of the rewards involved; doing what one is best suited to do or intended to do. Self-actualization is only attainable when all other needs have been met (*see* motivational hierarchy).

self-assertive *See* assertiveness.

self-attention The degree to which an athlete is concerned about the execution of his or her own skills. With some high-skilled performers, self-attention is higher at home matches than away ones. *See also* home-court advantage.

self-concept All the elements which make up a person's *self. Self-concept represents how a person sees himself or herself and is thought to be comprised of three components: the ideal self, which refers to the person one would like to be; the public self, the image one believes others have of oneself; and the real self, which is a sum of those subjective thoughts, feelings, and needs that the person sees as being authentically theirs. Sometimes there is a conflict between the real self and the others which results in *anxiety. To maintain good mental health, the public and ideal self should be compatible with the real self.

self-confidence A person's belief that he or she has the ability to succeed. Athletes who are self-confident and expect to succeed are often the same athletes who do succeed. *See also* self-efficacy.

self-control The ability of a person to exercise control over his or her own feelings and *behaviour.

self-directed relaxation An abbreviated form of *progressive muscle relaxation used in *stress management. The subject achieves full relaxation of the body by relaxing the *muscle groups while breathing slowly and evenly, and visualizing *tension flowing out of the body.

self-disclosure The sharing of one's feelings and thoughts with others. Self-disclosure is an important aspect of a coach's behaviour. Some coaches prefer being reserved, and wish to stay detached and objective; others prefer to be open and share with other athletes the way they feel about events, believing that self-disclosure generates trust.

self-efficacy A situation-specific form of *self-confidence. In sport, self-efficacy refers to the performer's belief that he or she can successfully execute a behaviour required to produce a certain outcome. Assuming an individual is capable of a response and there are appropriate incentives, self-efficacy theory asserts that the actual performance will be predicted by the individual's belief in his or her competence. *See also* Bandura's theory of self-efficacy.

self-esteem A person's inner conviction of his or her competency and worth as a human being. Positive self-esteem is viewing oneself as a competent and worthy person, however that is defined, and feeling good about that aspect of oneself.

self-focusing The process of *selective attention towards information that concerns oneself.

self-fulfilling prophecy A prediction which is confirmed solely because it was suggested. For example, potential spectators may not go to view a match because they have heard it will not be well supported.

self-image *See* self-concept.

self-orientation A psychological orientation in which an individual desires direct personal rewards regardless of the effects on others working with that individual. The self-oriented person may be dominating, introspective, and socially insensitive. Highly-successful athletes tend to be self-oriented while coaches tend to be lower in self-orientation. *Compare* task orientation.

self-paced task A *task or *skill, the initiation of which is determined by the performer. Self-paced tasks include a golf drive or tennis serve. Typically, they occur in stable, predictable environments in which the performer has plenty of time to respond. *Compare* externally-paced tasks.

self-perception The way a person sees himself or herself. Perceptions of oneself in any domain, such as physical or academic. *See* self-concept.

self-realization *See* self-actualization.

self-regulation The regulation of one's own goal-directed behaviour without immediate external control. In sport, self-regulation involves an athlete taking control of and responsibility for his or her own training, performance, and participation in sport.

self-report inventory *Questionnaire in which the respondents answer questions about themselves. Such inventories are commonly used to measure, among other things, *anxiety.

self-serving attributional bias The tendency to ascribe positive outcomes of performance to internal factors such as ability and effort, and negative outcomes to external factors such as luck and the weather, in order to maintain *self-esteem. *See also* functional model of attribution.

self-serving hypothesis An *hypothesis based on the observation that people will sometimes make illogical attributions to enhance or protect their *egos.

self-talk A mental preparation strategy in which individuals talk to themselves in an attempt to build up their *self-confidence and convince themselves that they can succeed.

self-theory An approach to the study of *personality and therapy which emphasizes the role of the individual in shaping his or her own destiny. Particularly important is the individual's *self-concept, which is that person's consistent, organized perception of himself or herself. Supporters of this theory stress the subjective side of human existence, and regard an individual's self-concept as more important than the conditions in the *environment.

self-worth A feeling of positive *self-esteem so that the person views himself or herself as competent and worthy.

semantic differential scale *See* Osgood's semantic differential scale.

semi-circular canal One of three fluid-filled canals in the *inner ear containing cells, sensitive to movement of the head, which serve as an *organs of *balance.

semi-lunar cartilage One of two crescent-shaped *cartilages in the *knee-joint between the *femur and *tibia. *See also* meniscus.

semi-lunar valve (pocket valve) A crescent-shaped valve, present in the *aorta and the *pulmonary artery, which prevents *blood returning to the *ventricles after *ventricular systole.

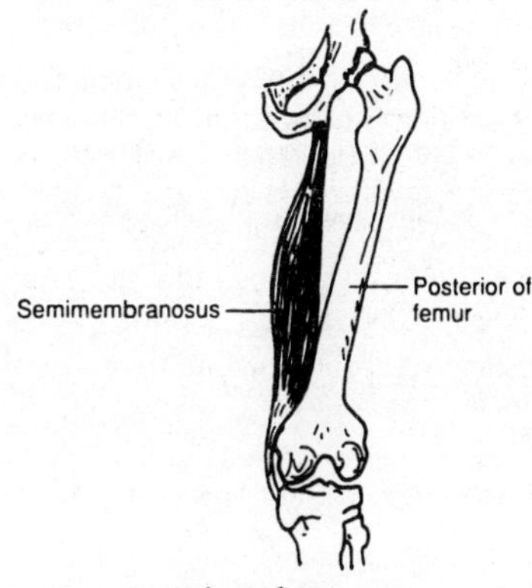

semimembranosus

semimembranosus One of three hamstring muscles which lies deep to the *semitendinosus muscle. The semimembranosus has its *origin in the *ischial tuberosity and its *insertion on the *medial *condyle of the *tibia. Its actions include *extension of the thigh on the hip, *flexion of the knee, and medial *rotation of the leg.

seminal vesicles Glands forming part of the male reproductive system that produce most of the fluid part of *semen.

semiology (semiotics) **1** The study of signs and symbols, especially the relationship between written and spoken signs. Semiology draws attention to the layers of meaning which may be embodied in a simple set of representations, such as the five interlocking rings of the Olympic flag. It is concerned with the meaning invested in the sign and the signifier, the physical representation of the sign. **2** The scientific study of the signs and symptoms of disease.

semiotics *See* semiology.

semi-permeable membrane A *membrane which allows only a solvent (in biological systems, usually water) to pass through.

semispinalis One of a pair of *composite muscles either side of the *vertebral column forming part of the deep layer of back muscles which extends from the *thoracic region to the head. The semispinalis has its *origin on the *transverse processes of *lumbar vertebrae 7 to 12 and its *insertions on the *occipital bone and the *spinous processes of *cervical and thoracic vertebrae. The semispinalis extends the vertebral column and head, and rotates them to opposite sides.

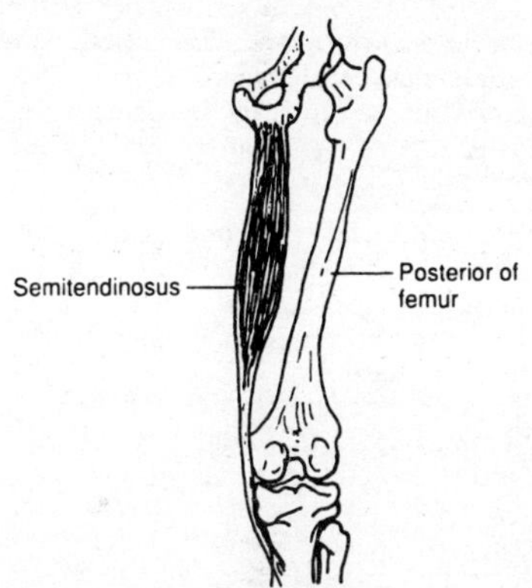

semitendinosus

semitendinosus One of three *hamstring muscles which lies medial to the *biceps femoris. The *origin of the semitendinosus is on the *ischial tuberosity (in common with the long head of the biceps femoris) and its insertion is on the medial aspect of the upper tibial shaft. The semitendinosus extends the thigh at the hip; flexes the knee; and, with the *semimembranosus, medially rotates the leg.

semi-vegetarian A person who has a diet mainly of plants supplemented with some animal products. *See also* vegetarian diet.

sensation An irreducible sensory experience such as might exist the first time a particular *receptor of a sense-organ is stimulated. Theoretically, a sensation is devoid of conscious meaning until the process of *perception occurs.

sense One of several faculties such as sight, touch, hearing, taste, and smell by which qualities of the internal and external *environment can be appreciated.

sense-organ An *organ in the body containing cells which respond to particular external or internal *stimuli. Messages from the sense-organ are conveyed by *sensory neurones to the *central nervous system where they are processed and where *perception takes place.

sensibility The capacity to be affected by, and to respond to, *stimuli.

sensible temperature The critical temperature range beyond which human beings feel too hot or too cold. The sensible temperature is affected by *relative humidity and *wind chill. *Compare* comfort zone.

sensitivity **1** The aspect of a measurement dealing with the possibility of detecting changes in a dependent measure in relation to varying experimental conditions. *See also* objectivity; reliability; and validity. **2** The ability to respond to *stimuli. The term is used especially for the ability to be affected by and to respond to stimuli of low intensity.

sensitization **1** A form of behavioural therapy in which anxiety-provoking *stimuli are associated with unwanted behaviour so that the unwanted behaviour can be suppressed. **2** The process which increases the *excitability of *receptors to sensory *stimuli.

sensorimotor *See* motor.

sensorimotor response Any overt *motor act initiated by *sensory processes.

sensory Pertaining to the *senses.

sensory adaptation Adaptation of some sensory function, as in dark adaptation where objects not seen at first in dim light gradually become visible. *See also* adaptation.

sensory area One of several areas of the *cerebral cortex of the *brain which process the incoming messages conveyed by *sensory neurones from *sense-organs.

sensory information store *See* sensory register.

sensory memory *See* short-term sensory store.

sensory nerve A *nerve that contains processes of *sensory neurones and carries *afferent nerve impulses to the *central nervous system.

sensory neurone (afferent neurone) A nerve cell that conveys impulses from a *receptor to the *central nervous system.

sensory reaction A component of *reaction time during which the subject's *attention is directed towards the *stimulus rather than the response.

sensory receptor Dendritic end-organs (*see* dendrites), or parts of other cell-types specialized to respond to a *stimulus.

sensory register *See* short-tem sensory store.

sensory store *See* short-term sensory store.

sensory transduction The transformation of the energy of a *stimulus into a *nerve impulse.

sentiment An *attitude that is expressed in *emotions.

separate frequency *Knowledge of results which refers to separate trials rather than to a summary of a number of trials. *Compare* accumulated knowledge of results.

separation *See* dislocation.

sepsis The breakdown of tissue by putrefying bacteria or toxins.

septic Pertaining to *sepsis.

septicaemia Blood-poisoning; a condition in which there is the presence of a large number of *pathogenic bacteria and their toxins in the blood.

septic arthritis A bacterial infection of a *joint marked by fever, and swelling and pain in the affected joint. It is associated with other infections and requires urgent medical attention. During the acute stage, the joint is relieved of any load, and the pathogenic organism identified and eliminated with *antibiotics. After the acute stage, *isometric exercises may be introduced to offset *muscle atrophy. Physical exertion should be resumed only with medical guidance.

septic bursitis *See* bursitis.

septum A partition or a dividing wall of a structure, such as that which divides the right and left sides of the heart.

sequencing A method of *learning a *motor skill in which the subject repeats the component movements in the proper order.

sequentially-dependent task A *delegated task in which group-members must execute their skills in a prescribed order. *Compare* sequentially-independent task. *See also* social facilitation.

sequentially-independent task A *delegated task in which group-members can execute their skills in any order, or at any time, in relation to one another. *Compare* sequentially-dependent task. *See also* social facilitation.

sequential stabilization In the human body, an increase in the *stability of some body-parts to stabilize the movement of other parts. During a golf swing, for example, the leading leg is stabilized to enable an effective *force to be produced by other body-parts. *See also* force summation.

serial-processing A pattern of *information-processing in which the stages of processing are arranged sequentially in time, as in *spinal reflexes. *Compare* parallel-processing.

serial skill *See* serial task.

serial task (serial skill) A task consisting of a series of several discrete elements strung together to produce an integrated movement. The order in which the elements are performed is important. In the high jump and triple jump, for example, the run-up and the take-off phases occur in a particular order. *See also* continuous task; and discrete task.

series elastic components (series elastic elements) The noncontractile body components which are in series with the *contractile elements of *muscles. Series elastic components are believed to be important for the storage of *elastic energy when an active muscle is stretched. *Tendons are major sites of series elastic components, but recent evidence suggests that the *cross-bridges between *actin and *myosin filaments may also contribute to series elasticity.

series elastic element *See* series elastic components.

serosa *See* serous membrane.

serotonin (entramine; 5-hydroxytryptamine; 5-HT) A *metabotropic *neurotransmitter belonging to the *biogenic amines. Serotonin is made from the *amino acid *tryptophan that serves as one of the *brain's principal neurotransmitters. It is secreted in some *neurones of the *brainstem, the *hypothalmus, *limbic system, *pineal gland, and spinal cord where its effects are generally inhibitory. Serotonin acts as a *vasoconstrictor and is thought to play an important role in the *inflammation response. When a person eats a meal, the level of serotonin is raised or lowered—depending on the amounts of *proteins, *carbohydrates, and other substances consumed—and this level may affect *mood and *motivation. The activity of serotonin is blocked by *LSD.

serous Pertaining to, secreting, or containing *serum.

serous fluid A clear, watery fluid secreted by cells of a *serous membrane.

serous membrane (serosa) A double-layered *membrane forming a sac which lines the large cavities of the body. The outer, *parietal membrane lines the walls of the cavity and the inner, *visceral membrane lines the organ. The inner surface of the sac is moistened by fluid which reduces friction of the organs within their cavities.

serratus anterior (anterior serrated muscle) *Muscle of the *anterior *thorax which lies deep to the *scapula and *inferior to *pectoral muscles on the *lateral ribcage. The serratus anterior forms the *medial wall of the *axilla. The muscle has its *origins (which resemble the teeth of a saw) on the first eight or nine *ribs, and its *insertions on the inner border of the scapula. The serratus anterior is the main muscle responsible for pushing and punching movements; consequently it is sometimes referred to as the boxer's muscle.

serum The clear watery body fluid exuded by a *serous membrane. Blood serum is the amber-coloured, noncellular, fluid part of *blood, excluding *fibrinogen and *platelets.

serum creatinin A *biochemical parameter used to measure the effects of *exercise. Normal levels are between 0.7 and 1.5 mg per cent; levels increase slightly after hard efforts.

serum urea The amount of *urea present in the *serum. The serum urea level is used as a *biochemical indicator of *protein *metabolism. The level is often increased by hard training and long-duration exercise. Its determination the day after intensive training or competition is used to estimate residual *metabolic fatigue and *metabolic recovery.

servo An abbreviation for servomechanism. *See* closed-loop system.

servomechanism *See* closed-loop system.

sesamoid bone A special type of short irregular *bone, such as the *patella, embedded within a *tendon or *joint capsule. Sesamoid bones vary in size and number in different individuals. Some clearly act to alter the direction of pull of a tendon (*see* pulley); the function of others is unknown.

set 1 In *interval-training, a group of work and relief intervals. 2 In mathematics, a set is a group of objects or elements sharing at least one common characteristic.

set point *See* norm.

severe strain (total muscle rupture) A *third-degree strain involving total *muscle-tear.

Sever–Haglund disease (calcaneal apophysitis; os calcis apophysitis; Sever's disease An *osteochondritis affecting the heel *apophysis in active adolescents (commonly the 12–14 age group). The disease is characterized by pain, when walking and running, at the point of *insertion of the *Achilles tendon into the *periosteum of the *calcaneus. The condition is probably caused by *overloading and overuse. It usually resolves spontaneously with reduction in vigorous activity, and will certainly do so when the sufferer reaches 16 to 18 years and *ossification of the bone is complete.

Sever's disease *See* Sever–Haglund disease.

sex The biological differences between males and females, especially differences in genitals and reproductive capabilities. *Compare* gender. *See also* sex determination; and sex differences.

sex chromosome A *chromosome that is involved in *sex determination. *See also* X chromosome; and Y chromosome.

sex determination Determining whether a person is male and female is not always easy because there is no precise definition of what is meant by male and female. There are a number of definable characteristics which most women share and other characteristics which most men share. The problem arises when an individual has some characteristics which have been designated male and some designated female. In humans, the genetic control of the production of male and female gametes is determined by two *sex chromosomes called X and Y. For most individuals, sex can be determined satisfactorily by discovering which two sex chromosomes their body cells have. Females, the homogametic sex, have XX chromosones, and males, the heterogametic sex, have XY chromosones. For these individuals, sex can be identified relatively easily by a chromatin test, a test which reveals their sex chromosomes. However, there remain a small proportion of individuals (approximately 6 in every 1000) of intersex, many of them women who would be labelled male by a chromatin test. They may have more than the normal complement of sex chromosomes (e.g., XXY, or XYY), they may lack a chromosome (e.g., XO), or they may be mosaics with a mixture of male and female cells. Some individuals possess both ovaries and testes. The situation is further complicated by hormonal and psychological disturbances which may result in an individual being ascribed as male in one test and female in another test. Athletes undergoing a test to determine their sex require sympathetic and delicate handling, and a single type of test is not sufficient to ascribe them to a sex. *See also* adrenal virilism; and testicular feminization.

sex differences In sport, differences in sporting performances and participation between males and females which may be due to cultural, physiological, biochemical, or hormonal distinctions. There is a wide variance of body-types in both males and females, and a degree of overlap, but there are certain physiological and physical characteristics in which women tend to differ from men and which may have an affect on sporting performance. These differences in women include the presence of breasts, a high proportion of *adipose tissue to *lean body-mass, relatively low bone strength, and greater pelvic tilt but higher flexibility.

sex discrimination The practice whereby an individual is disadvantaged or advantaged on the basis of *sex. *See also* sexism.

sex hormones A *steroid hormone, such as *oestrogen and *progesterone produced by the *ovary, or *testosterone produced in the *testes, necessary for normal reproductive function.

sexism Values, beliefs, and norms that supports the process of defining one *gender as less worthy and capable than the other, and discriminatory practices which support these beliefs. *See also* sex discrimination.

sex stratification A ranking system in which sex is the basis for making the evaluations, so that *gender becomes the basis for *social stratification. *See also* sex discrimination.

sex-typed An individual having the same *sex and *gender role orientation such as a sexual female with female gender role orientation. *Compare* cross-sex-typed.

sex-typing The process of ascribing certain activities as being appropriate for only one sex.

sexuality 1 The innate attributes of an individual, including sexual desires, roles, and identities, which find expression in sexual relationships and sexual activities with others. 2 An individual's preferences for specific forms of sexual expression; an individual's sexual orientation.

sexual orientation *See* sexuality.

shadowing A procedure, used to study *selective attention, in which a subject is exposed to two different spoken messages at the same time through earphones. The subject is instructed to repeat the messages coming through the right earphone and is later asked to recall the information received in the left ear.

shaft *See* diaphysis.

shapism An emphasis on body shape in the projection of a desirable body image by those with a vested interest in acceptance of this image. In western societies, the emphasis for women is on slimness; and for men the emphasis is on slim muscularity. Shapism is closely associated with *mesomorphism.

Sharpey's fibres Strong fibres which attach a *tendon and *ligament to the *periosteum, and secure the periosteum to the underlying *bone. Sharpey's fibres consist of dense tufts of *collagen fibres that extend from the fibrous layer into the bone *matrix.

shear An angular deformation without change in volume.

shear force 1 A *force applied to a body in the plane of one of its faces, which produces or tends to produce *shear. Shear forces cause an object to be twisted. 2 A *force identified on the basis of formula: force = mass×acceleration, in which the *mass component, or *resistance to be overcome, is more important than *acceleration. Shear force is particularly important in weight-lifting. *See also* absolute force; and relative force.

shear stress A system of *shear forces in *equilibrium producing or tending to produce a *shear.

sheath The layer of *connective tissue that surrounds structures such as *blood vessles, *muscles, *nerves, and *tendons.

Sheldon's constitutional theory A theory that proposes a strong link between body-type (*see* somatotype) and *personality (*see* Sheldon somatotype classification). *See also* cerebrotonic; somatonic; and viscerotonic.

Sheldon somatotype classification (Sheldon's somato-personality typology) A classification system of body-types which contains three basic types of physique: *ectomorph, *endomorph, and *mesomorph. Sheldon's method of somatotyping is based on photographs of an individual taken from three diferent perspectives. From these photographs a number of measurements are taken and with the aid of tables developed by Sheldon the *somatotype is determined and ascribed a three-figure classification. Each number has a value from one to seven which designates the degree of each of the three components. One represents least amount of the component and seven the maximal; the first number represent the degree of endomorphy, the second number the degree of mesomorphy, and the third number the degree of ectomorphy. Thus, 7–1–1 represents extreme endomorphy; 1–7–1 represents extreme mesomorphy; and 1–1–7 represents extreme ectomorphy.

Sheldon's somato-personality typology *See* Sheldon somatotype classification.

shin-bone *See* tibia.

shingles *See* herpes zostera.

shin splints A term used loosely to describe an *over-use injury characterized by a dull aching pain, associated with exercise, felt along the shins, either to the inside or outside of the main shin-bone (the *tibia). There are several causes of shin splints, as the term is applied to several conditions in which either soft tissues or bones (the tibia or *fibula) are damaged. These conditions include a *stress fracture of the tibia or fibula; *peroneal tendinitis; anterior or lateral *compartment syndrome; and medial tibial stress syndrome. In all cases of shin splints, the irritation and pain spreads, and continues as long as the athlete remains active; the shin splints stop when activity ceases. Treatment depends on the cause.

shock General term for a life-threatening state of weakness brought about by a circulatory disturbance when the *arterial *blood pressure is insufficient to maintain an adequate blood supply to the tissues. The sufferer has cold moist skin, a weak rapid pulse, irregular breathing, dilated pupils, and is distressed, thirsty, and restless. Shock may be induced by many causes including *dehydration, *heart attack, bacterial infection, allergic reactions, *drug overdosage, severe injury, or haemorrhaging.

shock-box *See* Buss aggression machine.

shoe-motif pain A pain associated with wearing training shoes with relatively inflexible motifs. A sore area of skin develops, usually on the inside of the shoe where the motif exerts pressure on the foot near the motif's attachment to the sole of the shoe.

short bone A small, roughly cube-shaped *bone, consisting mainly of *spongy bone with *compact bone providing a thin surface layer. Examples of short bones include the *sesamoid bones, and the bones of the wrist and ankle where they play an important role in movements of the hand and foot repsectively.

short saphenous vein A principal *vein at the back of the *calf.

short-sightedness *See* myopia.

short-term anaerobic performance Maximal exercise, lasting about 10s, which is supported by the *ATP–PC system.

short-term anaerobic performance capacity The total work output during maximal exercise lasting about 10s. Short-term anaerobic performance capacity is considered a measure of *alactacid *anaerobic performance supported by the *ATP–PC system.

short-term anaerobic test A test which generally lasts 10 s or less and is designed to evaluate the capacity of the *ATP–PC system in the *muscles used to accomplish the test. The *Margaria staircase test and the *Quebec ten-second test are short-term anaerobic tests.

short-term endurance An *endurance performance with a duration of 35 s–2 min. Short-term endurance is associated with a high activation of the *central nervous system, as indicated on *EEGs, and high recruitment of *fast twitch fibres. The energy for short-term endurance is supplied anaerobically with the *ATP–PC system being important for the initial 10 s of the exercise.

short-term memory (STM) According to the *black-box model of memory, short-term memory is a component of the *information-processing system in which new information must remain for a minimum of 20–30 s or the information will be lost. It acts as a link between the *short-term sensory store (STS) and the *long-term memory (LTM). The short-term memory is believed to be analogous to consciousness and has been described as the 'work space' where information from the STS and LTM can be brought together for processing.

short-term motor memory A short-term store for motor information or motor tasks which is analagous to verbal *short-term memory. Its functions include the storage for a short time of sensory information acquired from *feedback from movements.

short-term sensory store (STS) According to the *black-box model, the first of three memory compartments involved in *information-processing. It is regarded as a functionally limitless short-term store of massive amounts of sensory information presented to it for a brief period of time. It is believed that the short-term sensory store accepts the information without much recoding; that is, the information is recorded in the same way that it came into the system in terms of spatial location and form. Information is held by the short-term sensory store for perhaps as little as one second. Selected information may be passed on to the *short-term memory for further processing.

short-term store *See* short-term sensory store.

short-wave diathermy A form of heat treatment produced by a high-frequency alternating current passing through the body and generating heat in deeper tissues. It is used to treat both deep and superficial tissue injuries such as *chondromalacia patellae, but its claimed benefits have been doubted.

shoulder A body region where the arm joins on to the rest of the body. The shoulder includes the following joints: the *ball-and-socket joint between the *humerus and *scapula (*glenohumeral joint), the joint between the *clavicle and the scapula (*acromioclavicular joint), and the joint between the clavicle and *sternum (*sternoclavicular joint). The scapulae are not connected to each other or to the *vertebral column, but a connection of sorts occurs between the *anterior surface of the scapula and the tissues between it and the *ribs; this is often called the scapulothoracic articulation. *See also* shoulder-joint.

shoulder-blade *See* scapula.

shoulder-blade spine (spina scapula) A projection on the *scapula which acts as an attachment point for *muscles. The shoulder-blade spine forms the *origin of the *deltoideus and *supraspinatus muscles, and an *insertion for the *trapezius.

shoulder-girdle Two *gliding joints: the *sternoclavicular joint and *acromioclavicular joint. *See also* pectoral girdle.

shoulder-girdle abduction A movement of the *shoulder-girdle, primarily involving the *scapula and *clavicle, forward and away from the *spinal column. It is effected by the *serratus anterior, *serratus major, and *pectoralis minor muscles.

shoulder-girdle abductor A *muscle which effects *shoulder-girdle abduction.

shoulder-girdle adduction A movement of the *shoulder-girdle, primarily involving the *scapula and *clavicle, back towards the *spinal column. The movement is effected by the combined actions of the *trapezius and *rhomoideus muscles.

shoulder-girdle adductor A *muscle which effects *shoulder-girdle adduction.

shoulder-girdle anterior tilt Movement of the *inferior angle of the *scapula towards the *thoracic surface.

shoulder-girdle depression Movement, mainly of the *scapula and *clavicle, which results in returning shoulders from an elevated position during shrugging back to a normal position. The *pectoralis minor lowers the scapula.

shoulder-girdle depressor A *muscle which effects *shoulder-girdle depression.

shoulder-girdle downward rotation Movement of the shoulder, mainly involving the *scapula and *clavicle, which results in returning the *inferior angle of the scapula down towards the *spinal column and the *glenoid fossa to its normal position. Downward rotation usually accompanies *shoulder-girdle depression.

shoulder-girdle elevation Movement, mainly of the *scapula and *clavicle, which results in shrugging the shoulders. The *levator scapulae and the upper part of the *trapezius raise the scapula.

shoulder-girdle elevator A *muscle which effects *shoulder-girdle elevation.

shoulder-girdle movement A movement which is generally described with respect to the *scapula, which may be elevated, depressed, abducted, adducted, upwardly rotated, downwardly rotated, and tilted both posteriorly and anteriorly. Shoulder-girdle movements supplement those of the *glenohumeral joint (*see* arm movements) and, with movements of the *sternoclavicular joint, contribute to the extraordinary *range of movement of the shoulder-joint.

shoulder-girdle posterior tilt Movement of the inferior angle of the *scapula away from the *thoracic surface.

shoulder-girdle rotator A *muscle which rotates the shoulder-girdle. Rotation, which mainly involves the *scapula and *clavicle, may be either downward or upward. Downward rotation, effected by the *rhomboideus major, results in returning the *inferior angle of the scapula towards the *spinal column and the *glenoid fossa to its normal position. Upward rotation, effected by the upper fibres of the *trapezius and the lower fibres of the *serratus anterior, results in moving the inferior angle of the scapula away from the spinal column and returning the glenoid fossa to its normal position.

shoulder-girdle upward rotation Movement of the *shoulder-girdle, mainly of the *scapula and *clavicle, which results in an increase in the angle of the *glenoid fossa with respect to its normal position. It is brought about by the *rhomboideus major and the upper part of the *serratus anterior muscle. Upward rotation usually accompanies *shoulder-girdle elevation.

shoulder injuries The *shoulder-joint has a wide range of movement but *stability has been sacrificed to some extent for *flexibility, and it is susceptible to a number of injuries including *fractures, *dislocations, *ligament injuries, *muscle-tears, and inflammatory disorders.

shoulder-joint (glenohumeral joint) A *ball-and-socket joint formed by the *glenoid cavity of the *scapula and the *head of the *humerus. The shoulder-joint is the most freely movable joint of the body, and it allows all angular and rotational movements. Its *articular surfaces are shallow and its *capsule is lax and reinforced by *ligaments anteriorly and superiorly only. The *tendons of the *biceps brachii and *rotator cuff muscles help to stabilize it. All the muscles of the shoulder-joint are attached to the *humerus.

shoulder mover A *muscle which moves the shoulder. The chief shoulder movers are the *levator scapulae, *pectoralis minor, *rhomboids, *serratus anterior, *subclavius, and *trapezius muscles. The shoulder is a highly complex, very mobile region of the body containing several anatomically-distinct joints. However, the joints are functionally inseparable; movements of the *shoulder-girdle supplement the *range of movement of the *glenohumeral joint, for example, allowing movement of the arm around all three axes and, subsequently, *circumduction. All the muscles which move the shoulder combine to steady the shoulder when the arm is moved and to adjust the angle of the *glenoid cavity, allowing a great range of movement.

shoulder-pull An *isometric exercise for strengthening *muscles of the upper body. The subject stands or sits, with hands clasped together in front of the chest, and then attempts to pull the hands apart. The exercise is usually continued for 15–20 seconds.

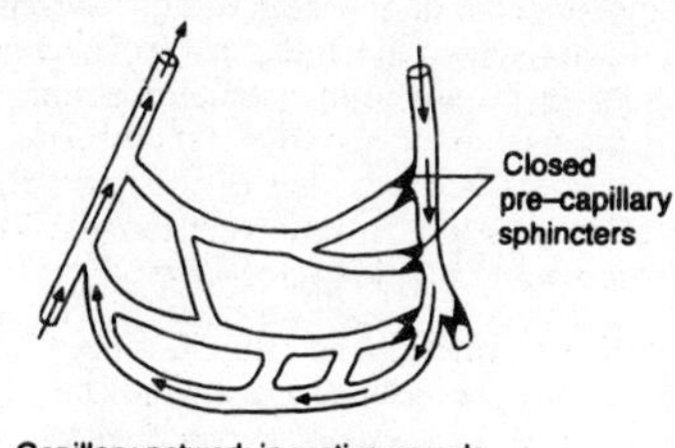

Capillary network in resting muscle

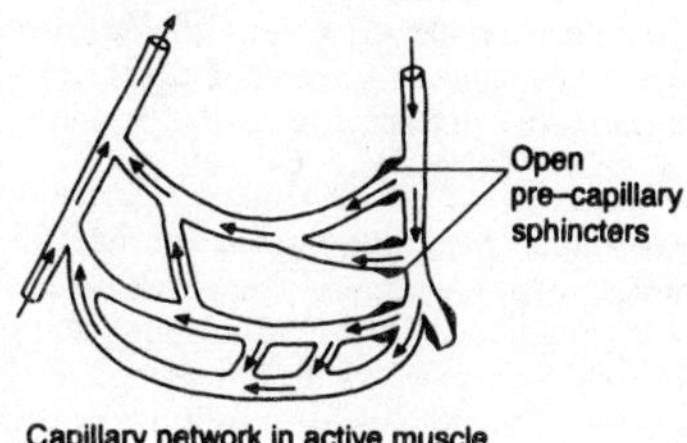

Capillary network in active muscle

shunting

shunting The diversitrengthening *muscles of the upper body. The subject stands or sits, with hands clasped together in front of the chest, and then attempts to pull the hands apart. The exercise is usually continued for 15–20 seconds.

shunting The diversion of *blood from one region of the body to another. During excercise, blood is shunted from vessels supplying the *intestines to vessels supplying *skeletal muscle. *Shunt vessels provide the means of shunting.

shunt muscle A *skeletal muscle which has its *proximal *insertions near the *joints at which it acts, and its *distal insertions at some distance from the joints, so that the greater part of the *force is directed along the *bones, tending to pull the joint surfaces together. This makes shunt muscles good stabilizers. *Compare* spurt muscles.

shunt vessel A *blood vessel which forms a by-pass channel in the *blood circulation, connecting two anatomical channels and diverting blood from one to the other. *See also* anastomosis

shuttle test(Leger test) A test of *aerobic fitness performed by running to and fro over a distance of 20m. The subject runs at a set pace which is increased at one minute intervals and the subject continues until exhaustion. The evaluation of *Vo_2max is based on the highest pace reached and maintained.

SI (Système Internationale d'Unites) An internationally agreed coherent system of units derived from the *mks system. The seven basic units are: *metre (m); *kilogram (kg); *ampere (A); *Kelvin (K); *mole (mol); candela (cd). Derived units that are important in sports science include the *newton, *joule, *watt, and *pascal.

sibling Brother or sister.

sibling influence The affect of a brother or sister on an individual's *socialization into sport. *See also* significant other.

sickle cell anaemia An hereditary blood disease characterized by abnormal *red blood cells which are sickle-shaped. The red blood cells are inefficient at carrying *oxygen and are rapidly removed from the circulation, causing *anaemia.

sickle cell trait An hereditary disease which is a mild version of *sickle cell anaemia. The *red blood cells of individuals with sickle cell trait appear normal and only about 40 per cent of the haemoglobin is abnormal. This produces only mild anaemia and those with the trait can usually lead a normal life as long as vigorous exercise and *cardiovascular stress is avoided. Carriers of the trait have a higher resistance to *malaria than noncarriers.

siderophilin *See* transferrin.

side spin *Spin which is imparted to a ball by an oblique impact which makes the ball kick or break to one side or the other. The spin may be to the left with the *angular rotation in a counter-clockwise direction around the horizontal axis, or to the right, with the angular rotation in a clockwise direction around the horizontal axis. A ball with a right side spin, on hitting a surface, will rebound to the left, while a ball with a left side spin will rebound to the right.

sign 1 An objective indication of a disease, physiological malfunction, or injury (that is, one found by examining a patient). *Compare* symptom. **2** A gesture or body movement which communicates an idea or intention.

signal 1 A variable parameter, such as frequency of *nerve impulses or *hormone levels, which serves as a means by which information is conveyed through a system. **2** A specific *stimulus. **3** A sign or gesture used to communicate information.

signal detection The ability to detect a particular *stimulus.

signal detection theory A theory which has been proposed to explain how a person is able to respond to one or more specific *stimuli, usually against a background of *noise. The theory suggests that individuals are actively involved in the response, which depends on both the subject's ability to discriminate between the signal and the noise (that is, sensitivity to the *signal) and the subject's response bias or response criterion. For example, in experiments where subjects are asked to respond 'yes' when they receive a signal and 'no' when they hear no signal or when there is only noise, some have a rigid response criterion and will respond 'yes' only when they are absolutely sure they hear the signal, while others are less rigid and respond even when they are not certain.

signal-to-noise ratio The ratio of one *parameter of a wanted *signal to the same parameter of *noise in a system. The signal-to-noise ratio has an important effect on the ability to detect a signal (*see* signal detection theory).

signal substance In the *nervous system, a *neurotransmitter substance.

significance In statistics, a description of an observed result that shows sufficient deviation from the expected or hypothetical result to be considered different from the expected result and not attributable to chance.

significant other A person in an individual's life, such as a family member, a close friend, a teacher, or a coach, who is likely to influence the individual's values, beliefs, and behaviour, and to act as a *role model.

simple carbohydrate A refined, highly-processed carbohydrate which has been broken down to a large extent into *disaccharides and *monosaccharides, lacking any associated *minerals, *vitamins, or *roughage. *Compare* complex carbohydrate.

simple fracture *Fracture in which the *bone breaks cleanly but does not penetrate the skin; sometimes called a closed fracture.

simple reaction time *Reaction time for a task in which a single known response is produced when a single stimulus is presented. An example of a simple reaction time is the time taken for a sprinter to respond to a starting pistol at the beginning of a race. *See also* choice-reaction time.

simple sugar A *monosaccharide. *See also* simple carbohydrate.

simulator A training device which provides specific, controlled conditions so that *skills can be practised under circumstances closely resembling those experienced in actual performance.

simultaneous conditioning A method of *classical conditioning in which the *conditioned stimulus and *unconditioned stimulus are always presented at the same time.

simultaneous force summation In humans, the production and combination of *forces from different parts of the body to work together at the same time.

sin (sine) A *trigonometrical ratio which, in a right-angled triangle, is the ratio of length of the opposite side to that of the hypotenuse.

sine *See* sin.

single-blind procedure In research, any method used to prevent the subject from knowing what treatment, such as a *drug, he or she has received.

single-channel hypothesis A theory of *attention which posits that the *information-processing system is structured as a single channel which can deal only with a single *stimulus leading to a response at any given time. The single-channel theory does not seem to account for the possibility of processesing in two stages simultaneously or for *parallel-processing of two signals in a given stage.

sinoatrial node (SA node; sinus node) The main *pacemaker region of the *heart. The sinoatrial node is a specialized area of *cardiac tissue, located in the right *atrium of the heart, which originates the electrical impulses to initiate heart contraction; it sets the pace of the heartbeat.

sinus **1** A cavity within a *bone filled with air and lined with *mucus. **2** A dilated channel allowing the passage of *blood, *pus, or *lymph from deeper tissues to the exterior.

sinusitis Inflammation of the paranasal sinuses due to bacterial infection. In order to avoid prolonging the illness, athletes suffering from sinusitis should not take part in hard physical activity until the illness is resolved. Swimmers susceptible to sinusitis may be advised to wear nose-clips during training and competition in water.

sinus node *See* sinoatrial node.

siri equation An equation for estimating percentage body fat from body density measurements: body fat percentage = (495/body density) – 450.

SIT *See* stress inoculation training.

sit-and-reach test *See* sitting toe-touch test.

sit-down-and roll principle Principle of maximizing the area of the body in contact with a landing surface such as a floor or gym mat, to spread the *force of landing over as wide an area as possible. It reduces the *pressure applied to any particular part of the body and so reduces the risk of injury on landing.

sitting height A *body height measurement taken from the *vertex to the base of the sitting surface when the seated subject is instructed to sit tall.

sitting toe-touch test (sit-and-reach test) An indirect test of *flexibility in which the subject sits on the floor with the legs straight and bends forwards as far as possible. The distance of the fingertips beyond a zero mark on the floor is used as a measure of flexibility.

situation The objective set of conditions towards which a person acts or reacts.

situational approach A theoretical viewpoint which emphasizes the importance of the environmental situation in determining a person's behaviour, rather than his or her innate *personality disposition.

situational behaviour A form of *leadership behaviour which is effective in one set of conditions but not in another.

situational factor (situational variable) Any factor, such as an environmental factor or the equipment a person is using, which contributes to the set of conditions to which a person acts or reacts. *See also* display.

situational trait A *leadership trait that is effective in one set of conditions but not in another.

situation variable *See* situation factor.

sit-up A *muscular endurance and *strength exercise for the *abdominal muscles. There are many variations of the sit-up, but typically the subject lies on his or her back, usually with hands on top of the head, with the knees slightly bent, and feet flat on the floor about a hip-width apart. The subject then curls up to a sitting position, touching the elbows to the knees.

sixty-second vertical jump A long-term *anaerobic test in which the subject performs consecutive vertical jumps continuously for a sixty-second period at maximum effort. The time in contact with a platform and the total flight time are measured electronically. The power output is computed as:

$$W = g \times T_f \times 60/4N(60 - T_f),$$

where W = mechanical power (W kg^{-1}), g = normal *acceleration of gravity (9.8 m s^{-2}), T_f = sum total of flight-time of all jumps, and N = number of jumps during 60 seconds.

skeletal Pertaining to the bony frame of the body.

skeletal age A measurement of maturity using *X-rays of bones, usually of the left hand or wrist; age approximations are based on the extent to which *ossification of the *epiphyses has occurred.

skeletal connective tissue *See* bone; and cartilage.

skeletal height *See* stature.

skeletal muscle *Voluntary muscle in the outer body which is attached to *bone or occasionally skin. When stimulated, skeletal muscle moves a part of the *skeleton, such as an arm or leg. *See also* striated muscle.

skeletomuscular system The body system which is composed of *muscles, *bones, and their attachments.

skeleton Any structure in an organism that maintains its shape, supports other structures, and facilitates locomotion. In humans, the skeleton consists of the hard structures that make up the rigid framework that supports and protects the soft tissues of the body. The skeleton includes *cartilage and over 200 *bones which make up the *appendicular and *axial skeleton, accounting for about 20 per cent of body-mass. In addition to support and protection, the skeleton also provides a large surface area for the attachment of *muscles and a system of *levers essential for locomotion. Some parts of the skeleton also manufactures *red blood cells and store materials, such as *fat, *calcium, and *phosphate.

skew A measure of dispersion which estimates how far a set of values varies from the symmetry of a *normal distribution curve. A deviation to the right of the curve indicates a negative skew value, deviation to the left indicates a positive value.

skewed distribution Distribution of a set of values which deviates from a normal distribution curve. *See also* skew.

skier's thumb A rupture of the *ulnar collateral ligament of the thumb adjacent to the web between the thumb and forefinger. Skier's thumb often occurs when a skier falls on an outstretched arm with the ski-pole forcing the thumb upwards and outwards.

skill Movement that is dependent on practice and experience for its execution, as opposed to being genetically defined. It is a learned movement, and is an essential com-

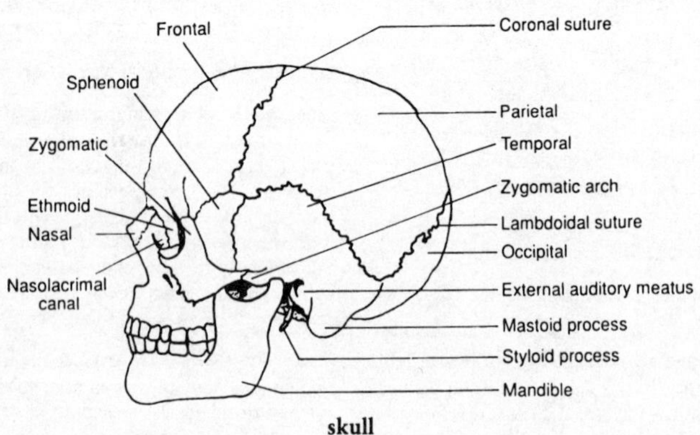

skull

ponent of sport which enables a person to bring about predetermined results with maximum certainty, often with the minimum expenditure of energy. Three important components of skill are *effectiveness, consistency (which relates to the ability to reproduce the skill), and *efficiency. *See also* closed skill; cognitive skill; continuous skill; discrete skill; motor skill; open skill; perceptual skill; and serial skill.

skill acquisition The *learning process by which a *skill is gained.

skill effectiveness A characteristic used to define *skill; it refers to the accuracy of a response and economy of effort in a *skill. *Compare* skill flexibility.

skill flexibility A defining characteristic of *skill; it is the ability to deal successfully with many different circumstances. *Compare* skill effectiveness.

skin Outer covering of the body that is external to the main *muscles. Skin consists of *epidermis and *dermis.

skin conductance The ability of the skin to conduct electricity, measured as the ratio of the current flowing through the skin to the *potential difference across it. Skin conductance varies with the moisture on the skin and has been used to measure *arousal level.

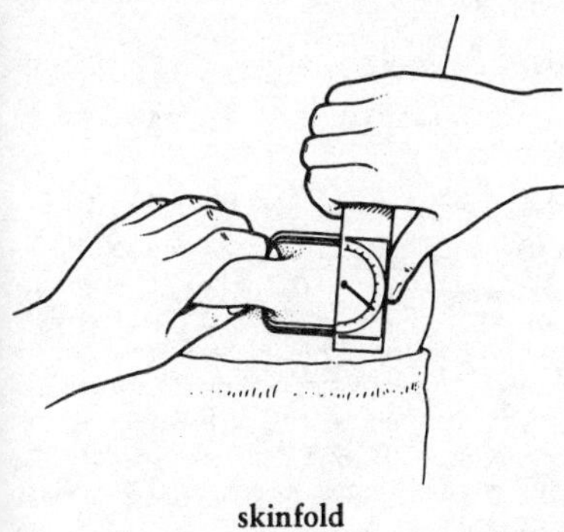

skinfold

skinfold A fold which includes a double layer of *skin and *adipose tissue, but no *muscle.

skinfold calipers *Calipers especially designed for measuring *skinfold.

skinfold measurement In *anthropometry, a measurement of *skinfold thickness. Usually the measurement is taken with *skinfold calipers of a vertical fold of tissue held by the left thumb and index finger at specific sites on the body.

skinfold test (fatfold test) Clinical test for *fatness. A skinfold on the back of the arm or below the *scapula is measured with a caliper. A fold of more than one inch indicates excess fat.

skin friction *See* surface friction.

skin temperature The temperature on the external surface of the body. Skin temperature varies considerably according to the environmental conditions and the degree of exercise. *Compare* core temperature.

skull Bones of the head and face. The skull is composed of cranial bones (*see* cranium) enclosing and protecting the *brain, and *facial bones.

sledge apparatus Equipment used to investigate the mechanical efficiency of isolated *concentric or *eccentric exercises, and exercises involving the *stretch-shortening cycles. The apparatus consists of a sledge with a mass of 33 kg to which the subject is fixed in a sitting position; a slow-friction aluminium track down which the sledge slides; a force plate placed perpendicular to the track; and apparatus for recording *oxygen consumption and *muscle fibre activity.

sleep A physiological condition of relative immobility and natural unconsciousness when there is an increased reluctance to respond to stimulation and when many bodily functions are maintained at a minimum level of activity. There is much controversy concerning the significance of sleep. Traditional views emphasize its restorative value; another view emphasizes the advantages of the associated immobility (for example, in conserving energy expenditure). *See also* REM sleep; and sleep deprivation.

sleep apnoea A potentially-dangerous condition in which breathing stops temporarily during *sleep. It is often associated with deep snoring when breathing resumes.

sleep deprivation A disruption and reduction in the number of hours of sleep that is normally needed by a person. There is no standard or minumum number of hours per night which is regarded as necesary for everyone. Lack of sleep is associated with impaired reaction time, reduced co-ordination, and poor vigilance; all of which adversely affect performances in sport. Sleep deprivation can produce distinct alterations in *personality. Exercise often restores normal sleep patterns in people who suffer sleep disorders.

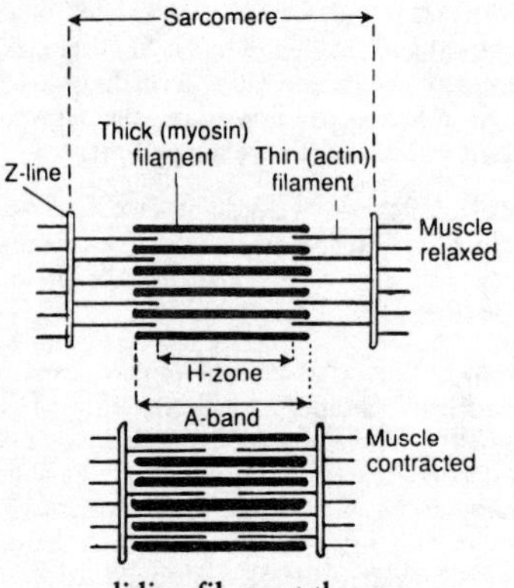

sliding filament theory

sliding-filament theory A theory which has been proposed to explain how muscle contracts. The functional unit of the muscle, the *sarcomere, contains overlapping thin and thick muscle filaments (*see* actin and myosin) which can be interconnected by *cross-bridges. It is suggested that a shortening of the sarcomere length is brought about by the filaments sliding past each other by means of a rachet-like mechanism of the cross-bridges. The thin filaments are pulled into the space between the thick filaments in each sacromere of a muscle fibre. The contraction is triggered by a stimulatory *nerve impulse which causes an *action potential to spread across the sarcomere. The action potential causes *calcium *ions to be released around the filaments, enabling the cross-bridges from myosin to attach onto the actin (in the absence of calcium, the attachment sites are blocked by *tropomyosin). *Adenosine triphosphate provides the energy used by the rachet mechanism.

sliding friction (dynamic friction) A form of *friction which develops when one body begins to slide across another. Until the body begins to slide, the magnitude of the friction is equal to the *force tending to cause the body to slide.

slipped disc A misnomer; discs do not slip, they herniate or rupture. The fibrous outer layer ruptures followed by protrusion of the spongy contents (the nucleus pulposus). If the protrusion presses on the *spinal cord or *spinal nerves exiting from the cord, numbness, excruciating *pain, or even permanent loss of function of the *nerve roots may result. A slipped disc is generally treated with bed-rest, traction, and pain-killers, but sometimes surgery may be necessary. *See also* prolapsed intervertebral disc.

slipped epiphysis *Over-training injury, occurring in young athletes, in which there is a disruption of the *epiphyseal plate. *See also* epiphysiolysis.

Sloan–Weir formula A formula which uses a combination of *anthropometric measures, including *skinfold measurements, for predicting body density and total body fat.

slope *See* gradient.

slow oxidative fibre *See* slow twitch fibre.

slow twitch fibre (red fibre; SO fibre; slow oxidative fibre) A *muscle fibre characterized by a relatively slow contraction time, low *anaerobic capacity, and high *aerobic capacity making the fibre suited for low power, long duration activities. Slow twitch fibres have a high density of *mitochondria, high *myoglobin content, and a rich blood supply. *Compare* fast twitch fibre.

small intestine Part of the *alimentary canal which is about 7 m long, and consists of the *duodenum, *jejunum, and *ileum. The small intestine is concerned with *digestion and *absorption. In addition to producing its own *enzymes and *mucus, it also receives enzymes from the *pancreas and *bile from the *gall-bladder.

smelling salts *See* ammonia salts.

Smith's fracture A fracture of the wrist caused by forward flexion (i.e., *palmar flexion) of the wrist resulting in *dislocation of the *distal *radius. *Compare* Colle's fracture.

smoking The act of inhaling the products of combustion from tobacco which contains *carbon monoxide and *nicotine. It is generally accepted that smoking is harmful to health and deleterious to athletic performances.

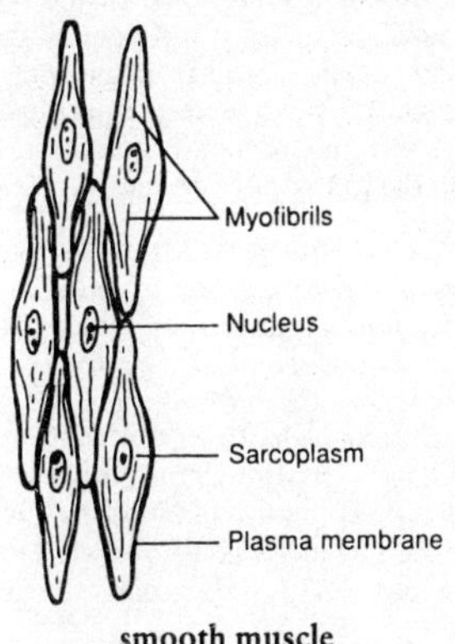

smooth muscle

smooth muscle (involuntary muscle) *Muscle consisting of spindle-shaped cells with no obvious striations. Smooth muscle lines the walls of hollow organs such as the stomach, intestines, and blood vessels, and is particularly well adapted to producing long, slow contractions which are not under voluntary control. *Compare* striated muscle.

snow-blindness Inflammation of the *cornea and *conjunctiva which arises in localities where sunlight is strongly reflected from the snow. Symptoms include *photophobia, a smarting pain, and an increased production of tears. The photophobia may be so great that the person may be rendered temporarily blind. Similar conditions may occur wherever sunlight is strongly reflected.

soccer toe *See* black nail.

sociability Any form of social interaction in which people become involved solely for its own sake, such as having a drink with a friend in the sports club bar. Although pursued for the sake of the pleasure it gives to the individual, sociability may have a serious underlying purpose.

social 1 Pertaining to the interaction humans have with one another, either as individuals or in groups. 2 Pertaining to mutual support and welfare.

social action theory The suggestion that a person has the capacity to make an individual interpretation of a situation and is not dictated to by circumstances, although the person is aware of the circumstances. *See also* role theory.

social actor *See* actor.

social adjustment The ability to integrate successfully with others. *See also* socialization.

social approval behaviour Behaviour which is directed at gaining approval from *significant others, such as coaches and parents. Social approval behaviour is particularly apparent in young children and is characterized by the way children often work hard for approval from significant others.

social behaviour Behaviour which is influenced by, or influences the behaviour of, others; behaviour involving the interaction of individuals or groups.

social bonding *See* bonding.

social categories theory A theory of *mass communication which argues that individuals within broad subgroups (such as age or gender groups, or social or educational classes) react similarly to the *mass media. *Compare* individual difference theory. *See also* mass communication theory.

social change Any major alteration in the pattern of social interactions in *society.

social class A division of *society which shares a similar social and economic status, and, in some societies, ancestry. Social class is used as an indicator of an individual's position, status, or power in society. Social mobility of individuals is generally easy within a given social class, but more difficult between different social classes.

social cohesion The degree to which the members of a team like each other and enjoy each other's company. Social cohesion is a major dimension of *team cohesion. *See also* cohesion.

social competence The ability to form social relationships easily and to mix with other people. It is often regarded as an objective of *physical education.

social conflict A struggle between two or more contesting groups over values or scarce resources.

social contagion The transmission of a corrupting influence from one person to another. Social contagion tends to occur when people are together in large crowds. When *aggression is carried out in a sports arena, there may be an urge in observers to join in and to complete the *hostility that has built up. *See also* audience effect.

social control The use of negative and positive sanctions (punishment and reward) by *control agents to enforce conformity with the *norms and expectations of *society. In sport, social control includes the means by which the rules are enforced.

social control agency An organized agency of *social control, such as the police. In sport, officials such as referees and umpires act as social control agencies.

social Darwinism Term, often used disparagingly, for any theory which attempts to apply Darwin's principles of natural selection to society.

social demarcation The *social separation of individuals on the basis of *social class. In English cricket, for example, there used to be a clear social demarcation between players who played professionally, and gentlemen, who were amateurs.

social development Any change in *society which leads to new or more complex relations between individuals or groups within that society. The decline of *apartheid in South Africa, for example, is resulting in greater social mixing, including participation in sport, of individuals from different ethnic and social backgrounds.

social distance The degree of separation of one group from another in terms of cultural development and social relationships, which may result in one group not joining in activities with another group. The term applies particularly to *social classes and is taken to its extreme in systems such as *apartheid.

social distribution In sport sociology, the extent to which a sport has permeated into a particular *society, and spread through different societies. Studies of social distribution usually include determining the origin of the sport, in terms of time and place, and tracing the pattern of *cultural diffusion.

social evaluation The evaluation of an individual's performance by others. Social evaluation has a powerful influence in sport especially for top-class sportsmen and women whose performances are scrutinized by the *mass media (*see* competitive stress). Individual sports which focus directly on personal performance tend to be more evaluative than team-sports in which the responsibility for performance and outcome is shared.

social exchange theory *See* exchange theory.

social facilitation The consequences upon behaviour which derive only from the presence of other individuals who do not interact verbally or emotionally with the performer. Social facilitation may have a positive or negative effect on athletic performance. It occurs whenever the individual in a group situation performs better or worse than when working alone. A better performance in terms of output may not necessarily mean that an individual is more efficient in the group situation, for the person may have an increased output but make more mistakes. *See also* audience effect; and coaction.

social gerontology theory *See* gerontological theory.

social identity (social self) The sense of *self, with respect to behaviour and development, derived from membership of, and interaction within a social group.

social imitation theory A theory which proposes that the process of *socialization is more or less passive. The individual learns how to behave in specific social situations by observing and modelling the *behaviour, perceived *values, *beliefs, and *norms exhibited by *significant others. *Compare* symbolic interaction perspective.

social indicator Statistics which relate to *society and are collected regularly (such as crime-rate or birth-rate figures) that can be used as general pointers to changes in society.

social interactive force An influence upon the learning and performance of a task which derives from a person doing the task in a group rather than in isolation. *See also* audience effect; coaction; competition; co-operation; and social facilitation.

socialization (enculturation) A complex process by which individuals learn skills, attitudes, values, and patterns of behaviour that enable them to function within a particular culture. These patterns are learned from agencies such as school and home. Socialization enables members of a *society to interact with one another and so pass on skills, values, beliefs, knowledge, and modes of behaviour pertaining to that society. Sport is generally regarded as playing a significant role in socialization.

socialization into sport 1 The learning process by which individuals acquire behaviour appropriate for a specific sport. This process includes the acquisition of attitudes, values, and beliefs, such as *sporting behaviour. 2 The process by which a person gets involved and assumes a particular role in sport as coach, athlete, or spectator.

socialization through sport The process of acquiring, by participating in sport, *beliefs, *values, *norms, and *dispositions, such as *sporting behaviour, that are applicable in other social situations.

socializing agent Any agent that brings about the process of *socialization.

socializing situation The setting or *environment in which social learning occurs. *See also* situation; and social-learning theory.

social-learning theory A theory which proposes that, within the constraints of the social environment, individuals behave according to how they have learned to behave by observing and interacting with others. Other people serve as models and the learner is prompted to imitate them, especially when the models' behaviour results in favourable consequences. The social learning theory supports the notion that an athlete's immediate and past experiences influence the athlete's behaviour more than his or her innate *physiological drives; for example, it is proposed that acts of *aggression which are rewarded or go unpunished beget more aggression, and that aggression in sport does not act as a catharsis against more aggression (*compare* frustration–aggression theory). *Compare* instinct theory.

social loafing The reduction in individual effort and motivation as group-size increases. Social loafing may help to explain the performance losses seen in the *Ringelmann's effect, and may be due to a diffusion of responsibility.

social mobility The process by which people move between different social layers such as *social classes or economic groups. High social mobility requires that there is a relatively open access to valued positions. Low social mobility exists where the valued positions are transmitted mainly through a system of inheritance.

social movement A collective action to promote or resist change. Social movements (such as feminist movements, civil rights movements, and fitness and health movements) are usually characterized by having either an organization with leaders, or a less structured organization but with role models. Followers of these leaders or role models share similar values and understandings, and possess a sense of shared membership. Sport has often been used by social movements to publicize their activities and policies.

social pathology A condition or phenomenon in *society, such as a widespread and deep civil unrest, generally regarded as unhealthy.

social problem Any aspect of society that might cause concern and a general desire for the society to intervene. Social problems in sport include inequality, oppression, discrimination, scandal, deviant behaviour, and violence. Social problems are usually a reflection of (and therefore a part of) the problems of society in general.

social psychology Study concerned with how a person's way of thinking or behaving is affected by others. Social psychology contains elements of both *sociology and *psychology.

social psychology of sport An area of *sport psychology which brings together a number of important topics which cannot be classified as either entirely psychological or entirely sociological. Social psychology of sport deals with areas in sport which affect both individuals and groups.

social reinforcement A form of *reinforcement that consists of nontangible, positive or negative evaluation, comments, and actions from others. Social reinforcement can take the form of verbal praise or criticism, or nonverbal communication such as smiles, frowns, and gestures.

social reinforcement theory A theory in which *social behaviour is believed to result from the *situations and encounters that are either rewarded or punished as an individual matures from *childhood to adulthood. Social reinforcement theory includes the idea that rewarded behaviours are likely to be repeated. *See also* classical conditioning; hedonism theory; and instrumental conditioning.

social relationship An interaction between individuals which affects every participant. Social relationships include the interactions which bind people together into *groups and *societies.

social relationships theory A theory of *mass communication which suggests that informal social relationships, particularly with *significant others, have an important effect on an individual's response to the *mass media.

social reproduction The processes by which *societies reproduce their *social structures and social institutions. *Socialization plays an important part in social reproduction.

social science A discipline which involves the systematic study of *society and individuals, or social phenomena. There is some disagreement as to how far some disciplines, such as the history of sport, can be regarded as a social science or can be studied in a scientific manner.

social scientist One who studies a *social science or who approaches a discipline concerned with some aspect of society in a scientific manner.

social self *See* social identity.

social setting A location defined in terms of both space and time, such as a particular football match, which provides the context in which *social interactions can occur.

social status A position to which an individual has been assigned in a social group and which is determined by the attitudes towards the individual of other members of the group. The attitudes may be influenced by a number of factors including the individual's income, occupation, and family.

social stratification The process by which people are assigned different social ranks in society. Social stratification forms the basis for the inequalities within a society; higher social ranks tend to have more power, prestige, and privileges than the lower ranks. Social stratification is based on social or biological characteristics (such as *social class, age, *gender, or *ethnic group) rather than natural ability. It is possible for a person to be assigned a high social rank with respect to one factor, such as economic status, and a lower rank with regards another factor, such as gender.

social stratum A distinguishable layer of people within a society. *See also* social stratification.

social structure The more or less enduring structural elements and cultural components of a sport or other social activity.

social support behaviour Coaching behaviour characterized by a concern for the welfare of individual athletes, a positive group atmosphere, and warm interpersonal relations with members of the group or team.

social theory Any theory which attempts to account systematically for the development and organization of the structure of a *society.

social thought The thoughts and views of different segments of *society concerning the social value and significance of a social activity such as sport.

society A group of people connected to one another by shared customs, institutions, *culture and, to a lesser extent, territory.

sociobiology The study of social organization and behaviour which uses biological explanations based on the premise that all behaviour is adaptive.

sociocultural aspects of sport Aspects of sport which focus on the interactions between sport, *society, and *culture.

socioeconomic status Categorization of an individual's position in *society by means of that person's level of education, income, and occupation. *See also* social status.

sociogram Diagrammatic representation of data gathered to show how individuals, such as team-members, relate to each other. *See also* sociomatrix; and sociometry.

sociologist A person who studies *sociology.

sociology The scientific study of every aspect and type of *society. Sociology encompasses elements of the other *social sciences, but views society in a holistic way. That is, sociology does not separate a study of society into areas such as history, economics, or politics but sees how all these aspects relate to one another.

sociology of sport *See* sport sociology.

sociomatrix A tabular representation in matrix form of data collected using a sociometric method (*see* sociometry) to measure interpersonal relationships. The information in the matrix is often transferred to and represented on a *sociogram.

sociometric cohesion The contribution to the *cohesion of a group made by the interpersonal attraction between members of the group. *See also* sociometry.

sociometric measurement *See* sociometry.

sociometric method *See* sociometry.

sociometry (**sociometric measurement; sociometric method**) An observational field-study method used mainly to measure what people in a group think and feel about each other. It uses a given criterion to gain a subjective measure of how members of a group view one another. For example, a question about who was the best player could be asked of each member of a team. The data gathered can be shown diagrammatically on a *sociogram and used to reveal who is generally highly thought of, which individuals form mutually supportive and attracted groups, and those individuals who are isolated.

SOD (superoxide dismutase) An *enzyme taken as an *ergogenic aid to protect the body against the *oxidative effects of *aerobic metabolism.

sodium (Na) A metallic *alkaline element which is an important constituent of the human body. Sodium is the most abundant *cation in extracellular fluid. It plays an important role in water balance. An excessive intake of sodium (usually in the form of common salt) has been implicated as a contributory cause of *hypertension and *oedema (*see* hypernatremia). Deficiency is rare, but it can occur if sodium losses during heavy sweating are not replaced, and leads to nausea, and muscular cramps (*see* hyponatremia). *See also* salt replacement.

sodium bicarbonate A *salt of *sodium that neutralizes *acids. Sodium bicarbonate is used in tablet-form as an *ergogenic aid in the hope that it will augment the body's *alkaline reserves against *lactic acid and thereby delay fatigue. Sodium bicarbonate is also taken to treat stomach disorders, *acidosis, and sodium deficiency.

sodium chloride (common salt) A *salt of *sodium which is an important constituent of the human body.

sodium cromoglycate (SCG) A *β_2 agonist *drug used in the treatment of *asthma and effective in the prevention of *exercise-induced asthma. Sodium cromoglycate has no reported effect on the *cardiovascular system and no *ergogenic value. Its use is permitted by the *IOC Medical Commission.

sodium pump An active mechanism by which sodium is transferred against a concentration gradient from the inside to the outside of cells to make the inside negative relative to the outside. It is essential in maintaining the *resting potential in *nerve cells. Its operation is dependent on the presence of *ATP and appropriate *enzymes.

SO fibres *See* slow twitch fibre.

soft tissue A tissue which has not been hardened (e.g., by *ossification). The soft tissues surrounding a *joint are *muscle, *tendons, *fascia, *ligaments, and *skin.

solanine A toxic substance found in the skin of damaged or green potatoes. In large amounts, solanine is a powerful *inhibitor of *nerve impulses.

solar plexus The network of *sympathetic nerves situated behind the *stomach that supply the organs in the *abdomen.

solar radiation Electromagnetic radiation, including light-waves within the visible spectrum, from the sun.

sole 1 The underside of the foot. 2 The underside of a shoe.

soleus A flat *muscle that extends along the back of the calf behind the *gastrocnemius with which it forms the *triceps surae. The soleus has extensive cone-shaped *origins on the *superior *tibia, *fibula, and *interosseus membrane. Its *insertion is on the *calcaneus via the *Achilles tendon. It has a high proportion of *slow twitch fibres which make it relatively fatigue-resistant. It contributes to *plantar flexion of the ankle, and it is also an important locomotor and postural muscle during walking, running, and dancing.

solid A substance, the constituent molecules or atoms of which are held in relatively fixed position by large attractive forces, causing the substance to resist changes in size and shape.

soluble fibre A form of dietary *fibre found particularly in oat bran. It is believed that when soluble fibre is ingested it chemically prevents or reduces the absorption of certain substances, such as *cholesterol, into the bloodstream. It may also help regulate *blood glucose levels.

solute A substance that is dissolved in a *solvent to form a *solution.

solution An homogenous mixture of two or more dissimilar substances. Most solutions are liquid and consist of a liquid *solvent and a solid *solute.

solvent A substance which has the power to dissolve a *solute. A solvent is the component of a *solution which has the same physical properties as the solution itself. Most solvents are liquid.

soma 1 The whole of a human excluding the gametes (eggs and sperm). 2 The cell body of a *neurone.

somatic Pertaining to the body.

somatic anxiety *Anxiety which is demonstrated by actual physiological responses such as increased heart-rate and sweating. *Compare* cognitive anxiety. *See also* somatic state anxiety.

somatic nervous system Portion of the *peripheral nervous system which carries *efferent motor nerves to the *skeletal muscles.

somatic pain *Pain arising from the *skin, *muscles, or *joints, as distinct from pain arising from the *viscera.

somatic sense Sense that enables people to feel *pain, temperature change, touch, pressure, and the body's position in space.

somatic state anxiety The somatic or bodily-related dimension of *state anxiety. Somatic state anxiety is increased when a person feels threatened, and the person becomes increasingly aware of his or her own *autonomic functions such as *heart-rate, *ventilation-rate, and sweating. *Compare* cognitive state anxiety.

somatic stress management A procedure, used to cope with *stress, which involves relaxing the body musculature (*see* progessive relaxation training). *Compare* cognitive stress management.

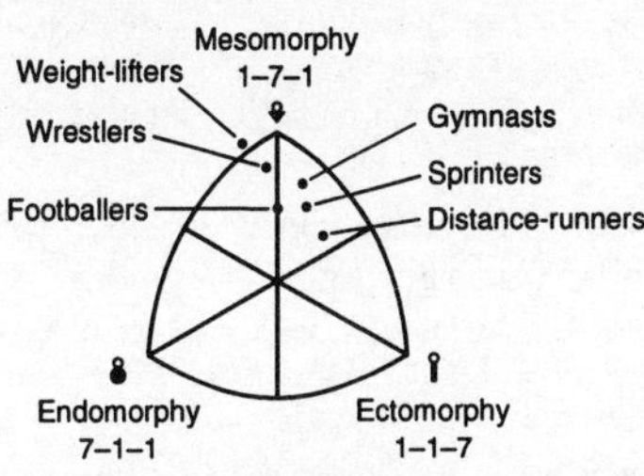

somatochart

somatochart A diagram used to describe *somatotypes in a sample by using the *mean and *standard deviation of each component. *See also* somatogram.

somatocrinin A *hormone which promotes the secretion of human *growth hormone from cells in the *anterior *pituitary gland. Somatocrinin is produced by the *hypothalamus.

somatogram A triangular pattern for recording individual physique using the three-figure classification system of *somatotyping. All possible somatotypes can be recorded.

somatomedin A growth-promoting factor released by the action of the human *growth hormone on *liver cells and possibly other cells. Somatomedins mediate many of the growth stimulating aspects of human growth hormone.

somatostatin A *peptide which is secreted in the *retina, the *hypothalamus and some other areas of the *brain where it may function as a *metabotropic neurotransmitter. Somatostatin is also secreted by the *pancreas and it inhibits the release of human *growth hormone.

somatonic trait A *personality-type which, according to *Sheldon's constitutional theory, has a strong correspondence with the *mesomorph somatype. Somatonics are claimed to be bold and competitive individuals who tend to be risk-taking, adventure-seeking *extraverts.

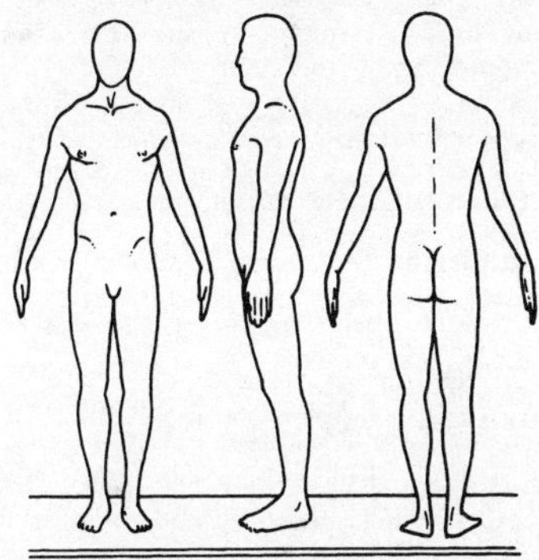

2-6-2 somatotype

somatotype (body-type) The characteristic shape and physical appearance of an individual, disregarding size. There are several methods of somatotyping (*see* Heath–Carter method and Sheldon's somatotype classification) but there are three main somatotypes (*endomorph, *mesomorph, and *ectomorph) based on the predominance of the structures derived from the three germ layers (endoderm, mesoderm, and ectoderm respectively). Generally, individuals are rated on a scale of 1 to 7 for each type, according to the degree of dominance. The descriptive sequence of numbers refers to components in the following order: endomorph, mesomorph, ectomorph. Thus 1–7–1 indicates extreme mesomorphy. There has been considerable research into the relationship between somatotype and suitability for particular sports events. One study indicated that competitors in particular events in the Olympic Games tended to share certain somatotypes: for example, discus-, shot-, and hammer-throwers tended to have a somatotype of about 3–6–2; while middle- and long-distance runners tended to have a somatotype of about 2.5–4–4. However, there were exceptions to these tendencies indicating that although a certain somatotype may contribute to success in specific activities, it is by no means essential. Skill attainment depends on many factors and a disadvantageous somatotype may be overcome by emphasis on other factors.

somatotyping Rating a person's physique along three dimensions of endomorphy (roundness), ectomorphy (linearity), and mesomorphy (muscularity). *See also* Heath–Carter somatotype; Sheldon's somatotype classification; somatotype.

somatroph *See* growth hormone.

somatropin *See* growth hormone.

sore Any open wound of the skin or mucous membranes.

sore throat *See* pharyngitis.

sotalol A *drug belonging to the *beta blockers which are on the *IOC list of *banned substances.

source trait *See* first-order trait.

spaced practice *See* distributed practice.

spasm (muscle spasm) A sudden, involuntary muscle twitch ranging in severity from merely irritating to very painful. A spasm may be due to chemical imbalance. Massaging the area may help to end the spasm.

spasmolytic A *drug which inhibits *spasms.

spatial Pertaining to space, the unlimited three-dimensional expanse in which all material objects are located.

spatial perception The ability to perceive or otherwise react to the size, distance, or depth aspects of the *environment.

spatial planes and axes Planes and axes identified according to their relationship with the ground. Axes are designated as the *x-axis, *y-axis, and *z-axis. The axes may be used to describe the direction of movement of a body.

spatial summation A phenomenon occurring at the *synapses between different *neurones and at *neuromuscular junctions in which the responsiveness of the *postsynaptic neurone or *muscle fibre depends on the additive effect of numerous *stimuli coming from different *afferent neurones or *dendrites. *See also* summation.

Spearman rank correlation coefficient A test which uses a ranking system to assess the degree of correlation existing between two sets of data. The two sets of data are placed in rank order next to each other so that they can be compared statistically.

special training (sport-related training) Training (e.g., hill-running for sprinters) aimed at perfecting individual components of sports techniques and sport-specific fitness.

specific adapatations to imposed demands principle *See* SAID principle.

specific dynamic action The elevating affect on *basal metabolic rate of eating a meal. The specific dynamic action results from the extra energy required to carry out the chemical changes on foods preparatory to their *oxidation. For example, if sufficient *protein is given to cover the calorie needs of basal metabolism of a fasting person, it is found that the *metabolic rate rises by about 30 kcal and the protein intake must be increased if it is to cover the metabolic requirements. There is a specific dynamic action for *fat and *carbohydrates, but these are lower than that for protein.

specific gravity The former name for *relative density.

specific heat capacity The quantity of heat required to raise the temperature of unit mass of a substance by one degree. It is measured in $J kg^{-1} K^{-1}$.

specificity principle A basic principle of training which states that in order to improve a certain characteristic of physical fitness, a person must *overload specifically for that characteristic. For example, exercises for *strength may do little to improve *flexibility, and exercises for improving *endurance of arm muscles may do little for the leg muscles. The specificity principle applies to the muscle groups, the movement pattern (e.g., single-joint or multi-joint movements), velocity range, and contraction type.

specific strength The strength of a particular type of muscle contraction (*see* eccentric contraction; isometric contraction; and isotonic contraction). A person who has a high level of strength for one type of contraction does not necessarily have a high level of strength for other types. *See also* specificity principle.

specific training (competition-specific training) Training in which techniques and skills are rehearsed in situations similar to those expected in competition.

spectator One of a group of individuals observing a sport. *See also* audience.

speed 1 Distance travelled per unit of time measured in $m s^{-1}$; it is a *scalar quantity. In running and walking, speed is the product of stride length and stride rate. *Compare* velocity. **2** The ability to perform a movement in a short period of time. **3** *See* amphetamines.

speed-accuracy trade-off The general principle that the accuracy of a movement tends to decrease when its speed is increased.

speed-of-arm movement A skill-oriented ability underlying tasks, such as a boxer's jab, for which a limb must be moved from one place to another very quickly.

speed of release The *speed of a *projectile at the instant of release. In throwing events (such as discus, shot, and javelin), the speed of release is proportional to the average *force exerted through the projectile's *centre of gravity. Generally, for a given angle and height of release, the distance reached by a projectile increases with the speed of release. As the angle of release becomes lower, the speed of release needs to be increased to reach the same distance. Speed of release depends on the speed of the last part of the body involved in the action at the time of release.

speed play *See* fartlek.

speed–time curve A curve or line which best fits the points on a graph on which speed is plotted on the *y-axis and time on the *x-axis. A speed–time curve may be used to identify different degrees of *acceleration; for example, during different phases of a 100 m race.

sperm Male *gametes.

spermatic cord The cord that runs through the *inguinal canal from the abdomen to the *scrotum. The spermatic cord consists of the *vas deferens, *nerves, and *blood vessels.

spermatogenesis The process by which sperm are formed.

SPF (sun-protection factor) An indicator on sunscreen products of the relative degree of protection it provides against sunburn as compared to using no sunscreen. A product with an SPF of 15, for example, is claimed to enable a person to be exposed to the sun fifteen times longer on average than if no sunscreen were applied.

sphincter A circular *muscle, the contraction of which can close an opening. Sphincters often function as valves.

sphygmomanometer (blood-pressure cuff) An instrument for measuring *blood pressure in the arteries. It usually consists of an inflatable cuff which incorporates a pressure gauge. The cuff is wrapped around the arm and pumped up sufficiently to stop the pulse as felt at the wrist or heard with a stethoscope placed on the *artery at the bend of the elbow. As the pressure is reduced, blood starts to flow again in the artery and the pressure at this point represents the *systolic pressure. The pressure at which there is a full flow of blood, indicated by a marked change in the sound heard through the stethoscope, represents the *diastolic pressure.

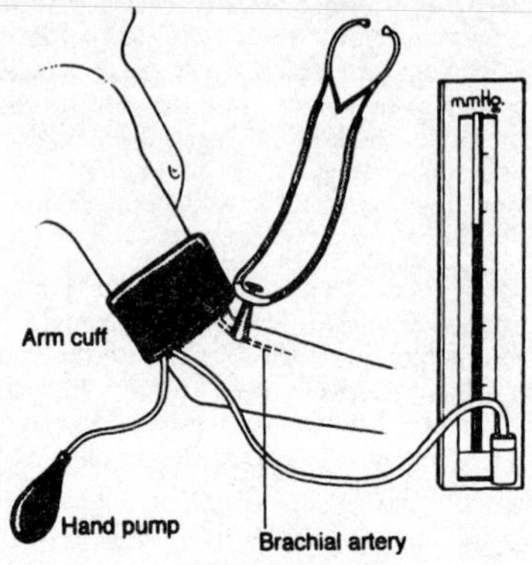

sphygmomanometer

sphyrion A *landmark which is the *distal tip, but not the outermost point, of the *malleolus.

spin Rotation of a ball or other projectile around its central *axis. *Friction tends to impart some spin on a ball. If a ball is spinning when it makes contact with a surface, the rate and direction of the spin will affect the magnitude of the friction. Consequently, the speed and direction of the ball after impact will also be modified. *See also* back spin; side spin; and top spin.

spina bifida A *congenital defect involving the *spinal canal. There are two main forms: spina bifida occulta and spina bifida cystica. In the former, a defect occurs in the posterior wall of the spinal canal. This is relatively common and may have no deleterious effect unless the spinal *cord is involved. In spina bifida cystica, a protrusion of the spinal cord occurs through a gap in the vertebrae. It varies in seriousness depending on how much the spinal cord is affected.

spinal canal Canal through which the *spinal cord passes.

spinal column *See* vertebral column.

spinal cord Part of the *central nervous system which extends down the back as a relatively uniform tube. The spinal cord is enclosed and protected by the *vertebrae. Pairs of spinal nerves leave the cord in each segment of the body. The cord is continuous with the *brain.

spinal curvature The normal S-shaped curvature in the *vertebral column which increases its strength, resilience, and flexibility. Viewed from the side, there are three principal curvatures that give the back its normal S-shape. The cervical and lumbar curvatures are convex anteriorly; the thoracic curvature is convex posteriorly. The *sacrum is also convex posteriorly. *See also* kyphosis; lordosis; and scoliosis.

spinale *See* iliospinale.

spinale height A *body height measurement made from spinale (*see* iliospinale) to base.

spinal generator A mechanism in the *spinal cord consisting of a complex network of *neurones capable of producing oscillatory behaviour (a rhythmical output of activity) thought to be involved in the control of certain basic movements in locomotion.

spinalis The most *medial *muscle of the *erector spinae group. The spinalis has its *origins on the *neural spines of the lumbar and lower thoracic vertebrae. Its *insertions are on the upper thoracic and *cervical vertebrae. The spinalis causes trunk extension.

spinal nerve A *nerve originating from the *spinal cord. There are 31 pairs of spinal nerves. Each contains thousands of afferent (sensory) and efferent (motor) fibres.

spinal process A projection rising from a bone. *See also* neural spine; and spine.

spinal reflex A *somatic reflex mediated by the *spinal cord. A spinal reflex may occur without the involvement of the higher brain centres. It is the simplest type of reflex and requires a minimum of two neurones. The *afferent neurone carries a sensory impulse via the *dorsal root of the spinal cord, and the impulse is transmitted along a *motor neurone to the *effector organs. Usually, a third neurone, the association neurone in the spinal cord, occurs between the sensory neurone and the motor neurone.

spinal stenosis An abnormal narrowing of the spinal canal.

spina scapula *See* shoulder-blade spine.

spindle *See* muscle spindle.

spine 1 *See* vertebral column. 2 Sharp, slender, often pointed projection of *bone used for *muscle attachment.

spinner's finger A cricket injury commonly occurring in spin bowlers and characterized by cracking of the *callosities which have developed in the fingers of the bowling hand.

spiral fracture Angulated break which occurs when excessive twisting forces are applied to a bone; a common sports *fracture.

spirometer A device for measuring the volume of gases inspired into and expired from the lungs during *ventilation.

spironolactone A *drug belonging to the *diuretics which are on the *IOC list of *banned substances. Spironolactone promotes the elimination of water and *sodium but encourages the retention of *potassium.

spleen A large *organ, situated beneath the stomach, which functions as part of the *reticuloendothelial system producing *white blood cells, and removing worn out *red blood cells and some foreign bodies. The spleen is highly *vascularized, consequently ruptures of the spleen result in potentially lethal massive haemorrhaging.

splenius A broad superficial muscle divided into two parts, the capitis and cervicis, extending from upper thoracic *vertebrae to the skull. The capitis portion is known as the 'bandage muscle' because it covers and holds down deeper neck muscles. Its *origin is on the ligamentum nuchae (the ligament which runs down the side of the neck) and the *neural spines from the seventh lumbar to the sixth thoracic vertebrae. The *insertions of the capitis are on a nipple-shaped extension (called the mastoid process) of the *temporal bone and the *occipital bone; the insertions of the cervicis are on the *transeverse processes of the second to fourth *cervical veretbrae. The splenius acts as a unified group on both sides of the neck simultaneously to extend or hyperextend the head; when the muscles on one side are activated, the head is rotated and bends laterally towards the same side.

splint A rigid device used to support or immobilize an injured body-part. Splints may be used to hold broken *bones or ruptured *ligaments in place and to ensure conformity between the broken ends during the healing process.

spondylitis Inflammation of the *synovial joints of the *vertebrae. *See also* ankylosing spondylitis.

spondylolisthesis Slippage of one *vertebra on another. Spondylolisthesis usually involves slippage of the fifth *lumbar vertebra on the first *sacral vertebra. It was thought that spondylolisthesis is *congenital but it is now known to be secondary to *spondylosis which is caused by injury and occurs most commonly in young people. Spondylolisthesis reduces *flexibility and usually results in tightening of the *hamstrings. It may preclude top-level gymnastic performance. Spondylolistheses has similar causes and treatment to *spondylolysis.

spondylolysis A split in a vertebral arch, the narrow bony neck in a *vertebra. The condition is characterized by acute pain in one side of the lower back, worsened by twisting and *hyperextension. Spondylolysis was previously thought to be a *congenital defect but it is now believed to be a *stress fracture. It is often caused by repeated hyperextension of the lumbar spine commonly carried out by, among other sportspeople, fast bowlers and weightlifters. There is a high incidence of spondylolysis in young, female gymnasts who perform front and back walk-overs, vaults, flings, and dismounts. Sufferers may require bed-rest followed by a special exercise programme including hamstring stretching.

spondylosis A degenerative condition of the *intervertebral discs causing pain and restricting movement.

spongy bone (cancellous bone) A type of *bone which has a honeycomb appearance. Spongy bone is composed of small needle-like or flat pieces of bone called trabeculae and has a good deal of open space.

sponsored mobility A process whereby a higher social status is acquired through the efforts and help of others. *Compare* contest mobility.

spontaneous behaviour A form of coaching behaviour initiated by the coach and which does not occur in response to player behaviour. *Compare* reactive behaviour.

sport Any highly structured, goal-directed physical activity governed by rules, which has a high level of commitment, takes the form of a struggle with oneself or involves competition with others, but which also has some of the characteristics of *play. Sport involves either vigorous physical exertion or the use of relatively complex physical skills by individuals whose participation is motivated by a combination of the intrinsic satisfaction associated with the activity itself and the external rewards earned through participation. *See also* recreation.

sport cohesion instrument Multidimensional questionnaire which measures four dimensions of *team cohesion: attraction to the group, sense of purpose, quality of team-work, and valued roles. It was originally designed for basketball but its versatility has allowed it to be used for other team-sports. *See also* sport cohesiveness questionnaire.

sport cohesiveness questionnaire A popular sport-related test of *team cohesion composed of seven questions. Two questions ask team-members to assess other members of the team relative to feelings of friendship and team influence; three questions ask each athlete to assess his or her relationship to the team in terms of a sense of belonging, value of membership, and enjoyment; and the remaining two questions ask the athlete to evaluate the team as a whole in terms of team-work and closeness. The findings of some studies indicate a strong association between cohesion and sport performance, and between cohesion and satisfaction.

sport competition anxiety test (SCAT) A test which measures the propensity of an athlete to experience *anxiety when competing in sport. It is used to measure *competitive trait anxiety. Test scoring is based on ten questions that ask people how they usually feel when competing in sports and games. Each item is answered on a three-point scale (often, sometimes, hardly ever) and a summary score ranging from 10 (low competitive trait anxiety) to 30 (high competitive trait anxiety) is computed for each respondent.

sport confidence The belief or degree of certainty individuals possess about their ability to be successful in sport. *See also* Vealey's sport-specific model of sport confidence.

sport consumer An individual who consumes sport either directly as a spectator attending a sporting event, or indirectly via the *mass media. The direct consumer tends to have an *audience effect. There is a strong relationship between *sport producers and sport consumers of a particular sport. A survey of adults in the United States concluded that people tend to watch what they play and play what they watch.

sport for all Slogan used in Britain to encourage physical performance opportunities for all members of the community, the emphasis being placed more on participation than performance standards.

sporting behaviour (sportsmanship; sportspersonship; sportswomanship) Behaviour exhibited by someone who respects and abides by the rules of a sport and responds fairly, generously, and with good humour whether winning or losing. Sporting behaviour is demonstrated by the competitor who chooses an ethically-correct strategy in preference to the success strategy which can be summed up as 'win at all costs'.

sport intelligence A concept recently introduced to describe the particular types of mental ability needed to complete the demands of a sport task successfully. Sporting intelligence includes knowledge of the sport; knowledge of where important cues are derived; ability to search for and detect task-relevant cues; identification of cue patterns; short-term memory recall; and decision-making ability.

sport mastery (sport orientation) The ability to perfect a skill and perform it well.

Sport mastery may form an intrinsically-motivated *achievement goal in which an athlete evaluates success or failure on how well he or she has performed, regardless of winning or losing in a performance against others.

sport orientation *See* sport mastery.

sport personology The study of the *personality of individuals involved in sport. The study may include three dimensions of personality: personality structure; personality dynamics; and personality development.

sport population The number of people within a country, community, or some other grouping who physically participate in sporting activities. Different criteria are used by different nations to calculate their sport population. In the former Soviet Union, the sport population was calculated on the basis of those engaged in organized physical activities more than two times a week, with each session being at least 1 hour long. In the United States of America and Europe the calculation is usually based on activities which are performed at least three times a week for more than 30 minutes each time.

sport producer Anyone actively involved in the production of a sporting event. Sport producers include coaches, managers, officials, team-doctors, promoters, and sponsors. They include direct producers who perform tasks that have direct consequences for the outcome of the sport (e.g., games officials, referees, coaches, and medical personnel), and indirect producers who have no immediate impact on the outcome of the sporting event (e.g., sponsors and ticket-sellers). *Compare* sport consumer.

sport psychologist A professionally-trained person who observes, describes, and explains the various psychological factors that influence diverse aspects of sport and physical activity. Sport psychologists support sportspersons with behavioural problems, but much of their time is devoted to helping psychologically well-balanced athletes to acquire extraordinary psychological skills in order to cope with the unusual demands of competition.

sport psychology The scientific study of behaviour in sport and the application of the principles of psychology to sport situations. These principles may be applied to enhance performance and improve the quality of the sport experience.

sports group A *group within sport which has a sense of unity or collective identity, a sense of shared purpose or objectives, structured patterns of interaction, structured modes of communication, personal and/or task interdependence, and interpersonal attraction.

sports injuries Damage to the body due to physical trauma associated with sport. Such damage varies little from injuries arising from domestic or industrial situations. However, there are subtle differences in the nature of the damage, and the form of treatment and rehabilitation due to the level of fitness an athlete has before injury, and the need to regain that high level of fitness after injury. There are also a number of *over-use injuries (including *shin splints, *spinner's finger, and *thrower's elbow) peculiar to certain sports which are rarely met elsewhere.

sportsmanship *See* sporting behaviour.

sports medical examination A medical examination of an athlete specifically to monitor the athlete's fitness to participate in a sport. Sports medical examinations usually include full personal details including competition and training performances as well as a a *clinical examination. The physician needs to know of such problems as *epilepsy, *asthma, and major allergies, not only because of periods of disablement but also because of any *drug therapy.

sports medicine A branch of *medicine which is concerned with the welfare of athletes and deals with the science and medical treatment of those involved in sports and physical activities. The objectives of sports medicine include the prevention, protection, and correction of injuries, and the preparation of an individual for physical activity in its full range of intensity. Sports medicine includes the study of the effects of different levels of exercise, training, and sport on healthy and ill people in order to produce information useful in prevention, therapy, and rehabilitation of injuries and illness in athletes. The information is used to optimize performance in sports. Sports medicine originally dealt with the medical aspects of sports, and its foremost objective was the welfare of the athlete. Recently, there has been an emphasis by some practitioners on the possible contribution of medical science to improving athletic performances, sometimes at the expense of morality and ethics.

sport socialization The process by which a person becomes involved in physical activity and sport. *See also* socialization.

sport sociology A young, dynamic subdiscipline of *sociology without a clear delineation. Sport sociology includes the study of sport in society as it affects human development, forms of expression, and value systems. It also includes the study of social systems and social relationships within sport settings.

sport-specific model of confidence *See* Vealey's sport-specific model of confidence.

sportspersonship *See* sporting behaviour.

sports science The pursuit of objective knowledge gleaned from the observation of sports and those taking part in sport whether as performers, coaches, or spectators. Sports science involves the systematic acquisition and evaluation of information about sport. It includes any discipline which uses the *scientific method and relies on observed information rather than biased judgement and vague impressions to explain and predict sports phenomena.

sportswomanship *See* sporting behaviour.

sprain An injury to a *joint or its associated structures in which joint movement is taken beyond its normal physiological range without *dislocation or *subluxation. Sprains usually arise from a sudden forceful movement that damages a *ligament or ligaments, as well as the *joint capsules, resulting in pain, swelling, and some loss of function. Sprains range from small tears to serious ruptures and the severity is graded by degree: with a first-degree sprain there is minimal damage; with a second-degree sprain, partial tearing of the ligament occurs; and with a third-degree sprain there is complete ligament disruption. *Compare* strain.

sprint A run of a short distance which can be covered at top speed in one continuous effort.

sprint-training A type of training system employing repeated *sprints at maximal speed.

sprue *See* coeliac disease.

spurt muscle A skeletal muscle which has its *origin at a distance from the *joint about which it acts and its insertion near the joint. It directs the greater part of the force across the bone rather than along it, and provides the force that acts tangentially to the curve traversed by the bone during movement. Spurt muscles also tend to be *prime movers. *Compare* shunt muscle.

squat Weight-training exercise for conditioning the muscles in the legs and buttocks in which the subject places a barbell on the shoulders either behind or in front of the neck and grasps the barbell with the palms-upward position of the hands. The subject then squats down to two-thirds of knee bend, keeping the back straight, and then returns to starting position.

squat jump A jump performed from a starting position in which the subject squats down to two-thirds of a knee bend before executing the jump. *See also* jump height.

squat thrust (burpee) An exercise used to develop lower-body muscles and *aerobic fitness. From a standing position, the subject moves to the squat position with arms outside the knees, then thrusts the legs to the rear into press-up position, keeping the back straight with the weight of the body on the hands and toes; then the subject returns to standing position.

squinting patellae *See* femoral torsion.

S–R approach (S–R viewpoint) An approach to behavioural research which focuses upon stimulus–response relationships. The approach, often adopted for the study of motor behaviour, focuses on the responses produced as a function of the *stimuli presented, without regard to the intervening mental events or processes.

S–R inventory A list of situations and the behavioural responses of an individual to each of the situations. Originally, the S–R inventory was designed to study general *anxiety but recently it has been used to study dominance, hostility, and interpersonal behaviour. Sometimes physiological responses, such as heart rate, are recorded in addition to the subjects being asked how they feel in different situations. An S–R inventory of anxiousness, for example, contains 11 anxiety-eliciting situations and 14 modes of response varying from 'heart beats faster' to 'feel anxious'. Each mode of response is paired with each of the eleven situations providing 154 inventory items.

S–R viewpoint *See* S–R approach.

stability 1 The tendency of an object to maintain its resting position or maintain a constant *linear velocity or *angular velocity. Factors affecting stability include the *mass and height of the object, and the position, size, and shape of its supporting base. Stability increases with the mass of the object and the area of the supporting base, and is inversely related to the height of its *centre of gravity above its supporting base. The body will also tend to be more stable as its *line of gravity falls closer to the centre of the base of its support. The further one part of the body moves away from the line of gravity, the less stable the body will be unless another part of the body makes compensatory movements. Stability of a body in motion is directly proportional to its *momentum. *See also* equilibrium. 2 A dimension in *causal attribution theory which extends from stable to unstable, indicating whether the attributions are liable to change or remain unchanged. Athletes tend to attribute stable factors, such as level of ability, to expected outcomes and unstable factors, such as luck, to unexpected outcomes. 3 In groups, the turnover rate for group-membership, and the length of time members of the group have been together. High stability is associated with high *cohesion. 4 The ability of a *joint to withstand shocks and motion without injury, especially *dislocation, to the joint. *See also* joint stability.

stabilizer *See* fixator.

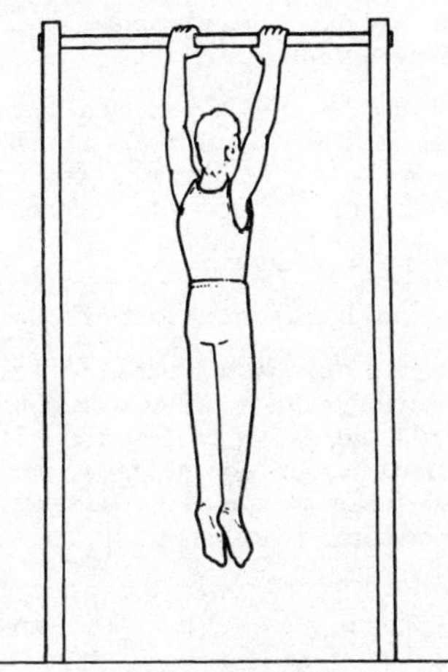

stable equilibrium

stable equilibrium The condition of a stationary body which tends to return to its original position of *equilibrium when slightly displaced. A body in stable equilibrium has a position of minimum *potential energy. *Compare* unstable equilibrium.

stable factor In *causal attribution theory, a factor which tends to remain relatively unchanged from competition to competition (e.g., the innate athletic ability of an individual).

stacking (positional segregation) The assignment of athletes to positions on a sports team on the basis of ascribed characteristics, such as ethnic group, rather than on the basis of merit. In North America, for example, *central positions tend to be assigned to white players and non-central positions to black players.

stage-training A variant of *circuit-training. Individuals perform exercises in sets with the same exercise repeated a number of times before moving on to the next exercise. Stage-training tends to make more demands on the *lactic acid system than circuit-training.

STAI *See* state trait anxiety inventory.

staleness A condition of mental fatigue and loss of enthusiasm, often associated with *over-training or unimaginative, repetitive training sessions.

stall angle A critical, maximum *angle of attack, beyond which a *projectile tends to fall toward the ground because *drag forces are increased and *lift forces are decreased.

stamina *See* endurance.

standard bicarbonate *See* alkali reserve.

standard deviation A statistical index of the variability of data within a distribution. It is the square root of the average of the squared deviation from the *mean; that is, it equals the square root of the *variance. *See also* descriptive statistics.

standard error A statistical measure of the dispersion of a set of values. The standard error provides an estimation of the extent to which the *mean of a given set of scores drawn from a sample differs from the true mean score of the whole population. It should be applied only to *interval measurements.

standard error of difference A statistical index of the probability that a difference between two sample *means is greater than zero.

standard error of the mean A statistical index of the probability that a sample *mean is representative of the mean of the population from which the sample was drawn.

standardization A criterion for effective testing or assessment of two or more test situations. Standardization demands that the test conditions need to be vigorously controlled and must be the same for each test situation. Thus, if the performance of one athlete is to be compared to that of another, or a comparison is to be made of performances of the same athlete at different times, all the test conditions should be the same.

standard temperature and pressure dry (STPD) A reference condition for comparing gas volumes. STPD is the volume occupied by all gas molecules, except molecules of water vapour, at the standard temperature of 0 °C and the standard pressure of 760 mmHg.

standing broad jump Test of muscular power in which the subject toes a line and jumps forward with both feet simultanously. The jump is measured from the take-off line to the nearest point touched by any part of the body at the end of the jump. *Compare* sargent jump.

standing toe-touch test An indirect test of flexibility (*see* flexibility test) in which the subject stands with hands by the side and knees straight, then leans slowly forward to touch the floor with the fingertips. In one test of minimal flexibility, men should be able to touch the fingertips to the floor and women should be able to touch the palms to the floor.

stanozolol A *drug belonging to the *anabolic steroids which are on the *IOC list of *banned substances. The drug achieved notoriety through its use by Ben Johnson in the Seoul Olympics of 1988. Johnson's gold medal was withdrawn. Stanozolol is an anabolic steroid which is relatively stable, relatively resistant to breakdown in the body, and *metabolites of which are relatively easy to recognize.

stapes One of the small bones in the middle ear which transmits vibrations from the *eardrum to the *cochlea. It is stirrup-shaped and articulates with the *incus and *oval window.

staphylococcus: A type of spherical *bacterium which occurs in grape-like clusters. Staphylococci are normally present in the skin and mucous membranes. Some species are pathogenic and cause diseases including *pneumonia and *osteomyelitis. One species, *Staphylococcus aureus* , causes boils and abscesses.

starch A *carbohydrate found as a storage product in many vegetables. It is a *polysaccharide made of *α glucose units, forming *amylose and *amylopectin. Starch is very difficult to digest, but heating breaks down the starch molecules to smaller compounds called *dextrins which are more digestible.

Starling's law A law which states that the *stroke volume of the heart increases in response to an increase in the volume of blood filling the heart *ventricles during *diastole.

starting strength The *strength recorded 30ms after the start of *contraction of a *muscle or *muscle group.

stasis Cessation of flow (e.g., of *blood or *lymph) resulting in congestion and accumulation of body fluids. Stasis is usually caused by an obstructed outflow.

state 1 A transitory emotional condition. 2 Government which exercises its authority over a particular territory, or the territory and society which is subject to such government.

state aggression A transitory emotional condition characterized by consciously-perceived feelings of *aggression, often resulting in overt aggressive acts against a human target. *Compare* trait aggression.

state anxiety A temporary emotional condition characterized by apprehension, tension, and fear about a particular situation or activity. State anxiety is usually accompanied by physiological *arousal and observable behavioural indicators which include nervous fidgeting, licking the lips, and rubbing the palms on a shirt or trousers. However, the correlation between physiological and psychological measures of state anxiety are quite low and can produce conflicting results.

state anxiety inventory (SAI) A test of *state anxiety which consists of twenty questions related to how the subject feels.

state trait axiety inventory (STAI) A standardized pencil and paper questionnaire which enables researchers to measure both *A-trait and *A-state levels of anxiety.

static contraction *See* isometric contraction.

static endurance The ability of a *muscle to remain contracted for a long period of time. This may be measured by the length of time an individual can hold a body position. *Compare* dynamic endurance.

static equilibrium The state of an object at rest when the *resultant forces acting on it are zero. A gymnast performing a handstand maintains a static equilibrium.

static flexibility The *range of motion about a *joint which is held in a position. It is measured using a *flexometer. *Compare* dynamic flexibility. *See also* flexibility.

static friction *See* limiting friction.

statics A division of *mechanics dealing mainly with the conditions under which objects remain at rest.

static strength (isometric strength) The ability to maintain an *isometric contraction and therefore hold a weight in a constant position. Static strength is important in events such as weight-lifting. It varies with the total number of *muscle fibres and their individual cross-sectional area.

static stretching A form of stretching in which a stretched position is held for a given amount of time (6–60s). Static stretching avoids forced movements which can elicit a *stretch reflex. During a static stretch, the *golgi tendon organs are stimulated resulting in relaxation of the muscles being stretched (*see* inverse stretch reflex). Therefore, there is a reduced danger of tissue damage. *Compare* dynamic stretching.

statistic A single piece of information capable of exact numerical representation, such as the arithmetic mean of a sample.

statistical significance A measure of the probability that an observed numerical result in a test occurred by chance. When a difference between two means is statistically significant to the 0.05 level then the probability of obtaining a difference this large or larger would occur by chance less than 5 times in a 100 trials.

statistics A branch of mathematics concerned with the collection, classification, and interpretation of numerical data. Statistics usually involves the application of *probability theory in the analysis of information.

stature (height; skeletal height) The height of a person. Stature is usually measured as the distance from the bottom of both feet with heels together to the highest point on the head. However, there are several techniques for measuring stature. The subject may be standing freely, stretching up, or even recumbent. Each technique gives slightly different measurements.

status A social position or rank held by a person in a group or society, and the respect, reputation, and power associated with the position. *See also* achieved status; ascribed status; horizontal status; and vertical status.

status reward Any form of nontangible *positive reinforcement which enhances a person's reputation and *status. Status rewards include the acquisition of a desirable nickname (e.g., 'Magic' Johnson) and the receiving of verbal praise from *significant others.

status symbol Any article or service whose intrinsic value is supplemented by the prestige it bestows on the person who acquires it, either in their own perception or the perception of others.

statute mile *See* mile.

staying power *See* endurance.

steadiness The ability to maintain the body or a limb in a fixed position, or to execute a smooth movement without any fluctuation from the desired course. Steadiness is a reflection of normal *muscle tremor and changes in the latter modify steadiness. Generally, as *muscle contraction increases, steadiness decreases. Steadiness is an important component of skills which require general immobility, such as pistol marksmanship.

steady state The condition of a system, or physiological function, such as oxygen uptake, which remains at a constant (steady) value, or which changes very little. After a few minutes submaximal exercise, a person reaches a steady state in which heart rate and rate of oxygen consumption tend to remain constant.

stenosis The abnormal constriction or narrowing of an opening such as a *blood vessel or *heart valve.

stepping-stone test A test of dynamic balance in which the subject leaps onto successive marked spots on the floor, maintains balance on the landing foot for a few seconds, then leaps again, and so on over an irregular pattern. Scoring for the test considers both the time taken and the error rate.

step test (bench test) A test of *cardiorespiratory fitness which utilizes *pulse rate responses to standard workloads. The step test is based on the ability of a person to recover from the workload as determined by the time required for the pulse rate to return to a predetermined percentage of the *resting pulse rate. *See also* Harvard step test.

stereotype Preconceived, simplistic description of all members of a given group which leads to certain expectations, often inaccurate and prejudicial, about members of that group without regard to individual differences.

stereotyping The process of ascribing a *stereotype to an individual.

sternal In anatomy, pertaining to the breastbone.

sternal body Mid-portion of the *sternum, the sides of which are notched where it articulates with the *cartilage of the third to the seventh ribs.

sternal notch A v-shaped space on the *sternum.

sternoclavicular joint The *synovial *gliding joint between the *sternum and *clavicle.

sternocleidomastoid muscle (sternomastoid muscle) A two-headed *muscle located deep on the anterolateral surface of the neck. The muscle has one of its *origins on the *manubrium of the *sternum, and the other on the *medial portion of the *clavicle; its *insertion is on the mastoid process (nipple-like extension) of the *temporal bone. The sternocleidomastoid muscle acts as a *prime mover of active head *flexion. When acting alone, the muscle rotates and laterally flexes the head. It also acts as an accessory inspiratory muscle, elevating the sternum.

sternocostal joint The cartilaginous, *amphiarthrotic joint between the *sternum and ribs 2 to 7. The joint allows slight movements only.

sternomastoid muscle *See* sternocleidomastoid muscle.

sternum (breastbone; breastplate) A *flat bone in the *anterior midline of the *thorax. The sternum consists of three parts: a *manubrium, the main sternal body, and the *xiphoid process. The sternum articulates with the collar-bone and the first seven pairs of ribs.

steroid One of a group of fat-souble, organic chemicals related to *cholesterol and derived from *lipids. Steroids include male and female sex hormones, such as *testosterone and *oestrogen, and the hormones secreted by the adrenal cortex (*see* corticosteroid). Steroids may occur naturally or they may be synthesized.

sterol A group of chemicals derived from the steroids. The most important are *cholesterol and the several compounds which make up *vitamin D.

STH *See* growth hormone.

stethoscope An instrument used for amplifying and listening to sounds within the body.

stiffness **1** A characteristic of muscles and springs defined as the change in *tension divided by the change in length. A very stiff spring requires a great deal of tension to increase its length. Muscle behaves in some ways like a spring by providing a compliant (springy) interface between the performer and the environment. **2** The subjective experience of restricted mobility caused, for example, by muscle over-use.

stigma **1** A mark or spot which acts as a *sign of a particular disease. **2** Any mark or lesion in the skin.

stimulants A pharmacological class of agents which are banned by the *International Olympic Committee (*see* doping classes). Stimulants have been used as appetite-repressants and weight-reducing drugs, and to obtain a feeling of well-being. They have been misused in sport, particularly in endurance events, to increase mental alertness, to conceal feelings of exhaustion, and to increase aggressiveness. Athletes using stimulants may force the body beyond safe limits. Several deaths have been associated with the use of stimulants such as *amphetamine. In addition, use of stimulants may result in loss of judgement and increase the risk of injury to both the user and others taking part in sport. Stimulants include *psychotonics and *analeptics. *See also* sympathomimetic amines.

stimulus (pl. stimuli) **1** Any factor inside or outside an organism, but external to the receptors of the living cell groups under consideration, which initiates activity of some kind. **2** An internal or external event that tends to alter the behaviour of an organism.

stimulus generalization *See* generalization.

stimulus identification (detection) The process of picking out a particular *stimulus among many other stimuli which may be present. *See also* cocktail party phenomenon.

stimulus-identification stage A stage of *information-processing in which a *stimulus is identified, and features or patterns are abstracted.

stimulus–response compatability The degree to which the set *stimuli and associated responses are naturally related to each other. For example, stimulus–response compatability occurs if, when coloured lights and coloured balls are presented to a subject, the response required is to hit the ball of the same colour as the flashing light rather than one of a different colour.

stitch A sharp pain, commonly in the side or ribcage. Stitch often occurs early during exercise and subsides as exercise is continued. However, a stitch may be so severe as to prevent continuation. Its exact cause is not known but a stitch may be due to lack of *oxygen in respiratory muscles, particularly the *diaphragm and *intercostals, due to insufficient blood flow. Stitches are also associated with jolting the body, and are made worse by eating a meal before exercising. There is no simple remedy but a stitch can sometimes be relieved by giving support to the abdomen wall. Although stitches have no serious medical significance, they are a great inconvenience to athletes. *See also* cramp.

STM *See* short-term memory.

Stockholm swimming flume A sophisticated *ergometer in which water moves under the thrust of propellers in a longitudinal direction. A swimmer, swimming against the current, remains in the same relative position to the outside.

Stokes–Adams syndrome Condition characterized by reduced *pulse rate and attacks of unconsciousness, dizziness, or blackout due to a lack of blood flow to the brain which may be caused by *ventricular fibrillation. The condition may be complicated by *heart block.

stomach An organ that forms part of the alimentary canal between the *oesophagus and duodenum. The stomach is a distensible, muscular chamber which continues digestion started in the mouth. The walls of the stomach secrete *mucus, pepsinogen (giving rise to *pepsin), *renin (in the young), and hydrochloric acid. The mixture of partly digested food, called *chyme, passes from the stomach to the duodenum through to pyloric *sphincter.

stomach ulcer *See* peptic ulcer.

storage fat *Fat contained within *adipose tissue which protects internal organs and is found beneath the surface of the skin. *Compare* essential fat.

storage problem A problem with early notions of *motor programs because the number of necessary programs required by early theories was so large that the storage of such programs in the *central nervous system seemed impossible.

strain 1 In *mechanics, the effect of a *stress on an object, measured as the ratio of the change to the total value of the dimension (e.g., the length) in which the change occurred. *See also* tensile strain. 2 An injury to *muscle caused by excessive stretching resulting in pain and swelling. A strain may result in various degrees of injury, from only a few *muscle fibres being torn, to the complete rupture of a muscle.

strain energy (elastic energy) The ability of a body to do *work because of its deformation and its tendency to return to its original shape. A fully extended bow, for example, has strain energy by virtue of the deformation it has undergone. Strain energy is measured in *joules and is given by:

$$S.E. = 1/2kd^2$$

where S.E. = strain energy, k = the spring contant of the material, and d = distance which the object is deformed.

strapping *See* taping.

strategic interaction Interaction, such as in a competition, where one participant must lose if another is to win.

strategy The art of planning a campaign. The term is usually applied to the planning of military campaigns, but it has been adopted in sport to describe the overall game plan of coaches and managers. *Compare* tactics.

stratified sample (stratified random sample) A *sample in which the *population from which the sample is drawn, is divided into tiers or strata specifically pertaining to the study being undertaken. For example, in a study of exercising habits, age, sex, and social class might be the relevant strata. A *random sample is then taken from each stratum to ensure greater precision in the results.

stratified random sample *See* stratified sample.

streamline A contour on a body that offers the minimum of *resistance to a fluid flowing around it. It is technically described as a line in a fluid such that the *tangent to it at every point is in the direction of the *velocity of the fluid particle at that point at the instant under consideration.

streamline flow Motion of a fluid in which, at any instant, *streamlines can be drawn through the whole length of its course. *Compare* turbulent flow.

streamlining The presentation of a body to a fluid so as to reduce the active surface area or to smooth the surface texture, thus

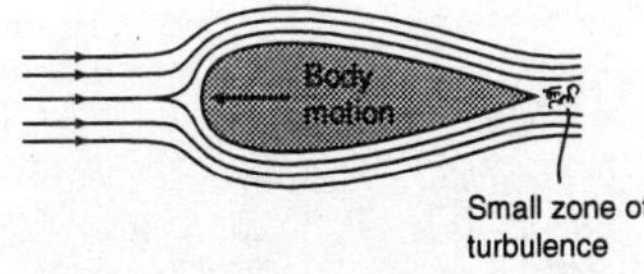

streamline flow

reducing *fluid resistance acting on the body.

strength The ability to apply *force and overcome *resistance. Strength is an essential element in physical performance. There are a number of different types of strength including *absolute strength, *dynamic strength, *elastic strength, *explosive strength, *isometric strength, *relative strength, *specific strength, *starting strength, *strength deficit, and *strength endurance.

strength deficit A strength parameter which is defined as the difference between maximum strength (when measured as a maximum voluntary contraction against an eccentric load) and maximum *isometric strength.

strength endurance The ability of an individual to withstand *fatigue. *See also* muscular endurance.

strength maximum *See* absolute strength.

strength tests A groups of tests which measure the peak capability of a *muscle or *muscle group to generate *force.

strength-training Exercises performed specifically to develop *strength. Strength-training can be achieved using a wide variety of exercises (including *body resistance exercise, exercises with a *medicine ball, *circuit-training, and *plyometrics) but it often involves weight-training using *progressive resistance exercises incorporating a *repetition maximum which ensures *overload. Other strength-training systems include the *pyramid system; *multi-set system; *super-set system; and *multi-poundage system. Strength-training results in both *myogenic and *neurogenic effects which are generally slow to develop. There are small or moderate gains in strength over several weeks dependent on inheritance, age, sex, and the muscle groups being exercised. The effects of strength-training include muscle *hypertrophy; increased muscle *capillarization; toughening of *connective tissue, joints (*see* joint stability), and *bones; and a reduction of fat in the muscle. To be effective, strength-training needs to take place at least two to three times a week for 45 minutes each time.

streptococcus A member of a group of nonmotile spherical *bacteria. Some streptococci are *pathogenic and cause *rheumatic fever and septic sores.

stress 1 The magnitude of a *distorting force, expressed as force per unit area of the surface on which it is applied. If the stress on an object, such as a bone, exceeds the tolerance load, a fracture may occur (*see also* stress fracture). **2** Any factor, physical or mental, that tends to disturb *homeostasis and has an adverse affect on the functions of the body. **3** A psychological condition which occurs when individuals perceive a substantial imbalance between demands being made on them and their ability to satisfy those demands, where failure to do so has important consequences. *See also* distress; eustress; general adaptation syndrome; and state anxiety.

stress fracture A microscopic break in a bone caused by repeated loading and unloading. The fracture occurs if the forces which are applied repetitively to a bone exceed the structural strength of the bone. Stress fractures are often not associated with a particular trauma and are characterized by local pain exacerbated by activity but relieved by rest. Stress fractures of the *tibia, *fibula, and *metatarsals are relatively common *over-use injuries in long-distance runners. They may be difficult to diagnose, except by a *bone scan, because they may not appear on an X-ray until very well established.

stress hormones *See* adrenergic stimulants.

stress injury *See* over-use injury.

stress inoculation training (SIT) A form of *cognitive stress management which has been applied to athletes to overcome *competitive stress. The athlete produces a hierarchy of *stressors and identifies the type of negative thoughts associated with each stressor. The athlete then develops positive self-statements as substitutes for the negative thoughts for each stressor. Finally, the athlete imagines each stressor, starting with the least stressful, and attempts to feel the stress while practising physical relaxation techniques as well as substituting the positive thoughts for the negative ones.

stress management Procedures designed to control or reduce *stress. *See also* autogenic training; biofeedback; imagery relaxation; intervention strategies; progressive relaxation techniques; and stress inoculation training.

stress-modelling The inclusion in a training programme of *stressors which an athlete is likely to encounter just before or during competition, so that the athlete can cope more easily with the stressors. *See also* isolation stress.

stressor An internal or external factor which makes demands on an individual and which tends to disrupt *homeostasis. Stressors include physical trauma, disease, social events and situations, and the demands of exercise and competition.

stress process The process by which the objective demands of a situation result in an increase in the *state anxiety of an individual if the situation is perceived as threatening. The stress process is dependent to a large extent on how the individual perceives the demands. This *perception will be a product of a variety of factors including the individual's emotional disposition, previous experiences, abilities, the need for success, and the perceived importance of the situation.

stress reaction A reaction in bones to a constant repetitive stressing resulting in the development of microscopic fractures called pre-stress fractures. These fractures generally heal if the athlete decreases the intensity of activities. However, if the *force on the bone is continued an actual *stress fracture may result.

stress test *See* electrocardiogram.

stretching A linear deformation of tissue that increases its length. Exercises involving muscle stretching are performed to maintain or improve *flexibility. *See also* ballistic stretch; prioprioceptive neuromuscular facilitation; and static stretching.

stretch receptor A *receptor which detects the degree of stretching in a *muscle. There are two main types of stretch receptor: the *muscle spindle organ in the belly of a muscle and the *Golgi tendon organ in the tendon of the muscle. Stretch receptors are essential for co-ordinated muscular activity, passing information about the state of the muscles to the *central nervous system through *sensory neurones.

stretch reflex (myotatic reflex) The *reflex contraction of a *muscle in response to a sudden longitudinal stretching of the same muscle. The stretch reflex is mediated by *proprioceptors and is an important mechanism for maintaining *muscle tonus, particularly in postural muscles. Neuromuscular functioning is sometimes tested by observing a stretch reflex exerted by a quick forceful tap with a rubber hammer to a *tendon, as in the *patellar reflex. *Compare* inverse stretch reflex. *See also* reciprocal inhibition.

stretch-shortening cycle A typical type of movement pattern that occurs in many sport movements including the countermovement or bob-down in jumping (*see* sargent jump) and the wind-up movement in throwing. The stretch-shortening cycle consists of a combination of three contraction types: an *eccentric contraction followed by a short *isometric contraction, and then a *concentric contraction of the same *muscle group. The combined action of eccentric and concentric contractions exerts greater *force or *power output than movements initiated by concentric contraction alone. The enhanced performance is believed to be due to the elastic behaviour of the *muscle during and immediately after the eccentric contraction.

stretch-shortening cycle test Measurements of the *strength and *power of movements which incorporate a *stretch-shortening cycle. Such movements include jumping, and the test may involve a subject jumping from a *force platform that can measure the *force, *work, and power produced during the jump.

stria In *anatomy, a stripe, line, or thin band.

striated muscle (skeletal muscle; striped muscle; voluntary muscle) Contractile tissue which consists of *fibrils with marked striations at right angles to the long axis. Each multinucleated *muscle fibre is made up of a number of *sarcomeres. The muscle fibre may be a *fast twitch fibre or a *slow twitch fibre. Striated muscle is involved in voluntary movement of skeletal parts.

stricture A constriction or narrowing of a tubular structure which may be caused by *muscle contraction, *inflammation, or the growth of tissue.

stride length The length between each step in running or walking. Stride length is an important component of *speed which is a product of stride length and *cadence. Stride length is dependent on a good *range of movement in *joints and an adequate strength of the *muscle groups involved in the action.

stridor A harsh, vibrating sound heard on breathing when the *larynx and *trachea are partially obstructed.

striped muscle *See* skeletal muscle.

stroboscope An instrument which produces intense flashes of light at a frequency which can be synchronized with movements of a body so that the movement can be analysed.

stroke (apoplexy) An interruption in the supply of blood to the brain. Causes include *cerebral thrombosis, a *head injury, or an *aneurysm, but the primary cause is usually disease of the heart or blood vessels with the effects on the head being secondary. The stroke results in a portion of the brain becoming deprived of *oxygen. The most common manifestation is some degree of *paralysis, but small strokes may occur without symptoms. Large strokes can result in severe paralysis or death. Regular exercise, by reducing *blood pressure and *blood cholesterol, can reduce the risk of a stroke.

stroke cycle 1 The complete cycle of a swimming stroke, including the propulsive and recovery phases. 2 Any one of the repeated movements used by a swimmer.

stroke length In swimming, the displacement of the body in the water produced by each complete *stroke cycle.

stroke mechanics The study of the mechanical principles which apply to swimming strokes.

stroke output *See* stroke volume.

stroke rate In swimming, the number of *stroke cycles per minute.

stroke velocity The *velocity of a swimmer in water.

stroke volume (stroke output) The volume of *blood pumped by the left *ventricle of the *heart per beat. A typical value for an untrained man at rest is 75 ml per beat, and for a trained man at rest a typical value is 105 ml per beat. The stroke volume varies according to whether the person is supine, sitting, or standing. *See also* Starling's law.

structural assimilation The incorporation into *society of an *ethnic group so that it has equal access to the major associations and institutions. *See also* cultural assimilation.

structural functionalism A theoretical approach to the study of *social systems in societies in which *social structures are described in terms of how they contribute to the maintenance of these systems. For example, sport may be described in terms of its contribution to social integration.

structural interference *Interference which occurs among tasks and is caused by the simultaneous use of *receptors, processing systems, and *effectors. A decrease in the quality of performance occurs when different tasks using these structures are performed simultaneously.

structural kinesiology The study of how *muscles and associated structures produce human movement.

structural protein *See* fibrous protein.

structural rating scale A structured method of measuring *causal attribution in which the subject is asked to rate several attributions, such as ability, effort, difficulty, and luck, in terms of how each applies to a particular outcome. It is felt by some researchers that this method is too constrained. *Compare* open-ended attributions.

structure **1** Any institutionalized social arrangement. The governing bodies of various sports can be regarded as structures. **2** The rules which underlie and create the outward features of a *society; the social relations which underpin these superficial features.

structured interview Type of *interview in which each interviewee is asked the same questions in the same way. Consistent responses are obtained by posing questions in such a way that the response to each question is limited to choices which can be recorded numerically through the use of a *scaled response system or checklists.

strychnine An alkaloid *drug belonging to the *stimulants which are on the *IOC list of *banned substances. Strychnine is obtained from the seeds of *Trychnos nux-vomica* and was formerly used in small amounts in 'tonics'. The drug blocks the action of *glycine, and high doses cause muscular spasms similar to those resulting from *tetanus; death can occur due to spasms of the respiratory muscles.

student's elbow An inflammation of the *bursa just behind the *olecranon of the elbow. It occurs commonly in sports such as soccer and rugby in which participants are not protected by elbow guards. The condition is known as student's elbow because it is commonly associated with students who rest their elbows on a desk and support their head in their hands while studying.

Student's *t* test A statistical significance test for comparing one set of data with another by comparing two *means to *see* if they are significantly different.

style An individual adaptation of a technique.

stylion A *landmark located at the most *distal point of the *styloid process of the *radius. It is located in the so-called *anatomical snuff box.

stylion height A *body height measurement made from *stylion to *base.

styloid process A pointed pen-like projection. Two examples are the process projecting from the *temporal bone and the process at the wrist end of the *ulna.

subacromial bursa A *bursa in the shoulder preventing the *greater tubercle from impinging on the undersurface of the *acromion process when the arm is fully abducted. *See also* calcification shoulder; and subacromial bursitis.

subacromial bursitis Inflammation of the *bursa between the *deltoid and *supraspinatus muscles due to excessive movement of the shoulder-joint. Sufferers include swimmers and javelin-throwers. Subacromial bursitis causes pain on elevation of the arm and the bursa is often very tender on *palpation. The condition is very common and is normally secondary to *strain of the *rotator cuff muscles.

subacute Applied to a disease or injury which develops more quickly than a *chronic condition but which does not become *acute.

subarachnoid space A space, containing *cerebrospinal fluid and large blood vessels, between the *arachnoid and *pia mater of the *brain and *spinal cord.

subclavian artery One of two arteries which supply blood to the neck and arms.

subclavian vein A vein which passes from the upper arm below the clavicle and joins the internal jugular vein to form the innominate vein.

subclavius Small, cylindrical *muscle extending from its *origin on the first rib to its *insertion on the *clavicle. The subclavius helps to stabilize and depress the *pectoral girdle.

subconscious In psychology, that part of the mind containing memories and motives of which the subject is not personally aware except with much effort.

subcultural resistance Opposition to a dominant culture which can occur when *subcultures are created. Subcultural resistance can occur, for example, when new or adapted forms of sport are created. People within the new sport subcultures may dislike or oppose the existing sporting opportunities.

subculture An identifiable subgroup of *society with a distinctive set of behaviour, *beliefs, *values, and *norms. A subculture is related to, but distinct from the dominant culture of a society and it sometimes allows individuals greater group identification. Those who take part in particular sports (for example, racing cyclists or professional footballers) are sometimes referred to as a subculture. *See also* idioculture.

subcutaneous In *anatomy, pertaining to areas beneath the skin.

subcutaneous administration Administration of a *medication by injection beneath the skin.

subcutaneous bursa Type of *bursa located between deep layers of skin and underlying bone.

subcutaneous tissue Tissue lying immediately beneath the skin which becomes exposed on laceration.

subjective competitive situation An athlete's thoughts and feelings about a particular *objective competitive situation. It refers particularly to whether or not the athlete perceives the situation as threatening. This will depend to a certain extent on the athlete's *competitive A-trait and will affect precompetitive anxiety.

subjective danger An avoidable and manageable danger that is potentially under the control of the person concerned (e.g., by the correct use and choice of equipment). *Compare* objective danger.

subjective fatigue (psychological fatigue) A condition characterized by a need for rest which is caused by psychological factors (such as boredom or mental stress), not physical ones. It is usually caused by repetition of the same behaviour. Fatigue is said to be subjective when a different response can be performed readily using the same muscles.

subjective reinforcement A form of *reinforcement, proposed by supporters of closed-loop theories of *motor-learning, which enables an individual to be able to report to himself or herself the errors made in the execution of a *skill. It is suggested that the subject acquires a reference of correctness (called the perceptual trace). When a movement is completed, the subject can compare the *feedback received against the perceptual trace; the deviation represents the error that the subject could report to themselves or an experimenter as subjective reinforcement.

subjectivity The perception an individual has about a situation or phenomenon. *Compare* objectivity.

subliminal Applied toa *stimulus below the level of awareness and below the absolute threshold of stimulation, as when an auditory or visual presentation is too weak to have an effect, or at least any effect of which the individual is aware.

sublimation A mechanism of *ego defence by which the energy of the *id is directed from a primary but unacceptable object to one that is socially acceptable. The term was originally conceived by Sigmund Freud (1856–1939) in relation to sex to describe behavioural mechanisms that channel sexual energies into more socially beneficial forms. In sport, sublimation may consist of directing energies to training hard and achieving excellence or seeking perfection in competition.

sublingual administration Administration of a tablet or some other medicine under the tongue, where it dissolves.

subluxation Movement of a *joint beyond its *maximum passive range distorting the alignment of the joint surfaces. Unlike a *dislocation, in a subluxatiom, partial contact is maintained between the articulating bones. It is often a transient condition with the joint going back to its normal position without any special treatment, but sometimes a deformity persists. A subluxation of the collar-bone at the *acromioclavicular joint as a result of a badly timed tackle in a contact sport, for example, commonly leaves a deformity.

submuscular bursa A *bursa found between muscles.

subroutine A component of a *motor program which consists of a group of commands for the execution of a simple, discrete element or movement that is thought to be combined with other subroutines to form the basis of larger, more complicated movements.

subscapularis A *rotator cuff muscle covering the front of the shoulder and forming part of the *posterior wall of the axilla (armpit). The subscapularis has its *origin in the *subscapular fossa of the *scapula and its *insertion is on the *lesser tubercle of the *humerus. It is an important internal *rotator of the humerus, and helps to hold the head of the humerus in the *glenoid cavity, stabilizing the shoulder-joint.

subscapularis tendon A *tendon which attaches the *subscapularis muscle high into the *anterior aspect of the head of the *humerus.

subscapular nerve One of three nerves supplying the *subscapularis, *teres major, and *latissimus dorsi muscles.

subscapular skinfold A *skinfold measurement of a vertical fold of tissue oblique to the inferior angle of the *scapula in a direction running obliquely downward and laterally at an angle of 45° from the horizontal.

substance P A *neuropeptide which functions as a *neurotransmitter through its *metabotropic effects. It is secreted in many areas of the brain and in *afferent neurones in the *dorsal root ganglia of the *spinal cord where it mediates *pain transmission.

substrate Particular chemical compound acted on by an *enzyme.

subungual exostosis A bony outgrowth under the nail usually caused by repeated impact to a toe (e.g., when the toe is trodden on repeatedly), commonly the big toe. It may be very painful and in many cases the nail or *exostosis has to be removed in order to relieve the pressure.

subungual haematoma The accumulation of blood resulting in a swelling at the base of a toe-nail. It is often caused by jamming the toe down into the front of a shoe. *See also* runner's toe.

success The achievement of a *goal. In sport, the concept of success can be very personal (*see* perceived success) and is not always dependent on winning a competition or obtaining a very high standard of performance (*see* absolute success).

successive force summation In the human body, the combination of *forces resulting from the sequential acceleration of different body parts. *See also* force summation.

succinic dehydrogenase An *enzyme found in *muscle fibres which plays an important role in *aerobic respiration in the *Krebs cycle. Succinic dehydrogenase occurs in higher concentrations in *slow twitch fibres than in *fast twitch fibres, and the concentration tends to increase with *endurance-training.

sucrase An *enzyme that catalyses the *hydrolysis of *sucrose into *glucose and *fructose.

sucrose A *disaccharide formed by the combination of *fructose and *glucose. Sucrose is a valuable energy source, but it can encourage the growth of oral bacteria which cause tooth decay. Refined sucrose, made from sugar cane and sugar beet, forms white table sugar which is added to foods as a flavour enhancer. Sucrose also occurs naturally in many other vegetables and fruits.

sudomotor Pertaining to the activation of the sweat glands.

sudor *See* sweat.

sudoriferous gland An *epidermal *gland that produces sweat. *See also* sweat gland.

sugar A group of simple carbohydrates which share the characteristics of being sweet, crystalline and soluble in water. Sugars are classified chemically as monosaccharides or disaccharides.

sugar malabsorption A partial or complete inability to breakdown complex sugars (*see* polysaccharides) into *simple sugars because of a lack of appropriate *enzymes. The complex sugars are retained in the intestine and cause diarrhoea. Bacterial decomposition of the complex sugars in the lower tract results in gas formation and abdominal pain. Many nutrients, including vitamins and minerals, and fluid are lost with the diarrhoea. Untreated malabsorption results in fatigue and deterioration in physical performance. Treatment, for example, by avoiding complex sugars, enables normal activity.

suggestibility The characteristic of readily accepting the suggestions of others.

sulcus **1** A groove of tissue on the surface of the *cerebral hemispheres. The most prominent sulci are similar in all people and are important anatomical *landmarks. **2** An infolding of soft tissue in the mouth.

sulpha drug *See* sulphonamide.

sulphonamide (sulpha drug) One of a group of bactericidal *drugs which are effective against a number of infections

sulphur A nonmetallic element which is an essential component of a healthy diet. Sulphur is readily available from meat, milk, eggs, and legumes. Sulphur forms part of a number of *proteins (e.g., *insulin) and *vitamins (e.g., *biotin and *thiamin). It is particularly abundant in *mucopolysaccharides, *cartilage, *tendons, and *bone.

sum *See* algebraic sum.

summation The phenomenon in nerves and muscles of the linear addition of responses elicited by *stimuli separated in space (*see* spatial summation) or time (*see* temporal summation). Summation may occur between two or more excitatory stimuli, between excitatory and inhibitory stimuli, or between inhibitory stimuli.

summatory interdependence *See* interdependent task.

sunburn Damage of the skin due to overexposure to the sun's rays. Sunburn may vary from a mild reddening to wide-spread blistering. *See also* SPF.

sun-protection factor *See* SPF.

sunstroke Overheating effect of the direct rays of the sun on the head or back of the neck. Symptoms include red skin, swollen face, buzzing in the ears, dizziness, nausea, elevated pulse rate, and rapid respiration. If overheating persists there is a risk of *heatstroke. People suffering from sunstroke should stop any activity and should rest in the shade, preferably with circulating cool air from a fan; they should have their clothes removed or loosened, and cold water applied to forehead and back of the neck.

superability A general ability thought to have a position above all specific abilities in a particular domain. In the motor domain, for example, it has been hypothesized that *general motor ability is a superability which lies above all the specific motor abilities and has relevance to any motor task.

supercompensation A physiological response to a special exercise-diet procedure in which the amount and rate of *glycogen resynthesis in *skeletal muscles during recovery from exercise is increased to values much higher than normal. *See also* carbohydrate-loading.

superego The part of the mind which acts as a moral conscience and controls the *ego by placing moral restrictions on it. It is maintained that the superego develops as an infant becomes aware of restrictions, controls, and reprisals emanating from parents and others close to the infant. Thereby, the child adopts for itself the moral standards of parents and society. The superego is one of the three chief psychic forces of Freud with the ego and the *id.

superficial In *anatomy, toward or at the body surface. *See also* directional terms.

superficial fascia The *hypodermis. *See also* fascia.

superficial muscle *Muscle lying close to the skin which can be easily palpated.

superficial palmar artery An *artery in the superficial layers of the palm of the hand.

superficial palmar network A network of *veins in the superficial tissues in the palm of the hand.

superior Toward the end or upper end of a structure or the body; above (e.g., the forehead is superior to the nose). *See also* directional terms.

superior gemellus *See* gemellus.

superior gluteal nerve A *nerve which arises from the lumbosacral region of the *spinal cord. It supplies the *gluteus maximus, *gluteus minimus, and the *tensor fasciae femoris.

superior mesenteric artery A *principal artery supplying the lower part of the abdomen.

superior vena cava A major *vein which conveys blood from the head, neck, thorax, and arms to the right *atrium of the heart.

superoxide dismutase *See* SOD

super-set system A *strength-training schedule in which two exercises are performed which develop opposing *muscle groups of the same limb (e.g., one exercise causing *flexion at a *joint, and the other *extension).

supination 1 Movements of the *radius and *ulna in the forearm so that palm faces anteriorly or superiorly (that is, forwards or upwards). *Compare* pronation. 2 Inward rotation of the foot combined with *plantar flexion; also known as inversion. *See also* supinator.

supinator 1 Runner who rotates the foot outwards during running; the foot makes contact with the ground with the inside edge of the heel, then the foot rolls towards the

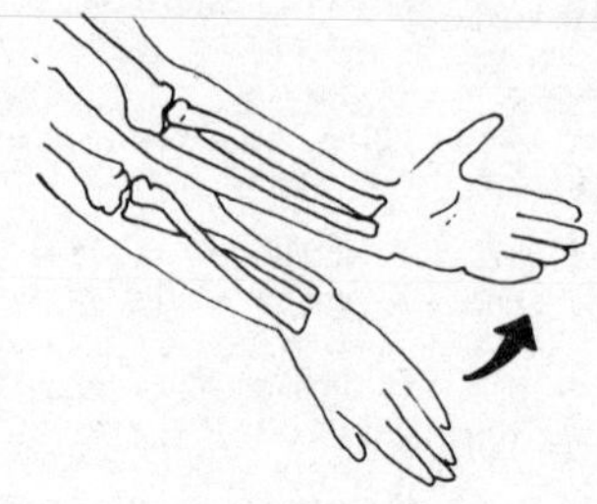

supination

outside edge of the toes to push off. *Compare* pronator. 2 A *deep muscle of the *posterior compartment of the forearm, at the posterior aspect of the elbow, which is largely overlayed by *superficial muscle. The *origin of the supinator is the *lateral *epicondyle of the *humerus and the *proximal *ulna. Its *insertion is on the proximal end of the *radius. It assists the *biceps brachii to supinate the forearm, acting as an *antagonist of *pronator muscles.

supine The position of a person lying horizontally on his or her back, with the face upward. *Compare* prone.

suppleness An ability to bend easily without causing damage, and to move easily and gracefully. *See also* flexibility.

suppository A medicinal preparation to be inserted into the *rectum, where it dissolves.

suppressor T-cell A regulatory *lymphocyte that suppresses the *immune response.

supra- A prefix used in *anatomy to denote above or over.

suprarenal gland *See* adrenal gland.

suprascapularis A muscle in the front of the shoulder which rotates the arm inwards. It has its *origin on the inner surface of the shoulder-blade and its *insertion on the *lesser tuberosity of the *humerus.

suprascapular nerve A *nerve which supplies the *supraspinatus and *infraspinatus muscles, and runs in a groove on the upper side of the *scapula. The suprascapular nerve is often damaged during *dislocation of the shoulder and by external pressures, including direct blows.

supraspinale skinfold A *skinfold measurement of a vertical fold of tissue at the intersection of the border of the *ilium (about 7cm above the *spinale) and a line from the spinale to the armpit.

supraspinatus A *rotator cuff muscle on the *posterior aspect of the *scapula deep to the *trapezius. The *origin of the supraspinatus is on the supraspinous *fossa of the *scapula and its *insertion is on the greater *tubercle of the *humerus. The supraspinatus stabilizes the shoulder-joint, helps prevent downward *dislocation of humerus (such as when carrying heavy weights), and assists *abduction.

supraspinatus tendinitis Inflammation of the *tendon of the *supraspinatus muscle. Supraspinatus tendinitis is a frequent cause of shoulder pain in throwers, wrestlers, racket players, and others who repeatedly use the shoulder muscles with the arm at or above shoulder level.

sural Pertaining to the calf region of the leg.

surface drag (skin friction) A *resistance exerted by a fluid on the surface of a body moving through it, due to the surface of the body slowing down the fluid and causing the layers within the fluid to mix (*see* turbulent flow). The magnitude of the surface drag depends on the velocity of flow relative to that of the body (that is, the relative motion of the fluid); the surface area of the body; the smoothness of the surface; and the type of fluid involved. The effect is generally more pronounced for bodies moving in air than for those moving in water. Some swimmers attempt to reduce surface drag by shaving the hair off their bodies. There is little evidence to suggest that this has any measurable effect on surface drag, but it may have a beneficial psychological effect by improving a swimmer's ability to feel the water and co-ordinate movements.

surface friction *See* surface drag.

surface tension A property of a liquid due to the forces of attraction existing between the molecules of the liquid. A surface tension exists at the boundary surface of a liquid and leads to the apparent presence of a surface film which has properties similar to those of a stretched elastic film. The surface tension is measured as the *tension across a unit length of a liquid surface.

surface traits *Personality characteristics which are readily apparent, such as sociability or shyness. *See also* second-order traits.

surfactant A substance which reduces *surface tension. Surfactants consisting of a mixture of *phospholipids are secreted by some alveolar cells in the lungs to reduce the surface tension of the watery fluid surrounding each *alveolus, thus preventing the alveoli from sticking together after each expiration.

surfer's ear *See* swimmer's ear.

surgery A branch of medicine which specializes in treating injuries and diseases by operative measures or manipulation

surgical Pertaining to surgery.

surgical decompression The reduction of pressure on an organ or body part by using a surgical procedure. For example, an abnormal pressure on a *nerve root by a *prolapsed disc may be released by excising the offending disc fragment.

surgical neck A *point just below the epiphysis at the head of the *humerus; so named because it is the most frequently fractured part of the humerus.

surgical spirit A liquid containing mainly *ethanol and *methanol, which is used to sterilize the skin before surgery and the administration of injections. Surgical spirit is also applied to the soles of feet to harden the skin and prevent blisters.

survey A research technique which is primarily descriptive. A survey is used most commonly to gather information about individuals. Surveys take many forms but often use *questionnaires and *interviews.

suspension A dispersion of fine particles throughout a body of liquid with the particles being supported by buoyancy.

sustained force contraction A *gross body movement which is made when a *force is applied against a *resistance by contracting *agonists while the *antagonists are relaxed. The initial leg thrust in a sprint start is achieved by a sustained force contraction.

suture 1 A surgical sewing thread or stitch. 2 An immovable *joint. Most of the bones of the skull are interconnected by sutures since any movement of the joints could severely damage the brain.

sway back *See* lordosis.

sweat (sudor) A clear watery fluid secreted by the sweat glands. Sweat is less concentrated than the *plasma and contains salts, mainly *sodium chloride, and *urea. Sweat plays a minor role in excreting nitrogenous wastes, but its main function is to provide a cooling effect when it evaporates from the skin surface. There is some evidence that urocanic acid in sweat may protect the skin against ultraviolet radiation.

sweat glands Coiled, tubular glands in the *dermis of the skin which secrete *sweat onto the surface of the skin. *See also* apocrine gland; and eccrine gland.

sweating (perspiration) The secretion of *sweat from the sweat glands onto the skin surface. Sweating plays an important part in thermoregulation during exercise and in hot environments. Because of the high latent heat of vaporization of water, sweat provides effective cooling as it evaporates. Evaporation of each litre of sweat removes approximately 580 kcal of heat from the body. Sweating can result in weight losses as high as 15–30 g per kg of body-weight per hour. Soccer players in hot climates have lost as much as 5 kg during one match. If sweating continues without water replacement, *overheating and *dehydration occurs. In addition to increasing with physical activity and body temperature, sweating also increases during periods of mental and emotional *arousal. *See also* water replacement.

sweet spot The spot on a racket or bat that produces the least initial shock to the hand of the player when a ball is hit; in physics it is termed the centre of percussion.

swimmer's ear (surfer's ear) A painful, itchy earache which commonly affects swimmers or surfers who neglect to dry the outer ear canal adequately after long periods of immersion. Water trapped in the ear canal breaks down the lining of the canal which becomes infected with bacteria or fungi.

swimmer's shoulder (impingement syndrome) An *over-use injury common in swimmers and other athletes, such as throwers, who make repetitive movements of the arms in or above the horizontal plane. Swimmer's shoulder is characterized by inflammation and intense pain especially when an examiner lifts the affected arm vigorously forwards and upwards (the impingement sign). It is caused by soft tissues (most commonly the *tendons of the *biceps brachii and *rotator cuff muscles) being trapped between the head of the *humerus and the space formed between the *acromion process of the *scapula and the *coracoacromial ligaments.

swimming efficiency The ratio of the *mechanical work performed by a swimmer to the *energy expended by the swimmer to do the work. The work is a product of the propulsive force and the distance the swimmer moves; the energy expenditure is usually determined indirectly by oxygen consumption. *See also* efficiency.

symbolic interactionism A study of communication between individuals, and between individuals and society, based on symbols and meanings, as in the use of language. Central to the concept of symbolic interactionism is that shared meanings are actively constructed through social interactions between people. Symbolic interactionism has made an important contribution to the analysis of *roles, *socialization, and communication and actions in sport. *See also* symbolic interaction perspective.

symbolic interaction perspective A viewpoint which emphasizes the importance of interpersonal interactions in *socialization. The perspective has as its basis the communication of symbols and shared meanings between individuals who tend to acquire more or less similar ways of behaving in specific social situations. Through talking with peers, for example, adolescents often reinterpret expectations of a coach and may publicly or privately question demands which in the past they had automatically accepted.

symbolic learning theory A theory, proposed to account for the effectiveness of *imagery, which suggests that the imagery helps to develop a mental blueprint by creating a *motor program in the *central nervous system. *See also* psychoneuromuscular theory.

sympathetic nervous system (adrenergic nervous system) Part of the *autonomic nervous system that prepares the body for action (e.g., immediately prior to a competition). Stimulation of the sympathetic nervous system results in a number of responses including constriction of *blood vessels supplying the skin and *viscera; dilation of blood vessels supplying the heart and the skeletal muscles (*see* shunting); dilation of *bronchioles to facilitate increased *ventilation; and mobilization of nutrients from the liver to increase *blood glucose. The nerve-endings use noradrenaline as a neurotransmitter. *Compare* parasympathetic nervous system.

sympathetic tone A state of partial *vasoconstriction of blood vessels maintained by impulses from *nerve fibres of the *sympathetic nervous system.

sympatholytic drug A *drug which opposes the effects of the *sympathetic nervous system.

sympathomimetic amines A group of *stimulants which include *ephedrine, *norpseudoephedrine, *phenylpropanolamine, and *pseudoephedrine. They have the effect of stimulating the *sympathetic nervous system, and are sometimes taken to increase muscular blood flow and to produce mental stimulation. Adverse effects of sympathomimetic amines include raised *blood pressure, increased *heart rate, and increased *anxiety.

sympathy 1 An emotional feeling of regret for a person experiencing troubles. *Compare* empathy. 2 In *physiology, the relationship between different parts of the body where a change in one part affects the other part or parts.

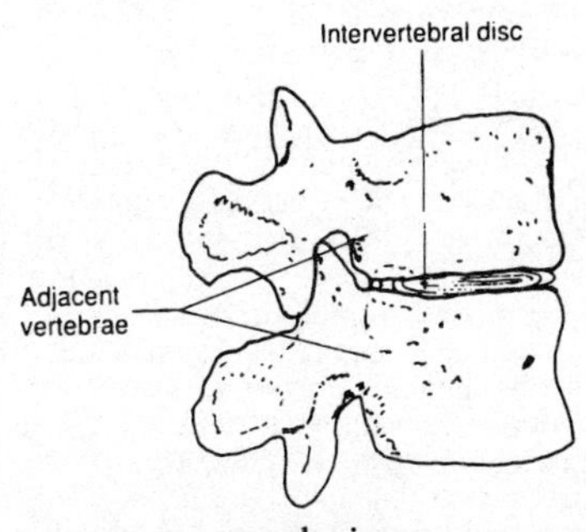

symphysis

symphysis 1 A *joint in which the bones are united by *fibrocartilage. Symphyses, such as the *pubic symphysis and the joints formed by *intervertebral discs, allow only a little movement. 2 The line of union between two bones which were separate during early stages of development.

symphysium A *landmark located on the *superior border of the *symphysis pubis at the mid*sagittal plane.

symptom Any indication of a disease or injury perceived by the patient. *Compare* sign.

symptomatic treatment The treatment of the symptoms of an illness.

synalgia *See* referred pain.

synality The relationship between, and similarity of, a social group to an individual's psychological and social functioning. Synality traits are analagous to *personality traits. *See also* group personality; and synergy.

synapse The connection or junction between one *neurone and another. Most synapses consist of a gap, the *synaptic cleft, across which a *neurotransmitter diffuses to facilitate transmission of a *nerve impulse, but some synapses are electrical (*see* electrical synapse). *See also* neuromuscular junction.

synaptic cleft A fluid-filled gap, approximately 40nm wide, which separates a *presynaptic membrane of one *neurone from a *postsynaptic membrane of another neurone or a *muscle fibre, and across which *neurotransmitter substances diffuse.

synaptic delay The time, typically lasting 0.3–0.5 ms, required for a *neurotransmitter to be released from a *presynaptic membrane, diffuse across the *synaptic cleft, and bind to a *receptor site on the *postsynaptic membrane. Synaptic delay is a rate-limiting step in the transmission of a *nerve impulse from one *neurone to another neurone or to an *effector cell, and is a component of *reaction time.

synaptic knob The expanded *distal end of the small terminal branches of a *neurone.

synarthrosis An immovable *joint formed of fibrous tissue connecting two bones. Examples occur between some bones of the *cranium, with the synarthroses forming the *sutures.

synchondrosis A slightly movable *joint in which the bones are united by *hyaline cartilage, such as the joint betwen the ribs and the sternum.

syncope (fainting) Loss of consciousness due to an insufficient blood supply to the brain. Syncope may occur in otherwise healthy people because of emotional *shock, *overheating, or because of a sudden reduction in *blood pressure on standing up quickly (*see* postural hypotension). However, it may also be due to severe injury or loss of blood. Syncope on exercise is a classical warning of severe *heart disease and may indicate a low fixed *cardiac output which cannot increase to compensate adequately for the increased *vascular load which opens up on exercise. Syncope can occur in normal, fit athletes after exertion due to *pooling of blood in the legs.

syndesmology A branch of *anatomy which deals with the study of joints and related structures.

syndesmosis An immovable *joint formed by *connective tissue between two bones. The *articulation between the *fibula and *tibia at the ankle, for example, is a syndesmosis formed by strong *ligaments.

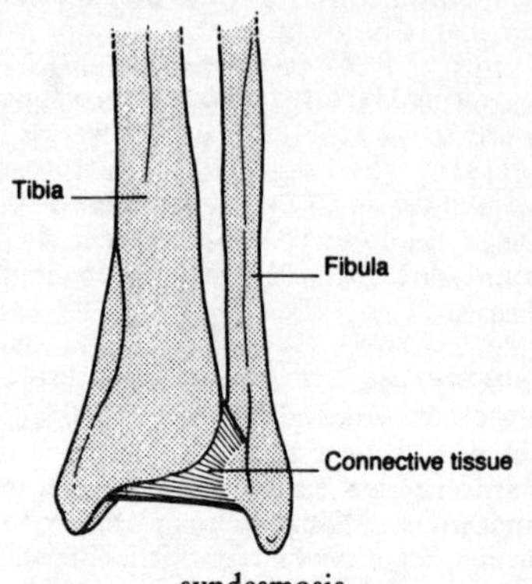

syndesmosis

syndrome A combination of *symptoms and *signs which form a distinctive clinical picture characteristic of a particular disease or injury.

synergist 1 A *muscle that aids the action of a *prime mover. The synergist may effect the same movement as the prime mover or it may stabilize the joints across which the prime mover acts, thereby preventing undesirable movements. **2** A *drug that interacts with another drug so that the combined effects of the two drugs is more than the sum of their separate effects.

synergy 1 The total *psychological energy available in a group. Synergy includes the energy needed to hold the group together (*see* maintenance synergy) and the energy exerted to meet outside goals (*see* effective synergy). In a sports team, if internal conflicts require that a lot of energy be used to keep the group together, there may be little effective energy left to deal with opponents. **2** Co-ordinated activity of *agonist and *antagonist muscles that results in smooth, well-controlled movements.

synostosis A completely ossified *joint; fixed joint.

synovia *See* synovial fluid.

synovial bursa A flattened sac found between two tissue surfaces which slide over each other; the synovial bursa reduces *friction.

synovial cavity *See* synovial joint.

synovial fluid (synovia) A transparent, viscous fluid contained within a *membrane enclosing a *movable joint or a *bursa, or within a *tendon sheath. Synovial fluid contains *hyaluronic acid, secreted by the *synovial membrane, which is diluted by *interstitial fluid derived from *blood plasma. The fluid has many functions: it lubricates and nourishes the *cartilages which provide the contact surface between the bones at the joint; it bears most of the weight at joint surfaces, preventing the *articular cartilages from touching one another, thereby preventing erosion, and minimizing *friction; and the fluid contains phagocytotic cells (*see* phagocytosis) that rid the *joint cavity of microbes and cellular debris resulting from wear and tear during joint activity.

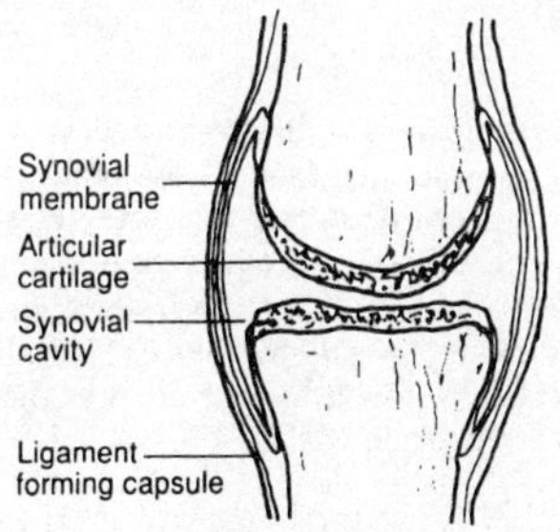

synovial joint

synovial joint (diarthrodial joint; diarthrosis) A *joint in which the articulating bones are separated by a fluid-containing *joint cavity which permits substantial freedom of movement. The ends of the bone are covered with *articular cartilage and the bones are interconnected by *ligaments lined with *synovial membrane. Synovial joints are classified according to the type of movement they allow (*see* ball-and-socket joint; condyloid joint; gliding joint; hinge-joint; pivot-joint; and saddle-joint).

synovial membrane (synovium) Loose *connective tissue lining the inside of a *joint capsule and covering all the internal joint surfaces not covered by *hyaline cartilage. The synovial membrane secretes *synovial fluid.

synovial sheath An elongated, closed sac forming a sleeve around a *tendon.

synovitis *Inflammation of the *synovial membrane of a *joint. A healthy joint has only a small volume of fluid present, but when the joint is inflamed (for example, as a result of a blow or infection), copious amounts may be produced, leading to swelling and limitation of joint movement.

synovium *See* synovial membrane.

synthesis The formation of a complex substance from simpler compounds.

syphillis A sexually-transmitted disease caused by a spiral-shaped bacterium (spirochaet), *Treponema pallidum* . Syphillis is characterised by flat, yellow-red sores at the site of infection, and destructive lesions in skin and bone. Treatment is with *antibiotics; untreated, the disease can have grave consequences. Physical exertion should be avoided if fever is present, otherwise the degree of exercise is determined by the severity of the symptoms.

syringe An instrument consisting of a hollow tube with a tight fitting piston. A syringe is used for injecting a fluid, washing out a body cavity, or removing substances from a part of the body.

system 1 Any kind of organized structure within a *society which contributes to that society (for example, the education system). **2** An organized set of interrelated and interactive parts which has a definite purpose. The human body can be viewed as a system in that it is a set of elements which work together, responding to changes in the *environment. *See also* systems theory.

systematic desensitization *See* desensitization.

system goal *See* norm.

systemic Pertaining to the whole body.

systemic circulation The flow of *arterial blood from the *heart to the body tissues (such as muscles) and of *venous blood from the tissues back to the heart.

systems theory An approach to sociological and behavioural studies which regards human beings as systems containing wholeness, organization, interactive parts, and the potential to interact with other systems. Systems can be closed or open. A closed system engages in repetitive activity and is rather limited. An open system is versatile and creative. A human being can be regarded as a hybrid system, capable of engaging in either type of activity depending on the demands of the task and the level of the skill.

systole The phase of the *cardiac cycle during which cardiac muscle contracts. Atrial systole concerns simultaneous contraction of the two *atria and produces the pressure which pumps blood into the *ventricles; ventricular systole concerns contraction of the ventricles which pumps blood to the lungs and rest of the body.

systolic blood pressure The maximum pressure in the *arteries during *systole. Systolic blood pressure is represented by the top number in the fraction of a *blood pressure reading. A typical value for a young adult at rest is 120mmHg.

T

tablet A small disc containing medicines which is taken orally.

tachycardia A rapid *heart rate which at rest is 20 to 30 beats per minute above normal. Simple sinus tachycardia occurs normally upon exercise or during periods of emotional excitement, as before a competition.

tacit knowledge Any knowledge a *social actor has which enables him or her to function successfully within a particular or general social context, but which the individual may not be able to communicate to others.

tactics The detailed directions and instructions which control movements or manoeuvres designed to achieve an aim. *Compare* strategy.

tactile Pertaining to the sense of touch.

TAI *See* trait anxiety inventory.

tailor's muscle The *sartorius muscle; so named because it helps effect the cross-legged position which was often adopted by tailors.

tail suction *See* eddy resistance.

TAIS *See* test of attentional and interpersonal style.

talar Pertaining to the *talus.

talent An individual's special aptitude or above-average ability for a specific function or range of functions. Physical talents may be functional, expressive, or athletic.

talus (ankle-bone; atragalus) A large *bone which forms part of the *tarsus. The talus articulates with the *tibia above, the *fibula to the side, and the *calcaneus below.

tan *See* tangent.

tangent (tan) **1** A geometric line, curve, or curved surface that touches another curve or surface at one point but does not intersect it. The tangent to a circle at any point is at right angles to the radius of the circle at that point. **2** A trigonometric function that in a right-angled triangle is the ratio of the length of the opposite side to that of the adjacent side; the ratio of *sine to *cosine.

tangential acceleration For an object moving along a curved path, the instantaneous *linear acceleration *vector acting at a *tangent to the curved path.

tangential component A component of a given *vector acting at right angles to a given radius of a given circle.

tangible reward A reward which has physical substance, such as money or a trophy. *Compare* status reward.

tannin Soluble, astringent yellow substance found in some plants. Tannins taken in the diet may reduce the absorption of iron and trace minerals.

taper down *See* cool down.

taping Use of tapes to support a weakened body-part without limiting its function, by preventing movements which stress the weakened area. The tapes generally used are rather inelastic and 38–50 mm in width. Taping may also be used as a preventative measure to improve stability and decrease injuries. There are two main views about preventative taping. One suggests that it is always wise to tape *joints for activity, thus preventing damage and maintaining joint stability by spreading the load onto other joints. The other view argues that joints should generally be left untaped because an immobilized joint cannot take its share of the load and therefore overloads other joints.

tapotement *Massage technique in which the fingertips, palms, or sides of the hands create tapping and slapping movements.

target cell A cell capable of being affected by a particular *hormone.

target game A game, such as darts or archery, in which an individual tries to hit an object or area with a projectile.

target heart rate A heart rate range reached during *aerobic training which enables the subject to gain maximum benefit. There are a number of methods of computing target heart rate; they include the *maximal heart rate reserve method, and the *heart rate method.

target organ Cell tissue or organ upon which a *hormone has an effect.

target zone *See* training zone.

tarsal 1 Pertaining to the ankle and *proximal part of the foot. 2 *See* tarsal bone.

tarsal bone One of seven bones in each *foot which forms part of the *tarsus. The tarsal bones are: the medial *cuneiform, *intermediate cuneiform, *lateral cuneiform, *navicular, *cuboid, *talus, and *calcaneus bones.

tarsalgia An aching pain in the ankle region and *proximal part of the foot.

tarsal tunnel A passage just below the *medial malleolus through which pass the *plantaris lateralis nerve and *plantaris medialis nerve.

tarsal tunnel syndrome A condition associated with excessive *pronation of the foot which causes tissues in the sole to become inflamed, swell, and press against the nerves within the *tarsal tunnel. A feeling of *pain follows the course of the nerves from the area of entrapment below the inside of the ankle and radiates along the sole of the foot towards the toes.

tarsometatarsal joint A *synovial, *gliding joint between the *tarsus and *metatarsals.

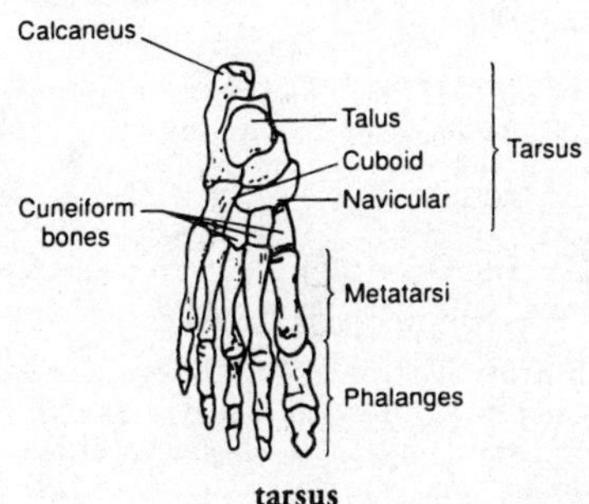

tarsus

tarsus (ankle-bone) The seven *tarsal bones of the ankle and *proximal part of the foot. The tarsus articulates with the *tibia and *fibula above, and the *metatarsals below.

task A specific activity which is to be completed. In sport, the completion of tasks usually requires the performance of specific *motor skills. The terms task and skill are often used synonymously.

task analysis A process of determining the underlying abilities required, and the structure of *motor skills that need to be performed to complete a *task.

task classification Classification of *tasks according to the types of *motor skills required for their completion. Several task classifications have been proposed but no one classification has gained general acceptance. Classifications include those based on pacing conditions (*see* externally-paced task; mixed-paced task; and self-paced task), the continuity of the tasks (*see* continuous task; discrete task; and serial task), and on the extent to which environmental conditions affect performance of the task (*see* closed task; and open task).

task cohesion The degree to which members of a group work together to achieve a specific identifiable *goal. Task cohesion is a major dimension of *team cohesion. *See also* sociometric cohesion.

task dependence The degree of interaction required between team-mates for a task to be completed. In baseball, pitching is an example of a task requiring low levels of interaction while a double play requires high interaction.

task-irrelevant cognitive activity (TICA) *See* cognitive state anxiety.

task motivation A style of *leadership behaviour in which the successful completion of the task is the critical factor. It is consistent with *initiating structure.

task orientation A *psychological orientation in which an individual is concerned primarily with completing a task, solving a problem, and with working persistently and doing the best job possible. Despite the fact that it seems to be a self-centred orientation, a person with high task orientation usually works well within a group, perceiving that a contribution to the group effort will contribute to overall success in the task. *Compare* interaction orientation; and self-orientation.

taste The sense of flavour in the mouth by which it is possible to identify food substances. There are four basic taste sensations: sweet, bitter, sour, and salt.

taste bud A *sensory receptor which lies on the tongue and is responsible for the sense of taste.

taste culture A *subculture which reflects the preference of a group for a particular cultural product. Membership of the group may be determined by many factors including the *ethnic origin, *social class, age, gender, and country or place of residence. In sport, preference for particular activities depends on the taste culture with which a person identifies. For example, polo and boxing may be the preferred sporting activities of particular social classes in certain countries. *See also* high culture; and popular culture.

taxis Manipulation by the hand to restore a body part to its normal position; used to treat a *dislocation or a *hernia.

Taylor manifest anxiety scale A means of measuring differences in chronic *anxiety between different subjects using a standardized paper and pencil questionnaire with statements such as 'I am easily embarrassed', and 'I have few headaches', to which the subject responds with the answer either true or false.

T-cell A type of *lymphocyte produced in *bone marrow that counteracts the presence of foreign *antigens by a process of cell-mediated immunity in which the antigen is slowly destroyed by the T-cell or by a *toxin released from T-cells.

team A social unit which has a relatively rigid structure, organization, and communication pattern. The task of each member of a team is usually well defined and the successful functioning of the team depends on the co-ordinated participation of all or several of its members. *Compare* group.

team-building The art of developing *team cohesion. Team-building depends on the ability to blend the various styles and temperaments of different people so that the skills of each can be used to the full.

team cohesion A dynamic process that is reflected in the tendency of a team to stick together and remain united in pursuit of its *goals and objectives despite difficulties or set-backs. Team cohesion is distinguished from *group cohesion by the importance, in team cohesion, of dynamic processes and the pursuit of team-goals. *See also* social cohesion; and task cohesion.

team-cohesion questionnaire A questionnaire incorporating a 9-point *Likert-type scale which measures six dimensions of *team cohesion including satisfaction, value of membership, leadership, task cohesion, desire for recognition, and affiliation cohesion.

team culture The *attitudes, *beliefs, and *norms of a team. The team culture is concerned with how the team operates, including its selection procedures and power structure; how rewards are given; practice procedures; game protocols; acceptable behaviour; and dress code. The team culture often depends on the traditions, or lack of them, within a team. *See also* idioculture.

team homogeneity Team-mate similarity in terms of such things as *culture, ethnic and religious background, and socioeconomic status. *See also* determinants.

team psyche The spirit of a *team, including a sense of loyalty and dedication among team-members, which is determined in part by the *team culture

team satisfaction A measurement of how satisfied a team feels, or how satisfied a team-member feels about being part of the team. *See also* consequences.

team stability The degree to which the membership of a team remains the same. Team stability can be defined in terms of the length of time that the team-members remain together.

technical competency An individual's knowlege and expertise in a specific group task and its processes; that is, knowledge of the skills, strategies, and tactics of a sport, and its rules and regulations. Technical competency is a managerial competency which a coach or other leader needs to possess to be successful.

technical model An exemplar, used in coaching, of a technique in action. Technical models may be visual, verbal, or written.

technique A pattern of movement which is technically appropriate for a particular *skill and which is an integral part, but not the whole part, of that skill. The Fosbury flop, for example, is a particular technique used in the skill of high-jumping.

tectorial membrane A membrane present in the *organ of Corti in the *cochlea of the *inner ear that runs parallel to the *basilar membrane. Sensory cells connected by *neurones to the auditory nerve span the gap between the basilar and tectorial membranes.

teeter-totter An unstable platform used to test *balance.

teleceptor *See* telereceptor.

telemetry The use of radio-waves to transmit the readings of measuring instruments to a device which can record the readings. Telemetry is used in *exercise physiology to monitor the heart rate and other functions of an athlete in motion.

telencephalon The *anterior part of the *forebrain which develops into the *olfactory lobes, *cerebral cortex, and corpus striatum (a part of the *basal ganglia).

teleological explanation An explanation (of human behaviour, for example) in terms of its outcomes or goals. Such explanations are usually given in terms of the purposes, reasons, or motives behind a particular behaviour.

teleology The concept that phenomena such as human behaviour are directed and determined by a goal or a purpose.

telereceptor (teleceptor) Specialized *sensory receptor, such as those in the eyes, ears, and nose, that responds to distant external stimuli.

temperament The emotional aspects of *personality such as joviality, moodiness, tenseness, or excitability.

temperature A measure of hotness; a property which determines the rate at which heat will be transferred between bodies which are in direct contact (heat flows from regions of high temperature to regions of low temperature). In science, temperature is expressed in terms of degrees *kelvin or degrees *Celsius.

temperature coefficient *See* Q_{10}.

temple Region of the head in front of and above the ears.

tempolauf A form of training which emphasizes high-intensity effort equalling or approaching that required in competition. Tempolauf may take the form of continuous or intermittent work, as in a *time trial, or brief repetitions at the competitive distance with adequate intervening rest periods. The aim of such training is to accustom the athlete to the tempo or pace of competition.

temporal 1 Pertaining to the *temple. 2 Pertaining to time.

temporal anticipation The *anticipation of when a given *stimulus will arrive or a movement be made.

temporal awareness An awareness of the passage of time; an essential ingredient of pace judgement and a sense of *rhythm.

temporal bone One of two bones on either side of the *cranium, and containing the middle and inner ears.

temporal summation The summative effect of repeated stimulation of one presynaptic neurone on the response of a *postsynaptic membrane. Each *stimulus causes a release of a *neurotransmitter from the presynaptic membrane which produces a *graded potential in the postsynaptic membrane. The graded potentials evoked by a rapid succession of two or more stimuli are added together until, in the case of excitatory stimuli, a *threshold level is reached and an *action potential occurs in the postsynaptic membrane.

temperomandibular joint A *synovial joint between the mandible (lower jaw) and the temporal bone at the base of the skull. It is capable of the following joint movements: *elevation, *depression, *protraction, and *retraction.

temperomandibular joint syndrome A painful condition of the *temperomandibular joint characterized by grinding, clicking, soreness, and limitiation of jaw movement when chewing.

tendinitis Inflammation of a *tendon that usually occurs from over-use especially in those who perform one sport or movement regularly and intensely. The tendon becomes swollen, red, and tender to the touch; motion may be impaired by *pain. Treatment may include rest and modification of tendon function by, for example, a heel pad, so that the *range of movement of the tendon is altered. Shock absorption in the lower limbs may also be improved by the use of shock-absorbing heel insets or full insoles and therefore the stress on the tendons is reduced. *Surgical decompression may be necessary. Treatment by the injection of *steroids such as *hydrocortisone into the *paratenon may be helpful, but injection into the tendons themselves can result in a *tendon rupture. *See also* Achilles tendinitis.

tendinosis A symptomatic *tendon degeneration due to ageing, accumulated *microtrauma, or both; it is subclassified into microscopical failures, central *necrosis, and partial *rupture.

tendocalcaneus The *tendon, common to the *soleus, *gastrocnemius, and *plantaris muscles, that inserts into the *calcaneus.

tendon A band of white tissue connecting a *muscle to a *bone. A tendon consists mainly of numerous bundles of parallel *collagen fibres, which provide mechanical strength, and a little *elastin which provides some elasticity. Tendons resist tensile stresses very well and have a tensile strength of about 50–100 *N mm^{-2}, but they resist *shear forces less effectively and also provide little resistance to *compression forces. Tendons contribute to effective muscle action by concentrating the pull of the muscle on a small area of bone.

tendon injury Damage to the tendon. Tendons have a poor blood supply and therefore injuries are generally slow to heal. Tendon injuries include *ruptures (which may be partial or complete), *tendinitis. and tendovaginitis or paratendinitis (i.e., inflammation of the sheath).

tendon organs *See* golgi tendon organs.

tendon rupture Loss of continuity of some or all fibres of a *tendon. Tendon ruptures commonly occur after the sudden application of an unbalanced load. The injury can be very dramatic with the victim feeling as if he or she has received a severe blow. A tendon rupture may be classified as complete ruptures (third-degree strain) resulting in loss of function, or partial ruptures (first-degree strain and second-degree strain). They heal slowly because of the poor blood supply to the tendon. *See also* peritendinitis; tendinitis; tenoperiostitis.

tendovaginitis A term which was formerly used for a thickening and inflammation of a *tendon sheath commonly caused by the cumulative effect of minor injuries. Its use has largely been replaced by the term *tenosynovitis.

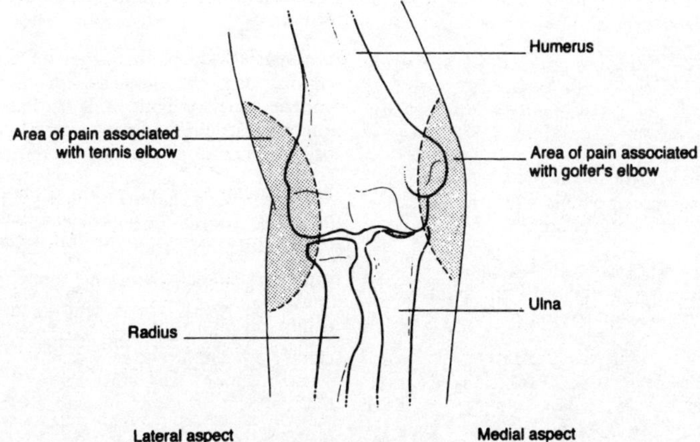

tennis elbow

tendon sheath A fibrous sheath lined with *synovial membrane which surrounds the *paratenon of some *tendons.

tennis elbow (enthesitis; lateral epicondylitis) A form of *tendinitis affecting the common *extensor tendon attached to the *lateral *epicondyle of the *humerus. Tennis elbow is characterized by a pain which originates in the outer part of elbow but which may pass from the shoulder to the wrist. Tennis elbow is a common *over-use injury of the elbow region which can occur in any sport in which the wrist is constantly bending while the hand is gripping; for example, canoeing, racket sports, baseball, ten-pin bowling, and fly-fishing. It is often caused by a technical fault.

tennis leg A condition characterized by a sudden sharp pain in the upper calf which feels like a 'shot in the leg'. It is due to a *rupture of the *musculotendinous junction of one of the heads (usually the *medial head) of the *gastrocnemius muscle. The injury is caused by a sudden *extension of the knee while the foot is dorsiflexed, or by a sudden *dorsiflexion of the ankle when the knee is extended. The injury occurs most often in middle-aged athletes, with some degeneration of the tendon, who play sports such as tennis, squash, and basketball.

tennis shoulder A condition caused by one-sided training, as in racket sports, which leads to an increase in the size of the bones and muscles; increased laxity of the *joint capsule and *ligaments; and over-use of the tendons of the racket arm. This can result in a dropping of the shoulder, a relative lengthening of the arm, and, in extreme cases, can cause *scoliosis.

tennis toe *See* black nail.

tenoperiostitis An inflammation at the point at which a *tendon inserts into, or originates from, *bone. Tenoperiostitis commonly arises from repeated strain on the attachment point of the tendon and *periosteum. A typical symptom is pain, during active motion, at the attachment point. It occurs most frequently in the elbow (*see* tennis elbow; and golfer's elbow); in the knee, at the *proximal attachment of the *adductor longus of the *Achilles tendon *insertion into the *calcaneus; and at the attachment of the plantar fascia into the calcaneus (*see* plantar fasciitis). *See also* Sever–Haglund disease.

tenosynovitis Inflammation of the *synovial membrane which forms a fibrous funnel through which a *tendon passes. It commonly occurs as a result of extended over-use of muscles.

TENS *See* transcutaneous electrical nerve stimulation.

tensile strain The effect of *tensile stress on an object. Tensile strain is expressed as the ratio of extension length to original length.

tensile strength The pulling *force, measured as force per unit area, that has to be applied to a body in order to break it.

tensile stress The *force applied per unit area of a cross-section of an object which stretches or tends to stretch the object.

tension 1 The state of an object being stretched or in the act of stretching. **2** *Force per unit area exerted by a stretched material on a support. **3** An *overt muscle contraction caused by an emotional state or an increased effort.

tensor A *muscle that stretches or tenses a body-part.

tensor fascia latae A muscle of the *anterior compartment of the thigh which has its *origins on the anterior aspect of the *iliac crest and the anterior, superior aspect of the *iliac spine, and its *insertion on the *iliotibial tract. The tensor fascia latae acts as a *synergist of the *iliopsoas, *gluteus medius, and *gluteus minimus muscles during *flexion and *abduction of the hip, steadying the trunk by making the iliotibial tract taut. It also takes part in knee *extension.

terbutaline A *drug belonging to the *β_2 stimulants. Its use in aerosol form only is permitted by the *IOC Medical Commission for the treatment of *asthma or other respiratory conditions. It may not be taken orally.

teres major A thick, rounded *muscle which, with the *latissimus dorsi and *subscapularis, helps to form the *posterior wall of *axilla. The teres major has its *origin on the posterior surface of the shoulder-blade, and its *insertion *tendon is fused to that of the latissimus dorsi and is attached to the crest of the lesser *tubercle of the *humerus. It acts as a *synergist of the latissimus dorsi and *pectoralis major in the *adduction, *extension, and inward *rotation of the arm.

teres minor A small, elongated, *rotator cuff muscle of the shoulder-joint which lies underneath the shoulder-blade. The teres minor has its *origin on the *lateral border of *scapula and its *insertion on the greater *tubercle of the *humerus. It acts with the *infraspinatus to hold the *humerus in the *glenoid cavity and to rotate the arm outwards.

terminal cisternae Sac-like channels of the *sarcoplasmic reticulum at the junction between the light and dark bands in a *sarcomere of a *muscle fibre. The terminal cisternae contain *calcium ions which are released from the sac immediately before *muscle contraction (*see* sliding-filament theory).

terminal feedback *Feedback given after a movement has been completed. *Compare* concurrent feedback.

terminal velocity A constant *velocity reached by an object falling through a resisting medium and being acted upon by a constant *force. A body falling through the atmosphere under the force of *gravity will accelerate until its *terminal velocity is reached. At this velocity, the upward *drag force is equal to the *weight of the falling object. The terminal velocity varies with the weight and orientation of the falling body. An ability to vary terminal velocity is very important in sky-diving.

terpenoids Compounds, including *steroids, made up of repeating units of *isoprene.

test 1 An examination designed to reveal the relative standing of an individual in a group (e.g., with respect to achievement or fitness). **2** A chemical or other form of analysis to determine the composition of a substance.

test-anxiety A fear of taking a test or of failing a test.

test-anxiety approach A theory of *achievement motivation which proposes that *test-anxiety is a critical factor in determining whether or not an individual approaches or avoids an achievement situation.

testicle One of a pair of male sex organs within the *scrotum which contain the *testes.

testicular feminization A rare condition in which a person has testes, is genetically male (having XY chromosomes), but has the hormonal responses of a female. The condition causes difficulties of *sex determination. The person is, by virtually all definitions, female but, having a testis and XY chromosomes, could be defined as a male.

testis (pl. testes) *Gamete-producing organ of the male which also produces male *sex hormones.

test of attentional and interpersonal style (TAIS) A self-report inventory which is used to assess *attentional style. The TAIS is based on the idea that attention has two independent dimensions: the first is width (narrow–broad), and the second is direction (internal–external). Several sport-specific tests have been developed from the TAIS. *See also* T-TAIS and B-TAIS.

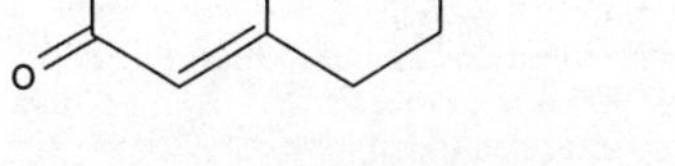

OH
CH_3
O

testosterone

testosterone An *androgenic and *anabolic *hormone which occurs naturally in both males and females. Testosterone is the main male *sex hormone, secreted by the testes, that induces and maintains the changes that take place in males at *puberty. The testes continue to produce testosterone throughout life, though there is some decline with age. Synthetic testosterone preparations have been designed to emphasize anabolic effects while minimizing androgenic properties. Injections of testosterone or related *drugs have been banned by the *IOC since 1984. Testosterone is usually excreted in the same amounts as *epitestosterone. Consequently, the ratio of testosterone to epistestosterone is used by the IOC as an indicator of testosterone misuse. The IOC regards a ratio of 6:1 (testosterone:epitestosterone) as indicating *doping. However, this level is not very reliable because alcohol can increase the ratio, and athletes trying to avoid detection may take mixtures of epitestosterone and testosterone. *See also* human chorionggonadotrophin.

tetanic contraction *See* tetanus.

tetanus 1 Lockjaw; a particularly dangerous infection by a bacterium *Clostridium tetani* , often following a laceration. Even when not fatal, this is a most unpleasant condition marked by muscle stiffness and rigidity requiring prolonged and painful treatment. The infective organism can be found anywhere but is most common on ground which has been used by animals. It is possible to use antitetanus serum but this carries the risk of allergic reactions and active immunity is better. **2** Sustained contraction of muscle due to the fusion of many small contractions (twitches) following one another in rapid succession.

tetany Spasm and twitching of a muscle due to a lack of *calcium which increases the excitability of nerves. Tetany usually affects the hands and feet. It may be caused by *alkalosis.

tethering scar A *scar which adheres to deeper structures. Tethering scars commonly occur around the eyes of boxers where the scar tissue adheres to underlying bone.

tetracosactrin A *drug belonging to the *peptide hormones and *analogues which are on the *IOC list of *banned substances.

tetracycline An *antibiotic derived from cultures of *Streptomyces* bacteria. Tetracyclines are effective against many microorganisms including certain *viruses.

thalamus A mass of *grey matter in the *diencephalon of the brain through which most sensory impulses pass before being transmitted to the *cortex.

thelion A *landmark located on the breast nipple.

thematic apperception test A personality test in which the subject is shown a particular picture and encouraged to make up an oral or written story about it.

thenar Pertaining to the thumb.

thenar muscles Four short muscles in the palm of the hand that act exclusively to circumduct and oppose the thumb.

theoretical mechanical advantage *See* mechanical advantage.

theoretical sampling *See* purposive sampling.

theoretical square law A law which states that the resistance a body creates in a fluid varies approximately with the square of its *velocity. The law applies to a swimmer who, by throwing his or her arm in the water twice as fast as before, increases by fourfold the resistance to forward progress.

theory A set of *hypotheses or propositions, logically or mathematically linked, which is offered as an explanation in general terms for a wide variety of connected phenomena.

theory of games A treatment of competitive games in which *probability theory is used in relation to the advantages and disadvantages of decisions that have to be made in situations involving conflicting interests.

therapy Treatment of an illness or injury.

thermic effect of food An increase in oxygen uptake, indicating an increase in *metabolic rate, due to an intake of food. *See also* specific dynamic action.

thermodynamic laws Laws which are believed to govern processes that involve heat changes. The two which are most relevant to sports science are the law of conservation of energy, and the law of entropy. Conservation of energy applies to a system of constant *mass in which energy can be neither created nor destroyed. A consequence of the law of entropy is that heat cannot be transferred by a continous, self-sustaining process from a colder to a hotter body. This means that the efficiency of energy transformation is imperfect as some *free energy will escape from the system, usually as heat.

thermodynamics The *science of the transformation of *heat and *energy.

thermography Use of infrared photography to measure thermal emissions from the *skin and *subcutaneous tissue. The thermograph is the picture produced. It provides a visual means of identifying areas of inflammation associated with some sports injuries and *ischaemia.

thermolysis The removal of body-heat (for example, by evaporation of body *sweat).

thermometer An instrument for measuring *temperature.

thermoreceptor A sensory nerve-ending sensitive to changes in *temperature. Skin thermoreceptors (cold and hot receptors) are thought by some to be *Ruffini's corpuscles and *Krause's end-bodies, but others are convinced that cold and heat receptors are naked nerve-endings and that Ruffini's corpuscles and Krause's end-bodies are *mechanoreceptors.

thermoregulation The regulation of body temperature. Thermoregulation can be by behavioural or physiological processes (*see* thermotaxis). Skin *thermoreceptors are involved in behavioural thermoregulation which is accomplished by voluntary responses initiated by the cortex of the brain, while the *hypothalamus contains thermoreceptors for physiological responses.

thermotaxis The normal physiological responses, such as changes in the rate of *sweating and in the *metabolic rate, which are used to keep a balance between heat losses and heat gains in the human body. *See also* thermoregulation.

thermotherapy *See* heat treatment.

thiamine *See* vitamin B_1.

thick filament The thicker of the two main types of filament within a *sarcomere of a muscle. Each thick filament contains approximately 200 *myosin molecules bundled together so that its central portion is smooth and its ends are studded with *cross-bridges. *Compare* thin filament.

thigh The body region between the *knee and *hip.

thigh abductor *See* hip abduction.

thigh adductor *See* hip adduction.

thigh extensor *See* hip extension.

thigh flexor *See* hip flexion.

thigh girth In *anthropometry, the circumference of the thigh (usually the right thigh) 1–2 cm below the protruberance of the *gluteal muscles. The measurement is taken when the subject is standing erect with feet slightly apart and with weight equally distributed on both feet.

thigh lateral rotation *See* hip lateral rotation.

thigh length In *anthropometry, either the difference between the *trochanterion height and the *tibiale (laterale) height, or the difference between the stretched stature, and the sum of the *sitting height and the *tibiale (laterale) height.

thigh medial rotator *See* hip medial rotation.

thigh movement A movement which occurs either at the knee (mainly *extension and *flexion) or at the hip (including *abduction, *adduction, *circumduction, *extension, *flexion, *inward rotation, and *outward rotation).

thigh rotator *See* hip rotation.

thin filament The thinner of the two main filaments which can be seen on *electron micrographs of a muscle *sarcomere. The thin filament is mainly composed of the helically-arranged *actin along with the regulatory proteins *tropomyosin and *troponin.

third-class lever A *lever which has its point of *effort between the *fulcrum and the *resistance or load. It is the most common type of lever in the human body. Since the distance between the resistance and fulcrum is always greater than the distance between the effort and the fulcrum, the effort is greater than the load but such levers provide a good *range of movement at speed.

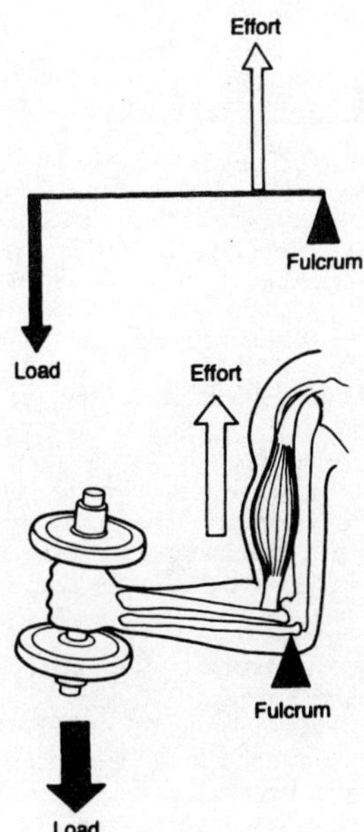

third-class lever

third degree strain A complete rupture of a *muscle or a *tendon which often occurs in athletes attempting a power activity. The tendons most commonly affected are the *Achilles tendon, the *biceps tendon, the *patellar tendon, the *quadriceps tendon, and the *supraspinatus tendon. *See also* strain.

thirst An uncomfortable feeling of dryness in the mouth and throat accompanied by a desire to drink. An athlete may need to replace water lost through *sweating before feeling thirsty in order to avoid *dehydration

thoracic Pertaining to the chest.

thoracic cage *See* bony thorax.

thoracic cavity The chest cavity (*see* thorax).

thoracic curvature *See* spinal curvature.

thoracic duct A large duct that receives *lymph drained from the lower body, the left upper extremity, and the left side of the head and *thorax; it drains into the left innominate vein (*see* subclavian vein).

thoracic injury Damage to the structures in the *thorax. Thoracic injuries are often serious since they can affect *vital organs. A fall from a horse, a crush in a rugby scrum, or any other direct hit on the thorax can result in fractured ribs with the potential risk of a *punctured lung. *Stress fractures of the rib occasionally occur especially in those, such as tennis players, who use mainly one arm.

thoracic vertebra One of twelve *vertebrae which articulate with the *ribs. Each thoracic vertebra has a roughly heart-shaped *centrum, a long *neural spine, and bears costal facets which receive the ribs.

thoracolumbar scoliosis *See* scoliosis.

thorax The chest; the portion of the body trunk above the *diaphragm and below the neck which contains the heart and lungs, and is enclosed by the *thoracic cage.

thorazine An *antipsychotic drug. *See also* dopamine.

Thorndike's stimulus–response theory of learning A theory which proposes that all *learning consists primarily of the strengthening of the relationship between a *stimulus and the *response. In developing this theory, Thorndike proposed three laws: the *law of effect, the *law of exercise, and the *law of readiness.

thought–stopping A technique used to overcome negative attitudes when performing. The performer is trained to recognize and become aware of negative thoughts and to replace them with constructive thoughts. At the start of a slalom, for example, a skier who starts to think about the consequences of misjudging turns, stops these thoughts and replaces them with thoughts of how the descent can be successfully completed. *See also* centring procedure; and refocusing.

threonine An *essential amino acid which is found in beans and other legumes, and corn and other cereal.

threshold (limen) 1 The weakest value of any *stimulus or other agency which will produce a specified effect. This is sometimes called the absolute threshold or stimulus threshold. 2 The smallest difference in intensity, magnitude, or pitch between two stimuli which can be discriminated (the just-noticeable difference). This is more precisely referred to as the difference threshold or differential threshold. 3 The upper limit of sensitivity, more precisely termed the terminal threshold; the point beyond which further increases in the intensity of stimulation have no typical effect (that is, the effect is different from that which a stimulus would normally have). Increases of light intensity above the terminal threshold may cause pain, for example, but this is not a typical effect of that stimulation.

threshold of training The minimum amount of exercise that will improve *physical fitness. For exercise to be effective, it must be done with sufficient frequency, intensity, and for a long-enough duration. As fitness improves the threshold level gets higher. *See also* overload principle; and principle of progression.

thrombin An *enzyme that accelerates the formation of *fibrin from *fibrinogen during the *clotting of blood.

thrombocytes *See* platelets.

thrombosis A condition in which a *thrombus forms in a *blood vessel.

thrombus A blood clot (*see* coagulation) that remains at its point of formation.

thrower's elbow (pitcher's elbow) A term given to a number of conditions of the *elbow associated with round-arm throwing. Thrower's elbow is characterized by damage to the triceps muscle, *ligaments (typically the medial ligaments), and the *olecranon process which may suffer a *stress fracture or an *osteochondritis. Thrower's elbow is caused by putting too great a load on the elbow (for example, in forceful straightening of the elbow when serving in tennis or when throwing a ball). It often requires correction of faulty technique as well as treatment of the damaged tissue. *See also* golfer's elbow.

thrower's fracture A fracture of the *humerus which occurs when the muscular force generated by a hard throw is enough to snap the bone.

thrust 1 A propulsive *force which produces motion. The most effective projections occur when the line of thrust coincides with the *centre of gravity of the body. A thrust which does not coincide with the body's centre of gravity will tend to cause rotation. **2** A continuous force applied by one object on another.

thumb *See* pollex.

Thurstone scales Measures of *attitude consisting of about twenty statements, each representing a different degree of favourableness or unfavourableness toward an attitude object, and arranged to present a continuum of equally-spaced levels of favourableness.

thymus An *endocrine gland in the neck which produces *lymphocytes active in the *immune response. Its function reaches a peak during puberty and then declines with age.

thyrocalcitonin An alternative name for *calcitonin.

thyroglobulin A *protein in the *thyroid gland from which the *thyroid hormones, *thyroxine and *triiodothyronine, are derived.

thyroid gland A large, bilobed *endocrine gland in the neck. The thyroid gland secretes *thyroid hormone which regulates the *metabolic rate.

thyroid hormone (TH) A *hormone produced by the *thyroid gland. Thyroid hormone is composed of at least two separate iodine-containing hormones: *thyroxine and *triiodothyronine. Thyroid hormone accelerates the *metabolic rate of every cell in the body except those of the *brain, *spleen, *testis, and *uterus. It is an important regulator of tissue growth and development, particularly of nervous and skeletal tissue. Deficient secretions result in sluggish muscle action, *cramps, and *myalgia; excessive secretions produce muscle *atrophy and weakness and, in adults, demineralization of bones.

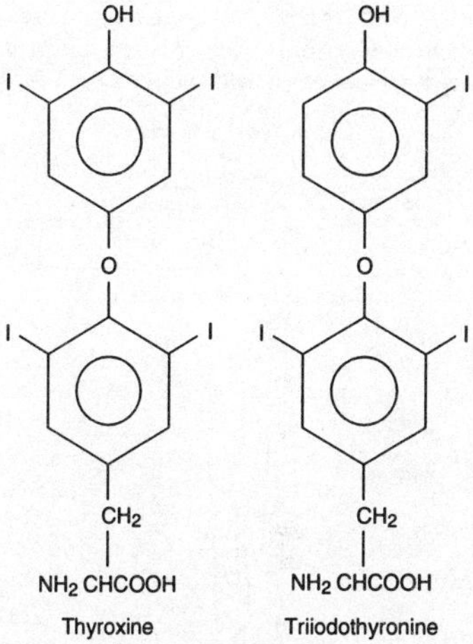

Thyroxine | Triiodothyronine

thyroid hormone

thyroid-stimulating hormone (thyrotropin; TSH) A *hormone secreted by the anterior *pituitary gland which stimulates the production of *thyroid hormone from the *thyroid gland.

thyrostatic Applied to a medication that reduces the production of *thyroid hormone.

thyrotoxicosis A condition, characterized by an increased *metabolic rate due to excessive secretion of *thyroid hormone. Thyrotoxicosis is usually accompanied by an enlargement of the *thyroid gland.

thyrotropin *See* thyroid-stimulating hormone.

thyroxine A complex *organic compound containing *iodine and secreted by the *thyroid gland. Secretion of thyroxine is increased with exercise and trained individuals have a higher concentration of thyroxine at rest, and a higher turnover during exercise, than untrained individuals.

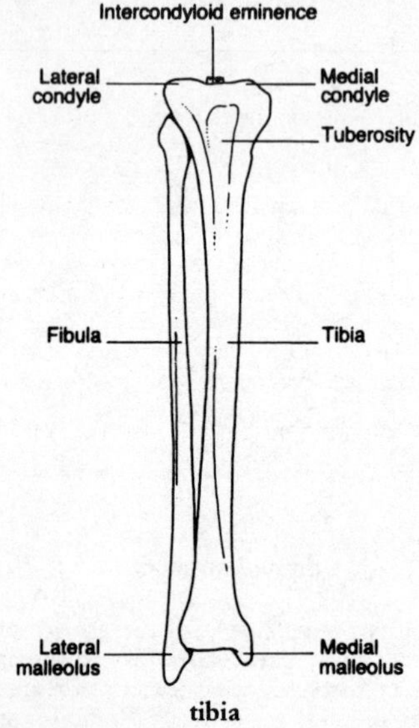

tibia

tibia (shin-bone) The inner and larger *bone of the lower leg. The tibia extends from the ankle to the knee, articulating with the *talus below and the *femur above. It is triangular in section. The sharp anterior crest and medial surface of the tibia are unprotected by muscle and can be felt just underneath the skin.

tibial collateral ligament tear A rupture of the *ligaments which make up the femoral-tibial aspect of the knee-joint.

tibiale laterale A *landmark located on the *superior extremity and the *lateral border of the head of the *tibia.

tibiale mediale A *landmark located on the *superior extremity and the *medial border of the head of the *tibia.

tibial height A *body height measurement made from *tibiale to *base.

tibialis anterior A long *superficial muscle in the *anterior compartment of the lower leg. The tibialis anterior has its *origin on the *lateral *condyle and the upper two-thirds of the *tibia. Its *insertion is by a *tendon into the *inferior surface of the first *cuneiform and *metatarsal bone. The tibialis anterior is a *prime mover of *dorsiflexion; it also inverts the foot and supports the *medial longitudinal arch.

tibialis anterior syndrome Pain and tenderness felt during ankle *dorsiflexion and when pressure is applied to the *lateral side of the *tibia at the front of the lower leg. The *syndrome is due to an acute inflammation of the *tendon sheath of the *tibialis anterior muscle which commonly arises from over-use of the ankle, such as from prolonged running or jumping on a hard surface.

tibialis posterior A thick, flat, *deep muscle of the posterior compartment of the lower leg. The tibialis posterior has extensive *origins on the *posterior, *proximal surface of the *tibia, *fibula, and *interosseus membrane. Its *insertion is via a *tendon which passes behind the *medial malleolus and under the arch of the foot to attach onto several *tarsal and *metatarsal bones. The tibilais posterior is a *prime mover of foot *inversion and of *plantar flexion of the ankle. It also helps to stabilize the longitudinal arch of the foot, especially during skating.

tibialis posterior syndrome A pain and tenderness associated with movement or loading of the *tendon of the *tibialis posterior muscle. The tendon runs behind the *tibia and the *medial malleolus, through a narrow groove to insert onto the *navicular bone. Overpronation of the foot results in an increase in pressure on the tendon which may lead to *inflammation of the tendon, its attachment, or its sheath. The injury is common in skating.

tibial nerve A *nerve derived from the *sciatic nerve just above the knee. The tibial nerve supplies the muscles within the posterior compartment of the lower leg. It subdivides into the medial plantar nerve and lateral plantar nerve which together supply the foot.

tibial torsion A condition in which the *femur and *tibia are rotated around their vertical axes. Internal *femoral torsion is usually associated with external tibial torsion. The condition may arise due to an imbalance of the *hamstring muscles. Tibial torsion increases stress on the medial structures of the *knee-joint and causes pain in the lateral aspect of the knee; it usually causes the toes to be pointed outwards (laterally) during weight-bearing.

tibial tuberosity A large rounded prominence on the *tibia.

tibial valgus Curvature of the *tibia outwards from its *proximal to its *distal end. The condition is usually combined with a *femoral varus and results in a knock-kneed appearance (*see* genu valgus). Tibial valgus results in extra *tensile stress being placed on the *medial side of the knee and the *lateral side of the ankle. However, this can be at least partly compensated for by strengthening the *quadriceps muscles which stabilize the knee, and by strengthening the muscles which support the lateral side of the foot.

tibial varus Curvature of the *tibia inwards from its *proximal to its *distal end. Tibial varus is often accompanied by *rearfoot valgus. It increases the *tensile stress on the lateral aspect of the knee-joint and may cause *iliotibial band friction syndrome.

tibiofemoral joint *See* knee-joint.

tibiofibular joint One of two fibrous joints (the superior and inferior tibiofibular joints) between the *tibia and *fibula (*see* syndesmosis). It is capable of only a little movement (for example, during ankle *dorsiflexion).

tic An involuntary spasmodic or sudden movement, generally of one of the face or head muscles, which varies in complexity from a simple *twitch to a complex, co-ordinated action. As a rule, tics originate in some *neurotic disorder.

TICA *See* cognitive state anxiety.

tidal volume The volume of air inspired into the *lungs or expired out of the lungs during each breath. The typical resting value for humans is about 500 ml but it increases dramatically during exercise.

tidal volume inspiratory capacity ratio The ratio of the volume of air actually breathed during one breath to the total lung capacity.

time A quantity measuring duration. The *SI unit for time is the *second. Time is often an *independent variable used in scientific investigations to which other physical magnitudes are related. An example is the change in oxygen consumption with respect to time where the origin in time can be any arbitrarily selected instant; negative values refer to events occurring before, and positive values to events occurring after, that instant.

time-dependent ageing The loss of function resulting from increasing chronological age.

time of flight (flight-time) The duration in time a projectile is airborne; it is equal to the sum of the time it takes the projectile to reach its peak and the time the projectile takes to return from the peak to the landing point. When release and landing points are at the same level, the projectile takes the same time to reach its peak as it does to return to its original level.

time trial Situation in which an athlete (e.g., a runner, swimmer or cyclist) races against the clock to establish how fast he or she can cover a given distance. Time trials may be performed at the competition distance, or above or below that distance, and they may be performed with or without the assistance of other athletes. Time trials form an important part of most training programmes, offering important *feedback about the value and effects of the training.

timing The ability to perform movements and actions of the body or body-part at a particular moment to produce the best effect. Timing is a quality which characterizes most *motor skills. Timing may be facilitated by external stimuli, such as visual or auditory stimuli caused by the movements of team-mates, or it may be facilitated by internal rhythmic stimuli. *See also* rhythm.

timolol A *drug belonging to the *beta blockers which are on the *IOC list of *banned substances.

tincture An alcoholic solution of a *drug.

tinnitus A ringing or buzzing sound in the ears. Tinnitus has many causes including damage to the *tympanic membrane, infection of the inner ear, and as a side-effect of *drugs such as aspirin.

tissue A group of cells with a similar structure performing a specific function. The primary types of tissue in the body are *epithelial tissue, *connective tissue, *muscle, and *nervous tissue.

tissue–capillary membrane The thin barrier dividing the capillaries and respiring tissues, such as those of a muscle. The tissue–capillary membrane is the site at which *gaseous exchange occurs.

tissue fluid A fluid formed by the *ultrafiltration of blood *plasma which surrounds cells. The tissue fluid acts as the internal environment of the cells.

TLC *See* total lung capacity.

TMAS (Taylor manifest anxiety scale) A scale, used to measure *anxiety, which is based on fifty items to which the subject answers either yes or no. It was most commonly used in the 1950s.

TNS *See* transcutaneous nerve stimulation.

tocopherol *See* vitamin E.

toe **1** A digit of the foot. **2** A region of a shoe covering the toes.

toe extension Upward movement of the toe effected by the *toe extensors.

toe extensor A *muscle which acts to raise the toe upwards. Toe extensors are the *extensor digitorum longus for the outer toes, and the *extensor hallucis longus for the great toe.

toe flexion Movement of the toe downwards accomplished by *toe flexors.

toe flexor A *muscle which causes a toe to move downwards. The *flexor digitorum longus is the *prime mover for *flexion of the outer toes and the *flexor hallucis longus flexes the big toe.

toe-joint *See* interphalangeal joint.

tolerance **1** The capacity to endure pain or hardship, such in harsh environmental conditions or psychological stress. **2** Condition in which increasing doses of a *drug are required to maintain the same response. *See also* drug tolerance. **3** Failure of a body to mount a specific *immune response against a particular *antigen. Such immunological tolerance usually results from the body having difficulty distinguishing between its own materials, which should be tolerated, and foreign materials, which should be attacked by antibodies.

tomogram The visual record produced by *tomography.

tomography A process by which an image is produced through different planes of a body part using *X-rays or *ultrasound. *See also* computerized tomography.

tone A state of tension, such as that caused by a sustained, partial muscle contraction. *See also* tonus.

tonic **1** A *drug used to give a sense of well-being. Tonics may contain *stimulants, banned by the *IOC. **2** Related to *muscle tone.

tonicity **1** The state of normal partial contraction of a muscle. *See also* tonus. **2** A measure of the ability of a solution to cause a change in the volume or tone of a cell by promoting osmotic flows of water (*see* osmosis).

tonic muscle *See* antigravity muscle.

tonic stretch The type of stretch placed on a *muscle because of a load which affects the final length of the *muscle fibres. A light load stretches the fibres less than a heavy load. *Compare* phasic stretch.

tonsillitis *Inflammation of the *tonsils usually caused by *bacteria. Physical exertion during infection can lead to complications.

tonsils A mass of lymphoid tissue (*see* lymph), particularly the glands at the back of the throat.

tonus (tone) The resistance (tension) developed in a *muscle as a result of a *passive stretch on a muscle. Tonus is due to a sustained partial contraction of the muscle and is essential for maintaining body posture. The term is frequently misused to refer to the voluntary strength of a muscle.

topical application Application of a *drug directly to the part of the body being treated, usually the skin surface.

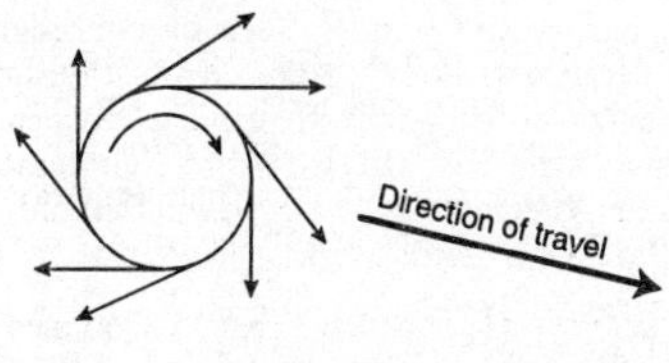

top spin

top spin A spin, typically of a ball, during which the top of the spinning body travels forward relative to the centre, and the bottom of the spinning body travels backward relative to the centre. The top spin modifies the *angular rotation in a clockwise direction around the *horizontal or *transverse axis. When a ball is hit by a bat, or some other implement, a top spin results from the back of the ball (that is, the part in contact with the bat) being lifted upward and forward during the strike. Generally, the spin will make the ball come off another surface with a greater *horizontal velocity than it possessed when it hit the surface, and the *angle of reflection is also greater than if no spin had been imparted to the ball.

torn cartilage *See* meniscus tear.

torn meniscus *See* meniscus tear.

torque (force moment; moment of couple; moment of force) A *force which produces a twisting or rotary movement in any plane about an *axis of motion. Torque occurs when bones move around each other at *joints which serve as the axes of movement. Thus, muscular force when applied over a *range of motion is measured as torque. Torque is a measure of the turning effect of a force on a lever given by: torque of lever = force × lever arm (or moment arm) distance, and also by: torque = moment of inertia×angular acceleration. A torque is sometimes referred to simply as a moment.

torque arm The force arm, lever arm, or moment arm. *See* force arm.

torr A unit of pressure equal to 1/760 standard atmospheric pressure, approximately 1 mmHg.

torsion Twisting of a part about an axis, produced by the application of two opposing *couples acting in parallel planes.

torsional modulus The ratio of *stress to *strain in an *elastic material when that material is being twisted. *See also* elastic modulus.

torsional rigidity The applied *torque needed to produce a unit angle of twist in a circular *elastic material; a measure of a body's resistance to *torsion.

torticollis (wryneck) A rigid *spasm of the *sternomastoid and *trapezius muscles causing the head and neck to be drawn painfully to one side. Torticollis may be *congenital but it can occur in young athletes after violent twisting of the neck (e.g., when heading in soccer).

torus fracture An outward buckling of the *cortex of the *distal end of a *bone shaft. The most common torus fracture is of the distal *radius. *See also* fracture.

total lung capacity (TLC) Volume of air in the lungs at the end of *maximal inspiration. It has a typical value of 5000 ml.

touch (tactile sense) The sense by which the size and shape of objects are perceived when they come into contact with the surface of the body. Touch popularly refers to a number of other senses which are diffused all over the body in addition to the touch sense proper. These are: the pressure sense, by which the heaviness and hardness of objects are perceived (*see* mechanoreceptors); the heat sense, by which increases in cutaneous temperature are perceived (*see* thermoreceptors); the cold sense, by which reductions in cutaneous temperature are perceived (*see* thermoreceptors); and the *pain sense, by which pricks, pinches, and other painful effects are perceived.

toxic Applied to poisonous substances.

toxicity The degree to which a substance is poisonous. Almost any substance in food, air, and water can become toxic if taken in a high enough concentration.

toxin A poisonous *protein formed by *bacteria, plants, and animals. Toxins act as *antigens in the body.

toxoid *Toxin which has had its poisonous element removed but which retains its ability to act as an *antigen and stimulate the production of *antibodies against the actual toxin.

trabecula (pl. trabeculae) **1** Small needle-like piece of *bone from which *spongy bone is formed. **2** A fibrous band of *connective tissue which supports functional cells and extends from the outer part into the interior of an *organ, dividing the organ into separate chambers.

trace-conditioning Method of *classical conditioning in which the *conditioned stimulus is removed before the appearance of the *unconditioned stimulus.

trace element An *element, usually a *metal, required by the body in minute amounts for health. These elements are required mainly as components of *enzymes, *vitamins, or *hormones, or are involved in the activation of enzymes.

trace mineral A *mineral salt which is required in very small amounts by the body to maintain health. *See also* trace elements.

tracer A material, usually a radioactive isotope, which can be used to trace the course of an *element or *compound through the body.

trachea (windpipe) A tube, reinforced with *cartilage and lined with ciliated *epithelium, which extends from the *larynx to the *bronchi.

tracking *See* guide movement.

tract **1** A group of *nerve fibres having the same origin, destination, and function in the *central nervous system. **2** A system of functionally-integrated structures (e.g., the *digestive tract).

traction The use of a pulling *force, especially referred to one used to counteract the *tension surrounding a broken bone (*see* fracture) so that the bone is kept correctly positioned during healing.

tragus The *cartilage which projects over the *external auditory meatus of the *outer ear.

trainability principle A principle of *training which suggests that the more extensively the body is trained for a given performance factor, the less there remains of that factor to be trained in the future.

training An exercise programme designed to assist the *learning of *skills, to improve *physical fitness, and thereby to prepare an athlete for a particular competition. Training includes *conditioning, specific technical training, and psychological preparation. *Compare* practice.

training dose *See* training impulse.

training duration **1** The length of time that a *training session lasts. The optimum duration of training will depend on the intensity of the session and the level of fitness of the individual, but a minimum period of 15 minutes is recommended for the improvement of health. **2** The length of time for a particular training programme. The minimum period required for improvements to occur varies considerably, but it tends to be longer for *aerobic activities (at least 12 weeks) than *anaerobic activities (at least 8 weeks).

training effects The functional physiological adaptations which have been linked with *training and physical exercise. Research has shown that regular training tends to increase the following: *articular cartilage thickness; *ATP in *muscle; *arterial–venous oxygen difference at maximal workload; *blood lactate at maximal workload; *blood volume; *capillarization of muscle (including *cardiac muscle); *creatine phosphate in *muscle fibres; *diffusing capacity of the lungs at maximal workload; *diphosphoglycerate in the blood; fibrolytic activity (*see* fibrolysis);

*haemoglobin content; heart volume; heart weight; *high density lipoproteins in the blood; *joint mobility; *lean body-mass; muscle cross-sectional area; *muscle glycogen content; *muscle strength; *myocardial contractility; *myoglobin in muscle; mitochondrial size and density in muscle cells; *phosphofructokinase activity in muscle *mitochondria; *potassium in muscle; *pulmonary ventilation at maximal workload; *respiratory rate at maximal workload; *speed of limb movement; *strength of *bones and *ligaments; *stress tolerance; *stroke volume; and *succinic dehydrogenase activity in mitochondria. Regular training tends to decrease *arterial blood pressure; *blood cholesterol; blood lactate at a given workload; *glycogen utilization; *heart rate at submaximal workloads; heart rate at rest; *low density lipoproteins in the blood; *myocardial infarction risks; *obesity; *oxygen uptake at a given workload; *platelet stickiness; pulmonary ventilation for a given workload; *stress; and *triglycerides in the blood. Many of the effects are produced by regular, progressive *aerobic training, but it must be emphasized that no one form of training will produce all the effects listed.

training frequency The number of times per week *training is undertaken. Some coaches advocate training on seven days in a week, but recommended frequencies vary considerably. As a rough guideline, it has been suggested that *aerobic training should occur at least four to five times a week, anaerobic training three times per week, and training for health at least three times per week.

training heart rate (THR; training target heart rate) The heart rate which indicates a level of intensity of exercise that produces maximum training effects. There are a number of methods of computing the training heart rate but the method commonly used is to take a range of 60–80 per cent of maximum heart rate. The target heart rate will vary for the type of activity and the fitness level of the individual. *Anaerobic training requires higher heart rates (up to 95 per cent maximum heart rate) sustained for short periods, while *aerobic training requires lower heart rates sustained for long periods. Unfit people should train at the lowest end of the range. Individuals with health problems need medical advice concerning their level of activity. *See also* maximum heart rate method.

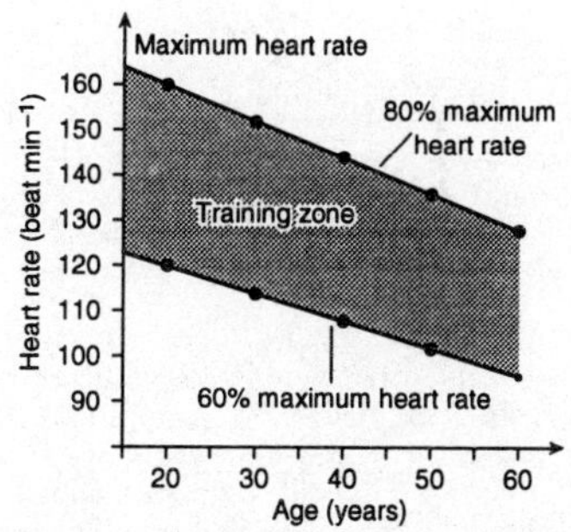

training heart rate

training impulse A measure of an athlete's level of training during a *training session assessed from the changes in *heart rate during the exercise, the duration of the training session, and the intensity of effort during the session. The training impulse is expressed in arbitrary units.

training intensity The effort of *training. A number of methods are used to establish training intensities which give maximum benefits. These include the *lactic acid method, *minute ventilation method, and *target heart rate.

training principles Basic principles which must be followed if improvements from training are to be maximized. *See also* overload principle; principle of progression; and specificity principle.

training programme A plan or schedule for *training. *See also* periodization.

training session A continuous period of time devoted to *training. A single session might include several *training units.

training shoe Footwear designed specifically for protection during *training. There are many different models and types but most incorporate features to cope with the

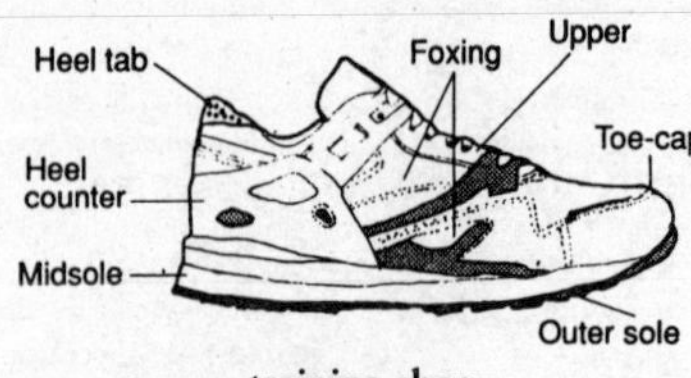

training shoe

*stress caused by the *forces which occur when the foot strikes the ground and the forces exerted by the sideways movements of the foot whilst still in contact with the ground. The parts of the training shoe include the *arch support, *external heel counter support, *heel-counter, *heel tab, *insock, *midsock, *midsole, and *outsole.

training target heart rate *See* target heart rate.

training time The rate at which exercise is to be accomplished during an exercise or work interval in an *interval training programme. A training time of 30s for 200m, for example, would mean that an athlete aims to complete the 200m in 30s.

training unit A single period of *training aimed at achieving a specified objective. The objective may be to develop *aerobic endurance in which case the unit might be a steady run of 16km. *See also* training session.

training zone A range of *heart rates indicating an intensity of effort which should be undertaken if training is to be beneficial. *See also* aerobic training zone; anaerobic training zone; and training heart rate.

trait A relatively stable predisposition to act in a certain way. Traits are usually applied to *personality and each trait is often represented as a two-dimensional construct (e.g., honest–dishonest, assertive–nonassertive) represented by a scale along which an individual can be rated. Traits are viewed as being consistent across a wide variety of different situations (*see* trait theory).

trait aggression A relatively stable *personality predisposition to respond to certain situations with acts of *aggression. *Compare* state aggression.

trait anxiety (general trait anxiety) A general tendency to exhibit *anxiety. Individuals with high trait anxiety are predisposed to perceive a wide range of situations as dangerous or threatening, and to respond to those situations with increased *state anxiety. *See also* competitive trait anxiety.

trait anxiety inventory (TAI) A measure of *trait anxiety which consists of twenty items to which the subject responds using a Likert-type scale. TAI is often used as a companion test to SAI (*see* state anxiety inventory).

trait perspective A view of *personality which suggests that personality traits are relatively enduring qualities which can be used to predict an individual's behaviour in a variety of situations.

trait theory A theory which describes individual differences of *personality in terms of *traits. *See also* trait perspective.

trait theory of leadership A theory which proposes that successful leaders have certain *personality characteristics or *leadership traits that make it possible for them to be successful leaders in any situation. This theory is also known as the 'great man' theory of leadership. There seems to be little support for a universal set of personality traits common to all successful leaders. *See also* universal behaviours.

trajectory The flight-path that a *projectile follows in its passage through the air.

tranquillizer A *drug that has a calming effect, reduces *anxiety, and relieves tension.

transcendental meditation A relaxation method that features the repetition of a *mantra. It has been used by some athletes to attain a state of calmness before competition.

transcutaneous electrical nerve stimulation *See* Trancutaneous nerve stimulation.

transcutaneous nerve stimulation (TENS; TNS; Transcutaneous electrical nerve stimulation) A technique used to relieve *pain. A weak electrical current is discharged through electrodes placed at strategic points on the skin in order to inhibit information about tissue injury from *pain receptors from reaching the *central nervous system. Research shows that transcutaneous nerve stimulation results in the release of *encephalins and *endorphins.

transducer A device that transforms energy from one form to another.

transfer design An experimental design for measuring learning effects in which all treatment groups are transferred to a common level of the *independent variable; that is, all groups practise the relevant task with the same value for the independent variable.

transfer of learning The effect that learning one *skill has on the subsequent learning of other skills. The learning of the new skill may be speeded up, slowed down, or may not be affected at all by previous learning. *See also* bilateral transfer; negative transfer; positive transfer; transfer of training; and zero transfer.

transfer of momentum The process whereby *momentum is transferred from one part of a body to another in accordance with the *conservation of momentum principle. Airborne movements which include somersaulting and twisting generally involve a transfer from the somersaulting *angular momentum, initiated during the take-off, for the twisting angular momentum performed during the flight.

transfer of training The effect of one form of *training on another form of training. *See also* transfer of learning; and transfer principle.

transfer principle A principle of training which states that the effects of one form of training on another will depend on the similarity between the two. The transfer principle emphasizes the independent nature of factors such as strength, endurance, and flexibility, and suggests that *positive transfer will only occur for those factors that are shared by the two forms of training.

transferrin (siderophilin) A *protein which transports *iron in the *blood.

transfusion The administration of a fluid (such as *saline, *plasma, or *blood) into the *circulatory system. The fluid is allowed to drip into the subject's *vein under gravity. *See also* blood doping.

transition period A period which allows an athlete to recover both physically and mentally following *training or *competition. During the transition period, there is a gradual reduction of training intensity but the athlete continues to exercise to maintain a reasonable level of general fitness. During this time emphasis is usually on physical and emotional relaxation involving leisure pursuits. *See also* periodization.

translation (linear motion; translatory motion) Form of motion in which all parts of a body travel exactly the same distance, in the same direction, in the same time. *Compare* angular motion. *See also* curvilinear translation; and rectilinear translation.

translatory motion *See* translation.

transmitter *See* neurotransmitter.

transverse In *anatomy, situated at right angles to the *longitudinal axis of a body or organ.

transverse axis *See* mediolateral axis.

transverse chest width The distance across the lateral aspect of the *thorax, at the level of the most lateral aspect of the fourth rib. *See also* body breadths.

transverse foramina *See* cervical vertebra.

transverse plane A plane which runs horizontally across the *longitudinal axis of a body or organ, dividing it into its *superior or *inferior parts. *See also* horizontal plane.

transverse process The long projections that extend laterally from each *neural arch of a *vertebra.

transversus *See* transversus abdominis.

transversus abdominis (transversus) The deepest of the four pairs of *abdominal muscles. The transversus abdominis has its *origins on the *inguinal ligament, lumbodorsal *fascia, and *cartilage of the last six ribs. It has its *insertion on the *linea alba and *pubic symphysis. The main action of the transversus abdominis is compression of the abdominal contents.

trapezium A wrist-bone which articulates with the first *metacarpal in front, the *trapezoid and second metacarpal on the side, and the *scaphoid bone behind.

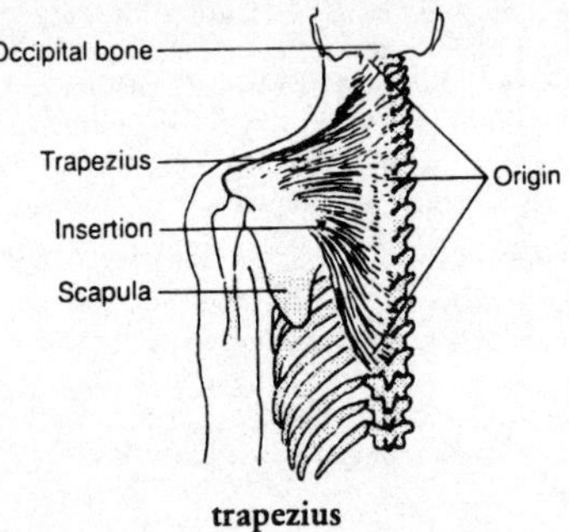

trapezius

trapezius The most *superficial muscle of the *posterior *thorax. The trapezius is flat and triangular in shape with its *origins on the *occipital bone, the *ligamentum nuchae, and the *spines of the *vertebrae. It has a continuous *insertion along the *acromion and spine of the *scapula, and the *lateral part of the *clavicle. The trapezius *adducts and rotates the scapula upwards (via the upper fibres) and downwards (via the lower fibres). It also assists in turning the head and extending the neck backwards.

trapezoid bone A wrist-bone which articulates with the second *metacarpal in front, the *trapezium on one side and the *capitate on the other, and the *scaphoid in front. *See also* carpus.

trauma 1 Physical damage caused by a blow, often the result of an external force. 2 An event causing psychological shock that may have long-lasting effects and which may lead to a *neurosis.

traumatic arthritis *Inflammation of a *joint due to an injury; it is the most common form of *arthritis in sport.

traumatic injury An *acute injury resulting in physical damage. *See also* trauma.

traumatic encephalopathy *See* encephalopathy.

traumatology The study of injuries, including recovery from injury. Sport traumatology is especially concerned with enabling an athlete to be sufficiently rehabilitated to participate in competitions at maximum capacity.

traveller's diarrhoea A notoriously disabling condition which often inflicts a touring sports team when the dietary and hygiene environment is poor. It is usually caused by an unaccustomed strain of the *bacterium, *Escherichia coli.* *Anxiety and change of *diet may also induce *diarrhoea.

travel sickness (motion sickness) A condition caused by stimulation of the organ of balance in the ear which gives rise to *nausea, *vertigo, and *vomiting. *Adrenergic and *anticholinergic drugs tend to diminish travel sickness. *Antihistamines, which have an anticholinergic effect, are commonly used to treat travel sickness but they can cause drowsiness which detracts from performance. Travel sickness can be a considerable handicap in sports such as sailing and motor-racing.

treadmill An *ergometer with a side-moving belt on which the subject walks or runs. The workload can be adjusted by changing the speed of the belt and the angle of inclination (gradient) of the belt.

tremor A rhythmical quivering movement that may affect any part of the body. Tremor may be a normal accompaniment of *isometric contractions which maintain *posture. These physiological tremors tend to increase in states of *fatigue or *anxiety. Tremor may also be due to *disease. *See also* essential tremor.

Trendelenburg's sign A *sign of *dislocation of the *pelvis. The subject stands on one leg while flexing (*see* flexion) the knee and hip of the other leg. Dislocation is indicated if the pelvis is lower on the side of the flexed leg, the reverse of the normal situation.

treppe The staircase effect of successive increases in the extent of contractions following rapid, repeated stimulation of a *muscle.

triad 1 Social interaction or relationship comprising three elements. *Compare* dyad. 2 In *medicine, a group of three closely-associated structures, or three symptoms which tend to occur together. *See also* triad response.

triad response A set of three nonspecific general responses to prolonged *stress observed in laboratory animals which has also been observed in some athletes under stress: enlargement of the *adrenal cortex, shrinking of *lymphatic tissue, and ulceration of the stomach-lining and duodenum (*see* peptic ulcer).

triad vesicle (T-vesicle) A *sac in a *muscle fibre which contains cellular secretions, such as *calcium ions, required to initiate *muscle contraction.

trial A single response in a test.

trial-and-error learning *Learning, common in nonhuman animals, which is marked by the performance of successive, apparently random responses to a situation until one response achieves a successful outcome. Trial-and-error learning is believed to involve *classical conditioning followed by *operant conditioning. *Compare* insight.

trials-delay technique Procedure in which *knowledge of results for a particular response are given after one or more other responses. Research has found that this has a detrimental effect on motor performance, but a positive effect on *motor-learning.

triamterene A *drug belonging to the *diuretics which are on the *IOC list of *banned substances.

triangle of forces A triangle which can be drawn when the magnitude and direction of three *forces, represented by the sides of the triangle, are in *equilibrium and acting at the same point. *See also* triangle of velocities.

triangle of velocities A triangle which can be drawn when the magnitude and direction of three component *velocities of a body at rest are represented by the sides of a triangle. *See also* triangle of forces.

tribology The science of *friction and lubrication.

tricarboxylic acid cycle *See* Krebs cycle.

triceps A muscle which has three heads of origin. *See also* triceps brachii.

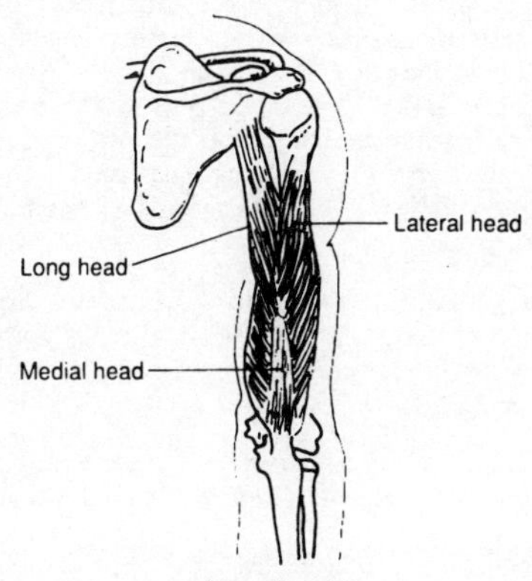

triceps brachii

triceps brachii (triceps) A large fleshy *muscle of the posterior compartment of the arm. It has three heads of *origin: the long head is attached to the infraglenoid tubercle of the *scapula; the lateral head is attached to the posterior *humerus; and the medial head is attached to the posterior humerus, *distal to the *radial groove. Its *insertion is by a common *tendon onto the *olecranon process of the *ulna. The triceps is a powerful *extensor of the forearm and is an *antagonist to the *flexors, such as the *brachialis. The long head helps to stabilize and adduct the scapula.

triceps skinfold A *skinfold measurement of a vertical fold of tissue midline between the *acromiale and the *radiale on the posterior surface of the arm.

triceps surae The name given by some anatomists to the *gastrocnemius and the *soleus muscles which shape the posterior calf and insert via a common *tendon into the *calcaneus of the heel. The gastrocnemius has two *heads and the soleus one head.

tricuspid valve A *valve with three flaps which occurs between the right *atrium and right *ventricle of the *heart. It ensures that blood flows from the atrium to ventricles by closing and preventing backflow during *ventricular systole.

Triesman model A complex model of *selective attention which contains elements of both the *Broadbent model and the *pertinence model. The model proposes that all sensory information reaches the memory for analysis, but that irrelevant cues are *attenuated while relevant information is attended to.

trigeminal nerve A *nerve supplying the side of the face. The trigeminal nerve consists of three branches of the fifth *cranial nerve.

triggered reaction A prestructured response to an environmental *stimulus that is thought to be triggered into action by the sensations produced by *stretch receptors. Triggered reaction time is faster than *reaction time.

trigger finger Thickening and hardening of the *flexor tendon or its *tendon sheath at a *metacarpophalangeal joint. The affected finger can flex but it then yields quickly and *extension is impaired.

trigger point A localized palpable spot of deep hypersensitivity which, when irritated, results in pain being referred to another area of the body (*see* referred pain). A trigger point in the shoulder, for example, might cause a headache. This condition is referred to as myofascial pain syndrome, and is often caused by *muscle tension, *fatigue, or *strain. The trigger point usually coincides with a tight band or knot in a *muscle or the *fascia of a muscle.

triglyceride (neutral fat) An *ester of three *fatty acids and *glycerol. Triglycerides are the main components of animal and plant *lipids. They are the most concentrated source of usable energy in the human body and are stored in *subcutaneous fat deposits where they contribute to insulation.

triiodothyronine *See* thyroid hormone.

triple-jumper's heel A *strain of the tissues in the heel, sometimes accompanied by a *bony spur in the *calcaneus. Triple-jumper's heel is commonly caused by banging the heel in the landing phase of a jump.

tritium A radioactive isotope of *hydrogen which has been used as a *tracer.

triquetral bone (triquetrum) A wristbone which articulates with the *hamate in front, the *lunate and *pisiform to the side, and the *ulna behind. *See also* carpus.

triquetrum *See* triquetral bone.

trochanter A large blunt, irregularly shaped prominence on the *femur. *See also* greater trochanter; and lesser trochanter.

trochanteric bursa A *bursa lying above the *greater trochanter.

trochanteric bursitis *Pain over the bony prominence on either side of the upper thigh due to *inflammation of the *bursa which is interposed between the *greater trochanter towards the top of the *femur and the overlying *muscle. Trochanteric bursitis usually results from poor *muscular co-ordination and an abnormal *gait during running.

trochanterion A *landmark which is the most *superior point on the *greater trochanter of the *femur.

trochanterion height A *body height measured from *trochanterion to *base.

trochlea A structure which is shaped like a *pulley or functions like a pulley. Examples are the trochleas, at the *distal ends of the *humerus and *femur, which are smooth depressions between the *condyles.

trochlear nerve A *nerve which supplies one of the eye muscles; the fourth *cranial nerve.

trochoidal In *anatomy, applied to a structure resembling, or functioning as, a *pivot or *pulley.

trochoides *See* pivot-joint.

trochoid joint *See* pivot-joint.

trophic Pertaining to nutrition or nourishment.

tropic hormone A *hormone which has a regulatory effect on another *endocrine gland.

tropomyosin A rod-shaped *protein found in *thin filaments of a muscle *sarcomere. Tropomyosin has a regulatory function on *actin. When *calcium ion concentration is low within a *muscle fibre, the tropomyosin inhibits *muscle contraction by blocking the binding site on actin, thereby preventing *myosin cross-bridges from attaching. *See also* troponin.

troponin A complex of three *polypeptides found in *muscle sarcomeres. One polypeptide (Tn1) binds to *actin, another (TnT) binds to *tropomyosin, and the third (TnC) binds to *calcium ions. When calcium ions bind to troponin, the troponin undergoes a shape-change that forces tropomyosin away from the actin filaments, allowing *myosin cross-bridges to bind onto the actin which allows contractions to occur. *See also* sliding-filament theory.

true ribs (vertebrospinal ribs) The upper seven *rib pairs attached to the *sternum by individual *costal cartilages. *Compare* false ribs.

trunk The human body excluding the head, neck, and limbs.

trunk circumduction A sequence of circling movements of the trunk occurring in the *sagittal plane, *frontal plane, and *oblique plane so that the movement as a whole describes a cone.

trunk extension (back extension) A movement which returns the *trunk to the *anatomical position from *trunk flexion, or which produces a backward movement of the *spine. Muscles involved include the *quadratus lumborum and *erector spinae.

trunk extensor A muscle which effects *trunk extension.

trunk flexion (back flexion) A movement which returns the *trunk to the *anatomical position from *trunk extension, or which produces a forward movement of the *spine. Muscles involved include the *obliquus externus abdominis, the *obliquus internus abdominis, and the *rectus abdominis.

trunk flexor A muscle which effects *trunk flexion.

trunk lateral flexion Movement of the *trunk to the left or right, which involves movement of the shoulder towards the hip on either side. The movement involves the action on one side of the body of the external and internal *oblique muscles, and the *quadratus lumborum.

trunk movements Movements of the trunk region of the body which can be effected by movements at the hip, and in the *lumbar and *thoracic regions of the *vertebral column. Trunk movements include *trunk circumduction, *trunk extension, *trunk flexion, *trunk lateral flexion, and *trunk rotation.

trunk rotation A rotary movement of the *spine in the horizontal plane. Trunk rotation may be to the left or to the right.

trunk strength The strength of muscles, particularly the *abdominal muscles, in relation to their ability to move the *trunk repeatedly or to support the trunk for a period of time. Trunk strength is an important component of physical fitness.

truth value The credibility of data acquired through a *naturalistic approach to research. To possess truth value, the interpretation of data must accurately reflect what the subjects have reported.

trypsin An *enzyme which acts in the *duodenum to continue the *digestion of *proteins into *amino acids.

trypsinogen An inactive precursor of *trypsin secreted by the *pancreas.

tryptophan An *essential amino acid found in some grains (such as corn) and some legumes (such as beans).

TSH *See* thyroid stimulating hormone.

T-system The network of *T-tubules within each *muscle fibre.

T-TAIS A sport-specific *test of attentional and interpersonal style which has been adapted for use in tennis. The inventory includes a series of questions which are specific to that sport. It is thought to have greater validity and predictive value than the more general TAIS.

***t* test** *See* Student's *t* test.

T-tubules Extensions of the *sarcolemma of a *muscle fibre that run between the *terminal cisternae of the *sarcoplasmic reticulum and protrude deeply into the muscle fibre. The tubules allow an electical *stimulus and extracellular fluid to come into close contact with the deep regions of the muscle fibre.

tubercle A nodule or small rounded process on a bone, smaller than a *tuberosity.

tuberosity A large rounded projection on a bone, larger than a *tubercle.

tumor A swelling; one of the signs of *inflammation. *See also* tumour.

tumour An abnormal swelling due to the growth of cells. Tumours may be *benign or *malignant.

tunica A membrane layer; a covering or *tissue coat.

tunica adventitia (tunica externa) The external covering of an *artery or *vein.

tunica externa *See* tunica adventitia.

tunica intima The inner lining of an *artery or *vein.

tunica media The middle layer of the wall of an *artery or a *vein. The tunica media contains *smooth muscle and *elastic fibrous tissue.

tunnel A canal or hollow groove which may form a passageway for *nerves or *blood vessels through a body structure.

turbulent flow The flow of a *fluid in which the motion at any point varies rapidly in both magnitude and direction. *Compare* laminar flow.

turf toe syndrome Swelling and pain at the base of the big toe (*see* hallux) caused by the foot sliding forward in a shoe (e.g., when stopping suddenly on artificial turf). The big toe is bent upward, stretching the *ligaments, and injuring the *articular surface and the *joint capsule. Sliding of the foot in the shoe may also result in *black nail and even a *fracture of the toe.

turgid Distended and congested, usually with *blood.

turgor The state of being distended and congested.

TV *See* tidal volume.

T-vesicle *See* triad vesicle.

T wave A deflection on an *electrocardiograph which follows the *QRS complex and represents *repolarization of the *ventricles.

twelve-minute test A test of *aerobic capacity in which the subject runs as far as possible in twelve minutes. *See also* Cooper test.

twin method The use of identical twins to study the effects of inheritance and environmental factors on an individual trait. This method may involve comparing the differences between identical twins who have been brought up in distinctly different environments, when differences in traits are hypothesized to be due to the effects of environmental factors. Another procedure involves subjecting one of the identical twins to a test while the other member is held as a control. The difference between the two during and after the test is used as a measure of the effect of the test (assuming other variables are constant). Genetic control of a trait may be studied by comparing a trait in a large sample of identical and nonidentical twins in comparable environments. If the similarity between the identical twins is greater than that between the nonidentical twins, the trait is assumed to be under genetic control.

twisting In a biomechanical system, a complex movement of rotation around the *longitudinal axis which is derived from rotation about the other two cardinal axes (*see* *x*-axis; and *y*-axis). In diving, the body may rotate around its own *transverse axis (rotation); the body's own axis of rotation may describe a curve round another axis (precession); and the angle between these axes of the body's own rotation and precession may vary (nutation).

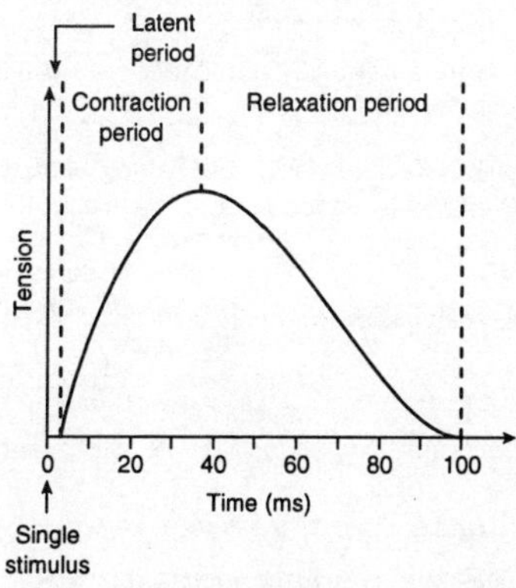

twitch

twitch 1 A brief contraction of muscle, for example, the solens muscle, in response to a *stimulus. 2 The response of a *motor unit to a single brief *threshold stimulus. A twitch has three phases: a *latent period; a period of contraction; and a period of relaxation. *See also* refractory period.

two-process theory A theory which proposes that both *classical conditioning and *operant conditioning are usually present in any learning situation, and that classical conditioning provides the motivation for operant conditioning.

two-tailed t-test Type of *t-test used when comparing the *means of two groups and it has not been anticipated which will be the greater or lesser.

tympanic membrane The eardrum; a tight membrane separating the *outer ear and *middle ear, and connected to the earbones. The membrane vibrates when sound pressure waves pass along the outer ear towards the middle ear.

type Any class or category with shared characteristics.

Type A behaviour A form of behaviour characterized by a high level of aggression, competition, drive, time urgency, and vigorous voice stylistics. Type A behaviour has been linked with increased risk of *coronary heart disease. *Compare* type B behaviour.

Type B behaviour A form of behaviour characterized by an easy-going, nonaggressive, and noncompetitive attitude. *Compare* type A behaviour.

type I fibre *See* slow twitch fibre.

type II fibre *See* fast twitch fibre.

type IIa fibre *See* fast oxidative glycolytic fibre.

type IIb fibre *See* fast glycolytic fibre.

type IIc fibre A *fast twitch fibre with contractile characteristics intermediate between *slow twitch fibres and *fast twitch fibres.

typical response The manner in which a person usually responds to particular environmental situations. Typical responses, when distinguished from play-acting, may be valid indicators of the *psychological core of an individual's *personality.

typical value In a pulmonary function test, the value obtained from a healthy, resting, recumbent young male ($1.7 m^2$ of lung surface area), breathing air at sea level. The results of pulmonary function tests vary with changes of position, age, size, sex, and altitude.

typology The study of symbolic representations.

tyramine An *amine, found in cheeses, game, broad bean pods, yeast extracts, wine, and strong beer, which has effects similar to those of *adrenaline.

tyrosine A nonessential *amino acid which can substitute for *phenylalanine.

U

ulcer *Lesion or erosion of the skin or *mucous membrane (e.g., of the *stomach). *See also* peptic ulcer.

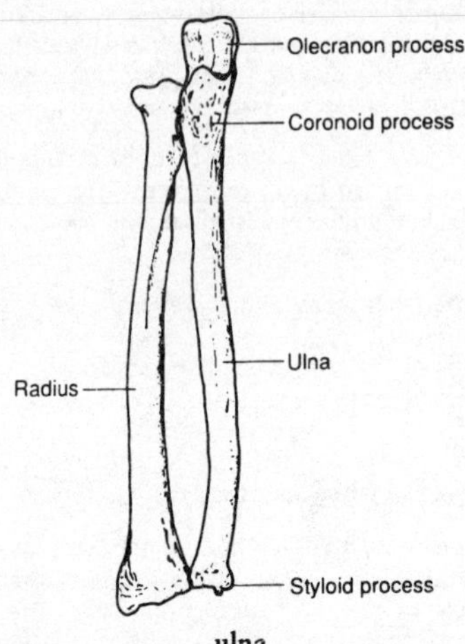

ulna

ulna A *long bone in the forearm which forms the *elbow-joint with the *humerus. In the *anatomical position, the ulna lies medially, away from thumb side. The ulna articulates proximally with the *radius and humerus, and distally with the radius and *carpals. A right ulna and radius (front view) is illustrated above.

ulnar Pertaining to the *ulna.

ulnar artery An *artery which runs alongside the *ulna in the forearm.

ulnar collateral ligament A triangular shaped band of ligamentous tissue which helps to stabilize the elbow-joint. The ulnar collateral ligament consists of three parts: an *anterior portion running from the *medial epicondyle to the *coronoid process; a *posterior portion which runs from the medial epicondyle to the *olecranon; and a *transverse band connecting the olecranon part of the posterior portion to the coronoid part of the anterior portion.

ulnar nerve One of three *nerves which supply the lower arm and hands. The ulnar nerve runs along the medial edge of the elbow just behind the *epicondyle to which the *flexor muscles of the wrist are attached. The ulnar nerve is susceptible to *entrapment in throwing or racket sports when the nerve can be compressed within its groove with subequent mechanical irritation.

ulnar neuritis *Inflammation of the *ulnar nerve which may occur when the nerve is subjected to *pressure. Vulnerable points are at the level of the elbow and where the nerve crosses the wrist on the inner aspect of the hand. The pressure can be caused by *friction of local tissues on the nerve, as happens during cycling. Ulnar neuritis is marked by muscular weakness on attempting to spread the fingers, tingling, and numbness in the little finger.

ulnar palsy *Paralysis or weakness in the hand due to pressure on the *ulnar nerve. *See also* ulnar neuritis.

ultimate strength *See* ultimate stress.

ultimate stress (ultimate strength) The load required to fracture a material expressed as *force per original unit area of its cross-section at the point of fracture.

ultracentrifuge Machine capable of spinning at more than 50000 revolutions per minute and of separating cellular components.

ultrafiltration Process by which small *molecules and *ions in blood are separated from larger molecules to form *glomerular filtrate or *tissue fluid.

ultrasonics The study and application of very high frequencies of sound beyond the limits of human hearing (frequencies of about 20kHz and above). *See also* ultrasound treatment.

ultrasonography The use of sound frquencies above 30kHz to produce images of structures within the human body. A beam of *ultrasound is directed into the body and its echoes are electrically analysed to produce the image.

ultrasound Sound frequencies beyond the limits of human hearing (frequencies above 20kHz).

ultrasound treatment The use of *ultrasonics in the treatment of disorders. Ultrasound is a popular treatment of deep, soft tissue injuries. It is believed to have a mechanical effect, accelerating the healing process; vibrating and loosening *scar tissue; and encouraging the reabsorption, at the cellular level, of blood or lymph which has escaped into surrounding tissue. The vibrations may reduce sensory stimulation and relieve *pain; they also produce heat at a deep level.

ultraviolet light *Electromagnetic radiation with short wavelengths and lying outside the visible spectrum of light. Sunlight contains ultraviolet light which causes *sunburn.

umbilical In *anatomy, pertaining to the navel.

umbilical cord Cord consisting of *blood vessels and *connective tissue, joining an *embryo to the mother's *placenta.

umbilicus (navel) A depression in the *abdomen which marks the site where the *umbilical cord was attached at the foetal stage.

unciform bone *See* hamate bone.

unconscious Part of the mind dealing with mental processes which are below the level of awareness. According to proponents of Freudian theory, the unconscious plays a major part in mental functioning and contains instincts, memories, and emotions which have been repressed (*see* repression). These repressed feelings are the stimuli for actions and *behaviour. *Compare* subconsious. *See also* id.

unconscious motivation Urges (such as fears, hopes, and desires) of which the individual is not aware and which are presumed to be repressed.

unconsciousness Loss of conciousness. It may be due to a head injury caused by a blow (e.g., in boxing). *See also* concussion.

unconditioned response An original or inborn response such as salivation stimulated by food in the mouth, withdrawal from an injurious *stimulus, or contraction of the pupil to light. In *classical conditioning, an unconditioned responsed is elicited by an *unconditioned stimulus.

underdetermination A view that the truth of a theory is underdetermined by the total evidence available; that is, a number of theories (technically, an infinite number) can equally, though differently, account for the same finite body of evidence.

underload principle A principle of *training which suggests that if regular muscular activity levels are less than normal, the *force capacity of the muscles decreases. *Compare* overload principle.

unfitness A condition in which an individual is unable to meet the demands of his or her work or way of life. Unfitness may be caused by an organic illness, physical defect, *malnutrition, lack of *muscular strength, or by social, emotional, and psychological maladjustment.

unhappy triad Classic *knee injury, first described as occurring in American Football, in which there is tearing of the *medial collateral ligament, the anterior cruciate ligament, and medial *cartilage.

uniarticular muscle A *muscle which takes part in the movement of one *joint only.

uniaxial movement Movement in one *plane only.

unidirectional information transmission The one-way transmission of informational *cues from one or more members of a *group to another member or members of the group. *Compare* omnidirectional information transmission; and social facilitation.

uniform acceleration The condition of a body which maintains the same magnitude and direction of *acceleration.

uniform angular motion The motion of a body which is rotating in such a way that equal angles are traversed in equal units of time.

uniform speed Speed of a body which is constant over a certain period of time.

unilateral Pertaining to one side of the body or body-part.

unilateral muscular hypertrophy Development of muscle bulk on one side of the body more than the other, commonly occurring in sportspeople with 'one arm' action; for example, shot-putters, tennis players, and oarsmen and women who row on one side of the body. *See also* tennis shoulder.

union The healing together of tissue, such as the broken ends of a fractured bone, which has been separated.

unipennate muscle *See* pennate muscle.

unipolar neurone A *neurone from which only one main process extends from the *cell body.

unisex reference human *See* phantom.

unit Quantity adopted as a standard for measurement. *See also* *SI unit.

unitary task *Task in which all participants perform in the same or a very similar manner. *Compare* divisible task.

universal behaviours A certain set of *leadership behaviours believed to be possessed by all successful leaders. Unlike traits, these behaviours can be learned. *See also* trait theory of leadership.

universal donor An individual with blood group O who has no A or B *antigens. Consequently, the blood type of a universal donor will not react with the recipient's and the blood can be given to any other ABO type. The term applies only to the ABO blood grouping; other blood groups are important in *blood transfusion and the term universal donor is, therefore, rather misleading.

universal functionalism *See* postulate of functional indispensibility.

universal trait One of a certain set of *personality traits believed to be shared by all successful leaders.

unmyelinated fibre *See* myelin sheath.

unobtrusive measure A research method, commonly used in qualitative sociological research, in which data is obtained without the knowledge of the subject and without affecting the data collected (e.g., the recording of player behaviour during a football match using hidden cameras).

unsaturated fat *Fat which contains one or more double or triple bonds and which is therefore able to incorporate additional *hydrogen atoms. Unsaturated fats are typically liquid (oil) at room temperature. The main dietary sources for unsaturated fats are plants and fish.

unstable equilibrium

unstable equilibrium The state of a body which, when slightly displaced, tends to be displaced further. *Compare* stable equilibrium.

unstable factor In *causal attribution theory, a factor which may be assumed to change over a period of time; for example, weather conditions, the amount of effort an individual applies to a task, or random chance (luck). *Compare* stable factor.

unstable joint A *joint in which there is abnormal movement and which is unable to support normal loads. An unstable joint may be due to ruptured or congenitally very lax ligaments, or to the malfunctioning of muscles which share a dynamic function by exerting gentle contractions, even at rest, to support the joint.

unstructured data Data which has been gathered without regard to the way it is to be analysed and interpreted. Much qualitative data, for instance, verbal answers to open-ended questions, are of this nature.

unstructured interview An interview in which the interviewer relinquishes control over the content and pattern of the questions, and in which the interviewee is not limited to a set of fixed responses. *See also* open-ended question.

upper limb Part of the body which includes the arm, forearm, and hand. The upper limb is relatively light compared with the lower limb, and is adapted for *flexibility rather than strength.

uppers *See* amphetamines.

upward mobility A form of *social mobility which results in a person moving to a higher *social class or socioeconomic status. The term is also applied to a sportsperson moving from a lower level of sport to a higher level at which there is an increase in *status among peers.

urea An organic molecule which is the major excretory product of *protein *metabolism. Urea is formed in the *liver from *carbon dioxide and *ammonia during the *ornithine cycle. It is eliminated in *urine and, to a much lesser extent, in *sweat.

ureter The duct which carries *urine from each *kidney to the *bladder.

ureteritis *Inflammation of the *ureter. Ureteritis commonly occurs with *cystitis.

urethra The duct which discharges *urine from the *bladder to the exterior.

urethritis *Inflammation of the *urethra commonly caused by bacterial *infection. Urethritis often occurs simultaneously with *cystitis. Athletes who suffer from urethritis are generally advised not to take part in physically demanding activities whilst undergoing treatment, and to resume training only when the infection clears.

uric acid An end-product of the *metabolism of *nucleic acids which is a normal constituent of *urine. Excessive amounts of uric acid in the blood are associated with *gout.

urinalysis The laboratory examination of a *urine sample to test for the presence of *bacteria or chemicals such as *sugar or *alcohol.

urination *See* micturition.

urine An *aqueous solution of inorganic and organic *salts, which include *urea, representing the *nitrogen waste products of *metabolism excreted by the *kidneys.

uriniferous tubule *Kidney tubule which extends from the *Bowman's capsule to the collecting duct.

urocamic acid An acid, present is *sweat, which is believed to offer some protection to the skin against ultraviolet radiation.

urokinase An *enzyme in *urine which causes the breakdown of *fibrin.

urticaria (hives; nettle-rash) An *acute or *chronic condition characterized by the appearance of itchy weals on the skin. The cause may be an allergy to certain foods (such as strawberries), *infection, *drugs, emotional stress, or local skin irritation resulting from contact with certain plants.

US RDA A version of the figures for *recommended daily allowances used by the United States *Food and Drug Administration for the legal regulation of food labelling in the United States. The values, based on RDAs, are expressed in percentages and are used for all persons over four years old.

uterine tube (fallopian tube) A tube through which the *ovum is transported to the *uterus.

uterus (womb) Enlarged posterior part of the *oviduct in which a fertilized egg implants. The main function of the uterus is to nourish and protect the *foetus during *pregnancy.

uvea The pigmented layer of the eye consisting mainly of the *iris with the *ciliary body and *choroid.

uvula The tissue tag which hangs from the soft palate.

V

V A symbol commonly used by pulmonary physiologists to refer to the volume of a gas.

V̇ A symbol commonly used by pulmonary physiologists to refer to the volume of a gas per unit time (usually 1 min).

v 1 A symbol commonly used by physiologists to refer to venous blood. **2** A symbol for voltage.

vaccination The administration of a *vaccine to confer *immunity against a specific *disease. Originally, the term was confined to the use of vaccinia (cowpox virus), but it is now used synomymously with *inoculation.

vaccine A preparation containing killed or attenuated microorganisms (i.e., microorganisms that have lost their virulence) such as *viruses, which is introduced into the human body to stimulate the formation of *antibodies and thereby confer *immunity against subsequent infections of the microorganism.

vacuum Space in which there are no molecules or atoms. In practice, a perfect vacuum is unobtainable and the term is generally applied to a space containing air, or other gases, at very low pressures.

vagina Lower part of the female reproductive tract which connects the *uterus to the exterior.

vaginitis *Inflammation of the vagina, accompanied by itching and pain, commonly caused by the microorganism *Trichomonas vaginalis* , the *fungus *Candida albicans* , dietary deficiencies (*see* balanced diet), or poor *hygiene. Vaginitis can be sexually transmitted. Usually, it does not hinder participation in sport although it may deter some sufferers from swimming.

vagus nerve One of a pair of *nerves which originate in the *medulla oblongata and extend down into the *thorax and *abdomen to innervate the *heart, *lungs, and parts of the *alimentary canal. The vagus nerve carries *motor neurones to the muscles which facilitate swallowing, and to both *afferent nerves and *efferent nerves of the *parasympathetic system.

valgus A condition in which a body-segment is curved outwards from its *proximal to its *distal end. *Compare* varus. *See* femoral valgus; forefoot varus; rearfoot valgus; and tibial varus.

valgus stress A *force applied to a *joint which causes the *distal aspect of a limb to be moved away from the midline of the body.

validation The process of determining the *validity of a test or investigation.

validity The extent to which a test, measurement, or other method of investigation possesses the property of actually doing what it has been designed to do.

valine An *essential amino acid found in grains (e.g., corn) and legumes (e.g., beans). Valine is a precursor of *pantothenic acid.

Valsalva's manoeuvre A technique, named after the Italian anatomist A. M. Valsalva (1666–1723), for increasing the *intrathoracic pressure by making a forced expiratory effort (*see* expiration) with the *glottis closed. Valsalva's manoeuvre occurs during the performance of *isometric contractions (e.g., during weight-lifting). Since the air cannot escape, pressure increases, causing an increase in systolic and diastolic blood pressure. Immediately after the event, a reflex *bradycardia can occur which may result in *dizziness and fainting (*see* syncope). Valsalva's manoeuvre can bring about *cardiac arrest in vulnerable heart patients.

value-added-theory of collective behaviour The theory that *collective behaviour develops only when several elements are present in a social situation. Each element adds to the likelihood of collective behaviour occurring, but all must be present for it to occur. The elements are structural strain (perceived or real *social conflicts); structural conduciveness (an acceptance by the collective, such as a crowd, that their grievance cannot be resolved through the normal channels); a shared belief about how to resond to the situation together with precipitating factors which reinforce the shared belief; mobilization of participants to action by leaders and by communication among the crowd; and a lack of adequate *social control.

value-alienation The way in which an individual's system of *values is in conflict with, or is inconsistent with a system of values the individual is expected to hold. Thus the individual develops feelings of estrangement from a situation, group, or culture because of the values he or she holds.

value-free approach 1 An approach to research which aims to exclude a researcher's own *values. Therefore, the aim of a value-free approach is to make the observations and interpretations as unbiased as possible. Some people believe that it is impossible for researchers to adopt a pure value-free approach. In this case, they argue, the researchers should at least make clear what their values are and how they affect their work. 2 An approach to research, particularly sociological research, which aims to establish facts and is not concerned with settling questions of values. *Compare* normative approach.

value-freedom *See* value-neutrality.

value-judgement An ethical or moral evaluation of what should be done.

value-neutrality (value freedom) Applied to a piece of research which has been conducted using a *value-free approach.

values The accepted standards or moral principles of a person or a group. Values are similar to *norms in having a moral and regulatory role, but values have a wider significance than norms in going beyond specific situations. Values are viewed as informing norms in different contexts.

valve A device which ensures that a fluid flows in one direction only. Valves in the blood circulatory system of the human body are flap-like structures that ensure that the blood maintains its unidirectional flow around the body and through the heart. Valves also occur in the *lymphatic system.

vanillylmandelic acid (VMA) An *acid which occurs as a *metabolite of *catecholamines in *urine. Levels of vanillylmandelic acid are used to estimate catecholamine levels; high values after exercise correlate with high physiological and psychological *stress which affects the *adrenal glands.

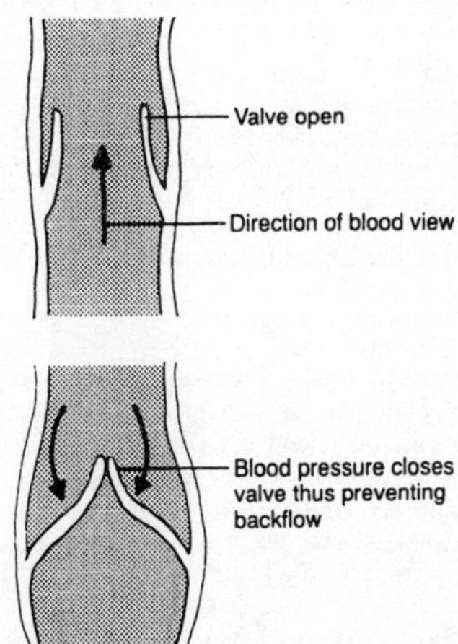

valve

variability The degree of variation in statistical data; measures of variability include *range, *standard deviation, and *variance.

variable (attribute) 1 A changeable aspect of a situation which can be manipulated or measured, as in the case of an *dependent variable and an *independent variable in an experiment. 2 A mathematical symbol which is used to represent some undetermined element from a given set.

variable error A measure of the inconsistency of responses produced by a subject who is striving for accuracy at some target (such as a force, a speed, or a location in space) with each response having a measurable dimension (e.g., kg, kms^{-1}, m). The variable error is expressed as a *standard deviation of a set of responses about a subject's own *constant error.

variable resistance exercise An exercise, usually performed on an exercise machine, in which the *resistance varies throughout the *range of movement of the *muscles involved. Since the difficulty of overcoming the load varies with the angle of the *joint, variable resistance exercise impose a relatively constant stress on the muscles.

variance A measure of the extent to which interval values are clustered around a *mean. Variance is calculated by averaging the squared deviations from the mean, and in so doing it takes into account both negative values, and the occurrence of unusually high and unusually low values. A low variance indicates high homogeneity and high variance low homogeneity of data.

varicella *See* chicken pox.

varices *See* varicose veins.

varicose veins (varices) *Veins, commonly in the legs, which have become abnormally distended and twisted as a result of incompetence of internal valves. Varicose veins may bleed heavily if ruptured, in which case the application of a firm pressure easily controls the bleeding. As long as varicose veins are not associated with other symptoms, a controlled programme of physical exercise may improve the circulation and benefit sufferers.

varix A varicose vein.

varus A curving inwards of a body-segment from its *proximal to its *distal end. In varus conditions, *tensile stress is placed on the *lateral side of the segment's proximal *articulation and on the *medial side of the segment's distal articulation. *Compare* valgus. *See also* femoral varus; forefoot varus; rearfoot varus; and tibial varus.

varus stress A *force, applied to a *joint, which causes the *distal aspect of a limb to be moved towards the midline of the body.

vas A duct or vessel.

vasa recta Capillary branches that supply the *loops of Henlé and collecting ducts of the *kidney. *Blood within the vasa recta is at a low pressure, adapting it for reabsorption of water.

vascular Pertaining to, or supplied with, blood vessels.

vascular system A system of the human body containing specialized *organs and *tissue for transporting substances. *See also* cardiovascular system.

vascularization The development of new *blood vessels within a *tissue.

vasoactive Applied to factors, such as *carbon dioxide, emotions, or pressure, which affect the diameter of *blood vessels.

vasoconstriction A decrease in the diameter of *blood vessels (usually *arterioles) resulting in a reduction of blood flow to the area supplied by the vessel. Factors causing vasoconstriction include *pain, loud noises, fear, a fall in temperature, and a fall in *blood pressure.

vasoconstrictor An agent, such as the *drug *epinephrine, that causes constriction of *blood vessels.

vasodilation An increase in the diameter of *blood vessels (usually *arterioles) resulting in an increase in blood flow to the area supplied by the vessel. Factors causing vasodilation include *exercise, high external temperatures, *stress, and a rise in *blood pressure.

vasodilator An agent that causes an increase in the diameter of a *blood vessel. *Drugs such as *calcium channel blockers, glyceryl trinitrate, and hydrazine, are vasodilators commonly prescribed for the treatment of cardiovascular disorders such as *hypertension.

vasomotion An increase or decrease in the diameter of a *blood vessel.

vasomotor Applied to factors acting on the *smooth muscles of *blood vessels, thus affecting the diameter of the vessels.

vasomotor centre An area in the *medulla oblongata of the *brain which contains *neurones concerned with the regulation of the diameter of *blood vessels and *heart rate so that *blood pressure can be controlled.

vasomotor fibres *See* vasomotor nerve.

vasomotor nerve A *nerve containing *sympathetic nerve fibres which regulates the contraction of *smooth muscle in the walls of *blood vessels, particularly the *arteries, thereby regulating blood vessel diameter and blood flow.

vasopressin *See* antidiuretic hormone.

vasospasm A *spasm in the *smooth muscle of a *blood vessel causing the vessel to constrict.

vastus intermedius A *muscle which is part of the *quadriceps femoris in the anterior compartment of the thigh. The vastus intermedius has its *origin on the *anterior and *lateral surfaces of the *proximal part of the *femur shaft, and its *insertion on the *tibia via the *patellar tendon. Its main action is as an *extensor of the knee.

vastus lateralis Part of the *quadriceps femoris muscle in the *lateral aspect of the thigh which has its *origin on the *greater trochanter, the intertrochanteric line of the *femur, and the *linea aspera of the *femur. It has its *insertion at the base of the patellar and *tibial tuberosity via the *patellar tendon. It is an *extensor of the knee.

vastus medialis A part of the *quadriceps femoris muscle in the *medial aspect at the front of the thigh. The vastus medialis has its *origin on the *linea aspera and intertrochanteric line of the *femur, and its *insertion at the base of the patellar and *tibial tuberosity via the *patellar tendon. Its main action is as an *extensor of the knee. Its lower fibres help to stabilize the *patella.

VC A symbol commonly used by pulmonary physiologists to refer to vital capacity.

V_D A symbol commonly used by pulmonary physiologists to refer to the volume of *dead space.

VE A symbol commonly used by pulmonary physiologists to refer to the volume of expired gas during *pulmonary ventilation.

Vealey's sport-specific model of confidence A theory of achievement motivation based on the concept of *sport confidence. It suggests that an athlete who is successful in one sport thereby enjoys a general feeling of sport confidence which he or she will be able to transfer to new sport situations. The theory predicts that an athlete will develop *self-confidence as he or she experiences task mastery and an expectation of success.

vector 1 An animal which carries a parasite from one host to another. 2 *See* vector quantity.

vector addition *See* vector composition.

vector-chain method Method of obtaining the *resultant vector of two or more *vectors by drawing the *component vectors to scale. The resultant vector is found by drawing a last vector from the finishing point to the starting point. *See also* vector, triangle law of.

vector composition (vector addition; vector sum) Method of determining the *resultant vector from two or more *component vectors. The component vectors are added together to give a single vector (the resultant vector) describing all the vectors added. *See also* vector-chain method.

vector quantity (vector) A *variable which requires direction as well as *magnitude in order to define it completely. *Velocity and *acceleration are examples of vectors. A vector is often represented graphically by an arrow drawn so that its length represents the magnitude of the vector, the tail of the arrow represents the origin of the vector, and the head represents the direction of *force. *Compare* scalar. *See also* component vector; and resultant vector.

vector resolution A method of determining *component vectors from a *resultant vector. *See also* vector-chain method.

vectors, parallelogram of *See* parallelogram of vectors.

vectors, triangle law of A law which states that if a body is acted upon by two vectors represented by two sides of a triangle taken in order, the *resultant vector is represented by the third side of the triangle.

vector sum *See* vector composition.

vegan A person who has a diet of plants only. A vegan eats no milk, milk products, or eggs.

vegetarian An individual who eats a diet that omits meat. The basic types of vegetarians include semi-vegetarians, who omit all animal foods except milk, milk products,

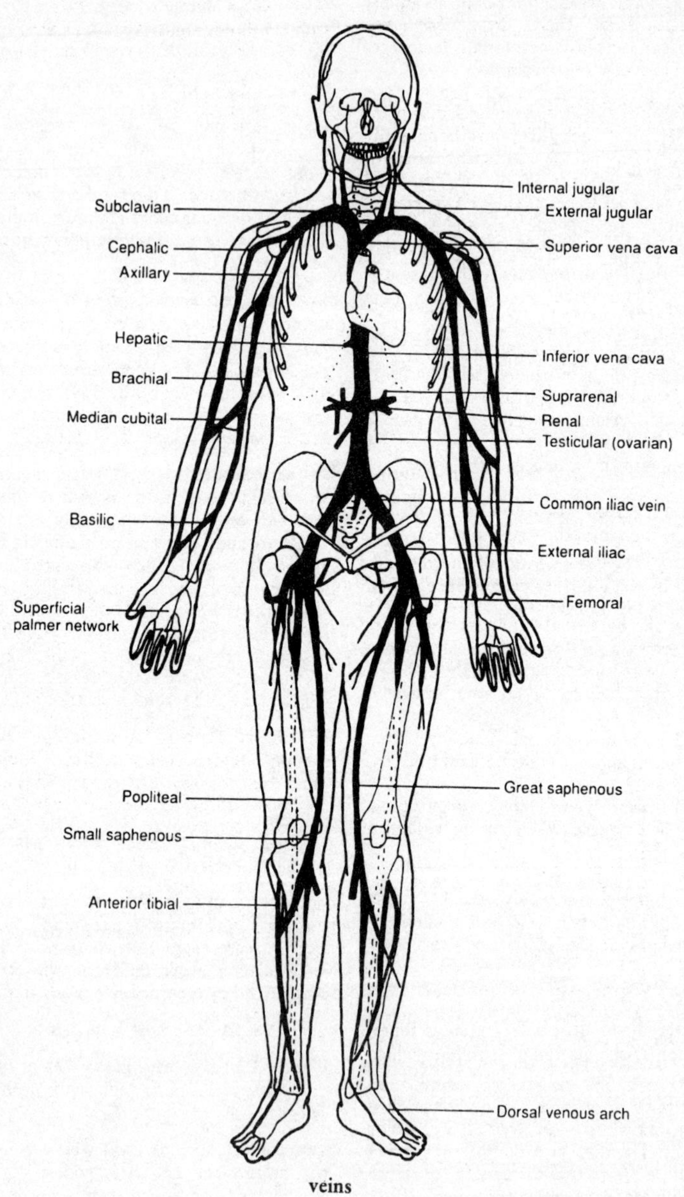
Internal jugular
Subclavian
External jugular
Cephalic
Superior vena cava
Axillary
Hepatic
Inferior vena cava
Brachial
Suprarenal
Median cubital
Renal
Testicular (ovarian)
Common iliac vein
Basilic
External iliac
Femoral
Superficial
palmer network
Great saphenous
Popliteal
Small saphenous
Anterior tibial
Dorsal venous arch

veins

and eggs; and vegans, who omit all animal products from their diets. *See also* fruitarian; lacto-ovo vegetarian; lactovegetarian; and new vegetarian.

vegetarian diet A diet composed of plant materials only. Such a diet must be carefully constructed to include a sufficient variety of cereals and legumes if all the *essential amino acids are to be provided. A vegetarian diet should also include nuts and pulses to provide sufficient vitamin B_{12}. A vegetarian diet is usually low in *calories because it is high in *dietary fibre.

vein Vessel carrying *blood to the *heart. A vein usually has thin walls and a series of one-way valves.

velocity Rate at which a body moves, measured as length per unit time, in a given direction. Velocity is a *vector quantity. *Compare* speed. *See also* angular velocity; and relative velocity.

velocity ratio The ratio of the distance moved by the effort, to the distance moved by the load in a *machine.

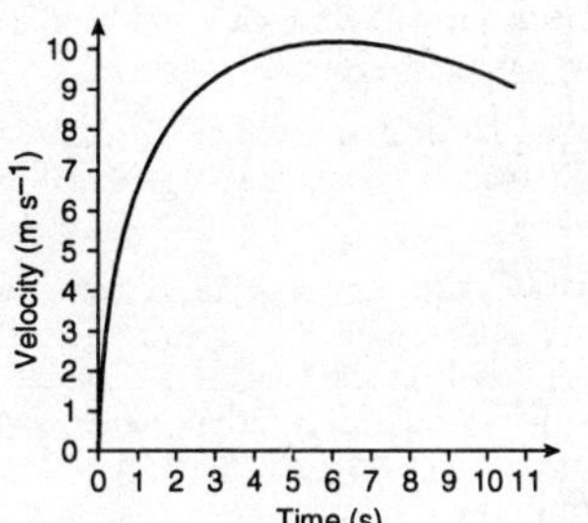

velocity–time graph

velocity–time graph A graphical representation of the motion of a body in which time is plotted on the x-axis of the graph and *velocity on the y-axis. In the velocity–time graph, *acceleration of the body is obtained from the gradient of the curve. The area beneath the graph represents the *distance travelled. The velocity–time graph for a sprinter in a 100 m race is shown above.

vena cava One of two major *veins leading into the right *atrium of the *heart. *See also* inferior vena cava; and superior vena cava.

venereal disease A sexually-transmitted *disease.

venoconstriction The reflex constriction of *veins occurring during exercise which forces *blood towards the *heart and contributes to an increase in *venous return.

venomotor control Regulation of *blood flow produced by changes in the shape of *veins. The *muscle coat of a vein receives *neurones from the *sympathetic nervous system and the *parasympathetic nervous system.

venomotor tone The degree of tension in the *muscle coat of a *vein which determines the shape of veins. Changes in venomotor tone produced by stimulation of the *autonomic nervous system can alter the capacity of the veins without affecting the veins' resistance to *blood flow.

venous return The volume of *blood returning to the right *atrium of the *heart. The heart can only pump as much blood as it receives, therefore increases in *cardiac output (for example, during exercise when cardiac output may exceed $30 l min^{-1}$) are dependent upon the venous return increasing to that amount. The *muscle pump, *respiratory pump, and *venoconstriction contribute to the increase in venous return during exercise. *See also* Starling's law.

ventilation The passage of air into (*see* inhalation) and out of (*see* exhalation) the lungs. *See also* alveolar ventilation; and pulmonary ventilation.

ventilation–perfusion ratio A ratio of the volume of air which reaches the *alveoli to the volume of *blood supplying the alveoli. Gas exchange in the lungs is most efficient when there is a good match between ventilation and *perfusion; an imbalance is a major cause of *anoxia and *cyanosis.

ventilation rate The volume of air breathed per minute. Ventilation rate is a product of the *tidal volume and the *respiratory frequency.

ventilatory breaking point *See* ventilatory threshold.

ventilatory buffering A homeostatic process (*see* homeostasis) which uses changes in *ventilation to minimize changes in the *pH of body fluids. Ventilatory buffering is particularly important during exercise. A decrease in pH (increased acidity) associated with exercise results in an increase in ventilation causing the *alveolar partial pressure of *carbon dioxide to decrease as carbon dioxide is expired from the *blood. The reduction in blood *plasma partial pressure of carbon dioxide causes *hydrogen ions and *bicarbonate ions to recombine thereby reducing hydrogen ion concentration in the blood.

ventilatory efficiency A measure of the amount of *ventilation required for each litre of *oxygen consumed. It is measured as the ratio of the volume of gas expired per minute to the volume of oxygen consumed per minute (i.e., $\dot{V}E/\dot{V}o_2$).

ventilatory equivalent The ratio of the volume of air breathed to the volume of *oxygen consumed. At rest, the ratio is about 20:1, but during exercise it can exceed 40:1.

ventilatory reserve (breathing reserve) The difference between maximal *ventilation rate (that is, a person's highest possible ventilatory rate) and the maximum ventilation rate during a particular activity . The ventilatory reserve indicates the potential for increasing the ventilation rate and therefore the potential for increasing the intensity of activity.

ventilatory threshold (ventilatory breaking-point) The intensity of exercise at which the rate of *ventilation sharply increases. The sharp increase is believed to be due to an accumulation of *lactic acid which stimulates an increase in ventilation which is out of proportion to the *oxygen uptake. *See* anaerobic threshold.

ventral (anterior) Pertaining to the front or belly.

ventricle 1 One of a pair of chambers in the *heart. The ventricles lie inferior to the atria. The right ventricle receives deoxygenated blood from the right *atrium and pumps this blood to the lungs. The left ventricle receives oxygenated blood from the left atrium and pumps the blood through the *dorsal aorta to the rest of the body. 2 A fluid-filled chamber in the brain.

ventricular ectopic beats Extra heartbeats due to impulses generated in the *ventricle rather than at the normal *pacemaker region in the *sinoatrial node. Ventricular ectopic beats which occur at rest, or only during recovery from exercise, in a person with an otherwise normal heart are quite common and do not usually indicate anything sinister. However, the occurrence of ventricular ectopic beats which increase with exercise severity are a cause for concern and merit expert medical attention. *See also* ectopic heartbeats; and extrasystoles.

ventricular systole The phase of the *cardiac cycle during which the *ventricles contract and empty themselves of blood. *See also* systole.

venule Small *vein which, unlike a *capillary, has some *connective tissue.

verbal feedback *Feedback presented in a form that is spoken or capable of being spoken.

verbal guidance Coaching technique in which athletes are instructed to do exactly what they hear the coach (or cassette, etc.) say they should do. Verbal guidance often involves the use of simple, clear, and meaningful *cues.

verbal pretraining 1 A pre-practice technique for improving *learning. Verbal pretraining is based on *stimuli being presented separately prior to practice so that the stimuli which are going to be experienced in the task can be learned before actual practice begins. Verbal pretraining is not, in fact, always verbal; a golfer walking around a course and becoming familiar with it before playing is also verbal pretraining, for example. 2 The use of simple words, given by a coach, to help remind an athlete of what to do next while the athlete is executing a complex skill. Once mastered, these labels identify the steps in the sequence simply and directly, and they make preparing for practice and learning skills easier.

verruca A round or oval shaped wart which has a crack or dark spot in the middle. Verrucas are caused by *viruses and can be transferred from one person to another via the contaminated floors of showers. They can be painful when pressed against underlying tissue.

verstehen A German word for 'understanding' which, in sociology, refers to the procedure by which sociologists and *social actors interpret and understand the meanings of the actions of others.

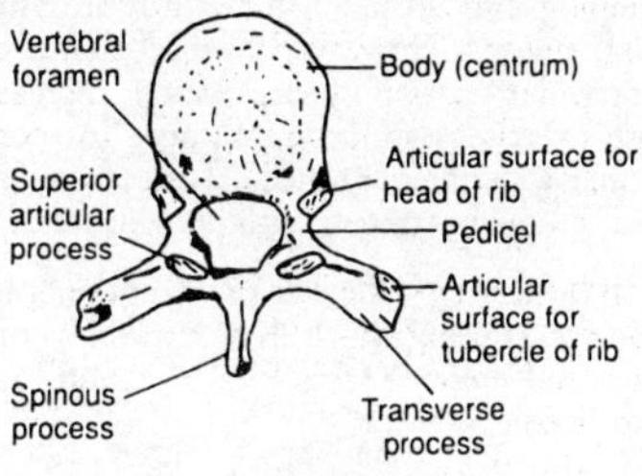

vertebra

vertebra One of 33 small *bones or *cartilage with collectively form the *spinal column. The vertebrae form a jointed rod, attached to the *skull and enclosing the *spinal cord. Each vertebra consists of a substantial mass (the *centrum) with an arch (the *neural arch) with a transverse process, and usually a *neural spine.

vertebral Pertaining to the *spinal column.

vertebral arch Composite structure in each *vertebra consisting of two *lamina and two pedicles which help to enclose and protect the *spinal cord. Pedicles are short bony cylinders projecting posteriorly from the vertebral body.

vertebral artery A branch of the *subclavian artery which ascends from the sixth *cervical vertebra through the *foramen (known as the foramina transversaria) of the *cervical vertebrae and the foramen magnum (the large opening in the skull through which the spinal cord emerges) to the front of the *medulla oblongata.

vertebral column (backbone) The *spine; formed of 33 individual bones called *vertebrae and two composite bones, the *sacrum and *coccyx.

vertebral rib *See* floating rib.

vertex In *anthropometry, a *landmark located at the most *superior point in the midsagittal plane on the skull when the head is held in the *Frankfort plane.

vertical displacement Total height reached by a *projectile measured at an angle of 90° to the ground surface.

vertical projection The upward displacement of a *projectile at 90° to the ground followed by the downward fall of the object.

vertical status The *status of a person in relation to others at a different hierarchical level. Vertical status on a team, for example, may involve a comparison of groundstaff to players, or players to administrators. *Compare* horizontal status. *See also* status.

vertical velocity The rate at which a body moves upwards at an angle of 90° to the ground. It is the component of a projectile's *velocity which is concerned with lifting the projectile. *Compare* horizontal velocity.

vertigo (dizziness) A feeling of unsteadiness. There are two main types of vertigo. In the first type the sufferer feels that his or her body or the environment is spinning. It is commonly caused by motion sickness or a viral infection of the organs of balance (*see* vestibular apparatus). The second type of vertigo is characterized by weakness and is commonly caused by low *blood sugar or low *blood pressure. As long as low blood pressure is not the result of *shock or blood loss, a sufferer of the second type of vertigo may benefit from physical activity. Anyone prone to vertigo should take great care when taking part in sports where a fall may be dangerous.

vertobrochondral rib *See* false rib.

vertobrocostal joint A *synovial, gliding joint between a vertebra and rib.

vertobrospinal rib *See* true rib.

very low calorie diet (VLCD) A diet containing less than 800 kcal per day specifically designed for the treatment of severe *obesity. Usually, food substitution in the form of a drink made from powder and water is used. Ingredients in the powder are designed to provide *nutrients in sufficient quantities to sustain *health, and consist mainly of high quality *protein such as egg whites, *minerals, and *vitamins. These diets require medical supervision and are not recommended for people with *BMI less than 30.

very low-density lipoprotein (VLDL) A specific kind of *lipoprotein that, when found in excessive amounts in the blood, is thought to increase the risk of *atherosclerosis by carrying *cholesterol to the tissues.

vesicle A small liquid-filled sac or bladder.

vested interest A strong personal concern in producing or maintaining a particular state of affairs. In sport, for example, coaches have a vested interest in maintaining a system of rewards so that they can maintain compliance from, and power over, their players.

vestibular apparatus The *equilibrium receptors of the *inner ear, consisting of the *utricle, *saccule, and *semicircular canals, that are sensitive to the orientation of the head with respect to *gravity, to rotation of the head, and to balance. Impulses from the vestibular apparatus are conducted along *vestibular nerve fibres to the *vestibular complex in the *brain stem and *cerebellum. The complex initiates visual and motor responses which help to maintain balance (*see* maculae and crista ampullaris).

vestibular canal Canal of the *cochlea of the *inner ear that connects to the *oval window.

vestibulocochlear nerve *See* auditory nerve.

vibration A repeated motion that moves back and forth over the same general path. *See also* angular vibration; harmonic motion; and linear vibration.

vibratory motion *See* harmonic motion.

vicarious experience Experience gained by watching another person perform a *skill.

vicarious learning *See* modelling.

vicarious punishment Refers to the tendency not to repeat behaviours that we observe others punished for performing. *See also* modelling; and vicarious reinforcement.

vicarious reinforcement Refers to a tendency to repeat behaviours that we see others rewarded for performing (for example, copying the *aggression of a player who is rewarded for that aggression by winning a match and gaining public acclaim). *See also* modelling; and vicarious punishment.

vicious circle (vicious cycle) A situation in which an action leads to another situation in which all gains brought about by the first action are lost. Typically, the initial problem may be worsened, or a series of actions and situations leads back to the initial problem. For example, an athlete with an *over-use injury wants to get back to fitness after a short period of rest so over-trains, leading to further over-use injuries. *See also* pain cycle.

vicious cycle *See* vicious circle.

victimization In sociology, the institutionalized pressure to participate in a form of violent behaviour which can be dangerous to health and safety. In some contact sports this is regarded as largely normative by those involved, and injuries are regarded as a natural consequence of participation.

victimology The study of victims of crime, including the relationship between the offender and victim.

view An attitude in which an abstract scheme dominates.

villus Finger-like projections from the surface of some *membranes (e.g., those of the *small intestine) that increase the surface area for the *absorption of *nutrients.

violence Infliction of physical damage on person or property. In sport, the term violence usually refers to serious types of overt *aggression.

viral myocarditis *Inflammation of the muscle wall of the *heart, caused by a viral infection. A cold or *influenza virus, for example, may attack, inflame, and irritate the *cardiac muscle causing varying degrees of pain and disturbance of the rhythmical beating of the heart. Viral myocarditis can cause circulatory collapse if the sufferer exercises at a high intensity, no matter how fit the person was before infection. *See also* myocarditis.

virilization *See* masculinization.

virulence The capacity of a *microorganism to generate *disease.

virus A member of a group of minute infectious agents which have a relatively simple structure and which can reproduce only within living cells. Viruses consist of genetic material (either *DNA or *RNA) surrounded by a *protein coat. They are responsible for many diseases including the common cold, *influenza, and *AIDS. They are not affected by *antibiotics, but many viral diseases can be effectively treated by *vaccines.

viscera (singular, viscus) Internal organs of the body cavity.

visceral Pertaining to the internal organs of the body or the inner part of a structure.

visceral fat deposition *Adipose tissue found within the body cavity surrounding the *liver and *intestines. This type of deposition is predominant in *android fat distribution, and has been linked with a higher metabolic risk and a higher incidence of *heart disease and *diabetes. The mechanisms of risk are unclear but the proximity of fat deposition to the hepatic vascular system is thought to be implicated.

visceral motor system *See* autonomic nervous system.

visceral pain A *pain which results from stimulation of *pain receptors in the *thoracic and *abdominal organs. *Stimuli include extreme stretching of tissue, *ischaemia, irritating chemicals, and *muscle spasms. *See also* referred pain.

visceral pericardium (serous pericardium) The inner part of the *pericardium which lies adjacent to the *myocardium. The visceral pericardium contains a small amount of fluid which reduces the friction between the two surfaces as the heart beats.

visceral pleura A thin *membrane lining the *lungs which secretes *serous fluid. *See also* pleura.

visceral reactions Responses of visceral organs, including contractions of the muscular wall of the stomach and secretion of *adrenaline from the *adrenal glands, which underlie such experiences as *nausea and *butterflies in the stomach.

visceroceptors *See* interoceptors.

viscerotonic An individual who exhibits *viscerotonic traits.

viscerotonic traits Psychological characteristics which are believed to correlate with *endomorphy. Viscerotonics are typically easy-going, sociable people who take pleasure in food and eating. *Compare* cerebrotonic traits; and somatonic traits. *See* Sheldon's constitutional theory.

viscoelastic substance A solid or liquid which can store and dissipate energy during mechanical deformation.

viscometer An instrument for measuring the *viscosity of a fluid.

viscosity A measure of the tendency of a *fluid to resist *relative motion within itself. A liquid with a high viscosity is sluggish and flows in a treacle-like manner. *See also* coefficient of viscosity.

viscous drag A form of *drag which is affected by the *viscosity of a *fluid. Viscous drag is analagous to *surface drag or skin friction.

vision 1 Sight; the ability to perceive with the eye. The eye is the most important sense-organ for supplying information about the external world and is classified as an *exteroceptor. It has also been shown to be an important proprioceptor (*see* visual proprioception). **2** The ability of a coach to set realistic goals and to understand the steps that lead to achieving these goals.

visual accommodation Changes in the lens of the eye so as to focus light from sources at different distances from the eye and thus form sharp images on the *retina. *See also* accommodation.

visual field The area in front of the eyes within which objects can be seen without moving the eyes. It is usually an advantage to have a wide visual field for sports involving *open skills, and a narrow visual field for sports involving *closed skills.

visual guidance A coaching technique in which the coach instructs athletes to copy the actions that they see someone else perform. It is a particularly effective form of training for young athletes.

visualization (imaging) A form of *mental practice in which an athlete creates a vivid, controlled image of a game situation and imagines how he or she will cope successfully with it. *See also* external imaging; and internal imaging.

visual proprioception Visual information about a person's own body movements in relation to the environment. *Vision can serve as a strong motion detector, particularly in balancing movements.

visuo-motor behaviour rehearsal (VMBR) A form of *stress management that uses *imagery and *relaxation techniques to help athletes reduce *anxiety, focus *attention, and enhance performance. The procedure involves the use of *mental practice in conjunction with *progressive muscle relaxation (PMR) then, when a relaxed state is established, the subject imagines himself or herself successfully performing a problem skill.

vital Pertaining to life.

vital capacity (VC) Maximum volume of air forcefully expired after *maximal *inspiration. Values vary from 3.5–6.0 l at rest. Normal values for a 40-year-old man, height 1.75 m and weight 60 kg is 4.75–5.85 l (*BTPS); the value decreases slightly during exercise.

vital centre Collection of nerve cells in the *medulla oblongata responsible for ensuring the maintenance of basic functions, such as heartbeat and ventilatory movements. Injuries to the vital centres are often fatal because of the nature of the activities for which they are responsible.

vital organ Any organ, such as the heart, brain, or kidneys, which is essential to life.

vital sign A measurable indicator, such as *heart rate or *body temperature, of essential bodily functions.

vitamin One of a group of potent nonprotein, organic compounds required in minute amounts for good health and growth. Vitamins cannot be synthesized by the body and are therefore essential constituents of the *diet. They are classified as *fat-soluble vitamins or *water-soluble vitamins. Many vitamins seem to act as *coenzymes or are involved in the production of coenzymes. Each vitamin has a specific function; one vitamin cannot substitute for another. Many metabolic reactions require several vitamins and lack of one vitamin may interfere with the activity of others. There is much disagreement about the effects of exercise on vitamin requirements. Many coaches believe that the added *stress experienced by élite athletes means that they need more vitamins than are required by other individuals; consequently it is thought that these athletes may be susceptible to *vitamin deficiency diseases. Currently, there is much research being undertaken to establish the precise vitamin needs of athletes.

vitamin A (retinol) A *fat-soluble vitamin concerned with the normal functioning of mucus membranes of the eye and respiratory tract, and for the formation of visual pigments in the eye. Vitamin A can be manufactured in the body from *β-carotene which is found in a variety of foods, particularly green vegetables and carrots; or it can be acquired preformed in animal products, such as fish-liver oils. Vitamin A deficiency causes night-blindness; changes to *epithelial tissue; increased respiratory, digestive, and urinogenital infections; drying of the *conjunctiva; and clouding of the *cornea. It is the most prevalent vitamin deficiency in the world. Excessive intakes of vitamin A can lead to *nausea, *vomiting, *anorexia, *headaches, hairlessness, *bone and *joint pain, and bone fragility. The recommended daily allowance is 750 μg *retinol equivalents.

vitamin B Any one of a group of *water-soluble vitamins which commonly occur in the same types of food such as milk, liver, and yeast.

vitamin B_1 (aneurine; thiamin) A *water-soluble vitamin obtained from lean meat, liver, eggs, wholegrains, and milk. Vitamin B_1 is rapidly destroyed by heat and is stored in only very limited amounts in the body. It plays an important role as a *coenzyme in *carbohydrate *metabolism. It is also required for the transformation of *pyruvic acid to *acetyl coenzyme A, for the *synthesis of certain sugars, and for the *oxidation of alcohols. Deficiency causes *beriberi. The recommended daily allowance is 1 mg for an adult.

vitamin B_2 (riboflavin) A *water-soluble vitamin which is quickly decomposed by visible light. Riboflavin is obtained from a wide variety of sources including wholegrains, yeast, liver, eggs, and milk. It is present in the body as the *coenzymes *FAD and *FMN which are involved in respiratory *metabolism. The recommended daily allowance for an adult is 1.7mg. A deficiency causes ariboflavinosis, characterized by *dermatitis and ocular problems including blurred vision.

vitamin B_3 (niacin; nicotinic acid) A *water-soluble vitamin obtained from grains, legumes, and yeast. Enteric bacteria also produce some vitamin B_3 in the intestine. It is quite stable; little is lost in cooking. Vitamin B_3 forms part of *coenzyme A, a key metabolic compound involved in the *oxidation and *synthesis of *fatty acids, and in the synthesis of *steroids and *haemoglobin. Deficiency causes vague symptoms including loss of appetite, mental depression, and pains in the arms and muscles.

vitamin B_6 (pyridoxine) A *water-soluble vitamin consisting of a group of three *pyridenes and obtained from meat, poultry, and eggs. The active form of vitamin B_6 is the *coenzyme pyridoxal phosphate which is involved in several reactions, including *amino acid *metabolism and *glycogenolysis, and in the formation of *antibodies and *haemoglobin. It is therefore essential for *protein metabolism and is also important for nerve and muscle function. Excessive intakes result in depressed tendon reflexes and loss of sensation in the extremities. Deficiency is relatively rare and causes nervous irritability, *anaemia, and convulsions in infants, and *lesions around the eyes and mouth (seborrhea lesions, resulting from excessive secretion of *sebum from the *sebaceous glands) in adults.

vitamin B_{12} (cobalamin; cyanocobalamin) A complex *water-soluble vitamin containing *cobalt which can be obtained from liver, fish, and some dairy products. Vitamin B_{12} is the only member of the vitamin B complex which cannot be obtained from yeast. *Intrinsic factor is needed for its absorption. It acts as a *coenzyme, involved in the synthesis of *DNA, *methionine, and choline (a component of *acetylcholine), and is essential for *erythrocyte manufacture. Vitamin B_{12} and *folic acid are interdependent. A deficiency of the vitamin can lead to *pernicious anaemia, weight-loss, and degeneration of the *nervous system. The recommended daily allowance for an adult is 3–4µg. There is much attention being paid to vitamin B_{12} as a possible *ergogenic aid because it is believed by many coaches to have a considerable effect on energy production in muscle cells.

vitamin B_{15} *See* pangamic acid.

vitamin C A *water-soluble, six-carbon crystalline compound destroyed by heat and light. In addition to being essential for the growth of healthy *connective tissue, vitamin C is important in other processes including the conversion of *cholesterol to *bile salts, and the protection of *vitamin A, *vitamin E, and dietary *fats from *oxidation. Vitamin C also enhances the absorption of *iron. Mild deficiency can cause fleeting joint pains, poor tooth and bone growth, poor wound-healing, and an increased susceptibility to infection. An extreme deficit causes *scurvy. The recommended daily allowance for an adult is 30 mg. which can be obtained from citrus fruits and vegetables.

vitamin D (antirachitic factor) A *fat-soluble vitamin that contains a number of chemically-distinct *sterols which enhance the absorption of *phosphorus and *calcium from the *intestine and, with *parathyroid hormone, mobilizes their deposition in *bone. Vitamin D is relatively stable when exposed to heat and light. It is stored in the *liver and, to a lesser extent, in the *adipose tissue of the skin. Vitamin D occurs in two forms: vitamin D_2 and vitamin D_3. Vitamin D_2 (ergocalciferol or calciferol) is obtained in the diet from foods such as oily fish, eggs, and margarine. Vitamin D_3 (cholecalciferol) is the main form of the vitamin and is produced in the skin by the action of ultraviolet light on 7-dehydrocholesterol. Vitamin D deficiency causes poor *muscle tone, restlessness, and irritability. Vitamin D deficiency also causes rickets in children and *osteomalacia in adults. The recommended daily allowance is 10 µg for children and 2.5 µg for adults

vitamin D_2 *See* vitamin D

vitamin D_3 *See* vitamin D.

vitamin deficiency disease A disease due to a lack of *vitamins in the body caused either by a dietary deficiency or as a secondary disease associated with *anorexia, *vomiting, or *diarrhoea. Vitamin deficiency diseases may also occur as a result of increased metabolic demands for vitamins imposed by *fever or *stress.

vitamin E (antisterility factor) A group of related compounds (including tocopherol and tocotrienole) which are believed to help maintain the integrity of *cell membranes. They may also act as *antioxidants of *vitamin A and *vitamin C. There is also a claim by some coaches that vitamin E increases muscle development and function; this claim is highly disputed. Vitamin E is widely available in the diet and deficiencies are probably rare, but such deficiencies may cause *haemolysis of *erythrocytes and *anaemia in humans. Deficiencies impair reproductive ability in rats and causes muscle wasting in pigs.

vitamin H *See* biotin.

vitamin K (coagulation vitamin) A *fat-soluble vitamin which is essential for the manufacture of *prothrombin and normal blood *clotting. It is also involved in *oxidative phosphorylation. Vitamin K consists of a number of related quinone compounds; the two main forms are phytomenadione and menaquinone. Vitamin K is obtained from foods such as green vegetables and liver. It is also synthesized by gut bacteria. Deficiencies, characterized by easy bruising and prolonged clotting time, are rare, but may result from taking *antibiotics which interfere with the activity of the bacteria, or from a lack of the vitamin in the diet.

vitamin supplements Additional vitamins taken to make up a deficit, to avoid a *vitamin deficiency disease, or in the belief that they act as an *ergogenic aid. There is much controversy concerning the value of vitamin supplements as ergogenic aids. Many nutritionists believe that the vitamin requirements of athletes, even those involved in strenuous sports, do not exceed the amount present in a normal balanced diet. It is generally agreed that taking additional *fat-soluble vitamins can be dangerous (*see* hypervitamonosis).

VLCD *See* very low calorie diet:

VLDL *See* very low-density lipoprotein.

VMA *See* vanillylmandelic acid.

VMBR *See* visuo-motor behaviour rehearsal.

vocal cords Laryngeal membranes which vibrate and produce sounds. The sound is altered by muscles changing the tension of the cords.

voice box *See* larynx.

volition In *decision-making, the conscious adoption by an individual of a line of action.

Volkmann's contracture Shortening of *muscles in the hand and forearm, with loss of power, caused by an inadequate *arterial *blood supply resulting from an injury or a constriction (e.g., from a *bandage that is too tight). A similar condition can occur in the foot. The condition is named after a German surgeon, R. von Volkmann (1830–89).

volt The *SI unit of *potential difference, *electromotive force, and *electric potential. One volt is the difference in potential between two conducting points carrying a current of 1A when the power dissipated between these points is 1W.

volume Measure of the amount of space occupied by a body.

volumeter A tank filled with water and used to measure the volume of a body. When the body (which may be a human body) is completely submerged in the water, the volume of the water displaced equals the volume of the body. The volumeter is usually combined with scales so that the weight of the body in and out of the water can be measured. The measurements are used to determine *density and *specific gravity.

volumetric analysis The measurement of the volume of a body or part of a body to estimate its *density. Volumetric analysis is based on *Archimedes' principle.

voluntary muscle *Muscle under conscious control. *See also* skeletal muscle.

voluntary reflex A *reflex which originates in the *motor cortex of the brain.

vomiting A reflex ejection of the stomach contents through the mouth. It is a common symptom of *gastrointestinal infections, abdominal disorders, and a number of diseases. Fluid-loss from vomiting can cause *dehydration.

Vo_2max *See* maximal oxygen consumption.

VT A symbol commonly used by pulmonary physiologists to refer to the *tidal volume.

W

W *See* watt.

waist girth In *anthropometry, the circumference of the waist at the level where the waist noticeably narrows, about midway between the *costal border and the *iliac crest. *See also* body girth.

waist–hip ratio The circumference of the body at the narrowest part of the waist divided by the circumference at the widest part of the hips. The waist–hip ratio is used as a convenient method of assessing *body fat distribution. The higher the figure, the greater the tendency towards the higher risk *android fat distribution. The lower the score, the greater the tendency towards *gynoid fat distribution.

waking hypnosis An hypnotic stage during which a subject is instructed to carry out suggestions that are alerting and arousing.

walking Locomotion in which the body is moved in a particular direction while maintaining foot-contact with the ground.

war Violent, open, armed conflict between two or more nations or peoples. Violent outbursts in sport have been linked with the start of war. In June 1969, Honduras played El Salvador in three World Cup soccer games. Riots occurred during the games and, following the games, diplomatic relations were severed between the two countries.

warm-down (cool-down) Gradual, controlled reduction of activity after *training or *competition. Swimmers may swim slowly in a warm-down, while runners may jog and perform flexibility exercises. The warm-down helps the body to eliminate waste products such as *lactic acid and to reduce the risk of *muscular stiffness.

warm-up A procedure, used prior to *competition or hard *training, by which an athlete attains the optimal *body core temperature and specific muscle temperature for performance, and prepares physically and mentally for the activity. A rise in temperature may be gained passively by taking a warm bath, but it more commonly involves light *aerobic exercise. There is a lack of general agreement about the effects of the warm-up, but the possible advantages include an increased *metabolic rate; increased *heart rate with improved oxygen and fuel transport to the tissues; increased speed of *nerve conduction; and increased speed of *muscle contraction. The warm-up procedure usually involves *static stretching and *callisthenics which reduces the risk of muscle and joint injury, and prepares the muscles for activity throughout their full range.

warm-up decrement The gradual loss of the effects of *warm-up during a period of inactivity between the warm-up and competition. Warm-up is usually most effective immediately before competition. A warm-up decrement may occur after only a few minutes of inactivity.

wart A raised, brownish area of skin caused by a *virus infection. *See also* verruca.

waste products Products of *metabolism which are eliminated from the body. Some waste products, such as *lactic acid, may be harmful if they accumulate in the body. *See also* excretion.

water A clear, colourless, tasteless liquid composed of *hydrogen and *oxygen. Water is an *essential nutrient, vital for the maintenance of life.

water balance (**fluid balance**) The relationship between the water taken into the body by all routes and the water lost by all routes. An inadequate water balance has immediate and serious debilitating effects on performances in sport. *See also* dehydration; and water intoxication.

water intoxication A condition of water imbalance which may result from a kidney disorder or from drinking extraordinary quantities of water very quickly. The *extracellular fluid component is diluted, decreasing the *sodium ion concentration causing a net osmotic inflow of water into the cells which consequently swell. This may cause *metabolic disturbances, *nausea, *vomiting, muscular *cramps, and in very extreme cases, death. Extreme cases are rare, but mild cases do occur in athletes who replenish water losses by drinking too much, too quickly. Water intoxication is also known as dilutional *hyponatraemia and *hypotonic hydration.

water potential The tendency of a system, usually a cell, to push water out through a *semi-permeable membrane. By convention, the water potential of distilled water at one *atmosphere of pressure, is given a value of zero and all other solutions are compared with this level. Thus water potential usually has a negative value.

water replacement The act of taking fluids into the body to replace those lost from the body through *sweating, urination, etc. Water replacement is important during sports which last longer than about 50 min if the risk of *dehydration is to be minimized. Replacement is best accomplished with a cold drink (8–13 °C), slightly *hypotonic, and low in *sugar (sugars retard gastric emptying). The replacement should not exceed the maximum absorption rate (about 800 ml per hour).

water retention *See* fluid retention.

water-soluble vitamins *Vitamins which dissolve in water. They include the *vitamin B complex and *vitamin C. Water-soluble vitamins are generally not stored in significant amounts because they tend to be eliminated through the *urine.

water tablets Tablets which are used to increase the elimination of water from the body. *See also* diuretics.

watt (W) A derived *SI unit of *power, equal to $1\,J\,s^{-1}$.

wave 1 An energy-carrying disturbance, either continuous or transient, travelling through a medium as a progressive local disturbance of the medium without an overall movement of matter. **2** A graphical presentation of an energy-carrying disturbance, plotted as the magnitude of the disturbance against time.

wave drag The *force that acts on a body which is at the interface between air and water. Movement of the body exerts forces which create waves; the reaction to these forces is the wave drag. It is a *resistance force additional to *form drag and *surface drag.

wave summation The combination of responses from a *motor unit which has had two or more stimuli applied to it in quick succession. A motor unit of a *muscle responds to a single *stimulus with a simple *twitch response. When a second stimulus is applied to the motor unit before the response to the first is completely lost, the two responses combine to produce a greater *muscle tension than that produced by a single response. If stimulation continues, the combination of the individual responses may result in *tetanus. *See also* temporal summation.

WBGT index (wet bulb globe thermometer index) An index developed by the US armed forces as a simple indicator of the relative severity of environmental temperature conditions. It is computed using the folowing equation: WBGT index = 0.7(WBT) + 0.2(GT) + 0.1(DBT), where WBT represents the wet bulb temperature (recorded from a thermometer with the bulb surrounded by gauze, moistened with distilled water, and ventilated by a fan or a whirling device such as a *swing psychrometer), GT represents the temperature recorded from a thermometer enclosed in a black or grey metal sphere and exposed to the full intensity of sunlight encountered by the athlete, and DBT is the dry bulb temperature recorded on a normal thermometer not exposed to direct sunlight. Temperature is measured in °F. The index takes no account of the *wind chill factor.

WBT index (wet bulb thermometer index) A simple measurement of environmental *heat stress recorded by spinning an ordinary thermometer with a wetted wick around the bulb. The temperature recorded by the wet bulb thermometer is usually less than that of a *dry bulb thermometer because of heat lost by evaporation. High wet bulb temperatures usually indicate high humidity when there is a greater danger of heat stress, and it has been suggested that the precaution of protective clothing should be taken by sportspeople when the WBT is above 60 °F.

weight The *force of attraction exerted on an object by the gravitational pull of the earth. Weight is often expressed in units of *mass, but this is not scientifically correct. Being a force, weight should be measured in N and a body of mass m will have a weight of mg, where g is the *acceleration of free fall.

weight-bearing exercise A physical activity, such as walking and running, in which the legs support the weight of the body.

weight control (weight management) The ability to control body-weight by the appropriate balance of weight-losses associated with the energy expended during exercise and weight-gains associated with the intake of food. *See also* energy balance.

weight density The *weight of an object expressed in terms of a given volume (e.g., Nl^{-1}). *Compare* density.

weight-lifter's blackout A loss of *consciousness which can occur in otherwise healthy athletes when the quick release of a great pressure in the *thoracic cavity causes a drop in *blood pressure which momentarily prevents the *heart from filling up with *blood.

weight-lifting strength Usually the heaviest weight that can be lifted once through a specified *range of movement. Weight-lifting strength is a measure of the strength of *isotonic contraction.

weight-loss maintenance Efforts to maintain weight after a successful weight-loss programme. Methods of fat loss are often fairly successful, but the difficulty of maintaining weight is reflected by a low success rate. Most dieters return to their original weight within a year. Efforts are now focusing on means of improving success in weight-loss maintenance. *Exercise, *cognitive behaviour therapy, and education are increasingly involved in multidisciplinary approaches to the problem.

weight management *See* weight control.

weight-training A form of *strength-training or *resistance-training using either *free weights or a *weight-training machine.

weight-training machine A specialized device which provides support while a person tries to overcome a resistance. Weight-training machines can be designed to produce resistances at a particular angle of pull for a specific *muscle or to provide resistances for *isokinetic exercises.

wellness A condition obtained when a person achieves a level of *health which minimizes the chances of becoming ill. Wellness is achieved by a combination of emotional, environmental, mental, physical, social, and spiritual health.

wet bulb globe thermometer index *See* WBGT index.

wet bulb thermometer An ordinary thermometer with a wetted wick wrapped around the bulb. The wet bulb's temperature is related to the amount of moisture in the air. When the wet bulb temperature and dry bulb temperature are equal, the air is completely saturated with water and the relative humidity is 100 per cent. *See also* WBT index.

wet bulb temperature index *See* WBT index.

wheel and axle A simple machine consisting of a larger wheel-like device rotating about a smaller central device called an axle. The radius of the wheel corresponds to the *force arm of a *lever. When a force is applied to the wheel in order to turn the axle, the *mechanical advantage favours force; when the force is applied to the axle in order to turn the wheel, the mechanical advantage favours speed. Most wheel and axle arrangements in the human body, such as the *trunk rotating around the *vertebral column, favour speed.

whiplash injury Damage to the structures in the neck region (usually the *cervical vertebrae and its *nerves and *ligaments) caused by a sudden, uncontrolled abnormal movement of the head and neck (for example, when a forward-moving body comes to a sudden stop). Rugby and American Football players may sustain a whiplash injury when tackled simultaneously from the front and back. Rear-end motor vehicle collisions, particularly when a stationary vehicle is hit from the rear, are notorious for causing neck strains as the vulnerable *cervical spine is first extended, then fully flexed.

white blood cell *See* leucocyte.

white fibre *See* collagen fibre.

white fibrocartilage Flexible, tough and elastic *cartilage consisting of a dense mass of *collagen fibres in a solid matrix with cells spread thinly among the fibres. White fibrocartilage forms a thin coating on some grooves in *bones through which *tendons glide. It is also found between the bodies of *vertebrae and in the *menisci.

white matter Regions of the *central nervous system which contain mainly *myelinated fibres and few cell bodies. *Compare* grey matter.

white muscle fibres *See* fast twitch fibres.

whitlow *See* felon.

whole method A method of *learning a *skill in which the skill is repeatedly practised until its performance is perfected. It is usually adopted when the skill is relatively simple.

whole-part-whole method A method of *learning a *skill in which the learner tries to perform the whole skill from time to time after practising parts of the skill, particularly those parts which are difficult.

whooping cough (**pertussis**) A *disease caused by bacterial *infection of the *mucous membranes lining the airway. It is characterized by short coughs followed by a noisy drawing in of breath (the 'whoop'). Exercise is *contra-indicated during the illness and may provoke coughing even 5 to 6 weeks after the onset of the illness.

Wilcoxon test A nonparametric statistical test for comparing two samples for overall *significant differences. The test is performed on paired-data which is of the *ordinal type so that the differences between the pairs can be ranked.

wind A movement of air horizontal in relation to the surface of the earth. In athletics, the wind is measured by an anemometer. If the velocity exceeds $2\,ms^{-1}$ (i.e., 4.473 miles per hour) at a height four feet above ground level in a direction which would assist competitors, the performances are not valid for establishing records.

wind chill The effect of cold winds which can lead to a lowering of *body core temperature and the onset of *hypothermia. *See also* sensible temperature.

winding A common sport injury resulting from an abdominal blow causing a *neurogenic shock due to stimulation of the *solar plexus. Typically, the winded person doubles up and has difficulty breathing because of a momentary *paralysis of the *diaphragm and *spasm of the *abdominal muscles. Drawing the sufferer's knees up to the abdomen is a popular treatment which may relax the abdominal muscles and assist return to normality, but even without special treatment the person usually recovers with no residual symptoms. Persistence of symptoms may indicate serious internal injury requiring expert medical attention.

windpipe *See* trachea.

wind tunnel A chamber in which the motion of a current of air can be regulated so that the *aerodynamic properties of objects can be studied. Wind tunnels are based on the idea that the aerodynamic effects of an object moving through a *fluid are identical to those produced if the object is stationary and the fluid moves past the object at the same relative speed. Wind tunnels have been used to analyse the flight of sports implements, such as the discus and javelin, and the flow of air over a human body (for example, a cyclist or skier). The body (implement or person) is placed in the wind tunnel and the airflow past the body is regulated so that the relative motion of the air is the same as it would have been in the natural environment.

Wingate anaerobic power test *See* Wingate thirty-second test.

Wingate thirty-second test (Wingate anaerobic power test) A test of *intermediate anaerobic performance in which a subject is instructed to pedal as fast as possible on a *bicycle ergometer for 30 s with a resistance load for the leg test of either 45 or 75 g per kg body-weight depending on the type of ergometer.

withdrawal A discontinuation of sport involvement. Factors causing withdrawal include loss of interest and injury. *See also* noninvolvement.

withdrawal symptoms Specific *symptoms associated with discontinuation of the use of a *drug on which the individual has become physically dependent.

withdrawal syndrome The combination of *symptoms and *signs in an indivdual who is deprived of a *drug on which the individual has become physically dependent.

Wolff–Parkinson–White syndrome (WPW syndrome) An abnormal *heart rhythm giving specific *electrocardiogram changes and attacks of paroxysmal *tachycardia. It is a *congenital condition caused by an accessory bundle between the *atria and *ventricles. There is no evidence that athletic exertion makes sudden death from WPW syndrome more likely. However, those with very low *resting pulse rates, such as distance-runners, may be more vulnerable to *ectopic beats.

Wolff's law A law which is applied to the development of *bone. Wolff (1836–1902) proposed that changes in the form and function of bones, or changes in their function alone, are followed by changes in the internal structure and the external shape of the bone in accordance with mathematical laws. Thus, in a mature bone where the general form is established, the bone elements place or displace themselves, and decrease or increase their mass, according to the mechanical demands imposed on them. The theory is supported by the observation that bones *atrophy when there is lack of *stress. *See also* bone remodelling.

work 1 The transfer of *energy expressed as the product of the *force and the distance a body moves in the direction of the application of the force, i.e., work (in *J) = force (in N)×distance (in m). The *SI unit for work is the joule; other units of work include the *erg, *foot-pound and *poundal. 2 A person's paid employment. 3 Any activity which occupies a person and which provides some service to others.

work- and family-orientation questionnaire A *questionnaire which uses *Likert-type scales to measure four components: work orientation (the desire to do one's best in whatever one undertakes);

mastery (persistence in accomplishing difficult tasks); competitiveness (enjoying challenging situations); and personal concern (lack of concern about what others think).

work ethic A code of conduct which emphasizes the value of being occupied. Those who adopt a work ethic generally view labour as a duty, and regard leisure and the pursuit of pleasure with suspicion and feelings of guilt. Those who adopt the work ethic in sport tend to have a high regard for work rate, discipline, and team effort, and have less regard for flair, spontaneity, and individualism.

working hypothesis A suggested explanation for a group of facts or phenomena provisionally accepted as a basis for further investigation and testing. *See also* hypothesis.

work interval Portion of *interval-training consisting of the work effort.

workload The total amount of *work completed in a specified period.

work rate *See* power.

work relief In *interval-training, a type of relief period involving light exercise such as rapid walking or jogging.

work–relief ratio In *interval-training, a ratio relating the duration of the *work interval to the duration of the *relief interval. Thus, a work:relief ratio of 1:1 means that the duration of the work and relief intervals are the same.

wormian bones Small irregular *bones sometimes formed in the sutures of the *cranium.

wound A break in the continuity of an *organ or *tissue by an external agent. Wounds include cuts and *lacerations.

WPW syndrome *See* Wolff–Parkinson–White syndrome.

wrestler's ear *See* cauliflower ear.

wrist The whole region in and around the *wrist-joint, including the more *distal parts of the *radius and *ulna, and the *carpus.

wrist abductor *Muscle which effects *abduction of the wrist. Wrist abductors include the *flexor carpi radialis in the anterior compartment of the forearm, and the *extensor carpi radialis longus, *extensor carpi radialis brevis, and *abductor pollicis longus in the posterior compartment.

wrist adductor Muscle involved in *adduction of the wrist. Wrist adductors include the *flexor carpi ulnaris in the anterior compartment of the forearm, and the *extensor carpi ulnaris in the posterior compartment.

wrist drop An inability to raise the wrist resulting from damage to the *radial nerve or from a *tendon injury.

wrist extensor Muscle involved in *extension of the wrist. Wrist extensors include the *extensor digitorum, *extensor carpi ulnaris, the *extensor carpi radialis longus, and the *extensor carpi radialis brevis in the posterior compartment.

wrist-finger speed A *skill which underlies tasks for which alternating movements of different fingers must be made as quickly as possible. Wrist-finger speed depends on the rapid co-ordination of muscles required for the up-and-down movements of the fingers and wrists.

wrist flexor Muscle involved in *flexion of the wrist. Wrist flexors include the *flexor carpi radialis, *flexor carpi ulnaris, and the *flexor digitorum superficialis in the anterior compartment of the forearm.

wrist girth In *anthropometry, the circumference of the right wrist *distal to the *styloid process.

wrist-joint The *joint formed by the *articulation of the *carpus with the *radius and *ulna of the forearm. *See also* radiocarpal joint.

wryneck *See* torticollis.

X

xamaterol A *drug belonging to the *stimulants which are on the *IOC list of *banned substances.

***x*-axis** 1 In *anthropometry, the *lateral axis formed by the intersection of the *frontal plane and *transverse plane. 2 A spatial axis parallel to the ground and directed to the observer's right and left, right being designated positive and left negative. 3 In mathematics, the horizontal axis of a graph.

X chromosome Sex *chromosome present in both sexes. In males, who have one X chromosome and one *Y chromosome, the *alleles carried on the X chromosomes are always expressed whether they are dominant or recessive. *See also* sex determination.

xerophthalmia A *disease characterized by drying and wrinkling of the *cornea and *conjunctiva, and caused by a deficency of *vitamin A.

xipamide A *drug belonging to the *diuretics which are on the *IOC list of *banned substances. Xipamide is used to treat *oedema and *hypertension.

xiphisternum *See* xiphoid process.

xiphoid process (xiphisternum) The inferior end of the *sternum which articulates with the sternal body and serves as an attachment point for the *diaphragm and *abdominal muscles.

X-rays (Roentgen rays) *Electromagnetic radiation of very short wavelength which can penetrate body structures to varying degrees. X-rays are used in *radiography to produce photographic images of body structures, and they are used in some forms of *radiotherapy.

xylose A *pentose sugar involved in *carbohydrate metabolism. It is found in some types of *connective tissue and in small amounts in the urine.

Y

yard A unit of length defined as 0.9144 m.

yaw 1 A movement in a fluid of a body, such as a swimmer, about the body's vertical axis. 2 The lateral deviation of an object moving in a fluid from a straight course.

***y*-axis** 1 In *anthropometry, the *longitudinal axis formed by the intersection of a *frontal plane and *sagittal plane. 2 A *spatial axis parallel to the ground, and directed forwards and backwards from the observer; forward being positive and backward, negative. 3 In mathematics, the vertical axis of a graph.

Y-chromosome The smaller of the two *sex chromosomes. It is normally found in males only and seems to carry few *genes. *See also* sex determination.

yellow bone marrow The fatty tissue which occupies the internal cavities of *long bones and begins to replace *red bone marrow soon after birth.

yellow elastic cartilage (elastic tissue) *Cartilage which consists of yellow elastic fibres (*see* elastic fibre) running through a a relatively solid *matrix with cells lying between the fibres. Yellow elastic cartilage occurs in the *pinna, *epiglottis, and *Eustachian tube.

yellow elastic fibre *See* elastic fibre.

yellow fibre *See* elastic fibre.

Yerkes–Dodson curve An inverted U-shaped curve showing a proposed relationship between *arousal and performance. One end of the curve indicates an unaroused condition, such as sleep, while the other end shows over-arousal. The curve suggests that there is an optimum level of arousal between the two extremes which maximizes performance. *See* inverted-U principle.

Yerkes–Dodson law A law which predicts an inverted-U relationship between *arousal and performance (*see* Yerkes—Dodson curve) and that the optimal level of arousal for a beginner is considerably less than that for an expert performing the same task. It also suggests that easily–acquired *skills not requiring difficult discrimination or complex association can be readily learned under conditions of high *arousal, whereas complex skills are more easily acquired under low levels of arousal.

young runner's heel An *over-use injury of the growing points of the heel-bone which results in pain as the heel strikes the ground. *See also* Sever–Haglund disease.

Young's modulus The *elastic modulus applied to tensional stress when the object concerned is not constrained. Young's modulus = (applied load per unit area of cross-section)/(increase in length per unit length). If the value is high, the material distorts only a little under the influence of the applied stress and the material is stiff.

Z

Zajonc's model A model of *social facilitation based on *drive theory. According to the model, the mere presence of others is psychologically arousing, and it is this arousal (loosely called drive) that causes the emission of the *dominant response. Thus, well-learned responses tend to be facilitated by the presence of an *audience, while the acquisition of new responses is impaired. *See* evaluation apprehension.

Zander apparatus Apparatus designed by the Swedish physician J. G. W. Zander for enabling a person to perform, within a gymnasium, various exercises that are usually performed only out of doors. The apparatus includes machines for exercising specific muscles used in rowing, bicycling, and horseback-riding. It also has components for moving *joints, to increase their suppleness after injury.

***z*-axis** **1** In anthropometry, the *sagittal axis formed by the intersection of the *sagittal plane and the *transverse plane. **2** A *spatial axis which is vertical to the ground and directed upward and downward from an observer, with upward being designated positive and downward, negative.

zeitgeist The spirit of the times; the dominant beliefs of a particular period. The term is usually applied to the study of literature, but it has also been applied to sport (for example, in connection with the current belief that winning is all that matters).

zero linear acceleration The *acceleration of a body which is moving in a straight line at a constant speed, or of a body which is at rest.

zero-sum competition A competition in which one participant wins totally and another loses without gaining any objectives. *Compare* nonzero-sum competition.

zinc A *trace element which is an *essential mineral constituent of a *balanced diet. Zinc can be obtained from seafood, cereal crops, legumes, wheatgerm, and yeast. Zinc works in close association with *vitamins and is important for the functioning of several *enzymes, including *carbonic anhydrase. Deficiencies can result in a retardation of wound-healing, retardation of growth in children, and a reduction in the sperm-count of adult males. The recommended daily allowance for an adult is 15 mg.

zinc oxide ointment An ointment which is used as a skin protector to prevent ultraviolet light from reaching the skin.

z-line (z-membrane; *zwischen*-line) A *protein band which defines the boundary betwen one *sarcomere and the next in a *muscle fibre. The 'z' is an abbreviation for the German word *zwischen* which means between.

z-membrane *See* z-line.

zoonosis An infectious *disease which can be transmitted to humans from animals.

***zwischen*-line** *See* z-line.

zwitterion An *amino acid or a *protein at its *isoelectric point which, although electrically neutral, has both positive and negative charges.

zygapophysis Any one of the facets of the *vertebrae which articulate with each other. The two prezygapophyses articulate with the two posterior zygapophyses.

zygoma (zygomatic arch) The arch formed by fusion between the molar bone and *temporal bone in front of the ear.

zygomatic arch *See* zygoma.

zygomatic bone One of a pair of bones which run between the cheeks and the ear, forming the prominent part of the cheek and contributing to the *orbits.